THE AMERICAN PAST

Part Two: A Survey of American History Since 1865

Third Edition

Joseph R. Conlin

California State University, Chico

Harcourt Brace Jovanovich, Publishers

San Diego   New York   Chicago   Austin   Washington, D.C.
London   Sydney   Tokyo   Toronto

A Note on the Paperbound Edition

This volume is part of a variant printing of *The American Past* in a two-volume paperbound format, which reproduces exactly the text of the one-volume version. A two-volume paperbound version is useful because it enables instructors to fit the text into the particular patterns of their teaching and scheduling. The first volume begins with the discovery of America and continues through Reconstruction. The second volume, repeating the chapter on Reconstruction (Chapter 26, "Bringing the South Back In: The Reconstruction of the Union"), carries the historical account forward to the present day. This variant printing, then, is intended as a convenience to those instructors and students who have occasion to use either one part or the other of *The American Past*. The pagination and index of the one-volume version, as well as its illustrations, maps, and sidebars, are retained in the new printing. The difference between the one-volume and two-volume versions of the book is a difference only in form.

To J. R. C. and L. V. C.

Cover photograph © David Muench.

Copyright © 1990, 1987, 1984 by Harcourt Brace Jovanovich, Inc.

ISBN: 0-15-502378-0

Library of Congress Catalog Card Number: 89-84687

Printed in the United States of America

Copyrights and Acknowledgments and Illustration Credits appear on pages 940–46, which constitute a continuation of the copyright page.

Preface to the Third Edition

As with the first and second editions of *The American Past,* I have tried to write this textbook without forgetting, for so much as a page, that a survey course *is* a survey course. The textbook is not primarily aimed at students training to be professional historians, but at budding accountants, engineers, physicians, and others. These students find themselves facing a historian's lectern under duress or by default, because they were required to "take history," or because they were unable to "find something else" to round out their class schedules.

Our colleges and universities offer and require survey courses in United States history because most of us believe that the knowledge and analytical skills to be gained in such courses are beneficial to all educated men and women and to the society of which we are members. But as self-evident as that assumption may be to historians and humanists generally, it is one which many of our students do not share.

The task facing the survey course instructor is to demonstrate to this captive audience that we were quite right to require their satisfactory completion of a course in American history. There are a good many classroom methods by which students are successfully wooed to such an appreciation of knowing their nation's past. If, in twenty-five years of teaching the survey course, I have learned one thing about doing it, it is not to disdain a method that works simply because it is not mine.

However, the only way, it seems, to perform the task facing the textbook author—to lure students into enjoying the *reading* of history—is by presenting them with a textbook that, however massive and forbidding it appears to be at first, proves over the semester to be attractive, vivid, colorful, alive, and enjoyable to read. For me, the mortification of receiving a colleague's utterly justified criticism of something about *The American Past* is greatly eased when the letter-writer adds, "The students really like this book."

In addition to writing a narrative that is engaging, I have striven to be comprehensive by providing a balanced treatment of such subdisciplines as political, economic, social, cultural, intellectual, constitutional, diplomatic, and military history. Writing attractively for nonhistorians seems to demand painting in broad strokes and avoiding the hyperspecialized bureaucratization of history that, to judge from the professional newsletters and scholarly journals, so troubles historians today. Individual lecturers will focus on the subjects and methods of analysis that they find most exciting and rewarding. A textbook should, I think, provide a general framework in which to understand these emphases and not try to sell the author's special interests to the exclusion of others.

Every chapter of this edition has been rewritten to brush up the prose, to correct lapses of knowledge or imagination that have been pointed out to me, and to incorporate insights gained since the publication of the second edition. The final group of chapters, dealing with the post-Second World War era, has been completely overhauled to reflect my own reconceptualizations of the period as well as the writings of others. A number of the special features, the boxed inserts and the essays titled "How They Lived" and "Notable People," are new with this edition.

I am indebted to a number of colleagues who have reviewed and used the textbook and made suggestions for its improvement: Charles W. Akers, Oakland University; Terry Alford, Northern Virginia Community College; Roy L. Askins, Missouri Western State College; Edward Beechert, University of Hawaii, Manoa; David Beesley, Sierra College; Thelma Biddle, Virginia Commonwealth University; N. Terry Bullock, Muscatine Community College; Ernest Cassara, George Mason University; Richard Chardkoff, Northeast Louisiana University; Martin B. Cohen, George Mason University; Virginia Crane, University of Wisconsin, Oshkosh; Mike Crow, Orange Coast College; Frank Dawson, Pennsylvania State University, Fayette; Roland DeLorme, Western Washington University; Eugene Dermody, Cerritos College; Jose Espinosa, Rancho Santiago College; William J. Fagan, Eastern Wyoming College; Robert Glover, Tyler Junior College; David Goldberg, Cleveland State University; John Hoeveler, University of Wisconsin, Milwaukee; Herbert T. Hoover, University of South Dakota; Joseph Logsdon, University of New Orleans; Everett L. Long, University of Wisconsin, Whitewater; Samuel T. McSeveney, Vanderbilt University; William F. Mugleston, Mountain View College; Patricia Mulvey, Bluefield State College; Lorraine Murray, Oakton Community College; Clifford Norse, Radford University; Albert Ortiz, San Joaquin Delta College; Mario Perez, Crafton Hills College; C. H. Peterson, California State University, Chico; Charles P. Poland, Northern Virginia Community College; Marlette Rebhorn, Austin Community College; Marilyn D. Rhinehart, North Harris County College; Elliott Schimmel, Longview Community College; Susan Schrepfer, Rutgers University; John H. Schroeder, University of Wisconsin, Milwaukee; Paul Siff, Sacred Heart University; Bernard Sinsheimer, University of Maryland, European Division; Pat Smith, Tulsa Junior College; Richard R. Sorrell, Brookdale Community College; George W. Spencer, Northern Illinois University; Leah Marcile Taylor, Wesleyan College; Thomas Wagstaff, California State University, Chico; Thomas R. Walther, Pittsburgh State University; and Stan Watson, Tyler Junior College.

Dale Steiner, California State University, Chico, prepared the Testbook, and Richard Mumford, Elizabethtown College, prepared the imaginative and innovative Study Guide.

Drake Bush, a friend as well as an editor, was patient with my crotchets. Manuscript Editor Robert Watrous rode herd on my stylistic lapses and excesses. Designer Martha Gilman Roach, Production Manager Lesley Lenox, Production Editor Leslie Leland, and Art Editor Avery Hallowell turned out a visually beautiful book.

J.R.C.

Contents

Maps

When the guns fell silent in 1865, the people of the South looked about them to see a society, an economy, and a land in tatters. Some southern cities, such as Vicksburg, Atlanta, Columbia, and Richmond, were flattened, eerie wastelands of charred timber, rubble, and freestanding chimneys. Few of the South's railroads could be operated for more than a few miles. Bridges were gone. River-borne commerce, the lifeblood of the states beyond the Appalachians, had dwindled to a trickle. Old commercial ties with Europe and the North had been snapped clean. All the South's banks were ruined.

Even the cultivation of the soil had been disrupted. The small farms of the men who had served in the

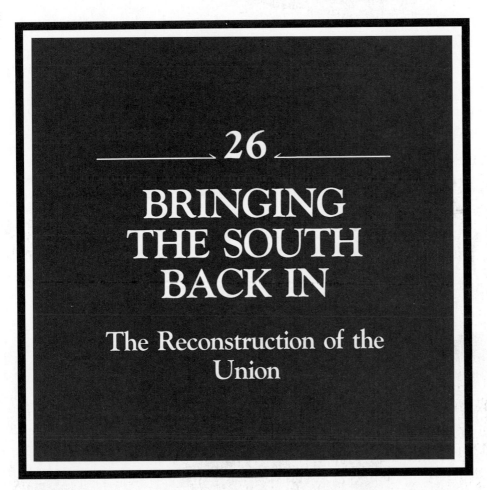

26

BRINGING THE SOUTH BACK IN

The Reconstruction of the Union

Freedmen pose for a photographer in Richmond, Virginia, with the ruins of the city in the background (1865).

ranks lay fallow by the thousands, many of them never to be claimed by their former owners. Great planters who had abandoned their fields to advancing Union armies discovered that weeds and scrub pine were more destructive conquerors. The people who had toiled in them, the former slaves, were often gone, looking elsewhere for a place to start new lives as free men and women.

THE RECONSTRUCTION DEBATE

In view of the widespread desolation, the word *reconstruction* would seem to be an appropriate description of the twelve-year period following the Civil War. But the word does not refer to the literal rebuilding of the South, the laying of bricks, the spanning of streams, the reclaiming of the land.

Reconstruction refers to the political process by which the 11 rebel states were restored to a normal constitutional relationship with the 25 loyal states and their national government. It was the Union, that great abstraction over which so many had died, that was reconstructed.

Blood was shed during Reconstruction too, but little glory was won. Few political reputations—northern or southern, white or black, Republican or Democratic—emerged from the era unstained. More than one historian has suggested that Abraham Lincoln comes down to us a heroic and sainted figure only because he did not survive the war. Indeed, the Reconstruction policy Lincoln proposed as early as 1863 was soundly repudiated by members of his own party. Lincoln anticipated the problems he did not live to face. He described as "a pernicious abstraction" the constitutional issue with which both sides in the bitter Reconstruction debate masked their true motives and goals.

Lincoln's Plan to Restore the Union

By the end of 1863, Union armies controlled large parts of the Confederacy, and ultimate victory was reasonable to assume. To provide for a rapid reconciliation of the sections, Lincoln declared on December 8, 1863, that as soon as 10 percent of the voters in

Prisoners from the Front, *by Winslow Homer (1866). As this painting depicts, Confederate soldiers were allowed to return home—to a shattered society and ruined economy.*

POCKET VETO

Section 7 of Article I of the Constitution provides that if a president vetoes an act of Congress, he shall return the act to Congress within ten days "with his Objections." If he fails to do so, the act becomes law without his signature.

However, if Congress enacts a bill and then adjourns before ten days have passed, as was the case with the Wade-Davis bill, the president can veto it without explanation simply by failing to sign it, figuratively leaving it in his coat pocket. Thus, the pocket veto.

any Confederate state took an oath of allegiance to the Union, the people of that state could organize a government and elect representatives to Congress. Moving quickly, Tennessee, Arkansas, and Louisiana complied.

Congress Checks the President

Congress refused to recognize the new governments, leaving the three states under the command of the military. Motives for checking Lincoln's plan varied as marvelously as the cut of the chin whiskers that politicians were sporting, but two were repeatedly voiced. First, almost all Republican congressmen were alarmed by the broad expansion of presidential powers during the war. No president since Andrew Jackson (still a villain to those Republicans who had been Whigs) had assumed as much authority as Lincoln had—at the expense of Congress. Few congressmen wished to see this trend continue during peacetime, as Lincoln's plan for Reconstruction promised to do.

Second, Radical Republicans, abolitionists who had been at odds with Lincoln over his reluctance to move against slavery, objected that Lincoln's plan made no allowances whatsoever for the status of the freedmen, as the former slaves were called. They took the lead in framing the Wade-Davis bill of July 1864, which provided that only after 50 percent of the white male citizens of a state swore an oath of loyalty to the Union could the Reconstruction process begin. Then, the Wade-Davis bill insisted, Congress and not the president would decide when the process was complete.

Lincoln responded with a pocket veto and, over the following months—the last of his life—hinted that he was ready for compromise. He said he would be glad to accept any former rebel states which opted to reenter the Union under the congressional plan and he let it be known he had no objection to giving the right to vote to blacks who were "very intelligent and those who have fought gallantly in our ranks." He urged the military governor of Louisiana to extend the suffrage to some blacks.

Stubborn Andy Johnson

Lincoln's lifelong assumption that blacks were inferior to whites and his determination to win back quickly the loyalty of southern whites prevented him from accepting black suffrage generally. However, he was willing to be flexible, which the man who succeeded him was not.

Andrew Johnson of Tennessee grew up in far more stultifying frontier poverty than Lincoln ever knew. Unlike Lincoln, who taught himself to read as a boy and was ambitious from the start, Johnson was illiterate as an adult, and working as a tailor when he swallowed his pride and asked a schoolteacher in Greenville, Tennessee, to teach him to read and write. She did, and later married him, encouraging Johnson to pursue a political career. Andrew Johnson had more political experience than Lincoln or, for that matter, most presidents. Johnson held elective office on every level, from town councilman to congressman to senator and, during the war, governor and, briefly, vice president.

Experience, alas, is not the same thing as aptitude. Whereas Lincoln was an instinctive politician who was

Obstinate, often vulgar, President Andrew Jackson was a self-taught student of the Constitution. Rigorous adherence to it, as he read it, and a reflexive distaste for the idea of black citizenship doomed his early friendly relationship with the Radical Republicans.

sensitive to the realities of what he could and could not accomplish, Johnson was unsubtle, insensitive, willful, and stubborn. He narrowly escaped assassination in the plot that felled Lincoln, was ill when sworn in, bolted several glasses of brandy for strength, and took the oath of office drunk and thick-tongued. Johnson had the goodwill of the Radicals because he had several times called for the harsh punishment of high ranking Confederates. (He wanted to hang Jefferson Davis.) But he quickly lost Radical support when, like Lincoln, he insisted that he, the president, possessed the authority to decide when rebel states were reconstructed. Thus he ensured the debate over what Lincoln had called "a pernicious abstraction."

Johnson: They Are Already States

Johnson based his case for presidential supervision on the assumption that the southern states had never left the Union because it was constitutionally impossible to do so: the Union was one and inviolable; it could not be dissolved. Johnson and the entire Republican party and most northern Democrats had held to that principle in 1861. He would stick by it in 1865.

There had indeed been a war and an entity known as the Confederate States of America. But individuals had fought the one and created the other; states had not. Punish the rebels, Johnson said—he approved several confiscations of rebel-owned lands—but not Virginia, Alabama, and the rest. They were still states in the United States of America. Seating their duly elected representatives in the Congress was a purely administrative matter. The president, the nation's chief administrator, would decide how and when to do it.

Logic versus Horse Sense

There was nothing wrong with Johnson's logic; he was an excellent constitutionalist. The president's problem was his inability or refusal to see beyond constitutional tidiness to the world of human feelings, flesh, and blood—especially blood.

The fact was that the senators and representatives from the rebel states—Johnson was an exception—had left their seats in the winter and spring of 1861, and Congress and president had functioned as the Union through four years of war. More than half a million people had been killed and a majority of northerners blamed these deaths on arrogant, antagonistic, rich southern slaveowners who, when Johnson announced that he would adopt Lincoln's plan of Reconstruction (with some minor changes), began to assume the leadership in their states that they had always held.

Nor did Johnson's reputation as a man who wanted rebels punished seem to hold up. By the end of 1865

he pardoned 13,000 Confederate leaders, thus making them eligible to hold public office. In elections held in the fall under Johnson's plan, southern voters sent many of these rebels to Congress, including four Confederate generals, six members of Jefferson Davis's cabinet, and a senator from Georgia, former Confederate vice president, Alexander H. Stephens.

The Radicals: They Have Forfeited Their Rights

To Johnson's argument, Thaddeus Stevens, Radical leader in the House of Representatives, replied that the former Confederate states had committed "state suicide" when they seceded. They were not states. Therefore, it was within the power of Congress to decide when the dead states might be resurrected. Senator Charles Sumner came to the same conclusion by arguing that the southern states were "conquered provinces" and therefore had the same status as the federal territories of the West.

These theories suited the mood of many northerners very well, but they were constitutionally indefensible. A rather obscure Republican, Samuel Shellabarger of Ohio, came up with the formula that appealed to angry, war-weary northerners and made constitutional sense: the rebel states had forfeited their rights as states. Congress's Joint Committee on Reconstruction found that "the States lately in rebellion were, at the close of the war, disorganized communities, without civil government, and without constitutions or other forms, by virtue of which political relations could legally exist between them and the federal government." Such a state of affairs meant that only Congress could decide when the eleven former Confederate states might once again function as members of the Union.

OLD THAD STEVENS

Few Radical Republicans were as sincerely committed to racial equality as Thaddeus Stevens of Pennsylvania. In his will he insisted on being buried in a black cemetery because blacks were banned from the one where he normally would have been interred.

Nevertheless, even Stevens came to terms with the racism of those northern whites who refused the vote to the blacks in their own states. In order to win their support for black suffrage in the South, Stevens argued that the situation was different in the South because blacks made up the majority of loyal Union men there. "I am for negro suffrage in every rebel state," he said. "If it be just, it should not be denied; if it be necessary, it should be adopted; if it be a punishment to traitors, they deserve it."

The Radicals

Congress refused to seat the senators and representatives who were sent to Washington under the Johnson plan. The leaders of the resistance, Radical Republicans, were determined to crush the southern planter class they had hated for so long and, with varying degrees of idealism, wanted to help the black freedmen who had, for so long, been victimized and exploited by the slaveowners.

Some Radicals, like Stevens and Sumner and Benjamin "Bluff Ben" Wade of Ohio, believed in racial equality. George W. Julian of Indiana proposed to confiscate the land of the planters and divide it, in 40-acre farms, among the blacks; with economic independence they could guarantee their civil freedom and political rights. Other Radicals wanted to grant the freedmen citizenship, including the vote, for frankly political purposes. Black voters would provide the backbone for a Republican party in the South, which did not exist before the war.

The Radicals were a minority within the Republican party. However, they were able to win the cooperation of party moderates because of Johnson's repeated blunders and a series of events in the conquered South that persuaded a majority of northern voters that Lincolnian generosity would mean squandering the Union's military victory and making a mockery of the cause for which so many soldiers had died.

Freedmen pose with their reading books in front of their log schoolhouse.

THE CRITICAL YEAR

The reaction of most blacks to the news of their freedom was to test it by leaving the plantations and farms on which they had lived as slaves.

Many flocked to cities that they associated with free blacks. Others, after a period of wandering, gathered in ramshackle camps in the countryside, eagerly discussing the rumor that each household would soon be alloted "forty acres and a mule." Without a means of making a living in a stricken land, these congregations of people were potentially, and in some cases in fact, dens of hunger, disease, crime, and disorder.

The Freedmen's Bureau

In order to prevent chaos in conquered territory, Congress had created the Bureau of Refugees, Freedmen, and Abandoned Lands, popularly known as the Freedmen's Bureau. Administered by the army under the command of General O. O. Howard, the Bureau provided relief for the freedmen (and some whites) in the form of food, clothing, and shelter; attempted to find jobs for them; set up hospitals and schools run by idealistic black and white women from the northern states, sometimes at the risk of their lives; and otherwise tried to ease the transition from slavery to freedom. When the Freedmen's Bureau bill was first enacted, Congress had assumed that properly established state governments would be able to assume responsibility for these services within a year after the end of the hostilities. The Bureau was scheduled to expire in March 1866.

In February 1866, however, the process of Reconstruction was at a standstill. Congress had refused to recognize Johnson's state governments but had not created any to its own liking. The former Confederacy was, in effect, still under military occupation. So, Congress passed a bill extending the life of the Bureau.

Johnson vetoed it and, a month later, he vetoed another congressional act that granted citizenship to the freedmen. Once again, his constitutional reasoning was sound. The Constitution gave the states the power to rule on the terms of citizenship within their borders, and Johnson continued to insist that the state governments he had set up were legitimate.

He might have won his argument. Americans took their constitutional fine points seriously, and Radical demands for black civil equality ran against the grain of white racism. However, the actions of the Johnson government toward blacks, and the apparent refusal of many southern whites to acknowledge their defeat in the war, nullified every point Johnson scored.

The Black Codes

Because blacks as slaves had been the backbone of the southern labor force, the southern legislatures naturally expected the blacks to continue to bring in the

Idealistic women, mostly former abolitionists from New England, were the unsung heroes of the work done by the Freedmen's Bureau. These were school teachers in Norfolk, Virginia, in 1865.

crops after the war. The freedmen wanted the work. Far from providing farms for them, however, the Johnsonian state governments did not even establish a system of employment that treated the blacks as free men and women. On the contrary, the black codes defined a form of second-class citizenship that looked to blacks and many whites like a step or two back into slavery.

In some states, blacks were permitted to work only as domestic servants or in agriculture, just what they had done as slaves. Other states made it illegal for blacks to live in towns and cities. In no state were blacks allowed to vote or to bear arms. In fact, few of the civil liberties listed in the Bill of Rights were accorded them.

Mississippi required freedmen to sign twelve-month labor contracts before January 10 of each year. Those who failed to do so could be arrested, and their labor sold to the highest bidder in a manner that (to say the least) was strongly reminiscent of the detested slave auction. Dependent children could be forced to work. Blacks who reneged on their contracts were not to be paid for the work that they already had performed.

The extremism of the black codes alienated many northerners who would gladly have accepted a less blatant form of second-class citizenship for the freedmen. (Only a few northern states allowed black people full civil equality.) Northerners were also disturbed when whites in Memphis, New Orleans, and smaller southern towns rioted, killing and injuring blacks, while the Johnson state governments sat passively by.

The Fourteenth Amendment

Perceiving the shift in mood, in June 1866, Radical and Moderate Republicans drew up a constitutional amendment on which to base congressional Reconstruction policy. The long and complex (and later controversial) Fourteenth Amendment banned from holding high federal or state office all high-ranking Confederates unless they were pardoned by Congress. This struck directly at many of the leaders of the Johnson governments in the South.

The amendment also guaranteed that all "citizens of the United States and of the State wherein they reside," in other words blacks, were to receive fully equal treatment under the laws of the states.

If ratified, the Fourteenth Amendment would preclude southern states from passing any more laws like the black codes. However, it also promised to cancel northern state laws that forbade blacks to vote, and in that aspect of the amendment Johnson saw an opportunity. Calculating that many northerners, particularly in the Midwest, would rather have Confederates in the government than grant full civil equality to blacks, Johnson decided to campaign against the Radicals on the amendment issue in the 1866 congressional election.

The Radical Triumph

The first step was the formal organization of a political party. Johnson, conservative Republican allies such as Secretary of State Seward and a few senators, and some Democrats therefore called a convention of the National Union party in Philadelphia. The message of the convention was sectional reconciliation; to symbolize it, the meeting was opened by a procession of northern and southern Johnson supporters in which couples made up of one southerner and one northerner marched arm in arm down the center aisle of the hall.

Unhappily for Johnson, the first couple on the floor was South Carolina governor James L. Orr, a huge,

DISCOURAGING REBELLION

Among other provisions of the Fourteenth Amendment, the former Confederate states were forbidden to repay "any debt or obligation incurred in aid of insurrection or rebellion against the United States." By stinging foreign and domestic individuals and banks that had lent money to the rebel states, the amendment was putting future supporters of rebellion on notice of the consequences of their actions.

fleshy mountain of a man, and Massachusetts governor John A. Andrew, a little fellow with a way of looking intimidated. When Orr seemed to drag the mousy Andrew down the length of the hall, Radical politicians and cartoonists had a field day. Johnson's National Union movement, they said, was dominated by rebels and preached in the North by cowardly stooges.

In the fall, Johnson sealed his doom. He toured the Midwest seeking support—he called it his "swing around the circle"—and from the start discredited himself. Johnson had learned his oratorical skills in the rough-and-tumble, stump-speaking tradition of eastern Tennessee. There, voters liked a red-hot debate between politicians who scorched each other and the hecklers that challenged them.

Midwesterners also liked that kind of ruckus, but not, it turned out, from their president. When Radical hecklers taunted Johnson and he responded gibe for gibe, Radicals shook their heads sadly that a man of so little dignity should be sitting in the seat of Washington and Lincoln. Drunk again, they supposed.

The result was a landslide. Most of Johnson's candidates were defeated. The Republican party, now led by the Radicals, controlled more than two-thirds of the seats in both houses of Congress, enough to override every veto that Johnson dared to make.

RECONSTRUCTION REALITIES AND MYTHS

The Republicans' Reconstruction program was adopted in a series of laws that were passed by the Fortieth Congress in 1867. These dissolved the southern state governments that had been organized under Johnson and partitioned the Confederacy into five military provinces, each commanded by a major general. The army would maintain order while voters were registered, blacks and those whites who were not specifically disenfranchised under the terms of the Fourteenth Amendment. The constitutional conventions that these voters elected were required to abolish slavery, give the vote to adult black males, and ratify the Thirteenth and Fourteenth Amendments. After examination of their work by Congress, the reconstructed states would be admitted to the Union, and their senators and representatives could take their seats in the Capitol. The Radicals assumed that at least some of these congressmen would be Republicans.

The Readmission of the Southern States

Tennessee complied immediately with these terms and was never really affected by the Radical experiment in

WAS JOHNSON IMPEACHED?

Andrew Johnson *was* impeached, the only American president to be so. *Impeachment* is not removal from office but the bringing of charges, the equivalent of indictment in a criminal trial. The official who is found guilty of the articles of impeachment is convicted and removed from office (and may be sent to prison or otherwise penalized if convicted in a subsequent criminal trial). Johnson was *not* convicted of the charges brought against him.

remaking the South. Ironically, it was Andrew Johnson, as military governor during the war, who had laid the basis for a stable government in the Volunteer State.

In 1868, thanks largely to the black vote, six more states were readmitted. Alabama, Arkansas, Florida, Louisiana, North Carolina, and South Carolina sent Republican delegations, including some blacks, to Washington. In the remaining four states—Georgia, Mississippi, Texas, and Virginia—because some whites obstructed every attempt to set up a government in which blacks would participate, the military continued to govern until 1870.

In the meantime, with Congress more firmly under Radical control, Thaddeus Stevens, Charles Sumner, and other Radicals attempted to establish the supremacy of the legislative over the judicial and executive branches of the government. With the Supreme Court they were immediately successful. By threatening to reduce the size of the Court or even to try to abolish it, the Radicals intimidated the justices. Chief Justice Salmon P. Chase decided to ride out the difficult era by ignoring all cases that dealt with Reconstruction issues, just what the Radicals wanted.

As for the presidency, Congress took partial control of the army away from Johnson and then struck at his right to choose his own cabinet. The Tenure of Office Act forbade the president to remove any appointed official who had been confirmed by the Senate without first getting the Senate's approval of the dismissal.

The Impeachment of Andrew Johnson

Although Johnson had attempted to delay and obstruct congressional Reconstruction by urging southern whites not to cooperate, the strict constitutionalist in him had come to terms with the fact of the Radicals' control of the government. He had executed the duties assigned him under the Reconstruction acts. However, he decided to defy the Tenure of Office Act for the same constitutional reasons. To allow Congress to decide if and when a president could fire a member of

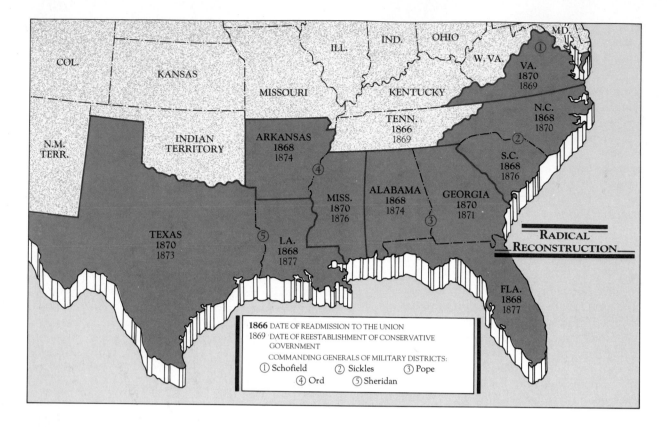

his own cabinet was a clear infringement of the independence of the executive branch of the government. In February 1868, Johnson dismissed the single Radical in his cabinet, Secretary of War Edwin Stanton.

Strictly speaking, the Tenure of Office Act did not apply to Stanton's dismissal because he had been appointed by Lincoln, not by Johnson. Nevertheless, as the Constitution provided, the House of Representatives drew up articles of impeachment, passed them, and appointed a committee to serve as Johnson's prosecutors. The Senate acted as the jury in the trial, and the Chief Justice presided.

A President on Trial

All but two of the eleven articles of impeachment dealt with the Tenure of Office Act. As expected, Johnson's defenders in the Senate argued that it did not apply to the Stanton case, and, in any event, its constitutionality was highly dubious. The other two articles condemned Johnson for disrespect of Congress. These charges were undeniably true; Johnson had spared few nasty words in describing the Radicals who seemed to dominate both houses. But the president's defenders argued that sharp and vulgar language did not approach being the "high crimes and misdemean-

ors" that the Constitution stipulates as the reason for impeachment.

Removal of an impeached federal official requires a two-thirds majority of the Senate. In 1868, that meant 36 senators had to vote for conviction, no more than 18 for acquittal. The actual vote against Johnson was 35 to 19. He remained in office by a single vote.

Actually, it was not so close. About six Moderate Republican senators had agreed privately that if they were needed to acquit, they would vote for acquittal.

A ticket of admission to the Senate gallery to witness the impeachment of Andrew Johnson.

They wanted to avoid going on record as favoring the president; Johnson had little support in the North in 1868, and they were practical politicians. However, they did not believe that the president should be removed from office simply because he was at odds with Congress. Moreover, if Johnson were removed from office, his successor would have been Ben Wade of Ohio, a Radical of such dubious deportment—he was a notorious foulmouth—that by comparison Johnson was a statesman. Finally, 1868 was an election year. Andy Johnson's days were numbered. The immensely popular Ulysses S. Grant would be the Republican nominee. Victory in November was a sure thing.

The Fifteenth Amendment

Grant easily defeated New York governor Horatio Seymour in the electoral college by a vote of 214 to 80. However, the popular vote was much closer, a hair's breadth in some states. Nationwide, Grant won by 300,000 votes, and, some rudimentary arithmetic showed, he got 500,000 black votes in the southern states. Grant lost New York, the largest state, by a very thin margin. Had blacks been able to vote in New York (they were not), Grant would have carried the state easily. In Indiana, Grant won by a razor-thin margin. Had blacks been able to vote in that northern state (they were not), it would not have been close.

This photograph of Ulysses S. Grant is a print from a restored glass plate negative.

WHAT IF JOHNSON HAD BEEN CONVICTED?

What would it have meant for the structure of American government if Andrew Johnson had been removed from office for, in effect, disagreeing with Congress? It might have been a major step toward the parliamentary form of government that is practiced in most representative democracies. Whereas in the United States the executive branch of government is separate from the legislative branch, in parliamentary systems like that of Canada and Great Britain, the prime minister, the head of government, must be a member of Parliament and have the support of a majority of the members of Parliament. If the prime minister loses that support, he or she loses the office and Parliament elects a new prime minister or is dissolved, and new elections held. The American presidency would still have been constitutionally independent had Johnson been removed, but the precedent probably would have emboldened later Congresses to remove presidents of whose policies they disapproved. As it was, Johnson's acquittal and, in 1974, Richard Nixon's resignation before he was impeached, have helped to preserve the independence of the executive branch.

In other words, the future of the Republican party seemed to depend on the black man's right to vote in the northern as well as in the southern states. Consequently, the Moderates in Congress supported Radicals in drafting a third "Civil War Amendment." The Fifteenth forbade states to deny the vote to any person on the basis of "race, color, or previous condition of servitude." Because Republican governments favorable to blacks still controlled most of the southern states, the amendment was easily ratified. The Radical Reconstruction program was complete.

Legends

By the end of the nineteenth century and increasingly after 1900, a legend of Reconstruction took form in American popular consciousness. Most white people came to believe that Reconstruction was a time of degradation and humiliation for white southerners. Soldiers bullied them, and they languished under the political domination of ignorant former slaves who were incapable of good citizenship, carpetbaggers (northerners who went south in order to exploit the tragedy of defeat), and scalawags (white southerners of low caste who cooperated with blacks and Yankees).

N   O   T   A   B   L   E   P   E   O   P   L   E

BLACKS IN CONGRESS

Better a white crook than a black crook; better a white grafter than a black of stature and probity. Such was the view of the "Redeemers," white Democrats who wrested control of southern state governments from the Republican party during Reconstruction. They depicted black officials as incompetent, corrupt, and uninterested in the welfare of the South as a whole. With most southern whites contemptuous of the recently freed slaves, it was an effective appeal. Other issues paled into near invisibility in what seemed the blinding urgency in asserting "white supremacy."

At low levels, many black officeholders were incompetent and self-serving. A few high in state administrations were venal grafters. That their Redeemer challengers were rarely better and often worse did not, however, lend a reflective bent to southern voting behavior. Rather, race was all.

While none of the blacks who sat in Congress in the wake of the Civil War may be said to have been statesmen of the first order, as a group they were as able and worthy a lot as the era's other "ethnic delegations" in the Capitol, any random selection of farmer-congressmen or businessmen-congressmen, any northern or western state delegation of either party, any random selection of 22 Redeemers.

Between 1869 and 1901, 20 blacks served in the House, two in the Senate. South Carolina, where blacks outnumbered whites, sent eight; North Carolina four; Alabama three; and Virginia, Georgia, Florida, Louisiana, and Mississippi one each. Both black senators, Hiram K. Revels and Blanche K. Bruce, represented Mississippi, where potential black voters also outnumbered whites.

Thirteen of the 22 had been slaves before the Civil War, the others were lifelong free blacks. Their educational attainment compared well with that of Congress as a whole. Ten of the black congressmen had gone to college, five had graduated. Six were lawyers (rather less than among all congressmen—nothing for which to apologize); three were preachers; four farmers. Most of the others were skilled artisans, by no means "the dregs of society" as the Redeemers ritually portrayed them.

Hiram Revels was a Methodist pastor. He was born in North Carolina in 1822 but, as a free black, prudently removed to Indiana and Ohio where, during the Civil War, he organized a black regiment. The end of the war found him in Natchez where a cultivated and conservative demeanor (and a willingness to defer to white Republicans) made him an attractive candidate for the Senate.

Blanche K. Bruce was born a slave in 1841, but he was well educated: his owner leased him to a printer. In 1861, he escaped from his apparently lackadaisical master and, in the wake of the Union troops, moved to Mississippi. His record in the Senate was conservative and quiet.

The most durable of the black congressmen was J. H. Rainey of South Carolina. He sat in Congress between 1869 and 1879, winning his last election in the year of the Hayes-Tilden debacle. In most of his district, blacks outnumbered whites by 6 to 1 and 8 to 1. He was retired in the election of 1878 only as a consequence of widespread economic reprisals against black voters and some little violence.

Rainey's parents had bought their freedom long before the Civil War but, in 1862, he was drafted to work on the fortifications in Charleston harbor, a condition that was tantamount to enslavement. However, Rainey escaped to the West Indies and worked his way to the North, returning to his home state early during Reconstruction.

Rainey was indeed vindictive toward the white South, exploiting racial hostilities as nastily as any Redeemer on the other side. Most of the black congressmen were, unsurprisingly, preoccupied with civil rights issues. No doubt, had South Carolina's blacks retained the franchise, Rainey would have exploited racial hostility as destructively as his opponents.

However, Rainey was by no means oblivious to other questions. By the end of the 1870's, he used his modest seniority to work for southern economic interests that transcended the color line. He defended the rights of Chinese in California on conservative "pro-business" Republican, as well as racial, grounds and attempted to improve relations with the black republic of Haiti.

George H. White was the last black to sit in Congress from a southern state before the passage of the Civil Rights Act of 1965. Born a slave in 1852, he attended Howard University in Washington (then a black institution), and practiced law in North Carolina.

In 1896, he won election to the House of Representatives by adding a number of white Populist votes to a black Republican bloc. At the time, some southern Populists, like Thomas Watson of Georgia, preached interracial political cooperation in an attempt to build a solid agrarian front to the "Bourbons" into which the Redeemers had been transformed. Unlike the northern Populists, who fastened on the Republican party as their chief enemy, southern Populists sometimes saw allies in black Republican voters. Their issues were agrarian: almost all southern blacks tilled the soil.

This put black politicians like White in an impossible situation. Preferment in the national Republican party required him to adhere to a line that, under President William McKinley, also elected in 1896, became conservative and imperialistic. White spoke out on behalf of a high tariff—albeit on the grounds that it favored the working man: "the ox that pulls the plow ought to have a chance to eat the fodder"—and favored the Spanish-American War.

Inevitably, his positions alienated those whites who had helped elect him. Moreover, southern Populism

A Currier and Ives print of the first black United States senator and black members of the House of Representatives in the 41st and 42nd Congresses. None were ignorant former fieldhands. Several were individuals of rare talent and accomplishment.

was undergoing a momentous transformation during the late 1890s. Shrewd Democratic party politicians like Benjamin "Pitchfork Ben" Tillman combined a populistic appeal to poor whites with an incendiary hatred of blacks.

Racial hatred was the staple of demagogues like Tillman (and, soon enough, Tom Watson in Georgia). However, they also hammered on the fact that southern blacks voted overwhelmingly Republican and that meant a "plutocratic" federal government.

Conservatives like White were easy targets and, in 1898, the North Carolina Populists switched sides, supporting the Democratic candidate and almost ousting White after only one term.

He knew his political future was doomed and compensated for "an organization man's" first term by speaking out loudly during his second about what was happening in the South (while most white Republicans merely shrugged). Only after 1898 did he fasten almost

exclusively on civil rights issues, describing himself as "the representative on this floor of 9,000,000 of the population of these United States."

By 1900, black voters in White's district had been reduced to a fragment. He did not even bother to stand for reelection and sure humiliation. Instead, in his farewell speech in 1901, he delivered his finest oration, an eloquent speech that served as the coda to Reconstruction's failure to integrate blacks into the American polity:

These parting words are in behalf of an outraged, heart-broken, bruised and bleeding, but God-fearing people, faithful, industrial, loyal people, rising people, full of potential force. The only apology that I have to make for the earnestness with which I have spoken is that I am pleading for the life, the liberty, the future happiness, and manhood suffrage for one-eighth of the entire population of the United States.

This cartoon from the British magazine Puck *illustrates the view many southerners held of Reconstruction as ordered by Ulysses S. Grant and the Republicans. It was, the southerners believed, a harsh and heavy burden forced upon a weary but solid South.*

The "Black Reconstruction" governments, the legend continued, were hopelessly corrupt as well as unjust. The blacks, carpetbaggers, and scalawags looted the treasuries and demeaned the honor of the southern states. Only by heroic efforts did decent white people, through the Democratic party, redeem the southern states once they had retaken control of them. Some versions of the legend glamorized the role of secret terrorist organizations, such as the Ku Klux Klan, in redeeming the South.

The Kernel of Truth

As in most legends, there was a kernel of truth in this vision of Reconstruction. The Radical governments did spend freely. In 1869, the state of Florida spent as much on its printing bill as had been spent on every function of state government in 1860. There was plenty of corruption in southern government; for example, the Republican governor of Louisiana, Henry C. Warmoth, banked $100,000 during a year when his salary was $8,000.

Sometimes the theft was open and ludicrous. Former slaves in control of South Carolina's lower house voted a payment of $1,000 to one of their number who had

lost that amount in a bet on a horse race. Self-serving carpetbaggers were numerous, as were vindictive scalawags and incompetent black officials.

The Legend in Perspective

Large governmental expenditures were unavoidable in the postwar South, however. Southern society was being built from scratch—an expensive proposition. It was the lot of the Radical state governments to provide social services—for whites as well as blacks—that had simply been ignored in the southern states before the Civil War. Statewide public school systems were not founded in the South until Reconstruction. Programs for the relief of the destitute and the handicapped were likewise nearly unknown before Republicans came to power.

Corrupt politicians are inevitable in times of massive government spending, no matter who is in charge; and shady deals were not unique to southern Republican governments during the 1860s and 1870s. The most flagrant theft from public treasuries during the period was the work of Democrats in New York, strong supporters of white southerners who wanted to reduce the blacks to peonage. In fact, the champion southern thieves of the era were not Radicals but antiblack, white Democrats. After a Republican administration in Mississippi ran a clean, nearly corruption-free regime, the first post-Reconstruction treasurer of the

Before the Civil War, Nathan Bedford Forrest had been a slave trader, an occupation of low social status in the South. He distinguished himself in battle, however, and founded the Ku Klux Klan after the war.

*Hiram Revels (left) and Blanche K. Bruce (right), both of Mississippi, were elected to the
United States Congress during Reconstruction.*

state absconded with $415,000. This paled compared
to the swag pocketed by E. A. Burke, the first post-
Reconstruction treasurer of Louisiana; he took
$1,777,000 with him to Honduras in 1890.

As for the carpetbaggers, many of them brought
much-needed capital to the South. They were hot to
make money, to be sure, but in the process of developing the South, not as mere exploiters. Many of the
scalawags were by no means unlettered "poor white
trash," as the legend had it, but southern Whigs who
had disapproved of secession and who, after the war,
drifted naturally, if briefly, into the Republican party
that their northern fellow Whigs had joined.

Blacks in Government

The blacks who rose to high office in the Reconstruction governments were rarely ignorant former field
hands, but well-educated, refined, even rather conservative men. Moreover, whatever the malfeasances
of Reconstruction, the blacks could not be blamed;
they never controlled the government of any southern
state. For a short time, they were the majority in the
legislatures of South Carolina (where blacks were the
majority of the population) and precisely one-half of
the legislature of Louisiana. Only two blacks served as
United States senators, Blanche K. Bruce and Hiram
Revels, both cultivated men from Mississippi. No
black ever served as a governor, although Lieutenant
Governor P. B. S. Pinchback of Louisiana briefly acted
in that capacity when the white governor was out of

the state. Whatever Reconstruction was, its color was
not black.

Redemption

The crime of Reconstruction in the eyes of most southern whites was that it allowed blacks the opportunity
to participate in government. The experiment failed
because black voters were denied an economic foundation on which to build their civil equality, and because northerners soon lost interest in the ideals of the
Civil War.

Because they had no land, the blacks of the South
were dependent on landowners for their sustenance.
When southern landowners concluded that it was to
their interest to eliminate the blacks from political
life, they could do so by threatening unemployment.

Unprotected former slaves could not command the
respect of poorer whites, who provided most of the
members of terrorist organizations like the Ku Klux
Klan, which was founded in 1866 by former slave
trader and Confederate general Nathan Bedford Forrest. These nightriders, identities concealed within
hoods, frightened, beat, and even murdered blacks
who insisted on voting. Congress outlawed and, within
a few years, effectively suppressed the Klan and similar
organizations like the Knights of the White Camellia,
but, in the meantime, many blacks had been terrorized
into staying home on election day.

Congress was unable to counter the conviction of
increasing numbers of white southerners that only

through "white supremacy," the slogan of the southern Democratic parties, could the South be redeemed. In most southern states, where whites were the majority, an overwhelming white vote on this issue alone was enough to install legislators and governors who promptly found effective ways to disenfranchise the blacks.

In the North and West, each year that passed saw the deterioration of interest in the rights of southern blacks. At no time had more than a minority of northern whites truly believed blacks to be their equals. As an era of unprecedented economic expansion unfolded in the wake of the Civil War, and unprecedented scandals rocked the administration of Ulysses S. Grant, to whom the protection of black civil rights was entrusted, support for Reconstruction dwindled. Albion W. Tourgee, a white northerner who fought for black civil equality in North Carolina, wrote that trying to enforce the Fourteenth and Fifteenth Amendments without federal support was "a fool's errand."

THE GRANT ADMINISTRATION

Ulysses S. Grant was the youngest man to be president to his time, only 46 years of age when he took the oath of office in 1869. In some ways, his appearance remained as unimpressive as when reporters caught him whittling sticks on the battlefield. Stoop-shouldered and taciturn, Grant has a peculiar frightened look in his eye in most of the photographs of him, as though he knew that he had risen above his capabilities.

In fact, Grant hated the duties and power of the presidency. It was the perquisites of living in the White House that he fancied. He took with relish to eating caviar and *tournedos béarnaise* and sipping the best French wines and cognac. The earthy general whose uniform had looked like that of a slovenly sergeant developed a fondness for expensive, finely tailored clothing.

Indeed, the elegant broadcloth on his back was the emblem of Grant's failure as president. Money and fame had come too suddenly to a man who had spent his life struggling to survive. Both he and his wife were overwhelmed by the adulation heaped on him. When towns and counties took his name, and when cities made gifts of valuable property and even cash— $100,000 from New York alone—Grant accepted them with a few mumbled words of thanks. He never fully understood that political gift givers were actually paying in advance for future favors. Or, if he did understand, he saw nothing wrong in returning kindness

with the resources at his disposal. Among the lesser of his errors, he gave federal jobs to any of his and his wife's relatives who asked and, a seedy lot, they were not bashful. Worse, Grant remained as loyal to them as he had been to junior officers in the army. In the military, backing up subordinates when they slip up is a virtue, essential to morale. Grant never quite learned that in politics backing up subordinates who steal is less than admirable.

Black Friday

Grant's friends, old and new, wasted no time in stealing. Unlucky in business himself, the president luxuriated in the flattery lavished on him by wealthy men. In 1869, two unscrupulous speculators, Jay Gould and Jim Fisk, made it a point to be seen in public with the president, schemed secretly with Grant's brother-in-law, Abel R. Corbin, and hatched a plot to corner the nation's gold supply.

That is, having won Corbin's assurance that he would keep Grant from selling government gold, Gould and Fisk bought up as much gold and gold futures (commitments to buy gold at a future date at a low price) as they could. Their apparent control of the gold market caused the price of the precious metal to soar. In September 1869, gold was bringing $162 an ounce. Gould's and Fisk's plan was to dump their holdings and score a killing.

Finally grasping that he was an accomplice, on Friday, September 24, Grant dumped $4 million in government gold on the market and the price collapsed. Gould and Fisk suffered very little. Jim Fisk simply refused to honor his commitments to buy at higher than the market price and hired thugs to threaten those who insisted. (High finance could be highly exercising during the Grant years.) But businessmen who needed gold to pay debts and wages were ruined by the hundreds, and thousands of workingmen lost their jobs. The luster of a great general's reputation was tarnished before he had been president for a year.

Other Scandals

During the construction of the Union Pacific Railway in the years following the Civil War, the directors of the U.P. set up a dummy corporation called the Crédit Mobilier. This company charged the U.P. some $5 million for work that actually cost about $3 million. The difference went into the pockets of Union Pacific executives. Because the U.P. was heavily subsidized by the federal government, and therefore under close scrutiny, key members of Congress were cut in on the deal. Among the beneficiaries was Schuyler Colfax, who was Grant's vice president. Speaker of the House James A. Garfield also accepted a stipend.

Three of Grant's appointees to the cabinet were involved in corruption. Carriers under contract to the Post Office Department paid kickbacks in return for exorbitant payments for their services. The secretary of war, William W. Belknap, took bribes from companies that operated trading posts in Indian reservations under his authority. He and his subordinates shut their eyes while the companies defrauded the tribes of goods that they were due under the terms of federal treaties. Grant insisted that Belknap leave his post, but since Belknap was Grant's old crony, the president refused to punish him on behalf of cheated Indians.

Nor did Grant punish his secretary of the treasury, Benjamin Bristow, or his personal secretary, Orville E. Babcock, when he learned that they had sold excise stamps to whiskey distillers in St. Louis. Whenever the president came close to losing his patience (which was considerable), Roscoe Conkling or another stalwart reminded him of the importance of party loyalty. Better a few scoundrels escape than party morale be damaged and the Democrats take over.

The Liberal Republicans

Although the full odor of the Grant scandals was loosed only later, enough scent hung in the air in 1872 that a number of prominent Republicans broke openly with the president. Charles Sumner of Massachusetts, a senator since 1851 and chairman of the Senate Foreign Relations Committee, split with the president over Grant's determination to annex the island nation of Santo Domingo to the United States. Without Sumner's opposition to imperialism and a land-grab by cynical Republican profiteers, Grant would surely have succeeded.

Carl Schurz of Missouri and the British-born editor of *The Nation* magazine, E. L. Godkin, were appalled by the steamy atmosphere of corruption in Washington and the treatment of public office as a way of making a living rather than as performing a public service. Schurz and Godkin (but not Sumner) had also given up on Reconstruction, which, whatever his personal sentiments, Grant enforced. Although not necessarily convinced that blacks were inferior to whites, they had concluded that ensuring civil rights for blacks was not worth the instability of government in the South, nor the continued presence of troops in the southern states. Better to allow the white Redeemers to return to power.

The Election of 1872

This was also the position of the man whom the Liberal Republicans named to run for president in 1872, the editor of the New York *Tribune*, Horace Greeley. It was a terrible choice, for Greeley was a lifelong

Grant's presidential campaign ribbon commemorated his march into Richmond, Virginia, during the Civil War.

eccentric. Throughout his 61 years, Greeley had clambered aboard almost every reform and far-out bandwagon that had rattled down the road, from abolitionism and women's rights at one end of the spectrum to vegetarianism, spiritualism (communicating with the dead), and phrenology (reading a person's character in the bumps on his or her head) at the other.

Even in his appearance, Greeley invited ridicule. He looked like a crackpot with his round, pink face exaggerated by close-set, beady eyes and a wispy fringe of white chin whiskers. He wore an ankle-length overcoat on the hottest days and carried a brightly colored umbrella on the driest. Sharp-eyed Republican cartoonists like Thomas Nast had an easy time making fun of Greeley.

To make matters worse, Greeley needed the support of the Democrats to make a race of it against Grant, and he proposed to "clasp hands across the bloody chasm." This was asking too much of Republican party regulars. Voters who disapproved of Grant disapproved much more of southern Democrats.

Moreover, throughout his editorial career, Greeley had printed just about every printable vilification of the Democrats—particularly southerners—that the English language offered. The Democrats did give him their nomination. But southern whites found it difficult to support such a leader. A large black vote for Grant in seven southern states helped give the president a 286 to 66 victory in the electoral college.

THE TWILIGHT OF RECONSTRUCTION

The Liberals returned to the Republican party. For all their contempt for the unhappy Grant, upon whom the scandals piled during his second term, the Liberals found their flirtation with the Democrats humiliating. Among them, only Charles Sumner remained true to the cause of the southern blacks. His Civil Rights Act of 1875 (passed a year after his death) guaranteed equal accommodations for blacks in public facilities such as hotels and theaters and forbade the exclusion of blacks from juries. Congress quietly dropped another provision forbidding segregated schools.

The Act of 1875 was the last significant federal attempt to enforce equal rights for the races for 80 years. Not only had northerners lost interest in Civil War idealism, southern white Democrats had redeemed most of the former Confederacy. By the end of 1875, only three states remained Republican: South Carolina, Florida, and Louisiana.

The Disputed Election

The Democratic candidate in 1876, New York governor Samuel J. Tilden, called for the removal of troops from these three states, which would bring the white-supremacy Democrats to power. The Republican candidate, Governor Rutherford B. Hayes of Ohio, ran on a platform that guaranteed black rights in the South, but Hayes was known to be skeptical of black capabilities and a personal friend of a number of white southern politicians.

When the votes were counted, Hayes's opinions seemed to be beside the point. Tilden won a close popular vote, and he appeared to have won the electoral college by a vote of 204 to 165. However, Tilden's margin of victory included the electoral votes of South Carolina, Florida, and Louisiana, where Republicans still controlled the state governments. After receiving telegrams from party leaders in New York, officials in those states declared that in reality Hayes had carried their states. According to these returns, Hayes had eked out a 185 to 184 electoral vote victory.

It was not really that easy. When official returns reached Washington, there were two sets from each of the three disputed states—one set for Tilden and one for Hayes. Because the Constitution did not provide for such an occurrence, a special commission was established to decide which set of returns was valid. Five members of each house of Congress and five members of the Supreme Court sat on this panel. Seven of them were Republicans; seven were Democrats; and one, David Davis of Illinois, a Supreme Court justice and once Abraham Lincoln's law partner, was known as an independent. Because no one was interested in determining the case on its merits, each commissioner fully intending to vote for his party's candidate, the burden of naming the next president of the United States fell on Davis's shoulders.

He did not like it. No matter how honestly he came to his decision, half the voters in the country would call for his scalp because he had voted down their candidate. Davis prevailed on friends in Illinois to get him off the hook by naming him to a Senate seat then vacant. He resigned from the Court and, therefore, the special commission. His replacement was a Republican, and the stage was set for the Republicans to "steal" the election.

The Compromise of 1877

The commission voted on strict party lines, eight to seven, to accept the Hayes returns from Louisiana, Florida, and South Carolina—thus giving Rutherford B. Hayes the presidency by a single electoral vote. Had that been all there was to it, there might have been further trouble. At a series of meetings, however, a group of prominent northern and southern politicians and businessmen came to an informal agreement that was satisfactory to the political leaders of both sections.

The "Compromise of 1877" involved several commitments, not all of them honored, for northern investment in the South. Also not honored was a vague agreement on the part of some conservative southerners to build a "lily-white" Republican party in the South based on economic and social views that they shared with northern conservatives.

As to the disputed election, Hayes would be permitted to move into the White House without resistance by either northern or southern Democrats. In return, he would withdraw the last troops from South

Carolina, Florida, and Louisiana, thus allowing the Democratic party in these states to oust the Republicans and destroy the political power of the blacks.

Despite the proclamations before Inauguration Day that Democrats would fight if Tilden were not elected, there was no trouble. This was not because the men who hammered out the Compromise of 1877 were so very powerful. It merely reflected the growing disinterest of Americans in the issues of the Civil War and Reconstruction and their increasing preoccupation with the fabulous economic growth of the country. The southern blacks, of course, were the casualties of this watershed year, but since the price they paid was suppression, few whites heard their complaints and fewer were interested.

For Further Reading

James McPherson, *Ordeal by Fire: The Civil War and Reconstruction* (1982) is the best recent account of Reconstruction. See William A. Dunning, *Reconstruction: Political and Economic* (1907) for the old, harshly critical view of the era's policies that dominated American historical thinking for half a century, and for a rejoinder, W. E. B. DuBois, *Black Reconstruction* (1935). John Hope Franklin, *Reconstruction After the Civil War* (1961) provides a briefer objective account, as does Herman Belz, *Reconstructing the Union* (1969). A splendid account of the reaction of blacks to freedom is Leon F. Liwack, *Been in the Storm So Long* (1979).

Valuable studies of special topics include Richard N. Current, *Three Carpetbag Governors* (1967); Stanley Kutler, *Judicial Power and Reconstruction Politics* (1968); Eric McKitrick, *Andrew Johnson and Reconstruction* (1960); Robert C. Morris, *Reading, 'Riting, and Reconstruction: The Education of Freedmen in the South, 1861–1870* (1981); Willie Lee Rose, *Rehearsal for Reconstruction* (1964); Hans A. Trefousse, *The Radical Republicans* (1969); A. W. Trelease, *KKK: The Ku Klux Klan Conspiracy and Southern Reconstruction* (1971); and C. Vann Woodward, *Reunion and Reaction: The Compromise of 1877 and the End of Reconstruction* (1951).

The presidents of the late nineteenth century were not an inspiring lot. Their portraits arranged side by side—Grant, Hayes, Garfield, Arthur, Cleveland, Harrison, Cleveland again—they resemble nothing so much as a line of mourners at a midwestern funeral. They were conscious of their dignity, to be sure, and grandly bewhiskered. They were competent to perform executive duties (except perhaps for Grant), devoted family men, sober-sided and drab (except for Chester A. Arthur), and unexciting across the board.

Their lack of charisma is one reason why twentieth-century Americans find them so uninteresting. In our age of instantaneous electronic media, it is the personable performer

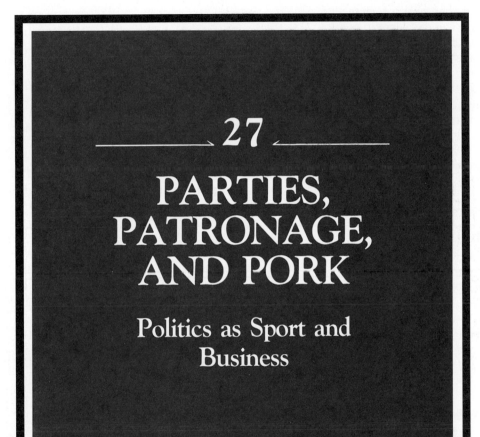

27

PARTIES, PATRONAGE, AND PORK

Politics as Sport and Business

This political cartoon of the 1880s shows Uncle Sam weighing the Democratic and Republican parties represented as roosters. Because they balanced, a few votes could, and did, win an election for either party.

who has the edge in winning elections. Moreover, twentieth-century Americans have gotten used to vigorous chief executives who seize the initiative in domestic and foreign matters alike, while, from Grant through William McKinley, whose election in 1896 ended a political era, just about everyone, including presidents, believed Congress should take the lead. The president was to execute laws, steer the government, and, when necessary, apply a constitutional brake.

Finally, there is no doubt that what was most vital in late nineteenth-century America lay not in politics but in the fabulous growth of American industry, the creation of big business, and the development of the great "Wild West" so central to American popular culture. The historian might easily be tempted to rush through the whole subject of politics with a few words—except for two striking facts.

First, politics was itself a business in the late nineteenth century, from White House down to city hall. Politics reflected the nation's preoccupation with getting ahead, with developing and organizing for material gain. Second, Americans loved the political game. In no other period of American history did a higher percentage of eligible voters actually exercise their right to vote. Despite the fact that their isolation made it difficult for many rural voters to get to the polls in wintry Novembers, and the fact that many blacks' constitutional right to vote was nullified in practice by fear of economic or violent reprisals, fully 80 percent of those who were eligible to vote in the 1870s, 1880s, and 1890s did vote. In the late twentieth century, by comparison, fewer than half the eligible voters turn out at a typical election.

HOW THE SYSTEM WORKED

Presidential elections brought out the most voters of all. In part this was because, nationally, the two major parties were so evenly matched. A man (and in a few states after 1890, a woman) found plenty of evidence that one vote really could make a difference. Between 1872, when Grant won reelection by a smashing 750,000 votes, and 1896, when William McKinley ushered in an era of Republican dominance with an 850,000 vote plurality, two presidential elections (1880 and 1884) were decided by fewer than 40,000 votes in a total of 9 to 10 million. In two elections (1876 and 1888), the winning candidates had fewer popular votes than the losers: the winners collected their prize in the electoral college.

In 1892, the victorious Democrat, Grover Cleveland, scored a respectable popular majority. Even then his share of the vote cast was well under half of the total, 46.1 percent. In fact, the only presidential candidate of either party between 1872 and 1896 to win a majority of the popular vote was Samuel J. Tilden, who lost the "Stolen Election" of 1876. (Tilden won a larger share of the popular vote than any Democratic presidential candidate between 1832 and 1932!)

Solid South and Republican Respectability

The parties were not so well balanced by region nor among distinct social groups. With the exception of Connecticut, which was evenly divided, New England dependably voted heavily Republican. In the section where Federalism, Whiggery, and abolitionism had been strongest, distaste for the party of Jefferson, Jackson, and the old slaveowners prevented Democrats from winning more than occasional elections.

The upper and middle classes of the Northeast and Midwest were generally Republican. They thought of the GOP, or the "Grand Old Party," as a bastion of morality and respectability, another legacy of the Whigs to the Republican party. Ironically, most big cities, run by cynical if not corrupt political machines, also voted Republican. (The most important exception was Democratic New York.) Finally, those blacks who retained the right to vote were staunch Republicans. Although they got scant attention from the GOP after 1877, it was still the party of Lincoln and emancipation.

The Democrats built their national vote upon the foundation of the "Solid South." Blacks and the white people of Appalachia who had opposed secession formed large Republican minorities in Virginia, North Carolina, and Tennessee. But not a single former slave state, Union or Confederate, including West Virginia, voted Republican in a presidential election during the late nineteenth century. The Democrats also invariably won New York City by appealing to immigrants, and they commanded a majority of immigrant and white ethnic votes elsewhere.

Swing States

As a result of these steady voting patterns, the outcome of national elections turned on the vote in a handful of "swing" states, particularly Illinois, Indiana, Ohio, and New York. In each of these states, with their large blocs of electoral votes, hard-core Republicans and Democrats were about equal in number; the decision was thus in the hands of independents who might swing either way depending on local issues, party organization, the personalities of the candidates,

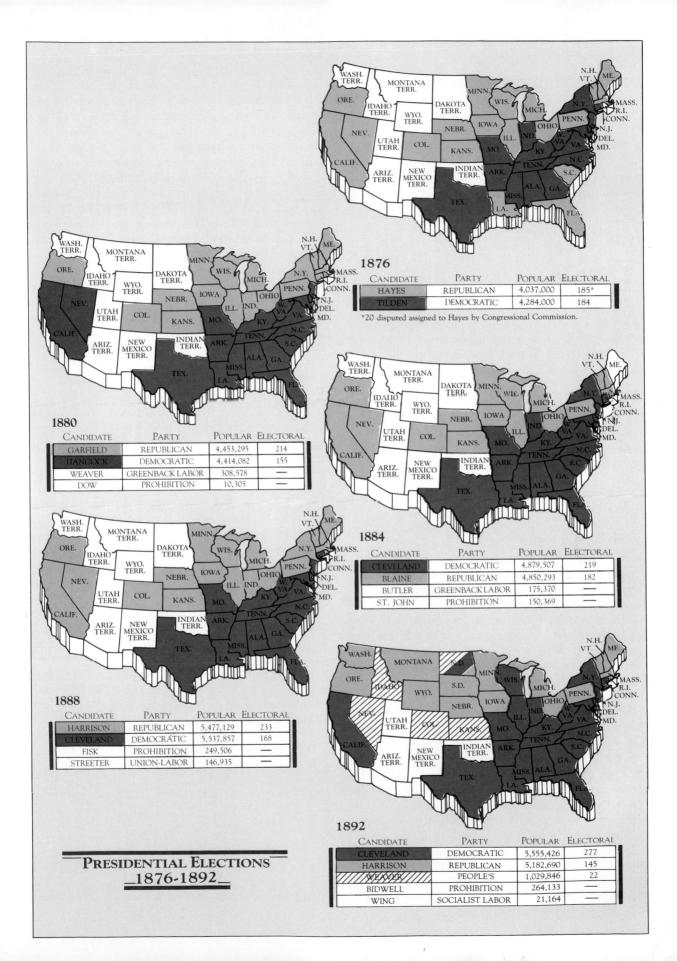

1876

CANDIDATE	PARTY	POPULAR	ELECTORAL
HAYES	REPUBLICAN	4,037,000	185*
TILDEN	DEMOCRATIC	4,284,000	184

*20 disputed assigned to Hayes by Congressional Commission.

1880

CANDIDATE	PARTY	POPULAR	ELECTORAL
GARFIELD	REPUBLICAN	4,453,295	214
HANCOCK	DEMOCRATIC	4,414,082	155
WEAVER	GREENBACK LABOR	308,578	—
DOW	PROHIBITION	10,305	—

1884

CANDIDATE	PARTY	POPULAR	ELECTORAL
CLEVELAND	DEMOCRATIC	4,879,507	219
BLAINE	REPUBLICAN	4,850,293	182
BUTLER	GREENBACK LABOR	175,370	—
ST. JOHN	PROHIBITION	150,369	—

1888

CANDIDATE	PARTY	POPULAR	ELECTORAL
HARRISON	REPUBLICAN	5,477,129	233
CLEVELAND	DEMOCRATIC	5,537,857	168
FISK	PROHIBITION	249,506	—
STREETER	UNION-LABOR	146,935	—

1892

CANDIDATE	PARTY	POPULAR	ELECTORAL
CLEVELAND	DEMOCRATIC	5,555,426	277
HARRISON	REPUBLICAN	5,182,690	145
WEAVER	PEOPLE'S	1,029,846	22
BIDWELL	PROHIBITION	264,133	—
WING	SOCIALIST LABOR	21,164	—

PRESIDENTIAL ELECTIONS 1876-1892

THE ONLY WAY

A. Oakey Hall, mayor of New York under the Tweed Ring, explained why a machine was necessary: "This population is too hopelessly split up into races and factions to govern it under universal suffrage, except by the bribery of patronage, or corruption."

or a passing whim. Several presidential elections during the period were decided in New York state, where the result depended on how big a majority the New York City Democrats could gather in order to counterbalance the Republican edge upstate.

Party leaders believed that the personal popularity of a candidate in the swing states could make the difference. Consequently, a disproportionate number of late nineteenth-century presidential and vice-presidential nominees came from Indiana, Ohio, and New York.

In the elections held between 1876 and 1892, the major parties filled 20 presidential and vice-presidential slots. Eighteen of the 20 (or 90 percent) were filled by men from the four key states. Eight were from New York alone, and five more from Indiana. Neither party was particularly interested in finding "the best man" for the job. They wanted to win an election. To do so they had to carry the swing states.

Bosses at Conventions

National conventions, which met every four years, played a much more important role in party politics than they do today. The difference was communications. Today, political leaders from every part of the country can discuss affairs with any other by picking up the phone or by hopping on a plane. In the late nineteenth century, congressmen saw one another in Washington on a regular basis. However, governors and state and city political bosses, who were often the real powers in party politics, did not.

When they did gather at their quadrennial meetings, they wheeled and dealed, bargained and traded, made and broke political careers. There was no army of pushy television reporters around to shove a microphone in the midst of every group of politicians who gathered on the floor of the barn-like convention halls. Newspaper reporters could be kept away by strongarm bodyguards, often ex-boxers, when the discussion promised to be interesting.

Today, the primary system almost inevitably assures that a party's presidential candidate will be known long before the delegates answer the roll call at the conventions. In the late nineteenth century, nominations were more likely to be decided at the convention, perhaps on the floor, or just as likely by bosses in hotel corridors and suites over oysters, beefsteak, and free-flowing whiskey. Delegates, whose livelihood depended on party bosses, did as they were told.

In the Democratic party, the most important bosses were the head of New York's Tammany Hall, who reliably delivered that city's vote, and the Bourbon leaders of the Solid South. (They were named for their extreme conservatism, like that of the Bourbon kings of France—not after Kentucky's famous corn liquor, although most liked it well enough.) In the Republican party, men like Boss Matthew Quay of Pennsylvania and Boss Thomas C. Platt of New York traded the support of their delegations for the promise of a prestigious cabinet post or a healthy share of the lucrative government offices and contracts that a victorious party had at its disposal.

The Patronage

The spoils system had come a long way since the days of Andrew Jackson and William Marcy. The United States was a big country. There was a lot of patronage—government jobs for the party faithfuls—to go around: 50,000 in Grant's time, 250,000 by the end of the century. Some government jobs involved real work. There was a postmaster in every town and hundreds of postal employees in the cities. Indian agents administered the government's treaty obligations to the tribes. In some federal bureaucracies like the Customs Service, there was enough paperwork to bury thousands of clerks wearing green visors and plastic cuffs to protect their white shirts from smudges of ink and graphite.

Who got these jobs? For the most part, they were filled by supporters of the party in power. Political activists who worked to get the vote out were rewards with government employment. In return, in election years their party assessed them a modest percentage of their income to finance the campaign. The result was politics for its own sake. The party scratched the jobholder's back; the jobholder reciprocated.

ONE-PARTY POLITICS

When M. B. Gerry sentenced Alfred E. Packer to death for murdering and eating five companions during a blizzard in Colorado in 1873, he stated as the reason for his decision: "There were seven Democrats in Hinsdale County, but you, you voracious, man-eating son-of-a-bitch, you ate five of them."

Campaign songs and songbooks were popular in the late nineteenth century, when election campaigns were fought with slogans and sentiments.

Pork

Other party supporters were rewarded with contracts for government work in "pork-barrel" bills. At the end of each congressional session, congressional coalitions pieced together bills to finance government construction projects in each member's district—a new post office here, a government pier there, the dredging of a river channel somewhere else. The idea was not so much to get needed work done, but to reward businessmen who supported the proper party.

Thus, the River and Harbor Bill of August 1886 provided for an expenditure of $15 million to begin over 100 new projects, although 58 government projects that had been started two years before remained unfinished.

Of course, there was not a job or contract for every voter. In order to turn out the vast numbers they did, the parties exploited the emotional politics of memory, the very rational politics of pensions, and ballyhoo that would have horrified Washington, Adams, Jefferson, and even William Henry Harrison.

The Politics of Memory

If most Republicans forgot the blacks, they remembered the Civil War. GOP orators specialized in "waving the bloody shirt," reminding northern voters that

The higher ranking the party official, the more rewarding the job. Not only was corrupt income possible in some positions, but it was possible to grow modestly rich legally in government service. The post of Collector of Customs in large ports was particularly lucrative. In addition to a handsome salary, the collector was paid a share of all import duties on goods reclaimed from smugglers who had been caught at their work. This curious incentive system made for a remarkably uncorrupt Customs Service; there was more to be made in catching violators than in taking bribes from them.

Thus, Collector of the Port of New York Chester A. Arthur earned an average $40,000 a year between 1871 and 1874, and in one big case he shared a bounty of $135,000 with two other officials. He was the best paid government official in the country, earning more than even the president. And he was assessed a handsome sum for the privilege by the Republican party. On a rather more modest level, a handful of Southern blacks benefited from the patronage when the Republican party was in power. Some federal appointments in the South went to black people.

For Americans of the late nineteenth century, even the nursery was a fit place for presidential politics. This toy scale weighed the comparative merits of Democrat Grover Cleveland and Republican Benjamin Harrison.

Democrats had caused the Civil War. Lucius Fairchild, a Wisconsin politician who had lost an arm in battle, literally flailed the air with his empty sleeve during campaign speeches. With armless and legless veterans hobbling about every sizable town to remind voters of the bloodletting, it was an effective technique. Robert G. Ingersoll, perhaps the greatest Republican orator of the era, pulled no punches in using it:

Every man that lowered our flag was a Democrat. Every man that bred bloodhounds was a Democrat. Every preacher that said slavery was a divine institution was a Democrat. Recollect it! Every man that shot a Union soldier was a Democrat. Every wound borne by you Union soldiers is a souvenir of a Democrat.

The Civil War loomed over the period. Between 1868 and 1901, every president but the Democrat Grover Cleveland had been an officer in the Union Army. When Cleveland, believing that sectional bitterness was fading, issued an order to return captured Confederate battle flags to their states for display at museums and war monuments, an angry protest in the North forced him to back down and contributed to his failure to win reelection the next year.

The man who defeated Cleveland in 1888, Benjamin Harrison, was still waving the bloody shirt after 20 years and not apologizing for it. "I would a thousand times rather march under the bloody shirt, stained with the lifeblood of a Union soldier," Harrison told voters, "than march under the black flag of treason or the white flag of cowardly compromise." Dwelling on the past could not possibly be constructive, but it won elections, even for the Democrats in the South. They waved the Confederate Stars and Bars, reminding voters of the nobility of the lost cause and of the white supremacy that the Democratic Redeemers had salvaged from that cause and from the "Black Republicans."

Vote Yourself a Pension

In their pension policy, the Republicans converted the bloody shirt into dollars and cents. Soon after the war ended, Congress had provided for pensions to Union veterans who were disabled from wartime wounds and diseases. The law was strictly worded, excessively so. Many genuinely handicapped veterans did not qualify under its terms. Instead of changing the law, however, northern congressmen took to introducing special pension bills that provided monthly stipends for specifically named constituents who had persuaded them that their case was just.

By the 1880s, the procedure for awarding the special pension had become grossly abused. Congressmen took little interest in the truthfulness of the petitioner or the worthiness of his grievance. (One applicant for a pension had not served in the army because, he said, he had fallen off a horse on the way to enlist.) They simply introduced every bill that any constituent requested. When almost all Republicans and many northern Democrats had a few special pension bills in the hopper, the bills were rushed through collectively by voice vote. Instead of declining as old veterans died, the cost of the pension program actually climbed to $56 million in 1885 and $80 million in 1888. Pensions made up one of the largest line items in the federal budget, and a veterans' lobby, the Grand Army of the Republic (GAR), came to serve effectively as a Republican political action committee.

The GAR

In 1888, Congress passed a new general pension bill that granted an income to every veteran who had served at least 90 days in the wartime army and was disabled for any reason whatsoever. An old soldier who fell off a stepladder in 1888 was eligible under its terms.

President Cleveland vetoed the law and was sustained. The Republicans ran against him that year with the slogan "Vote Yourself a Pension" and won the election. The next year, the new president, Benjamin Harrison, signed an even more generous Dependent Pensions Act and appointed the head of the GAR, James "Corporal" Tanner, to distribute the loot. "God help the surplus," Tanner said, referring to the money in the U.S. Treasury. He meant it. By the end of Harrison's term, Tanner had increased the annual expenditure on pensions to $160 million. Local wits took wry notice of young women who married doddering old Billy Yanks who had a gleam in their eyes and a check in the mail.

Northern Democrats posed as the party of principle in the controversies over the bloody shirt and pen-

In 1902, forty years after Antietam and Shiloh, members of the Grand Army of the Republic were still a staple of Memorial Day parades. They were almost always Republican voters.

sions. In the South, however, Democrats played the Civil War game in reverse. State governments provided benefits for Confederate veterans.

PRESIDENTS AND PERSONALITIES

As a legacy of the Grant scandals, a presidential candidate's reputation for honesty was a popular campaign cry. In 1876, the Republicans turned to Rutherford B. Hayes, and the Democrats to Samuel J. Tilden—in part because, as governors of Ohio and New York respectively, they had never stolen a cent. When Hayes's supporters stole the election of 1876, the Democrats delighted in calling him "His Fraudulency" or "Rutherfraud" B. Hayes.

Hayes, Integrity, and Oblivion

In truth, Hayes was an honest man, amiable and obliging within the law. A Civil War hero who was twice seriously wounded, he was the first president who traveled for pleasure rather than on military or diplomatic missions. Perhaps most interesting about Hayes, who

Looking like anything but "His Fraudulency," Rutherford B. Hayes was in fact a politician of scrupulous honesty.

was president during a severe depression and widespread violence between workers and employers, he had serious reservations about the desirability of the capitalist system. His wife had very serious reservations about alcoholic beverages. She would not serve them at the White House, earning the by-no-means affectionate nickname, "Lemonade Lucy."

As president, Hayes pleased virtually no one but Lucy. Old Radical Republicans were angered by his abandonment of southern blacks (to which he was bound by the Compromise of 1877). Both the Republican party's two major factions, the "Stalwarts" (Grant supporters) and the "Half-Breeds" (critics of Grant) believed that Hayes allotted them less patronage than they deserved. There never was a question of renominating him; even Hayes yearned to hit the tourist road. Long before his term ended, two prominent Republicans announced their intention of succeeding him. One was James G. Blaine of Maine, leader of the Half-Breeds. The other was Ulysses S. Grant, out of office four years, just back from his own world tour, and nearly bankrupt. He needed the salary; he resented the fact that in becoming president earlier

ORDINARY PEOPLE

Presidents were not so remote and sheltered from the people in the late nineteenth century, as Garfield's assassination shows. When he was shot, the president of the United States was waiting for a train on a public platform.

An incident that involved Rutherford B. Hayes after he left the White House illustrates the point more amusingly. While attending a GAR encampment, Hayes was stopped by a policeman, who brusquely pulled him back to a pathway, and gave him a finger-shaking lesson because he was walking on the grass. Likewise, President Grant, who never lost his love for fast horses, was written a ticket by a Washington officer for speeding.

he had been obligated to give up his lifetime pay as a general. And the leader of the Stalwarts, an old Radical who despised Blaine, Roscoe Conkling of New York, persuaded Grant that it was his duty to run.

Garfield: A Dark Horse

Neither Blaine nor Grant was able to win a majority of the delegates to the Republican convention. They were frustrated by the ambitions of several "favorite son" candidates, men who came to Chicago backed only by their own states. The hope of "favorite sons" is that there will be a deadlock between the front runners, which would force the tired delegates to turn to them as compromise candidates.

Finally, after 34 ballots, the Blaine men recognized that the cause of their hero was lost. Instead of turning to one of the favorite sons whom they held responsible for their disappointment, they switched their votes to a man whose name was not even in nomination, James A. Garfield of Ohio. On the thirty-sixth ballot, he became the Republican candidate.

SPIKED ORANGES

Lucy Hayes allowed no alcoholic beverages in the White House—or so she thought. According to Washington newspapermen, a bibulous lot, they bribed White House servants to serve them punch and oranges spiked with rum—or so they thought. After he left the presidency, Hayes insisted that the joke was on the drinkers. He said that he and his wife knew of the journalists' plan and had their servants spike the drinks and fruit with a nonalcoholic beverage that tasted like rum.

James Garfield had served as president for only four months when he was shot and incapacitated.

Garfield tried to placate both wings of the party. But when he handed the choicest plum of all, the post of Collector of Customs of the port of New York, to a Blaine man, Roscoe Conkling openly broke with the president. He and his protégé in the state Republican machine, Thomas Platt, resigned their seats in the Senate. Their intention was to remind Garfield of their power in the New York Republican party by having the state legislature reelect them.

By the summer of 1881, it appeared that Conkling and Platt had lost their battle. The Garfield—Blaine Half-Breeds had succeeded in blocking their reelection. But the issue was finally resolved by two gunshots in a Washington, D.C., train station. On July 2, 1881, Charles Guiteau, a ne'er-do-well preacher and bill collector who had worked for the Stalwarts but had not been rewarded with a government job, walked up to Garfield as he was about to depart on a holiday and shot him twice in the small of the back. After living in excruciating pain for eleven weeks, the second president to be murdered died on September 19.

"I am a Stalwart! Arthur is president!" Guiteau shouted when he fired the fatal shots. He meant that the new president was none other than Conkling's longtime ally, Vice President Chester A. Arthur. The deranged Guiteau expected Arthur to free him from prison and reward him for his patriotic act.

Once in office, however, Chet Arthur, recently the "prince of spoilsmen," proved to be an able and uncorrupt president who signed the first law to limit a party's use of government jobs for political purposes.

Garfield was a Half-Breed, a Blaine supporter, but he played on Roscoe Conkling's bottomless vanity by traveling to New York to seek the boss's blessing and to promise him a share of the patronage. Garfield went to the polls with a united party behind him.

The Democrats, having failed to win with an antiwar Democrat in 1868 (Seymour), a Republican maverick in 1872 (Greeley), and a reformer in 1876 (Tilden), tried their luck with their own Civil War general, Winfield Scott Hancock. An attractive if uninspiring man, he made the election extremely close. Garfield drew only 10,000 more votes than Hancock, just 48.3 percent of the total.

Another President Is Murdered

Garfield was a much more intelligent and substantial man than his opportunistic career would indicate. Whether or not he would have blossomed as president cannot be known for he spent his four short months as an active chief executive sorting out the claims of Republican party workers to government jobs. At one point he exclaimed in disgust to Blaine, his secretary of state who wanted very badly to be president, that he could not understand why anyone pursued the post, considering all its trivial, tawdry concerns.

How They Spoke, How They Listened

George Washington was no orator. Other delegates to both the Continental Congress and the Constitutional Convention are almost apologetic in their strident assertions that his contributions lay in other realms. Contemporaries compared him to Cincinattus. No one ever mentioned Cicero.

John Adams was a passionate courtroom lawyer, but his platform manner was fussy and irritable.

Thomas Jefferson's conversation sparkled like his prose. However, Jefferson suffered from a lisp and was painfully sensitive to his impediment. He hated to speak before a crowd. He mumbled his famous first inaugural address so incoherently that many people in the small chamber understood nothing until they had a chance to read it in print.

James Madison cut an even weaker figure on a podium. Small in stature, crinkled of face by the time he became president in 1809, Madison was also a hypochondriac, constantly complaining of aches, pains, and imminent collapse.

He did not have to beg off speaking to Congress. Washington had set the precedent of delivering presidential messages in writing. Not until 1913, when Woodrow Wilson, confident of his presence after a lifetime in the lecture-hall, strode into the Capital, would a president actually address a "State of the Union" speech to Congress.

The fact is, mastery of oratory was not the road to the White House. The two finest orators of the antebellum period, Henry Clay and Daniel Webster—both Whigs—never became president. Inferior, long-winded speeches delivered out of doors in extreme weather killed the two Whigs who did, William Henry Harrison and Zachary Taylor. (Harrison's was a suicide; he gave the longest and perhaps the most pompous inaugural address in presidential history during a frigid March storm; he died of pneumonia a month later.)

If Americans did not demand a silver tongue in their chief executives, the paintings of George Caleb Bingham, the perennial success of histrionic revivalist preachers, Ralph Waldo Emerson's long and lucrative career as a lecturer, and the inscription of "Rhetoric" and "Declamation" in every college curriculum remind us that Americans did love to hear others hold forth in public.

In the late nineteenth century they liked their political oratory "spread-eagle." Memorial Day, Confederate Day, the Fourth of July—all were occasions in city and country alike of long, gymnastic disquisitions on American heroism, sacrifice, and greatness.

The orator who did not run on for hours was not doing his job. (Lincoln's Gettysburg Address was faulted for its brevity.) The orator who did not work up a sweat flailing the air, shaking his fist, and beating his breast was a cold fish. (Armless Republican Lucius P. Fairchild had a technique by which he could release the empty sleeve of his coat—he had lost an arm in the Civil War—at climactic moments in damning Democrats; socialist Eugene V. Debs would fall to his knees in his revolutionary maledictions.) The orator who did not lace his speeches with allusions from the Bible, the classics, modern literature, the Declaration of Independence, was accounted superficial.

Americans of the late nineteenth century also wanted to be told, over and over, the stories of Concord Bridge, Cowpens, New Orleans, Vicksburg, Grant Before Richmond. They would even sit still to hear a politician explain—perhaps slyly, perhaps without shame—why his own august behind would honor the chair of Washington, Jefferson, Jackson, Lincoln.

And yet, with the possible exception of Benjamin Harrison, none of the presidents of the late nineteenth century were very good at pleading for themselves or some other grand old cause. In 1896, when the Republicans were faced with an opponent who could mesmerize an audience, William Jennings Bryan, party leader Mark Hanna instructed his candidate, William McKinley, to stay at home in Canton, Ohio. The Republicans contrasted McKinley's dignity with the unseemly behavior of his rival, rushing about the country *chasing* the presidency.

Nevertheless, Mark Hanna also made sure that a corps of Republican tub-thumpers followed Bryan wherever he went! He understood American ambivalence in the matter of oratory. Americans loved a rip-roaring speech—but as entertainment; they wanted their presidents dignified. The lesson had been taught at the beginning of the era, in 1866, by President Andrew Johnson. Johnson was trained in the Tennessee hills school of oratory, as entertaining a method as there was. He returned heckler's vulgarity with vulgarity, insult with insult. "Giving 'em hell" had brought him a long way.

During a presidential speaking tour in 1866, however, when he fought a running battle with Radical Republican hecklers, his opponents shook their heads, sadly and loudly, at his lack of dignity. Some privately stated that Johnson's greatest asset as a politician, his mastery of bumptious stump-speaking, had as much to do with his destruction as a president as his policies.

The Verdict of the People, *detail of a painting by
George Caleb Bingham.*

Civil-Service Reform

The Pendleton Act of 1883 established the Civil Service Commission, a three-man bureau that was empowered to draw up and administer examinations that applicants for some low-level government jobs were required to pass before they were hired. Once in these civil-service jobs, employees could not be fired simply because the political party to which they belonged lost the presidency.

At first, only 10 percent of 131,000 government workers were protected by civil service. But the Pendleton Act also empowered the president to add job classifications to the civil-service list at his discretion. Ironically, because the presidency changed party hands every four years between 1880 and 1896, each incumbent's desire to protect his own appointees in their jobs—a violation of the spirit of civil-service reform—led by the end of the century to a fairly comprehensive civil-service system.

After the Democrat Grover Cleveland was elected in November 1884, but before he took office in March 1885, outgoing President Chester Arthur protected a number of Republican government employees by adding their jobs to the civil-service list. Cleveland did the same thing for Democratic government workers in 1888, Benjamin Harrison for Republicans in 1892, and Cleveland again for Democrats in 1896. By 1900, 40 percent of the federal government's 256,000 employees held civil-service positions. About 30 percent of government clerks were women, an unlikely proportion at a time when jobs were given out in order to win votes.

Another provision of the Pendleton Act was the abolition of the assessment system. That is, the parties were forbidden to insist that those of their members who held government positions "donate" a percentage of their salaries for political campaign chests each election year. Until the presidency of Benjamin Harrison (1889–93), the professional politicians were at a loss as to how to replace these revenues. Harrison's Postmaster General John Wanamaker came up with the solution. He levied "contributions" on big businessmen who had an interest, direct or ideological, in Republican victory at the polls. This method, with the Democrats finding their share of big business support, and later drawing from the treasuries of labor unions, remained the chief means of financing national political campaigns until the 1970s.

Honest Chet Arthur

Chester A. Arthur may have been president illegally. Enemies said he was not born in Fairfield, Vermont, as he claimed, but in a cabin a few miles north—in

Chester A. Arthur, Collector of the Port of New York from 1871 to 1878, and later, James A. Garfield's successor as president.

Canada. However that may have been, the urbane and elegant Arthur, resplendent in his furs and colorful waistcoats compared to the gray dour look of the Republicans around him, did a good job in the White House.

Arthur wanted a second term. He tried to mend fences with the Stalwarts by twice offering Roscoe Conkling (a superb lawyer) a seat on the Supreme Court. He tried to woo the Half-Breeds by deferring to Secretary of State James G. Blaine's judgment in foreign affairs. Blaine would have none of it and resigned from the cabinet. With Conkling's political career in eclipse, Blaine easily won the Republican nomination for the presidency, again at Chicago, in the summer of 1884.

1884: Blaine versus Cleveland

Blaine expected to win the election as well. As usual, New York state seemed to be the key to victory, and Blaine believed that he would run more strongly there than most Republicans. Some old Liberal Republicans, now known as Mugwumps (an Algonkian word for "big chief," a reference to their self-righteous pomposity), had deserted the party, announcing that the Democratic candidate, Grover Cleveland, was the more honest man.

Blaine expected to make up this defection and more by winning the Irish vote, which usually did not go Republican. He was popular in the Irish-American community because, in an era when Republican leaders frequently disdained the Catholic Church, Blaine had Catholic relatives. Moreover, for reasons of his own, Blaine liked to "twist the lion's tail," taunt the British, the ancestral enemy in many unsmiling Irish eyes. Finally, news broke that seemed a bonus: it was revealed that while he was a lawyer in Buffalo, Grover Cleveland had fathered an illegitimate child. The stringent sexual code of the period seemed to dictate that such a libertine should not be president.

Cleveland nimbly neutralized the morality issue by publicly admitting the folly of his youth and explaining that he had tried to make amends by financially sup-

Grover Cleveland was the only Democratic president of the late nineteenth century, elected in 1884 and 1892. He was defeated in 1888.

porting the child. Indeed, the Democrats turned the scandal to their advantage when they argued that if Cleveland had been indiscreet in private life, he had an exemplary record in public office, whereas Blaine, who was admirable as a husband and family man, had engaged in several dubious stock deals as a congressman from Maine. Put Cleveland into public office where he shined, they said, and return Blaine to the private life that he richly adorned.

How Little Things Decide Great Elections

Just a few days before the election, disaster struck the Blaine campaign. The confident candidate made the mistake of dining lavishly with a group of millionaires in Delmonico's, the most regal restaurant in New York City. It was not a good idea when he wanted the votes of poor men. Before another group, he ignored the statement of a Presbyterian minister, Samuel Burchard, who denounced the Democrats as the party of "rum, romanism, and rebellion," that is, of the saloon, the Roman Catholic Church, and southern secession.

This was pretty ordinary stuff in Republican oratory of the period, but Blaine was not fighting the campaign with an ordinary strategy. He was wooing Irish-American votes, and the Irish were sensitive about their Catholic religion. When Democratic newspapers plastered the insult "romanism" across their front pages, Blaine rushed to express his sincere distaste for this kind of bigotry and to explain that had he heard Burchard's words, he would have called him on them. But the damage was done. The Irish voters trundled back into the Democratic column and blizzards upstate snowed many Republican voters in. New York state and the presidency went to Grover Cleveland.

In 1888, four years later, Cleveland was undone in his bid for reelection by a similarly trivial incident. A Republican newspaperman, pretending to be an Englishman who was a naturalized American citizen, wrote to the British ambassador in Washington asking which of the two candidates, Cleveland or Benjamin Harrison of Indiana, would be the better president from the British point of view. Foolishly, the ambassador replied that Cleveland seemed to be better disposed toward British interests. The Republican press immediately labeled Cleveland the British candidate. Thousands of Irish Democrats in New York, who were reflexively hostile to anything or anyone the British favored, voted Republican and helped give that swing state to Harrison.

This sort of folderol, and the color and excitement of political rallies, seemed to make the difference in an era when the two parties were so evenly balanced. Unlike late twentieth-century Americans, who are flooded with entertainment from a dozen media and to whom elections are just one show among many, late nineteenth-century Americans enjoyed politics as a major diversion. They flocked to rallies in numbers almost unknown today in order to hear brass bands, swig lemonade or beer, and listen to speeches that were more show than statement of principle.

ISSUES

Principles and issues did play a part in late nineteenth-century politics. Within the Republican party, a shrinking minority of leaders tried to revive the party's commitment to protecting the welfare of southern blacks until as late as 1890. When President Grant tried to seize Santo Domingo in 1870, he was frustrated by the resistance of senators from his own party who were impelled by old antiexpansionist prejudices.

However, both episodes illustrate the fact that differences of principle and opinion were more likely to lie within the parties rather than to distinguish one from the other. The political party's business was to win power. Having cooperated in that effort, politicians lined up on issues with only casual or self-serving nods toward the organization to which they belonged.

Even the question of the tariff, the nearest thing to an issue that distinguished Republicans from Democrats, found members of both parties on each side. The level at which import duties were set could inspire orators to sweating, thumping, prancing paroxysms of holy passion. But their position on the issue, low tariff or high protective tariff, depended on the place their constituents occupied in the economy, not on the party to which they belonged, an abstract principle, or even social class.

The Tariff

With the exception of the growers of a few crops that needed protection from foreign producers—like Louisiana's sugar cane planters—farmers inclined to favor a low tariff. Corn, wheat, cotton, and livestock were so cheaply produced in the United States that American farmers were able to undersell local growers of the same crops in large parts of Europe and Asia—if other countries did not levy taxes on American crops in response to high American duties on the goods that those countries shipped to the United States. Moreover, low duties on imported manufactured goods meant lower prices on the commodities that consumers of manufactured goods, such as farmers, had to buy.

The interest of agriculturalists in keeping import duties down meant that the Democratic party, with its powerful southern agrarian contingent, was generally the low-tariff party. However, Republican congressmen representing rural areas also voted for lower rates.

While industrialists, who wanted to protect their factories from foreign competition, were generally Republican and set the high-tariff tone of that party, equally rich and powerful railroad owners and bankers often supported lower duties. Some remained contentedly within the Republican party in the company of other wealthy capitalists; others—the grand financier August Belmont, for example—were Democrats. As far as bankers like Belmont were concerned, the more goods being shunted about the country the better, no matter whether they were foreign or domestic in origin. Railroaders had an added incentive to support a low tariff. They were huge consumers of steel for rails, which was one of the commodities that received the most protection.

In the late nineteenth century, high-tariff interests had their way. After bobbing up and down from a low of 40 percent (by no means a "low" tariff) to a high of 47 percent, rates were increased to about 50 percent in the McKinley Tariff of 1890. That is, on the average, an imported item was slapped on average with a tax that was equivalent to half of its value.

When a depression followed quickly on the act, Grover Cleveland and the Democrats campaigned against the McKinley rates and won the election of 1892. But the tariff that Congress prepared, the Wilson-Gorman bill, lowered duties by only 10.1 percent—to a level of 39.1 percent of the value of imports. This rate was good enough for Cleveland's supporters in commerce and finance, but too high for the farmers who had voted for him. The president's rather wishy-washy way out of his quandary encapsulates the fact that tough issues were intra-party problems, not questions that divided the two parties. Cleveland did not sign the Wilson-Gorman bill; he did not veto it; he let it become law by ignoring it. When a party was sharply divided on an issue, the president had to play to both sides.

Money

The issue that would, in the 1890s, shatter the political equilibrium of the 1870s and 1880s was money. The question was: what should be the basis of the circulating currency in America's rapidly expanding economy? Should it be gold and paper money redeemable in that metal from the bank that issued the note? Or should the supply of money be monitored and regulated by the government in such a way as to adjust to changing economic needs?

The controversy had its roots in the Civil War. In 1862, in order to help finance the war effort, the Union government authorized the printing of about

$450 million in paper money that was not redeemable in gold. The greenbacks, so called because they were printed in green ink instead of gold on the obverse, were accepted at face value by the federal government. That is, their value in payment of taxes or other obligations was established in the law.

As long as the war went badly and the government's word was of dubious value, individuals involved in private transactions insisted on discounting the greenbacks, redeeming them in gold at something less than face value. Even after the war was won, bankers remained suspicious of any paper money that was not redeemable in gold. The secretaries of the Treasury, who shared the conservative views of the bankers, determined to retire the greenbacks. When the notes flowed into the Treasury in payment of taxes, they were destroyed and were not replaced by new bills.

The result was deflation: a decline in the amount of money in circulation and, therefore, an increase in the value of gold and of paper money that was redeemable in gold. Prices dipped; so did wages. It took less to buy a sack of flour or a side of bacon than it had when the greenbacks had flowed in profusion. That meant that the farmer who grew the wheat and slopped the hogs received less for his efforts.

Farmers, who were usually in debt, were hit hardest by deflation. They had borrowed heavily to increase their acreage and to purchase machinery when the greenbacks had been abundant and prices therefore high. After the Treasury began to retire the greenbacks, the farmers found themselves obligated to repay these loans in money that was more valuable and more difficult to get. For example, a $1,000 mortgage taken out on a farm during the 1860s represented 1,200 bushels of grain. By the 1880s, when a farmer might still be paying off his debt, $1,000 represented 2,300 bushels.

The Greenback Labor Party

Protesting the retirement of the greenbacks as a policy that enriched banker-creditors at the expense of producer-debtors, farmers formed the Greenback Labor party in 1876. In an effort to convince industrial wageworkers that their interests also lay in an abundant money supply, the party chose as its presidential candidate Peter Cooper, New York philanthropist and an exemplary, popular employer.

Cooper made a poor showing, but in the congressional race of 1878, the Greenbackers elected a dozen congressmen, and some Republicans and Democrats rushed to back their inflationary policy. However, President Hayes's monetary policy was as conservative as Grant's had been, and in 1879, retirement of the greenbacks proceeded apace. In 1880, the Greenback Labor ticket, led by a Civil War general from Iowa, James B. Weaver, won 309,000 votes, denying Garfield a popular majority but, once again, failing to affect policy.

In 1884, Benjamin J. Butler led the Greenbackers one more time, but received only one-third of the votes that Weaver had won in 1880. The demand to inflate the currency was not dead. Indeed, within a decade the structure of American politics was turned upside down and inside out because of it. But the greenbacks were gone. Just as, after all the fuss and fury had died down, industrialists had their way on the tariff, banking interests got the money policy they wanted. When political parties are not built around principles and issues, the best organized interest groups within the parties usually prevail.

POLITICS IN THE CITY

By 1896, silver had replaced the greenbacks as the talisman of those Americans who wanted to inflate the nation's money supply. Both the Republican and Democratic parties were shaken by a fierce debate in which gold and silver became sacred symbols. The political atmosphere was religious, evangelical, even fanatical. "Gold bugs" and "free silverites" both believed they were engaged in a holy war against the other in which there could be no compromise, no quarter. The political equilibrium of the 1870s and 1880s were shattered, not to mention the minor role issues had played in distinguishing the parties.

The Democratic party convention of 1896 was the most tumultuous since the party of Jefferson and Jackson destroyed itself at Charleston in 1860. Richard Croker, the leader of New York City's Democrats, was bewildered by the fury in which the members of his party were running about, arguing, shaking their fists. He listened to an agitated gold versus silver debate and impatiently shook his head. He could not understand what the fuss was about. As far as he was concerned, gold and silver were both money, and he was all for both kinds.

CITIZENSHIP

The New York machine naturalized newly arrived immigrants almost as soon as they stepped off the boat. The record day was October 14, 1868, when a Tweed judge swore in 2,109 new citizens, 3 a minute. One James Goff attested to the "good moral character" of 669 applicants. Two days later, Goff was arrested for having stolen a gold watch and two diamond rings.

The Political Machine

Urban politics in the late nineteenth century resembled national politics in some ways. Issues were of secondary importance. What counted first was winning elections. The big city political party existed, like a business, for the benefit of those who "owned" it. The technique of election victory, therefore, was the profession of the political leader. His skill and willingness to work for "the company," and his productivity in delivering votes, determined how high he rose in an organization as finely tuned as any corporation.

The chairman of the board of the urban political company was "the boss." He was by no means necessarily the mayor, who was often a respectable " front man." The boss coordinated the complex activities of the machine. Voters had to be aroused by the same sort of emotional appeals and hoopla that sustained national political campaigns. The machine was expected to provide small material incentives to more demanding citizens comparable to the GOP's pensions program. The party activists (the company's "employees"), who worked to get the voters out to the polls and kept them happy between elections, were "paid" with patronage and pork courtesy of the city treasury. Control of the municipal treasury was the purpose of politics, not the service of principles or the implementation of a program for the public good.

"You are always working for your pocket, are you not?" an investigator into government corruption asked Richard Croker, thinking to embarrass him. Croker snapped back, "All the time, the same as you." On another occasion, he told the writer Lincoln Steffens, "Politics is business, and reporting—journalism, doctoring—all professions, arts, sports—everything is business." Candor as blunt as the prow of a ferryboat

was one quality that distinguished municipal politicians from national politicians in the late nineteenth century. Another was that the control of cities that many political machines exercised was so nearly absolute that profiteering in government sometimes took the form of blatant thievery.

The Profit Column

The political machine in power controlled law enforcement. In return for regular cash payments, politicians winked at the operations of illegal businesses: unlicensed saloons, gambling houses, opium dens, brothels, even strong-arm gangs. "Bathhouse" John Coughlan and "Hinkey-Dink" Kenna, Chicago's "Gray Wolves," openly collected tribute from the kings and queens of Chicago vice at an annual ball.

The political machine in power peddled influence to anyone willing to make a purchase. Although he was no lawyer, William Marcy Tweed of New York, the first of the great city bosses, was on Cornelius Vanderbilt's payroll as a "legal adviser." What the Commodore was hiring was the rulings of judges who belonged to Tweed's organization. In San Francisco after the turn of the century, Boss Abe Ruef would hold office hours on designated nights at an elegant French restaurant; purchasers of influence filed in between appetizer and entrée, entrée and roast, and made their bargains.

Kickbacks and Sandbagging

The rapid growth of cities in the late nineteenth century provided rich opportunities for kickbacks on contracts awarded by city governments. In New York, Central Park was a gold mine of padded contracts. The most notorious swindle of all was the New York County Courthouse, a $600,000 building that cost taxpayers $13 million to erect. Plasterers, carpenters, plumbers, and others who worked on the building had standing orders to bill the city two and three and more times what they actually needed to make a reasonable profit and kick back half the padding to Tammany Hall, the "men's club" that controlled the Democratic party in New York. For example, 40 chairs and 3 tables cost the city $179,000. The most intriguing item was "Brooms, etc.," which cost $41,190.95.

Then it was possible to do business directly with the city at exorbitant prices. Boss Tweed was part owner of the stationery and printing companies that supplied and serviced the New York City government at ridiculous prices—$5 for each bottle of ink, for example.

Another technique for getting rich in public office was called "sandbagging." It worked particularly well in dealing with traction companies, the streetcar lines that needed city permission to lay tracks on public streets. It goes without saying that paying bribes was necessary to get such contracts in machine-run cities. Moreover, the most corrupt aldermen, such as Coughlan and Kenna in Chicago, would grant a line the rights to lay tracks on only a few blocks at a time; thus the Chicago "Traction King," Charles T. Yerkes, would be back for a further franchise at an additional cost.

Another variety of sandbagging involved threatening an existing trolley line with competition on a nearby parallel street. Rather than have their traffic decline by half, traction companies coughed up the money to prevent new construction.

It was not necessary to break the law in order to profit from public office. A well-established member of a political machine could expect to be on the city payroll for jobs that did not really exist. In one district of New York City where there were four water pumps for fighting fires, the city paid the salaries of 20 pump

inspectors. Probably, none of them ever looked at the pumps. Their purpose was to keep the political machine in power at taxpayer expense.

Even holding several meaningless city jobs simultaneously was possible. Cornelius Corson, who kept his ward safe for the New York Democratic party from an office in his saloon, was on the books as a court clerk at $10,000 a year, as chief of the Board of Elections at $5,000 a year, and as an employee of four other municipal agencies at $2,500 a year per job. Another ward boss, Michael Norton, held city jobs that paid him $50,000 a year.

This was a munificent income in the late nineteenth century, but the bosses at the top of the machine did much better. Altogether, the Tweed Ring, which controlled New York City for only a few years after the Civil War, looted the city treasury of as much as $200 million. (Nobody really knew for sure.) Tweed went to jail, but his chief henchman, Controller "Slippery" Dick Connolly, fled abroad with several million. Richard Croker, head of Tammany Hall at the end of the century, retired to Ireland a millionaire. Timothy "Big Tim" Sullivan also rose from extreme poverty to riches as well as adulation; when he died as the result of a streetcar accident, 25,000 people attended his funeral.

Staying in Business

Big Tim's sendoff illustrates that despite their generally obvious profiteering, machine politicians stayed in office. Although few of them were above stuffing ballot boxes or marching gangs of "repeaters" from one polling place to the next, they won most elections fairly; the majority of city voters freely chose them over candidates who pledged to govern honestly.

The machines acted as very personalized social services among a hard-pressed people. During the bitter winter of 1870, Boss Tweed spent $50,000 on coal that was dumped by the dozens of tons at street corners in the poorest parts of the city. Tim Sullivan gave away 5,000 turkeys every Christmas. It was the duty of every block captain to report when someone died, was born, was making a First Holy Communion in the Catholic Church, or was celebrating a Bar Mitzvah in the Jewish synagogue. The sensible ward boss had a gift delivered.

Ward bosses brought light into dismal lives by throwing parties. In 1871, Mike Norton treated his constituents to 100 kegs of beer, 50 cases of champagne, 20 gallons of brandy, 10 gallons of gin, 200 gallons of chowder, 50 gallons of turtle soup, 36 hams, 4,000 pounds of corned beef, and 5,000 cigars.

Ward bosses fixed up minor (and sometimes major) scrapes with the law. In control of the municipal government, the machines had jobs at their disposal, not

Boss Richard Croker of New York's Tammany Hall made enough money in politics to own thoroughbred Irish racehorses. Here he poses with his trainer.

Everyone blames everyone else for the looting of New York City's treasury. William Marcy "Boss" Tweed is at left. Notice the Irish stereotypes at right.

only the phoney high-paying sinecures that the bosses carved up among themselves, but jobs that required real work and that unemployed men and women were grateful to have. Boss James McManes of Philadelphia had more than 5,000 positions at his disposal; the New York machine controlled four times that number. When the votes of these people were added to those of their grateful relatives and friends, the machine had a very nice political base with which to fight an election.

The Failure of the Goo-Goos

Not everyone brimmed with gratitude. The property-owning middle classes, which paid the bills with their taxes, periodically raised campaigns for Good Government—the bosses called them "Goo-Goos"—and sometimes won elections. The Tweed Ring's fall led to the election of a reform organization, and in 1894, even the powerful Richard Croker was displaced. Chicago's "Gray Wolves" were thrown out of city hall, and a major wave of indignation swept Abe Ruef and

Mayor Eugene Schmitz out of power in San Francisco in 1906. But until the turn of the century, reform governments were generally short lived. The machines came back.

One political weakness of the Goo-Goos was that they did not offer an alternative to the informal social services that the machine provided. They believed instead that honest government was synonymous with very inexpensive government. Faced with their great material problems and inclined from their European backgrounds to think of government as an institution that one used or was used by, the immigrants preferred the machines.

Indeed, Goo-Goos often combined their attacks on political corruption with attacks on the new ethnic groups, not a ploy that was calculated to win many friends among recent immigrants. In the persons of the successful machine politicians, however, the ethnics could take a vicarious pleasure in seeing at least some Irishmen, Jews, Italians, Poles, or blacks making good in an otherwise inhospitable society.

Erin Go Bragh

"The natural function of the Irishman," said a wit of the period, "is to administer the affairs of the American city." In fact, a few bosses had other lineages: Cox of Cincinnati and Crump of Memphis were WASPs; Tweed was of Scottish descent; Ruef was Jewish; and Schmitz was German. But a list of nineteenth-century machine politicians reads like a lineup of marchers in a St. Patrick's Day parade: Richard Connolly, "Honest" John Kelley, Richard Croker, George Plunkitt, Charles Murphy, and Tim Sullivan of New York; James McManes (unlike the others, a Republican) of Philadelphia; Christopher Magee and William Finn of Pittsburgh; Martin Lomasney of Boston.

The Irish were so successful in politics in part because they were the first of the large ethnic groups in the cities, and in part because they had been highly political in their homeland as a consequence of rule by Great Britain. Moreover, the Irish placed a high premium on eloquent oratory, which led naturally to politics, and, most important of all, the Irish spoke the English language, a headstart in the race to succeed over the other major immigrant groups of the late nineteenth century.

Ethnic Brokers

The primacy of the Irish did not mean that the New Immigrants were shut out of politics. On the contrary, the political machine lacked ethnic prejudice. If a ward became Italian and an Italian ward boss delivered the votes, he was welcomed into the organization and granted a share of the spoils commensurate with his contribution on election day. In many cities, while the police forces retained an Irish complexion, sanitation departments and fire departments often were highly Italian.

After the turn of the century, it became the unwritten law among New York Democrats that nominations for the three top elective offices in the city (mayor, president of the city council, and controller) be divided among New York's three largest ethnic groups—Irish, Italians, and Jews. Later, with the arrival of Puerto Ricans and of blacks from the South, certain public offices were assigned to their leaders—for example, president of the borough of Manhattan to a black and political leadership of the borough of the Bronx to a Puerto Rican. Other cities worked out similar arrangements.

For Further Reading

The best survey of politics during "the gilded age," the late nineteenth century, is H. Wayne Morgan, *From Hayes to McKinley: National Party Politics, 1877–1896* (1969). For a more jaundiced and once the traditional view, see Matthew Josephson, *The Politicos, 1865–1896* (1938). Also valuable are John A. Garraty, *The New Commonwealth, 1877–1890* (1968); Ray Ginger, *Age of Excess* (1965); Vincent P. DeSantis, *The Shaping of Modern America, 1877–1916* (1973); and Robert H. Wiebe, *The Search for Order* (1967).

On prominent politicians and individual administrations, see Harry Barnard, *Rutherford B. Hayes and His America* (1954); R. G. Caldwell, *Gentleman Boss: The Life of Chester A. Arthur* (1975); D. B. Chidsey, *The Gentleman from New York: A Life of Roscoe Conkling* (1935); Justus T. Doenecke, *The Presidencies of James A. Garfield and Chester A. Arthur* (1981); J. R. Hollingsworth, *The Whirligig of Politics: The Democracy of Cleveland and Bryan* (1963); David S. Muzzey, *James G. Blaine: A Political Idol of Other Days* (1934); Allan Nevins, *Grover Cleveland: A Study in Courage* (1932); Alan Peskin, *Garfield: A Biography* (1978); Harry J. Sievers, *Benjamin Harrison: Hoosier Statesman* (1959).

Concentrating on specific political issues and institutions are A. B. Callow, Jr., *The Tweed Ring* (1966); M. R. Dering, *Veterans in Politics: The Story of the G.A.R.* (1952); Ari Hoogenboom, *Outlawing the Spoils: A History of the Civil Service Reform Movement, 1865–1883* (1961); Morton Keller, *Affairs of State: Public Life in Late 19th Century America* (1977); Paul Kleppner, *The Third Electoral System, 1852–1892* (1979); J. Morgan Kousser, *The Shaping of Southern Politics* (1974); Seymour Mandelbaum, *Boss Tweed's New York* (1965); R. O. Marcus, *Grand Old Party: Political Structure in the Gilded Age, 1889–1896* (1971); Samuel T. McSeveney, *The Politics of Depression: Political Behavior in the Northeast, 1893–1896* (1972); Horace L. Merrill, *Bourbon Democracy of the Middle West* (1953); Walter T. K. Nugent, *Money and American Society, 1865–1880* (1968); D. J. Rothman, *Politics and Power: The United States Senate, 1869–1901* (1966); John G. Sproat, *The Best Men: Liberal Reformers in the Gilded Age* (1968); Tom E. Terrill, *The Tariff, Politics, and American Foreign Policy, 1874–1901* (1973).

In 1876, the American people celebrated their nation's centennial. It was a hundred years since the Founding Fathers had pledged their lives, their fortunes, and their sacred honor to the causes of liberty and independence. The birthday party, called the Centennial Exposition, was held in Philadelphia, where the Declaration of Independence had been signed, and it was a splendid success. Sprawling over the gentle hills of Fairmount Park, housed in more than 200 structures, the great show dazzled 10 million visitors with its displays of American history, ways of life, and products.

The emphasis was on the products and the processes for making them. The center of the fair was not the hallowed Declaration, but a building that covered 20

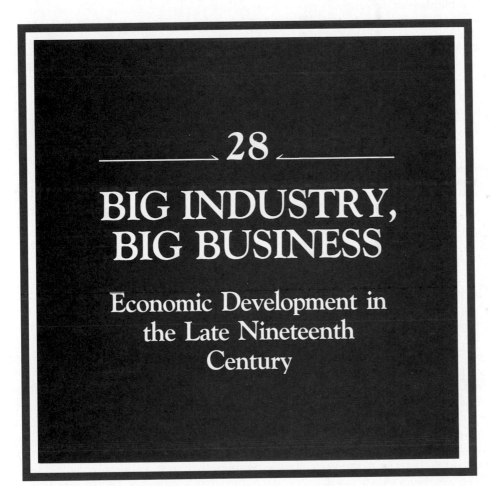

28

BIG INDUSTRY, BIG BUSINESS

Economic Development in the Late Nineteenth Century

Andrew Carnegie's steel plant at Homestead, Pennsylvania, was the largest in the world.

acres and housed the latest inventions and technological improvements: from typewriters and the telephone through new kinds of looms and lathes and a dizzying variety of agricultural machines.

Towering above all the pulleys and belts, five times the height of a man, and weighing 8,500 tons, was the largest steam engine ever built, the giant Corliss. Hissing, rumbling, chugging and gleaming in enamel, nickel plate, brass, and copper, the monster powered every other machine in the building. It was literally the heart of the exposition. It was to the giant Corliss that President Ulysses S. Grant came to open the fair. When he threw the switch that set Machinery Hall in motion, he wordlessly proclaimed that Americans were not just free and independent, but they were hitching their future to machines that made and moved things quickly, cheaply, and in astonishing quantities—industry!

A LAND MADE FOR INDUSTRY

Between 1865 and 1900, the population of the United States more than doubled from fewer than 36 million to 76 million people. The wealth of the American people grew even more rapidly than their numbers. At the end of the Civil War, the annual production of goods was valued at $2 billion. It increased more than six times in 35 years, to $13 billion in 1900.

Even in 1860, the United States had been the fourth largest industrial nation in the world with more than 100,000 factories capitalized at $1 billion. But before the Civil War there was no doubt that the United States was primarily a farmer's country. More than 70 percent of the population lived on farms or in small farm towns. In 1860, scarcely more than a million people worked in industrial jobs. Because many of them were women and children who did not vote, factory workers were an inconsequential force in politics.

By 1876, change was everywhere. Railroads were so central to the national economy that a strike by railway workers the next year shook the country to its foundations. By 1900, $10 billion was invested in U.S. factories, and 5 million people worked in industrial jobs. During the first years of the 1890's, the industrial production of the United States surpassed that of Great Britain to put the United States in first place in the world. Industrial workers were quickly becoming a social force with which to reckon.

The Corliss steam engine was the centerpiece of the Centennial Exposition of 1876. No larger steam engine was ever built.

An Embarrassment of Riches

Viewed from the late twentieth century, this success story seems to have been as predestined as John Winthrop's salvation. All the ingredients of industrial transformation were heaped upon the United States in an abundance that no other country has enjoyed.

In contrast to the plight of the people if the undeveloped countries today, Americans were rich in capital and able to welcome money from abroad without losing control of their own destinies. Once the Union victory in the Civil War assured foreign investors that the U.S. government was stable and friendly to commercial and industrial interests, the pounds, guilders, and francs poured in. By 1900, over $3.4 billion in foreign wealth fueled the U.S. economy. Thanks to investors from abroad, Americans had to divert only 11 to 14 percent of their national income into industrial growth, compared with 20 percent in Great Britain half a century earlier and in the Soviet Union some decades later. As a result, the experience of industrialization was far less painful in the New World than in the Old. Americans sacrificed less on behalf of the future than other industrial peoples.

The United States was also blessed in both the size and character of its labor force. The fecund and adaptable farm population provided a pool of literate and mechanically inclined people to fill the skilled jobs the new industry created. Unlike peasants of Asia and Europe who were attached to an ancestral plot of ground and often suspicious of unfamiliar ways, U.S. farmers had always been quick to move on at opportunity's call. In the late nineteenth century, not only did the opportunity of the new industry beckon seductively, but the labor-saving farm machinery that factories sent back to the farm made it possible for farm families actually to increase production of crops while their sons and daughters packed themselves off to the city.

During these same years, Europe's population underwent a spurt of growth with which the European economy could not keep pace. Cheap American food products undersold crops grown at home, helping to displace European peasants. They emigrated to the United States by the hundreds of thousands each year, filling low-paying, unskilled jobs. At every level

in the process of industrialization, the United States was provided a plenitude of clever hands and strong backs.

A Land of Plenty

No country has been so blessed with such varied and abundant natural resources as the United States: rich agricultural land producing cheap food; seemingly inexhaustible forests supplying lumber; deposits of gold, silver, semiprecious metals, and dross such as phosphates and gravel. Most important of all in the industrial age were huge stores of coal, iron, and petroleum.

The gray-green mountains of Pennsylvania, West Virginia, and Kentucky seemed to be made of coal, the indispensable fuel of the age of steam. In the Marquette range of Michigan was a mountain of iron ore 150 feet high. The Mesabi range of Minnesota, just west of the birdlike beak of Lake Superior, was opened in the 1890s to yield iron ore richer and in greater quantity than any other iron mining region in the world.

The United States had a huge, ready-made market for mass-produced goods in its constantly growing population. And with the growth of industry (and the political influence of the industrial capitalist class), government in the United States proved quick to respond to the needs of manufacturers.

"Yankee Ingenuity"

So were inventors. "As the Greek sculpted, as the Venetian painted," wrote an English visitor to the Centennial Exposition, "the American mechanizes." Actually, the new invention that turned the most heads at the great fair, the telephone, was the brainchild of a Scot who came to the United States via Canada, Alexander Graham Bell. Millions of people picked up the odd looking devices he had set up and, alternately amused and amazed, chatted with companions elsewhere in the room. Young men at the fair dropped a hint of what was to come by "ringing up" young ladies standing across from them, casually striking up conversations that, lacking proper introductions, would have been unacceptable face to face.

It was probably true that only in the United States could Bell have parleyed his idea into the gigantic enterprise it became, the American Telephone and Telegraph Company. As a writer in the *Saturday Evening Post* at the end of the century put it,

the United States is the only country in the world in which inventors form a distinct profession. . . . With us, inventors have grown into a large class. Laboratories . . . have sprung up almost everywhere, and today there is no great

New inventions such as the phonograph were sold through another new invention—the mail-order catalog.

Young women quickly monopolized the profession of telephone operator when Bell's companies found "boys" to be imprudent and impolite.

manufacturing concern that has not in its employ one or more men of whom nothing is expected except the bringing out of improvements in machinery and methods."

The Telephone

Bell was a teacher of the deaf who, while perfecting a mechanical hearing aid, realized that if he linked two of the devices by wire, he could transmit voice over distance. Unable to interest the communications giant Western Union in his telephone, he set up a pilot company in New York, and the telephone seized the American imagination. Rutherford B. Hayes put a telephone in the White House in 1878. By 1880, only four years after they first heard of the thing, 50,000 Americans were paying monthly fees to hear it jangle on their walls. By 1890, there were 800,000 phones in the United States; by 1900, 1.5 million people in the tiniest hamlets knew all about "exchanges," "party lines," and bored, nasal-voiced "operators."

Many systems were useful only locally. But as early as 1892, the eastern and midwestern cities were connected by a long-distance network, and rambunctious little western desert communities noted in their directories that "you can now talk to San Francisco with ease from our downtown office." Instantaneous communication was an invaluable aid to business and, important to some entrepreneurs, it left no written records of dubious transactions such as letters and telegrams did.

The Wizard of Menlo Park

Even more celebrated than Bell was Thomas Alva Edison. Written off by his boyhood teachers as a dunce, Edison was, in fact, befuddled throughout life by people who pursued knowledge for its own sake. He was the ultimate, practical American tinkerer who looked for a need—an opportunity to make money from it—and went to work. Despite his hideous personality, Edison became a folk hero because he approached invention in a no-nonsense all-American way. He said that genius was 1 percent inspiration and 99 percent perspiration. He took pride in his work, not his thoughts. With a large corps of assistants sweating away in his research and development laboratory in Menlo Park, New Jersey, he took out more than a thousand patents between 1876 and 1900.

Most of these patents were for improvements in existing processes. (He perfected a transmitter for Bell.) However a few of Edison's inventions were seedbeds for wholly new industries: the storage battery, the motion-picture projector, and the phonograph. The most important of his inventions was the incandescent light bulb, a means of converting electricity into stable, controllable light.

Electric Light

Edison solved the theoretical principle of the electric bulb—the 1 percent inspiration—almost immediately. Within a vacuum in a translucent glass ball an electrically charged filament or thread should burn (that is, glow) indefinitely. The perspiration part was discovering the fiber that would do the job. In 1879, after testing 6,000 materials, Edison came up with one that burned for 40 hours, enough to make it practical. Before he patented the incandescent light bulb early the next year, Edison improved the filament enough to make it work for 170 hours.

The financier, J. P. Morgan, who loathed the telephone, was fascinated by Edison's invention. His house and bank were among the first electrically illuminated structures in the United States. Morgan re-

Inventor Thomas A. Edison at work in his laboratory.

CLOUDED CRYSTAL BALLS

The fabulous success of Americans in exploiting technology can obscure the fact that technological pioneers often faced massive resistance in selling their inventions, and often themselves failed to understand the potential of what they had done.

This has been vividly true in the communications field. Thus, in 1845, the Postmaster General rejected an opportunity to purchase the patent for the telegraph for $100,000 because "under any rate of postage that could be adopted, its revenues could [not] be made equal to its expenditures." Within a generation, a private telegraph company, Western Union, was one of the most profitable giants of American business. In 1876, Western Union's president, William Orton, turned down an opportunity to buy Alexander Graham Bell's telephone, saying "What use could this company make of an electrical toy?"

In 1907, a businessman told radio pioneer, Lee De Forest that "all the radio . . . apparatus that the country will ever need" could be put in a single room. In 1985 there were 500 million radio receivers in the United States. If they were spread out evenly throughout the country, no person, even in the wilderness of Alaska, would be more than 233 feet from the chatter of a disc jockey.

In 1926, De Forest himself said of television that while it was theoretically and technically workable, "commercially and financially I consider it an impossibility, a development of which we need waste little time dreaming." As for the phonograph, its inventor Thomas Edison said it was "not of any commercial value." Today—every day in the United States—Americans buy 50,000 TV sets (and throw out 20,000 old ones). The record industry manufactures 574,000 record albums daily, 342,000 "singles," and imports another 66,000 disks.

alized that many people disliked gas, the principal source of nighttime light. Although clean enough (unlike kerosene), gas could be dangerous. Hundreds of fires were caused when, in a moment of ignorance, forgetfulness, or drunkenness, people blew out the flame instead of turning off the gas. Hotel managers nervously plastered the walls of rooms with reminders that the lights were gas.

The incandescent bulb succeeded as dramatically as the telephone. From a modest start in New York in 1882 with about 80 customers, Edison's invention spread so quickly that by 1900, more than 3,000 towns and cities were electrically illuminated. Within a few more years, the gaslight disappeared, and the kerosene lantern survived only on farms and in the poorer sections of the cities.

No single electric company dominated the industry, as American Telephone and Telegraph controlled Bell's patents. Nevertheless, like the railroads, the great regional companies were loosely associated by interlocking directorates and the influence of the investment banks. Edison, a worse businessman than scholar, saw most of his profit go to backers like Morgan. He ended his working life as an employee of mammoth General Electric, the corporate issue of his inventive genius.

The Problem of Bigness

George Westinghouse became a millionaire from his invention of the air brake for railroad trains. By equipping every car in a train with brakes, operated from a central point by pneumatic pressure, Westinghouse solved the problem of stopping long strings of railroad cars. Not only did his air brake save thousands of lives, but it led to bigger profits for railroads by making longer trains possible.

Well established, Westinghouse turned his inventive genius to electricity and capitalized on Edison's stubborn resistance to alternating current. Edison's direct current served very well over small areas, but it could not be transmitted over long distances. By perfecting a means to transmit alternating current, Westinghouse leapt ahead of his competitor by fully utilizing massive natural sources of power at isolated places such as Niagara Falls.

Westinghouse's invention confronted the single impediment Americans faced in their drive toward massive industrial development. The very vastness of the country was an impediment as well as a blessing. The United States spanned a continent that was dissected by rivers, mountains, and deserts into regions as large as the other industrial nations of the time. If geography had the last word, the United States would have remained a patchwork of distinct manufacturing regions in which small factories produced goods largely for the people of the vicinity alone. Indeed, this is a fair description of manufacturing in the United States through the period of the Civil War.

Chicago's proximity to major railroads helped make it the beef capital of the United States.

THE RAILROAD REVOLUTION

The steam railroad conquered America's awesome geography. The steam-powered locomotive, belching acrid smoke, its whistle piercing the air of city and wilderness, tied the country together on its "two streaks of rust and a right of way." Railroads made it possible for Pittsburgh steel makers to bring together the coal of Scranton and the iron of Michigan as if both minerals were found just across the county line. Thanks to the railroad, the great flour mills of Minneapolis could scoop up the cheap spring wheat of the distant Northwest, grind it into flour, and put their trademarked sacks into every cupboard in the country.

Because so many western railroads found their way into Chicago, the Windy City quickly eclipsed river-based Cincinnati as "hog butcher to the world" and the nation's dresser of beef. Livestock fattened on rangeland a thousand miles away rolled bawling into Chicago in rickety railroad cars and then rolled out—

packed in cans, barrels, and refrigerator cars—to the east coast and from there around the world.

Inefficiency and Chaos

By 1865, the United States was already the world's premier railway country with about 35,000 miles of track. With a few exceptions, however, individual lines were short, serving only the hinterlands of the cities in which they terminated. In the former Confederacy, there were 400 railroad companies with an average track length of only 40 miles each. It was possible to ship a cargo between St. Louis and Atlanta by any of 20 routes. Competing for the business in cutthroat rate wars, not a single southern line was financially secure.

Few lines actually linked up with one another. Goods to be shipped over long distances, and therefore on several lines, had to be unloaded (hand labor added to costs), carted across terminal towns by horse and wagon (another bottleneck), and reloaded onto another train. No two of the six railroads that ran into Richmond shared a depot. Before the Civil War, Chicago and New York were linked by rail on the map, but a cargo going the entire distance had to be unloaded and reloaded six times.

NARROW GAUGE

The short, narrow-gauge feeder lines that snaked into canyons and around mountains to bring out ore or logs were not so colossal as the great trunk lines, but the engineering required to build them was often more demanding. For example, the California Western that brought redwood logs down to the port of Fort Bragg, California, was only 40 miles long but never ran in a straightaway for as much as a mile, crossed 115 bridges, and went through one tunnel 1,122 feet long.

Early railroaders actually encouraged inefficiency in order to discourage takeovers by companies interested in consolidation. They deliberately built in odd gauges (the distance between rails) so that only their own locomotives and rolling stock could run on their tracks. As narrow as two feet apart in mountainous areas, the distance between rails ran to five feet in the South. Until 1880, the important Erie Railroad clung to a monstrous six-foot gauge. The Illinois Central, the nation's third largest railroad, employed two different gauges.

Lack of coordination among railroads presented shippers and passengers with another headache. Each railway company scheduled its trains according to the official time in its headquarters city. But local time varied even in cities just a few miles apart. When it was noon in Washington, D.C., it was 12:24 P.M. in Baltimore, 70 miles away (and 11:43 in Savannah, Georgia). The Baltimorean in Washington who tried to catch a 12:00 train home might discover that his watch was quite right for Baltimore, but that he was nearly half an hour too late to make the trip that day. In the train station in Buffalo, which served the New York Central and the Michigan Southern, three clocks were necessary: one for each railroad, and one for local time, which was different yet. In the Pittsburgh station there were six clocks. Traveling from Maine to California on the railroad, one passed through 20 "time zones." In fact, there were 80 such zones in the United States.

The Consolidators

Charles F. Dowd introduced the idea of four official times zones in 1870; his plan was enacted into law at the behest of the railroads in 1883. Long before that, men like J. Edgar Thomson of the Pennsylvania Railroad and Cornelius Vanderbilt of the New York Central labored outside the law, and often in conflict with it, to bring order out of the chaos of independently owned "short lines."

They secretly purchased stock in small railroad companies until they had control of them, then drove other competitors out of business by means of ruthless rate wars. They built the "Pennsy" and the New York Central ever westward from New York to Chicago and, thus, connections with lines that ran to the Pacific. All along their "main lines," feeders tapped the surrounding country.

Thomson was all business, a no-nonsense efficiency expert with little celebrity outside railroad and government circles. Vanderbilt, who began his working

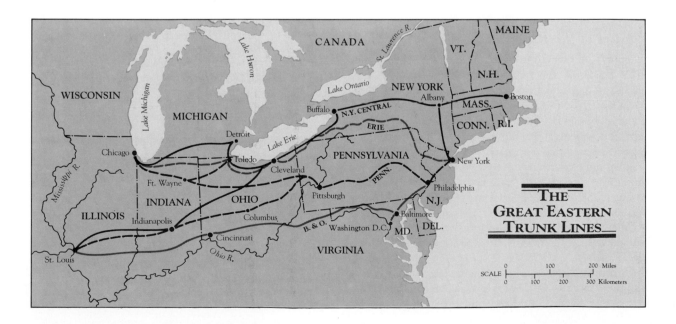

THE GREAT EASTERN TRUNK LINES

life as a ferryman in New York City's crowded harbor, was colorful and often in the news. Ferrying was a rough business, no place for a milquetoast, and as a young man, the Commodore, as Vanderbilt styled himself (dressing in a mock naval uniform), fired more than one cannon at a competitor's harbor barge.

Vanderbilt gave up brawling as his shipping empire and responsibilities grew, but he was as tough and unscrupulous behind a broad oak desk as he had been at the tiller of a ferry. Once, when a reporter suggested that he had broken the law in a conflict with a rival, Vanderbilt snapped back gruffly, "What do I care about the law. Hain't I got the power?"

He had, and he used it masterfully to crush competition. By the time of the Civil War, Vanderbilt had a near-monopoly of New York harbor commerce. He even controlled the business that hauled New York City's monumental daily production of horse manure to farms in Staten Island. Vanderbilt's waterborne transportation empire led him naturally into moving the commerce of America's greatest city overland, too.

The Commodore was never quite respectable. His rough-and-tumble origins resonated in his speech. He was a friend of Victoria Woodhull and Tennessee Claflin, two eccentric sisters who preached free love. The mention of his name caused ladies and gentlemen of genteel New York society to shudder—for a while. Because he said out loud what other businessmen did quietly—that ethics and social responsibility did not always make good business—he was an easy target for moralists. Vanderbilt could not have cared less. Like many of the great capitalists of the era, he regarded his fortune—$100 million when he died—as adequate justification for what he did.

Pirates of the Rails

Compared to another breed of early railroader, men like Thomson and Vanderbilt can be justified very easily. In addition to making millions for themselves, they built transportation systems of inestimable social value. The Pennsy was famous for safe roadbeds in an age of frequent, horrendous railroad accidents. The New York Central pioneered the use of steel rails and was equipped with the life-saving Westinghouse air brake while other lines halted (or failed to halt) their trains mechanically. The Commodore's son and heir, William Vanderbilt was best known for saying "The public be damned!' but he also played a major part in standardizing the American gauge at the present 4 feet, 8 1/2 inches.

In contrast, some early railroaders simply took, making their fortunes by destroying what others had built. The most famous of these pirates were a trio that owned the Erie Railroad and actually succeeded in bilking Cornelius Vanderbilt. The senior member of the "Erie Gang" was Daniel Drew, a pious Methodist who knew much of the Bible by heart, but put a very liberal interpretation on the verse in Exodus that said "Thou shalt not steal."

James Fisk, only 33 years old in 1867, was another sort altogether. No Bible for "Jubilee Jim"; he was a stout, jolly extrovert who fancied garish clothing, tossed silver dollars at street urchins, and caroused openly in New York's gaslit restaurants and cabarets with showgirls from the vaudeville stage who, at the time, were considered little better than prostitutes. (One of them, Josie Mansfield, was his undoing; in 1872, Fisk was murdered by another one of her suitors.)

Jay Gould was a man of the shadows. When Drew went to church and Fisk slapped on cologne, Gould slipped home to his respectable Victorian family. Furtive in appearance as in fact, tight fisted, and close mouthed, Gould was probably the brains of the Erie Ring. Certainly he lasted the longest, becoming almost respectable and marrying a daughter to a European nobleman. But when it came to making money, Gould was at one with his partners in the Erie Gang: the consequences of their piracy for others, let alone society, were quite beside the point.

The Erie War

In control of the Erie Railroad, the three men knew that Vanderbilt wanted their property and was secretly making large purchases of Erie stock. In order to separate him from as much of his fortune as possible, they watered Erie's stock; that is, they marketed shares in the dilapidated railroad far in excess of the Erie's real assets, from $24 million to $78 million in a few years when virtually nothing was done to improve the line. As Vanderbilt bought, they pocketed the money that should have gone into expanding the Erie's earning power.

WATERING STOCK

Daniel Drew was notorious for watering the stock in companies he owned. A popular story about him had it that he had started young. As a young drover, Drew would bring his cattle to the New York market, where he would pen them up with salt and no water. The next morning, before he sold them, he would drive them into a creek, where the groaning beasts bloated themselves. At market, they were fat, sleek, and largely phony.

THE GREAT RACE FOR THE WESTERN STAKES 1870

*"Commodore" Cornelius Vanderbilt races James Fisk for control of the Erie R.R. in this
1870 cartoon. Newspaper readers followed the financial struggle as avidly as a fictional serial.*

The Commodore came to his senses and went to the judges, whom he regularly bribed, to indict the trio. Forewarned, Drew, Fisk, and Gould escaped to New Jersey, where they owned the judges. (It was said in the streets that they rowed across the Hudson River in a boat filled with bank notes.) A settlement was pieced together. In the meantime, the Erie amassed the worst accident record among world railroads and the company was devastated as a business. The Erie did not pay a dividend to its stockholders until the 1940s. For 70 years, what profits there were went to make up for the thievery of three men over six years.

THE TRANSCONTINENTAL LINES

In the Northeast and South, the creation of railroad systems was partly a matter of consolidating short lines that already existed. This movement peaked during the 1880s, when the names of 540 independent railway companies disappeared from the business registers. In the West, railroad lines were extensive, integrated transportation systems from the start. Beyond the Mississippi, creating railroad systems was a matter of construction from scratch.

Public Finance

The great transcontinental railroads were built and owned by private companies but (with one exception: James J. Hill's Great Northern) financed by the public. The sparsity of population between the Mississippi Valley and the western states of California and Oregon (and Washington after 1889) made it impossible to attract private investors. Railroad building was expensive. To lay a mile of track required bedding more than 3,000 ties in gravel and attaching 400 rails to them by driving 12,000 spikes. Having built that mile in Utah or Nevada at considerable expense, a railroader had nothing to look forward to but hundreds more miles of arid desert and uninhabited mountains.

Ten thousand immigrant Chinese laborers built the Central Pacific Railway across the West.
Here workers complete the Secrettown Trestle in the Sierra Nevada.

With no customers along the way, there would be no profits and, without profits, no investors. The federal government had political and military interests in binding California and Oregon to the rest of the Union, and, in its land, the public domain, the government had the means with which to subsidize railroad construction.

The Pacific Railway Act of 1862 granted to two companies, the Union Pacific and the Central Pacific, a right of way of 200 feet wide between Omaha, Nebraska, and Sacramento, California. For each mile of track that the companies built, they were to receive, on either side of the tracks, ten alternate sections (square miles) of the public domain. The result was a belt of land 40 miles wide, laid out like a checkerboard on which the U.P. and C.P. owned half the squares. (The rest was reserved for disposition under the Homestead Act or by direct government sale.)

The railroads sold their land, thus raising money for construction and creating customers. Or, just as important, they could use the vast real estate as collateral to borrow cash from banks. In addition, depending on the terrain, the government lent the two companies between $16,000 and $48,000 per mile of track at bargain interest rates.

The Romance of the Rails

As in the consolidation of eastern trunk lines, the business operations of the transcontinentals was sometimes a wee bit shady—as in the case of the Crédit Mobilier. However, the actual construction of the line was a heroic and glorious feat. The Union Pacific, employing thousands of Civil War veterans and newly immigrated Irish pick-and-shovel men, the "Paddies," laid over a thousand miles of track. The workers lived in shifting cities of tents and freight cars built like dormitories. They toiled by day, and bickered and brawled with gamblers, saloon keepers, and whores by night. Until the company realized that it was more efficient to hire professional gunmen as guards, the workers kept firearms with their tools in order to fight off those Indians who may have sensed that the "iron horse" meant the end of their way of life.

The builders of the Central Pacific had no trouble with Indians, but a great deal with terrain. Just outside Sacramento rose the majestic Sierra Nevada. There were passes in the mountains through which the line could snake, but they were narrow and steep. Under the direction of a resourceful engineer, Theodore D. Judah, 10,000 Chinese chipped ledges into the slopes,

built roadbeds of rubble in deep canyons, and bolted together trestles of timbers two feet square.

The snows of the Sierra proved to be a difficult problem, not only for the builders but for the eventual operation of the line. To solve it, the workers constructed snowsheds miles long. In effect, the transcontinental railroad crossed part of the Sierra Nevada indoors. Once on the Nevada plateau, the experienced C.P. crews built at a rate of a mile a day for an entire year.

The U.P. and C.P. joined at Promontory Point, Utah, on May 10, 1869. The final days were hectic. Because the total mileage that each company constructed determined the extent of its land grants, the

TRANSCONTINENTAL RAILROADS

CANADA

GREAT NORTHERN (no land grant)

MONTANA
TERRITORY

IDAHO
TERR.

Helena

Butte

NORTHERN PACIFIC

NORTH
DAKOTA
TERR.

SOUTH
DAKOTA
TERR.

SCALE   0   100 Miles
         0   100 Kilometers

WYOMING
TERRITORY

ONE-HALF OF ALL LAND IN
AN 80-MILE-WIDE AREA WAS
GRANTED TO **NORTHERN
PACIFIC**

LAND GRANTS
TO
RAILROADS

two companies raced around the clock. The record was set by the crews of the Central Pacific. They built 10.6 miles of more-or-less functional railroad in one day (just about the same length of track the company laid down during the whole of 1864). That involved bedding 31,000 ties, and connecting 4,037 iron rails to them with 120,000 spikes!

Railroad Mania

Seeing that the owners of the U.P. and C.P. had become instant millionaires, other ambitious men descended on Washington, D.C. in search of subsidies.

LAND FOR SALE

In order to promote land that it owned in Nebraska, the Burlington and Missouri River Railroad offered a number of come-ons. A would-be purchaser had to pay his own fare to go out to look at the land, but the railroad would refund his fare if he bought. Once a landowner, he would receive a free railroad pass, as well as "long credit, low interest, and a twenty percent rebate for improvements." Prices were not extravagant. The Union Pacific disposed of pretty good Nebraska land at $3 to $5 an acre.

In the euphoria of the times, Congress in 1864 was doubly generous to the Northern Pacific, which planned to build from Lake Superior to Puget Sound. In the territories, the N.P. received 40 alternate sections of land for every mile of railway built! The Atchison, Topeka, and Santa Fe ran from Kansas to Los Angeles. The Texas Pacific and Southern Pacific linked New Orleans and San Francisco at El Paso, Texas (Jefferson Davis's route in the days before the Kansas-Nebraska Act). In 1884, the Canadians (who were even more generous with government land) completed the first of their two transcontinental lines, the Canadian Pacific. Never before had there been such an expenditure of effort and wealth to accomplish the same purpose in so short a time.

The costs were considerable. The federal government gave the land-grant railroads a total of 131 million acres. To this, the state governments added 45 million acres. Totaled up, an area larger than France and Belgium was given to a handful of capitalists. In addition, towns along the proposed routes enticed the builders to choose them as sites for depots by offering town lots, cash bounties, and exemption from taxes.

These gifts were not always offered with a glad hand. If a railroad bypassed a town, the town fathers knew, the town might die, their fortunes and status with it.

Aware of this, railroaders did not hesitate to set communities against one another like roosters in a cock fight. The Atchison, Topeka, and Santa Fe, popularly known as "the Santa Fe," did not originally enter the city of that name. Nearby Albuquerque offered the better deal and got the major depot.

The Panic of 1873

Western railroaders made money by building railroads with public and borrowed money, not by actually operating them. As a result, they built too much railroad too soon. When the time came to pay the high operating costs and to pay off loans out of fees paid by shippers and passengers, many of the new companies found that there were just not enough customers to go around. In 1872, only one railroad in three made a profit.

On September 18, 1873, a Friday, the chickens came home to roost. Jay Cooke and Company, a bank that had loaned heavily to western railroads, including the richly endowed Northern Pacific, announced that the firm was bankrupt. Jay Cooke and Company was not an ordinary bank. It was the most prestigious house of finance in the United States, the government's chief agent during the Civil War. Its failure caused a panic: speculators rushed to sell their stocks and the market crashed. By the end of 1873, 5,000 businesses had declared bankruptcy and a half million workers were jobless. The depression of the 1870s was the worst in American history to that time.

It would not be the last. A by-product of fabulous economic growth was a wildly erratic "business cycle." For a time the industrial capitalist economy boomed, luring investment and speculation, encouraging expansion and production. Sooner or later, the capacity of railroads to carry freight and factories to produce goods outpaced the capacity of the market to absorb their services and products. When that happened, banks closed, investments and savings were wiped out,

A construction crew in the Montana Territory in 1887 is shown laying track for the Manitoba Railway which ran between Seattle, Washington and St. Paul, Minnesota.

factories locked their gates, workers lost their jobs, the shops they frequented went broke.

THE ORGANIZERS

In a free, unregulated economy, the cycle of boom and bust was inevitable and, since the age of Jackson, Americans as a people had been committed to the ideal of a free and unregulated economy. They believed that their country's peculiar virtue lay in the fact that competition was open to everyone having the will and wherewithal to have a go at it.

Once a businessman reached the top of the economic pyramid, however, he was apt to become disenchanted with the competitive ideal. To the entrepreneur who was no longer scrambling, but in charge of a commercial or industrial empire valued at millions of dollars and employing thousands of people, free-wheeling competitors threatened stability and order, like so many dogs yapping at his heels. In the late nineteenth century, Andrew Carnegie in steel, John D. Rockefeller in oil, and other canny businessmen

---

BUILDING THE RAILROADS

"Track-laying is a science. A light car, drawn by a single horse, gallops up to the front with its load of rails. Two men seize the end of a rail and start forward, the rest of the gang taking hold by twos. They come forward at a run. At a word of command the rail is dropped in its place, less than thirty seconds to a rail for each gang, and so four rails go down to the minute: Close behind come the gangers, spikers, and a lovely time they make of it."

William Bell

BIG BUSINESS AT THE DINNER TABLE

Technology and big business reached into the American home with more than the telephone during the latter part of the nineteenth century. Several inventors and business organizers devised new ways to process food that scrambled ancient patterns of marketing and cooking and, within a generation, changed the way Americans ate.

The first of these remakers of food was Gail Borden (1801–74). Living on the Texas frontier, Borden was aware of the monotony of the diets of overland travelers, and he began to experiment with ways to preserve and make more portable one of the most perishable and bulkiest of foods, milk. Borden's solution was condensation and canning. In 1856, he took out a patent on a process for evaporating milk in a vacuum and preserving the product in cans. Union soldiers in the Civil War did not find Borden's "Condensed Milk" particularly tasty, but it was more or less milk and healthful too, as many military rations were not. Back home again, they continued to use it because, except on the farm where cows could be milked daily, that perishable food was risky eating. Before the pasteurization process, which came to the United States only at the end of the century, fresh milk was the source of several diseases, some serious.

Condensation became an obsession with Borden. "I mean to put a potato into a pill box," he said, "a pumpkin into a tablespoon, the biggest sort of watermelon into a saucer. . . . The Turks made acres of roses into attar of roses. . . . I intend to make attar of everything." He never had a success to rival his milk, but did condense fruit and vegetable juices with his process.

H. J. Heinz of Pittsburgh calculated that by using industrial methods, he could sell preserved foods such as were put up in many American homes at a price that would tempt buyers, particularly in the cities, to forgo that tedious task. He went bankrupt once but stuck by his idea, canning and bottling pickles, vegetables, fruits, and the mainstay of his prosperous company, ketchup or catsup. Before Heinz, the word *ketchup* referred to any number of sauces and relishes. Only after the success of Heinz's *tomato* ketchup did Americans forget how to make the others.

Much more fundamental was the revolution in processing America's staples, wheat flour and meat. The bread and fresh meat that Americans ate always had come from the region in which they lived. Local or regional millers gathered in the grain and ground it into flour, returning some to the grower and selling the rest. The butcher shops in every town and city were also slaughterhouses. Without refrigeration, the only fresh meat was meat that had been on the hoof a day or two earlier in the butcher's backyard.

The railroad was the key to changing this. Reaching westward into lands where wheat and livestock could be grown on a larger scale and, therefore, much more

cheaply than in the East, the trains funneled grain and cattle into Minneapolis-St. Paul, Chicago, St. Louis, and other cities that had railroad connections with the east coast. In the transfer cities, gigantic processing companies such as General Mills, Ralston, Purina, Swift, Armour, Wilson, and Cudahy turned the raw materials into consumer goods.

Using huge steam-driven steel rollers instead of the slow and cumbersome water-powered grindstones, the great milling corporations were able to undersell and quickly destroy local millers almost everywhere in the country. Their flour did not spoil because the living germ had been refined out of it. Although refined flour was fine and white, therefore a much more elegant baking ingredient than previously had been available to ordinary people, it was, as numerous critics pointed out then and in the twentieth century, far less nutritious than unrefined flour.

Chicago was the center of the new meatpacking industry. From vast corrals in the yards of the western railroads, cattle and hogs were processed by applying industrial methods to slaughtering and butchering. The mass-produced meat sold so cheaply in the East that the combination slaughterhouse-butcher shop became a thing of the past. However, during their unsuccessful campaign to fight the Chicago packers, local butchers contributed to American tastes: to this day Americans want their beef blood-red—fresh—in sharp contrast to the preference for aged, brown beef in other countries.

The Swift meat packing "disassembly line."

devoted their careers to minimizing the threat of competition. Carnegie organized his company so efficiently that he could determine the price structure of the entire steel industry without regard to what other steel makers did. Rockefeller destroyed his competitors by fair means and foul, and simply gobbled them up.

Steel: *The Bones of the Economy*

Steel is the element iron from which carbon and other "impurities" are burned out at high temperatures. Engineers were well aware of its potential in construction. Steel is much stronger than iron per unit of weight. Produced in quantity, steel could be used in buildings, bridges, and, of particular interest in the late nineteenth century, superior rails for trains. Until the mid-nineteenth century, however, the costs involved in producing this "super-iron" were so great that steel was used mostly in small, expensive items: knives and other blades, precision instruments, bearings for machinery, and the like.

By the time of the Civil War, working independently of each other, two ironmakers, Henry Bessemer of England and William Kelly of Pennsylvania and Kentucky, developed a method by which steel could be made in quantity at a reasonable price. No one grasped the significance of their discovery more quickly than Andrew Carnegie, an immigrant from Scotland who, beginning as a telegrapher, became a high-ranking executive of the Pennsylvania Railroad. Already a rich man by the end of the Civil War as a result of speculations in oil and the manufacture of iron bridges (his company built the first span across the Mississippi), he decided to sell everything and concentrate on steel, "putting all his eggs in one basket, and then watching that basket." In 1873, he began construction of a huge Bessemer plant in Braddock, Pennsylvania, outside Pittsburgh.

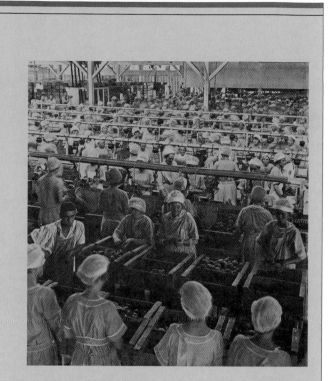

Canning peaches in Fresno, California, around 1900.

The pioneers of centralized meatpacking were Gustavus Swift (1839–1903) and Philip D. Armour (1832–1901). Armour perfected the "disassembly line," a continuously moving chain in which hogs ran in one end under their own power, and pork packed for retailing came out the other. Armour kept his prices down by using what previously had been waste: bones, blood, hides, and even bristle (which was made into hairbrushes). It was said that he made money on every part of the pig but its squeal, and he was working on that.

Gustavus Swift pioneered the use of ice and, later, refrigerator cars to ship fresh sides of beef from Chicago to the east coast. He had to overcome popular suspicions of any meat from animals that had been slaughtered more than a few days before it was set on the table and the resistance of local butchers. By opening his own shops in the major cities of the East and underselling even locally raised steers with his Texas, Wyoming, and Montana beef, Swift had his way.

By the end of the nineteenth century, a middle-class family in Portland, Maine, would likely sit down to a loaf of bread baked with flour from Minneapolis, a beefsteak from Chicago seasoned with Heinz ketchup from Pittsburgh, and oranges from Florida or California for dessert. Vegetables alone were local. Maine produced plenty of potatoes, and it was only in the twentieth century that the food revolutionaries shipped greens any considerable distance.

STEEL AT ONE CENT A POUND

Just as John D. Rockefeller liked to point out that kerosene was cheaper after Standard Oil came to monopolize the refining industry, Andrew Carnegie had a neat justification of his organization of the steel industry:

Two pounds of ironstone mined upon Lake Superior and transported nine hundred miles to Pittsburgh; one pound and one half of coal, mined and manufactured into coke, and transported to Pittsburgh; a small amount of manganese ore mined in Virginia and brought to Pittsburgh—and these four pounds of materials manufactured into one pound of steel, for which the customer pays one cent.

A Head for Business

Carnegie knew apples as well as eggs—how to polish them. He named his factory after J. Edgar Thomson, the president of the Pennsy, which would be a major customer of Carnegie Steel. But Carnegie also knew to locate the great works outside of Pittsburgh, which was served by the Pennsylvania Railroad alone. In Braddock, Carnegie could play several railroads against one another, winning the most favorable shipping rates. Nor was it luck that Carnegie built his mill during the depression of 1873. For the next 25 years, he took advantage of hard times, when the price of everything was down, to expand his factories, scrap old methods, and introduce new technology.

Carnegie also prided himself on spotting talent, putting it to work for him, and rewarding it. Charles Schwab, later the president of United States Steel and the founder of Bethlehem Steel, was an engineer's helper at Carnegie Steel whom Carnegie promoted and made a partner.

"Vertical Integration"

Carnegie's major contribution to business organization was his exploitation of the principle of "vertical integration." That is, in order to get a leg up on his competitors, he expanded his operation from a base of steel manufacture to include ownership of the raw materials from which steel was made and the means of assembling those raw materials at the factory. For example, Bessemer furnaces were fueled by coke, which is to coal what charcoal is to wood, a hotter-burning distillation of the mineral. Rather than buy coke from independent operators, Carnegie absorbed the 5,000 acres of coalfields and 1,000 coke ovens owned by Henry Clay Frick, who became a junior partner in Carnegie Steel. Carnegie and Frick then added iron mines to their holdings.

While never completely independent of trunk-line railroads, Carnegie controlled as much of his own shipping as he could. He owned barges that carried iron ore from Michigan and the Mesabi to his own port facilities in Erie, Pennsylvania. He owned a short-line railroad that brought the ore from Erie to Homestead. By eliminating from his final product price the profits of independent suppliers, distributors, and carriers, Carnegie was able to undersell competing companies that were not vertically integrated and, therefore, had to include the profits of independent suppliers in their final product price.

Vertical integration served Andrew Carnegie very well. His personal income rose to $25 million a year. He lived much of the time in a castle in Scotland not far from where his father had worked as a weaver. His company steadily assumed a more dominant role in the steel business. In 1870 there were 167 iron and steel firms around Pittsburgh. By the end of the century there were 47.

In 1901, 66 years old and bored with business, Carnegie threatened to combine most of these into a behemoth that would threaten companies organized by the banker J. P. Morgan with an all-out price war. Morgan was persuaded to buy Carnegie out for $500 million, the largest personal commercial transaction ever made. Morgan then created the first billion dollar corporation, United States Steel.

The Corporation

Carnegie was progressive in many ways, always open to the new. But he organized his company as a partnership, disdaining the business structure that was the chief means consolidation in the late nineteenth century, the corporation. Corporate structure—selling small "shares" in a company on the open market—was advantageous to both investors and business organizers. Widely dispersed ownership meant widely dispersed risk. The investor who owned some shares in a number of companies did not lose everything if one of those companies failed. American law also provided investors with the privilege of "limited liability." That is, the corporation's legal liability was limited to the assets of the corporation, and did not extend to

Andrew Carnegie, steel manufacturer and master of vertical integration.

A ladle used in a nineteenth-century steel mill dwarfs the men standing nearby.

the assets of shareholders. (If an individually owned business or partnership went bust, creditors could seize the other assets of the owners, including home and personal property.)

These inducements made it possible for entrepreneurs to raise the huge amounts of capital needed to finance expensive industrial enterprises. However, by reserving controlling interest to themselves, they did not have to share decision making with small investors. Abuses were common enough. Pirates like the Erie Ring could drain a corporation of its assets, enrich themselves personally through their control of corporate policy, allow the company to go under, and walk away with their ill-gotten personal fortunes.

New Uses for Equal Rights

The Fourteenth Amendment to the Constitution, designed to secure equality under the law to all citizens, proved to be more valuable to corporations than to the black former slaves for which it was written. After dodging the question for several years, the Supreme Court ruled in *Santa Clara County* vs. *the Southern Pacific Railroad* (1886) that a corporation was a "person" under the meaning of the Fourteenth Amendment. The states were forbidden to pass laws that applied specifically to corporations and not to flesh-and-blood persons because such laws denied corporate persons civil equality.

However, while corporations enjoyed the civil rights of citizens who walked and talked, it was difficult to exact the same responsibilities of it. Men and women could be sent to jail for violating the law. Corporations could not.

John D. Rockefeller

While thousands of businessmen organized corporations, they all fade from sight in the shadow of the solemn, muscular, well-dressed, and deeply religious person of John Davison Rockefeller. Beginning his career as an accountant, Rockefeller avoided service in the Civil War by hiring a substitute. He made a small fortune selling provisions to the Union Army, but a small fortune was only an appetizer. Rockefeller had a voracious appetite for riches. Outside of home and Sunday School, which he taught, he talked of little but business. After swinging a lucrative deal as a young man, he danced a two-step jig and exclaimed "Bound to be rich! I'm bound to be rich!"

Rockefeller disapproved of smoking and drinking, in part because of his Baptist faith, but in part because cigars and whiskey cost money that could be invested to make more money. He carefully recorded how he spent every dime; he spent few frivolously. He would remove his stovepipe hat and bend down to pick up a penny. John D. Rockefeller would have succeeded no matter what his business. The one he chose proved to be as basic to modern society as steel.

Black Gold

Crude oil has been seeping to the surface of the earth since before there were human beings to step into it and growl. Europeans used it as a lubricant. Some American Indians ate it as a laxative. That classical American huckster, the snake-oil salesman, bottled the stuff, flavoring it with sugar and spices and tossing in a healthy shot of alcohol, thence claiming it cured everything from "female weakness" to rainy days. The farmers who lived around Titusville in western Pennsylvania were more likely to hate the gunk. It fouled the soil, polluted streams, and, if it caught fire, it filled the air with billows of noxious smoke.

In 1855, an organic chemist, Benjamin Silliman, discovered that one of the components into which crude oil could be broken down was kerosene, a liquid that could be safely burned to heat a house or cookstove, or illuminate the night. It was a timely discovery. In the 1850s, overharvesting had desolated the world's population of whales. Whale oil, used to illuminate

---

INC. AND LTD.

In the United States, a limited liability corporation is distinguished by the word "Corporation" in its name or the abbreviation "Inc.," meaning "incorporated." in Great Britain, the comparable designation is "Ltd.," meaning "limited."

middle and upper-class homes—the poor used candles or went to bed—had soared in price. Kerosene was cheap; even the poor could afford it. In 1859, seeing the opportunity, a former army officer named Edwin Drake went to Titusville, Pennsylvania, and devised a drill and pump system by which crude oil could be extracted in commercial quantities.

The Pennsylvania oil rush that followed was as wild as the gold rush of 1849. Drilling for oil, like panning for gold, required only modest capital, so thousands of men dreaming of instant riches descended on the "oil fields" of western Pennsylvania. John D. Rockefeller, living in nearby Cleveland, Ohio, came and looked. But he did not like what he saw, neither the social disorder and moral laxity, nor the fact that the independent drillers, competing fiercely to stay afloat, repeatedly declared price wars on one another, slashing the price at which they sold their black gold to refiners. A few drillers got rich; many more went broke. It was not Rockefeller's kind of business.

"Horizontal Integration"

Oil refining was a fragmented business too; there were 250 companies engaged in it as late as 1870. However, operating a refinery called for rather more capital than sinking a drill-bit into the ground and saying a prayer. Rockefeller recognized that—unlike drilling, which would always attract "wildcatters" who might get lucky, hit a gusher, and become a major competitor overnight—the refining end of the business was manageable. It was a kind of "narrows" on the river of oil that flowed from well to consumers. Like the robber barons of medieval Europe who built castles at narrow places on the Rhine and Danube, thence deciding which boat might pass and which might not, the company that controlled the narrows of the oil business—refining—would be able to determine production and prices. It did not matter how many wild-eyed visionaries roamed the countryside with a drilling rig. If there was one refiner, they would sell their crude at the price the refiner was willing to pay.

Controlling an entire industry by controlling a key phase of its process is known as horizontal integration. Instead of setting the standards for an industry by integrating a portion of the business from top to bottom—from source of raw materials to market (as Carnegie did in steel)—horizontal integration meant establishing an effective monopoly across the industry.

This is what Rockefeller and his associates—his brother William, Samuel Andrews, and Maurice Clark—accomplished. In 1870, their Standard Oil Company of Ohio refined 3 or 4 percent of the nation's oil. Within 20 years, Standard Oil controlled 90 percent of U.S. refining capacity. They worked this magic by persuading strong and cooperative competitors to throw in with them and by driving weak and uncooperative refiners out of the business.

Rebates

Rockefeller ground some refineries down by attacking them in cutthroat rate wars. With generally superior facilities, Standard Oil was able to take losses over the short term that less efficient competitors could not bear. On one occasion, Rockefeller bought up every barrel stave and hoop in the oil region. Competitors could not ship their products for lack of containers. On another, a private army of 250 Standard Oil men forcefully prevented a refining company from building a pipeline to New York City.

Much more effective was the "draw-back" or "rebate." Because Standard Oil could promise railroads a fixed, large amount of oil to carry east each day, Rockefeller demanded of them and got a refund of part of their published rate list—under the table. With smaller competitors paying the published rates, Rockefeller had a huge advantage when it was time to sell. For a short period, Rockefeller got a rebate from the Erie Railroad for each carload of kerosene his competitors shipped! This was his price to the Erie for continuing to use the line himself. The rebate was particularly effective in fighting the refiners of Pittsburgh,

John D. Rockefeller and his attorneys.

who were served by only one railroad which, therefore, did not have to bargain.

The Standard Oil Trust

In order to win these wars, Rockefeller had to occupy a commanding position in the refining industry. At the beginning of the consolidation, however, he and his associates lacked the vast capital resources that would have been necessary to buy out other large producers. The solution, designed by Rockefeller's lawyers, Samuel C. T. Dodd and John Newlon Camden, was to adapt the ancient legal device of the trust to the running of a business.

Traditionally, the trust was the means by which the property of a minor or an incompetent was managed on his or her behalf. That property was put into the care of a trustee whose obligation was to see to it that the property was well administered. Rockefeller, Andrews and Clark, and Henry Flagler explained to their major competitors that if they surrendered control of their refineries to the Standard Oil Trust, for which they would receive trust certificates, they would be spared the duties of management and the risks of com-

petition while, because the trustees would coordinate the use of the combined facilities, their income would soar. The wiser refiners saw the point and agreed (and became very wealthy).

Rockefeller, once in control of a near monopoly, was able to mop up those refiners who held out and to calculate precisely how much oil the market could absorb, how much, therefore, to produce, and at what price to sell.

The goal of the trust was not to drive prices up to extortionate levels. Rockefeller enjoyed telling hostile interogators that with each step toward monopoly, Standard had reduced the retail price of a gallon of kerosene. The goal of the trust, he said, was economic order, not rapacious profiteering.

Rockefeller had no apologies for what he did. He remained a scathing critic of the gospel of competition to the end of his days. However, the fact that a handful of men could dictate the doings of an entire, vital industry—Standard Oil was run by only nine trustees—aroused a storm of fear and resentment in the land.

For Further Reading

For overviews of American economic development, see the following books: Elliott Brownlee, *Dyanmics of Ascent: A History of the American Economy* (1974); Thomas C. Cochran and William Miller, *The Age of Enterprise* (1942); Vincent P. DeSantis, *The Shaping of Modern America, 1877–1916* (1973); John A. Garraty, *The New Commonwealth, 1877–1890* (1968); Samuel P. Hays, *The Response to Industrialism, 1885–1914* (1957); Robert Higgs, *The Transformation of the American Economy* (1971); Matthew Josephson, *The Robber Barons* (1934); Glenn Porter, *The Rise of Big Business, 1860–1910* (1973); Robert H. Wiebe, *The Search for Order* (1967).

Valuable special studies include Roger Burlingame, *Engines and Democracy: Inventions and Society in Mature America* (1940); A. D. Chandler, Jr., *The Visible Hand: The Managerial Revolution in American Business* (1977); Thomas C. Cochran, *Railroad Leaders, 1845–1890*

(1953); Robert W. Fogel, *Railroads and American Economic Growth* (1964); Edward C. Kirkland, *Dream and Thought in the Business Community, 1860–1900* (1956) and *Men, Cities, and Transportation* (1948); Gabriel Kolko, *Railroads and Regulation* (1965); James McCague, *Moguls and Iron Men* (1964); Elting E. Morison, *From Know-How to Nowhere: The Development of American Technology* (1974); Walter T. K. Nugent, *Money and American Society, 1865–1880* (1968); George R. Taylor and R. D. Neu, *The American Railroad Network, 1861–1900* (1956).

One of the finest recent biographies is Robert V. Bruce, *Alexander Graham Bell and the Conquest of Solitude* (1973). For other personages mentioned in this chapter see Matthew Josephson, *Edison* (1959); Harold C. Livesay, *Andrew Carnegie and the Rise of Big Business* (1975); Alan Nevins, *A Study in Power: John D. Rockefeller* (1953); and J. F. Wall, *Andrew Carnegie* (1971).

In *Democracy in America*, written more than 20 years before the Civil War, Alexis de Tocqueville admired the equity with which wealth was distributed in the United States. Except for slaves, as he saw it, few Americans were so poor that they could not hope to improve their situation; few were so rich that they had coalesced into an aristocracy, a privileged social class permanently entrenched above the mass of the population. Many well-to-do people whom Tocqueville observed seemed to fear that one adverse stroke of fortune would send them tumbling down into the world of hard work, sore backs, and calloused hands. The many, in the Age of Jackson, seemed confident that their country

29

LIVING WITH LEVIATHAN

Reactions to Big Business and Great Wealth

Members of America's leisure class flaunted their wealth and devoted themselves to idle pursuits. This painting by John Singer Sargent, The Wyndham Sisters, portrays three members of this privileged class.

was indeed the promised land of opportunity, where their fate lay entirely in their own hands.

Today, it is clear that Jacksonian America did not apportion its wealth so equitably as Tocqueville and others believed. Nevertheless, the gap between dirt poor and filthy rich was not nearly so yawning then as it was in the late nineteenth century. Industrialization and the growth of big business created a class of multimillionaires whose fortunes were so great that it was absurd to imagine them slipping into the anonymous masses. Cornelius Vanderbilt amassed $100 million in his lifetime. His son, William, doubled that to $200 million in a few years. By 1900, Andrew Carnegie was able to pocket $480 million in a single transaction. John D. Rockefeller gave away such a sum within a few years, all the while his family grew richer.

Rather more worrisome, the industrial and financial aristocracy's control of technology, transportation, industry, and money made a mockery of the American dream of equality of opportunity. How could an ordinary fellow succeed against such entrenched power and privilege? Social critics railed at the new elite; substantial social movements protested the new inequities. But, in the end, Americans came to terms with a society that was both richer and poorer than that which Alexis de Tocqueville had chronicled.

REGULATING THE RAILROADS AND TRUSTS

Railroads, the first big businesses, were the target of the first significant social protests of America's industrial era. Poets and philosophers saw "the machine in the garden" as a defilement of what was good and vital in American life. Some city dwellers banded together to fight plans to run tracks down the streets on which they lived and shopped.

But such nay-sayers were few. Most Americans welcomed the iron horse at first, especially those who lived in isolated rural areas. To them the railroad offered the possibility of shipping their produce to market, thereby earning money with which to escape a life of mere subsistence.

A Short Honeymoon

The honeymoon was brief. It was not difficult to see that pirates like Drew, Fisk, and Gould made money only to the extent that they abused the railroad as a means of transportation. Western townspeople discovered that the railway barons' arrogance did not end

with their demands for free sites for depots. Along the transcontinental lines, virtually every important piece of business had to be "cleared" with the local railway manager. Farmers learned that the railroads were less their servants, carting their produce to market, than the masters of their fate.

California's "Big Four"—Collis P. Huntington, Leland Stanford, Mark Hopkins, and Charles Crocker—it was said, "owned" the state, thanks to their control of the Southern Pacific Railroad, which absorbed the Central Pacific. In addition to its stranglehold on transportation, the S.P. was, next to the federal government, California's biggest landowner. Indeed, instead of disposing of its land grant cheaply, as the transcontinental lines did, the S.P. held tight to its holdings in California's fertile Central Valley, driving the price of an acre to ten times and more than the $3 to $5 charged elsewhere in the West.

By the end of the century, the S.P. actually used its tremendous leverage to drive small farmers and ranchers out of business. The line's political officer, William F. Herrin, was widely considered to be the boss of the state legislature, monitoring every law that was passed in the interests of the S.P. Novelist Frank Norris summed up the Southern Pacific for many Californians in the title of his novel, *The Octopus* (1901), its tentacles reaching into every corner of the Golden State.

The Farmer's Grievances

The farmers of the Mississippi Valley also discovered that the railroad did not necessarily usher in a golden age. The problem, as they saw it, was monopoly. In most areas, one line handled all the traffic. Consequently, the rates at which farmers shipped their wheat, corn, or livestock to markets in the East were at the mercy of the shippers. Too often for goodwill to prevail, farmers saw their margin of profit consumed by transportation costs.

Most infuriating was the railroads' control of storage facilities, the grain elevators that stood close to the depot in every railway town. The farmer had to pay the company storage fees until such time as the railroad sent a train to haul away his grain. Obviously, it was often to the railroad's interests to delay scheduling shipment as long as possible. The company alone determined how long a farmer had to store his produce and, therefore, how large his fee was. Within a few months, a railroad could gobble up a year's income.

Attempts to Regulate

In the early 1870s, an organization of farmers, the Patrons of Husbandry (or Grangers, as members were called) won control of the state legislature of Illinois and considerable influence in adjoining states. Allied

Gift for the Grangers, *a lithograph made in 1873
celebrates the Patrons of Husbandry, a farmers'
organization.*

with small businessmen, who also felt squeezed by railroads, they passed a series of "Granger laws" that set maximum rates that railroad companies could charge both for hauling and storing. Several other state governments followed Illinois's lead.

The railroad barons launched a legal counterattack, hiring clever and high-powered corporation lawyers like Richard B. Olney and Roscoe Conkling to challenge state regulatory legislation before the Supreme Court. At first, the Grangers prevailed. In the case of *Munn* vs. *Illinois* (1877), the Supreme Court dominated by old-fashioned Lincoln Republicans declared that when a private company's business affected the public interest, the public had the right to regulate that business for the common good.

Nine years later, the times and the personnel of the Supreme Court had changed. In 1886, justices on cordial terms with the new order wrote several pro-railroad doctrines into the law of the land. The most important was handed down in the Wabash case of 1886 (*Wabash, St. Louis, and Pacific Railway Co.* vs. *Illinois*). In its decision, the Court reinterpreted the interstate-commerce clause of the Constitution in such a way as to protect large railroad companies. That is, the Constitution provides that only Congress can reg-

ulate commerce between and among states. In the Wabash case, the Court ruled that because the Wabash Railroad ran through several states, the Illinois legislature could not regulate freight rates even between two points within the state. The Wabash decision left state governments with authority over only short, generally insignificant local lines that were rarely exploitative in the first place.

The Interstate Commerce Commission

The decision was not popular. Rural politicians and urban reformers condemned the Court as the tool of the railway barons. If only Congress could bridle the iron horse, they shouted from Grange halls and from the stages of city auditoriums, let Congress do so. In 1887, Congress did, enacting the Interstate Commerce Act.

On the face of it, the law brought the national railroads under control. It required railroads to publish their rates and to charge them; under-the-table rebates were forbidden. Railroads were forbidden to charge less for long hauls along routes where there was competition than for short hauls in areas where a company had a monopoly. The act also outlawed the pooling of business by railroads, a practice by which, many shippers believed, they were controlled and fleeced. To enforce the act and to regulate rates, Congress created a permanent independent federal commission, the Interstate Commerce Commission (ICC).

The Interstate Commerce Act calmed antirailroad protest, but it did not have much effect on railroad policy. The ICC, simply, did not have any real power. If the Commissioners wished to compel a railroad to comply with their regulations, they had to take the company to the same courts that had favored the railroads over the state legislatures. Commissioner Charles A. Prouty commented, "If the ICC was worth buying, the railroads would try to buy it. The only reason they have not is that the body is valueless in its ability to correct railroad abuses."

In fact, the railroads did not have to buy the ICC because it was given to them. The Harrison, Cleveland, and McKinley administrations (1889–1901) were all sympathetic to big business and packed the Commission with railroaders and lawyers friendly to them.

The Money Power

By the early 1890s, the trunk lines of the country had been consolidated into five great systems. By 1900, these had effectively fallen under the control of two large New York investment banks, J. P. Morgan and Company and Kuhn, Loeb and Company, the latter in league with the Union Pacific president, Edward H. Harriman.

This development was due to the fact that, when the government ceased to subsidize construction, the railroads had to look to other sources in order to mobilize the huge amounts of capital needed to lay second tracks, modernize equipment, and buy up competitors. The companies often needed more money than their profits provided. Capital was even more serious a problem during the recurrent business recessions of the period when income sank, while fixed costs (such as maintenance) remained the same.

The traditional means of raising capital—offering shares of stock to the public—was simply not up to these needs, particularly during recessions. Into the gap stepped the investment banks. These institutions served both as sales agents, finding moneyed buyers for railway stock at a commission, and as buyers themselves. In return for these services, bankers such as John Pierpont Morgan insisted on a say in the formation of railroad policy, placing a representative of the bank on the client's board of directors.

Because every large railroad needed financial help at one time or another—every transcontinental but the Great Northern went under during the depression of 1893–97—Morgan's and Kuhn Loeb's men soon sat on every major corporate board, creating an interlocking directorate. Like all bankers, their goal was a steady, dependable flow of profit, and their means to that end was to eliminate wasteful competition. They called a halt to the periodic rate wars among the New York Central, Pennsylvania, and Baltimore and Ohio railroads in the eastern states. In 1903, J. P. Morgan tried to merge the Northern Pacific and the Great Northern, two systems with parallel lines between the Great Lakes and the Pacific Northwest. Competing for traffic, he believed, hurt them both.

Banker control also had its benefits. No more did unscrupulous pirates like the Erie Gang ruin great transportation systems for the sake of short-term killings. The integration of the nation's railways also resulted in a gradual but significant lowering of fares and freight rates. Between 1866 and 1897, the cost of shipping a hundred pounds of grain from Chicago to New York dropped from 65 cents to 20 cents, and the rate for shipping beef from 90 cents per hundred weight to 40 cents. J. P. Morgan's self-justification was identical to that of John D. Rockefeller: competition was wasteful and destructive; consolidation better served the nation as a whole, as well as the cream of its capitalists.

J. P. Morgan

But the control of so important a part of the economy by a few men with offices on Wall Street called into question some very basic American ideals. Where was individual freedom and opportunity, many people asked, when a sinister "money power" headed by the imperious Morgan could decide on a whim the fate of millions of farmers and workingpeople?

A resplendent and cultivated man who owned yachts that were larger than the ships in most countries' navies and collections of rare books and art that were superior to those in most countries' national museums, Morgan never attempted to disguise his power or his contempt for ordinary mortals. In return he was feared, held in awe, and hated.

Morgan shook off all such criticism. In the end, he was vulnerable only to ridicule. An affliction of the skin had given him a large, bulbous nose that swelled and glowed like a circus clown's when he was angry. Making fun of it, however, was the only foolproof way to make it light up, and Morgan rarely rubbed elbows with the kind of people who would notice his single human weakness.

An Age of Trusts

In addition to railroaders, Morgan found plenty of company among the industrialists whose trusts and

*J. Pierpont Morgan, by Edward Streichen (1906).
Collection, The Museum of Modern Art, New York.
Gift of A. Conger Goodyear.*

An overfed monopoly demands tribute from workers, farmers, and merchants in the cartoon from the British magazine Puck.

other devices for doing business he organized for fees of a million dollars and more. The trust was most useful in industries in which, like oil, there was a single critical stage of manufacture that involved relatively few companies. Some of John D. Rockefeller's most successful imitators were in sugar refining (the sugar trust controlled about 95 percent of the nation's facilities) and whiskey distilling. In 1890, James Buchanan Duke of Durham, North Carolina, founded the American Tobacco Company, a trust which coordinated the activities of practically every cigarette manufacturer in the United States. In effect, he dictated the terms by which tens of thousands of tobacco growers did business.

By 1890, many Americans had become convinced that when a few men could control a whole industry, the principle of economic opportunity and the foundations of American democracy were in jeopardy.

The Sherman Antitrust Act

Responding to public pressure in that year, Congress passed the Sherman Antitrust Act, which declared that "every contract, combination, in the form of trust or otherwise, or conspiracy, in restraint of trade or commerce among the several states, or with foreign nations, is hereby declared to be illegal." The Sherman Act authorized the Attorney General to move against such combinations and force them to dissolve, thus reestablishing the independence of the companies that had formed them.

The Sherman Act was no more successful in halting the consolidation movement than the Interstate Commerce Act was in controlling the power of the railroads. Critics said that the Sherman Act was a sham from the beginning, designed to quiet unease but not to hurt big business. In fact, the weakness of the law lay in the inability of congressmen to comprehend this new economic phenomenon. Real monopoly was so unfamiliar to the lawmakers that they were unable to draft a law that was worded well enough to be effective. The language of the Sherman Act was so ambivalent that a shrewd lawyer—and the trusts had the best—could usually find a loophole.

Moreover, while congressmen could take fright at a popular uproar, the courts were immune to it. The Wabash case was only one of a series of decisions by

NOTABLE PEOPLE

THE FIELD BROTHERS

The Field brothers: (left to right) Cyrus, Henry, Matthew, David, Jonathan, and Stephen.

The economic explosion of the late nineteenth century created opportunities from the bottom to the top of American society. Immigrants who had flirted with starvation in the old country found subsistence and comfort. Ordinary Americans moved up into the middle class as skilled workers, managers, and small businessmen. Scions of the old elite, of comfortably fixed, educated, and genteel families who would have been content to have been local eminences in the early nineteenth century found that, in the new America, they had a vast, national arena in which to make their marks.

The Field family of Connecticut is a case in point. Of *Mayflower* vintage, the Fields had produced generation upon generation of farmers, Congregationalist ministers, merchants, and local political leaders. The family was ancient and respectable, but quite unknown beyond its township. Opportunity for the reverend David Field, born in 1781, meant a midlife exchange of a pulpit in tiny Haddam, Connecticut, for one in Stockbridge, Massachusetts, a scarcely larger town. Four of his six sons, by way of contrast, became national figures in the law, business, technology, and popular culture.

The eldest of them, David Dudley Field (1805–94), was America's foremost legal reformer. As a lawyer in

New York, he observed that the century-old tangle of ordinances that had worked well enough in a small commercial city were inadequate in a burgeoning metropolis and commercial empire. He labored, much of the time drawing on his own resources, to sift, reform, and codify city and state law. Late in his life, he turned to international law, particularly rules governing the conduct of nations during wartime.

New York state adopted David Dudley Field's codification of criminal law in 1881, but not the reforms of the civil code which he proposed. By the 1880s, his influence had been somewhat tarnished by his political and business associations. Field had defended "Boss" William Marcy Tweed, the head of the corrupt political machine that governed New York City during the 1860s, as well as the notorious robber barons Jim Fisk and Jay Gould. However, many of his proposals were incorporated into the English Judicature Acts of 1873–75, which later spread to British colonies throughout the world.

David Dudley Field had the curious experience of arguing cases before the Supreme Court when his younger brother was an associate justice. Stephen Johnson Field (1816–99), also an attorney, was a Forty-Niner, rushing off to California in search of gold or, perhaps, litigants.

He settled in the boomtown of Marysville, was elected mayor and, in 1857, was named Justice of the California Supreme Court in 1857. Stephen Field was a Democrat but also a staunch supporter of the Civil War. In 1863, Abraham Lincoln named him to the U. S. Supreme Court.

On the high court, he proved to be conservative in cases involving business, but also a defender of civil liberties. Indeed, his insistence on defending the rights of Chinese immigrants in Calfornia may have cost him further advancement in public life. He was several times considered as a favorite-son candidate for the presidency, but was denied the prize because he had offended white workingmen with his "pro-Chinese" judicial decisions.

Cyrus Field (1819–92) was a technological visionary of extraordinary persistence. A successful paper manufacturer before he was 30, in 1854 he turned to promoting the idea of a cable between Europe and North America over which telegraphic messages could be sent. Such a device would obviously be of inestimable value to business, but the difficulties of laying such a cable seemed overwhelming. Indeed, Field's first attempt at laying a cable between Ireland and Newfoundland in 1857 broke and a second, in 1858, lasted just three weeks.

In 1865, Cyrus Field tried again, this time using the largest ship in the world, the British-built *Great Eastern*. Almost 700 feet long and 120 feet across, the "great iron ship" was an engineering marvel that was never used properly. Able to power itself by sail, paddle wheel, or screw, it could carry 4,000 passengers and 2,000 crew. Instead of exploiting its size in long voyages, such as between Britain and Australia, the *Great Eastern*'s owners put it on the Atlantic run, where it did not compete well with smaller ships. Repeatedly, its owners went bankrupt.

Cyrus Field saw the *Great Eastern* as a massive cable factory with enough power to run all the mills of Manchester. He outfitted the ship to reel out the continuous, fragile wire that would tie together Old World and New. In 1865, he lost a cable once again but, on July 27, 1866, the connection was made. Despite his achievement, Cyrus Field did not die wealthy. A bit too trusting of his business associates, including Jay Gould, he saw his fortune evaporate by the time of his death.

The youngest Field brother, Henry Martyn Field (1822–1907), was a Presbyterian minister who wrote adulatory biographies of David Dudley and Cyrus (but not, oddly, Stephen). However, he too made his mark as a communicator. During the 1890s, with the American middle class large, energetic, and curious, he wrote best-selling travel books for vicarious sojourners.

the Supreme Court that ensured the survival of the biggest of businesses. In the first major case tried under the Sherman Act, *U.S.* vs. *E. C. Knight Company* in 1895, the Court found that a nearly complete monopoly of sugar refining in the United States did not violate the law because manufacture, which the sugar trust monopolized, was not a part of trade or commerce, even though its sugar was sold in every state.

Nor was the executive branch keen to attack big business. President Grover Cleveland's Attorney General, Richard B. Olney, was a former corporation lawyer. Under Benjamin Harrison and William McKinley, the other presidents of the 1890s, the Justice Department was similarly probusiness. During the first ten years of the Sherman Act, only 18 cases were instituted and 4 of these were aimed at labor unions, also "conspiracies in restraint of trade."

Consequently, rather than heralding doomsday for the trusts, the years between 1890 and 1901 were a golden age. The number of state-chartered trusts actually grew from 251 to 290. More telling, the amount of money invested in trusts rose from $192 million to $326 million. By the end of the century, there was no doubt that the demands of modern manufacturing meant that massive organizations were here to stay. But whether they would continue to be the private possessions of a few Bells, Morgans, Carnegies, and Rockefellers was still open to debate.

RADICAL CRITICS OF THE NEW ORDER

The Interstate Commerce and Sherman Antitrust laws were enacted by mainstream politicians who believed that the individual pursuit of wealth was a virtue, men who wished only to restore the opportunity to succeed and the possibility of competing that the big business combinations had apparently destroyed. Outside the mainstream, sometimes radical critics of the new industrial capitalism raised their voices and wielded their pens in opposition to the new order itself. At least briefly, some of them won large followings.

Henry George and the Single Tax

A lively writing style and a knack for simplifying difficult economic ideas made journalist Henry George and his single tax the center of a short-lived but momentous social movement. In *Progress and Poverty*, published in 1879, George observed what was obvious, but also bewildering to many people. Instead of freedom from onerous labor, as the machine once seemed to promise, the machine had put millions to work under killing conditions for long hours. Instead of making life easier and fuller for all, the mass production of goods had enriched the few in the "House of Have," and impoverished the millions in the "House of Want."

George did not blame either industrialization or capitalism as such for the misery he saw around him. Like most Americans, he believed that the competition for comfort and security was a wellspring of the nation's energy. The trouble began only when those who were successful in the race grew so wealthy that they ceased to be entrepreneurs who built, and became parasites who lived off the "rents" their property generated.

George called income derived from mere ownership of property "unearned increment," because it required no work, effort, or ingenuity of its possessors. Property grew more valuable and its owners richer only because other people needed access to it in order to survive. Such value was spurious, George said, government had every right to levy a 100 percent tax on it. Because the revenues from this tax would be quite enough to pay all the expenses of government, all other taxes could be abolished. "The single tax" became the rallying cry of George's movement. It would destroy the idle and parasitic rich as a social class. The entrepreneurship and competition that made the country great would flourish without the handicaps of taxation.

George's gospel was popular enough that in 1886 he narrowly missed election as mayor of New York, a city where real-estate values and "unearned increment" from land were as high as anywhere in the world.

Edward Bellamy Looks Backward

Another book that became the Bible of a protest movement was Edward Bellamy's novel of 1888, *Looking Backward, 2000–1887*. Within two years of its publication, the book sold 200,000 copies (the equivalent of more than a million in 1990) and led to the founding of about 150 "Nationalist clubs," made up of people who shared Bellamy's vision of the future.

The story that moved them was simple and soon to be rather conventional in its gimmick. A proper young Bostonian of the 1880s succumbs to a mysterious sleep and awakes in the United States of the twenty-first century. There he discovers that technology has produced not a world of sharp class divisions and widespread misery (as in 1887), but a utopia that provides abundance for all. Like George, Bellamy was not opposed to industrial development in itself.

Capitalism no longer exists in the world of *Looking Backward*. Through a peaceful democratic revolution—won at the polls—the American people have abolished competitive greed and idle unproductive living because they were at odds with American ideals.

American writer Edward Bellamy, author of the widely read novel, Looking Backward.

Instead of private ownership of land and industry, the state owns the means of production and administers them for the good of all. Everyone contributes to the common wealth. Everyone lives decently, and none miserably or wastefully, on its fruits.

Bellamy's vision was socialistic. However, because he rooted it in American values rather than in the internationalism of the Marxists, he called it "Nationalism." The patriotic facet of his message made his gospel palatable to middle-class Americans who, while troubled by the growth of fantastic fortunes and of wretched poverty, found foreign ideologies and talk of class warfare obnoxious and frightening.

Socialists and Anarchists

Nevertheless, Marxist ideology, including the doctrine of class conflict, found adherents in the United States. Some old-stock Americans were converted to Marxian socialism. For the most part, however, Marxism found its followers among immigrants and the children of immigrants. Briefly after 1872, the General Council of the First International, the official administration of world socialism, made its headquarters in New York, where Karl Marx sent it to prevent the followers of his anarchist rival, Mikhail Bakunin, from winning control of it.

The Marxists taught that the capitalist system of wage slavery—workers laboring for wages in the employ of a capitalist class that owned the means of production, the factories and machines—would fall under its own weight to socialism and then to communism, under which, respectively, the state and the workers themselves would own the factories and machines, administering them for the good of all.

Some Marxist socialists held that in democratic countries like the United States, this social revolution would be voted in peacefully. Social Democratic movements flourished in a number of cities, most notably in Milwaukee, where an Austrian immigrant, Victor L. Berger, built a party that, after 1900, would govern the city for several decades.

Other Marxian socialists held that the overthrow of capitalism would inevitably be violent. The most extreme of these revolutionaries were the anarchists, some of whom held that individuals could hasten the great day through "the propaganda of the deed," acts of terrorism against the ruling class. Anarchists figured prominently in an incident in Chicago in 1886 in which, ironically, they were not responsible for the bloodshed that occurred.

Haymarket

In May 1886, workers at the McCormick International Harvester Company, the world's largest manufacturer of farm machinery, were on strike. The Chicago police were blatantly on the side of the employers, and over several days they killed four workers. On May 4, a group of anarchists, mostly German but including a Confederate Army veteran of some social standing, Albert Parsons, held a rally in support of the strikers at Haymarket Square, just south of the city center.

The oratory was red-hot; but the speakers broke no laws, and the crowd was orderly. Indeed, the rally was about to break up under the threat of a downpour when a platoon of police entered the square and demanded that the assembly disperse. At that instant, someone threw a bomb into their midst, killing seven policemen and wounding 67. The police fired a volley, and four workers fell dead.

News of the incident fed an antianarchist hysteria in Chicago. Authorities rounded up several dozen individuals who were known to have attended anarchist meetings, and authorities brought eight to trial for the murder of the officers. Among them was Parsons and a prominent German agitator, August Spies.

The trial was a farce. No one on the prosecution team knew or even claimed to know who had thrown the bomb. (His or her identity is still unknown.) Nor did the prosecution present evidence to tie any of the eight to the bombing. One, a deranged young German named Louis Lingg, was a bomb maker, although even he had a plausible alibi. Several of the defendants had not been at the rally. Parsons had been ill in bed that evening and, indeed, had been ill since before the rally was called.

All these facts proved to be irrelevant. Chicago was determined to have scapegoats, and, although the charge was murder, the Haymarket anarchists were tried for their ideas and associations. Four were hanged. Lingg committed suicide in his cell. Three were sentenced to long prison terms.

The Social Gospel

Taking a more moralistic approach to the tensions of the late nineteenth century were a number of influential Protestant clergymen. Troubled by the callousness of big business, preachers of the "Social Gospel" emphasized the Christian's social obligations, his duty to be his brother's keeper.

Walter Rauschenbusch began his ministerial career on the frontiers of Hell's Kitchen, one of New York City's worst slums. "One could hear human virtue cracking and crushing all around," he wrote in later years. To Rauschenbusch, poverty was the cause of the crime and sin, and mass poverty was the result of allowing great capitalists a free hand in enriching

A New York tenement photographed by Jacob Riis.

themselves. Later, as a professor at Rochester Theological Seminary, Rauschenbusch taught the obligation of the churches to work for both the relief of the poor and a more equitable distribution of wealth.

Washington Gladden, a Congregationalist, called unrestricted competition "antisocial and anti-Christian." He did not propose the abolition of capitalism, but he did call for regulation of its grossest immoralities. He was highly moralistic. Late in life, Gladden described John D. Rockefeller's fortune as "tainted money" and urged his church not to accept contributions from the millionaire.

The Social Gospel appealed to many middle-class people, often modestly well-to-do themselves, who did not suffer directly from the power of the very wealthy but who were offended by the extravagance and idleness of their lives. William Dean Howells, the editor of the *Atlantic Monthly*, wrote a novel about a successful manufacturer of paint (*The Rise of Silas Lapham*, 1885) who finds the idleness of wealth discomfiting. He "rises," finds purpose and happiness again, only when he loses his fortune and is forced to return to productive work. Howells even convinced an old friend from Ohio, former president Rutherford B. Hayes, to go on record late in his life as an advocate of the peaceful abolition of capitalism.

DEFENDERS OF THE FAITH

Such a barrage of criticism did not, of course, go unanswered. At the same time that great wealth was taking its knocks, it was reaping the praise of defenders. In part, like the critics, they drew on traditional American values to justify the new social system. In part, also like the critics, the defenders created new philosophies, original with the era of industrial capitalism.

Social Darwinism

Thoughtful and reflective people who were at peace with their era found a justification for great wealth and even dubious business ethics in a series of books, essays, and lectures by the British philosopher Herbert Spencer. Because Spencer seemed to apply Charles Darwin's celebrated theory of biological evolution to human society, his theory is widely known as "Social Darwinism."

According to Spencer, as in the world of animals and plants, where species compete for life and those best adapted survive, the "fittest" people rise to the top in the social competition for riches. Eventually, in the dog-eat-dog world, they alone survive. "If they are

sufficiently complete to live," Spencer wrote, "they do live, and it is well that they should live. If they are not sufficiently complete to live, they die and it is best they should die."

The intellectual tough-mindedness of Social Darwinism made Spencer immensely popular among American businessmen who were proud of their practicality. The Englishman was never so celebrated in his own country as he was in the United States. Although a vain man, Spencer was positively embarrassed by the adulation heaped on him at banquets sponsored by American academics and rich businessmen. Social Darwinism accounted for brutal business practices and underhand methods, justifying them as the natural "law of the jungle."

The language of Social Darwinism crept into the vocabulary of both businessmen and politicians who represented business interests. John D. Rockefeller, Jr., told a Sunday school class that "the growth of a large business is merely the survival of the fittest. The American Beauty Rose can be produced in the splendor and fragrance which bring cheer to its beholder only by sacrificing the early buds which grow up around it. This is not an evil tendency in business. It is merely the working out of a law of nature and a law of God."

But few American millionaires were true Social Darwinists. The very ruthlessness of the theory made it unpalatable to rich families who, in their personal lives, were committed to traditional religious values. Moreover, businessmen are rarely intellectuals, and Spencer's philosophy and writing style were as thick and murky as Rockefeller's crude oil. Understanding Spencer demanded careful study, such as businessmen rarely had the time to do. As a result, his explanation of the new society was more influential among scholars.

William Graham Sumner

The most important of these was a Yale professor, William Graham Sumner. He was uncompromising in his opposition to aiding the poor, putting government restrictions on business practices, and interfering in any way whatsoever with the law of the jungle. "The men who are competent to organize great enterprises and to handle great amounts of capital," he wrote, "must be found by natural selection, not political election."

Sumner's rigorous consistency also led him to oppose government on behalf of capital. He opposed protective tariffs. To subsidize American manufacturers by taxing imports was just as unnatural to him as was regulating the growth of trusts. If American manufacturers were not fit to compete with European manufacturers in a free market, Sumner said, they were not fit to survive. Likewise, Sumner opposed government intervention in strikes on behalf of employers. He believed that the strike was a natural test of the fitness of the employers' and the workers' causes. The outcome of a strike determined which side was "right."

To businessmen who used government trade policy and courts to their own purposes, Sumner's impartial applications of "natural law" were going too far. They had no objection to the right kind of government action.

After the turn of the century, the principles of Social Darwinism were turned on their head by the sociologist Lester Frank Ward of Brown University. Whereas Sumner argued that nature in society must be allowed to operate without restraint, Ward suggested that human society had evolved to a point where natural evolution could be guided by government policy. Just as farmers improved fruit trees and ranchers improved livestock through selective breeding, government could improve society by intervening in the naturally slow evolutionary process. Ward's "Reform Darwinism" influenced two generations of twentieth-century liberals.

The Success Gospel

The Gospel of Success had far more influence among nineteenth-century capitalists than Social Darwinism did. The United States had been built on the desire to prosper, Success Gospellers said. Therefore, if competition for riches was a virtue, what was wrong with winning? Far from a reason for anxiety or evidence of social immorality, the fabulous fortunes of America's wealthy families were an index of their virtue. The Rockefellers, Carnegies, and Morgans deserved their money.

Success manuals, books purporting to show how anyone could become a millionaire, were read as avidly as the works of George and Bellamy, and by far more people. All much the same, the manuals drew on the widespread assumptions that hard work, honesty, frugality, loyalty to employers and partners, and other "bourgeois virtues" drawn from Benjamin Franklin inevitably led to success. Having succeeded, America's millionaires deserved not resentment but admiration and imitation.

Shrugging off his enemies, John D. Rockefeller said flatly, "God gave me my money." A Baptist minister from Philadelphia, Russell B. Conwell, made a fortune delivering a lecture on the same theme. In "Acres of Diamonds," which the eloquent preacher delivered to paying audiences more than 6,000 times, Conwell said that great wealth was a great blessing. Not only could every American be rich, but every American should be rich. If a person failed, the fault lay within, not

with society. "There is not a poor person in the United States," Conwell said, "who was not made poor by his own shortcomings." The opportunities, the "acres of diamonds," were everywhere, waiting to be collected.

Conversely, those who already were rich were by definition virtuous. "Ninety-eight out of one hundred of the rich men of America are honest. That is why they are rich."

Horatio Alger and "Ragged Dick"

Through the 130 boys' novels written by another minister, Horatio Alger, the Success Gospel was conveyed to the younger generation. Alger's books sold 20 million copies between 1867 and 1899, and a battalion of imitators accounted for millions more.

He enjoyed this success despite the fact that he was no writer. His prose was wooden, his characters were snipped from cardboard, and his plots were variations on two or three simple themes. All assume as a given that one of the paramount goals of life is to get money. All teach that wealth is within the grasp of all because almost all Alger's heros are lads grappling with destitution. They are also honest, hard working, loyal to

Thrifty, hard-working, idealized boys were the staple of Horatio Alger's novels.

their employers, and clean living. "Ragged Dick," Alger's first hero and the prototype for "Tattered Tom," "Lucky Luke Larkin," and dozens of others, is insufferably courteous and always goes to church.

Curiously, Ragged Dick and the other heroes do not get rich slowly through hard work. At the beginning of the final chapter, the hero is usually as badly off as on page one. Then, however, he is presented with what amounts to a visitation of grace, a divine gift that rewards his virtues. The child of a rich industrialist falls off the Staten Island Ferry; or a rich girl stumbles into the path of a runaway brewery wagon drawn by panicked horses; or she slips into the Niagara River just above the falls. Because the Alger hero acts quickly, rescuing her, the heroic lad is rewarded with a job, marriage to the daughter, and eventually the grateful father's fortune. While appealing to the adolescent boy's yen for adventure, the novels also touched the American evangelical belief in divine grace. Just as he did with Rockefeller, God gave Ragged Dick his money as reward for his virtues.

Philanthropy

The flaw in the Success Gospel as a justification of great fortunes was the obvious fact that many rich men got their money by practicing the opposite of the touted virtues—dishonesty, betrayal of partners and employers, reckless speculation; and they grew richer while living a life of sumptuous, even decadent ease. The ethics of John D. Rockefeller's business practices were not so bad as his many enemies said, but there was no question that he cut corners. Similar suspicions surrounded practically every rich family in the country.

Booker T. Washington (center) won the support of many wealthy benefactors with his "Atlantic Compromise." To his left is steel magnate, Andrew Carnegie at the dedication of Tuskegee Institute.

Perhaps in part to compensate for the negative marks on their reputations, many wealthy businessmen turned to philanthropy as a kind of retroactive justification of their fortunes. Horatio Alger supported institutions that housed homeless boys in New York City. Russell B. Conwell founded Temple University, where poor young men could study very cheaply and improve themselves. Leland Stanford built a wholly new "Harvard of the West" in California. Rockefeller and other industrial millionaires gave huge sums to their churches and to universities. In retirement, Rockefeller took particular interest in helping American blacks to break out of the prison that racial discrimination had built around them.

Andrew Carnegie devised a coherent theory that justified fabulous fortunes on the basis of stewardship. In a celebrated essay entitled "Wealth," he argued that the unrestricted pursuit of riches made American society vital and strong, but it also made the man who succeeded a steward, or trustee. He had an obligation to distribute his money where it would provide opportunities for poor people to join the competition of the next generation. Indeed, Carnegie said that the rich

---

PRIVATE CARS

Partial to yachts, J. P. Morgan never owned a private railroad car, which was one of the status symbols of the late nineteenth century. In George Gould's, guests for dinner were expected to dress formally; Gould's liveried waiters served the food on solid gold plates. The Vanderbilt family's car, called the "Vanderbilt," could not accommodate all the guests whom they wished to entertain, so they had a new one built and called it "Duchess" after Consuelo. At Palm Beach, a favorite pleasuring ground of the rich, twenty to thirty private cars were sometimes parked in a special section of the train yard. When Morgan wished to go to a place he could not reach by water, he had to rent an opulent private car. On one occasion, he rented a whole train of private cars to transport east coast Episcopalian bishops to a conference in San Francisco.

man who died rich, died a failure. He retired from business in 1901 and devoted the rest of his life to granting money to libraries, schools, and useful social institutions. He was so rich, however, that despite extraordinary generosity, he died a multimillionaire.

HOW THE VERY RICH LIVED

Probably nothing reconciled ordinary Americans to the existence of multimillionaires more than the sheer fascination of the multitudes with the splendor in which the very rich lived. As Thorstein Veblen, an eccentric sociologist observed in several books written at the end of the century, the very wealthy literally lived to spend money for the sake of proving that they had money. Veblen called this showy extravagance "conspicuous consumption," and the propensity to throw it away, "conspicuous waste."

Conspicuous Consumption

Having much more money than they could possibly put to good use, the very rich competed in spending it by hosting lavish parties for one another, by building extravagant palaces, by purchasing huge yachts that were good for little but show, by adorning themselves with costly clothing and jewelry, and by buying European titles for their daughters.

The Waldorf-Astoria Hotel was decorated to resemble the palace at Versailles for the Bradley Martin Costume Ball. It was held, according to Mrs. Martin's brother, to provide employment to seamstresses during the depression of the 1890s.

There could be only one reason for dining on horseback: the diners could afford to do it. This was at Sherry's Ballroom in New York in 1903.

Some high-society parties lasting but a few hours cost more than $100,000. At one, hosted by the self-proclaimed prince of spenders, Harry Lehr, 100 dogs dined on "fricassee of bones" and gulped down shredded dog biscuit prepared by a French chef. The guests at one New York banquet ate their meal while mounted on horses (trays balanced on the animals' withers). The horses munched oats out of sterling-silver feedbags, possibly making more noise than their riders. At the Bradley Martin Costume Ball, guests boasted that they had spent more than $10,000 each on their fancy dress.

It was the golden age of yachting. Cornelius Vanderbilt's *North Star* was 250 feet long. Albert C. Burrage's *Aztec* carried 270 tons of coal; it could steam 5,500 miles without calling at a port for fuel. As on land, J. P. Morgan was champion at sea. He owned three successively larger, faster, and more opulent yachts called *Corsair*. Morgan had a sense of humor; a corsair is a pirate's vessel.

Nowhere was consumption more conspicuous and lavish than at upper-class resorts such as Newport, Rhode Island. A summer "cottage" of 30 rooms, used for only three months a year, cost $1 million. Coal

The lavish interior of "The Breakers," built by Cornelius Vanderbilt as his summer house, in Newport, Rhode Island.

Thus, heiress Alice Thaw was embarrassed on her honeymoon as countess of Yarmouth when creditors seized her husband's luggage. She had to wire her father for money to get it out of hock. Helena Zimmerman, the daughter of a coal and iron millionaire from Cincinnati, married the duke of Manchester. For 20 years their bills were paid by the father of the duchess out of the labor of workers living on subsistence wages.

The most famous American aristocrats were the heiresses of two of the original robber barons, Jay Gould and Cornelius Vanderbilt. Anna Gould became the Countess Boni de Castellane. Before she divorced him in order to marry his cousin, the higher-ranking Prince de Sagan, the count extracted more than $5 million from Jay Gould's purse. Consuelo Vanderbilt was married against her wishes into the proudest family in England. Both when Consuelo married the duke of Marlborough and when she divorced him, the payoff ran to several million. The duke may have been the only individual ever to get the better of the Vanderbilt family.

Women as Decor

The role of young heiresses in the game of conspicuous waste helps to illustrate the curious role of the women of the new social class. They were idler than their menfolk. A role in business or public life was denied them and they had none of the homemaking duties of middle-class women to occupy their time.

baron E. J. Berwind spent $1.5 million to build "The Elms." William K. Vanderbilt outdid everyone with "Marble House." That cottage cost $2 million; the furniture inside, $9 million.

Those places were for vacations. At home in the cities, the millionaires created neighborhoods of mansions such as New York's Fifth Avenue, a thoroughfare given over to grand houses for 20 blocks; Chicago's Gold Coast, which loomed over the city's lakeshore; and San Francisco's Nob Hill, from which palaces looked down on the city like the castles of medieval barons.

A Lord in the Family

A fad of the very rich that aggravated many Americans was the rush during the 1880s and 1890s to marry daughters to European nobles. Nothing more clearly dramatized the aristocratic pretensions of the new elite. Wealthy families took pride in the price that they paid to have an earl or a duke as a son-in-law.

It was a two-way bargain. An American daughter got a title to wear to Newport; an impoverished European aristocrat got money with which to maintain himself in fine wines, horses, and hounds.

moments when she entered ballrooms, all eyes on her pearls.

Women's fashions were designed to emphasize their wearers' idleness. Indeed, fashion, by its very nature, is conspicuously wasteful. In keeping up with changes, the whole point of fashion, the wealthy woman demonstrated that it made no dent in her husband's fortune if she annually discarded last year's expensive clothing to make room in her closet for the latest from Paris.

Fashion reflects social status in other ways. When wealthy women laced themselves up in crippling steel and bone corsets, which made it difficult for them to move, let alone perform any physical work, they were making it clear that they did not have to do such work and were purely decorative. They had servants to care for every detail of their lives.

Men's clothing reflected social status, too. The tall silk hat, the badge of the capitalist, was a completely useless headgear. It offered neither protection nor

Consuelo Vanderbilt's marriage to the Duke of Marlborough marked the epitome of "buying titles" among American millionaires. The unhappiness of the Duchess, which led to divorce, is obvious even in the first photograph of her in her robes.

What, then, to do? In effect, the women of the wealthiest classes became their families' chief conspicuous consumers. The rich woman's role was to reflect her husband's accomplishment in amassing wealth; she was a glittering display piece for costly clothing and jewelry. Mrs. George Gould, daughter-in-law of the crusty Jay, went through life known for nothing but the fact that she owned a pearl necklace that was worth $500,000. No one ever mentioned Mrs. Gould in any other context. Her life revolved around the

Mrs. George Gould's identification with her half-million dollar pearl necklace was so total that she was never-photographed without it.

LELAND STANFORD

When he was president of the Southern Pacific Railroad, Leland Stanford ordered that all employees of the company stand at attention in a line along the track when his private trains passed through. All Southern Pacific locomotives traveling in the other direction were to blow their whistles in salute.

warmth. But it did prevent a man from so much as bending down to dust his patent-leather shoes. "White collar," displaying clean linen at wrist and neck, made it clear that the wearer did no work that would soil his clothing.

Unlikely Neighbors

For the most part, ordinary Americans knew of the shenanigans of the very rich only through hearsay and the popular press. Farmers and factory workers did not vacation at Newport or attend costume balls and ducal weddings at Blenheim palace. The nature of urban life in the late nineteenth century was such, however, that the idle rich could not conceal their extravagance from the middle and lower classes.

The rich employed legions of servants to maintain their mansions. The grandeur and waste of upper-class life was well known to these poorly paid people. (Two million women worked in domestic service at the end of the century.) More important, because it was impossible to commute long distances in the congested cities, whether for business or social life, the wealthy lived not in isolated suburbs but close to the centers of New York, Boston, Philadelphia, Chicago, and other great cities.

The tradesmen who made daily deliveries of groceries, meat, vegetables and fruit, ice, coal (for heating), and other necessities, not to mention repairmen and those who delivered durable goods, were intimately familiar with the kind of wealth that their customers enjoyed. Marginal workers who were employed by the service and the light manufacturing industries of the center city walked daily past palaces and saw the rich come and go in lacquered carriages tended by flunkies in livery.

YOU CAN TAKE IT WITH YOU

At the Vanderbilt family tomb on Staten Island, watchmen punched a time clock every hour on the hour around the clock. William Vanderbilt, son of the Commodore, had a deathly fear of graverobbers.

Popular Culture

In newspapers aimed at a mass readership, in popular songs, and in the melodramas favored by workingpeople, the idleness and extravagance of the "filthy rich" were favorite themes. The wealthy were depicted with a mixture of envy and resentment. New York's Tin Pan Alley, the center of the sheet-music industry, preached a combination of pity for the "bird in a gilded cage," the wealthy woman, and the traditional moral that because poor people worked, they were more virtuous.

In the popular melodramas of the day, simple plays with no subtlety of character and a completely predictable plot, right-living poor people were pitted against an unscrupulous rich villain. "You are only a shopgirl," said the high-society lady in a typical play. "An honest shopgirl," replied the heroine in stilted language, "as far above a fashionable idler as heaven is above earth!" (The poor but virtuous shopgirl was often rewarded in the final act by marriage to a rich young man; she consequently took up the life of idle-

Readers of sensationalist newspapers were awed by the beauty of Evelyn Nesbit and titillated by the sex scandal in which she was involved.

ness that she had condemned through two and a half acts.)

Juicy Scandals

Ordinary people studiously followed the scandals that periodically rocked high society. In 1872, "Jubilee Jim" Fisk was shot to death by a rival for the affections of his showgirl mistress, Josie Mansfield. Newspaper readers could find a moral in the fact that Fisk's great wealth and power could not save him from a violent death at the age of 38. Nevertheless, a good part of the story's appeal were the details of Fisk's sumptuous personal life, on which the newspapers lovingly dwelled.

Even more sensational was the 1906 murder of architect Stanford White by millionaire Harry Thaw. During his trial, Thaw accused White of having seduced his beautiful fiancée, Evelyn Nesbit. Her testimony concerning the famous White's peculiarities behind closed doors simultaneously titillated the public and served as a moral justification for the murder. (Thaw went free.) Such scandals were the stock in trade of nationally circulated periodicals, such as the *Police Gazette* and *Frank Leslie's Illustrated Newspaper*, that appealed to the working classes. By the end of the century, many large daily papers also took to bumping conventional news to the back pages when an upper-class scandal came up in the courts.

For Further Reading

Most of the works cited at the conclusion of Chapter 28 are relevant here, particularly Vincent P. DeSantis, *The Shaping of Modern America, 1877–1916* (1973); John A. Garraty, *The New Commonwealth, 1877–1890* (1968); Samuel P. Hays, *The Response to Industrialism, 1885–1914* (1957); Glenn Porter, *The Rise of Big Business, 1860–1910* (1973); and Robert A. Wiebe, *The Search for Order* (1967). Also see Sigmund Diamond, *The Reputation of American Businessmen* (1959), and L. Galambos, *The Public Image of Big Business in America* (1975).

Justifications and defenses of the new order are studied in John G. Cawelti, *Apostles of the Self-Made Man in America* (1966); Sidney Fine, *Laissez-Faire and the Welfare State: A Study of Conflict in American Thought,* 1865–1901 (1956); Richard Hofstadter, *Social Darwinism in American Thought* (1944); Edward C. Kirkland, *Dream and Thought in the Business Community* (1956); and Irwin Wyllie, *The Self-Made Man in America* (1954).

Criticisms of the new commonwealth are the focus in C. A. Barker, *Henry George* (1955); Gabriel Kolko, *Railroads and Regulation* (1965); Samuel T. McSeveney, *The Politics of Depression: Political Behavior in the Northeast, 1893–1896* (1972); Andrew Sinclair, *Corsair: The Life of J. Pierpont Morgan* (1981); John L. Thomas, *Alternative America: Henry George, Edward Bellamy, Henry Demarest Lloyd* (1983); and Thorstein Veblen, *The Theory of the Leisure Class* (1899).

Leland Stanford and James J. Hill thought of themselves as the men who had built the railroads. So did most Americans. John D. Rockefeller took pride in the majesty of the Standard Oil Company as his personal creation, and, whether they liked the results or not, Americans agreed with him. Newspapers and magazines referred to Andrew Carnegie as the nation's greatest steelmaker. In the popular mind, vast industries were associated with powerful individuals, just as battles were identified with generals: Sherman had marched across Georgia; Grant had taken Richmond; Vanderbilt ran the New York Central. J. P. Morgan even spoke of his hobby, yachting, in personal terms. "You can do

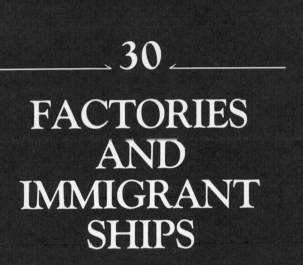

30

FACTORIES
AND
IMMIGRANT
SHIPS

The People Who Built
Modern America

Immigrants, identification tags pinned to their clothes, arrive at Ellis Island, New York, in 1907.

business with anyone," he huffed, "but you can only sail a boat with a gentleman."

In reality, Morgan and his friends merely decided when and where the boat was to go. It took 85 grimy stokers and hard-handed sailors to get Morgan's *Corsair* out of New York harbor and safely into Newport or Venice. In the same way, Stanford, Hill, Rockefeller, Carnegie, and other great businessmen supervised the creation of industrial America, but the edifice was built by anonymous millions of men and women who wielded the shovels and needles and tended the machines that whirred and whined in the factories and mills.

Girls work at a thread-winding machine at the Loudon Hosiery Mill in London, Tennessee, in 1910.

A NEW WAY OF LIFE

America's workingpeople could not be kept below decks like the crew of the *Corsair*. While the population of the United States rose rapidly during the last part of the nineteenth century, more than doubling between 1860 and 1900, the size of the working class quadrupled. In 1860, 1.5 million Americans made their living in workshops and mills, and another 700,000 in mining and construction. By 1900, 6 million people worked in manufacturing and 2.3 million in mining and construction, increases of 4 times and 3.3 times, respectively. Wageworkers, once a decided minority, now constituted a distinct and significant social class.

Bigger Factories, Better Technology

The size of the work place also grew, a fact of profound importance for the quality of workingpeople's lives. In 1870, the average workshop in the United States em-

ployed eight people and was owned by an individual or by partners who lived nearby and who personally supervised the business, sometimes working at the bench with their employees. Like it or not, generous, peevish, or cruel, such bosses were personally involved in the lives of their workers. They heard of events in their lives ranging from the birth of a child to the death of a parent, and they discussed matters such as wages, hours, and shop conditions face to face with the people who were affected by them. Even Pittsburgh's iron and steel mills, the largest factories in the country, employed on average just 90 workers.

By 1900, the average industrial worker labored in a shop with 25 employees. Plants employing a thousand men and women were common. The average payroll of Pittsburgh steel plants was 1,600 and a few companies listed 10,000 people on the payroll; Carnegie Steel employed 23,000. The men who directed the affairs of such concerns rarely stepped on the floor of a shop. They were interested in wages, hours, and conditions only insofar as entries in the ledgers that lined the walls of their offices.

The increased application of steam power and improved machinery affected workers in other ways. The highly skilled craftsman, trained for years in the use of hand tools, ceased to be the backbone of the manufacturing process. Not many crafts actually disappeared (as they would in the twentieth century), and

JOHN HENRY

Ironically, considering that few blacks held industrial jobs in the nineteenth century, a black man became the symbol of the decline of the skilled worker in the face of the new machines. "The Ballad of John Henry," written about 1872 and immediately popular among workingpeople, told the story of a black miner's contest with the newly introduced steam drill. There are several versions. Most of them end in tragedy for the human being. John Henry might defeat the steam drill in a contest to sink steel in rock, but he dies from the pace, "with his hammer in his hand."

some, like the machinist's trade, increased in importance. But in most areas, steam-powered machines took over from artisans, performing their jobs more quickly and often better.

Many machines were tended by unskilled or semiskilled men, women, and children who merely guided the device at its task. Unlike craftsmen, these workers were interchangeable, easily replaced because their jobs required little training. Consequently, they could be poorly paid, and they commanded scant respect from employers, small businessmen, professionals, politicians, and skilled workers. "If I wanted boiler iron," said one industrialist, "I would go out on the market and buy it where I could get it cheapest; and if I wanted to employ men I would do the same."

Wages

In dollars, the wages of many workers declined during the final decades of the nineteenth century. However, real wages, or purchasing power, generally rose as the cost of food, clothing, and housing dropped more radically than did hourly pay. Taken as a whole, the industrial working class enjoyed almost 50 percent more purchasing power in 1900 than in 1860.

But this statistic can be misleading because the skilled "aristocracy of labor"—locomotive engineers, machinists, master carpenters, printers, and other highly trained craftsmen—improved their earnings much more than did the unskilled workers at the bot-

AVERAGE ANNUAL EARNINGS FOR SELECTED OCCUPATIONS—1890	
Farm laborers	$233
Public school teachers	256
Bituminous coal miners	406
Manufacturing employees	439
Street railway employees	557
Steam railroad employees	560
Gas & electricity workers	687
Ministers	794
Clerical workers in manufacturing & Steam RR	848
Postal employees	878

tom of the pile. The average annual wage for all manufacturing workers in 1900 was only $435, or $8.37 a week. Unskilled workers were paid about 10 cents an hour on the average, about $5.50 a week. A girl of twelve or thirteen, tending a loom in a textile factory, might take home as little as $2 a week after various fines (for being late to work, for example) were deducted from her pay. As late as 1904, sociologist Robert Hunter estimated that one American in eight lived in poverty, and he almost certainly hit below the true figure.

Hours

Hours on the job varied. Most government employees had enjoyed an eight-hour day since 1840. Skilled workers, especially in the building trades (bricklayers, carpenters, plumbers), generally worked ten. Elsewhere, a factory worker was counted lucky if he or she worked a twelve-hour day. During the summer months, many mills ran from sunup to sundown, as long as 16 hours—with only one shift.

The average workweek was 66 hours long in 1860, and 55 hours in 1910. People were on the job five and a half or six days a week; half-day Saturday was considered a holiday. In industries that were required to run around the clock, such as steel (the furnaces could not be shut down), the workforce was divided into two shifts on seven-day schedules. Each shift worked for twelve hours. At the end of a two-week period, the day workers switched shifts with the night workers. This meant a "holiday" of 24 hours once a month. The price of the holiday was working for 24 hours two weeks later while the other shift enjoyed its vacation.

True holidays were few. However, because of the erratic swings in the business cycle, factory workers had plenty of unwanted time off. Some industries were highly seasonal. Coal miners, for example, could expect to be without wages for weeks or even months

WEEKENDS OFF

The necessity of taking a break from toil was recognized at the dawn of history. The western tradition of one day off a week derives from the sabbath of the ancient Hebrews, a day—Saturday—when the Lord forbade work. The Christians made Sunday their sabbath, in part to distinguish themselves from their Jewish origins and the medieval church forbade "servile labor" on the sabbath as one of its precepts. The longer weekend is of English origin. In 958 A.D., the Saxon King Edgar ordered that peasants cease working at noon on Saturday. In the United States, the five-day workweek became general only in the twentieth century. Scheduling certain holidays—most notably Labor Day, a legal holiday since 1894—created the occasional "three-day weekend" but as high absenteeism rates on Fridays and "Blue Mondays" tell, personally proclaimed three-day weekends occur more frequently. During the 1970s, there was a flurry of enthusiasm in some industries for a four-day workweek and a three-day weekend as a means of saving jobs for more people in troubled industries, but the movement did not have much effect.

during the summer, when city people did not heat their homes. In times of depression, unemployment soared. During the depressions of the 1870s and 1890s, about 12 percent of the working population was jobless for extended periods.

Conditions

While some employers attended to safety conditions, a safe workplace was far from the rule in the nineteenth century. Between 1870 and 1910, there were 10,000 major boiler explosions in American factories, or just under one per workday. Between 1880 and 1900, 35,000 American workers were killed on the job, an average of one about every two days. Railroads had a particularly horrid record. Every year, one railroad worker in 26 was injured seriously, and one in 400 was killed. Textile workers without some fingers and ex-textile workers without hands were fixtures in every mill town. In lumber mill towns, the old-timer with all his digits was a marvel.

In many cases, injured workers and the survivors of those who were killed on the job received no compensation. In others, employer compensation amounted to little more than burial expenses. In the coal fields, the mine owners thought themselves generous if they allowed a dead miner's son, who was younger than the regulation age, to take a job in the mines in order to support his mother.

Employer liability law was stacked against workers. Most courts insisted that employers were not liable for an employee's worker injury unless the plaintiff bore no responsibility whatsoever for the accident in question. Short of the collapse of a factory roof, a complete lack of culpability was difficult to prove, particularly by a worker who could not afford a skilled lawyer. Courts ruled that if an employee was hurt because his machine was dangerous and he knew it, the employer was not liable. It did no good to plead that the injured worker would have been fired had he refused to tend the device; under the law, the choice to stay on the job, and therefore part of the responsibility for his injury, was his.

Occupational diseases—the coal miner's "black lung," the cotton-mill worker's "white lung," and the hard-rock miner's silicosis—were not recognized as the employer's responsibility. Poisoning resulting from work with chemicals was rarely identified as job-related.

WHO WERE THE WORKERS?

Skilled workers inclined to be males of old-stock British or Irish origin. Unskilled jobs were generally filled by children, women, and recent immigrants. In some industrial towns, half to three-quarters of the workforce was foreign-born.

Child Labor

In 1900, the socialist writer John Spargo estimated that 1.8 million children under 16 years of age were employed full time. They did all but the heaviest kind of work. Girls as young as twelve tended dangerous looms and spinning machines in textile mills. "Bobbin boys" of ten hauled heavy wooden boxes filled with spindles from spinning rooms to weaving rooms and back again. Children swept filings in machine shops. Boys of eight were found working the "breakers" at coal mines, hand picking slate from anthracite in filthy, frigid wooden sheds.

In city tenement "sweat shops," whole families and their boarders sewed clothing or rolled cigars by hand, and children worked as soon as they were able to master the simplest tasks. In cities, children practically monopolized messenger-service work, light delivery, and some kinds of huckstering.

In part, child labor was the fruit of greed. On the grounds that children had no nonworking dependents to support and accomplished less, employers paid them less than they paid adults. Even that justification was not always valid. In southern textile towns, the "Mill Daddy" became a familiar figure. Unable to find work

A newsboy peddles papers in St. Louis, Missouri.

Mostly women and children, these cannery workers prepare beans under the strict eyes of the supervisor.

because his own children could be hired to do his job for less, the Mill Daddy was reduced to carrying lunches to the factory and tossing them over the fence each noon.

But the phenomenon also provides an example of "cultural lag." Children had always worked and it took time for society to face up to the reality that industrial labor was something new in the world; factory work was different from chores on a family farm or in a small workshop. Where relations in the small shop were personal, the sharply limited capacity of children, particularly fatigue when set to tedious, repetitive tasks, was easy to recognize and take into account. Placed in a niche in a massive factory, the child laborer became nothing but a number on an accountant's sheet.

Women Workers

Cultural lag also played a part in the large numbers of women in industry. The first industrial workers had been female, partly because women had always been the mainstay of cloth making in western culture, partly because the founders of the first American textile mills—like the Lowells—had not been able to imagine factory work as a suitable lifetime career for the head of a family. In devising the "Lowell system," the well-meaning pioneers of the factory system had believed that they had reconciled industrialization with the old way of life.

The increasing demands of growing industry, and the heavy nature of much factory work, soon resulted in a work force that was predominantly male. Nevertheless, the difficulty of supporting a family on one person's income forced working-class women to continue to labor for wages even after they married. In 1900, almost 20 percent of the total work force was female. About half the workers in textiles were women, and the percentage in the needle trades and other home manufactures was much higher.

With few exceptions, women were paid less than men for performing the same tasks for the same number of hours, sometimes half as much. Abysmally low pay was particularly characteristic of the largest female

Women factory workers, being paid less than men, were more economical to employ.

occupation. In 1900, 2 million women were employed for subsistence wages or less in domestic service: cooking, cleaning, and tending the vanities and children of the well-to-do.

No Blacks Need Apply

While a few blacks found factory jobs in the most menial positions—as floor sweepers, for example—industrial work went mostly to whites. Blacks remained concentrated in agriculture and in low-paying service occupations: domestic servants, waiters, porters, and the like. In 1900, more than 80 percent of the black population lived in the South, most of them on the land.

The industrial color line was most clearly drawn in the South. When the cotton textile industry moved south at the end of the century, the millowners drew on the poor white population for its work force. Implicitly, and sometimes explicitly, employees were informed that if they proved troublesome (that is, if they complained about wages, hours, and conditions), the companies could always tap the huge and poor black population. Racism served to keep southern workers the poorest industrial work force in the country. Rather than risk the loss of poorly paid jobs to blacks, they accepted their low wages and standard of living.

ORGANIZE!

However poorly industrial work paid, it was preferable to other alternatives open to people on the bottom of society. The majority of workers, most of the time, tacitly accepted unattractive wages, hours, and conditions of labor. They expressed their discontent (or desperation) as toilers have done since ancient times. Absenteeism was high in factories, particularly on "Blue Monday" after beery Sunday. And in good times, when getting another menial job was not difficult, workers unable to take holidays sufficient to health and sanity simply quit on a minute's notice.

Sabotage was a word yet to be invented, but the practice was well understood. When the pace of work reached the dropping point, or a foreman stepped beyond the bounds of tolerable behavior, it was easy enough to jam or damage a machine so that it appeared to be an accident—and take a break while it was fixed. An angry worker who had made up his mind to quit might decide literally to "throw a monkey wrench into the works" or to slash the leather belts that turned the looms, drills, stampers, and lathes—that ran the entire factory.

A Heritage of Violence

When workers were powerless to remedy their conditions "through channels," violence was common. During the nationwide railroad strike of 1877, an unorganized, spontaneous outbreak that had its roots in a

---

DIVIDE AND CONQUER

A western lumber magnate explained that in order to have a tractable work force, an employer should hire from several ethnic groups: "Don't get too great a percentage of any one nationality. For your own good and theirs mix them up and obliterate clannishness and selfish social prejudices."

WOMEN IN THE WORK FORCE

There was at least one woman in each occupation listed by the Census Bureau in 1890. More than 225,000 were running farms, and 1,143 listed their occupation as clergyman. Women outnumbered men as teachers and as waiters (the latter by five to one). There were 28 female lumberjacks. In all the United States, however, out of 12,856 wheelwrights (makers and repairers of wagon wheels) there was only one woman.

SABOTAGE

Sabotage is thought of as violent, but it is not necessarily so, and the origin of the word, at the end of the nineteenth century, is ambivalent. The word comes from the French word for the wooden shoes many peasants still wore, *sabots*. One explanation of its beginnings is that when a worker threw a sabot into a machine, like a monkey wrench, the machine would be damaged. Another is that sabotage was nonviolent: it meant the conscious withdrawal of efficiency; that is, angry French stevedores—men who load and unload ships—decided to work as if they were peasants in the clumsy *sabots*—in other words, not very well. In any case, while some American labor leaders called only for the peaceful form of sabotage, which they called "striking on the job," it was the other meaning that stuck.

serious depression, workers did not merely walk off the job, but they stormed in mobs into railroad yards and set trains and buildings on fire. In a few places they fought pitched gun battles with company guards and, toward the end of the unsuccessful strike, with troops who had been called out to put them down.

At Andrew Carnegie's Homestead Works in 1892, a strike led by the Amalgamated Association of Iron and Steel Workers actually besieged the giant factory and forced the withdrawal of a barge bringing 300 armed guards into the town. Less colossal conflicts characterized labor disputes in many industries. They were nowhere more bloody and bitter than in the coal mines of Pennsylvania and in the hard-rock gold and silver mines of the mountainous West.

The Molly Maguires

During the early 1870s, many Irish coal miners in northeastern Pennsylvania gave up on the possibility of improving the conditions of their unhealthful and dangerous work through peaceful means. Within the semisecret atmosphere of a fraternal lodge, the Ancient Order of Hibernians, they formed a secret society called the Molly Maguires. The Mollys then launched an effective campaign of terrorism against the mine owners and particularly the supervisors. They systematically destroyed mine property and murdered loyal company men rather than merely beating them up. (In which case, the victims could have identified their attackers.)

Because of the ethnic dimension of the conflict— almost all the miners were Irish; almost all the bosses were American or Cornish—the Molly Maguires were able to maintain an effective secrecy. Their enemies did not know who they were, how numerous they were, how much support they had in the community. To this day, historians must conjecture a good deal when discussing the Mollys.

In any case, the mine owners had the last word. They brought in an Irish-American undercover detective, James McParland, an employee of the Pinkerton Agency, which specialized in breaking up unions. McParland infiltrated the Mollys and gathered evidence that led to the hanging of 19 men and the end of terrorist action in the mines.

The Union Makes Us Strong

At best, violence is a risky mode of protest and resistance. In a stable and free society, organizing or strength seemed more appropriate and more likely to yield results. "One out of many," "in numbers there is strength," the sacredness accorded to the federal union in the Civil War—all such American mottos and ideals fed the imaginations of workingpeople who were determined to improve their lot.

The first American union dated from before 1800, an association of shoemakers in Philadelphia, the Knights of St. Crispin. Workingmen's associations had been the backbone of the Jacksonian political movement in the eastern states. By the early 1870s, skilled workers such as machinists, iron molders, carpenters, and locomotive engineers and firemen had formed thousands of local trade groups that totaled about 300,000 members.

For the most part, these scattered organizations had little to do with one another. Developing at a time when industry was decentralized, the unions inevitably lagged behind the employers in recognizing the need for national organization. By the end of the Civil War, however, the outlines of the new industrial order had been sketched in. In 1866, William Sylvis, a visionary iron puddler (a man who made castings from molds), founded the National Labor Union (NLU) and devoted the last three years of his life to its cause, traveling by foot around the northeastern states and rallying workers of every occupation in churches, in fraternal lodges, or under the stars.

Sylvis believed that the workers' future depended on political action. He formed alliances with a number of reform groups, including the woman-suffrage movement and farmers' organizations that were lobbying for a cheap currency. The National Labor party put up candidates in the presidential election of 1872 but with so poor a showing that the party and the NLU folded. From a membership of 400,000 in 1872, the NLU disappeared within two years.

Women delegates to a Knights of Labor convention held in 1886.

The Knights of Labor

A different kind of national labor organization already had emerged to take the place of the National Labor Union. Organized in 1869 by a group of tailors led by Uriah P. Stephens, the Noble and Holy Order of the Knights of Labor spread its message much more quietly than Sylvis had done, indeed, secretly. Stephens was aware that an employer's usual reaction, when he discovered a union man in his midst, was to fire him. When the Knights announced meetings in newspaper advertisements, therefore, they did not reveal their meeting place or even their name, but identified the group as "* * * * * * *."

The Knights of Labor also differed from the NLU in their disinterest in political action as an organization. Members were urged to vote, but Stephens believed that the interests of workingpeople would ultimately be served by solidarity in the work place, not at the ballot box.

Some Knights spoke as if they believed in class conflict, irreconcilable differences between producers and parasites, workers and farmers on the one hand; capitalists, on the other. But their concept of class lines was far less precise than that of the Marxists; they barred from membership only saloonkeepers, lawyers, and gamblers, hardly professions that included all the bosses of industrial America. In fact, Stephens himself disliked the idea of class conflict and looked forward to a day when all men and women of good will would abolish the wage system and establish a cooperative commonwealth.

Women were welcome in the Knights; so were blacks and unskilled workers, who usually were overlooked as union material in the nineteenth century. However, the Knights failed to appeal to one group that was essential to the success of any labor organization. Roman Catholics, particularly Irish-Americans, were the single largest ethnic group in the working class.

As the name of his organization implies, Stephens surrounded the Knights of Labor with the mystery, symbolism, ritual, secret handshakes, and other rigamarole that was common to American fraternal organizations. A lifelong Freemason, Stephens based the Knights' ritual on that of his own lodge. The trouble was that in Europe, the Masons were an anti-Catholic organization, and the pope forbade members of the Church to join secret societies of any sort. The Catholic suspicion of the Knights was a serious drawback. Without Catholic support, no labor organization could prosper.

Enter Terence Powderly

In 1879, Stephens was succeeded as Grand Master Workman by Terence V. Powderly, a misleadingly mild-looking man with a handlebar moustache. Himself a Roman Catholic, Powderly brought the Knights into the open and toned down the Masonic flavor of their rituals. He then persuaded an influential Catholic bishop, James Gibbons, to prevail on the pope to remove his prohibition of Catholic membership in the union.

The Knights grew at a dazzling rate under Powderley. With 110,000 members in 1885, the organization claimed 700,000 the next year. Ironically, for Powderly disliked strikes, the major impetus of this growth was a remarkable stirke victory by the Knights against Jay Gould's Missouri Pacific Railroad. Gould had vowed to destroy the union. "I can hire half the working class

THE YELLOW-DOG CONTRACT

Yellow-dog contracts, which were forced on employees by some companies, were meant to intimidate as much as anything else. The penalty for violating such a contract was dismissal, which employers did often enough without such documents. Employees had to agree that "in consideration of my present employment I hereby promise and agree that I will forthwith abandon any and all membership, connection, or affiliation with any organization or society, whether secret or open, which in any way attempts to regulate the conditions of my services or the payment therefor."

to kill the other half," he growled. But when he tried to cut wages, the Knights closed down his line and forced him to meet with their leaders and agree to their terms.

The easy victory and the explosive growth of the union proved to be more curse than blessing. Powderly and the union's general assembly were unable to control the new members. Instead of working together according to a national policy, which was the rationale of a national labor organization, local leaders, who were often new to the concept of unionism, were encouraged by the victory in the Missouri Pacific strike to go it alone in a dozen unrelated directions. Powderly fumed and sputtered and refused to back the rash of strikes in 1885 and 1886. But he could not stop them.

Jay Gould got his revenge, completely crushing a strike against the Texas Pacific Railroad, another of his many properties. Then, in 1886, the Haymarket tragedy was unfairly but effectively imputed to the Knights. Membership plummeted. Workers wanted union; not many wanted chaos.

Samuel Gompers and the AFL

In the same year as Haymarket, a national labor organization dedicated to union and stability for *some* workers was put together by a few dozen existing associations of skilled workers—the American Federation of Labor (AFL). Its guiding spirit was a cigar maker, born in London of Dutch-Jewish parents, an emigrant to the United States as a boy.

Samuel Gompers astonished his fellow workers (and their employers) with his intelligence, learning, toughness in bargaining, and eloquence on the soapbox. He was a homely, even ugly man, squat and thick of body with a broad, coarse-featured face. But this uncomely character had very definite ideas about how labor organizations could not only survive in the United States, but become one of the interlocking forces that governed the country.

Practicality

First of all, Gompers believed that only skilled craftsmen could effectively force employers to negotiate with them. When bricklayers refused to work, and all the bricklayers in a locality stuck together, the employer who wanted bricks laid had no choice but to talk. When the unskilled hod carriers (workers who carried the bricks to the bricklayers) went out, however, employers had no difficulty in finding other men with strong backs and empty stomachs to take their place. Therefore, Gompers concluded, the AFL would admit only skilled workers.

Second, the goal of the AFL unions was "bread and

Samuel Gompers was elected head of the American Federation of Labor every year but one until his death in 1924.

butter," higher wages, shorter hours, better working conditions. Gompers had no patience with utopian dreamers, particularly socialists. What counted was the here and now, not "pie in the sky." Unions with utopian programs not only distracted workers from the concrete issues that counted, but were easy targets for suppression by the bosses who were able (as in the Haymarket incident) to convince Americans that labor organizations threatened the very foundations of their society.

Third, while Gompers believed that the strike, as peaceful coercion, was the union's best weapon, he made it clear that AFL unions would cooperate with employers who recognized and bargained with them. Make unions partners in industry, he told employers, meaning AFL unions that supported the capitalist system, and radical anticapitalist organizations would wither and die.

The Friends of Friends

Gompers, who lived until 1924, served as president of the AFL every year but one (when AFL socialists defeated him). He did not see his hopes come to fruition, but he made a start. With his carrot-and-stick approach to dealing with employers—striking against those who refused to deal with the AFL, cooperating with those who accepted unions—he saw the AFL grow from 150,000 members in 1888 to more than 1 million shortly after the turn of the century.

Most employers continued to hate him and the AFL as dearly as they hated socialists and revolutionary labor unions. "Can't I do what I want with my own?" Cornelius Vanderbilt had asked years before about his company's policies. The majority of American industrialists continued to believe that the wages they paid and the hours their employees worked were no one's business but their own. Their argument was that the worker who did not like his pay had the right to quit. In 1893, such hard-nosed antilabor employers formed the National Association of Manufacturers (NAM) to destroy unionism wherever it appeared. The NAM remained the most important antiunion organization into the twentieth century.

In 1900, a more enlightened group of manufacturers led by Frank Easley and Marcus A. Hanna, a former Rockefeller associate, came to the conclusion that labor unions were a permanent part of the American industrial scene. The choice was not between unions and no unions. The choice was (as Gompers had preached for more than a decade) between conservative, procapitalist unions that were willing to cooperate with employers and desperate, revolutionary unions that were determined to destroy capitalism. Easley and his associates chose Gompers's AFL and joined with him in 1900 to form the National Civic Federation, which was to work for industrial peace through employer—union cooperation.

Conservative Unionism

By the turn of the century, Gompers' anti-radicalism and opposition to organizing the unskilled, once practical policies, hardened into ideology and prejudice. On more than one occasion, Gompers actually used AFL unions to destroy promising unions formed by unskilled workers.

The AFL's opposition to unrestricted immigration began as a hard-headed bread-and-butter policy—to keep wages up—and took on a racialist aspect. Gompers, though himself a Jewish immigrant, denounced Jews from Eastern Europe as being incapable of becoming good American citizens. His opinions of the Japanese and Chinese on the West Coast were rabid.

The AFL unions generally opposed the organization of women (20 percent of the work force) and blacks, who were not numerically important outside of agriculture but were potentially of supreme interest to any working-class movement because they could be used as strikebreakers. The result was that while the lot of the skilled workers steadily improved in the late nineteenth and early twentieth centuries, only 3 percent of "gainfully employed" Americans were members of labor organizations. A union movement, the AFL was; a working-class organization, it was not.

THE NATION OF IMMIGRANTS

"So at last I was going to America! Really, really going at last!" These words were written by Mary Antin, recalling her feelings as a girl in a *shtetl*, a Jewish village in the Russian Empire, when her family decided that their future lay in the United States. "The boundaries burst!" she went on. "The arch of heaven soared! A million suns shone out for every star. The winds rushed in from outer space, roaring in my ear, 'America! America!'"

No one ever caught the thrill of moving to the New World with such exuberance. It may have been Mary Antin's genius with her adopted language. Americans thought so: they bought 85,000 copies of *The Promised Land* when it was published in 1912. Or her joy may have been because, as Jews, her mother and father had come to the United States not merely to improve their standard of living, but to survive.

In 1881, a czar who had relaxed anti-Jewish laws in Russia was assassinated. His dim-witted son, Alexander III, persecuted the Jews and encouraged Christian peasants to rampage through the *shtetls* on bloody *pogroms* (from the Russian word meaning "riot" or "devastation"). Frustrated by the poverty and desperation

---

HOLD FAST!

Some immigrants may have believed that the streets of the United States were paved with gold, but there is no sign of that fantasy in an immigrants' manual of 1891 that advised:

Hold fast, this is most necessary in America. Forget your past, your customs, and your ideals. Select a goal and pursue it with all your might. No matter what happens to you, hold on. You will experience a bad time, but sooner or later you will achieve your goal.

of their own lives in that oppressive and poor country, they beat and killed Jews with no fear of the law. As they had before and would again, the Jews moved on. Between about 1881 and 1914, fully one-third of the Jewish population of Russia left the country, most of them bound for the United States. It was one of the greatest relocations of a people in such a short period in the history of the world.

The Flood

And the Jews were not the largest ethnic group to come to the United States during the late nineteenth and early twentieth centuries. Between 1890 and 1914 (when the outbreak of the First World War temporarily choked off immigration), some 3.6 million Italians cleared the Immigration Service. And there were others: Irish, Scots, Welsh, English, Scandinavians, Germans—the so-called "Old Immigration" that continued in large numbers through the late nineteenth century—and Poles, Lithuanians, Ukrainians, Russians, Serbians, Croatians, Slovenes, Armenians, Greeks, and, from Asia, Chinese and Japanese.

Immigration was part and parcel of the American historical experience (and is so again). The word itself, meaning movement to a place, was coined by an American, as more appropriate to Americans than emigration, movement from a place. Not even the Indians, the "Native Americans," had originated in the Western Hemisphere. Throughout most of the colonial period, immigrants were as important to American growth as the natural increase of population. The Revolution and the uncertain period that followed slowed down the flow of newcomers, but not even the dangers of sea travel during the War of 1812 could quite close it down. After 1815, Europeans came over in numbers that increased almost annually. Only during serious depressions, when jobs were scarce, and during the Civil War, when a young man might be drafted before he shook down his sea legs, did the influx slow down.

From 10,000 in 1825, immigration topped 100,000 in 1845. Except for the first two years of the Civil War, the annual total never dipped below that figure. In 1854, 428,000 foreigners stepped ashore, a record that fell only in 1880 when 457,000 immigrants made landfalls in Boston, New York, Philadelphia, Baltimore, New Orleans, and dozens of smaller ports. Only a crippling depression during the 1890s pushed the annual total below 300,000. After the turn of the century, during each of 6 years, more than 1 million people arrived to make homes in the United States. Always an abundant stream, sometimes swollen, immigration had become a flood.

A sign in four languages helps immigrants at Ellis Island.

Old Immigrants, New Immigrants

But there was more to the immigration after 1880 than a mere increase in numbers. Before 1880, a large majority of immigrants listed the British Isles, Germany, or Scandinavia as their place of birth. While these northern and western Europeans continued to arrive in large numbers after 1880, an annually larger proportion of newcomers after that year originated in southern Italy; the Ottoman (Turkish) Empire; Greece; and the Slavic, Hungarian, and Rumanian parts of the Austro-Hungarian Empire. And from Russia, which then included much of Poland, came both Christian and Jewish Russians, Poles, Lithuanians, Latvians, Estonians, and Finns.

Before 1880, only about 200,000 people of southern and eastern European origin lived in the United States. Between 1880 and 1910, about 8.4 million arrived. In 1896, this New Immigration exceeded the Old for the first time. By 1907, New Immigrants were almost the whole of the influx. Of 1,285,349 legal immigrants who were registered that year, just about 1 million began their long, difficult journey in southern and Eastern Europe.

Birth Pains of a World Economy

Although only parts of Europe, North America, and Japan may be described as having been "industrialized"

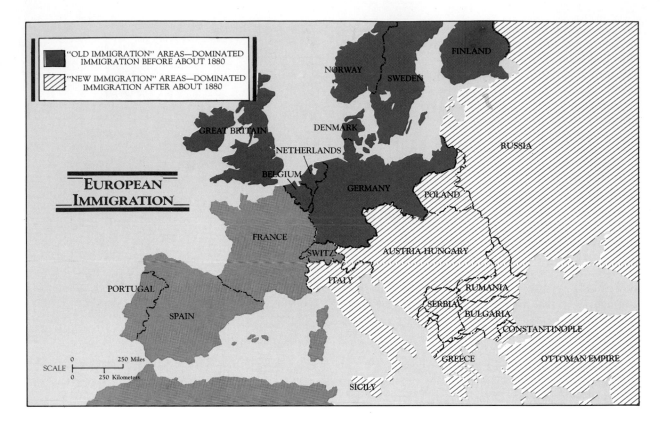

in the nineteenth century, the effects of this economic revolution were felt everywhere save the most remote jungles and mountain valleys. A decline in infant mortality and an increase in life expectancy, side effects of the new technology, resulted in a giant leap in population in agricultural lands as well as in the industrial countries.

World production of foodstuffs soared too, but unequally. The biggest gains were made where agriculture was itself becoming mechanized, as in the United States. In those parts of the world where peasants remained the agricultural work force, food production did not keep up with population growth. Thus, the grain from the broad American prairies and increasingly from Canada undersold grain raised on small plots by peasants in countries such as Italy and Poland, the granary of Eastern Europe. Even in Italy and Poland, American and Canadian grain was cheaper than the home-grown product.

The bottom fell out of the standard of living in the industrial world's hinterlands. During the latter decades of the nineteenth century, southern Italian farm workers made between $40 and $60 a year, Polish farm workers about the same. The cash income of peasants in southern China was too small to be worth calculat-

ing. When large landowners in Europe attempted to consolidate and modernize their holdings, the result was to push people off the land even more efficiently than declining incomes had.

The Jews of Russia felt the effects of the worldwide Industrial Revolution in their own way. Generally forbidden by Russian law to own land, most of them were old-fashioned artisans who handcrafted goods. Others were peddlers, some fixed in one place, others wanderers. Both craftsmen and peddlers found that their way of life was undercut by modernization. The shoes made by a Warsaw cobbler could not compete with cheap, machine-made shoes from England. The peddler who wandered around Russian Poland trying to sell handmade clothing learned the same lesson.

Fleeing Militarism

Finally, people on the bottom in Germany, in the Austro-Hungarian, Russian, and Ottoman empires, and in some smaller nations were cursed by the drive to build up modern military forces. In the period before the First World War, conscription into the army could mean a life sentence. Terms of service were ten to twelve years in Austria-Hungary. They could be 25 years in Russia. Even when the term was just a few

Rural vs Urban

The change from a rural to an urban environment was a gradual process that gained increasing momentum as the population of the country increased. Landscape (detail) *by Thomas Cole (1825) depicts an early pioneer's homestead.* The Minneapolis Institute of Arts.

Philadelphia was the largest colonial city with a population of over 28,000 by 1770. This print by William Birch views Second Street North from Market with Christ Church.

During the heyday of steamboats, St. Louis became the gateway to the West for thousands of settlers.

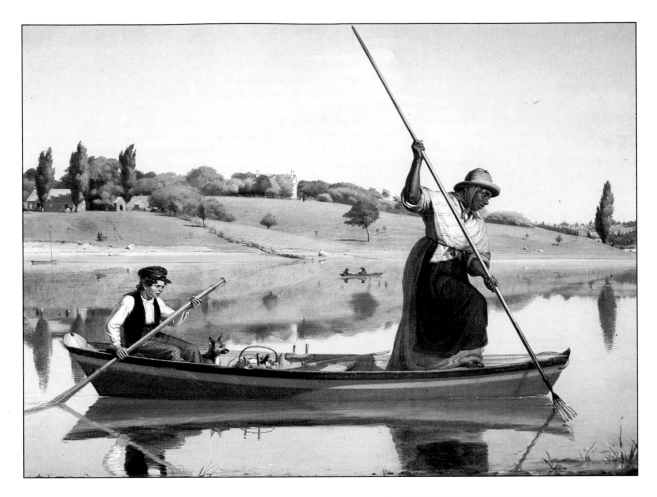

Tranquil rural life before the Civil War was portrayed by
William Mount in Eel Spearing at Setauket (*above*)
and Long Island Farmer Husking Corn (*right*).

Although it was the capital of the nation, in 1851 Washington, D.C., was still a small southern town.

As factories grew, they often became the sole source of employment for people living in the area.

Gift for the Grangers, *a lithograph made in 1873, celebrates the virtues of the Patrons of Husbandry, a farmer's organization.*

An elevated train moves above street traffic in this 1895 painting by W. Louis Sontag, Jr.,
The Bowery at Night.

Alexander Hogue captures the abandonment and despair of the Dust Bowl in Drought Stricken Area *(1934).* Dallas Museum of Art, Dallas Art Association Purchase.

American Gothic *by Grant Wood is a vivid study of determined, hardworking farm people and their entire way of life.* Art Institute of Chicago.

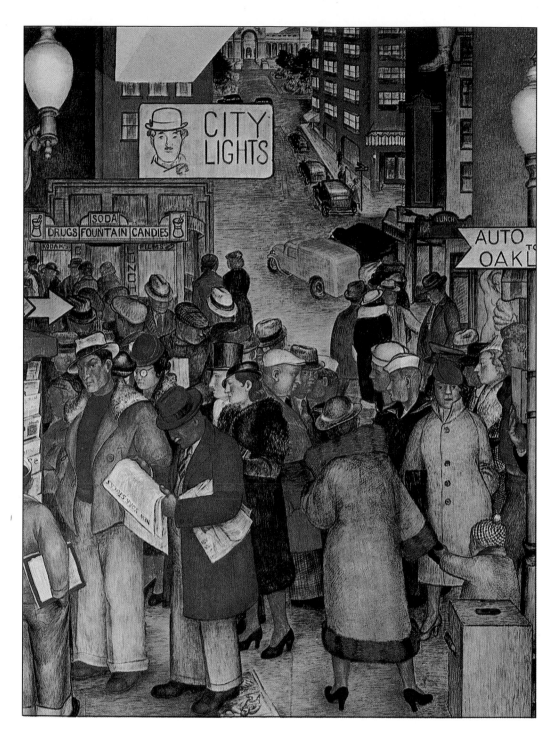

"Street Scene" from the mural Metropolitan Life *was painted by Victor Arnautoff in 1934 for the WPA.*

years, army life was brutalizing. For generations, peasants and immigrants to the United States related chilling tales of self-mutilation by young men who were trying to escape the press gangs; they chopped off their toes or fingers, or blinded an eye. Clearly it was better to go to the United States.

Promoting Immigration

Many American industrialists encouraged immigration. Until the Foran Act of 1885 made it illegal to do so, some companies paid immigrants' fares if they signed contracts agreeing to work for their patrons when they arrived in the United States. James J. Hill plastered every sizable town in Sweden and Norway with posters that described the richness of the soil along his Great Northern Railroad. (South Dakota was nicknamed the "Sunshine State" in a promotional campaign; some advertisements had palm trees swaying in the balmy Dakotan breezes.) The American Woolens Company circulated handbills in southern Italy that showed an immigrant worker with a sleek, perfumed handlebar moustache carrying a heavy sack of money from a mill to a *banco* across the street. In the West, railroaders and other employers handsomely paid Cantonese labor recruiters to import gangs of Chinese coolies to do heavy construction work at minescule wages.

Posters like this—"Direct to America"—caught the eye of farmers in even the smallest villages of Scandinavia.

GOING HOME

The immigrant ships were not empty when they steamed eastward across the Atlantic. Plenty of immigrants returned to Europe disillusioned or in quite a good mood because they had intended to go home once they had made money in the land of opportunity. It is estimated that 370,697 British nationals, including Irish people, returned during the 1880s. Between 1875 and 1910, 18 percent of Swedish immigrants went home. In the depression year of 1875, about half the German immigrants to the United States turned around. Many Italian emigrants were virtual commuters known as "birds of passage." They shipped to the United States (or South America), worked for six months or so, living frugally and saving, and then returned to *bel' Italia* where they lived on their earnings until they were broke and it was time to commute once again. After the turn of the century, about one Italian returned to Italy for every three that arrived in America. The Greeks were thought to be the most likely to return. Between 1908 and 1931, about 40 percent of Greek immigrants made the trip back home.

Employers liked immigrant labor because it was invariably cheaper than American labor, because immigrants would take menial, dirty jobs that Americans shunned, and because the newcomers were almost always more docile than old-stock Americans. So far from familiar surroundings and customs, they hesitated to complain. Since many intended to work in America only temporarily, a few months or a few years, and then return to their homelands, they were likely to accept very low wages, live on next to nothing, and take no interest in joining a union or going on strike.

From the national perspective, immigrant labor was pure asset. On the average, more than 60 percent of the arrivals on late nineteenth-century immigrant ships were able-bodied males; the percentage was higher among Italians and Greeks. The "old country" had borne the expense of supporting them during their unproductive childhood years and was still, often enough, supporting their women and children. In the United States, immigrants were producers pure and simple. It was a very profitable arrangement.

THE IMMIGRATION EXPERIENCE

The immigrants' trek began with a walk. Most of the people who came to the United States after 1880 were peasants, from rural villages that were far from a seaport or a railroad line. So they walked, a circumstance that put a stricter limit on the amount of baggage they could carry to America than did the rules of the steamship companies. Some might fill a handcart and sell it in a buyer's market when they reached their port of embarkation. More commonly, they carried a cheap suitcase or a bundle filled with their few possessions: clothing; a down-filled pillow or comforter; perhaps a favored cooking pot; a treasured keepsake; sometimes a vial of the soil of the native land that they would never see again.

In Italy, they usually walked all the way to the seacoast, to Genoa in the north or to Naples in the south. In Greece, which is made up of peninsulas and islands, there would usually be a ferry ride to Piraeus, the port of Athens. From deep within Russia, Lithuania, Poland, and Germany, there would be a train ride—more likely in boxcars than in passenger wagons. Even the Russians and Poles headed for a German port, Bremen or Hamburg, because while the czarist government provided both Christian peasants and Jews with excellent reasons to leave, the absence of a first-class commercial port in Russia prevented exploitation of the emigrant trade at home. Indeed, despite the threat of persecution, Russian and Polish Jews often had to enter Germany illegally, paying people who lived on the frontier to smuggle them across and secure a semblance of legal passports and exit visas.

Tickets, at least, were cheap. By the 1890s, heated competition among steamship companies in both northern and southern Europe pushed the price of transatlantic passage in steerage (the lowest class) below $20 and sometimes as low as $10. There were humiliating but important ceremonies on departure day: a rude bath and fumigation for lice on the docks, and a more than casual examination by company doctors for contagious diseases (especially tuberculosis), insanity, feeble-mindedness, and trachoma (an inflammation of the eye that leads to blindness and was common in Italy and Greece at the time). On the other side of the Atlantic, United States immigration authorities would refuse entry to anyone who suffered from these diseases, and the company that had brought them over was required to take them back. With paying passengers waiting in New York for passage home—there was a reverse migration too—captains were careful to make sure that they would not lose money on the return voyage. Moreover, while the horrors of shipboard epidemic were considerably reduced from what they had been in the age of sail, highly contagious diseases were not to be taken lightly.

The immigrants were crowded together. Immigrant ships held as many as a thousand people in steerage. There were no cabins, only large compartments formed by bulkheads in the hull. The only privacy was the minimum that could be created by hanging blankets around the few square feet of deck to which a family could enforce its claim. Bickering was constant, and fist fights were common. Except when the weather was bad, almost everyone preferred sitting on the open deck to huddling in the hold.

Most captains prohibited cooking of any kind, except perhaps the brewing of tea on the open deck. Meals were included in the price of passage and were taken in shifts; the last breakfast ran into the first dinner, and so on. Despite the efforts of the German and Italian governments to regulate the quality of food and cookery, the ship at sea was pretty much on its own, and emigrants were unlikely to complain about the quality of service once they arrived in America. Food was cheap, and the cause of constant complaint. Even when meals were good and prepared in sanitary galleys, the ship's cook could not please every passenger; the immigrants tended to be conservative in their culinary tastes, and devoted to a regional or village cuisine. Immigrant manuals recommended the smuggling on board of a sausage or two, or some fruit and vegetables, in order to escape from the poor fare.

Between meals the travelers chatted, sewed, played games, sang, danced, studied English in small groups, read and reread manuals and letters from friends and relatives who were already in the United States, exchanged information and misinformation about their new home, and worried that they might have made a mistake. Days could be interminable, but the voyage was not a long one by steamship. Depending on the port of embarkation and the size of the ship, it took from eight days to two weeks to arrive in New York harbor.

Indeed, an immigrant steamer that arrived at the same time as many others might lie at anchor in lower New York harbor for almost as long as it had taken to cross the Atlantic. In 1892, the United States Immigration Service opened a facility designed specifically for the "processing" of newcomers on Ellis Island, a landfill site in New York harbor that had served as an arsenal. Laid out so that a stream of immigrants would flow in controlled lines through corridors and examination rooms to be inspected by physicians, nurses, and officials. Ellis Island, its architects boasted, could handle 8,000 people a day. Fifteen thousand immigrants passed through on some days, and thousands more had to wait before they could be checked.

Processing at Ellis Island was an experience that few immigrants ever forgot. Crowds milled and shoved for position before they entered the maze of pipe railings that took them from station to station. Instructions boomed over loudspeakers in half a dozen languages;

Immigrants huddled on the steerage deck of the S.S. Pennland, bound for the United States in 1893.

children wailed; and anxious parents called for their lost children.

The first person to examine the immigrants was a doctor who was expected to make an instant diagnosis of afflictions for which the newcomers might be denied entry. If he saw a facial rash, he marked a large *F* on the immigrant's clothing with a piece of soft white chalk. People so marked were cut out of the herd and examined more closely. *H* meant suspected heart disease; *L* meant limp and examination for rickets (children were made to do a little dance); and a circle around a cross meant feeble-mindedness and thus immediate return to the ship. Thousands of families were faced with the awful decision, which had to be made within moments, whether to return to Europe with a relative who had been forbidden entry or to push on.

Those who pushed on were quickly examined for trachoma and other eye diseases and brusquely interviewed by an immigration officer. Everyone was prepared for the trick question: "Do you have a job waiting for you?" Immigrant manuals cautioned readers in capital letters *NOT* to reply in the affirmative. The Foran Contract Labor Law of 1885 forbade the making of pre-arrival agreements to work. Previously—and surreptitiously after 1885—labor jobbers had impressed immigrants into jobs under virtually slavelike conditions, or, at least, many immigrants believed that they had no choice but to work for what the Italians called the *padrone*, or "master."

About 80 percent of those who had entered the building were given landing cards that enabled them to board ferries to the Battery, the southern tip of Manhattan Island. The United States government was through with them, and the horde of agents who made their living by offering "services" now took charge. Again in a babel of languages, previously arrived countrymen shouted that they could offer jobs, provide train tickets, change currency, recommend an excellent boarding house. Some, but not many, were honest. Every large ethnic group in the United States eventually founded aid societies to provide newcomers such services and to protect them from being swindled within hours of their arrival in the land of opportunity.

ETHNIC AMERICA

In addition to the general push and pull that affected all immigrants to some degree, each ethnic group had its unique experience that strongly influenced both the decision to make a home in a new land and the reception that greeted them.

The Smooth Road of the British

The people of England, Scotland, Wales, and the Protestant north of Ireland continued to be among the major immigrant groups of the nineteenth century. Between the Civil War and the turn of the century, 1.9 million Britons came to the United States. They were almost immediately at home among a people who derived primarily from their stock: in appearance they were indistinguishable from the vast majority of white Americans; they practiced the religious faiths that were most common in the United States, were familiar with the basic culture and folkways, and spoke the language.

To be sure, they spoke with identifiable accents that distinguished them from native-born Americans. But those accents are so rarely mentioned in the historical sources that it seems clear that the foreign birth of English, Scottish, and Welsh immigrants separated them in no meaningful way from the mainstream of American society. Andrew Carnegie, Alexander Graham Bell, James J. Hill, and several of John D. Rockefeller's associates were British, but their places of birth were of no consequence to their careers or historical images.

Among the most significant as a group in the building of the American economy were the Cornish "Cousin Jacks." Miners in their homeland in England's southwest, the Cornish brought skills that were indispensable to the development of American mining for coal, iron, lead, and precious metals. The English and Scots and Welsh eased into positions at every level in every occupation and industry.

PADDY'S LETTER

A favorite Irish-American story that reflects the abundance that Irish immigrants found in the United States concerned "Paddy," who was writing to relatives back in Ireland with the help of his parish priest. (Most Irish immigrants were illiterate.)

"Why do you say you have meat on the table twice a week, Paddy," the priest asks, "when you know very well you have it twice a day."

"Because," Paddy replies, "if I said twice a day no one would believe me."

A MODEST PROPOSAL

In 1881, during a lecture tour of the United States, a famous Professor of History from England's Oxford University, Edward A. Freeman, commented within earshot of a journalist that "the best remedy for whatever is amiss in America would be if every Irishman should kill a Negro and be hanged for it."

The Catholic Irish

The story is a little different for the people of southern Ireland, then officially a part of Great Britain but far from British in sentiment. Almost all of the 3.4 million Irish who came to the United States between 1845 and 1900 spoke English, and they too were familiar with the rudiments of Anglo-American culture. However, they differed from the British in two important ways.

First, they were members of the Roman Catholic Church, which many nineteenth-century American Protestants feared and hated out of historical memory. Indeed, in 1887 anti-Catholic prejudice was revived with the formation of the American Protective Association (APA), which was especially strong in the Midwest. Members of the APA took an oath to "strike the shackles and chains of blind obedience" to the Roman Catholic Church from the minds of communicants, but their chief activity seemed to be discrimination against ordinary Catholics.

Second, the Irish arrived not only much poorer than other Britons, but practically starved. Their land had been exploited by England for centuries. Brutalized by poverty, the Irish were considered by their English lords to be semibarbaric, stupid, and addicted to drunken riot as their recreation. Many Americans, especially the WASPs (white Anglo-Saxon Protestants) who dominated American society, culture, and economy, adopted the common English prejudice. Although Irish behavior was little different from the behavior of any people ground down by poverty, many of the idealistic Republicans who had fought against similar stereotypes when they had been applied to blacks were the most extreme Irish-baiters. Employers hung the sign "NINA" (No Irish Need Apply) on their gates and in their shop windows.

And yet, Irish-Americans took with zest to their adopted home. Numerous enough that they could insulate their personal lives from anti-Catholic prejudice, the Irish parlayed their cohesiveness and natural bent for oratory into a formidable political force. By the time of the Civil War, the Democratic party organizations in heavily Irish cities such as Boston and New York were catering to the interests of the Irish community and reaping rewards in an almost unanimous Irish vote. By the 1880s, Irish immigrants and Irish-Americans dominated urban politics in much of the East and Midwest, and in San Francisco. Ironically, it was their considerable power on the West Coast that led to the first legislation to restrict immigration—of the Chinese.

Guests of the Golden Mountain

In 1849, seamen brought the news to the Chinese port of Canton that a "Mountain of Gold" had been discovered in California. In a country plagued by overpopulation, flood, famine, epidemic disease, and civil warfare, the people of southern China listened avidly to the usual distortions of life across the ocean. "Americans are a very rich people," one promoter explained. "They want the Chinaman to come and will make him welcome. . . . It will not be strange company."

By the time the Chinese arrived in any numbers, the rich mines had been exhausted. Accustomed to working communally, they often made a living taking over diggings that Caucasians had abandoned and found employment in the menial jobs that whites disdained: cook, laundryman, farm worker, domestic servant. By 1860, there were 35,000 Chinese immigrants in California. Most of them were young men who hoped to return home after they had made their fortune; there were only 1,800 Chinese women in the state, a good many of them prostitutes. In San Francisco, Sacramento, Marysville, and most mining camps of any size, lively Chinatowns flourished.

Race and a radically different culture kept the Chinese separate. "When I got to San Francisco," wrote Lee Chew, later a wealthy businessman, "I was

A Chinese immigrant posed with his possessions to prove to relatives back home that he had been successful in America.

half-starved because I was afraid to eat the provisions of the barbarians. But a few days living in the Chinese Quarter and I was happy again."

Leaders of the Gum Shan Hok—the Guests of the Golden Mountain—also encouraged the immigrants to stick to themselves. "We are accustomed to an orderly society," explained a leader of the San Francisco Chinatown, "but it seems as if the Americans are not bound by rules of conduct. It is best, if possible, to avoid any contact with them."

After the construction of the transcontinental railroad began in 1864, Chinese immigration stepped up. Previously about 3,000 to 6,000 a year had come to California; after 1868, the annual number jumped to 12,000 and 20,000, peaking at 23,000 in 1872.

Keeping John Chinaman Out

As long as there was plenty of work, hostility to the Chinese was restrained. But in 1873, the West lapsed

---

SUI GENERIS

The population of Ireland in 1840 was estimated to have been 8 million. In 1980, the population of the country was a bit less than 4 million. Surely the Emerald Isle is the only part of the world with fewer people today than 140 years ago, let alone less than half the number. Leaving is, perhaps, the central fact of Irish culture.

IRISH-AMERICAN PATRIOTISM

In 1835, John England, the Roman Catholic bishop of Charleston, provided an explanation of why the Irish took so adeptly to politics: "The Irish are largely amalgamated with the Americans, their dispositions, their politics, their notions of government; their language and their appearance become American very quickly, and they praise and prefer America to their oppressors at home."

into a depression along with the rest of the country. In 1877, when the Chinese represented 17 percent of California's population, a San Francisco teamster named Denis Kearney began to speak to white workingmen at open-air rallies in empty sandlots. He blamed the joblessness not on impersonal economic forces but on the willingness of the Chinese to work for less than an American's living wage. Kearney led several rampages through Chinatown, but, much more important, the anti-Chinese movement inspired politicians to choke off the Asian immigration. In 1882, Congress enacted the Exclusion Act, which forbade the Chinese to come. A few hundred continued to enter legally every year (mostly women to become wives of Gum Shan Hok already here), and illegal immigration via Canada helped somewhat to augment the Chinese-American population.

To some extent, Filipinos and Japanese replaced the Chinese in the Asian immigration. Filipinos had free access to the United States after their country was made an American colony in 1898. Japanese began to trickle in, usually via Hawaii, where they were an important factor in the agricultural labor force. Caucasians resented them as much as they had disliked the Chinese, but because Japan had a strong government that was sensitive to racial slights, the U.S. Congress did not adopt a Japanese exclusion law until 1924, when most immigrant groups were shut out.

The Germans and the Political Motive

In general, the large German immigration to the United States owed to the same worldwide economic forces that displaced other peasant peoples. After 1848, however, there was also a strong political dimension to the German removal. The failure of a series of liberal revolutions in several German states—revolutions aimed at establishing a democratic system and individual rights much like those that existed in the United States—forced the exile of many leading German liberals. The most famous German exile in the United States was Carl Schurz, who became a senator from Missouri and a member of Rutherford B. Hayes's cabinet.

Many of the 4.4 million ordinary Germans who came to the United States between 1850 and 1900, an average of about 100,000 a year, were also influenced by fears that life would be intolerable under the new reactionary governments in their homeland.

Because many of them had been landowners in Europe, albeit not rich ones, German immigrants generally had enough money when they reached the United States to move west and take up free or cheap land. Wisconsin became heavily German in the last half of the nineteenth century. By 1900, more Mil-

waukeeans spoke German, at least as their first language, than spoke English. There were other heavily German areas in Missouri and Texas.

Adapting to America

Like the Germans, Scandinavians inclined to become farmers in the United States. Norwegians predominated in whole counties in Wisconsin and Minnesota. Swedes were numerous in other parts of Minnesota and in the Pacific Northwest. Finns, who speak an entirely different language from the Swedes but are historically tied to them in many respects, were important in yet other regions, particularly in logging country and in the iron mines of the Mesabi Range.

Ethnic groups that predominated over large areas found adaptation to the New World comparatively easy since they could approximate familiar Old World ways of life. They founded schools taught in their native languages, newspapers and other periodicals, European-style fraternal organizations (the Germans' athletically oriented *Turnverein*, or the Norwegians' musical Grieg Societies, named after their national composer), and so on. They continued to eat familiar food and raise their children by traditional rules. They were numerous enough to deal with "Americans" from a position of strength.

The problems that such immigrants faced were common to all settlers of a new land. Olë Rolvaag, a gloomy Norwegian-American writer, focused on the loneliness of life on the northern prairies, an experience that was shared by all pioneers there regardless of ethnic background; he did not write about cultural alienation. Indeed, he wrote in Norwegian and, like Isaac Bashevis Singer in the late twentieth century, became known as an American novelist only in translation.

Sephardic and German Jews

Other immigrant groups had a comparatively easy time adapting because they were few and cosmopolitan. The best example is the Sephardic Jews (Jews descended from and still somewhat influenced by the customs of Spanish and Portuguese forebears). Small in numbers, generally well educated and well fixed, they eased into middle and upper-class society even before the Civil War, particularly in Rhode Island, New York, Charleston, and New Orleans. Considering the fewness of their numbers, they contributed a remarkable number of prominent citizens. Jefferson Davis's strongest supporter in the Confederacy was Judah P. Benjamin, a Sephardic Jew who served in three cabinet posts. Supreme Court Justice Benjamin Cardozo had a Sephardic background. So did the twentieth-century financier and presidential adviser, Bernard Baruch of South Carolina.

By 1880, there was also a small German Jewish community in the United States, perhaps 150,000 people. The majority were small-scale tradesmen or businessmen—rare was the southern town without its Jewish-owned drygoods store. Some German Jews, such as Levi Strauss, pioneered in the founding of the ready-made clothing industry; others carved out places for themselves in finance, usually independent of the long-established American banking community, which was WASP and generally closed to outsiders (August Belmont was the most successful). The Guggenheim syndicate was one of the nation's leading owners of metal mines by the turn of the century.

The German Jews clung to their religious heritage, but otherwise quickly adopted American mores and customs. Indeed, led by Rabbi Isaac Mayer Wise of Cincinnati, German Jews in the United States preferred Reform religious observance, which is highly secular and closely equivalent to liberal Protestantism, to the Orthodox, fundamentalist Judaism of the Jews of the New Immigration.

The Trauma of the New Immigration

Adapting to their new homes was not so easy for most of the New Immigrants who arrived after 1880. Very few of the newcomers from southern and Eastern Europe had much money when they arrived. Most were illiterate, and their Old World experience in peasant villages and shtetls did not prepare them for life in the world's greatest industrial nation during its era of most rapid development.

However serious the immigrants' reasons for leaving ancestral homes, the homes were still ancestral, the rhythms of life familiar, the customs second nature. Wherever their origins, the New Immigrants had been accustomed to a rural and traditional way of life that was the very antithesis of life in the United States, whether on a commercial farm or in the crowded streets of the big city.

Not only was the circle of friends and acquaintances small in the Old World, but the number of people with whom the peasant or Jewish shopkeeper dealt in the course of life was limited to a comparative few who, in any case, spoke a familiar language and thought according to similar (or, at least, well understood) values.

In the United States, however, all but a very few landsmen or campagni were alien, and everyone spoke incomprehensible languages. The immigrants, at home for better or for worse in Europe or Asia, were foreigners, a minority in the United States.

Strangest of all for people who came from traditional, preindustrial cultures where life was regulated and slowed by the seasons, the weather, the use of hand tools, American life was regulated and rushed by the tyrannical clock and powered by the relentless churning of the dynamo. In the industrial society of the late nineteenth century, Americans were even more self-driven than they had been when Alexis de Tocqueville's head had been set spinning by the American pace. This was particularly true in the big cities where a majority of the New Immigrants settled and which, in the minds of other Americans, were intimately associated with the newcomers.

For Further Reading

The general histories listed in the bibliographies of Chapters 27–29 are all pertinent to this chapter as well. Specifically dealing with immigrants are: Rowland T. Berthoff, British Immigrants in Industrial America (1953); Leonard Dinnerstein and David Reimers, Ethnic Americans: A History of Immigration and Assimilation (1975); Nathan Glazer and Daniel P. Moynihan, Beyond the Melting Pot (1970); Oscar Handlin, The Uprooted (1951); Marcus L. Hansen, The Immigrant in American History (1940); John Higham, Send These to Me: Jews and Other Immigrants in Urban America (1975); Maldwyn A. Jones, American Immigration (1960); Dale Steiner, Of Thee We Sing (1986); and Philip A. M. Taylor, The Distant Magnet (1970).

Books with a focus on working people include David Brody, Workers in Industrial America (1979); Robert V. Bruce, 1877: Year of Violence (1959); Melvyn Dubofsky, Industrialism and the American Worker, 1865–1920 (1975); Foster R. Dulles and Melvyn Dubofsky, Labor in America (1984); Herbert G. Gutman, Work, Culture, and Society in Industrializing America (1976); Harold C. Livesay, Samuel Gompers and the Origins of the American Federation of Labor (1978); David Montgomery, Workers' Control in America: Studies in the History of Work, Technology, and Labor Struggle (1979); Daniel Nelson, Managers and Workers: Origins of the New Factory System in the United States, 1880–1920 (1975); Henry Pelling, American Labor (1960); Daniel T. Rogers, The Work Ethic in Industrial America, 1850–1920 (1974); and Philip Taft, The A. F. of L. in the Time of Gompers (1929).

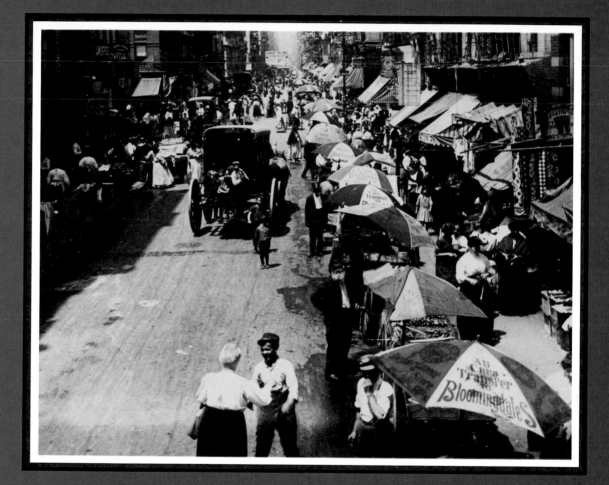

Once in the United States, the New Immigrants discovered that their most ordinary practices—even the way they looked!—struck Americans of older stock as exotic. Even WASPs who had grown accustomed to the restrained Roman Catholic worship of the Irish and the Germans found themselves troubled by the mystical Catholicism of the Poles and the public ceremonies of the Italians. Indeed, Irish Catholic bishops joined Methodists in worrying about the "paganism" implied in the magnificently bedecked statues of the Madonna and the gory, surrealistic representations of the crucified Christ that peasants from Sicily and the Campania carried through the streets of San Francisco, Chicago,

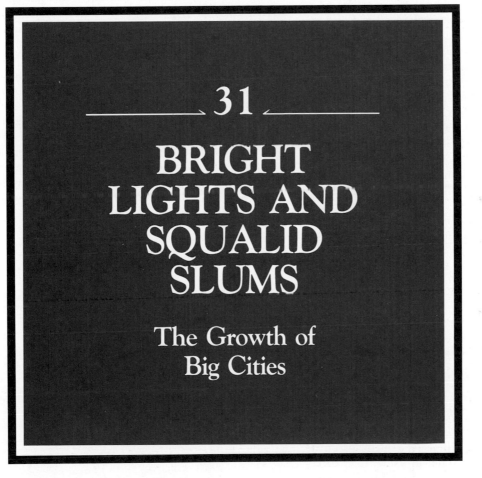

31

BRIGHT LIGHTS AND SQUALID SLUMS

The Growth of Big Cities

The first step for an independent-minded immigrant was a rent-free peddler's cart parked by the curb as in this view. They lined the streets in the ethnic communities.

New Orleans, and New York accompanied by the music of brass bands.

The Orthodox services of the Greeks, Russians, some Ukrainians, Serbians, and other Balkan peoples seemed even more extravagant. The Jews and the Chinese, of course, were not even Christian and therefore all the more out of line with American traditions.

The newcomers looked different from Americans. The Greeks, Armenians, Assyrians, Lebanese, and Italians were swarthy in complexion, a formidable handicap in a nation that had long since drawn a sharp color line. Polish women often arrived clad in colorful babushkas, aprons, and billowing ground-length skirts of the eastern European peasant. The impoverished Jews dressed drably enough for late-nineteenth-century American taste, but the men, if religious, wore full beards and never removed their hats. Their Saturday sabbath attracted attention principally because the Jews turned Sunday into a combination holiday and major market day, which offended the sabbatarian sensibilities of some Protestants.

Americans who visited immigrant neighborhoods were unsettled because the smells in the air were alien. Clinging to their traditional diets, which were often based on pungent seasonings and the use of much more onion and garlic than old-stock Americans deemed humane, the immigrants seemed determined to resist American ways all the while they lived in the country.

CITIES AS ALIEN ENCLAVES

I n his novel of 1890, *A Hazard of New Fortunes*, William Dean Howells sent Basil March, a genteel and educated middle-class American, on a ride on an elevated train in New York City. March "found the variety of people in the car as unfailingly entertaining as ever," but he felt like a foreigner in his own country. Even the Irish, who ran the city, were outnumbered by

the people of Germanic, Slavonic, of Pelagic [Mediterranean], of Mongolian stock. . . . The small eyes, the high cheeks, the broad noses, the puff lips, the bare, cue-filleted skulls, of Russians, Poles, Czechs, Chinese, the furtive glitter of Italians, the blonde dullness of Germans; the cold quiet of Scandinavians—fire under ice—were aspects that he identified, and that gave him abundant suggestion for the . . . reveries in which he dealt with the future economy of our heterogeneous commonwealth.

A Patchwork Quilt

The cities, particularly in the Northeast and Midwest, where 80 percent of the New Immigrants settled, seemed to be salients established and secured by invading armies. By 1890, one-third of the population of Boston and Chicago had been born abroad, and one-quarter of Philadelphia's people. When their children, who seemed to old-stock Americans as obdurately align as their parents, were added to this total, the anxiety of "American" residents and visitors to the cities is easy to understand.

In fact, the immigrants threatened no one. Members of each ethnic group clustered together into "ghettos" that were exclusively their own. A map of New York, wrote journalist and photographer Jacob Riis, himself a Danish immigrant, "colored to designate nationalities, would show more stripes than the skin of a zebra and more colors than the rainbow." Jane Addams sketched a similar patchwork in the poor part of Chicago, where she established one of the first American settlement houses, agencies to help the immigrants, Hull House. The same was true of most large eastern

A Russian immigrant in native dress, photographed by R. F. Turnbull in 1900.

Early Chinese immigrants to San Francisco, most of them men, lived in a segregated section of town dubbed Chinatown, shown here in a photograph by Arnold Genthe.

and midwestern cities and of many smaller industrial towns. In Lawrence, Massachusetts, a woolens manufacturing town, more than 20 languages and probably twice that many distinctive dialects were spoken by the immigrant population.

There were ghettos within ghettos. In New York City's Greenwich Village, an Italian community, people from the region of Calabria effectively controlled housing on some streets, and immigrants from Sicily on others. On such regional blocks, Italians from a specific village would sometimes be the sole occupants of an "Agrigento tenement," and so on. Grocery stores and restaurants advertised themselves not as Italian but as purveyors of Campanian or Apulian food. Priests frequently ministered to the same people whom they had known back in Italy; lawyers often represented the same clients.

The same held true for Jewish neighborhoods, where Galician Jews (Galicia was a province of Poland) looked with suspicion on Jews from Russian-speaking areas. Rumanian Jews fastidiously set up their own communities, and the better established and assimilated German Jews wondered what the world was coming to. Christian Germans divided on Lutheran and Catholic lines. Serbians and Croatians from what is now Yugoslavia divided on whether they wrote their language in the Latin or the Cyrillic alphabet.

The Impulse to Assimilate

The desire to assimilate, to become "American," varied in intensity from group to group, and among individuals within a group. Some immigrants found solace in the familiar language, familiar customs, familiar foods, and fellowship of "Little Italy," "Jewville," and "Polack Town," and clung tenaciously to the neighborhood. The ethnic ghetto was a buffer against the prejudice of old-stock Americans and the hostility of other ethnic groups with whom its inhabitants competed for the lowest-level jobs. Even an educated immigrant from the Austro-Hungarian Empire found himself disoriented in his attempts to "shift" from old to new ways of thinking and reacting.

I never knew if my reactions would be in line with the new code of conduct and had to think and reflect. Whenever I decided on the spur of the moment I found myself out of sympathy with my environment. I did not feel as they felt and therefore I felt wrongly according to their standards. To act instinctively in an American fashion and manner was impossible, and I appeared slow and clumsy. The proverbial slowness of foreigners is largely due to this cause.

Others seized avidly on what they took to be "American" ways with an extraordinary enthusiasm. This was perhaps best illustrated in the large Jewish community of New York's Lower East Side, which in its earliest years was sharply divided between those who clung to the medieval ways of the Russian and Polish *shtetls* and the big city-wise and sophisticated younger immigrants and children of immigrants who often scorned their elders' "greenhorn" ways.

Avenues of Advancement

Hard work at menial jobs was the economic lot of most immigrants. The urban political machine, which had room at or near the top for anyone who could deliver votes, provided an avenue of advancement for a few who recognized the opportunities it provided for the "boss" of the ethnic ghetto. Others joined the American quest for material success by pursuing careers in areas that were not quite respectable, and, therefore, less attractive to members of established social groups—show business, professional sports, and organized crime, that is, illegal business. The roster of surnames of leading entertainers, boxers, baseball players, and gangsters over a period of decades reads like the strata of a canyon that geologists read, each layer dominated by members of a new, aspiring ethnic group.

Immigrant Aid Institutions

The ethnic groups themselves established institutions to assist their countrymen in adjusting to the new life. Some encouraged assimilation, some clannishness. Sephardic and German Jewish families who were comfortably established in the United States founded the Hebrew Immigrant Aid Society to minister to the needs of the penniless eastern European Jews who flocked into the cities. The Young Men's and Young Women's Hebrew Associations, dating back to 1854, expanded several times over during the last decade of the century.

Among the Catholic population, which grew from 6 million in 1880 to 10 million in 1900 (making Roman Catholicism the country's largest single denomination), traditionally charitable religious orders such as the Franciscans and the Sisters of Mercy established hospitals and houses of refuge in the slums. The St. Vincent de Paul Society functioned much like the Salvation Army, providing food, clothing, and shelter for the utterly desperate, but without the military trappings.

Curiously, a sort of ethnic prejudice helped to hamstring the older Jewish and older Catholic communities in responding to the needs of the New Immigrants. Sephardic and German Jews worried that the numbers, poverty, and provincialism of the eastern European newcomers would arouse an anti-Semitic spirit among Christians that would be turned on them too. The American Catholic Church was dominated by Irish-Americans who were little more cordial toward Italians, Poles, and other new Catholic nationalities than were old-stock Protestants. Only after an encyclical of 1891, *Rerum Novarum*, in which the pope proclaimed a Catholic Social Gospel, did the Church hierarchy take much interest in the material well-being of its communicants.

Then the Church was torn between serving as an agency of assimilation and maintaining its high standing among Catholic immigrants—who often clung to their religion with more piety than they had in Europe—by encouraging a "fortress mentality" toward the dominant Protestant culture. Indeed, the Church approved of parishes organized along ethnic rather than geographical lines. In places like Detroit and New Orleans, there might be an Italian, a Polish, a Lithuanian, and a geographical parish church—that is, an Irish-German one, within a few blocks of one another.

Settlement Houses

Old-stock Americans created the settlement house, patterned after Toynbee Hall, in a notorious London slum, to assist immigrants in coming to terms with their new country.

During the 1880s, a number of middle-class Americans who were imbued with the New England conscience that dictated concern for others traveled to England to learn how Toynbee worked. They found that the house provided food and drink to the disinherited, as traditional charities had, but also child care for working mothers, recreational facilities, and courses of study in everything from household arts to the English language and social skills needed for self-improvement. The young men and women who

Hester Street in New York City was home to a large community of Jewish immigrants in the early 1890s.

worked at Toynbee Hall also told the Americans that they had been morally elevated by their sacrifices and exposure to a misery that they had not known in their own lives.

The first American settlement house was the Neighborhood Guild, set up in New York City in 1886. More famous, however, because of the powerful personalities of their founders, were Jane Addams's Hull House in Chicago (1889), Robert A. Woods's South End House in Boston (1892), and Lillian Wald's Henry Street Settlement in New York (1893). From comfortable middle-class backgrounds, well-educated, and finely mannered, Addams, Woods, and Wald were exemplars of the American middle class who were determined to fight the materialism of their own people, the misery suffered by poor city dwellers, and to keep traditional American values alive. What they did

not always understand was that in the great metropolises that took shape in the late nineteenth century, a new American culture and code of values was emerging.

THE GROWTH OF GREAT CITIES

Americans had an ingrained prejudice against cities that dated back to Thomas Jefferson, but they were also, by the end of the nineteenth century, one of the world's most urban peoples. The proportion of city dwellers in the total population, the number of cities, and the size of cities all increased at a faster rate in the United States than in any other country in the world.

BIG CITY SWEATSHOPS

In the early nineteenth century, four Americans in five wore clothing that had been made to order. The wealthy took their wants to the little shops in every town and city where fine garments were expertly made by hand from fabric to finished product. With great skill, tailors and seamstresses worked not from patterns, as someone interested in sewing would do today, but from fashion plates, carefully drawn pictures in magazines of people dressed in the latest styles. By the early nineteenth century, Paris was already considered the authority in such matters.

The middle classes, which began to pay more attention to "fashion" in the nineteenth century, depended on their womenfolk for their garb. That is why needle-craft learned at a mother's knee was such an important part of a young girl's education; clothing her family would be one of her most important duties as a wife and mother.

As for the poor, they made do with castoffs either scavenged or purchased from merchants who specialized in buying and reconditioning used clothing. The fact that most garments were made to fit an individual did not mean that any particular item had been made to fit the person who, at a given time, was wearing it.

Only sailors, slaves, and—after 1849—miners in the West were likely to wear clothing such as virtually everyone does today, ready-made in quantity to standard sizes and sold "off the rack." Sailors were not generally in a port long enough to be fitted and a garment sewn. (The first ready-made clothing stores were called "sailors' shops.") The slaves had no choice in the matter of what they put on their backs, and their owners, wanting to provide them some protection from the elements at a minimum cost, became an attractive market for enterprising tailors who abandoned the custom trade and took to producing rough, cheap garments in quantity. Miners, like sailors, were in a hurry, and they lived in an almost entirely masculine society. Their demand for sturdy, ready-made clothing provided the impetus for the founding in 1850 of the Levi Strauss Company of San Francisco, today perhaps the best-known manufacturer of ready-made clothing in the world.

By 1900, things had changed. Nine Americans in ten were wearing ready-made togs. A "Clothing Revolution," as historian Daniel Boorstin has called it, had taken place as a consequence of technology with, curiously, a boost from the American Civil War.

The technology was supplied by inventions such as the sewing machine, patented by Elias Howe in 1846, and powered scissors that could cut through eighteen pieces of fabric at once, thus making the parts for eighteen garments of exactly the same size. The standard sizes were provided by the United States government when the Civil War made it necessary to buy uniforms for hundreds of thousands of men. The army's Quartermaster Corps measured hundreds of recruits and arrived at sets of proportions that provided a fit for almost all. It was a simple step to do the same for women's sizes after the war ended, and ready-made clothing shops began to displace tailors and seamstresses. The department store, which appeared at the end of the century, was built around its selection of every kind of clothing. The great mail-order houses such as Montgomery Ward and Sears Roebuck were able, with everyone knowing his or her size, to sell garments by mail.

How were the new ready-made clothes manufactured? Not, ironically, in factories. There was little outsize machinery involved in the making of garments (sewing machines were treadle or electrically powered) and a great deal of handwork (finishing buttonholes, installing linings). Thus it was possible to farm out the work to people in their homes, just as, before the invention of cloth-making machinery, spinning and weaving had been farmed out.

Whereas the old putting-out system usually had involved the wives and daughters of farmers, leaving people on the land, the new putting-out system engaged people who lived in city slums and who depended exclusively on needlework for their livelihood.

The system was called "sweating," and the places in which the garmentmakers worked were called "sweatshops" because of the peculiarly exploitative character of the system. A manufacturer of clothing kept a small headquarters; at the most, the material was cut to pattern in his "factory." Then, the pieces of a garment were handed out on a weekly or daily basis to people, usually Jewish or Italian immigrants, who took them home to their tenement apartments. There the whole family—perhaps some boarders, perhaps even some neighbors—sat down during all the daylight hours to make up the garments. Sometimes a household saw a coat (usually called a cloak in the nineteenth century) or a gown through from components to completion. Other households specialized in different phases of the process, such as roughing the garment in, or finishing work. Some sweatshops made buttonholes, others sewed pockets, and so on.

The key to the system was that everyone involved was paid by the piece—so much per jacket, so much per lining. A complex hierarchy of subcontracting developed in which it was to the interest of all to pay those below them in the chain as little for their work as possible. That is, a man who provided finished cloaks to the manufacturer received a fixed rate for each garment that he delivered. In order to make a profit, he had to pay less than that rate to those households that had done the work. If the head of a household sweatshop had boarders or neighbors sewing, he had to pay them even less. Everybody was "sweating" their income out of somebody else.

Moreover, just as in factories, employers were inclined to cut the piece rate as a worker's productivity

The tenement sweatshop was an avenue out of poverty for a few, but a squalid, oppressive, unhealthy workplace for most. Here workers make neckties in this photograph by Jacob Riis.

increased or when someone else told the manufacturer whom he supplied (who sweated him) that others were willing to work for less. In order to compete, he sweated the people under him.

In turn, everyone in the chain had to take less for their work. The operator of a Chicago sweatshop explained the results to a Congressional committee in 1893:

Q. *In what condition do you get the garments?*
A. *They come here already cut and I make them up.*
Q. *What is the average wage of the men per week?*
A. *About $15 a week.*
Q. *How much do the women get?*
A. *About $6. They get paid for extra hours. . . .*
Q. *Are wages higher or lower than they were two years ago?*
A. *Lower. There are so many who want to work.*
Q. *How much do you get for making this garment?*
A. *Eighty cents.*

Q. *How much did you get for making it two years ago?*
A. *About $1.25.*
Q. *Is the help paid less now?*
A. *Yes, sir.*

A cloakmaker, Abraham Bisno, told the same panel that he had earned about $20 a week in 1885 for completing fewer garments than he had sewn in 1890, when he had made $13 to $14 a week. In 1893, he was being paid $11 a week for even greater productivity.

As the rate per piece fell, sweatshop workers increased their hours in the unhealthful, poorly ventilated tenements. Only when urban states such as New York and Illinois passed laws that forbade such work in residences was there any improvement in conditions. But, often as not, the driving exploitation of the sweat system was merely transferred to an unhealthful, poorly ventilated factory that was little different from a tenement flat.

POPULATION OF TEN LARGEST AMERICAN CITIES—1880

City	Population
New York	1,773,000
Philadelphia	847,000
Chicago	503,000
Boston	363,000
St. Louis	351,000
Baltimore	332,000
Cincinnati	255,000
Pittsburgh	235,000
San Francisco	234,000
New Orleans	216,000

In 1790, when the first national census was taken, only 3.4 percent of Americans lived in towns of 8,000 people or more. By 1860, the eve of the Civil War, 16 percent of the population was urban, and by 1900, 33 percent.

The increase in the number of cities is rather more striking. In 1790, only 6 American cities boasted populations of 8,000 or more. The largest of them, Philadelphia, was home to 42,000 people. In 1860, 141 municipalities had at least 8,000 people within their limits; by 1890, 448 did, and by 1910, 778! Fully 26 cities were larger than 100,000 in 1900, and 6 of them topped 500,000. Philadelphia counted 1.3 million people at the turn of the century and, at that, had slipped to third place behind New York and Chicago.

From Country to City

Although the influx of immigrants was largely responsible for the tremendous growth of cities at the end of the century, Americans migrated from country to city too. Dismayed by the isolation of farm life, ground down by the heavy, tedious labor, and often as not reaping few rewards for their toil, they heard of well-paying jobs for literate, mechanically inclined people. Or they visited cities and were dazzled by the bright lights, the abundance of company, the stimulation of a world in constant motion, and the stories of the fortunes that might be made in business.

Parents, rural ministers, and editors of farm magazines begged, threatened, and cajoled in an effort to keep the children of the soil at home, but their efforts met with limited success. While the total number of farm families grew during the late nineteenth century, the proportion of farmers in the total population declined, and in some regions, with a nearby city beckoning, even the numbers dropped. During the 1880s, more than half the rural townships of Iowa and Illinois declined in population, while Chicago underwent its miraculous growth. In New England, while the overall population of the region increased by 20 percent, three rural townships in five lost people to the dozens of bustling mill towns that lined the fast-moving rivers and to the metropolises of Boston and New York.

For the most part, the American migration from farm to city was a white migration. Only 12 percent of the 5 million blacks in the United States in 1890 lived in cities. Nevertheless, about 500,000 blacks moved from the rural South to the urban North during the final decade of the century, foreshadowing one of the most significant population movements of the twentieth century.

The Walking City

While rapid growth was the rule in cities large and small, the most dramatic phenomenon of American urbanization in the late nineteenth century was the emergence of the gigantic metropolises, the six cities of more than 500,000 people that dominated the regions in which they sat like imperial capitals. Philadelphia doubled in size between 1860 and 1900, when William Penn's "green countrie towne" claimed 1.3 million people. New York, with 33,000 people in 1790, and over 1 million in 1860, quadrupled its numbers until, by 1900, 4.8 million lived within its five "boroughs." New York was the second largest city in the world, smaller only than London.

Chicago's crazy rate of growth as the hub of the nation's railroad system amazed Americans and foreigners alike. With only a little more than 100,000 people in 1860, Chicago increased its size 20 times in a generation, numbering 2.2 million inhabitants in 1900.

Before the 1870s, cities so vast were unimaginable. When the mass of a city's population moved around by foot, city growth was limited in area to a radius of a mile or two, as far as a worker could walk to work or a housekeeper could walk to market in an hour or

POPULATION OF TEN LARGEST AMERICAN CITIES—1900

New York	3,437,000
Chicago	1,699,000
Philadelphia	1,294,000
St. Louis	575,000
Boston	561,000
Baltimore	509,000
Pittsburgh	452,000
Cleveland	382,000
Buffalo	352,000
San Francisco	343,000

Grid-lock in the horsedrawn age. Because a horse could panic or collapse, traffic jams in the late nineteenth century were often worse than they are today.

so. To be sure, the well-to-do owned horses and carriages in the walking city and could, therefore, live a greater distance from their places of business and entertainment. But not too far. A horse moves only marginally faster than a pedestrian and rather more slowly when the streets are choked with people wending to and fro. Indeed, the most common layout of a mill town was a factory or two at the geographical center of the city and residential areas surrounding it in concentric circles or, more likely, because mills were generally located near rivers, in semicircles fronting the water. The workers clustered close by; with a twelve-hour day to work, there was little time for commuting. The small businessmen who owned the shops lived behind them. The millowners, their top supervisors, and professionals lived on the outskirts. They were not strangers to the crowding, noise, dirt, and turmoil of the walking city, but when the opportunity to flee presented itself, they were quick to seize it.

Farthest out of all, beyond the built-up neighborhoods, paved streets, and sewers, were ramshackle shantytowns inhabited by people with only a marginal role to play in the city's life. Unlike today, when the homeless crowd into the core cities, in the nineteenth century, the limitations inherent in foot and horse travel left the suburbs, a form of banishment, to them.

Getting Around

The first means by which wealthy and middle-class people could put some distance between their residences and center city was the horsecar line. With charters from city hall, entrepreneurs strung light rails down major thoroughfares and ran horse-drawn streetcars with seats open to the public. Cheap as the fares were, usually five cents, they were still too expensive for most workingpeople, who continued to walk to work. However, skilled artisans, white-collar workers, and small businessmen took advantage of the quick, cheap transportation to move away from their places of business: north on the island of Manhattan in New York, west across the Schuylkill River in Philadelphia, north and west in Chicago, and west out of Boston.

Making possible even more distant residential neighborhoods was the steam-powered elevated train, or El, which ran at high speeds above the crowded streets on ponderous and ugly steel scaffolding. In 1870, New York completed the first El on Ninth Avenue, and the range of the trains, soon up to the northern tip of Manhattan, encouraged the middle classes to move even farther away from Wall Street and the once leafy, now crowded Bowery. In making the suburbs more accessible, the Els also served to begin the process of pushing the residents of the shantytowns into inner-city housing abandoned by the middle classes.

Electric Trolleys

The utility of elevated trains was limited by the high cost of constructing them. Only the richest, largest (and most corrupt) cities were able and willing to shoulder the expense. Moreover, no sooner did the Els stimulate residential construction along their routes, where they ran at ground level, than the noisy, dirty, and dangerous locomotives roused the ire of the very people who rode on them to work and recreation.

Consequently, it was the electric trolley car, pioneered by inventor-businessman Frank J. Sprague, that really turned the walking city into a memory and ensured the sprawl of the great metropolises. Economical, fast but easy to stop, clean, quiet, even melodious in their rattling and ringing of bells, the trolleys were the key to the growth of big cities and assets to smaller ones. Richmond was the first to build a system in 1887. By 1895, fully 850 lines crisscrossed American cities

on 10,000 miles of track. They were as important to the urbanization of the United States as the railroads were to the settlement of the West.

Building Up

By enabling the construction of residential neighborhoods miles from city business districts, the trolleys made it possible for many more people to congregate in city centers for work, business, and entertainment. This caused real-estate values in the city centers to soar to absurd heights.

The practical solution was obvious enough: multiply the square footage of midtown properties by building multistoried structures such as the electric-powered elevator theoretically made possible. Even with the elevator at hand, however, there was still a catch in vertical construction. In order to support the weight of tall buildings built of stone or brick, the weight-bearing walls had to be so thick on the lower floors, virtually solid like the pyramids of Egypt, as to defeat the whole purpose of building up.

Once again, technology provided the solution in the form of extremely strong I-shaped steel girders. With these at their disposal, architects were able to abandon the very concept of weight-bearing walls and design skeletons of steel on which, in effect, they hung decorative siding of cast iron or of stone. The potential height of steel buildings seemed almost limitless. They

Elevated trains, or Els, were unsightly, noisy, and dirty, but they enabled cities to expand by providing fast, unimpeded transit.

The Flatiron Building, an early skyscraper, photographed around 1905. Today it is dwarfed by its neighbors.

could rise so high as to scrape the sky. Indeed, once the method was perfected, corporations competed to erect the tallest tower, as medieval cities had competed to build the tallest cathedral spire.

In time, New York was to become the most dramatic of the skyscraper cities; but Chicago architects pioneered in the design of "tall office buildings," as Louis H. Sullivan, the most thoughtful of architects, rather prosaically described his graceful structures. In an article in *Lippincott's Magazine* in 1896, Sullivan explained how through the use of "proud and soaring" vertical sweeps, "a unit without a single dissenting line," the artistic form of the skyscraper reflected the essence of its construction. In the twentieth century, Sullivan's even more imaginative protégé, Frank Lloyd Wright, was to apply the principle of "form following function" to a wide variety of structures.

Building Over

Another technological innovation that contributed to the expansion of cities was the suspension bridge, which erased wide rivers as barriers to urban growth. Its pioneer was a German immigrant, John A. Roebling, who came to the United States in 1831 as a

canal engineer and set up the first American factory for twisting steel-wire into cable. Roebling's associates scoffed at his contention that if a bridge were hung from strong cables instead of built up on massive pillars that had to stand in the water, much broader rivers could be spanned. Obsessed with the concept of a suspension bridge, Roebling devoted his life to perfecting a design. Before the Civil War, he had several to his credit, including an international bridge over the Niagara River near the Falls.

Roebling planned his masterpiece for the East River, which separated downtown New York, a city bursting at the seams, from the roomy seaport of Brooklyn on Long Island. While working on the site in 1869, he was injured, contracted a tetanus infection, and died. Without delay, his equally devoted son, Washington A. Roebling, carried on the work. He, too, received serious injuries; he was crippled from the "bends," later associated with deep-sea divers, as a result of working too long below water level on the foundations of the towers. Nevertheless, from a chair in a room overlooking the great span, now called the Brooklyn Bridge, he saw it completed in 1883. It was admired for its beauty as well as its engineering.

In providing easy access to Manhattan—33 million people crossed it each year—the bridge ignited a residential real-estate boom in Brooklyn; within a few years, Brooklyn was the fourth largest city in the United States. But the bridge also spelled the end of Brooklyn as an independent city. A satellite of Manhattan in fact, Brooklyn was incorporated into the city of New York by law in 1898.

The Great Symbol

The Brooklyn Bridge was dedicated with a mammoth celebration. President Chester A. Arthur proclaimed it "a monument to democracy"; sides of beef were roasted in the streets; oceans of beer and whiskey disappeared; brass bands competed in raising a din; races were run; prizes were awarded; dances were danced; and noses were punched. A fireworks display of unprecedented magnificence topped off the festivities, illuminating the fantastic silhouette from both sides of the East River. The Brooklyn Bridge was a celebration of the city.

It was also an indictment of the city. On the morning of the gala, one dissenting newspaper editor groused that the Brooklyn Bridge had "begun in fraud" and "continued in corruption." It was no secret to anyone that much of the $15 million that the project had cost had gone not into concrete, steel, and Roebling cable, but into the pockets of crooked politicians.

This 1877 engraving from Harper's Weekly depicts construction of the Brooklyn Bridge. As skyscrapers allowed cities to expand vertically, suspension bridges allowed cities to sprawl even beyond rivers.

The glories of the bridge were also marred by its cost in human lives. At least 20 workers were killed building it, and others just vanished, probably falling unnoticed, Many more were maimed. Then, just a few days after the dedication, a woman stumbled while descending the stairs that led from the causeway to the ground, and someone shouted, "The bridge is sinking!" In the stampede that followed, 12 people were trampled to death.

THE EVILS OF CITY LIFE

City people died at a rate not known in the United States since the seventeenth century. At a time when the national death rate was 20 per 1,000 (20 people in each 1,000 died annually), the death rate in New York City was 25. In the slums, it was 38, and for children under 5 years of age, 136 per 1,000. The figures were only slightly lower in the other big cities, and in parts of Chicago they were higher. In one Chicago slum as late as 1900, the infant mortality rate was 200; 1 child in 5 died within a year of birth. By way of comparison, the infant mortality rate in the United States today is less than 20 per 1,000, and the total death rate is less than 9.

Too Many People, Too Little Room

City people died primarily because of impossibly crowded living conditions, another consequence of high real-estate values. In Philadelphia and Baltimore, the poor crowded into two- and three-story brick "row houses" that ran for 200 yards before a cross street broke the block. In Boston and Chicago, typical housing for the New Immigrants was in old wooden structures that had been comfortable homes for one family; in the late nineteenth century, they were crowded by several families, plus boarders. In New York, the narrow confines of Manhattan Island made the crowding even worse. Former single-family residences were carved into tenements that housed a hundred and more people.

In 1866, the New York Board of Health found 400,000 people living in overcrowded tenements with no windows, and 20,000 living in cellars below the water table. At high tide, their "homes" filled with water. The board closed the cellars and ordered 46,000 windows cut in airless rooms; but in 1900, people whose memories dated back to 1866 said that conditions were even worse than ever.

Jacob Riis, a newspaper reporter who exposed urban living conditions in a book of 1890, *How the Other Half Lives*, estimated that 330,000 people lived in a square mile of slum; 986.4 people an acre. New York was more than twice as crowded as the London that had turned Charles Dickens's stomach, and parts of it were more populous than Bombay, the American's image of a living hell. On one tenement block in the Jewish section of the Lower East Side, just a little larger than an acre, 2,800 people lived. In one apartment of two tiny rooms there, Riis found a married couple, their twelve children, and six adult boarders.

When architect James E. Ware designed a new kind of building to house New York's poor, he worsened the situation. His "dumbbell" tenement, named for its shape, ostensibly provided 24 to 32 apartments, all with ventilation, on a standard New York building lot of 25 by 100 feet. However, when two dumbbells were constructed side by side, the windows of two-thirds of the living units opened on an air shaft, sometimes only two feet wide, that was soon filled with garbage, creating a threat to health worse than airlessness. Nevertheless, the dumbbells met city building standards, and by 1894, there were 39,000 of them in New York, housing about half the population of Manhattan.

Health

Such crowding led to epidemic outbreaks of serious diseases like smallpox, cholera, measles, typhus, scarlet fever, and diphtheria. Quarantining of patients, the indispensable first step in dealing with highly contagious diseases in the nineteenth century, was out of the question in slums: where were the unafflicted people to go? Even less dangerous illnesses like chicken pox, mumps, whooping cough, croup, and the various influenzas were killers in the crowded cities. Common colds were feared as the first step to pneumonia.

In his famous book, Jacob Riis took readers on a tour of a tenement: "Be a little careful, please! The hall is dark and you might stumble. You can feel your way, if you cannot see it. Close? Yes! What would you have? All the fresh air that enters these stairs comes from the hall-door that is forever slamming." He paused at the entrance to a windowless apartment. "Listen! That short, hacking cough, that tiny, helpless wail. . . . The child is dying of measles. With half a chance it might have lived; but it had none. That dark bedroom killed it."

Lewis W. Hine's photograph of a rear tenement bedroom on New York's Lower East Side shows the crowded conditions in which poor city dwellers lived.

Sanitation

The crowding itself was the chief cause of poor sanitation. Whereas free-roaming scavengers—chickens, hogs, dogs, and wild birds—handily cleaned up the garbage in small towns, and backyard latrines were adequate in disposing of human wastes, neither worked when more than a hundred people lived in a building and shared a single privy. City governments provided for waste collection, but even when honestly administered (which was the exception), sanitation departments simply could not keep up.

Horses compounded the problem. They deposited tons of manure on city streets daily, and special squads could not begin to keep pace. Moreover, on extremely hot and cold days, old and poorly kept horses keeled over by the hundreds; sometimes in New York the daily total topped 1,000. Although by law the owner

Dead horses left to rot in the streets compounded New York's growing sanitation problems at the turn of the century.

of the dead beast was required to dispose of the carcass, this often meant dumping it into the river. More often, because the task was so formidable, owners of faltering nags cut their horses out of harness and vanished in the teeming crowds. In summer, the corpses bloated and began to putrefy within hours.

In the poorest tenements, piped water was available only in shared sinks in the hallways, which were typically filthy. Safe water had been so heavily dosed with chemicals that it was barely palatable. The well-to-do bought bottled "spring water" that had been trucked into the cities. Other people depended on wells in the streets that were inevitably fouled by runoff.

Tenement apartments did not have bathrooms. Children washed by romping in the water of open fire hydrants or by taking a swim in polluted waterways. If you did not come home tinged gray or brown, one survivor of New York's Lower East Side remembered, you had not washed. When a bath was necessary, adults went to public bathhouses where there was hot, clean water at a reasonable price. Many of these es-tablishments were quite respectable. Others became known as dens of immorality.

Vice and Crime

As they always are, slums were breeding grounds of vice and crime. With 14,000 homeless people in New York City in 1890, many of them children—"street Arabs"—and work difficult to get and uncertain at the best of times, many found the temptations of sneak thievery, pocket picking, purse snatching, and, for the bolder, violent robbery too much to resist. As early as the 1850s, police in New York were vying with (or taking bribes from) strong-arm gangs that were named after the neighborhoods where they held sway: the Five Points Gang, Mulberry Bend, Hell's Kitchen, Poverty Gap, the Whyo Gang.

They occasionally struck outside their areas, robbing warehouses and the like, and preying on the middle- or upper-class fops who took to slumming in these neighborhoods. But the gangs' typical victims were slum dwellers struggling to survive and escape the

HORSE AND BUGGY DAYS

A horse dead was a sanitation problem in big cities, but so was a horse alive. Each horse produced as much as 25 pounds of manure each day. In New York City in 1900 there were about 150,000 horses. The potential litter problem, therefore, weighed about 1,800 tons. Most manure merely dried and crumbled where it dropped, blowing or washing away in time. Some was scooped up by the city or private entrepreneurs and sold to farmers on the outskirts of the city as fertilizer.

slum: the workingman who paused for a beer before he took his pay envelope home or the small businessmen who were forced to make regular payments or risk physical violence. Whereas the homicide rate declined in German and British cities as they grew larger, it tripled in American cities during the 1880s. Although the prison population rose by 50 percent, the streets in some sections grew more dangerous.

By the end of the century, the more sophisticated gangs moved into vice, running illegal gambling operations, opium dens, and brothels. Prostitution flourished at every level in a society where sex was repressed, and there was a plentiful supply of impoverished girls and young women who had no

other way to survive. The lucky ones set themselves up as mistresses or in fancy houses that catered to the wealthy. More common was the wretched slattern who plied her trade in the slums under the "protection" of a gang.

An Urban Culture

And yet, for all the horror stories, which no one savored more than the people who lived in the cities, for all the lurid accounts of urban life in books, newspapers, magazines, sermons, lectures, plays, and scandalized reports by people who visited New York, Chicago, Kansas City, or other "dens of pestilence," a vital, exciting, and excited urban culture developed in American cities. City people compared rural "yokels" and "hayseeds" unfavorably to themselves. Once established, city people were unlikely to move to the country or even to be attracted by jobs beyond the municipal limits.

The cities continued to grow at an extraordinary rate, both from immigration and the influx from the towns and countryside. Indeed, had it not been for the existence of a more traditional American frontier larger than any that had gone before, it is likely that the rural population would have declined in the late nineteenth century, as it was to do in the twentieth century.

For Further Reading

Again see the overviews listed after several of the chapters immediately preceding this one: Vincent P. DeSantis, *The Shaping of Modern America, 1877–1916* (1973); John A. Garraty, *The New Commonwealth, 1877–1890* (1968); Samuel P. Hays, *The Response to Industrialism, 1885–1914* (1957). Even allowing that urbanists have been among the most productive of historians in recent decades, A. M. Schlesinger, *The Rise of the City, 1878–1898* (1933) is still an essential source.

To augment and correct Schlesinger in particulars, see Robert H. Bremner, *From the Depths: The Discovery of Poverty in America* (1956); Howard Chudakov, *The Evolution of American Urban Society* (1975); John Higham, *Send These to Me: Jews and Other Immigrants in Urban America* (1975); Blake McKelvey, *The Urbanization of America, 1860–1915* (1962); Zane L. Miller and Patricia Melvin, *The Urbanization of Modern America* (1987); Thomas L. Philpott, *The Slum and the Ghetto* (1978); Barbara Rosenkrantz, *Public Health and the State* (1972); Stephan Thernstrom, *The Other Bostonians: Poverty and Progress in the American Metropolis* (1973); Sam B. Warner, *Streetcar Suburbs: The Process of Growth in Boston, 1870–1900* (1971) and *The Urban Wilderness: A History of the American City* (1972); and Morton White, *The Intellectual Versus the City* (1962).

Books focusing on immigrants but with a special concern for urban life include Nathan Glazer and Daniel P. Moynihan, *Beyond the Melting Pot* (1970); Oscar Handlin, *The Uprooted* (1951); Leonard Dinnerstein and David Reimers, *Ethnic Americans: A History of Immigration and Assimilation* (1975); John B. Duff, *The Irish in the United States* (1971); Irving Howe, *World of Our Fathers* (1976); Alan Kraut, *The Huddled Masses: The Immigrant in American Culture, 1880–1921* (1982); Humbert Nelli, *The Italians of Chicago* (1970); Moses Rischin, *The Promised City: New York's Jews* (1962); Thomas Sowell, *Ethnic America: A History* (1981); Virginia Yans-McLaughlin, *Family and Community: Italian Immigrants in Buffalo* (1977).

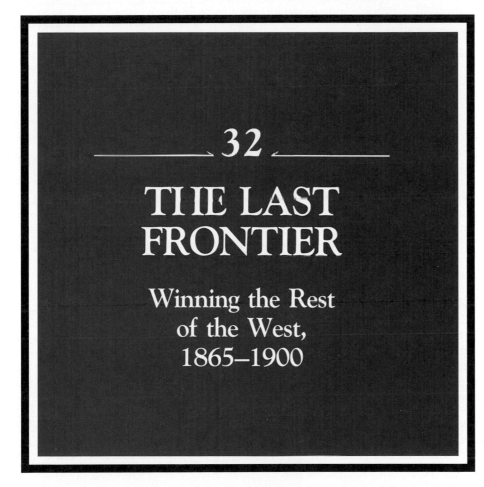

32

THE LAST FRONTIER

Winning the Rest of the West, 1865–1900

In long-settled parts of the world, the frontier is the place where the territory of one sovereign state comes to an end and the territory of another state begins. In Europe, the crest of the Pyrenees mountains marks the frontiers of Spain and France, the Rhine River the frontiers of France and Germany. The novelist's and film-maker's vision of such frontiers is a place of locomotives hissing on sidings, customs guards interrogating travelers, zebra-striped barricades lowered across tracks and roadway.

European frontiers have been moved about frequently enough as a consequence of dynastic marriages, wars, and treaties. But redrawing a frontier in Europe has long meant detaching from one country lands that are already populated, often densely, and attaching them to another sovereignty.

The typical crew of cattle-herding cowboys included black and Mexican cowboys.

In the United States, the word *frontier* came to mean something entirely different. To Americans, the frontier was the vaguely demarcated zone where the nation's settled lands ended and its undeveloped region began. Because the course of American expansion had begun on the eastern rim of the continent, the frontier was usually a line that ran from north to south and more or less constantly moving westward. On and beyond that line was not a rival sovereign state but a wilderness to be conquered and developed, what Americans called "the West."

THE LAST FRONTIER

The Census Bureau's definition of "settled land" was not very rigorous. While Americans of the late twentieth century would consider a square mile on which only 2, 3, or 4 people lived to be something on the order of howling wilderness, the Census Bureau defined a square mile as "settled" if 2.5 persons lived there. Even at that, at the time of the Civil War, the part of the United States that was beyond the frontier comprised roughly half the nation. With the exception of California, Oregon, and Washington Territory on the West Coast, where 440,000 people lived; the Great Salt Lake basin, where the Mormon Zion had grown to be home to a population of 40,000; and New Mexico, which was the seat of a gracious culture and home to 94,000 mostly Spanish-speaking citizens, the American frontier ran north to south about 150 to 200 miles west of the Mississippi River. Settlers had barely spilled over the far boundaries of Minnesota, Iowa, Missouri, and Arkansas. Half of the state of Texas was beyond the frontier at the end of the Civil War.

An Uninviting Land

Rather more striking in view of what was to happen in the late nineteenth century, most Americans believed that this West would never be settled. Americans thought agriculturally; pioneering meant bringing land under tillage, and, except for isolated pockets of fertile, well-watered soil, none of the three geographical regions of the West was suitable to agriculture. And those isolated pockets of good land were too far from the markets and the sources of manufactured goods that any settlers would need in order to prosper.

In the middle of the last West lay the majestic Rocky Mountains, which range from Alaska to New Mexico. The snowy peaks of the Rockies were familiar to easterners from landscape paintings by artists who had

accompanied the transcontinental wagon trains or military expeditions, or, having learned of the natural glories of the American landscape, had traveled west on their own, easel and canvas packed in their lumbering wagons. The very grandeur of the Rockies, however, told Americans that the mountains could not support a population living as people did in the older regions.

West of the Rockies and east of California's Sierra Nevada lay the high desert and the Great Basin—the mountainous and arid home of birds, snakes, rodents, comical armadillos, cactus, creosote bush, and sagebrush. The soil was rocky, thin, and often alkaline. This region is called a basin or sink because its rivers lose heart in their search for an outlet and pool up in the desert, disappearing into the earth and evaporating in the sun. The Mormons had worked miracles in one of those sinks, the Great Salt Lake basin. But no part of the West seemed less inviting to Americans than this genuine desert.

East of the Rockies stretched the Great Plains, also a land of little rain and no trees. A short grass carpeted the country, and rivers like the Missouri and the Platte meandered through it, making the Great Plains less forbidding than the Great Basin. Nevertheless, there was simply not enough rainfall on the plains to support staple agriculture as Americans knew it.

The Native Peoples of the West

Some people did live in this last great region, of course. In addition to the Mormons and the *nuevos mexicanos*, hundreds of thousands of Indians continued to cling proudly to traditional, sometimes ancient ways of life. Even the most forbidding parts of the Great Basin supported the Ute, Paiute, and Shoshone who

A WOMAN OF THE WILD WEST

In several instances during the Civil War, women were discovered posing as men—soldiers in the army. No doubt, many more maintained such an imposture throughout the war. "Charlie" Parkhurst was a woman who lived as a man in one of the West's toughest professions. Beginning in 1851, Charlie drove a stage coach through the California gold country. During "his" career, Charlie built a reputation as an expert with the whip. He chewed tobacco, squandered money at the gaming tables, and put in as hard a day's work as was expected of any man. Charlie shot at least one would-be bandit who stopped the stage. In 1879, Charlie's neighbors in Watsonville, California, remarked on his absence and went to his cabin where they found the old teamster dead. Only then was it discovered Charlie Parkhurst was a woman.

coped with the torrid summers by dividing into small foraging bands and seeking higher elevations.

Farther south, in the seemingly more hostile environment of present-day Arizona and New Mexico, the Pima, Zuñi, and Hopi had been farming the desert intensively for centuries before the explorations of Francisco de Coronado. Their *pueblos* (a Spanish term, of course), communal houses or groups of apartments, sometimes perched high on sheer cliffs, were home to a delicately integrated quasi-urban culture. The Navajo, more numerous than the other peoples in the desert south of the Grand Canyon (and comparative newcomers there) lived in family groups spread out over the country. The Navajo were skilled weavers of cotton when the introduction of Spanish sheep provided them with the opportunity to raise their craft into a durable art. Both the Navajo and the Pueblo Indians feared the warlike raiders of the Apache tribes, who dwelled farther south but ranged widely in search of booty.

In what was then called Indian Territory, present day Oklahoma, the "civilized tribes," which had been forced out of Georgia, Alabama, and other eastern states during the age of Jackson, had rebuilt their amalgam of native and European cultures: an intensive

Navajo weaving techniques predated white settlement in the Southwest.

cash-crop agriculture, a town life, a written language, a school system, and newspapers. Indian Territory came to loom large in the American imagination after the Civil War because, beyond the pale of state and effective federal law, it was an attractive sanctuary for some of the most famous outlaws and "badmen" of the era.

But the Indians who most intrigued easterners were, curiously, those who were most determined to resist the whites and their ways, the tribes of the Great Plains. Thanks to the writings of intrepid travelers such as historian Francis Parkman and painters Alfred J. Miller, Karl Bodmer, and George Catlin, the Comanche, Cheyenne, and Arapaho peoples of the central and southern plains, and the Mandan, Crow, Sioux, Nez Percé, and Blackfoot peoples of the northern half of the grasslands were a source of awe and admiration to easterners and of apprehension to those whites who came into their country to compete with them.

Plains Culture

Everything in the lives of the Plains Indians—economy, social structure, religion, diet, dress—revolved around two animals: the native bison and the horse, which was introduced to the Plains by Mexicans. The bison not only provided food, but its hides were made into clothing, footwear, blankets, portable shelters (the conical tepees), bowstrings, and canvases on which artists recorded heroic legends, tribal histories, and genealogies. The bison's manure made a tolerable fuel for cooking and warmth in a treeless land where winters were harsh.

The Plains Indians were nomadic. Except for the Mandan, they grew no crops but trailed after the herds of bison on their horses, to southern grazing grounds in the winter, and back north to fresh grass in the summer. It was not an ancient way of life, like that of the southwestern pueblos. Runaway horses from Mexican herds had been domesticated only about 150 years before the Plains Indians were confronted by white Americans. Nevertheless, in that short time the Indians had developed their stirrup-less, saddle-less, and bit-less mode of riding, which was quite independent of Mexican example and awe-inspiring to American observers. "Almost as awkward as a monkey on the ground," wrote painter George Catlin in 1834, "the moment he lays his hand upon a horse, his face even becomes handsome, and he gracefully flies away like a different being."

The wandering ways of the Plains tribes brought them into frequent contact with one another and with Indians who had developed different cultures. While they traded and could communicate with remarkable

Sioux Indians, camouflaged by animal skins, stalk buffalo in this painting by George Catlin.

subtlety through a common sign language, the tribes were just as likely to fight one another. Since the Indians had no concept of private ownership of land, their wars were not aimed at territorial conquest, but at capturing horses, tools, and sometimes women, and at demonstrating courage, the highest quality of which a Great Plains male could boast. The English word *brave*, given to Plains warriors as a noun, was not chosen on a whim.

With only about 225,000 Native Americans roaming the Great Plains in 1860, war was not massive, but it was chronic. A permanent peace was as foreign to the Indians' view of the world as the notion that an individual could claim sole ownership of 80 acres of grassland.

By 1860, every Plains tribe knew about the "pale-faces" or "white-eyes." They did not like the wagon trains that had traversed their homeland for two decades, and they occasionally skirmished with the white wayfarers. But the outsiders did move on and were

welcome to the extent that they traded, abandoned, or neglected to secure horses, textiles, iron tools, and rifles, all of which improved the Indians' standard of living.

The Destruction of the Bison

This state of coexistence began to change when Congress authorized the construction of the transcontinental railroad. The crews that laid the tracks of the

---

WHOSE LAND?

Bear Rib, chieftain of the Hunkpapa Sioux, during treaty talks at Pierre, South Dakota, in 1866: "To whom does this land belong? I believe it belongs to me. If you asked me for a piece of it I would not give it. I cannot spare it, and I like it very much. . . . I hope you will listen to me."

Union Pacific and Kansas Pacific across the plains were not interested in staying. But unlike the California and Oregon emigrants, their presence led directly to the destruction of the bison.

The killing of the bison began harmlessly enough. In order to feed the big work crews cheaply, the Union Pacific Railroad hired hunters like William F. "Buffalo Bill" Cody to kill the beasts. The workers could hardly consume enough of the lean, beeflike meat to affect the size of the herds, which numbered perhaps 15 million bison in 1860. However, when a few of the hides were shipped back east and caused a sensation as fashionable "buffalo robes," wholesale slaughter began.

A team of marksmen, reloaders, and skinners could down and strip a thousand bison in a day. Living in huge herds, the animals were not startled by loud noises and stood grazing, pathetically easy targets, as

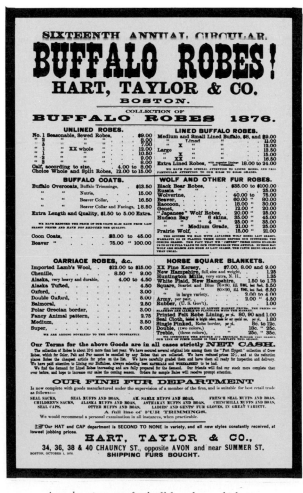

An advertisement for buffalo robes, which were fashionable in the 1870s.

long as they did not scent or see human beings. With dozens of such teams at work, the bison population declined at a startling rate.

The railroad companies encouraged the slaughter because, merely by crossing over the flimsy iron tracks, a herd of bison could obliterate the line. To apply the finishing touches, wealthy eastern and European sportsmen chartered special trains and, sometimes without stepping to the ground, they shot trophies for their mansions and clubs. By the end of the century, when preservationists stepped in to save the species, only a few hundred American buffalo remained alive. It was the most rapid extinction of a species in history, but no more rapid than the extinction of the culture of the people whose fate was tied to the bison.

The Cavalry

The United States cavalry accompanied the railroad's construction crews, ostensibly to enforce the Indians' treaty rights as well as to protect the workmen. Some of these troops were captured Confederate soldiers who elected to take an oath of loyalty and serve in the West as preferable to languishing in prisoner camps. After the war, they were joined by northern whites and former slaves who had enlisted and found army life preferable to hard-scrabble farming back home.

Some soldiers and officers learned to respect the tribes and tried to deal fairly with them. General George Crook, who is remembered as the ablest of the army's Indian fighters, preferred being known for his just dealings with the natives. Other officers shared the opinion of General Philip H. Sheridan, who was reputed to have told a Comanche chief at Fort Cobb in 1869, "The only good Indian is a dead Indian."

Overall, of course, the sympathies of the army were with the the railroaders, miners, cattlemen, and eventually farmers who intruded on Indian lands. Whites believed in an elaboration of Manifest Destiny, that because the Indians, like the Mexicans, used the land so inefficiently, their claim to it was not equal to their own. From 1862, when the final era of Indian wars began with a Sioux uprising in Minnesota, to 1890, when the power of the last untamed tribe was shattered at Wounded Knee, South Dakota, the United States cavalry joined with the buffalo hunters to destroy a way of life.

The Last Indian Wars

As in the eastern woodlands, Indian war was a war of small skirmishes and few pitched battles. Between 1869 and 1876, for example, the peak years of the fighting, the army recorded 200 distinct "incidents," a number that did not include many unopposed Indian raids and confrontations between civilians and the tribes. But the total casualties on the army's side (and possibly the Indians') was less than in any of several Indian-white battles in the 1790s.

The army preferred to fight decisive battles. But the Indians generally clung to traditional hit-and-run attacks that exploited their mobility and allowed them to escape fights in which, with their inferior arms and numbers, they were at a disadvantage. The result was frequent frustration among the soldiers and a cruelty toward the enemy such as had not been seen in the Civil War. In 1871, Commissioner of Indian Affairs Francis Walker explained that "when dealing with savage men, as with savage beasts, no question of national honor can arise. Whether to fight, to run away, or to employ a ruse, is solely a question of expediency."

By 1876, the army's victory seemed complete. Little by little, the soldiers in their ever-dusty blue had hemmed in the wandering tribes and whittled away at their ability to subsist. The typical state of a surrendering tribe was near-starvation, with a goodly proportion of the young men dead. But Indian resistance was not quite at an end.

Custer's Last Stand

In June of the centennial year, an audacious Civil War hero and colonel of the Seventh Cavalry, George Armstrong Custer, led 265 men into a battle with the Sioux on Montana's Little Bighorn River. In a rare total victory for the Indians, every one of Custer's men was killed. Although a completely unexpected defeat, "Custer's Last Stand" thrilled Americans. Denied in life the advancement that he believed his record and talents had merited, "Yellow Hair," as the Sioux called him, became a romantic hero in death. A brewery

A drawing of the battle of Little Bighorn by Red Horse, 1881.

MOVING AMIDST THE HOSTILES

A cavalry detachment in the West, unlike its movie versions, was accompanied by huge wagon trains of equipment, often 150 vehicles. In addition to a rider, each horse carried 80 to 90 pounds of equipment. With such a load, a horse needed to be rested frequently. This was accomplished without arresting progress by dividing the soldiers on the march into two troops. One troop walked until it was half a mile ahead of the plodding wagon train. Then, the soldiers dismounted to rest and graze their horses until the wagons were half a mile ahead. As they caught up, the other troop moved on ahead and repeated the maneuver. In this way, there was always a troop, in two columns, on either side of the precious supplies to warn off raiders.

Helen Hunt Jackson, author of Ramona *and* A Century of Dishonor.

commissioned an imaginative painting of the Battle of the Little Bighorn by Cassilly Adams and within a few years distributed 150,000 reproductions of it.

Senior officers who had disapproved of the flamboyant and impetuous Custer, and thought him to blame for the disaster, kept their mouths shut. Only in the next century would the episode be fully appreciated from the Indians' point of view, as a final great military victory brilliantly engineered by Sioux war-chiefs. At the time, however, the tribes' joy was short-lived. Most of the victors were under control within the year.

Good Intentions, Tragic Results

In 1881, a Colorado writer, Helen Hunt Jackson, published *A Century of Dishonor*, one of the decade's best-sellers. In meticulous detail and with little distortion of fact, she detailed the cynicism with which the United States government had dealt with the Indians

A CENTURY OF DISHONOR

"It makes little difference . . . where one opens the record of the history of the Indians; every page and every year has its dark stain. The story of one tribe is the story of all, varied only by differences of time and place; but neither time nor place makes any difference in the main facts. Colorado is as greedy and unjust in 1880 as was Georgia in 1830, and Ohio in 1795; and the United States Government breaks promises now as deftly as then, and with added ingenuity from long practice."

Helen Hunt Jackson,
A Century of Dishonor (1881)

since independence. The list of Indian treaties was the list of broken treaties. Time and again, according to Jackson, "Christian" whites had cheated "savage" Indians of their land, had herded them onto reservations on lands judged to be the least useful, and then had chipped away at those.

By 1876, the government had ceased to make treaties with the Indians. Those Indians who did not resist American control were defined as wards of the federal government; they were not citizens but were under Washington's protection and enjoyed a few special privileges. After the publication of *A Century of Dishonor*, many easterners demanded that the government use this wardship in a just manner.

In 1887, Congress approved the Dawes Severalty Act. Intentions were of the best. Assuming that the traditional Indian life was no longer feasible, the supporters of the Dawes Act argued that the Indian peoples must be Americanized; that is, they must become self-sustaining citizens through adoption of the ways of the larger society. Under the Dawes Act, the tribes were dissolved and the treaty lands were distributed, homestead-style, 160 acres to each head of the family (itself not a plausible concept to most tribes), and an additional 80 acres to each adult member of the household. Lands left over were sold to whites. In order to

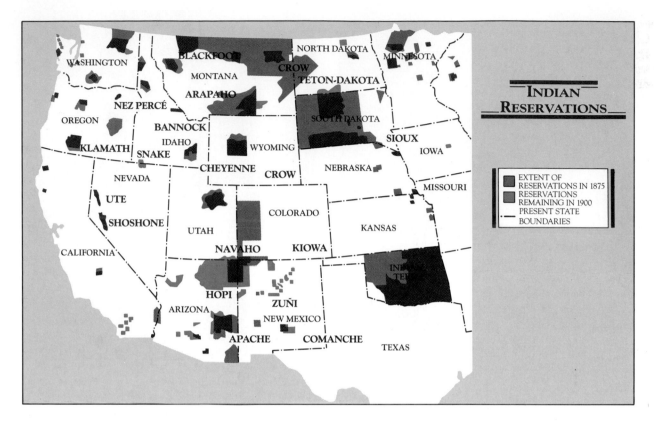

avoid further despoliation, remaining Indian land could not be sold or otherwise disposed of for 25 years.

The supporters of the Dawes Act overlooked a number of vital facts. First, few of the western Indians were farmers; traditionally they had been hunters, gatherers, and traders. Second, the reservation lands were rarely suited to agriculture; they had been allotted to the Indians precisely because they were unattractive to white farmers. Third, tracts of a few hundred acres in the arid West were rarely enough to support efficient white farmers, let alone novices at tillage. Finally, no western tribe thought in terms of private ownership of land as vested in a nuclear family. The tribe, which the Dawes Act aimed to relegate to the dustheap, was the basic social unit to which the native Americans looked. The defeated Indians were demoralized by the forced disintegration of their culture and individuals too often were debauched by idleness and alcohol. When it was again permitted by law, they would be stripped of much of their land too.

Wounded Knee

Among these desperate people appeared a religious teacher in the tradition of Tecumseh's brother, The Prophet. Jack Wilson, or Wovoka, a Paiute who had lived with a white Christian family and had been fascinated by the doctrine of redemption, wandered

the West preaching a religion that appealed to thousands of Indians. His message was that by performing a ritual dance, the Indians, who were God's chosen people, could prevail on the Great Spirit to make the white man disappear. This "Ghost Dance" would bring back to life the buffalo herds and the many Indians who had been killed in the wars. The old way of life, which in the 1880s most adult Indians remembered, would be restored.

This sort of belief, simultaneously edifying and pathetic, is common among peoples who have seen their world turned upside down. In parts of the Southwest that were untouched by Wovoka's religion, defeated Indians turned to peyote, a natural hallucinogenic drug, as a way to escape a bewildering, intolerable reality.

To understand the appeal of the Ghost Dance religion, it is necessary to recall just how rapidly the culture of the Plains Indians was destroyed. The Dakota Sioux, for example, did not go to war with the whites until the end of the 1860s. Within another decade, the survivors had been herded on the Pine Ridge Reservation in South Dakota. There, on Wounded Knee Creek, when the Dakotas took avidly to the Ghost Dance religion, and the soldiers guarding them heard that there were guns in the camp, a war of nerves set in. In December 1890, after a shoving incident, the soldiers opened fire with rifles and artillery. About 200 people, half of them women and children, were killed. For the Indians there was no escape, even in mystical religion.

THE CATTLE KINGDOM

As the Indians lost the West, white Americans won it. Indeed, the final decades of the nineteenth century stand as the greatest era of economic expansion in American history.

In 1870, American forests yielded about 12.8 billion board feet of lumber. By 1900, this output had almost tripled to about 36 billion. Although this increase reflects in part the development of forest industries in the southern states, the region of greatest expansion was a new one, the Pacific Northwest.

In 1870, Americans were raising 23.8 million cattle. In 1900, 67.7 million head of the stupid, bawling creatures were fattening on grasslands, mostly in the West, and in western feedlots.

Annual gold production continued only slightly below the fabulous levels of the gold-rush era, until the end of the century, it was nearly double the totals of 1850. Annual silver production, only 2.4 million troy ounces in 1870, stood at 57.7 million in 1900.

The First Buckaroos

Acre for acre, cattlemen won more of the West than any other group of pioneers. They were motivated to bring the vastness of the Great Plains into the American economy by the appetite of the burgeoning cities for cheap meat, and they were encouraged in their venture by the disinterest in the rolling, arid grasslands of anyone save the Indians. Their story thrills Americans (and other peoples) to this day partly because it was romanticized, partly because the cattle kingdom was established so quickly and just as quickly destroyed.

The cowboy first rode into American legend just before the Civil War. In the late 1850s, enterprising Texans began to round up herds of the half-wild longhorns that ranged freely between the Nueces River and the Rio Grande. They drove them north over a trail that had been blazed by Shawnee Indians to Sedalia, Missouri, a railroad town with connections to Chicago. Although the bosses were English-speaking,

The Sioux camp near Pine Ridge, South Dakota, in 1891.

HOW THEY LIKED TO REMEMBER THE WEST

Jane Russell as Belle Star.   *Belle Starr.*

Americans were introduced to the Wild West of legend when the last frontier was still a going concern. Beginning in 1872, when the cattle and mining frontiers were at equinox, the racy *Police Gazette*, a magazine aimed at the all-male preserves of livery stables and barbershops, published accounts of intrepid sheriffs and federal marshalls single-handedly bringing law, order, and decency to chaotic cowtowns. The stories were purveyed not as history, but as "current events." The *Gazette* and writers of popular fiction for boys, such as Ned Buntline, churned out thrilling tales of superhuman heroes and heroines like Wild Bill Hickok when, in a real and thriving Deadwood, South Dakota, a real Hickok was luring miners into high-stakes games of poker.

Like the sensationalist supermarket tabloids of the 1980s ("Amazon Tribe Worships Elvis, Sings His Songs in Religious Ceremonies"), the journalistic mythmakers of the late nineteenth century spun their fantastic epics around tiny kernels of fact. For example, Hickok became a national celebrity when, as marshall of Abilene, Kansas, in 1871, he really did, without help, kill three toughs, members of the McCanless gang, who were gunning for him. In the popular account of the incident, the shootout was a high-noon showdown on Main Street such as is familiar to every movie and television viewer. In reality, Bill was less knightlike (but more sensible) in Abilene. He hid behind a curtain to shoot the leader of the gang, Dave McCanless, and behind a door to bag the second villain. Bill shot the third McCanless in the back as he was running away.

Hickok's subsequent career as a peace officer was rather more dubious. On October 5, 1871, he shot a drunken cowboy, heard someone coming toward him from behind, wheeled and fired and discovered he had plugged his own deputy. He was relieved of his duties several weeks later, news that was not reported in the *Police Gazette*.

Writer Peter Lyon codified the traits of the heroic western lawman as shaped in the pages of the *Gazette*. He was prodigiously accurate with a gun: Wild Bill could shoot an even spaced row of holes in the rim of a sombrero thrown into the air; Wyatt Earp could kill a coyote with a Colt 45 revolver at 400 yards. The hero's bravery was boundless: Wild Bill cleaned up Hays and Abilene single-handedly; Earp outdid him by making Ellsworth, Wichita, Dodge City, and Tombstone, Arizona, fit for women and Presbyterian preachers. The hero's vices were minor: "Wild Bill found relaxation and enjoyment in cards, but he seldom drank." His gallantry beggared Lancelot's; he was courteous to all women regardless of their social status, age, or physical attractions. He was gentle and modest, stunningly handsome, with blue eyes that turned steel-gray when aroused by the sight of injustice and foul play. He protected the poor, weak, and exploited against the rich and powerful. Could a formula more likely to appeal to modern male fantasies be devised?

The cinema adopted the western hero as its own and permanently fixed it in the American imagination. Hickok was gone when moving pictures were introduced (he was shot in the back by 1876) but the frontier was not quite dead during the infancy of film. The first "feature film"—a movie made to serve as a show in itself—depicted the robbery of a train by "baddies" and the restoration of law and order by "goodies" at a time when western railway companies were still vexed by mounted robbers who stopped trains in the middle of nowhere.

Men with real experience in the real Wild West played a significant part in celluloid mythmaking. William S. Hart, one of the first actors to specialize in playing western superheroes, had grown up a neighbor of the Sioux (he spoke the language) during years the tribe was still powerful and warring with the United States Cavalry. His chief rival on the silver screen, Tom Mix, had been an authentic working cowboy. They knew of what they portrayed, but they were not particularly observant of what they knew.

One of the most durable western heroes was Wyatt Earp, who actually appeared as an extra in a film of 1916, *The Half Breed*, unsuccessfully auditioned as a supporting actor, and spent his last years hanging around Hollywood studios advising film people, including the great director John Ford about the Wild West and his own part in taming it. Earp was a featured character in a dozen films (future president Ronald Reagan portrayed him in 1953), and the central figure in an immensely popular television series of the 1950s. Until *Hour of the Gun* in 1967, Earp was invariably depicted as a peace- and justice-loving idealist who anguished over the necessity of using violence but, in the end, oiled his gun.

In fact, the real Wyatt Earp had not been trigger-happy, but neither did his career much resemble the one depicted on film and television. He had been a policeman in Wichita—one of several, not sheriff or marshall—and he served two four-month terms as *Assistant* Marshall of Dodge City. He did not "clean up" either town. Indeed, the city council of Wichita fired him after he was a year in his low-level job and recommended that he be arrested as a vagrant. During a month in Dodge when, Earp later claimed, he personally arrested 400 rambunctious cowboys, he was not a law officer at all. He was, in fact, himself arrested during that month for punching a dancehall girl. (So much for gallantry towards the fair sex; later, in Tombstone, Earp deserted his wife and may, indeed, have been a bigamist.)

Wyatt Earp, like his equally romanticized friend, Bat Masterson, and like Wild Bill before him, was first and foremost a professional gambler. Such men lived by separating recently paid cowboys and miners from their wages. They sought out jobs wearing badges because, as peace officers, they alone were entitled to wear firearms in the saloons and casinos. A revolver provided a dandy psychological edge in the psychological game of poker.

Professional gamblers were closely allied with the owners of saloons, casinos, and whorehouses, a group perpetually involved in political struggles against "the better element" for control of the railhead towns. When the saloon-keepers were riding high, the likes of Hickok and Earp were lawmen. When the better element took control—when a town was in reality "cleaned up"—the likes of Hickok and Earp and Masterson were asked to leave.

One of the foremost historians of the late nineteenth-century frontier, Elliott West, helps to explain why the heroic representations of such characters seized on the American imagination by isolating four defining traits of the television western of the 1950s. First, he writes, the television West was a man's world: men did the big things, little things, good things, and bad things; women were present in the legendary West only as background or as helpless creatures to be rescued and protected. It was just the sort of thing to appeal to men in a society that was in the process of demasculinization.

Second, West writes, "pioneers of the picture tube were almost entirely of Anglo-Saxon origin" (old blue-eyes of the *Police Gazette*). Mexicans, Chinese, and Europeans, in reality major elements of the population of the last frontier, played little part in the television West. Again, it was a world calculated to appeal to American whites in a time of rising racial tensions and adjustment of interracial relations.

Third, virtually all the problems of the television West were ironed out in gun battles, in other words, decisively and finally. Nothing could be more reassuring to a people whose nation's problems seemed eternally beyond resolution. Finally, problems were ultimately quite simple, a confrontation of clear good and palpable evil, the way everyone in every time wishes problems could be.

Gary Cooper as Wild Bill Hickok.

Wild Bill Hickok.

Skills now exhibited at rodeos were once the cowboy's everyday activity.

many of the actual workers were Mexican. They called themselves *vaqueros*.

Vaquero, "cowboy," entered the English language as buckaroo. Indeed, while Anglo-Americans soon comprised the majority of this mobile work force, and former black slaves were a substantial minority of it, much of what became part of American folklore and parlance about the buckaroos was of Mexican derivation. The cowboy's colorful costume was an adaptation of functional Mexican work dress. The bandana was a washcloth that, when tied over the cowboy's mouth, served as a dust screen, no small matter when a thousand cattle were kicking up alkali grit. The broad-brimmed hat was not selected for its picturesque qualities but because it was a shield against sun and rain. Manufactured from first-quality beaver felt, the *sombrero* also served as a drinking pot and washbasin.

The pointed, high-heeled boots, awkward and even painful when walking, were designed for riding in the stirrups, where a *vaquero* spent his workday. The "western" saddle was of Spanish design, quite unlike the English tack that Americans in the East used. Chaps, leather leg coverings, got their name from chaparral, the ubiquitous woody brush against which they were designed to protect the cowboy.

Meat for Millions

The Civil War and Missouri laws against importing Texas cattle (because of hoof-and-mouth disease) stifled the cattle-driving business before it was fairly begun. However, in 1866, when the transcontinental railroad reached Abilene, Kansas, a wheeler-dealer from Illinois, Joseph G. McCoy, saw the possibilities of underselling steers raised back East with Texas longhorns. McCoy built a series of holding pens on the outskirts of the tiny Kansas town, arranged to ship cattle he did not then have with the Kansas Pacific Railroad, and dispatched agents to southern Texas to induce Texans to round up and drive cattle north to Abilene on a trading route called the Chisholm Trail.

In 1867, McCoy shipped 35,000 "tall, bony, coarse-headed, flat-sided, thin-flanked" cattle to Chicago. In 1868, 75,000 of the beasts, next to worthless in Texas, passed through Abilene with Chicago packers crying for more. In 1871, 600,000 "critters" left the pens of several Kansas railroad towns to end up on American dinner tables.

The profits were immense. A steer that cost about $5 to raise on public lands could be driven to Kansas at the cost of one cent a mile ($5 to $8) and sold for $25 or, occasionally, as much as $50. Investors from as far as England went west to establish ranches that were as comfortable as big-city gentlemen's clubs. The typical cattleman at the famous Cheyenne Club never touched a gun, and he sat on a horse only for the photographer. Instead, he sank into plush easy chairs, ignited a Havana cigar, and discussed account books, very often in a proper English accent, with his fellow businessmen.

The railhead continued to move westward, and with it went the destination of the cowboys, who were soon arriving from the North as well as the South. The migration of the railhead was alright with most of the citizens of towns like Abilene. They concluded after a few seasons that the money to be made as a cattle trading center was not worth the damage done to their own ranches and farms by hundreds of thousands of cattle. The wild atmosphere given their towns by the rambunctious cowboys, many of them bent on a blow-out after months on the trail, was even less conducive to respectable civic life. As a cow town grew, its "better element" demanded churches and schools in place of saloons, casinos, and whorehouses. The stage was set for the "taming" of a town, which is the theme of so many popular legends.

Never, though, did the cowboys lack for someplace to take their herds. There were always newer, smaller towns to the west to welcome them. In Kansas alone, Ellsworth, Newton, Wichita, Dodge City, and Hays had their "wide-open" period.

Disaster

The cattle kingdom lasted only a generation, ending suddenly as a result of greed in collaboration with two natural disasters.

The profits to be made in cattle were so great that exploiters ignored the fact that grassland has its limits as the support of huge herds. Vast as the plains were, they were overstocked by the mid-1880s. Unlike the bison, which had migrated vast distances each season, allowing the Plains to rest, the cattle stayed put. Clear-running springs were trampled into unpotable mudholes. Weeds never before noticed replaced the grasses that had invited overgrazing. Hills and buttes were scarred by cattle trails. Some species of migratory birds that once passed through twice a year simply disappeared; the beefsteaks on hoof had beaten them to their food.

Then, on January 1, 1886, a great blizzard buried the eastern and southern plains. Within three days, three feet of snow drifting into 20- and 30-foot banks suffocated the range. Between 50 and 85 percent of the livestock froze to death or died of hunger. About 300 cowboys could not reach shelter and were killed; the casualties among the Indians never were counted. When spring arrived, half the American plains reeked of death.

The summer of 1886 brought ruin to many cattlemen who had survived the snows. Grasses that had weathered summer droughts for millennia were unable to do so in their overgrazed condition; they withered and died, starving cattle already weakened by winter. Then, the next winter, the states that had escaped the worst of the blizzard of 1886 got 16 inches of snow in 16 hours and weeks more of intermittent fall.

The End of a Brief Era

The cattle industry recovered, but only when more prudent and methodical businessmen took over the holdings of the speculators of the glory days. Cattle barons like Richard King of southern Texas foreswore risking all on the open range. Through clever manipulation of land laws, King built a ranch that was as large as the state of Rhode Island. If not quite so grandiose in their success, others imitated King's example in Texas, Wyoming, Montana, and eastern Colorado.

Even more important in ending the days of the long drive and the cowboy as a romantic knight-errant was the expansion of the railroad network. When new

The blizzard of 1886 froze millions of cattle. This illustration is from Harper's Weekly.

east-west lines snaked into Texas and the states on the Canadian border, and the Union Pacific and Kansas Pacific sent feeder lines north and south into cow country, the cowboy became a ranch hand, a not-so-freewheeling employee of large commercial operations.

The Cowboy's Life

Even in the days of the long drive, the world of the cowboy bore scant resemblance to the legends that came to permeate American popular culture. Despite the white complexion of the cowboys in popular literature and in Western films of the twentieth century, a large proportion of cowboys were Mexican or black. In some cases, these workers and the whites acted and mixed as equals. Just as often, however, they split along racial lines when they reached the end of the trail, frequenting segregated restaurants, barber shops, hotels, saloons, and brothels.

Black, white, or Hispanic, they were indeed little more than boys. Photographs that the buckaroos had taken in cow towns like Abilene and Dodge City (as well as arrest records, mostly for drunk and disorderly conduct), show a group of very young men, few apparently much older than 25. The life was too arduous for anyone but youths—days in the saddle, nights sleeping on bare ground in all weather. Moreover, the cowboy who married could not afford to be absent from his own ranch or farm for as long as the cattle drives required.

The real buckaroos were not constantly engaged in shooting scrapes such as made novels and movies so exciting. Their skills lay in horsemanship and with a rope, not with the Colt revolver that they carried to signal co-workers far away. Indeed, toting guns was forbidden in railhead towns. With a drunken binge on every cowboy's itinerary, the sheriff or marshal in charge of keeping the peace did not tolerate shooting irons on every hip. Those who did not leave their revolvers in camp outside town checked them at the police station.

THE WILD WEST IN AMERICAN CULTURE

The legend of the cowboy as a romantic, dashing, and quick-drawing knight of the wide-open spaces was not a creation of a later era. On the contrary, all the familiar themes of the Wild West were well formed when the cold, hard reality was still alive on the plains. Rather more oddly, the myths of the Wild West were embraced not only by easterners in their idle reveries, but by the cowboys themselves.

Play-Acting

The most important creator of the legendary Wild West was a none-too-savory character named E. Z. C. Judson. A former Know-Nothing who was dishonorably discharged from the Union Army, Judson took the pen name Ned Buntline, and between 1865 and 1886, churned out more than 400 romantic, blood, guts, and chivalric novels about western heroes. Some of his characters he invented; others were highly fictionalized real people. Called pulps after the cheap paper on which they were printed or dime novels after their price, the books by Judson and his many competitors were devoured chiefly but not exclusively by boys.

Buntline's mythical world appealed even to those who should have known better. During the 1880s, while living as a rancher in North Dakota, future president Theodore Roosevelt helped capture two young cowboys who had robbed a grocery store. In their saddlebags, Roosevelt found several Ned Buntline novels that no doubt featured outlaws who were unjustly accused. The tiny town of Palisade, Nevada, on the Central Pacific Railroad line, won the reputation in eastern newspapers as a den of cutthroats because brawls and gunfights broke out so regularly when passengers left the train for refreshment. In fact, the fights were staged by locals in part to twit eastern fantasies, in part because they were just plain bored.

American Heroes

In the pulps and later in films, Americans discovered that the bank and train robbers Jesse and Frank James, and several cohorts from the Clanton family, were really modern-day Robin Hoods who gave the money they took to the poor. When Jesse was murdered, his mother made a tourist attraction of his grave, charging admission and explaining that her son had been a Christian with an inclination to read the Bible in his spare time.

Belle Starr, the moniker of one Myra Belle Shirley, was immortalized as "the bandit queen," as pure in heart as Jesse James was socially conscious. Billy the Kid (William Bonney), a Brooklyn-born homicidal maniac, was romanticized as a tragic hero who had been forced into a life of crime by a callous society. James Butler "Wild Bill" Hickok, a gambler and clothes-horse who killed perhaps six people before he was shot down in Deadwood Gulch, South Dakota, in 1876, was attributed with dozens of killings, all in the cause of making the West safe for women, children, and psalmbooks. Calamity Jane (Martha Cannary),

Primarily a showman, "Buffalo Bill" Cody was transformed into a chivalric hero in pulp novels.

romantics, were talented artists; Owen Wister, an aristocratic easterner, created the finest prototype of the western knight without armor in *The Virginian*, published in 1902. If the cowboy gave you his word, Wister wrote, "he kept it; Wall Street would have found him behind the times. Nor did he talk lewdly to women; Newport would have thought him old-fashioned."

THE MINING FRONTIER

The folklore of the precious-metal mining frontier is second only to the legend of the cowboy in the American imagination. Deadwood Gulch, for example, where Wild Bill Hickok was gunned down and Calamity Jane spent much of her life, was no cow town but a gold-mining center.

Gold and Silver Rushes

After the richest of the California gold fields played out, prospectors in search of "glory holes" fanned out over the mountains and deserts of the West. For more than a generation, they discovered new deposits almost

later said to have been Wild Bill's paramour, wrote her own romantic autobiography in order to support a drinking problem.

Calamity Jane and other "living legends" of the West personally contributed to the mythmaking by appearing in Wild West shows that traveled to cities in the East and in Europe, where they dramatized great gun battles. The most famous of these shows was the creation of "Buffalo Bill" Cody, who easily made the transition from hunter to impresario. Among his featured performers was Sitting Bull, the Hunkpapa Sioux chief who had overseen the defeat of George Custer. Reality and myth were cruelly confused in Sitting Bull's life. After a successful career in show business, he returned to the Rosebud Reservation where, during the Ghost Dance excitement, he was accidentally killed by Indian policemen who were arresting him on suspicion of fomenting rebellion.

Some creators of the legendary West were conscientious realists; Frederic Remington, whose paintings and bronze statues of cowboys and Indians are studiously representative, is a fine example. Others, while

Sitting Bull, a squaw, and three of his children pose with two white visitors to the Standing Rock reservation in 1882.

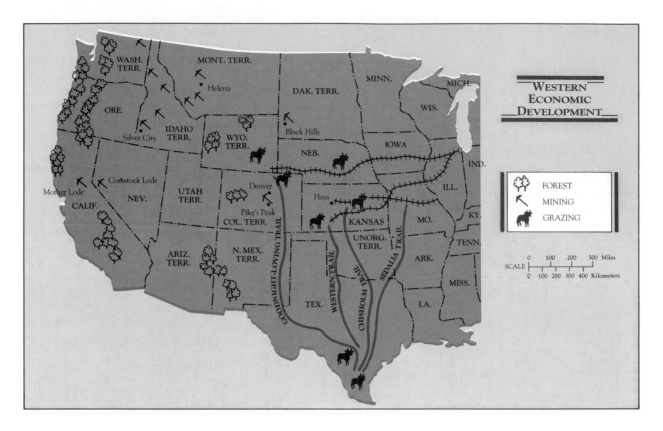

annually and very rich ones every few years. In 1859, there were two great strikes. A find in the Pike's Peak area of Colorado led to a rush that was reminiscent of that of 1849. At about the same time, gold miners in northern Nevada discovered that a "blue mud" that had been fouling their operations was one of the richest silver ores ever discovered. This was the beginning of Virginia City and the Comstock Lode. Before the Comstock pinched out in the twentieth century, it yielded more than $400 million in silver and gold.

In 1862, Tombstone, Arizona, was founded on the site of a gold mine; in 1864, Helena, Montana, rose atop another. In 1876, rich placer deposits were discovered in the Black Hills of South Dakota (then forbidden to whites by Indian treaty). The next year, silver was found at Leadville, Colorado, almost two miles above sea level in the Rockies.

During the 1880s, the Coeur d'Alene in the Idaho panhandle drew thousands of miners, as did the copper deposits across the mountains in Butte. In 1891, the Cripple Creek district in Colorado began to outproduce every other mining town. In 1898, miners rushed north to Canada's Yukon, Alaska's Klondike, and then to Nome, where the gold was on the beach. As late as 1901, there was an old-fashioned rush when the classic grizzled old prospector in a slouch hat, Jim Butler, drove his pick into a desolate mountain in

southern Nevada and found it "practically made of silver." From the town of Tonopah, founded on its site, prospectors discovered rich deposits in Goldfield, a few miles away.

Of Mining Camps and Cities

Readers of the dime novels of the time and film viewers since have avidly savored the vision of boisterous, wide-open mining towns, complete with saloons rocking with the music of tinny pianos and the shouts of bearded men. The live-for-today miner, the gambler, the prostitute with a heart of gold are permanent inhabitants of American folklore. Nor is the picture altogether imaginary. The speculative mining economy fostered a risk-all attitude toward life and work.

However, efficient exploitation of underground (hard rock) mining required a great deal of capital and technical expertise, both to finance the operation and to build the railroads that hauled ore out. Consequently, the mining camps that were home to 5,000 or even 10,000 people within a short time of their founding were also cities with a variety of services and a social structure more like that of older industrial towns than the towns of the cattleman's frontier.

In 1877, only six years after it was founded on a vein of gold, Leadville, Colorado boasted several miles of paved streets, gas lighting, a modern water system,

Mining was a dangerous occupation in the West. Here a mucker moves a load of silver ore to the surface.

characters like Wild Bill Hickok and Wyatt Earp discharged their revolvers; but they were also the sites of huge stamping mills (to crush the ores) that towered over the landscape, and of busy exchanges where mining stocks were traded by agents of San Francisco, New York, and London bankers.

In Goldfield, the last of the wide-open mining towns, one of the most important men in the camp was the urbane Wall Street financier Bernard Baruch (who may have been outdressed by some of the locals). The Anaconda Copper Company of Butte, Montana, was one of the nation's ranking corporate giants. The Guggenheim mining syndicate was supreme in the Colorado gold fields. Rockefeller's Standard Oil was a major owner of mines in the Coeur d'Alene. If it was wild, the mining West was no mere colorful diversion for readers of dime novels, but an integral part of the national economy. In fact, the gold and silver that the hard-rock miners tore from the earth stood at the very center of a question that divided Americans more seriously than any other after the end of Reconstruction—what was to serve as the nation's money?

The miners and mine owners alone could not make an issue of the precious metals from which coins were minted, goods bought and sold, and debts incurred and paid off—or not paid off. There were too few of them. However, as the century wound to a close, the money question became of great interest to a group of people who formed a major part of the American population, and who had once been its most important segment, the farmers on the land.

thirteen schools, five churches, and three hospitals. It was hardly the tiny, false-front set that is used to represent mining towns in Hollywood films.

"Camps" such as Virginia City in Nevada, Deadwood Gulch in South Dakota, and Tombstone in Arizona are best remembered as places where legendary

---

For Further Reading

Three good books deal with "the West" in general from rather different perspectives: Ray A. Billington, *Westward Expansion: A History of the American Frontier* (1967); Thomas D. Clark, *Frontier America: The Story of the Westerward Movement* (1969); and Frederick Merk, *History of the Westward Movement* (1978). Also valuable is Robert A. Wiebe, *The Search for Order* (1968). An essential book is that by the "founding father" of frontier history, Frederick Jackson Turner, *The Frontier in American History* (1920). Also see Billington's *Frederick Jackson Turner* (1973) and *America's Frontier Heritage* (1967).

Useful special studies include Allan C. Bogue, *From Prairie to Corn Belt* (1963); E. Dick, *The Sod-House Frontier* (1937); Dee Brown, *Bury My Heart at Wounded Knee* (1970); E. E. Dale, *The Range Cattle Industry* (1930); David Day, *Cowboy Culture: A Saga of Five Centuries* (1981); Robert R. Dystra, *The Cattle Towns* (1968); Gilbert C. Fite, *The Farmer's Frontier, 1865–1900* (1966); Joe B. Frantz and J. E. Choate, *The American Cowboy: The Myth and the Reality* (1955); William S. Greever, *The Bonanza West: The Story of the Western Mining Rushes* (1963); William T. Hagan, *American Indians* (1961); E. S. Osgood, *The Day of the Cattleman* (1929); Rodman W. Paul, *Mining Frontiers of the Far West, 1848–1880* (1963); J. M. Shagg, *The Cattle Trading Industry* (1973); Fred A. Shannon, *The Farmer's Last Frontier* (1967); Duane A. Smith, *Rocky Mountain Mining Camps* (1967); Henry Nash Smith, *Virgin Land: The American West as Symbol and Myth* (1950); J. R. Swanson, *The Indian Tribes of North America* (1953); Robert M. Utley, *Last Days of the Sioux Nation* (1963); Wilcomb E. Washburn, *The Indian in America* (1975); Thomas H. Watkins, *Gold and Silver in the West* (1960); and Walter P. Webb, *The Great Plains* (1931).

Ever since the world's first farmer poked a hole in the ground and inserted a seed, tillers of the soil have understood that they were engaged in a game of chance with nature. Farming was a gamble, betting a year's living on such uncertainties as the day of winter's final frost and summer's yield of sunshine and rain. Farmers were at the mercy of capricious insects and birds. They knew that illness at harvest time could mean twelve months of privation. But farmers have also known that their work was the bedrock on which civilization was based. After all, it was they who produced the first necessity of life after air and water. The farmer was the man, in the words of a song of the 1890s, "who feeds them all." American farmers were, perhaps, particularly

33

STRESSFUL TIMES DOWN HOME

The Crisis of American Agriculture, 1865–1896

The grandeur and isolation of a plains farm are captured in this traveling photographer's masterpiece.

conscious of their role in society. They believed they were the nation's most valuable citizens, the "bone and sinew" of the republic. So they were told by Thomas Jefferson and succeeding generations of politicians fishing for their votes.

In the final decades of the nineteenth century, the staple farmers of the West and South discovered that the grand old truisms were not necessarily so. In the new America of gigantic railroads, multimillion-dollar corporations, mighty investment banks, and a marketplace that extended to the obscurest corners of the earth, the powers of nature could seem to be secondary, almost innocuous by comparison with diabolical economic forces—and the power of people whom farmers came to think of as parasites, sucking them dry. In the 1890s, welling anger and resentment down on the farm culminated in a radical political movement that shook the confidence of the conservative men who had governed the United States since the end of the Civil War.

THE BEST OF TIMES, THE WORST OF TIMES

Farmers rarely led the way on the last frontier. Miners and cattlemen and soldiers clearing the land of Indians were the usual pioneers. Subsistence agriculture attracted no one. Commercial agriculture was feasible in the late nineteenth-century West only after the railroad arrived to connect field and barnyard to hungry eastern and foreign cities. Once the railroad made its appearance, however, settlers with plow and little more fairly inundated the last frontier.

Success Story

Never in the history of the world have people put new land to the plow as quickly as Americans (and many immigrants) did in the final three decades of the nineteenth century. As of 1870, when the railway building boom was at full tilt, Americans had brought a total of 408 million acres of land under cultivation, an average of 1.6 million acres of new farmland a year. Between 1870 and 1900, a single generation of farmers put 431 million acres of virgin soil to the plow, more than between 1607 and 1870, and an average of 14.4 million acres each year.

Crop production increased just as sharply. By 1900, American farmers were producing up to 150 percent

more of the staple grains—corn and wheat—than they had in 1870. Hogs, a by-product of corn, numbered 25 million in 1870 and 63 million in 1900.

The ravenous appetites of American and foreign city dwellers encouraged this amazing growth. The expansion of the railroads made it possible for crops raised by a Great Plains farmer to feed the inhabitants of Chicago and New York, London and Warsaw. Even at that, however, the pioneer farmers of the West had to overcome formidable difficulties to accomplish what they did.

Cool, Clear Water

American farmers and immigrants from northern Europe were accustomed to summer rains nourishing their crops. From the Atlantic Seaboard to as far west as Missouri and eastern Kansas, 32 to 48 inches of rain fell each year, more in the deep South. West of about Wichita, Kansas, however, annual precipitation declined to 16 to 32 inches a year, with much of it during the winter. Yet farther west in the "rain-shadow" of the Rocky Mountains, at about the eastern boundary of Colorado, rainfall dropped to 16 inches or less per year. This was the "Great American Desert," which an early explorer had called "almost totally unfit for cultivation." The central valley of California was just as arid with, in some years, no rain at all during the summer months.

The Californians solved their problem with large-scale irrigation. They formed cooperative "ditch companies" that tapped the water of the San Joaquin, Sacramento, and numerous other rivers that rose in the Sierra Nevada, channeling it to their crops. Irrigation brought them into conflict with hydraulic miners who, in washing down whole mountainsides to win their grains of gold, clogged the rivers and irrigation ditches with mud. The more numerous farmers won the contest in California's courts, shutting down the hydraulic operations.

To some extent, "dry farming" on the Great Plains was based on a delusion. The summers of the 1870s and early 1880s, when cultivators arrived in the region, were abnormally rainy. This convinced the settlers and some experts, such as Charles Dana Wilber, that "rain follows the plow." When they broke the primeval sod, farmers believed, they permanently altered the climate by liberating moisture from the earth that would return indefinitely in the form of heavier rains.

There was nothing to this theory, as the devastating drought of 1887 was to show, but Great Plains farmers did make the most of what moisture they had by

Wearing masks so they won't be recognized, settlers cut fifteen miles of Brighton Ranch fence in 1885. Note the fencepost, a mere brittle branch of a tree.

plowing more deeply than Eastern farmers did. The thick layer of dust that settled in the foot-deep furrows acted as a kind of mulch.

Large California-style ditch companies were out of the question on most of the Great Plains. The level of the largest rivers dropped too low to be drained; smaller streams dried up by mid-summer. Some farmers individually irrigated their fields from wells on which they mounted prefabricated windmills. However, the cost of the windmills and of drilling a well, between $1 and $2 a foot, was too much for most settlers to risk when they had no idea whether they would hit water at 25 feet or 200.

A Treeless Land

Save for groves of cottonwood and poplar along the muddy rivers, there were no trees on the Great Plains and, therefore, no lumber with which to build. Importing wood for a respectable frame house had to be delayed until after a family had harvested a few crops and squirreled some money away. In the meantime, pioneers lived in sod houses, which were constructed of blocks cut from the tangled plains sod. Sod houses

were rather snug in the winter, but they dripped mud in the spring thaw and became hellholes of choking dust during the long arid summers. Many western farmers died in them after many years, still just dreaming of clapboards and windows.

MAKING A SOD HOUSE

To make a sod house, pioneers mowed about an acre of grassland, preferably when it was slightly moist, and hitched mules or oxen to a "grasshopper plow" that turned up the sod in strips about a foot wide and 4 to 5 inches thick. These were chopped into blocks with a spade and, grass side down, the "Nebraska marble" was laid like bricks. The walls of a sod house had to be two to three feet thick in order to support the roof, which was made of wooden rafters with a layer of sod grass-side up on top. Door and window frames were made from old packing crates.

A sod house was fireproof, quite snug in winter and cool in summer, but it dropped dirt and dust constantly and, in heavy rains, it might be necessary to cook, eat, and sleep with an umbrella overhead.

A couple stand with their prized possessions in front of their sod house in Custer County, Nebraska, about 1886.

Building fences was more urgent. Crops needed to be protected from open-range cattle, and the settler's own livestock kept under control. But cheap as fence lumber was, the cost of ringing a 160 acre farm with wooden posts and rails was beyond the means of nearly all. The solution to their problem came in 1872 when Joseph Glidden of Illinois perfected a machine that mass-produced cheap barbed wire. With the flimsiest of scavenged fenceposts, a Great Plains farmer could erect a steel "hedge" so efficient that a starving cow would lie down and die rather than push through it.

Barbed wire's effectiveness was the cause of numerous clashes between settlers who used it (sometimes called "nesters"), and open-range cattlemen accustomed to running their animals freely on the plains. When fences prevented their cattle from reaching streams and water holes, cattlemen retaliated by damming up streams above nester land, cutting fence wire into useless shreds, and, in Johnson County, Wyoming, hiring gunfighters to terrorize the nesters.

Machines in the Land

Barbed wire was but one of hundreds of technology's contributions to the fabulous expansion of agriculture. A chilled steel plow invented by Oliver Evans in 1877

sliced through sod and heavy soils. Disc harrows cultivated wide swaths with each pass, allowing "dry farmers" to tend more acres than eastern farmers needed. Manufacturers like John Deere and International Harvester developed machines that planted seeds, shucked corn, threshed wheat, bound shocks, and shredded fodder for livestock. The value of farm machinery in use in the United States increased from $271 million in 1870 to $750 million in 1900.

Machinery made the American farmer of the late nineteenth century the most productive in the world and, potentially, able to cultivate six times as much land as his father had farmed back East before the Civil War. That is, plowing and seeding wheat by hand, harvesting it with a sickle, and threshing with a flail, a prewar farmer had to spend between 50 and 60 hours to harvest about 20 bushels of wheat per acre. With a gang plow and a horse-drawn seeder, harrow, reaper, and thresher—all of which were in widespread use by 1890—a farmer produced a much larger crop after only eight to ten hours of work per acre.

Hard Times

On the other hand, machinery cost money that most farmers simply did not have. Already short-term debtors, borrowing each year for seed and provisions during the growing season, the typical farmer of the late nineteenth century was also a long-term debtor, owing money for his machines even if he got his land or free.

What was worse, beginning about 1872, the western growers of wheat, corn, and livestock watched their incomes sag and, by the 1890s, utterly collapse. A crop that in 1872 brought a farmer $1,000 in real income (actual purchasing power) was worth only $500 in 1896. A man who was 48 years of age in 1896, still an active working farmer, had to turn out twice as many hogs or double the bushels of corn or wheat as he had produced as a young man of 24, just to enjoy the same standard of living that he had known in 1872. It was not comforting to know that a quarter century of backbreaking toil had yielded nothing but the prospect of more struggle. By the 1890s, the price of corn was so low (8 cents a bushel) that some farmers had to forgo buying coal and to burn their grain for winter warmth.

Those that were unable to pay their debts went under. Between 1889 and 1893, some 11,000 Kansas farm families lost their homes when they failed to make their mortgage payments. In several western counties of Kansas and Nebraska during the same period, nine out of every ten farmsteads changed hands. The number of farm tenant families—those that did not own the land they worked—doubled from 1 to 2 million between 1880 and 1900, most of the increase coming after 1890. For every three landowning farm families in the North and West, there was one tenant family.

STOVEPIPING

In the autumn of 1893 there was so much rain in the wheatbelt of eastern Washington State that much of the year's crop was ruined. Some farmers tried to stave off disaster by means of a technique called "stovepiping." A length of stovepipe was inserted into an upright sack and filled with the rotten grain. Then the rest of the sack—top and sides—was filled with good wheat, and the stovepipe was removed. When the purchasing agent opened the sack, the grain looked good. It did not work for long. Buyers learned to use their own hollow tube to dig for samples deep within each sack.

For them, farming was no longer the basis of independence and hope for the future, but grinding toil for the sake of putting a meal on the table and keeping the banker from the door.

The South: Tenants and Sharecroppers

Tenancy was far more common in the South, particularly in the cotton belt. Below the Ohio River, there were as many tenant farmers as there were families working land they owned. Among blacks, tenants and sharecroppers outnumbered landowners by almost five to one.

The South's tenancy problem had different origins, dating to Reconstruction. Having freed blacks from bondage, the then-dominant Republicans failed to

Mechanization on the farm—horse-drawn reapers like this did the work of many men.

BLACK SODBUSTERS

With the collapse of Reconstruction, Benjamin "Pap" Singleton, a black carpenter from Nashville, concluded that blacks could make decent lives for themselves only by doing what so many whites were doing—moving West. He came to be known as the "Moses of the Colored Exodus" by traveling throughout the South urging blacks to migrate to Kansas and found black colonies. His message touched a chord in some communities. By the end of 1878, more than 7,000 "Exodusters" took out homesteads in Kansas. In 1879, another 20,000 arrived, founding communities such as Nicodemus, which still preserves its black pioneer heritage.

At first glad for the emigrants, Kansas soon launched a campaign of discouragement to counter Singleton's work. While propagandists publicized the usual rosy lies among potential white emigrants, they told southern blacks about the hardships and risks of farming on the Great Plains (all true enough), for fear that the state would become a black refuge.

provide the freedmen the means to survive on their own. After some consideration, the Republicans rejected proposals to confiscate the large plantations and divide them into 40-acre farms for the blacks who had worked them as slaves. With a few exceptions, land was left in the hands of those who owned it before the war.

But how were the crops to be got in? The former slaves refused to work in gangs for wages; it was too reminiscent of the patterns of life under slavery. Even if they had been willing, the landowning planters had no money with which to pay wages. They were themselves impoverished; the blacks had been their capital.

The solution to the problem was a system of cultivation that, on the face of it, seemed fair to both landowner and worker, sharing the crop. Plantation owners partitioned their land into family-farm-sized plots on which a cabin, usually quite rude, was constructed. In return for the use of the house and the land, sharetenants, who provided their own daily bread, mule, plow, and seed, turned over to the landlord one-quarter to one-third of each year's crop. Sharecroppers were tenants who were too poor to supply mule, plow, and seed. The landlord provided everything in return for one-half of the crop.

As a means of production, the system worked. Southern cotton production reached its 1860 level in 1870 and exceeded the prewar record (1859) a few years later. As in the West, however, greater production was accompanied by a drastic decline in wholesale prices. The price of a pound of cotton fell to 6 cents by the 1890s, and briefly in 1893 to a nickel, $30 for a bale that took six strong men to lift.

Debt Bondage

One result of declining prices was a physically and morally debilitating poverty. Pellagra, a fatal niacin-deficiency disease unknown even in slavery times, became a problem of epidemic proportions in the South. Another consequence was a form of debt bondage that, wrote Charles Oken in 1894, "crushed out all independence and reduced its victims to a coarse species of servile labor."

The victims were white as well as black, for many farmers with modest holdings lost them to creditors, usually merchants. The ledgers of one southern merchant, T. G. Patrick, show that during one season he provided about $900 worth of seed, food, tools, and other necessities to a farm owner named S. R. Simonton. When the price of cotton dropped well below Simonton's expectations that fall, he was able to repay only $300, leaving Patrick with a lien against his property of $600. Simonton cut his costs drastically the following year to just $400, but the accumulated debt of $1,000 was too much for Patrick to carry. He took Simonton's land, and Simonton became his tenant.

In southern agriculture, a system of sharecropping replaced slavery. Here, sharecroppers pick cotton in the 1890s.

Once a tenant or sharecropper, the southern farmer's debts bound him to the land as if he were a medieval serf. Tenants and sharecroppers also bought their necessities on credit from a general merchandiser, often their landlord, putting up as collateral their share of the crop. If the income from their share did not cover the year's debt, the merchandiser put a lien on the next year's harvest, quite effectively binding the cropper to work for him indefinitely. There was no quitting and moving out. To try to flee such a debt was a criminal offense punishable by imprisonment.

There was, of course, an element of security in debt bondage; the cropper who owed money to his landlord was not likely to be evicted. But there had been such an element of security in slavery too.

Hayseeds

Southern black farmers needed no tutoring to know that their race excluded them from full participation in the mainstream of American politics and social life. The color line was drawn ever more clearly in the South as the nineteenth century waned. White farmers of the South and West experienced a more subtle deterioration in their political power and status. Not only did the proportion of agriculturalists in the population decline annually, but the legislators whom farmers sent to Washington and the state capitals seemed all too often to forget their grimy constituents once they made the acquaintance of back-slapping lobbyists for railroads, industry, and banks.

A newly confident urban culture depicted the man of the soil in popular fiction, songs, and melodramas as a thick-skulled yokel, a ridiculous figure in a tattered straw hat with a hayseed clenched between his teeth, who allowed traveling salesmen to sleep with his daughter. Rather more serious chroniclers of rural life, such as Hamlin Garland, sympathized with farmers but

wanted no part of their lives. In his popular book of 1891 *Main-Travelled Roads*, Garland depicted rural life as dreary and stultifying.

Tens of thousands of farmers' sons and daughters followed Garland in his flight to the city. In part, they despaired of ever making a living on the land. In part, they were lured by the social and cultural attractions of the city. "Who wants to smell new-mown hay," playwright Clyde Fitch wrote in 1909, "if he can breathe gasoline on Fifth Avenue instead?" With each son and daughter who opted for urban fumes, farmers who clung to the Jeffersonian image of themselves became further dejected, agitated, and demoralized.

PROTEST AND ORGANIZATION

To ward against jokes and jeers, farmers could repair to the good old gospel of agrarianism, the confidence that they were peculiarly valuable to society. They could and did disdain the cities as sinks of iniquity and sin. In speech and sermon, and in the pages of magazines catering to country people, politicians, preachers, and journalists repeated the old shibboleths. In sturdy pillars of American popular culture, like the McGuffey's Readers in which urban and rural schoolchildren alike learned their ABCs, and values on the side, the ennoblement of farm life was alive and well.

Rural Renaissance

And yet, American farm life was undeniably isolated, arduous, and often dreary. The winds on the Great Plains dispatched men and women to the state asylum in numbers high enough to worry the doughtiest Jeffersonian. Aside from church—which was not for everyone—and moments snatched on shopping trips to town, there was little to relieve the tedium and monotony, especially for farm women, whose lives were far more isolated than those of their menfolk.

In the 1870s, farmers and their wives joined the Patrons of Husbandry, called simply the Grange, which sponsored dances, fairs, lecturers who spoke on everything from the date of creation to the habits of the people of Borneo. In the 1880s, new organizations—the Agricultural Wheel, the Texas State Alliance, The Southern Alliance, the Colored Farmers' National Alliance—mushroomed all over the countryside to take over many of the same functions.

Their value was inestimable, particularly for women. A leader of the Southeren Alliance, the largest of the regional organizations, declared that it "redeemed woman from her enslaved condition, and placed her

---

THE FARMER FEEDS THEM ALL

When the Lawyer hangs around and the Butcher cuts
*   a pound,*
Oh the farmer is the man who feeds them all.
And the preacher and the cook go a-strolling by the brook
And the farmer is the man who feeds them all.

Oh the farmer is the man, the farmer is the man,
Lives on credit 'till the fall.
Then they take him by the hand and they lead him from
*   the land*
And the middle man's the one that gets them all.
                                    Song of the 1890s

in her proper sphere." Indeed, women were to play an active role in the agrarian movement at every level.

Originally, both the Grange and the Alliances were avowedly nonpolitical. Inevitably in the hard times, however, farmers getting together asked themselves what—or who—was to blame for their woes? The Grangers attacked the railroads for exploiting them and successfully regulated their rates by electing sympathetic politicians to state legislatures. Then they saw their work wiped out by the Wabash decision of 1886. The Alliances and Wheels taught that the truculent individualism of the farmer in a highly organized society contributed to their distress and encouraged members to form cooperatives and other economic combinations.

The Co-op Movement

In consumer cooperatives, farmers banded together to purchase essential machinery in lots and therefore more cheaply. Money pools, associations much like contemporary credit unions, sprouted all over the Midwest. Through these associations, which were capitalized by members and operated on a nonprofit basis, farmers hoped to eliminate their dependence on banks. While many survived to serve the credit needs of their members for generations, money pools suffered from the opposition of bankers and the inexperience of their own amateur administrators. Farmers too often put

Mary Elizabeth Lease, one of America's first women lawyers and a leader of protesting farmers.

friends rather than professionals in charge of the money pools, and the rate of mismanagement and embezzlement was sadly high.

Producer cooperatives were designed to counter the power of the railroads over farmers' lives after the Supreme Court's decision in the Wabash case of 1886 struck down the Granger laws regulating charges for storing grain. Corn-belt farmers pooled funds and built their own grain elevators in the expectation they could keep their crop off the market until they liked the selling price.

But co-ops could not remedy the problem that was at the root of agricultural distress: American staple farmers were too many and too good for their own good. Too much land had been opened to settlement by too many railroads too quickly. Improvements in farm machinery and new methods resulted in far more grain, livestock, and fiber than the market could absorb.

Sinister Forces

Some agrarian leaders recognized overproduction as a problem. Canadian-born "Sockless Jerry" Simpson of Kansas called on the federal government to carve out new markets for American farm goods abroad. Mary Elizabeth Lease of Kansas, one of the nation's first women lawyers and an orator of fiery intensity, told farmers to "raise less corn and more hell." But that was a slogan, not a program. To the individual farmer, the only solution to declining prices was not to plant less corn but more, thus worsening the situation.

Moreover, few farmers believed that overproduction was the sole or even the chief cause of agrarian distress. Mother Lease herself pointed out that the streets of American cities teemed with hungry, ill-clad people while foodstuffs rotted in Kansas and cotton went unsold in Alabama. She and other agrarian leaders—Simpson, Ignatius Donnelley of Minnesota, William Peffer of Kansas, Thomas Watson of Georgia—said that sinister, parasitical forces were at work like thieves in the night to enrich themselves at the expense of men and women who produced wealth. Their villains included the great railroaders, politicians and judges pliantly in their employ, and most of all the "money power," a conspiracy of bankers and lawyers who manipulated the nation's currency.

THE MONEY QUESTION

Money is a medium of exchange, a token that the people of a society agree represents value. It makes the exchange of goods and services more workable than

"Sockless Jerry" Simpson reveled in his homey nickname, but he was no "hick." He was a sophisticated thinker and shrewd politician.

simple barter: so much grain in return for so many pairs of shoes or so many hours of labor. Obviously, money is essential to all but the most primitive economies. The value of money can change. At the time of the first European settlements in North America, the tribes of the Eastern Woodlands used wampum, or strings of beads made of shell, to represent value when they exchanged corn, hides, and other goods. Strings of wampum were difficult to make and, therefore, scarce.

When Europeans introduced glass beads in great quantity into this economy at little cost to themselves, buying valuable pelts for a pittance, but refusing to accept the beads in return when the Indians tried to purchase iron tools, weapons, and other European products, wampum was soon worthless to everyone.

Wampum, Gold, and Silver

Rather than wampum, the economically sophisticated nations of the world used precious metals—gold and silver—as their medium of exchange. They were rare, durable, limited in supply. There was little danger that the world would suddenly be flooded with either.

Thus, the value they represented was stable and dependable. The farmer who received gold for his crop knew that the suppliers of the goods his family needed would accept the gold at the value he put on it. It did not even matter which country's emblem was stamped on a coin. The weight of the gold in it determined its worth. In the United States, the Treasury minted coins of large denomination in gold: $5 coins, $10 coins (called "eagles"), and $20 coins ("double eagles").

Coins of smaller denomination (dimes, quarters, dollars) were minted in silver, which was more common than gold and therefore less valuable, but also limited in quantity. In 1837, Congress determined that the value of silver as money would be pegged to that of gold at a ratio of 16:1. That is, an ounce of gold was legally worth 16 ounces of silver, it being estimated that there was in the world just about 16 times as much silver as gold. Put another way, for every 16 ounces of silver a miner presented to the mint for sale, he would receive one ounce in gold.

Large commercial transactions were carried out in paper money issued by banks pledged to redeem it in

THE NEW SOUTH: THE PROPHET AND THE BUILDER

In speech after speech throughout the South, he told the story of a funeral that he had attended in rural Georgia. "They buried him in a New York coat and a Boston pair of shoes, and a pair of breeches from Chicago and a shirt from Cincinnati." The coffin, continued Henry W. Grady (1851–89), the wisecracking editor of the Atlanta *Constitution*, was made from northern lumber and hammered together with northern-forged nails. "The South didn't furnish a thing on earth for that funeral but the corpse and the hole in the ground."

Grady's point, to which he devoted most of his short life, was that the South must abandon its traditional reliance on agriculture and promote industrialization. The North's industry explained why the Confederacy had been defeated and why, in the wake of the war, the South suffered in company with the agricultural Plains. Only by accepting the realities of the modern world would the South prosper and escape its status as a backwater.

Although Grady lived to see few of his ideas come to fruition, during the very period that southern agrarians like Thomas E. Watson were vilifying urban, industrial America, southerners scored the kind of successes that Grady had called for. Beginning with a federal grant of almost 6 million acres of forest land in 1877, southern syndicates laid the basis of a thriving lumber and turpentine industry in the vast pine woods of the section. Birmingham became the "Pittsburgh of the South," the center of a booming steel industry, following the discovery of coal and iron in northern Alabama in the early 1870s. By 1890, Birmingham was making more pig iron than was Pittsburgh. ("Pigs" are iron ingots, intermediate products ready for further processing.)

The southern oil industry was largely a twentieth-century development; the great Texas gusher, Spindletop, came through in 1901. Likewise the southern textile industry. Most of the New England textile mills migrated to the South after 1900, although, even before Grady died in 1889, the trend of "bringing the factory to the fields" was to some degree under way.

The southerner who was most successful in bringing the factory to the fields was not a maker of cloth but a maker of cigarettes and bad habits. James Buchanan "Buck" Duke (1856–1925) started out as a tobacco grower, a good southern agrarian on the face of it. In 1881, he was shown a new machine that rolled cigarettes by the hundreds per minute, and his head began to spin in contemplation of its possibilities. All cigarettes were then rolled by hand, mostly by the smoker. Like a chess player, Duke had to see several moves ahead. To make money from manufacturing cigarettes, it was necessary not only to mass-produce them cheaply, but also to change Americans' tobacco habits.

In the late nineteenth century, "decent" women did not smoke (at least in public), upper- and middle-class

Newspaper editor Henry W. Grady.

men smoked cigars or pipes, and workingmen and the lower classes in the South were inclined to chew tobacco. Cigarettes were around. The soldiers in the Civil War had taken to them because they could carry papers and a pouch of tobacco but not cigars. After the war, however, the white cylinders were considered to be effete, a boy's smoke behind the barn. Duke would have to change that image, and he did.

Buying the patent to the cigarette-rolling machine, he encouraged adolescents to cultivate the habit by selling a pack of twenty for only a nickel and by including inside each pack a "trading card" that featured pictures and brief biographies of military heroes and popular athletes, mostly boxers and baseball players. No one better understood the wisdom in putting together a long-term market than "Buck" Duke. All the while he created his consumers, he improved machinery and bought out competitors. By 1889, his company accounted for half the cigarettes sold in the United States, and Duke had only begun.

In 1890, he set up a trust along the lines laid out by John D. Rockefeller. Through it he gained control of his major competitors, R. J. Reynolds and P. J. Lorillard, and built an almost perfect monopoly. Indeed, through loose arrangements with British cigarette manufacturers, Duke had a major say in the tobacco-processing industry on two continents. Only federal an-silver or gold. The value of this paper depended, of course, upon people's confidence in the ability of the bank in question to hand precious metal over the counter when presented with its own notes.

The Greenbacks

During the Civil War, finding itself with too little gold and silver to support the army, the Lincoln administration issued a new kind of paper money, some $433 million in bills called "greenbacks" because they were printed on the obverse (like our own money) in green ink. The greenbacks were not redeemable in gold or silver. Their value depended entirely upon the government's agreement to accept them in payment of most obligations, such as taxes.

Government acceptance of the greenbacks gave them value as a medium of exchange. However, no one considered them "as good as gold" (or silver), and their value fluctuated, sometimes wildly, depending on the success or failure of the Union Army or a twist in federal financial policy. At the end of the Civil War, it took $157 in greenbacks to buy $100 in coin.

Inflation or Deflation

Discounted as they were, the abundant greenbacks nevertheless circulated; the Union did, after all, survive and continue to accept them. Indeed, the greenbacks won many friends because, by increasing the amount of money in circulation, they inflated wages and prices, including prices at which farmers sold their crops. The Civil War was a prosperous time down on the farm. Looking back on it in bleaker days, many farmers associated the good times with the greenbacks. They argued that the federal government should continue to use them to regulate the amount of money in circulation in order to accommodate the needs of a dynamic people. The supply of gold and silver did not expand rapidly enough to keep up with the explosive economy of the United States.

Bankers and big businessmen thought otherwise. They dealt in large sums of money and feared having the value of their vast properties—and the money others owed to them—reduced in value by politicians seeking favor with voters. These monetary conservatives insisted that money had absolute, natural value, determined by the amount of gold in existence and, until the 1870s, by the amount of silver.

With their close ties to the executive branch of the government in the wake of the Civil War, the conservatives generally had their way. By February 1868, $45 million in greenbacks had been retired from circulation, simply burned when paid to the government

titrust action in 1911 forced him to disband his gigantic corporation. By that year, he controlled 150 factories, and, even at that, his reputation as the South's greatest home-grown business mogul was being challenged by the directors of the recently founded Coca-Cola Company of Atlanta.

Like the Yankee moguls whose methods he adopted, "Buck" Duke was a generous philanthropist. His most enduring monument is Duke University, which had been a small, local college before it received an endowment from Duke and changed its name; it is now an architecturally magnificent Gothic-style campus in Duke's hometown of Durham, North Carolina. Until the militant antismoking campaigns of the 1970s, Duke was one of the few universities in the United States where students and faculty could light up the "coffin nails" that had built the institution wherever and whenever they chose. That practice has been abandoned, but his statue, which stands in front of the university's cathedral-size chapel, portrays James Buchanan Duke gently tapping the ash from his cigar.

James Buchanan "Buck" Duke, the father of the modern cigarette industry and the philanthropist after whom Duke University is named.

in taxes. Money grew scarcer and therefore more valuable: deflated. Wages and prices, including the prices at which farmers sold their crops, declined.

The protest was so widespread that, in October 1868, Congress ordered the Treasury Department to stop retiring the greenbacks. But the inflationist victory was short-lived. In 1875, ascendant conservatives ordered that for every $100 issued by banks (money theoretically backed by gold), $80 in greenbacks be retired. In 1879, secretary of the Treasury John Sherman ordered that all payments to the government be made in specie, or coin, effectively destroying the greenbacks. Between 1865 and 1878, the amount of all kinds of money in circulation in the United States shrunk from $1.08 billion to $773 million. Whereas in 1865 there had been $31.18 in circulation for every American, in 1878 there was $16.25.

The Greenback Party

In an attempt to stem this deflation, many farmers, workingpeople, and some small businessmen joined together to form the Greenback Labor party, which was dedicated to the single issue of inflating the currency. Like most third parties in American history, the Greenbackers attracted few voters. In the presidential election of 1880, Civil War General James B. Weaver of Iowa won 308,578 votes. In 1884, Greenback candidate Benjamin F. Butler won just 175,370 votes, not much more than the Prohibitionist party candidate received. By 1884, people who wanted the currency inflated had turned to another form of money for their salvation—silver coin.

Silver to the Fore

Between 1837 and 1873, the price of silver was legally pegged to the price of gold at a ratio of 16:1. During the 1860s, however, American mines produced proportionately less silver than gold. Therefore, mine owners preferred to sell not to the United States Mint, which paid the official price, but to private or foreign buyers, who were willing to pay more, an ounce of gold for just 14 ounces of silver or less.

In 1873, confronted with the fact that little silver was being presented to the Mint, Congress enacted the Demonetization Act, ceasing the purchase of silver. The silver dollar was dropped from the list of coins the government minted. Silver became an ordinary commodity like wheat, hogs, lumber, or petticoats, its value (in gold) set by the laws of supply and demand. President Grant signed the bill without ado.

Already as the ink was drying, however, the relative supply of silver and gold was changing again. New silver strikes and new methods of mining it were resulting in a vast increase in production of the white metal. In 1861, only $2 million worth of silver had been mined in the United States compared to $43 million worth of gold. In 1873, the value of silver and gold mined was about equal, $36 million each. During the rest of the 1870s, silver production increased so rapidly that its price on the private market, the only market now open to miners, collapsed.

Politician friends of mining interests like the excitable Democrat Richard "Silver Dick" Bland of Missouri and Senator Henry W. Teller of Colorado began to denounce the Demonetization Act as "The Crime of '73." They accused the government of conspiring with bankers to punish silver miners for their very success. There was no "Crime of '73"; no one could have anticipated the explosive growth of silver production when the Demonetization Act was passed but the most sanguine western prospector.

Nevertheless, when silver production did rise, monetary conservatives were undoubtedly relieved that the government was no longer buying and minting it, thus inflating the currency and reducing the value of their property. The "Gold Bugs," as Bland and Teller called them, began to look upon abundant silver as a threat to the value of their money as serious as the greenbacks.

By themselves, mine owners and miners would have been powerless to force the government to resume the purchase and minting of silver. Even after the admission of mineral-rich Colorado in 1876, mining interests were significant in only a handful of states. However, inflationist congressmen from agricultural states—mostly southern and western Democrats, but also including Republicans—seized on silver coinage as a way to get more money in circulation. In the depression year of 1878, they forced the conservatives to agree to a compromise. The Bland-Allison Bill of that year required the secretary of the Treasury to purchase between $2 and $4 million of silver each month for minting into money. The silver dollar was back.

The Sherman Silver Purchase Act

The silver dollar was back, but the principle of bimetalism (both gold and silver as money, the value of one pegged to the other) was not. In both the Republican and Democratic administrations of the 1880s, the Treasury was safely in the hands of conservatives dedicated to gold as the sole standard of value. The government almost invariably bought the minimum $2 million in silver required by law. In effect, the silver

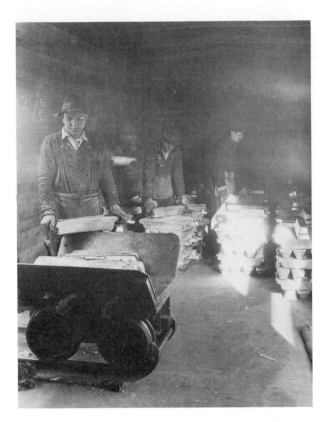

Loading silver bullion into a freight car in Leadville, Colorado, a silver boomtown until the Sherman Act was repealed.

dollars that were minted were tokens akin to paper money, themselves backed by gold.

Meanwhile, the national production of silver continued to grow and the market price of the metal plummeted. By 1890, it took nearly 20 ounces of silver to buy an ounce of gold. In the minds of inflationists and silver producers, the old lost ratio of 16:1 took on a mythic, sacred significance.

In 1889 and 1890, the balance of power tipped to the side of the inflationists. Two states in which silver was an important commodity (Montana and Idaho) and four in which inflationist farmers were a majority (the two Dakotas, Washington, and Wyoming) entered the Union, bringing twelve new silver senators to Washington.

The result was the Sherman Silver Purchase Act of 1890. Like the Bland-Allison Act, it was a compromise. The Sherman law required the secretary of the Treasury to purchase 4.5 million ounces of silver each month, in effect the entire monthly production of the nation's silver mines at that time. However, the government bought silver at the market price, which con-

tinued to decline, from a ratio of 20:1 in 1890 to 26.5:1 in 1893. Consequently, the Sherman Act failed to relieve discontent in the mining regions and led to violent strikes as mine owners attempted to cut costs by forcing down wages.

Farmers, who favored silver coinage as a means of inflating the currency and raising prices, were also disappointed. Although he signed the Sherman Act, President Benjamin Harrison favored the gold standard. He treated siver coins as if they were tokens— paper money—instructing the secretary of the Treasury to pay all the government's bills in gold. To distressed farmers already inclined to look for sinister forces at work in the night, the presidency itself seemed in the employ of the money power.

THE POPULISTS

By 1890, the Alliance movement was at flood tide. The Southern Alliance had 1.5 million members, the Colored Farmers Alliance a million, other groups combined about the same. Feeling their strength, the leaders of the various regional organizations gathered in Ocala, Florida, in December to draw up a list of grievances and consider the possibility of organizing a third party.

Hesitation

By December 1890, Kansas farmers had already organized a statewide People's Party, calling themselves Populists after the Latin word for people, *populus*, and winning control of the state legislature. At Ocala, however, old Republican and Democratic loyalties were too strong, and racial anxieties too gnawing for the delegates to take the same leap.

Southern white farmers hesitated because they had made inroads in the Democratic party and feared that if they split the white vote in the South by forming a new party, blacks would regain the political equality they had held through the Republican party during Reconstruction. Indeed, the leaders of the Colored Farmers Alliance were reluctant to give up their allegiance to the Republican party, which had, however uncertainly, defended black civil rights.

But events were already underway to undermine old loyalties. In July 1890, the same month the Silver Purchase Act was passed, the Republican majority in the United States Senate failed to enact the Force Bill, a law designed to protect the right of southern blacks to vote. In effect, the Republicans abandoned

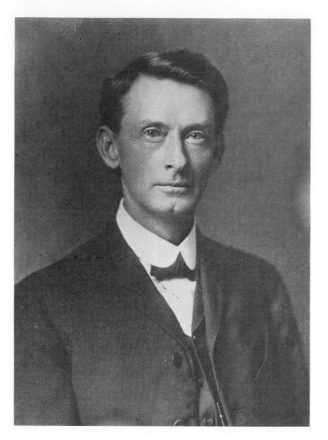

Thomas E. Watson, a Populist from Georgia, advocated the principle that social class was more important than race. He had a knack for inflammatory journalism and oratory.

southern blacks to their own fate. Some black southerners called for a new party. Some southern whites like Tom Watson of Georgia, a diminutive lawyer who had been cheated out of elective office by the Democratic machine, called for an alliance between black and white farmers. In a magazine article published in 1892, he told white and black farmers,

You are kept apart that you may be separately fleeced of your earnings. You are made to hate each other because upon that hatred is rested the keystone of the arch of financial despotism which enslaves you both. You are deceived and blinded that you may not see how this race antagonism perpetuates a monetary system which beggars both.

The Omaha Convention

In February 1892, delegates from the various Alliances and Wheels, and more than a few self-appointed spokesmen for the farmers and silver miners, met in Omaha, Nebraska, to form a new party. They gladly adopted the name "Populist" from the Kansas party that had already sent several congressmen and Senator William Peffer to Washington.

To symbolize the fact that farmers of North and South had bridged the sectional chasm that had made them enemies, the Populists nominated former Union General and Greenbacker James B. Weaver for president, and former Confederate General James G. Field for vice president. No one expected them to win, and they did not. Grover Cleveland, the Democratic candidate, won a comfortable victory in the electoral college despite carrying only 46 percent of the popular vote. And Weaver did well enough, winning more than a million votes and carrying Kansas. At Omaha, the Populists were planning for November 1896, not 1892, when they expected to restore democracy and justice to a corrupted country.

Indeed, what most struck observers about the Omaha convention was the evangelical fervor with which the Populists addressed public questions, as if they were embarked not on a political campaign, but on a crusade against satanic evil itself. "We meet on the verge of a nation brought to the verge of moral, political, and material ruin," Ignatius Donnelley of Minnesota wrote in the preamble to the party platform, "Corruption dominates the ballot box, the legislatures, the Congress, and touches even the ermine of the bench." William Peffer, looking like a biblical prophet with his waist-length beard, railed like one about the iniquities of the land.

"Conspiracy" was a word on everyone's lips, the conspiracy of the great railroads to defraud the shipper, the conspiracy of politicians to destroy democracy, the conspiracy of the money power, even the conspiracy of Jews.

"The people are at bay," Mother Lease said, "let the bloodhounds of money beware." When the platform was finally approved, according to one not too sympathetic reporter, "cheers and yells . . . rose like a tornado . . . and raged without cessation for thirty-four minutes, during which time women shrieked and wept, men embraced and kissed their neighbors, locked arms, marched back and forth, and leaped upon tables and chairs in the ecstasy of their delirium."

A Far-Reaching Program

The atmosphere was, no doubt, disarming. And yet, the platform the Populists wrote was far from lunatic. On the contrary, it was a comprehensive program for reform that, if enacted intact, would have transformed American development, and not necessarily for the worse.

Indeed, the Populists' political reforms were in large part, although not by them, to become the law of the land. They called for the election of United States senators by popular vote, rather than by state legislatures, a reform instituted in the Seventeenth Amendment to the Constitution in 1913. They demanded the universal use of the Australian, or secret ballot, to prevent landlords and employers from intimidating their tenants and workers into voting as the bosses chose. By the early twentieth century, public ballots had been abolished everywhere but in New England town meetings.

The Populists introduced the concepts of the initiative, recall, and referendum to American government. The initiative allows voters, through petition, to put measures on the ballot independent of action by legislatures and thus, in theory, free of manipulation by professional lobbyists and their accomplices. The recall allows voters, also through petition, to force a public official to stand for election before his or her term is up. The Populists hoped that the recall would discourage politicians from backing down on campaign pledges. The referendum allows voters to vote directly on laws rather than indirectly through their representatives; it is the means by which initiative measures and recall petitions are decided. All three are accepted procedure in many states today.

The most controversial Populist demand was for the abolition of national banks and for government ownership of railroads and the telegraph. Enemies pointed to this plank as evidence that the Populists were socialists. They were not; virtually all of them were

---

THE POLLOCK CASE

In the Wilson-Gorman Tariff of 1894, provision was made for an income tax of 2 percent on all incomes of $4,000 or more, a pretty modest tax by today's standards. It was widely condemned by men of means, and in the case of *Pollock v. Farmers' Loan and Trust Co.* (1895), the Supreme Court ruled that because the tax was a direct tax that did not fall on all equally, it was unconstitutional. Only after the Sixteenth Amendment was adopted in 1913 was it constitutional to tax the wealthy at a higher rate than the poor.

---

landowners or tenants who aspired above all to own land. However, they believed that "natural monopolies"—huge enterprises that could be run efficiently only under a single management—should not be in private hands. To the Populist mind, decisions that affected the interests of all should be made democratically, not by combinations of private parties interested only in their own enrichment.

The Populists also called for a postal savings system, so that ordinary people might avoid depositing their money in privately owned banks, and for a graduated income tax. In 1892, the federal income tax was 2 percent for all; the Populists wanted the wealthy to pay a higher percentage of their income than the modest farmer or wageworker paid.

Finally—as only one plank of many—the Populists addressed the silver question. They called for an increase in the money in circulation of $50 per capita. This inflation was to be accomplished through the free and unlimited coinage of silver, its value pegged to that of gold. In the summer of 1892, this was perhaps the mildest of the Populist demands. It represented only an adjustment of the Sherman Act then in effect. In just over a year, however, "Free Silver" was to become the Populists' obsession, nearly destroying their ardor for the rest of the Omaha platform.

The Panic of 1893

In February 1893, ten days before Grover Cleveland took the oath of office, the Reading Railroad, a major eastern trunk line, announced it was bankrupt. For two months the stock market was jittery, and then it collapsed. Hundreds of banks and thousands of businesses joined the Reading in receivership. By November, the country was sunk in a depression greater than that of the 1870s.

Needing money or fearing for the safety of their government bonds, both American and British financiers rushed to redeem them. Cleveland, who was

---

POPULIST ANTI-SEMITISM?

The hatred of farmers for bankers sometimes took the form of anti-Semitism, hatred of Jewish bankers. One book that blamed Jews particularly for the ruination of the American farmer was Ignatius P. Donnelly's novel *Caesar's Column.* One character's explanation of why Jewish bankers were exploiting farmers is curious: past anti-Semitism with a Darwinian twist:

Christianity fell upon the Jews, originally a race of agriculturists and shepherds, and forced them, for many centuries, through the most terrible ordeal of persecution the history of mankind bears record of. Only the strong of body, the cunning of brain, the long-headed, the persistent, the men with capacity to live where the dog would starve, survived the awful trial. Like breeds like; and now the Christian world is paying, in tears and blood, for the sufferings inflicted by their bigoted and ignorant ancestors upon a noble race. When the time came for liberty and fair play the Jew was master in the contest with the Gentile. . . . They were as merciless to the Christians as the Christians had been to them.

Coxey and his secretary leading his army to Washington, D.C.

more firmly committed to the gold standard than Harrison, was true to his word. He instructed the secretary of the Treasury to redeem all demands in gold alone. By fall, the government's gold reserve—the actual metal in its vaults—sunk to below $100 million, the level regarded by conservatives as the absolute minimum for maintaining the government's credit.

A Most Unpopular Man

Cleveland blamed the crisis and the panic that led up to it on the Sherman Act. "To put beyond all doubt or mistake" the commitment of the United States to the gold standard, the president called for its repeal and a frightened Congress obliged him. That lost him the support of Democrats from the mining states. Then the news leaked that, at the height of the crisis, Cleveland had called on J. P. Morgan for help in increasing the government's gold reserve. Throughout the South and Midwest, more Democrats denounced him.

In 1894, Cleveland's Attorney General, a former railroad attorney, Richard B. Olney, crushed a strike of railway workers led by a charismatic former brakeman, Eugene V. Debs, turning industrial workers against him. He blundered even in his treatment of Jacob Coxey, an Ohio businessman who led a march of unemployed men to Washington to ask for relief. Coxey was arrested for walking on the grass.

Few presidents have been so unpopular as was Grover Cleveland in his second term. And with each blow to his prestige, the Populists celebrated. In their eyes, Cleveland's Democrats and the Republicans were indistinguishable. Both parties were the puppets of the money power. The people did indeed seem to be at bay. The Populists expected to come to power in 1896. The word "revolution" was being voiced in many gatherings of "the bone and sinew of the republic."

For Further Reading

For background and context, see Vincent P. DeSantis, *The Shaping of Modern America, 1877–1916* (1973), and Robert H. Wiebe, *The Search for Order, 1880–1920* (1967). The genuinely classic studies of the subject, with contrasting visions, are Gilbert C. Fite, *The Farmer's Frontier, 1865–1900* (1966), and Fred A. Shannon, *The Farmers' Last Frontier: Agriculture 1860–1897* (1945). Also see Allan C. Bogue, *From Prairie to Corn Belt* (1963); E. Dick, *The Sod-House Frontier* (1937); and Walter P. Webb, *The Great Plains* (1931).

On farmers' movements, see Solon J. Buck, *The Granger Movement* (1913); R. F. Durden, *The Climax of Populism* (1965); Lawrence Goodwyn, *Democratic Promise: The Populist Movement in America* (1976); John D. Hicks, *The Populist Revolt* (1931); the appropriate chapters of Richard Hofstadter, *Age of Reform* (1955); J. Morgan Kousser, *The Shaping of Southern Politics: Suffrage Restriction and the Establishment of the One-Party South, 1880–1910* (1974); Walter T. K. Nugent, *Money and American Society, 1865–1880* (1968) and *The Tolerant Populists: Kansas Populism and Nativism* (1963); Norman Pollock, *The Populist Response to Industrial America* (1966); Theodore Saloutos, *Farmer Movements in the South, 1865–1933* (1960); Irwin Unger, *The Greenback Era: A Social and Political History of American Finance, 1865–1879* (1964); Allen Weinstein, *Prelude to Populism: Origins of the Silver Issue, 1867–1878* (1970); and C. Vann Woodward, *The Strange Career of Jim Crow* (1974).

P. E. Coletta, *William Jennings Bryan: Political Evangelist, 1860–1908* (1964) and Louis W. Koenig, *Bryan: A Political Biography of William Jennings Bryan* (1971) present somewhat different views of the man who came to personify agrarian aspirations. The model biography of the leading southern Populist is C. Vann Woodward, *Tom Watson: Agrarian Rebel* (1938).

Only a few presidential elections have been held amidst such anxiety and tension as swirled about the election of 1896. Even as the year began, politicians were describing the contest as more critical than any since 1860, when the survival of the Union itself hung in the balance. This time the fissure in American society was social rather than sectional, country arrayed against city, social class arrayed against social class. The terrible depression, the "revolt of the hayseeds," the violent strikes, the mass demonstrations, and the passions the silver issue had engendered lent a sense of foreboding to every political discussion.

34

THE DAYS OF McKINLEY

The United States Becomes a World Power, 1896–1903

Taking It Easy During a Lull, a photo of American troops in the Philippines taken around 1899 by Perley Freemont Rockett.

WATERSHED

The election of 1896 was a watershed of American history. When it was over, the political era that had begun with the end of Reconstruction would be dead, and a new one underway. No one knew what the new era would be like when the campaign began. That depended upon which party and which candidate won the electoral college in November. Thus the anxiety.

Mark Hanna and Bill McKinley

Meeting in St. Louis in June, the Republican convention was placid on the surface. Most Republican agrarians had long since bade farewell to the Grand Old Party and signed on with the Populists. A small free-silver contingent from the mining states, led by Senator Teller of Colorado, caused a minor ruckus trying to win concessions for their cause. But the convention was dominated by "Gold Bugs." When they rebuked Teller, rather gently, he and his followers walked out. The convention was left to people of like mind and, with little folderol, they chose as their presidential candidate a man who was a model of conservatism, prudence, respectability, and sobriety, William McKinley of Ohio. Or, rather, as the Populists and Democrats were soon to claim, they sat back and allowed a beefy Cleveland industrialist, Marcus Alonzo Hanna, to choose their candidate for them.

Bald, scowling Mark Hanna was nearly 60 years of age in 1896. He had made a fortune in coal and iron, was close to the Rockefellers, and was well known in industrial circles as a feisty spokesman for moderation and flexibility in dealing with employees and labor unions. Hanna railed against exploitative capitalists and labor radicals alike.

Only in the 1890s, after the descent of the depression, did Hanna take an interest in national politics. He had ambitions of his own, but also the realism to know that he could not move in one jump from board room to Executive Mansion. Instead, he devoted his energies to promoting the candidacy of his fellow Ohioan, former representative and governor William McKinley of Canton.

McKinley, the Republican party's chief expert on the tariff, was himself ambitious. Theodore Roosevelt later said that McKinley looked into every introduction and conversation for the advantage it might mean to him. And yet, without Hanna clearing the way and pushing him on, it is unlikely that McKinley would

Industrialist Marcus Alonzo Hanna was the kind of man who walked into an office and got what he wanted.

have won the Republican nomination in 1896. The issue that was tearing the country apart—gold standard versus free silver—simply did not interest him very much.

Moreover, while his studiousness and dignity commanded respect, McKinley lacked the presence and personality that made people stand up and applaud. William Allen White said that "he was destined for a statue in the park and he was practicing the pose for it." McKinley was easy to overlook and underestimate. Mark Hanna was the wheeler-dealer who marched into an office, cigar blazing, and planted a hefty haunch on the desk of the person he wanted to see. Republicans and Democrats alike assumed that McKinley was his puppet.

The Frightening Boy Bryan

The partnership of energy and solemnity proved indispensable to the Republicans in 1896 because the Democratic party candidate, nominated at a frenzied convention in July, was a tornado of energy with a singular lack of dignity. William Jennings Bryan, scarcely beyond the 35 years of age the Constitution requires a president to be, was a two-term congressman from Nebraska, a newspaperman, and regionally famous as a platform orator. His one and only subject for four years had been the free coinage of silver, and Bryan had polished a single speech, the "Cross of Gold," to a mathematical perfection in phrasing, timing, and theatrical gesture. Deeply religious himself, Bryan enlisted God in the cause of silver coinage. He identified the gold standard with the crucifiers of Christ, silver with democracy and Christianity.

If the intensity with which he spoke was set aside, Bryan was a rather conservative man. He did not approve of much of what the Populists held dear except for free silver. But his language and apparently irresponsible youth were enough to frighten Republicans. They called him "Boy Bryan" and "the boy orator of the Platte," scornfully but also with trepidation. The Democrats, committed to the cause of silver when the Chicago convention was planned, gladly scheduled him and his Cross of Gold to close out the debate on the currency question.

Later it would be said that when Bryan spoke he transformed himself from an obscure delegate into a presidential candidate by acclamation. In fact, he and

William Jennings Bryan carries a cross of gold in this cartoon by Grant Hamilton, who viewed Bryan as a despoiler of the Bible.

his supporters had paved the way for his nomination as carefully as Mark Hanna had worked for McKinley. And yet, his speech and the Democratic party's ringing endorsement of free silver were so electrifying that the western farmers began to celebrate a November victory in July. For, late in the month, the Populists nominated Bryan too.

The Populists Join the Democrats

Meeting in St. Louis, the Populists were presented with a difficult decision. If they maintained their party's independence by nominating a candidate of their own, they would split the free silver vote and put Bill McKinley in the White House. If they nominated Bryan—and just about everyone but Mark Hanna agreed on this in July—they would easily elect a man whose evangelical style suited them and whose position on free silver was perfect.

However, Bryan was pointedly clear in his opposition to the comprehensive Populist program for reform. For the sake of a free silver president, the Populists would throw away their grand plans for America and, fused to the older, larger Democratic party, their very identity.

Urban Populists like Henry Demarest Lloyd urged the party to think in long-range terms. He told the Populists to maintain their independence and the integrity of their program, accept defeat in 1896, and

William Jennings Bryan was famous for his impassioned oratory.

work toward 1900. Some southern Populists like Tom Watson of Georgia had another reason for opposing fusion. In the South, the conservative enemy was not Republican but Democratic. To fuse with the Democrats in the South meant suicide, and breaking the connections that Watson had been trying to forge between white and black farmers. Southern blacks would not vote for the Democratic party, the party of white supremacy.

But midwestern Populists like Jerry Simpson wanted fusion. "I care not for party names," he said, "It is substance we are after, and we have it in William J. Bryan." The Populists from the mining states agreed; free silver had always been the heart of their rebellion. The party nominated Bryan and, to seal the partnership, nominated Tom Watson for vice president, asking the Democrats to accept him as their candidate too. Bryan ignored them. He accepted Populist support but made no concessions to them, not even the symbolic one of taking a Populist for vice president.

Waves against a Rock

Rallying voters was Bryan's forte. Handsome, tireless, and completely at home among ordinary, hardworking farm people—whether exhorting them or gobbling up potato salad and chowchow after a speech—Bryan revolutionized presidential campaigning in the United States.

With a few exceptions, presidential nominees had been quiet, as though it were an insult to the dignity

Candidate William McKinley between speeches on his front porch in Canton, Ohio.

THE CROSS OF GOLD

The following lines are the first and last from William Jennings Bryan's electrifying speech at the 1896 Democratic convention:

I would be presumptuous, indeed, to present myself against the distinguished gentlemen to whom you have listened if this were a mere measuring of abilities; but this is not a contest between persons. The humblest citizen in all the land, when clad in the armor of a righteous cause, is stronger than all the hosts of error. I come to speak to you in defense of a cause as holy as the cause of liberty—the cause of humanity. . . .

If they dare to come out in the open field and defend the gold standard as a good thing, we will fight them to the uttermost. Having behind us the producing masses of this nation and the world, supported by the commercial interests, the laboring interests, and the toilers everywhere, we will answer their demand for a gold standard by saying to them: you shall not press down upon the brow of labor this crown of thorns, you shall not crucify mankind upon a cross of gold.

---

of the office to woo votes like a candidate for town councilman in an Appalachian hollow. Not Bryan. His speaking tour took him more than 13,000 miles by train. He delivered 600 speeches in 29 states in only 14 weeks, more than 6 speeches a day. The roaring enthusiasm of the crowds that greeted him, at least in the West and South, confirmed him in his zeal and threw bankers and industrialists into a panic.

Panic was what Mark Hanna wanted to see. He pressured wealthy Republicans (and more than a few conservative Democrats) into making large contributions to McKinley's campaign. By the time of the election, Hanna had spent more on posters, buttons, rallies, picnics, advertisements, and a corps of speakers who dogged Bryan's steps than had been spent by both parties in every election since the Civil War. (The Republicans printed five pamphlets for every American voter.) Hanna was so successful a fund-raiser that, before election day, he began to return surplus contributions.

Knowing that the phlegmatic McKinley could not rival Bryan on the stump, Hanna kept the candidate at his modest home in Canton, Ohio, instructing Republican speakers to compare McKinley's self-respect with Bryan's huckstering. In fact, McKinley's campaign was as frantic as Bryan's and nearly as tiring. Delegations of party faithfuls came in a steady stream to Canton, where they marched through the town behind a brass band and gathered on McKinley's front lawn. McKinley delivered a short speech from the porch, answered a few prearranged questions, and invited "all his friends" to join him for lemonade or beer, depending on the delegation's attitude toward alcohol (which had been discreetly ascertained by party workers when the visitors arrived at the railroad depot). About 750,000 friends visited McKinley's home that summer and fall, trampling his lawn "as if a herd of buffalo had passed through."

Momentous Results

Bryan won more votes, 6.5 million, than any candidate in any previous election. But McKinley won 7 million and, in the electoral college, gathered 271 votes to Bryan's 176. It was the first time in a quarter of the century that any presidential candidate had won an absolute majority. What happened? As late as September, professional politicians believed that Bryan was well ahead.

First, although Bryan's supporters were noisy, his appeal was fatally limited to Democrats from the Solid South, hard-pressed staple farmers of the West, and to a few numerically insignificant groups like western metal miners. McKinley swept the Northeast, includ-ing the swing states, and also the largely agricultural states of North Dakota, Minnesota, Wisconsin, Iowa, Michigan, and Illinois. Many farmers whose conditions were not desperate accepted the Republican contention that Boy Bryan was a dangerous radical, never a desirable label in American politics.

Nor did Bryan win much support among factory workers and city people generally. He hardly tried. Imbued with rural prejudices against big cities and the "foreigners" who lived there, he made only one speaking tour in vital New York state and was quoted as having called New York City "the enemy's country," as though it were inhabited solely by bankers and grain speculators. Fourteen of the fifteen biggest cities were controlled by Republican machines and they delivered the vote to William McKinley.

Some industrialists tried to intimidate their employees into voting for the Republican candidate. The Baldwin Piano Works posted notices on the eve of election day to the effect that if Bryan won, the plant would close for good the day following. But Bryan's weakness in the industrial districts was not due to such tactics. His single-issue free-silver campaign offered little to factory workers. They found more convincing the Republican claim that a high-tariff policy protected their jobs.

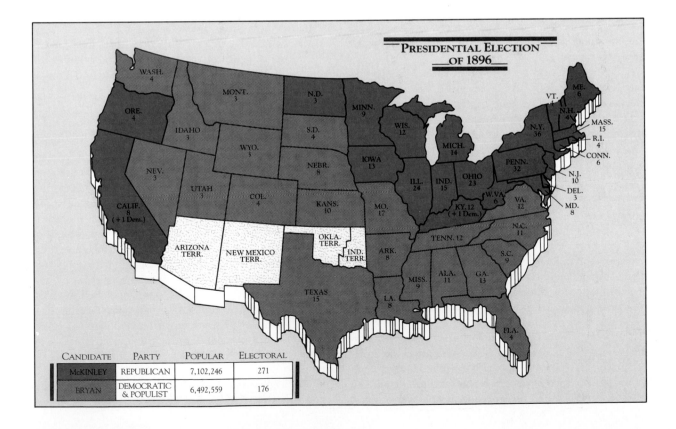

PRESIDENTIAL ELECTION OF 1896

CANDIDATE	PARTY	POPULAR	ELECTORAL
McKINLEY	REPUBLICAN	7,102,246	271
BRYAN	DEMOCRATIC & POPULIST	6,492,559	176

Finally, Mark Hanna shrewdly judged the instincts of a newly important element in American politics, the growing middle class of small businessmen, professional people, salaried town dwellers, and highly skilled, well-paid workingmen. Preoccupied with their respectability and considering themselves to be the new bone and sinew of the American republic, they were frightened by Bryan and the ragged, restive farmers whom he represented. These people committed themselves to the Republican party as "the party of decency." For 40 years after 1896, they made the Republican party the majority party.

The End of Populism

As Watson and Lloyd had feared, fusion with the Democrats meant extinction for the Populists. Having sacrificed their comprehensive reform program for the chance of winning free silver with Bryan, they had nothing left when the votes were counted against him. In the South, Populists who had worked to build a party based on interracial cooperation turned against the blacks (most of whom voted Republican in 1896) to become prominent exponents of white supremacy. In the West, the party withered away, in part because of the electoral rebuke, and in part because, slowly under McKinley, the wholesale prices of farm products began to rise.

The agricultural depression lifted for a number of reasons. Newly discovered gold deposits in Canada and Alaska inflated the currency somewhat and helped raise prices. Several poor growing seasons in Europe created an increased demand for American farm products. Finally, farmers, like most of the American people, were distracted in 1898 by the McKinley administration's decision to win the United States a place among the empires of the world. Tom Watson was to say, "The blare of the bugle drowned the voice of the reformer."

AMERICAN IMPERIALISM

McKinley hoped to have a quiet presidency, watching over the retrenchment of the nation after the years of depression and agitation. His confidence in the vitality and resilience of American business convinced him that prosperity was just around the corner. All he had to do was wait patiently.

McKinley got his prosperity. Even before he was inaugurated in March 1897, the economic indicators began to show improvement. Peace and quiet were more elusive. Little as the role suited him, McKinley led the American people into a series of overseas adventures that transformed a nation that had been born in an anticolonial revolution into an empire with colonies in both hemispheres.

The Myth of Isolationism

Not that the United States had been isolated from world affairs before McKinley became president. Far from it. The American government maintained busy missions in all important capitals, had fought a war with Mexico in the interests of expansion, and several times came close to war in defense of American prestige. In 1889, only a typhoon that had sunk German and American warships near Samoa prevented a full-scale naval encounter with a major European power.

Trade made the United States an active participant in world affairs. American ships and sailors were a common sight in the world's most exotic ports. As early as 1844, the United States had signed a trade treaty with the Chinese Empire, as far off and foreign a place as Americans could imagine. In 1854, a naval squadron under Commodore Matthew Perry had anchored off Yokohama, Japan, and had threatened to bombard the city unless the Japanese agreed to abandon their country's genuine isolationism and begin to purchase American goods.

By 1870, American exports totaled $320 million, mostly agricultural produce bound for Europe. By 1890, $857 million in goods was sold abroad, with American manufacturers competing with European industrialists in peddling steel, textiles, and other products in Pacific countries, Latin America, and Europe itself.

Anticolonialism

If Americans were not isolationists, neither were they imperialists. Neither the people nor most statesmen wanted anything to do with the scramble for colonies that engrossed Europe and newly powerful Japan in the late nineteenth century. To Americans, there was a difference between taking the West from a handful of Mexicans and Indians, and establishing suzerainty over distant and densely settled lands with long cultural traditions. Repeatedly, attempts to annex Cuba and the Dominican Republic were squelched in Congress. With the exceptions of Alaska and the tiny Pacific island of Midway, both acquired in 1867 and neither with much population, the United States possessed no territory that was not contiguous to the states.

Two deep convictions worked against the occasional proposals that the United States take such colonies.

A pro-expansion cartoon shows a sword-bearing Uncle Sam rolling up his sleeves for a fight.

First, the country had been founded in a war against an empire. Could the heirs of the first great anticolonial rebellion take over the lands of other peoples? Second, the vastness of the American continent provided a more than adequate outlet for American energies. There was plenty of work to be done at home. William McKinley shared these assumptions. In all sincerity, he said in his inaugural address that "we must avoid the temptation of territorial expansion."

The Nature of Imperialism

But times were changing. By 1897, the United States was the single most important industrial power in the world. Consciousness of this greatness stirred many people to believe that the United States should assume its rightful place among the great nations, and in the 1890s, the great nations were imperialist nations.

The European powers were partitioning Africa so that only two countries there maintained their independence, ancient Ethiopia and Liberia, a republic that had been founded by former American slaves. Indochina was a French colony. The Dutch flag flew over Indonesia. The Japanese were in the process of securing Korea and the Chinese island province of

Taiwan, which they renamed Formosa. Russia had designs on northern China. Germany and Italy, latecomers to the scramble, looked in Africa and Asia for areas to annex. India, the finest prize of all, save China, was British.

The initial impulse toward empire was economic. Colonies were a source of raw materials and a market for the products of the mother country. Colonialism also generated an emotional justification of its own. Colonies were a source of pride. British imperialists took pleasure in seeing "all that red on the map." (Mapmakers usually colored British possessions in red.) The Germans seized parts of Africa that had little economic value just for the sake of having colonies.

In England and later in the United States, this bumptious chauvinism was known as "jingoism," from a British song of 1877, "We do not want to fight, But by jingo, if we do. . . ." To the jingoes, being strong enough to overcome less-advanced peoples was reason enough to do so. Finally, imperialism fed on itself like a sport. Nations seized colonies simply to prevent competitors from doing so.

Some young American politicians such as Henry Cabot Lodge of Massachusetts and Theodore Roosevelt of New York itched to join the scramble. They worried publicly that, in their wealth and prosperity, Americans were becoming soft and flabby. The country needed war now and then in order to toughen up. Roosevelt, a bodybuilding enthusiast, often drew analogies between individuals and nations, between boxing matches and battles.

Anglo-Saxons

Lodge, Roosevelt, and other expansionists were influenced by a theory of race that had evolved in part out of Social Darwinism. Whereas Herbert Spencer had applied his doctrine of "survival of the fittest" to relationships within a society, disciples such as Harvard historian John Fiske and Congregationalist minister

---

AMERICAN EMPIRE

"The West Indies drift toward us, the Republic of Mexico hardly longer has an independent life, and the city of Mexico is an American town. With the completion of the Panama Canal all Central America will become part of our system. We have expanded into Asia, we have attracted the fragments of the Spanish dominions, and reaching out into China we have checked the advance of Russia and Germany."

Brooks Adams,
The New Empire (1902)

Josiah Strong applied it to relationships among different races and cultures. In separate publications of 1885, Fiske and Strong wrote that the Anglo-Saxons (British and Americans) were obviously more fit to govern than were other peoples. According to Strong's *Our Country*, the Anglo-Saxons were "divinely commissioned" to spread their institutions. It was not a betrayal of American ideals to take over other lands. There was a racial and religious duty to do so.

Strong believed that inferior races eventually would die out. An influential political scientist at Columbia University, John W. Burgess, stated flatly in 1890 that the right of self-determination did not apply to dark-skinned peoples. He wrote that "there is no human right to the status of barbarism."

Alfred Thayer Mahan

Also in 1890, the expansionists found a highly calculating spokesman in naval captain Alfred Thayer Mahan. In *The Influence of Sea Power Upon History*, a bestseller in both Europe and America, Mahan argued that the great nations were always sea-faring nations possessing powerful navies. He chided Americans for having allowed their own fleet to fall into decay. (In 1891, jingoes who wanted war with Chile had to quiet down when they were informed the Chilean navy would humiliate the American fleet.) Mahan urged a massive program of ship construction, and Congress responded with large appropriations.

A modern steam-powered navy needed coaling stations at scattered points throughout the world. That in itself required taking colonies, even if they were only dots on the globe like Midway, or building bases in ostensibly independent countries like Hawaii, where in 1887, the United States cleared a harbor at the mouth of the Pearl River on the island of Oahu.

Fears for an America without a Frontier

Another theory of history that fired up the expansionist movement was based on the announcement of the Director of the Census in 1890 that the frontier no longer existed. In 1889, Congress opened Oklahoma to white settlement; the last large territory that had been reserved for the sole use of Indians was occupied by whites literally overnight.

At the 1893 meeting of the American Historical Association, a young historian named Frederick Jackson Turner propounded a theory that the frontier had been the key to the vitality of American democracy, social stability, and prosperity. Turner was interested in the past, but the implication of his theory for the future was unmistakable. With the frontier gone, was the United States doomed to stagnation and social

upheaval? To some who found Turner convincing, the only solution was to establish new frontiers abroad. Throughout the 1890s, American financiers pumped millions of dollars into China and Latin America because they felt that investment opportunities within the United States were shrinking.

By 1898, America's attitude toward the world was delicately balanced. Pulling in one direction was the tradition of anticolonialism. Tugging the other way were jingoism, Anglo-Saxonism, and apprehensions for the future. All it took to decide the direction of the leap was a sudden shove. That was provided by a Cuban war for independence that began in 1895.

THE SPANISH-AMERICAN WAR

On a map, Cuba looks like an appendage of Florida, a geographical curiosity that frequently excited the interest of American expansionists. Cuba was also a historical curiosity because, along with Puerto Rico, it alone had remained under Spanish control after the Latin American wars of independence. Rebellion was chronic in Cuba, but weak as Spain was, the archaic monarchy was able to hold fast to its last American jewel.

The uprising of 1895 was more serious. Smuggling in arms and munitions provided by Cuban exiles in the United States, the rebels won the support of a large number of ordinary Cubans, perhaps the majority. Until the 1890s, the island had been rather prosperous, exporting sugar to the United States, but the Wilson-Gorman Tariff of 1894 practically shut out Cuba's sole export and caused an economic crisis.

It was a classic guerrilla war. The Spanish army and navy controlled the cities of Havana and Santiago and most large towns. By day, Spanish soldiers moved with little trouble amongst a seemingly peaceful peasantry. By night, however, docile field workers turned into fierce rebels and sorely punished the Spanish troops. As in most guerrilla wars, fighting was bitter and cruel. Both sides were guilty of atrocities.

Americans were generally sympathetic to the Cubans. Their interest in the conflict was excited into near hysteria when two competing newspaper chains decided that the rebellion could be used as ammunition in their circulation war.

The Yellow Press

William Randolph Hearst's New York *Journal* and Joseph Pulitzer's New York *World* were known as the "yellow press" because they relied on gimmicks to appeal to readers. The nickname came from one of those gimmicks: "The Yellow Kid," the first comic strip to appear in a newspaper. The Hearst and Pulitzer chains could squeeze the most lurid details out of celebrated murder and sex cases, and they pioneered the "invented" news story. In 1889, Pulitzer's *World* sent Elizabeth S. "Nellie" Bly around the world in an attempt to break the record of the fictional hero of Jules Verne's novel, *Around the World in Eighty Days*. (She did it, completing the trip in 72 days, six hours, and eleven minutes.)

It was easy to move from this kind of promotionalism to exploiting Spanish atrocities. The yellow press dubbed the Spanish military commander in Cuba, Valeriano Weyler, "The Butcher" for his repressive policies, which included the establishment of concentration camps. Warring against a whole population, Weyler tried to stifle the uprising by herding whole villages into camps; everyone who was found outside the camps could be defined as enemies to be shot on sight. This strategy was inevitably brutal, and Cubans died in the camps by the thousands from malnutrition, disease, and abuse.

Real atrocities were not enough for Hearst and Pulitzer. They transformed innocuous incidents into horror stories and invented others. When Hearst artist Frederic Remington wired from Havana that everything was peaceful and he wanted to come home, Hearst ordered him to stay: "You furnish the pictures. I'll furnish the war." One sensational drawing showed Spanish officials leering at a naked American woman. In fact, the woman had been searched quite properly in private by female officers.

McKinley's Dark Hour

McKinley tried to calm tempers. The business community had substantial investments in Cuba, about $50 million in railroads, mines, and sugar cane plantations, and they feared the revolutionaries more than the Spanish. McKinley and his advisers wanted Spain to abandon its harsh policies and placate both Cubans and bellicose Americans by liberalizing government on the island.

The Spanish responded to his pressure. In 1898, a new government in Madrid withdrew Weyler and proposed autonomy for Cuba within the Spanish Empire. McKinley's administration was satisfied. But the war came anyway, largely because of two unforeseeable events.

On February 9, Hearst's New York *Journal* published a letter that had been written by the Spanish ambassador in Washington, Enrique Dupuy de Lome. In it, Dupuy told a friend that McKinley was "weak, a bidder

The February 17, 1898, edition of William Randolph Hearst's New York Journal *reported the destruction of the U.S.S.* Maine *and suggested it was sunk by Spaniards.*

for the admiration of the crowd." It was by no means an absurd assessment of the president, but it was insulting. McKinley himself was riled, and war fever flared higher.

Six days later, on February 15, 1898, the battleship U.S.S. *Maine* exploded in Havana harbor with a loss of 260 sailors. To this day, the cause of the disaster is unknown. The explosion may have been caused by a coal fire that spread to the magazine. A bomb may have been planted by Cuban rebels in an attempt to provoke the United States into declaring war on their behalf. Or it may have been the work of Spanish diehards who opposed the new liberal policy in Cuba. So charged was the atmosphere that some people suggested that William Randolph Hearst had planted the bomb for the sake of a headline!

In any case, with the yellow press raging, many Americans accepted the least credible explanation: the Spanish government, which was trying to avoid war at all costs, had destroyed the Maine.

McKinley vacillated for a month and a half. He flooded Spain with demands for a change of policy. As late as March 26, Mark Hanna urged him to keep the peace, and on April 9 the Spanish government gave in to every demand McKinley had made on them. In

REMEMBERING THE MAINE: SOLDIERS IN THE SPANISH-AMERICAN WAR

Secretary of State John Hay called it "a splendid little war." Undersecretary of the Navy Theodore Roosevelt resigned his post in order to fight in it. William Allen White remembered the glad excitement with which the declaration of war had been received in the Midwest: "Everywhere over this good, fair land, flags were flying, . . . crowds gathered to hurrah for the soldiers and to throw hats into the air." The celebrants' favorite cry was, "Remember the *Maine*; to hell with Spain." Americans regarded the occasion as an opportunity to prove the arrival of the United States as a world power and, at home, as a chance to seal the reunion of North and South by having northern and southern boys join together to fight Spain. While McKinley would not allow political rival William Jennings Bryan to go abroad and make a military reputation, he was delighted to appoint old Confederate officers like Fitzhugh Lee and General Joseph Wheeler to active command.

But, as historian Frank Freidel points out, for the soldiers in the ranks "It was as grim, dirty, and bloody as any war in history." He adds: "Only the incredible ineptitude of the Spaniards and the phenomenal luck of the Americans" kept the Spanish-American War small and short—splendid.

While the navy proved ready to fight on an instant's notice, the army was not ready for anything. In 1898, the army was only 28,000 strong, and those troops were scattered the length and breadth of the country. Congress had authorized increasing this force to 65,700 in wartime, but despite a rush of enlistments, the army never grew this large. The young men who rallied to arms in every state preferred to join the state militias or new units of volunteers, in which enlistments were for two years unless discharged earlier (as almost all would be).

In 1898, the militias numbered 140,000 men, but regular army officers justly suspected their training and equipment and generally preferred volunteer units in the regular army. Indeed, training was generally inadequate across the board because of the rush to get into action, and supplies were worse. Companies mustering, mostly in the southern states, were issued heavy woolen winter uniforms and Civil War-vintage Springfield rifles. Much meat that was provided the recruits was tainted and sanitary conditions in the crowded camps were such that filth-related diseases such as typhoid and dysentery ravaged them. When the dead were counted at the end of 1898, 379 men were listed as killed in combat, while 5,083 men were listed as dead of disease.

There was no difficulty in getting volunteers. While 274,000 eventually served in the army, probably an equal number were turned down. Among these rejects were Frank James, brother of the late train robber Jesse James, and William F. "Buffalo Bill" Cody, who annoyed the War Department by writing a magazine article entitled "How I Could Drive the Spaniards Out of Cuba with Thirty Thousand Indian Braves." Martha A. Chute of Colorado was discouraged in her offer to raise a troop of women, as was William Randolph Hearst in his suggestion to recruit a regiment of professional boxers and baseball players. "Think of a regiment composed of magnificent men of this ilk," the editor of the *New York Journal* wrote "They would overawe any Spanish regiment by their mere appearance." Nevertheless, the "Rough Riders," a motley collection of cowboys, athletes, and gentlemen like Colonel Theodore Roosevelt, was mustered. But because of shipping problems, the Riders had to leave their horses in Florida when they sailed for Cuba and fight on foot.

In fact, there were few battlegrounds in Cuba or in the Philippines that were suited to cavalry attack. Both are tropical countries, and most of the fighting was done in summer and much of it in jungle. The army tried to prepare for jungle warfare by authorizing the recruitment of up to 10,000 "immunes," young men who were thought to be immune to tropical diseases. However, medicine's comparative ignorance of the nature of tropical diseases combined with racism to make the immune regiments no more serviceable than any others. Whereas the original idea had been to fill these units with men who had grown up in marshy areas of the Deep South, within months recruiters were turning away white Louisianians from the bayous and accepting blacks from the upcountry South and even urban New Jersey. They were believed to possess a genetic immunity to malaria, yellow fever, and other afflictions of the tropics.

Blacks played a large part in both the Cuban and the Philippine campaigns. When the war broke out, there were four black regiments in the regular army: two infantry and two cavalry, the Ninth and the Tenth Horse Regiments. All four saw action. In fact, while Theodore Roosevelt was describing the capture of San Juan Hill as an accomplishment of the Rough Riders, other witnesses believed that the Rough Riders would have been devastated had it not been for the Tenth Negro Cavalry, which was immediately to their left during the charge. While the Rough Riders made a lot of noise, the Tenth simply did their job. In the words of the restrained report of their commander, later to be General of the Armies, John J. "Black Jack" Pershing: "The 10th Cavalry charged up the hill, scarcely firing a shot, and being nearest the Rough Riders, opened a disastrous enfilading fire upon the Spanish right, thus relieving the Rough Riders from the volleys that were being poured into them from that part of the Spanish line."

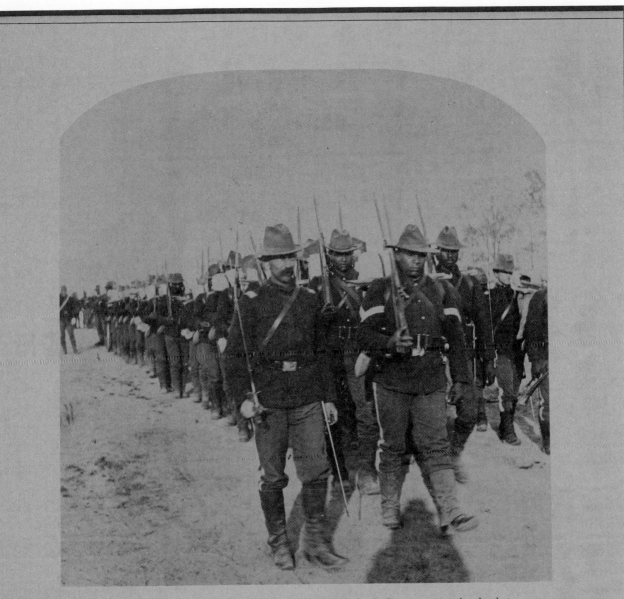

Black soldiers, members of the Twenty-fourth U.S. Infantry Division assigned to battle in Cuba, in an 1898 stereographic image by B. L. Singley.

About 10,000 blacks served in the war, 4,000 of them in the "immunes." A study done of white regiments indicates that the Spanish-American War was generally a poor man's fight and, rather more surprising, a city man's fight.

From largely rural Indiana, for example, of those volunteers who listed their occupation, only 296 were farmers. There were 322 common laborers, 413 skilled laborers, and 118 white-collar workers (clerks). Only 47 in the regiment were professional men, and 25 were merchants. A survey of a Connecticut volunteer unit reveals similar figures. Several historians state that the army was far less representative of the occupations of the general population than were the armies of the two world wars.

In age, it was typical, however. The average age of the soldiers was 24. Their average height was 5 feet 8 inches, and their average weight was 149 pounds, both less than the averages today.

the meantime, however, fearing that to continue resisting the war fever would cost the Republicans control of Congress in the fall elections, McKinley caved
in. On April 11, practically ignoring the Spanish ca-
pitulation, the president asked Congress for a declaration of war and got it.

The "Splendid Little War"

Declaring war was one thing. Fighting the Spanish was
quite another. The U.S. Army numbered only 28,000
men, most of whom were in the West keeping an eye
on Indians. The army was not up to launching an
invasion even just a hundred miles from Florida.

The spanking new navy was ready, however, but it
struck first not in Cuba but halfway around the world
in Spain's last Pacific colony, the Philippines. On May
1, acting on the instructions of undersecretary of the
Navy Theodore Roosevelt (the secretary of the Navy

was ill), Commodore George Dewey steamed a flotilla
into Manila Bay and completely surprised the Spanish
garrison. He destroyed most of the Spanish ships before
they could weigh anchor.

But Dewey had no soldiers with which to launch an
attack on land. For more than three months, he and
his men sat outside Manila harbor, baking in their
steel ships, while Filipino rebels struggled with the
Spanish garrison. In August, newly arrived troops finally took the capital. Although they did not know
it, a peace treaty had been signed the previous day.

For, by that time, American troops had also conquered Cuba and Puerto Rico. Secretary of State John
Hay called their campaign a "splendid little war" because so few Americans died in battle. In order to
celebrate so gaily, however, it was necessary to overlook the more than 5,000 soldiers who died from typhoid, tropical diseases, and poisonous "embalmed

Theodore Roosevelt and his "Rough Riders" cavalry unit.

beef," tainted meat that had been supplied to the soldiers because of corruption or simple inefficiency.

Although the Spanish army in Cuba outnumbered the Americans until the last, both commanders and men were paralyzed by defeatism. They might have been overcome more easily than they were but for the ineptitude of the American commanders, General Nelson A. Miles and General William R. Shafter, who was so fat that he had to be helped into the saddle of an extremely large horse when it was time to move.

Despite shortages of food, clothing, transport vehicles, medical supplies, ammunition, and horses, an army of 17,000 was landed in Cuba in June and defeated the Spanish outside Santiago at the battles of El Caney and San Juan Hill. (With 200,000 soldiers in Cuba, the Spanish foolishly stationed only 19,000 in Santiago.)

The victory allowed Americans to forget the poor management of the war and gave them a popular hero. Theodore Roosevelt had resigned from the Navy Department to accept a colonelcy in a volunteer cavalry unit called the "Rough Riders." It was a highly unmilitary group, made up of cowboys from Roosevelt's North Dakota ranch, show business fops, upper-class polo players and other athletes, and even some ex-convicts. The Rough Riders had to fight on foot because the army had been unable to get their horses out of Tampa, Florida, but they fought bravely in the hottest action on San Juan Hill.

EMPIRE CONFIRMED

In August, the Spanish gave up. American troops occupied not only Manila in the Philippines and much of Cuba, but also the island of Puerto Rico, which had been seized without resistance. But what should be done with these prizes? Suddenly, the imperialism controversy was no longer an academic debate. It involved three far-flung island countries that were inhabited by millions of people who spoke Spanish or Malayan languages, who clung to traditions very different from those of Americans, who were not Caucasian for the most part, and who did not want to become colonial subjects of the United States.

To the dismay of the imperialists, the independence of Cuba had been guaranteed before the war had begun. In order to get money from Congress to fight Spain, the administration had accepted a rider drafted by Senator Teller of Colorado. The Teller Amendment forbade the United States to take over the sugar island. Therefore, the great debate over imperialism centered on Puerto Rico and the Philippine Islands.

The Debate

The anti-imperialists were a disparate group, and their arguments were sometimes contradictory. In Congress, they included idealistic old Radical Republicans like George Frisbie Hoar of Massachusetts, former Liberal Republicans like Carl Schurz, and much of the old Mugwump wing of the party. Some Republican regulars also opposed taking colonies; among them was Thomas B. Reed of Maine, the no-nonsense, dictatorial Speaker of the House who otherwise despised reformers. Finally, a substantial part of the Democratic party, led by William Jennings Bryan, opposed annexation of any former Spanish lands. Henry Teller himself became a Democrat in 1900 because of his opposition to imperialism.

The anti-imperialists reminded Americans of their anticolonial heritage. "We insist," declared the American Anti-Imperialist League in October 1899, "that the subjugation of any people is 'criminal aggression' and open disloyalty to the distinctive principles of our government. We hold, with Abraham Lincoln, that no man is good enough to govern another man without that man's consent."

Some of the anti-imperialists appealed to racist feelings. With many people ill at ease because of the nation's large black population, was it wise to bring millions more nonwhite people under the flag? When Congress finally decided to take the Philippines and pay Spain $20 million in compensation, House Speaker Reed resigned in disgust, grumbling about "ten million Malays at two dollars a head."

But racist feelings worked mostly in favor of the imperialist group. Shrewd propagandists like Roosevelt, who was now governor of New York; Henry Cabot Lodge; and the eloquent Albert J. Beveridge, senator from Indiana, preached that the white race

Sanford B. Dole, a businessman and the first governor of the territory of Hawaii, seated next to Queen Liliuokalani, the last monarch of Hawaii.

had a duty and a right to govern inferior peoples. "God has not been preparing the English-speaking and Teutonic peoples for a thousand years for nothing but vain and idle self-contemplation and self-admiration," Beveridge told the Senate. "No! He has made us the master organizers of the world to establish system where chaos reigns."

Well-grounded fears that if the United States abandoned the Philippines, Japan or Germany would seize them motivated other politicians to support annexation. Such anxiety was especially significant in deciding McKinley's mind on the question. But most of all, the American people were in an emotional, expansive mood. Coming at the end of the troubled, depressed, and divided 1890s, annexation of colonies seemed a way to unite the country.

Hawaii

McKinley found it easier to come out for annexation of the Philippines and Puerto Rico because the United States already had taken its first real overseas colony.

In July 1898, shortly after the Spanish-American War began, Congress had annexed the seven main islands and 1,400 minor ones that made up the mid-Pacific republic of Hawaii. Shortly thereafter, Guam, Wake, and Baker islands were added as coaling stations for the navy.

The annexation of Hawaii was long in the making. The descendants of American missionary families in the islands had grown rich by exporting sugar to the United States, and they had won the confidence and support of the Hawaiian king, Kalakaua. Until 1890, they were content with their independent island paradise.

Then, the McKinley Tariff of 1890 introduced a bounty of 2 cents per pound on American-grown sugar. This encouraged enough mainland farmers to produce cane or sugar beets that Hawaiian imports declined sharply. Unable to affect American tariff policy from outside, the Hawaiian oligarchy concluded that it must join the islands to the United States and benefit from the subsidy.

The plan was squelched before it got started. In 1891, Kalakaua died and was succeeded by his sister, Liliuokalani, who was determined to maintain the independence of the islands. She announced that the theme of her reign would be "Hawaii for the Hawaiians" and introduced a series of reforms aimed at undercutting *haole* or white control of the economy and legislature.

Alarmed, the oligarchy acted quickly with help from the American ambassador in Honolulu. He declared that American lives and property were in danger and landed marines from the U.S.S. *Boston* who quickly took control. Back home, imperialists in the Senate introduced a treaty of annexation, but before they could push it through, Grover Cleveland was sworn in as president (March 4, 1893), and he withdrew the proposal.

Cleveland was not opposed to annexation on principle. But he wanted to know how the Hawaiian people felt, and he sent an investigator, James H. Blount, to the islands. Blount reported that very few nonwhite Hawaiians wanted to be part of the United States; they wanted independence and the restoration of Queen Liliuokalani. Cleveland ordered the marines to return to their ships and to the naval base at Pearl Harbor.

The Hawaiian whites had gone too far to chance restoring Queen Liliukalani. They maintained control and declared Hawaii a republic. As long as Cleveland sat in the White House, they bided their time and quietly cultivated Republican senators. In the excitement of the Spanish War, Hawaii was annexed by means of a joint resolution of the American Congress and Hawaiian legislature, the same device under which Texas had joined the Union.

Many Hawaiians continued to resent the takeover. Liliuokalani spent much time in the United States trying to win financial concessions for herself and the islands' natives. But as the white population grew and the islands attracted Japanese and Chinese immigrants, the native Hawaiians declined into a weak minority. Like the American Indians, they became foreigners in their own homeland. The famous islands' anthem, *Aloha Oe*, which was written by Liliuokalani, translates as "Farewell to Thee."

The Philippine Insurrection

Taking over the Philippines was not so easy. If the war with Spain had been something like splendid, the war that followed was a great deal like ugly. Like the Cubans, the Philippine people were experienced in guerrilla warfare. Led by Emilio Aguinaldo, a well-educated patriot who was as comfortable in the jungle as he was in the library, the rebels withdrew from the American-occupied cities to the jungle and fought only when the odds favored them.

In response, the American army of occupation was expanded to 65,000 men by early 1900, but even then the troops could make little progress outside the cities. The American commanders were unable to draw the *insurrectos* into a conventional battle in which superior fire power told the tale.

The fighting took a vicious turn. The Filipinos frequently decapitated their captives. The Americans, frustrated by their failures, the intense tropical heat, insects, and diseases, retaliated by slaughtering whole villages that were thought to be supporting the rebels. The army never did defeat the Filipinos. The rebellion ended only when, in March 1901, General Arthur MacArthur succeeded in capturing Aguinaldo. Weary of the bloodshed, Aguinaldo took an oath of allegiance to the United States and ordered his followers to do the same. (He lived quietly and long enough to see Philippine independence established in 1946.) More than 5,000 Americans died in the cause of suppressing a popular revolution, a queer twist in a conflict that had begun, three years before, in support of a popular revolution.

Emilio Aguinaldo, well-educated Philippine patriot.

The China Market

The Philippines provided a superb base for Americans engaged in the China trade and investors interested in developing the large but weak and impoverished "Middle Kingdom." On the face of it, China too was ripe for imperialist plucking. The emperor had little power outside Beijing (Peking); powerful regional warlords battled one another in the provinces; and most of the imperialistic nations of Europe, plus Japan, had carved out "spheres of influence" in China where their own troops maintained order and their own laws governed their resident citizens' behavior.

However, the most powerful of the powers in China, Great Britain, opposed the partition of China. Longer an imperial power and therefore more conscious than Japan, Russia, Germany, and Italy of the headaches and expense that attended imperial glory, the British believed that with their efficient industrial complex they could dominate the market of an independent China.

American businessmen disagreed with the British assessment of how economic competition in China would turn out, believing that they would win the lion's share of the prodigious purchases 160 million

Chinese Boxers captured by soldiers of the U.S. Cavalry in Tianjin, China.

Chinese were capable of making. However, this projection put them in complete agreement with the British policy of preventing the other imperialist nations from turning their spheres of influence into full-fledged colonies and shutting the door on free competition.

The Open Door Policy

Just as John Quincy Adams had beaten the British to promulgating the Monroe Doctrine, McKinley's secretary of state, John Hay, rushed ahead of Great Britain to circulate a series of memoranda called the "Open Door notes." These declarations pledged the imperial powers to respect the territorial integrity of China and to grant equal trading rights in their spheres of influence to all other countries.

Anticolonialist as it was, the Open Door policy by no means established the self-determination of the Chinese people, nor ended military intervention by outsiders. In 1900, when antiforeign rebels known as Boxers (the Chinese name of their religious movement was "Righteous Harmonious Fist") besieged 900 foreigners in the British legation in Beijing (Peking), American troops joined the soldiers of six other nations in defeating them. The victory encouraged beliefs in white superiority (despite the Japanese contribution) and convinced other nations that cooperation in maintaining the Open Door was the best policy in China.

McKinley Reelected, McKinley Murdered

In 1900, the Democrats again nominated William Jennings Bryan to run against McKinley. Bryan tried to make imperialism the issue but the campaign fizzled. Americans were either happy with their overseas possessions or simply uninterested. McKinley sidestepped the issue and pointed to the nation's new prosperity; the Republican slogan was "Four More Years of the Full Dinner Pail." Prosperity carried the day. Several states that had voted for Bryan in 1896 went Republican in 1900, including Bryan's own home state of Nebraska.

A new vice president stood at McKinley's side on Inauguration Day. Theodore Roosevelt had moved quickly from his exploits in Cuba to the governorship of New York. There, however, he alienated the Republican boss of the state, Thomas C. Platt, by refusing to take orders and even attacking some corrupt members of Platt's machine. When McKinley's vice president, the obscure Garrett Hobart of New Jersey, died in 1899, Platt saw a chance to get rid of the troublesome Rough Rider. He would banish him to the political burial ground of the vice presidency.

Mark Hanna, who was accustomed to consider all contingencies, had his reservations. What would happen to the country, Hanna asked McKinley, if something happened to him, and the manic Roosevelt became president? The president was almost 60 at a time when that was a ripe old age.

Something did happen to McKinley. On September 6, 1901, the president paid a ceremonial visit to the Pan-American Exposition in Buffalo. Greeting a long line of guests, he found himself faced by a man who extended a bandaged hand. The gauze concealed a pistol of large bore and Leon Czolgosz, an anarchist who "didn't believe one man should have so much service and another man should have none," shot the president several times in the chest and abdomen. Eight days later, McKinley died. "Now look," Hanna shook his head at the funeral, "that damned cowboy is president."

A Flexible Imperialist

Unlike every "accidental president" who preceded him, "Teddy" Roosevelt was to leave an indelible mark on the office. The young New Yorker (42 years old when he took office) knew only one way to do anything: rush into the lead and stay there. Nowhere was his assertive personality more pronounced than in his foreign policy, a peacetime extension of the zest that had taken him bellowing up San Juan Hill.

Roosevelt's actions varied according to the part of the world with which he was dealing. With the European nations, he insisted that the United States be accepted as an equal, active imperial power. Although friendship between Great Britain and the United States had been long in the making, Roosevelt sped it along by responding cordially to every British request for cooperation. Toward Latin America, Roosevelt was often arrogant. He told both Latin Americans and Europeans that the whole Western Hemisphere was an American sphere of influence. Toward Asia, Roosevelt continued to practice the "Open Door."

During Roosevelt's presidency, American capital poured into China. International consortia developed mines, built railways, and set up other profitable enterprises. In 1905, the president applied his policy of equilibrium in China by working through diplomatic channels to end a war between Russia and Japan. Much to the surprise of most Europeans, Japan handily defeated Russia and threatened to seize complete control of Manchuria and other parts of northern China. Through a mixture of threats and cajolery, Roosevelt got both sides to meet at Portsmouth, New Hampshire, to work out a treaty that maintained a balance of power in the area and guaranteed Chinese independence.

High-Handedness in Latin America

In Latin America, Roosevelt was not so compromising. He made it clear to the European nations that the United States held a preeminent position in the Western Hemisphere. In 1904, when several European nations threatened to invade the Dominican Republic to collect debts owed to their citizens, Roosevelt proclaimed what came to be called the Roosevelt Corollary to the Monroe Doctrine. In order to protect the

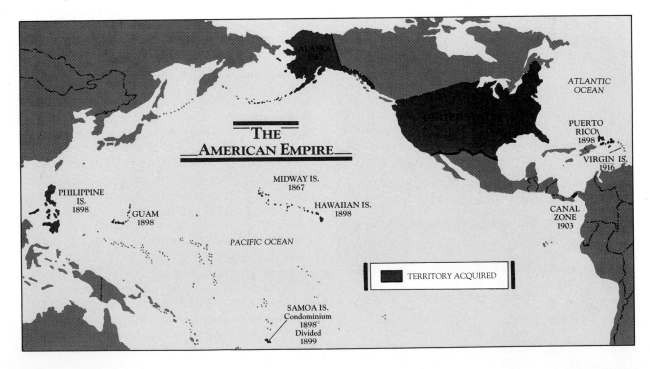

independence of American states, the United States would, if necessary, exercise an "international police power" in the Western Hemisphere. In other words, while European nations still had to keep out of the Americas, the United States would intervene south of the border if circumstances called for such action.

Roosevelt wasted no time putting his corollary to work. United States Marines landed in the Dominican Republic and took over the collection of customs, seeing to it that European creditors were paid off. From 1904 until the 1930s, the United States intervened in a number of Latin American countries: Cuba, Nicaragua, the Dominican Republic, and Haiti. These actions may have pleased European investors, but they created a reservoir of ill will among Latin Americans who felt bullied by the great Anglo colossus of the north. No action offended Latin Americans more than Roosevelt's high-handed seizure of the Panama Canal Zone, which the president considered his greatest achievement.

In 1911, when the construction of the canal was nearly complete, Roosevelt reflected (quite accurately) that only his decisiveness had moved the project along. "If I had followed traditional, conservative methods," he said, "the debates on it would have been going on yet. But I took the Canal Zone and let

Congress debate; and while the debate goes on the Canal does also."

A Path between the Seas

Naval officers had long recognized the value of a quick route between the Atlantic and the Pacific. During the Spanish-American War, the battleship *Oregon*, stationed in San Francisco, took 67 days to steam the 12,000 miles to Cuba via Cape Horn. Had there been an isthmian canal, the voyage would have been but 4,000 miles.

A French company had started to dig a canal across Panama, then part of Colombia, in the 1880s. But the project was abandoned because of financial and engineering difficulties and the ravages of malaria and yellow fever among the builders. Three out of five Frenchmen and women in Panama died; the mortality was undoubtedly higher among the laborers, mostly blacks from Jamaica. The horrors of the French experience convinced most American experts that the "path between the seas" should be dug not in Panama, but in Nicaragua, which was more healthful and provided the lowest crossing of the American landmass from the Arctic to Tierra del Fuego.

It was a Nicaraguan canal that Secretary of State Hay had in mind when he negotiated a treaty with Britain, promising the United States full control of the project. Congress also favored the Nicaragua route. Then, however, two of the most effective lobbyists of all time, an agent of the French company that held rights to the Panama route, Philippe Bunau-Varilla, and an American wheeler-dealer, William Nelson Cromwell, went to work in Washington's restaurants, the cloakrooms of Congress, and in the White House itself.

Their goal was win approval of the Panama route, then sell the assets of the French company in Panama, including an American-built railroad, to the United States. There was no good reason why their proposal should have been accepted. Even if the United States opted for the Panama route, the French company's rights on the isthmus were due to expire and most of its equipment was useless. Nevertheless, Bunau-Varilla and Cromwell somehow won over President Roosevelt and key members of Congress.

Roosevelt Takes Panama

Then the project stalled in Bogota. The Colombian government turned down the American offer to pay Colombia $10 million and an annual rental fee of $250,000. (The Colombians wanted $25 million.) Rather than take a step backward, Roosevelt conspired with Bunau-Varilla to start a revolution in Panama.

Theodore Roosevelt took immense personal satisfaction in securing American rights to dig the Panama Canal and in 1906 traveled to Panama to inspect the construction project.

OLD BOYS

Most of Theodore Roosevelt's advisors were drawn from his own social class. They were gentlemen of old, genteel families who assumed without much reflection that they were the people intended to govern the United States. They wore their duties lightly. Cabinet meetings could seem like a clubroom full of joshing old boys.

When T. R. asked Attorney-General Philander C. Knox to prepare a legal justification of his actions in the detachment of the Isthmus of Panama from Colombia, Knox replied, "Oh Mr. President, do not let so great an achievement suffer from any taint of legality." After a long, blustering explanation of his actions to the cabinet, T. R. asked, "Well, have I defended myself?" secretary of war, later of state, Elihu Root, replied, "You certainly have, Mr. President. You have shown that you were accused of seduction and you have conclusively proved that you were guilty of rape."

On November 2, 1903, the president moved several warships to the vicinity, and the next day, the province erupted in riots and declared its independence. On November 6, the United States recognized the new republic of Panama. On November 18, the first foreign

minister of Panama, none other than the Frenchman Bunau-Varilla, signed a treaty with the United States that granted perpetual use of a ten-mile-wide "canal zone" across the isthmus on the terms that Colombia had refused.

None of Roosevelt's successors in the presidency were quite so arrogant in dealing with Latin America. For example, Roosevelt's hand-picked successor, William Howard Taft, tried to replace "gunboat diplomacy" with "dollar diplomacy," the attempt to influence Latin America (and China) through investment rather than armed force. In 1921, over the protests of Roosevelt's old ally Henry Cabot Lodge, the United States attempted to make amends to Colombia for Roosevelt's high-handed actions by paying the $25 million that the Colombians originally had demanded for the right to dig the Panama Canal.

But such gestures could not change America's "big brother" behavior or the simmering resentment of the Latin American people. The plunge into imperialism established intervention as an essential part of American diplomacy. Every president from Theodore Roosevelt to Herbert Hoover (1929–33) used troops to enforce their wishes in Latin America. Lyndon B. Johnson (1963–69) and Ronald Reagan (1981–89) revived the policy.

For Further Reading

The essential background of the political upheaval at the end of the nineteenth century can be found in Vincent P. DeSantis, *The Shaping of Modern America, 1877–1916* (1973); H. Wayne Morgan, *From Hayes to McKinley: National Party Politics, 1877–1896* (1971); Robert H. Wiebe, *The Search for Order, 1880–1920* (1967).

Valuable special studies include Howard K. Beale, *Theodore Roosevelt and the Rise of America to World Power* (1956); Robert L. Beisner, *From the Old Diplomacy to the New, 1865–1900* (1975); C. S. Campbell, *The Transformation of American Foreign Relations, 1865–1900* (1976); Robert F. Durden, *The Climax of Populism: The Election of 1896* (1965); Frank Freidel, *The Splendid Little War* (1958); Lloyd Gardner, Walter Le Feber, and Thomas McCormick, *The Creation of the American Empire* (1973); Ray Ginger, *Altgeld's America: The Lincoln Ideal and Changing Realities* (1958); Paul F. Glad, *McKinley, Bryan, and the People* (1964) and *The Trumpet Soundeth* (1960); G. Grunder and W. E. Livezey, *The Philippines and the United States*

(1951); S. L. Jones, *The Presidential Election of 1896* (1964); Walter R. Le Feber, *The New Empire: An Interpretation of American Expansion, 1860–1898* (1963); Ernest R. May, *Imperial Democracy: The Emergence of America as a Great Power* (1961); David McCullough, *The Path Between the Seas* (1977); Dwight C. Miner, *Fight for the Panama Canal* (1966); Thomas J. Osborne, *American Opposition to Hawaiian Annexation, 1893–1898* (1981); J. W. Pratt, *America's Colonial Experiment* (1950) and *Expansionists of 1898: The Acquisition of Hawaii and the Spanish Islands* (1936); William A. Russ, Jr., *The Hawaiian Republic, 1894–98* (1961); William A. Williams, *The Tragedy of American Diplomacy* (1959).

See the biographies of Bryan by P. E. Coletta and Louis W. Koenig listed at the conclusion of Chapter 33; Margaret Leech, *In the Days of McKinley* (1959); H. Wayne Morgan, *William McKinley and His America* (1963); and Edmund Morris, *The Rise of Theodore Roosevelt* (1979).

As 1899 drew to a close, editors and writers of letters to editors bickered about the significance of the New Year's Day that was approaching. One faction declared that New Year's Day 1900 would mark the beginning of a new century. Another rushed to point out that the first century A.D. had not ended with the last day of A.D. 99, but with the last day of A.D. 100. Therefore, the twentieth century would begin at the stroke of midnight on January 1, 1901, a year in the future. They were quite right, of course. The year 1900 was the last year of the nineteenth century, not the first year of the twentieth. Nevertheless, the titillation of writing such a portentously sounding date as 1900 on their next letter to the editor meant more to people than did the

---

35

GAY NINETIES AND GOOD OLD DAYS

American Society in Transition, 1890–1917

Men and women bicyclists riding at the turn of the century.

dictates of arithmetic. Americans would ring out the old century on December 31, 1899, and ring in the new in the wee hours of January 1, 1900. The newspapers say that the celebrations were particularly festive that night.

MIDDLE AMERICA

Many political historians have celebrated 1900 as the dividing line between an age of conservative hegemony and an age of reform, the Progressive Era. Culturally, however, 1900 seems less a watershed year than the midpoint in a quarter-century era when the American middle class, as we know it, came into its own and brimmed with confidence.

Dark Corners

To a black, to an Indian of the Plains or a Mexican-American of the Southwest, to a white workingman in a marginal job, or to many of the nearly 12 million immigrants who came to the United States between 1890 and 1910, the decades that spanned the year 1900 were not rosy. During most of the 1890s, the United States languished in hard times. It was the decade of Wounded Knee and bloody labor battles, an era when the lynching of blacks in the South reached epidemic proportions. In 1899, a mob in Palmetto, Georgia, could announce in advance that a man would be burned alive so that thousands could flock aboard special excursion trains to witness the spectacle.

Life expectancy at birth for native-born white Americans was about 45 years, lower for blacks and immigrants, much lower for Indians. Infant mortality in New York City was worse than it had ever been. Nationwide, people were 6 times more likely to die of influenza than they are today, 60 times more likely to die of syphilis, and more than 80 times more likely to die of tuberculosis. Diseases that are minor health problems in the late twentieth century—typhoid, scarlet fever, strep throat, diphtheria, whooping cough, measles—were common killers in the 1890s and 1900s.

And yet, when people who lived through the years around the turn of the century remembered them, they were apt to call the final decade of the nineteenth century the "Gay Nineties," to recall a time of nickelodeon music and days at Coney Island, of nights at vaudeville shows and a week at the seaside, of beer gardens and ice cream parlors, of the bicycle craze and winsome Gibson Girls.

A white mob preparing to lynch a black man in Paris, Texas, in 1893.

The first years of the twentieth century have lived on in popular consciousness as the original "good old days." The era before the First World War is the slice of time to which popular novelists and film makers repair when they want to portray an America that is recognizable but unmistakably better. Life was less complex in this engaging vision. The summer sun was warmer, the hot dogs tastier, the baseball more exciting, the cars adventurous, the boys more gallant, the girls prettier, the songs lilting and cheering the heart with sprightly melody.

A Golden Age

The turn of the century has cast such an alluring glow over time because middle-class values and aspirations have dominated American culture in the twentieth century, and in the 1890s and early 1900s the modern middle class came into its own. The troubles of poor farmers, factory workers, blacks, Indians, Mexican-Americans, and recent immigrants were real and often tragic. But the class of people who, while not rich, did not have to struggle in order to survive reached unprecedented numbers at the turn of the century. The middle class became numerous enough to create and sustain a distinctive lifestyle and to support a bustling consumer economy and technology devoted to physical comfort, convenience, individual self-improvement, and the enjoyment of leisure time.

Increasingly well educated, the new middle class quietly shelved the zealous, religious piety of their parents and grandparents. They embraced instead the proper pleasures of their rich nation. The people of the "good old days" were by no means oblivious to social evils. Far from it; they were also the citizens of the "Progressive Era," a time of rampant reform. But progressivism was itself the manifestation of a confident people. War and revolution were not yet constant companions.

Teddy

The buoyant temper of the period was personified in the man who succeeded William McKinley as president, in September 1901. Theodore Roosevelt was climbing a mountain in the Adirondacks when he received the news of McKinley's death. He rushed to Buffalo, took the oath of office, and confided to a friend, "It is a dreadful thing to come into the presidency in this way. But it would be a far worse thing to be morbid about it." Roosevelt intended to enjoy the presidency, as his fellow Americans intended to make the most of life. And no other chief executive before or since has had such a "bully" time living at 1600 Pennsylvania Avenue.

Both critics and friends of the president poked fun at his personal motto: "Walk softly and carry a big

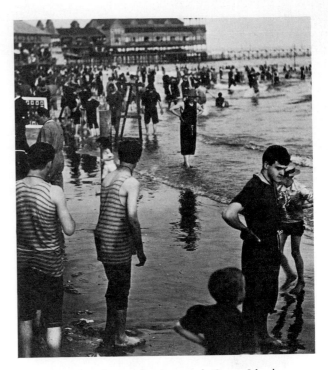

By 1896, cheap trolley fares made Coney Island a popular destination with middle- and working-class people.

stick." They said that they observed Roosevelt wildly waving clubs around often enough, but rarely knew him to walk softly. Quite the contrary. Everything that Roosevelt did was accompanied by fanfare. He seemed to swagger and strut about like an exuberant adolescent, hogging center stage and good naturedly drowning out anyone who dared to compete for the spotlight. He insisted on being, as one of his children put it, the bride at every wedding and the corpse at every funeral. "The universe seemed to be spinning round," wrote Rudyard Kipling, "and Theodore was the spinner."

Roosevelt shattered the image of solemn dignity that had been nurtured by every president since Rutherford B. Hayes. He stormed about the country far more than had any predecessor, delivering dramatic speeches, mixing gleefully with crowds of all descriptions, camping out, climbing mountains, and clambering astride horses and atop farm and industrial machines. When a motion-picture photographer asked him to move for the ingenious new camera, Roosevelt picked up an ax and furiously chopped down a tree.

The Strenuous Life

Of an old aristocratic Dutch family, Roosevelt had been sickly as a youth. He was hopelessly nearsighted and suffered from asthma. As an adolescent, however,

---

HOT DOG

The hot dog is second only to the hamburger as a symbol of *cuisine americaine*, but its origins are hotly disputed. Not the origins of the mild sausage itself: it was being made commercially in Frankfurt, Germany, and Vienna, Austria, in the early nineteenth century. (Thus the alternative names, frankfurter and wiener—Vienna in German is *Wien*.) The disputed point is: who first put one of the things in a soft roll and provided the classic condiments of yellow mustard, chopped onion, and sweet pickle relish?

Some partisans claim that the deed was first done at the amusement park at Coney Island; hot dogs were once called "coney islands," too. Others credit Anton Feuchtwanger, who sold the sausages so quickly at the St. Louis World's Fair in 1904 that he had to add the roll so that his customers did not burn their hands. Yet others say the roll was first added at a New York Giants baseball game in April 1900 where they were first called "dachsund sausages." A popular cartoonist of the time who liked his baseball, Tad Dorgan, provided the more durable name "hot dog."

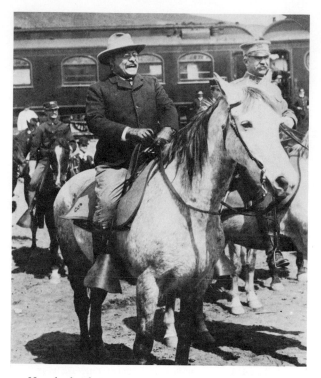

Horseback riding was one of Theodore Roosevelt's many athletic pursuits.

he took up body-building and unfettered his tremendous inner energy. He fought on the Harvard boxing team, and rode with cowboys on his North Dakota ranch. As Police Commissioner of New York City, he accompanied patrolmen on night beats as dangerous as any in the world. When the war with Spain broke out, he left his office job and joined the army. In dozens of articles and books, he wrote of the glories of "the strenuous life."

Roosevelt liked to show off his large, affectionate, and handsome family with himself at stage center, a stern but generous patriarch. He sported a modest paunch (fashionable at the turn of the century), a close-snipped moustache, and thick pince-nez that dropped from his nose when he was excited, which was often. His teeth were odd, all seemingly incisors of the same size and about twice as many as normal. He displayed them often in a broad grin that he shed only when he took off after enemies whom middle-class Americans also found it easy to dislike: Wall Street bankers, Socialists, impudent Latin Americans.

William McKinley had concealed his fondness for cigars so as not to be a bad example to young men. Roosevelt had no compunctions about puffing away in public. What was the harm in a minor vice that brought a man pleasure? More than any other individual, he taught Americans to believe that their president should be a good fellow and part showman.

The Symbol of His Age

Roosevelt had many critics. But most Americans, especially those of the vibrant new middle class, found him a grand fellow indeed. They called him "Teddy" and named the lovable animal doll they bought for their children, the teddy bear, after him. He was the first president to be routinely identified in newspapers by his initials, T.R. Even Elihu Root, a stodgy eastern aristocrat who served as both secretary of war and secretary of state, waxed playful when he congratulated the president on his forty-sixth birthday in 1904. "You have made a very good start in life," Root said, "and your friends have great hopes for you when you grow up." The British ambassador quipped, "You must remember that the president is about six years old."

Kansas journalist William Allen White, the archetype of the middle-class townsman, wrote that "Roosevelt bit me and I went mad." White remained a lifelong devotee of "the Colonel," as did Finley Peter Dunne, the urbane Chicagoan who captured the salty, cynical humor of the big-city Irish in his fictional commentator on current events, Mr. Dooley. Radical dissenters hated Roosevelt (who hated them back with interest). But they were at a loss as to how to counter his vast popularity. Labor leaders and Socialists stuck to the issues when they disagreed with him. There was no advantage in attacking Teddy Roosevelt personally.

Although Roosevelt was a staunch believer in Anglo-Saxon superiority, he won the affection of blacks when he ignored the squeals of southern segregationists and invited Booker T. Washington to call on him in the White House. Woman suffragists, gearing up for the last phase of their long battle for votes, petitioned rather than attacked him. Elizabeth Cady Stanton addressed him from her deathbed in 1901 as "already celebrated for so many deeds and honorable utterances."

Much mischief was done during Theodore Roosevelt's nearly eight years in office. He committed the United States to a role as international policeman that damaged the nation's reputation in many small countries. He was inclined to define his opponents in moral terms, a recurring and unfortunate characteristic of American politics since his time.

But the happy symbiosis between the boyish president and the majority of the American people may be the most important historical fact of the years spanning the turn of the century. Like the man who was their president between 1901 and 1909, the worldly middle class of the Gay Nineties was confident, optimistic, and glad to be alive.

An Educated People

The foundation of middle-class vigor was wealth. American society as a whole had grown so rich that despite the disproportionate fortunes of the great multimillionaires, millions of people in the middle could afford to indulge interests and pleasures that had been the exclusive property of tiny elites in earlier epochs and other countries. Among these was education beyond "the three r's"—"readin', 'ritin', and' rithmetic." During the final third of the nineteenth century, and especially after 1890, the American educational system expanded and changed to accommodate the numbers and aspirations of the new class.

There were no more than about 300 secondary schools in the United States in 1860 (a country of 31.4 million people), and only about 100 of them were free. While girls were admitted to most public elementary schools, very few attended beyond the first few grades.

Colleges and universities—about 560 in 1870—catered to an even more select social set. They offered the traditional course in the liberal arts (Latin, philosophy, mathematics, and history) that was designed to polish young gentlemen rather than to train people for a career. The handful of "female seminaries" and colleges that admitted women before the Civil War also taught the ancient curriculum mixed with a strong dose of evangelical religion.

After about 1880, educational facilities rapidly multiplied and changed character. By 1900, there were 6,000 free public secondary schools in the United States, and by 1915, there were 12,000, educating 1.3 million pupils. Educational expenditures per pupil increased from about $9 a year in 1870 to $48 in 1920.

Secondary schools no longer specialized in preparing a select few for university, but offered a wide range of courses leading to jobs in industry and business, from engineering and accounting to agriculture and typing.

A New Kind of University

The Morrill Land Grant Act of 1862 and the philanthropy of millionaires combined with the middle class's hunger for learning to expand the opportunities for higher education. The Morrill Act provided federal land to the states for the purpose of serving the educational needs of "the industrial classes," particularly in "such branches of learning as are related to agri-culture and mechanic arts." Thus it not only fostered the founding of technical schools in which middle-class youth might learn a profession, but put liberal-arts training within the reach of those who sought it. Many of the great state universities of the West owe their origins to the Morrill Act.

Gilded Age millionaires competed for esteem as patrons of learning by constructing buildings and by endowing scholarships and professorial chairs at older institutions. Some even founded completely new universities. The story was told that railroad king Leland Stanford and his wife traveled to Harvard with the notion of erecting a building in memory of their son, who had died. As President Charles W. Eliot was explaining how much it had cost to construct each of Harvard's splendid buildings, Mrs. Stanford suddenly exclaimed, "Why, Leland, we can build our own university!" And they did; Stanford University in Palo Alto, California, was founded in 1885.

Cornell (1865), Drew (1866), Johns Hopkins (1876), Vanderbilt (1872), and Carnegie Institute of Technology (1905) were universities that bear the names of the moguls who financed them. In Philadelphia, Success Gospel preacher Russell B. Conwell established Temple University in 1884 explicitly to educate poor boys ambitious to rise in social station. John D. Rockefeller pumped millions of dollars into the University of Chicago (1890), making it one of America's most distinguished centers of learning within a decade. George Eastman, who made a fortune from Kodak cameras, contributed heavily to the University of Rochester.

The midwestern and western state universities, beginning with Iowa in 1858, generally admitted women to at least some programs. In the East, however, separate women's colleges were founded, again with the support of wealthy benefactors. Georgia Female College (Wesleyan) and Mount Holyoke dated from before the Civil War. In the later decades of the century they were joined by Vassar (1861), Wellesley (1870), Smith (1871), Radcliffe (1879), Bryn Mawr (1880), and Barnard (1889). Vassar's educational standards rivaled those of the best men's colleges, but it was necessary to maintain a kind of "head start" program in order to remedy deficiencies in the secondary education provided even well-to-do girls.

Studying for Careers

The transformation of higher education was not simply a matter of more colleges, universities, and students. While some institutions, such as Yale, clung tenaciously to the traditional liberal-arts curriculum, the

Stanford University, constructed by railroad baron Leland Stanford in memory of his son.

majority of schools adopted the "elective system" that was pioneered by the College of William and Mary, Washington College in Virginia, and the University of Michigan, and most effectively promoted by President Eliot of Harvard. Beginning in 1869, Eliot abandoned the rule that every student follow precisely the same sequence of courses. Instead, he allowed individuals to choose their field of study. "Majors" included traditional subjects but also new disciplines in the social sciences, engineering, and business administration. The new emphasis on university education as preparation for a career reflected the aspirations of middle-class students who had not yet arrived financially and socially.

From Germany, educators borrowed the concept of the professional postgraduate school. Before the 1870s, young people who wished to learn a profession attached themselves to an established practitioner. A would-be lawyer agreed with an established attorney to do routine work in his office, sweeping floors and helping with deeds and wills, in return for the right to "read law" in the office and to observe and question his teacher. After a few years, the apprentice hung out

his own shingle. Many physicians were trained the same way. Civil and mechanical engineers learned their professions "on the job" in factories. All too often, teachers received no training and were miserably paid, about $200 a year in rural states.

Women, Minorities and the New Education

Exceptional women who were dauntless enough to shake off the ridicule of their male classmates could be found in small numbers at every level of the new system. By the mid-1880s, the word *coeducational* and its breezy abbreviation, "coed," had become part of the American language. The first female physician in the United States, Elizabeth Blackwell, was accredited only in 1849. In 1868, she established a medical school for women in New York City. By that date, the Woman's Medical College of Pennsylvania already was recognized, however grudgingly, as offering one of the nation's most effective programs of medical education.

Female lawyers were unusual at a time when women were not considered equal to men before the law. In

1873, the Supreme Court approved the refusal of the University of Illinois to admit women by declaring that "the paramount mission and destiny of women are to fulfill the noble and benign offices of wife and mother." By the end of the century, dozens of women practiced law, among them the Populist wife and "Mother" Mary Lease. Antoinette Blackwell, sister-in-law of Elizabeth, paved the way for the ordination of women ministers, and by the turn of the century, the more liberal Protestant denominations, such as the Unitarians and Congregationalists, had ordained some women.

Also in small numbers, well-to-do Jews and Catholics began to take advantage of the new educational opportunities. The Sephardic and German Jews were a secular people who preferred to send their sons to established institutions rather than found their own. The Catholic Church, on the other hand, the largest religious denomination in the United States but mainly a church of the lower classes, preferred to found its own colleges. Church policy was to prepare the sons and daughters of the Catholic middle class for active careers in business and the professions while simultaneously shoring up their loyalty to their faith by means of rigorous schooling in Church doctrine, history, and observance.

The most famous Catholic colleges dated from before the Civil War: Notre Dame had been founded in 1842; Holy Cross (1843) and Boston College (1863) were explicitly created as foils to aristocratic Harvard.

W. E. B. Du Bois, a founder of the National Association for the Advancement of Colored People.

Thomas Jefferson and John Quincy Adams's dream of a national university was fulfilled by the Roman Catholic Church with the founding in 1889 of the Catholic University of America in Washington, D.C. It is difficult to imagine either the Virginian or the New Englander quite happy about the sponsor.

On a much smaller scale, educational opportunities for blacks also expanded. The traditional universities in New England and many of the sectarian colleges of the Ohio Valley continued to admit a small number of very well-qualified blacks. W. E. B. Du Bois, a founder of the National Association for the Advancement of Colored People, earned a Ph.D. at Harvard. Hamilton S. Smith earned a law degree from Boston University in 1879 (the first black to do so), and when he could not make a living as an attorney, attended the Howard University School of Dentistry.

Howard was a private university educating the small but dynamic black middle class. In the North as well as the South, philanthropists and state governments founded institutions for blacks only. Beginning with Lincoln University in Pennsylvania (founded as the Ashmun Institute in 1854), idealistic benefactors supported schools such as Howard in Washington (1867) and Fisk in Nashville (1866). After Booker T. Washington's Atlanta Compromise speech of 1895 and the Supreme Court's decision in *Plessy* vs. *Ferguson* (1896)

Thomas Eakins' The Gross Clinic, *painted in 1875, shows young physicians learning their trade from more experienced colleagues.*

PUBLIC WOMEN

Elizabeth Cochran, alias Nellie Bly.

The 1890s were a watershed decade in the public status of women in the United States. Led by the methodical Carrie Chapman Catt, the American Woman Suffrage Association began to win the vote for women where the movement of Elizabeth Cady Stanton and Susan B. Anthony had met only frustration. Social workers like Jane Addams and Lillian Wald proved too assertive and effective to be written off as eccentric spinsters. In the popular press, Charles Dana Gibson celebrated "the Gibson girl," an assertive, independent young lady who bore little resemblance to the frail violet who had been the ideal of the Gospel of True womanhood.

At the very beginning of the decade, Elizabeth Cochran, the orphan daughter of a Pennsylvania miller, came to personify the "new woman" while remaining rather distant from the organized woman movement. Cochran's aloofness toward the feminists may have owed to a childhood of struggle. (Feminists were overwhelmingly middle-class.) Born in 1864, she was forced by her father's death to go to work. Almost entirely self-educated, Cochran was to parlay her talents and a knack for self-promotion into international celebrity and, via an odd route, riches.

In 1885, while working at a menial job to support her mother, Cochran wrote a letter to a Pittsburgh newspaper editor who had helplessly bemoaned the fact that women who did not marry seemed useless to society. Eloquently and forcefully, Cochran called for opening employment opportunities for girls (who were "just as smart" as boys and "a great deal quicker to learn"). In that way, the single woman could prove herself, be independent, and cease to concern gentlemen like the editor of the *Pittsburgh Dispatch*.

The editor (who became a lifelong friend) was sufficiently impressed that he hired Cochran as a reporter. Using the pen name Nellie Bly (from a Stephen Foster song), she wrote a series of exposés of working and living conditions in the city ten years before the age of the muckraker is said to have begun. Nellie Bly also pioneered the technique of the undercover reporter, actually taking jobs in factories and writing her articles in the first person.

When pressure was brought on the *Dispatch* to relegate Nellie to the society pages, where women "belonged," she moved to New York and pushed her way into a job with Joseph Pulitzer's booming *World*. She was an immediate sensation when she managed to have herself committed to a municipal asylum for insane women. She lived as an inmate for ten days, and penned another blistering first-person exposé.

Nellie was sincerely interested in social reform but far from oblivious to her own interests. Her most famous project for Pulitzer was a masterpiece of self-promotion and one of journalism's first manufactured stories. As a girl, Nellie had read Jules Verne's novel *Around the World in Eighty Days*, in which a British dandy and his valet girdled the globe with unbelievable speed. A number of adventurers had tried to beat the fictional record and failed. Nellie locked herself up with train and steamship timetables and told the *World* that she could make the trip in 75 days. The editors were interested but said that if they financed such a project, a man would have to carry the banner. A woman on such a journey would "need a protector" anyway, her editor said. "Even if it were possible for you to travel alone, you would have to carry so much baggage that it would detain you in making rapid changes." Nellie replied, "Very well. Start the man and I'll start the same day for some other newspaper and beat him."

Nellie Bly left Jersey City under the *World's* auspices on November 14, 1889 and, after a trip that sometimes seemed leisurely as she waited for steamships to depart, returned to her point of departure via a special transcontinental train on January 25, 1890. Her trip took 72 days.

Suffragists courted Nellie Bly for their cause, but she was uninterested. As early as 1885, when she brought herself to the attention of the *Pittsburgh Dispatch* with her plea on behalf of employment opportunities for women, she expressed oblique disdain for organized feminism. Fighting for jobs for women, she wrote, "would be a good field for believers in women's rights. Let them forego their lecturing and writing and go to work; more work and less talk." After her famous journey, Nellie declined to join the Women's Suffrage Party. "If I became a suffragette," she wrote, "I would play into the hands of my critics. They may not like me, but they respect me. Joining your group would identify me as a partisan. I can help your movement more by putting into practice what you've been preaching."

Again Nellie expressed her disdain for "mere talk." She also disliked what she regarded as the feminists' lack of feminity, remembering late in life that "they looked to be neither men nor women, so queer and nondescript was their attire." She told Susan B. Anthony that "if women wanted to succeed, they had to go out as women. They had to make themselves as pretty and attractive as possible." On rather a different level, Nellie Bly was arguing for what Carrie Chapman Catt was effecting of the American Woman Suffrage Association, espousing expanded rights for women because they were different from men, rather than because they were the same.

The fact was, Nellie Bly was a loner, marching to her own drummer. Shortly after her return from her world trip, she quit journalism to marry a well-to-do manufacturer, 72 years of age to her 31. When he died in 1904, she ran his factory, designed a steel barrel, provided social and medical services and recreational facilities for her employees, and paid women the same wages received by men, a practice then almost unheard of. Unfortunately, her Iron Clad Manufacturing Company went bankrupt because of theft by an employee with whom Nellie was having an affair. She was absolved of complicity in the corruption but was soon broke herself, writing in 1919 that "I have exactly $3.65 and a trunk full of Paris evening dresses." William Randolph Hearst gave her a job writing a column for the New York *Journal* but she never regained her celebrity. She died in 1922.

gave the go-ahead to segregation at all levels of education, southern state governments founded "agricultural and mechanical" schools patterned after Alabama's Tuskegee Institute (1881), at which blacks could train for manual occupations.

The accomplishments of these institutions should not be underestimated. Few scientific researchers of the time were more productive than Tuskegee Institute's great botanist, George Washington Carver. Nevertheless, the educational level of blacks lagged so far behind that of whites that in 1910, when only 7.7 percent of the American population was illiterate (the figure includes the millions of recent immigrants), one black in three above the age of ten could neither read nor write.

A LIVELY CULTURE

Americans continued to buy the books of European authors and the works of the older generation of American poets—Emerson, Longfelow, Whitman, Whittier Emily Dickinson of Amherst, Massachusetts, a recluse who was virtually unknown until after her death in 1886, was immediately recognized as one of the country's finest writers. But it was first of all an age when novelists flourished, some growing quite rich from the demand for their books.

Twain and James

Samuel Langhorne Clemens, or Mark Twain, was quintessentially and comprehensively American. A Missourian, he deserted a Confederate militia unit to go west to Nevada, and eventually settled in Hartford, Connecticut, when he became able to choose his style of life. Brilliantly capturing both the hardships and ribald humor of frontier life in *Roughing It* (1872), he earned an international reputation with *The Adventures of Tom Sawyer* (1876) and *The Adventures of Huckleberry Finn* (1885). Readers sometimes missed the profound and subtle social criticism in Twain's work (as an old man, he grew melancholy and cynical), but they read him with pleasure for his wit and mastery of the American language.

Twain's favorite settings and themes were robustly western. The other great novelist of the period, Henry James, settled in England because he found American culture stultifying, and he set most of his novels in the Old World and peopled them with cultivated, cosmopolitan characters. But like Twain, his goal was to define America. In *The American* (1877), *The Europeans* (1878), and *Daisy Miller* (1879), James dealt with the relationship of open, albeit less cultivated,

Samuel L. Clemens, known to his wide readership as Mark Twain.

American characters with a jaded and decadent European culture.

Realism and Naturalism

An able novelist in his own right, William Dean Howells presided over the American literary establishment as editor of the *Atlantic Monthly*. Like *Harper's*, *Forum*, and *The Arena*, the *Atlantic* published a mix of poetry, stories, and elegant essays that sometimes dealt with contemporary issues but usually at a fastidious distance.

Howells was a realist. He had no patience with the high-flown, preposterous motives and beliefs that sentimental writers imputed to their characters. In *The Rise of Silas Lapham* (1885), a novel about a successful industrialist, when one sister loses a suitor to another, she does not react selflessly, nor does the sister who gets her man think seriously of sacrificing herself. Nevertheless, neither Howells nor the *Atlantic* would have considered dealing graphically with sexual matters or the degradation that poverty and squalor created. Because the proper upper and middle classes themselves considered such discussions unacceptable, the writings of realists like Howells are sometimes lumped with romanticism and sentimentalism as part of "the genteel tradition."

Naturalistic writers defied the taboos, some of them

with considerable success. In *Maggie: A Girl of the Streets* (1893), Stephen Crane depicted the poor not as noble and selfless but as miserable and helpless. In *The Red Badge of Courage* (1895), the Civil War is described as something other than glory, bugles, bravery, and flying colors (if anything, a more daring venture than a book about a prostitute). In *McTeague* (1899) and *The Octopus* (1901), Frank Norris dealt with people driven almost mechanically by animal motives.

The most popular of the naturalists was Jack London. His *Call of the Wild* (1903) is comparable to *Huckleberry Finn* in that it is simultaneously a grand tale of adventure (about a dog) and, at a deeper level, a profound commentary on the human condition. Theodore Dreiser broke with a moralistic literary convention (that nevertheless survived) by allowing characters like *Sister Carrie* (1900) to enjoy rich lives despite sinful pasts. Dreiser's success was doubly remarkable because, from a midwestern German household, his treatment of the English language was adversarial at best, and more often downright cruel.

A Hunger for Words

The genteel tradition was also challenged by a new type of magazine that made its appearance in the 1880s and 1890s. Catering to the new, hungry, but not so ethereally intellectual middle classes, these periodicals illustrate the interaction of industrial technology, the larger reading public, and the emergence of modern advertising that was first exploited in 1883 by Cyrus H. K. Curtis and his *Ladies' Home Journal.*

Improved methods of manufacturing paper, printing, and photoengraving, as well as cheap mailing privileges established by Congress in 1879, inspired Curtis to found a magazine for women who were hungry for a world beyond the kitchen and parlor but who found few opportunities in business and the professions. The *Ladies' Home Journal* sold for only 10 cents (compared with the 35 cent *Atlantic* and *Harper's*) and emphasized women's interests. It was not a feminist publication. On the contrary, editor Edward Bok preached a conservatism that reassured homemakers that their conventional prejudices were proper and right and middle-class people generally that they were a "steadying influence" between "unrest among the lower classes and rottenness among the upper classes."

Somewhat more daring were the new general-interest magazines of the 1890s, such as *McClure's, Munsey's,* and *Cosmopolitan.* They too cost a dime, thus putting them within reach of a large readership. (The *Saturday Evening Post,* which Cyrus Curtis bought in 1897, sold for only a nickel.) Without stooping to sensationalism, they presented readers with a livelier writing style than the established journals and a lavish use of photographs and illustrations.

McClure's and *Munsey's* pioneered the curious but successful economics of selling their publications for less than it cost to print and mail them. They made their profit from building up big subscription lists and selling advertising to manufacturers of consumer goods wanting to reach people who had extra money to

The cover of a 1910 copy of The Ladies' Home Journal.

spend. The subscription list of *McClure's* increased from 8,000 in 1893 to 250,000 in 1895 (with $60,000 in advertising per issue), and that of *Munsey's* grew from 40,000 to 500,000 during the same two years. By 1900, the combined circulation of the four largest magazines totaled 2.5 million per month, more than all American magazines combined only 20 years earlier.

Libraries and Lyceums

The cultural hunger of the middle class was also expressed in the construction of free public libraries. Again, men suddenly grown rich gave millions to build them. Enoch Pratt donated $1 million to Baltimore for its library. Wealthy lawyer and presidential candidate Samuel J. Tilden gave New York City $2 million, and William Newberry founded one of the nation's greatest collections of books and valuable manuscripts in Chicago with a munificent bequest of $4 million. Beginning in 1881, the self-taught Andrew Carnegie

---

POP TUNES

Two musical classics, one now international, were written in 1893. *Happy Birthday to You* began as *Good Morning to You* and was written by Patty Smith Hill, a pioneer of the kindergarten movement who taught at the Teacher's College of Columbia University. Irving Berlin tried to steal it from Hill in 1921, but she sued and won.

The lyrics of *America the Beautiful* were put to the music of a hymn by Katherine Lee Bates, a professor of English at Wellesley College. Congress annually receives petitions demanding that the song, which celebrates American beauty and natural grandeur, replace the militaristic (and unsingable) *Star-Spangled Banner* as the national anthem.

made libraries his principal philanthropy. Before his death in 1919, Carnegie helped found 2,800 free public libraries.

The old lyceum idea of sending lecturers on tour to speak to people who lived far from big cities was revived in 1868 by James Redpath. Offering large fees, Redpath persuaded the most distinguished statesmen, ministers, and professors of the day to deliver highly moral and usually informative addresses in auditoriums and specially erected tents in hundreds of small cities and towns.

Chautauqua

The lyceum movement was a throwback to the antebellum period, when only the very wealthy traveled away from home and the middle class still held fast to the Calvinist beliefs that constant work was the human fate and idleness such as casual travel was a sin. The lyceum scheduled programs in the evening, when the day's toil was done.

The phenomenon that was born in 1874 at Lake Chautauqua in New York's Allegheny Mountains was more characteristic of the new age. The "Chautauquas" originally were eight-week summer training programs for Sunday-school teachers. During the 1890s, however, cheap excursion fares on the trains made it feasible for people who might have little interest in active church work to make the trip for the sake of the cool mountain air and relaxation. To accommodate them, the Chautauqua organizers broadened their program to include lecturers on secular subjects.

By the turn of the century, a middle-class family spending a few weeks at Lake Chautauqua could expect to hear lectures by individuals as prominent as William Jennings Bryan and to watch "magic-lantern" (slide) shows about the Holy Land, Persia, or China presented by professional world travelers. Distinguished professors (including quacks) expounded on their theories about human character, happy marriage, or childrearing. German oom-pah bands, Hawaiian dancers, trained dogs, Italian acrobats, and Indian fire-eaters provided lighter entertainment.

AMERICANS AT PLAY

Promoters founded more than 200 Chautauqua-type resorts, some in the mountains, some at the seaside. Enough people could afford to take a holiday from work that a flourishing tourist economy based on leisure time soon grew up.

Nevertheless, old assumptions died hard. Resort promoters found it advisable to provide at least the appearance of "usefulness" for the vacations they offered.

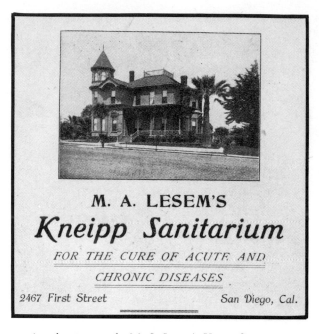

An advertisement for M. S. Lesem's Kneipp Sanitarium in San Diego.

If the middle class trekked to Lake Chautauqua or Lake George in New York and to Long Beach or Atlantic City in New Jersey primarily for rest and relaxation, they could tell others and convince themselves of the cultural and educational aspects of their holiday. They were not just wasting time.

Taking the Cure

A similar conjunction of relaxation and constructive use of time underlay the resorts that were devoted to good health. Owners of mineral springs claimed miraculous powers for their waters. Baths in naturally heated mineral waters or in hot mud were prescribed as nostrums for dozens of afflictions. "Hydropathy," a nineteenth-century medical fad, taught that virtually constant bathing and drinking water improved health. For decades, the wealthy had made prosperous summer resorts of places like Saratoga Springs in New York and White Sulphur Springs in Virginia where "taking the cure" could be done in pleasant surroundings among congenial people. Now thousands of middle-class people followed them, again rationalizing their desire for relaxation by extolling the health benefits of their holiday.

Leisure and the Working Class

Working people could not afford to take off a week for the mountains or seaside. However, leisure came to play a part in their lives, too. Great urban greens, beginning with New York's magnificent Central Park, provided free relief on weekends for the teeming masses of the city's slums. Working people in large cities were also able to enjoy themselves at the commercial "amusement parks" that sprang up as a means by which trolley car companies could exploit their investments to the fullest.

Traction companies made a profit only from those parts of their lines that traversed the crowded parts of the cities and then only on workdays. However, the expense of center-city real estate required them to build their sprawling car barns (storage and repair facilities) outside the city. If they were not required by law to run trolleys on Saturday and Sunday, they still wanted to make constant use of their expensive equipment.

In order to encourage people to ride the trolleys beyond the city centers, the traction companies encouraged the construction of amusement parks "at the end of the line" or, in many cases, built "playlands" themselves. Perhaps the most famous was New York's Coney Island, located on the ocean in Brooklyn. The fare from downtown New York was 5 cents with children riding free. Once there, for a dollar or two, a large family could ride the mechanical amusements, such as George C. Tilyou's Bounding Billows, Barrel

of Love, and Human Roulette Wheel. They could imitate Buffalo Bill at shooting galleries, visit sideshows and exotic "Somali Villages," or simply loll on the beach with a picnic lunch or "a weird-looking sausage muffled up in two halves of a roll"—a hot dog.

These homely pleasures were as exciting to working people as was a trip to Saratoga to the new middle class. Most important, Coney Island, Philadelphia's Willow Grove, Boston's Paragon Park, and Chicago's Cheltenham Beach represented an organized industry, manufacturing, packaging, and merchandising leisure time.

Working-class leisure was more frankly devoted to simple "fun" than were the middle-class Chautauquas. Nevertheless, insistence that even a day at Coney Island was educational and healthful demonstrated the pervasiveness of traditional ideals. Sordid sideshows were touted with moralistic spiels. Knocking over weighted bottles for a prize of a Kewpie doll was defined as honing a valuable skill. Even suggestive dancing by "hoochie-koochie girls" such as Fatima, the sensation of the Chicago World's Fair of 1893 who toured the country for a decade, was described as glimpses into the culture of the Turkish Empire. A writer in prim *Harper's Weekly* approved of the "trolley parks" because they were "great breathing-places for millions of people in the city who get little fresh air at home." In a nation not quite free of its Calvinistic past, every hour must have a purpose.

The First Fitness Craze

Good health was also the rationale for a series of sporting manias that swept over the United States at the turn of the century. To some extent, the concern for bodily health was a contribution of German immigrants, whose *Turnvereins*, clubs devoted to calisthenics, were old-country carry-overs like democratic socialism and beer gardens. However, it was obvious as early as the mid-nineteenth century that the urban population walked less and got less exercise generally than had its farmer forebears. In the first issue of the *Atlantic Monthly* in 1858, Thomas Wentworth Higginson asked, "Who in this community really takes exercise? Even the mechanic confines himself to one set of muscles; the blacksmith acquires strength in his right arm, and the dancing teacher in his left leg. But the professional or businessman, what muscles has he at all?" Only a society with plenty of spare time could take Higginson's question to heart.

Croquet, archery, and tennis, all imported from England, enjoyed a vogue in the 1870s. Roller skating was even more popular. Great rinks like San Francisco's Olympian Club, with 5,000 pairs of skates to rent and a 69,000-square-foot floor, charged inexpensive

New York's Coney Island amusement park in 1896.

fees that were within reach of all but the poorest people. But no sporting fad was so widespread as bicycling.

Bicycles

Briefly during the 1860s, French "dandy horses" were seen on American city streets. These crude wooden vehicles were powered by pushing along the ground. About 1876, the "bone crusher," with its six-foot-high front wheel, made its appearance; by 1881, when the League of American Wheelmen was founded, more than 20,000 intrepid young Americans were devoting their idle hours to pedaling furiously about parks and city streets.

While some praised bicycling as a "health-giving outdoor exercise," moralists condemned the sport for promoting casual relations between young people of the opposite sex. While young men and ladies might leave home for a Sunday ride in proper groups of their own sex, they found it easy to strike up acquaintanceships in parks far from the eyes of parents and chaperone aunts. More than one worried preacher thought that the bicycle was a first step toward moral chaos.

Indeed, it was on the pneumatic tires of the bicycle that many emancipated young women of the 1890s escaped into a refreshing new freedom. The "safety bicycle," which had much the same design as bicycles today, took the risk of broken bones out of the sport. On Sundays, the streets were full of bicycles, and a goodly number carried young women in candy-striped blouses with billowing sleeves, sporty broad-brimmed hats, and full free-flowing skirts.

The Gibson Girl

The "new look" woman of the 1890s took the name of the "Gibson Girl," after the popular magazine illustrator, Charles Dana Gibson, who "invented" her. Gibson's vision of ideal American womanhood charmed the nation from Newport high society to working-class suburbs. The Gibson Girl was by no means a feminist. She took little interest in woman's suffrage or other political issues. Essentially she remained an object of adoration—fine-featured, trim, coy, flirtatious, even seductive.

The Gibson Girl was novel: she was no shrinking violet. She did not faint after the exertion of climbing a staircase. She played croquet, golf, and tennis. She rode a bicycle without chaperones. She was quite able to take care of herself; one of Gibson's favorite themes was the helplessness of young men in the hands of his self-assured young ladies.

Theodore Roosevelt's daughter, Alice, who became a national sweetheart when the popular waltz "Alice

---

WOMEN IN GOVERNMENT

Just as the black cowboy virtually has been forgotten, few historians have noted that women played an important part in government long before they could vote. At the turn of the century, nearly one government worker in three was female. The federal bureaucracy was very much a woman's world.

Blue Gown" was named for her, might have been sculpted by Gibson, and middle-class women adopted her style. Photographs of mill girls leaving textile factories in Massachusetts and of stenographers in offices in New York reveal an air of Gibson Girl self-assurance. The new independence of women was also indicated by the fact that they were marrying later. In 1890, the average age for a woman on her wedding day was 22, two or three years older than it had been in 1860.

Technology and the Lives of Women

Technology played a part in creating the new, active, and independent woman. The telephone, for example, permitted a familiarity with men that was forbidden to "young ladies of breeding" face to face.

Also much noted by people of the time was the fact that Bell's American Telephone and Telegraph Company turned to young ladies to handle the job of connecting callers to each other. The company fired the young men whom it originally had hired because their conversation on the wires was flippant and occasionally obscene; also anticipating the future, they took advantage of anonymity to shock or insult proper middle-class subscribers.

Unlike factory work, which was menial and "dirty," a job as an operator was socially acceptable or middle-class girls. In addition to finding an escape from the plush and velvet prison of the parlor, thousands of women earned an income independent of their parents and husbands. Alexander Graham Bell, unknown to both parties, was a partner with American feminists in their movement to emancipate women.

The Changing Office

Another invention that created jobs for women, and therefore a sense of independence, was the typewriter. Because handwriting was often illegible and potentially costly in business, dozens of inventors had taken a stab at creating a "writing machine." But the first practical "type-writer" was perfected only in 1867 by Christopher Latham Sholes, and first marketed in 1874 by the Remington Arms Company, a firearms manufacturer in search of a product with which to diversify its interests.

Before the use of the machine became standard in business, almost all secretaries were men. They not only wrote letters for their employers, but they ran various errands and sometimes represented the boss. The typewriter made it possible for businessmen to split the secretarial profession into assistant and typist. Men continued to perform the more responsible and better-paid job, rising to a status that would be described as "junior executive" today. The mechanical task of transcribing letters and business records into type went to women.

Like the job of telephone operator, that of typist did not require the higher education that was available only to women determined to the point of eccentricity. It was not heavy labor, an important consideration in an age that defined respectable young ladies as "delicate." And the job did not usually involve much responsibility, which nineteenth-century men were disinclined to allot to women. By 1890, 15 percent of clerical workers were female, by 1900 almost 25 percent.

SPORTS

The turn of the century was also a golden age of organized sport. Although football (with somewhat different rules from today's) was a game played almost exclusively by university students, people of all social classes avidly followed the fortunes of the nearest "Ivy League" team. Basketball, which was invented in Springfield, Massachusetts, in 1891 by Dr. James Naismith, a physical-education instructor who was looking for a sport that his students could play during the rigorous New England winter, was still in its infancy. The spectator sports that obsessed Americans were baseball and boxing. Both had evolved from traditional folk recreations, but by the end of the nineteenth century, both already were organized as money-making enterprises.

The National Pastime

Baseball developed out of two ancient children's games, rounders and town ball, which had been brought to the United States by English immigrants.

The typewriter created secretarial jobs for women in large business offices where formerly all employees were male.

According to Albert G. Spalding, a professional pitcher for clubs in Boston and Chicago, systematic rules for the sport were first drafted by Abner Doubleday of Cooperstown, New York, in 1839. The story was poppycock. There is no evidence Doubleday invested a minute thinking about the game. Spalding devised the tale to promote the sporting goods manufacturing company that made him a millionaire. In reality, baseball "just growed"; there was little agreement on a number of important rules until after the Civil War.

While many towns organized teams to play neighbors on special occasions, the professional sport emerged from upper-class baseball "clubs" such as the New York Knickerbockers. Soon concerned more with defeating rivals than with enjoying an afternoon of exercise, the clubs began to hire (at first secretly and despite noisy protest) long-hitting and fast-pitching working-class boys to wear their colors ("ringers"). In 1869, the first openly professional team, the Cincinnati Red Stockings, went on tour and defeated all comers.

When people proved willing by the thousands to pay admission fees to see the difficult game played well, businessmen in most eastern and midwestern cities, feeling exploited, tried to organize a cooperative association. The National League was founded in 1876, the American League, "the junior circuit," dates from 1901. The first World Series between the champions of both leagues was played in 1903.

Teams were focal points of civic pride. Important games often received more attention in the newspapers than did foreign wars. After Brooklyn became a borough of New York City in 1898, its baseball team, the Trolley Dodgers, became the former city's sole symbol of an independent identity, its antidote to the Brooklyn Bridge.

Boxing and Society

Watching a fight between two strong men may be humanity's oldest diversion. In 1867, because boxing was becoming a "manly art" practiced by the upper class, an English sportsman, the Marquis of Queensberry, devised a code of rules that was quickly adopted throughout Europe and the United States. The Queensberry rules hardly made for a gentle sport. One read that "all attempts to inflict injury by gouging or tearing the flesh with the fingers or nails and biting shall be deemed foul."

As with baseball, the opportunities to make money from paid admissions encouraged promoters to search out popular heroes. The first to win a national reputation was a burly Boston Irishman named John L. Sullivan, who started out by traveling the country and offering $50 and later $1,000 to anyone who could last four rounds with him. Between 1882 and 1892, "the Boston Strong Boy" bloodied one challenger after another, personally collecting as much as $20,000 a fight and making much more for the entrepreneurs who organized his bouts.

The first World Series in 1903 was played between Boston and Pittsburgh.

CONSUMER GOODS

By 1909, thirteen of the largest industrial firms in the United States were involved in the production of consumer goods, including tobacco, whiskey, meat, petroleum products, and tires for automobiles.

The crowds that watched great championship bouts and most baseball games included comparatively few working people. However, they followed their heroes in the new sports pages of the newspapers, which, as with baseball, devoted column after column to important fights. Because Sullivan and his successor as heavyweight champion, Gentleman Jim Corbett, were Irish, they became objects of ethnic pride. So entangled in the culture did the sport become that when a black boxer rose to the top, he caused an anxiety that reached into the halls of Congress.

Jack Johnson

Blacks played baseball with whites during the earliest professional years. The catcher on a team that toured the world in the 1880s was black. However, the same wave of racism that initiated the Jim Crow Laws in the 1890s led to the segregation of the sport. A first baseman from Iowa, Adrian "Cap" Anson, led the fight to keep black players out of the two major leagues.

Black boxers did fight whites and, in 1908, one of them, Jack Johnson won the heavyweight crown and proceeded to batter every challenger who stepped forth. Such a feat by a black man rankled many white Americans. Johnson aggravated the hatred for him by gleefully insulting every "great white hope" who challenged him. A tragically indiscreet man, he flaunted his white mistresses at a time when the color line was being drawn across practically every American institution.

Southern states, which had been the most hospitable to professional prize fights, forbade Johnson to fight within their borders. Politicians raved at every Johnson victory and gaudy public appearance. Congress actually passed a law that prohibited the interstate shipment of a film of Johnson's victory over former champion Jim Jeffries in Reno in 1910. Finally, in 1912, racism defeated him not in the ring but through an indictment under the Mann Act, which forbade "transporting women" across state lines "for immoral purposes." (Johnson had taken his common-law wife to another state.)

Johnson fled to Europe, but was homesick and agreed to fight the white boxer Jess Willard in Havana in 1915. He lost, and it was widely believed that he threw the match as part of a deal with the Justice Department by which he could reenter the United States without fear of arrest. A famous photograph of the knockout shows Johnson on his back, apparently relaxed and unhurt, and shielding his eyes from the Caribbean sun. Jack may have had his last jibe at good-old-days America, but the days were good enough for the white middle class that few people noticed.

For Further Reading

Overviews of the era are Vincent P. DeSantis, *The Shaping of Modern America, 1877–1916* (1973); Ray Ginger, *The Age of Excess* (1965); William L. O'Neill, *The Progressive Years: America Comes of Age* (1975); and Robert H. Wiebe, *The Search for Order, 1880–1920* (1967). On general social and cultural history, students should look at Frederick Lewis Allen, *The Big Change* (1952); Van Wyck Brooks, *The Confident Years, 1885–1915* (1952); and the classic Mark Sullivan, *Our Times* (1926–35).

Studies of special topics include G. W. Chessman, *Governor Theodore Roosevelt* (1965); Carl M. Degler, *At Odds: Women in the Family in America from the Revolution to the Present* (1980); Ann Douglas, *The Feminization of American Culture* (1977); Foster R. Dulles, *America Learns to Play* (1940); Ray Ginger, *Altgeld's America: The Lincoln Ideal and Changing Realities* (1958); Otis L. Graham, Jr., *The Great Campaigns: Reform and War in America, 1900–1928* (1971); Jack D. Kirby, *Darkness at the Dawning: Race and Reform in the Progressive South* (1972); J. R. Krout, *Annals of American Sport* (1924); Margaret Leech, *In the Days of McKinley* (1959); Henry F. May, *The End of American Innocence* (1959); H. Wayne Morgan, *William McKinley and His America* (1963); George E. Mowry, *The Era of Theodore Roosevelt* (1958); Steven A. Reiss, *Touching Base: Professional Baseball and American Culture in the Progressive Era* (1980).

Three fine books about "Teddy" are John M. Blum, *The Republican Roosevelt* (1954); W. H. Harbaugh, *Power and Responsibility: The Life and Times of Theodore Roosevelt* (1961); and, best of all, Henry F. Pringle, *Theodore Roosevelt* (1931).

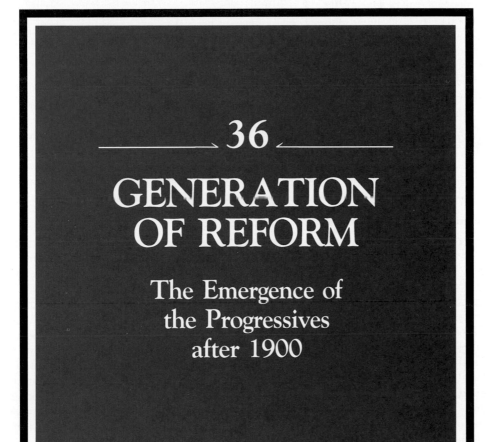

36

GENERATION OF REFORM

The Emergence of the Progressives after 1900

In 1787, when his contemporaries were launching the Constitution, in part because they feared social turmoil, Thomas Jefferson was in France. The Bastille had not yet been attacked, Paris was peaceful, and Jefferson still had plenty of the revolutionary fire in his blood. During this period, he wrote several letters in which he said that periodic revolution was essential to the health of a free society. "A little rebellion, now and then, is a good thing," he wrote to James Madison, "as necessary in the political world as storms in the physical." To another friend a few months later he added, "The tree of liberty must be refreshed from time to time with the blood of patriots and tyrants."

Does political progress depend upon violent uprising by the oppressed masses, or the fear of revolution among society's leaders? The history of the United States seems to say not. During a 200-year epoch of world history that has been marked by just such instability and tumult, only once has the United States been shaken by a revolution, the secession of the southern states in 1861; and it was neither progressive nor successful.

A mechanism for peaceable change was, of course, written into the Constitution in the form of the amendment process. The strictest adherence to the basic instrument of government in America means (or should mean) a readiness to change. More important, periodically in American history—in rather predictable cycles, some historians think—people whose means and privileges put them far above the masses have themselves risen up, quite without violence, to rid themselves of political and social abuses, pruning the deadwood and disease from Jefferson's tree of liberty. Such a welling of the reform spirit was the "Progressive Era," spanning roughly the first two decades of the twentieth century.

THE PROGRESSIVES

The far-reaching reforms that the people calling themselves "progressives" demanded and, for the most part, put into effect after 1900 were not original with the new century. The movement inherited impulses and ideas from the Mugwumps, the Social Gospel, the half-century-old women's movement, urban social workers, Populism, and even the sundry varieties of socialism expounded in the late nineteenth century.

What was new about the progressives was that they rallied a generation of Americans to most of their causes, while their predecessors appealed to relatively small groups and antagonized (or simply did not interest) the majority.

Middle America

Their chief appeal, however, and the source of almost all progressive leaders, was the new middle class of small businessmen and professionals: lawyers, physicians, ministers, teachers, journalists, social workers, and the wives and daughters of the middle classes whose first reform was personal—to break free of the nursery, parlor, and chapel. Few progressive leaders came from the industrial and financial elite, and few rose from the masses of laboring people and poor farmers. The progressive movement was middle class in its heart and head.

PROGRESSIVES

It makes a difference whether the word *progressive* is written with a lowercase *p* or a capital *P*. In the lowercase, *progressive* refers to the broad impulse that motivated all the many kinds of reformers during the first couple of decades of the twentieth century. A *Progressive*, however, was a member of the Progressive party, an offshoot of the Republican party, which was organized in 1912. Because there were progressives in the Democratic party—and some historians consider the Socialist party to be part of the movement—not every progressive, in a word, was a Progressive.

The progressives were acutely aware that they were "in between." Eternally knocking about in the back of the progressive mind were the assumptions that what was best about America was its middle class—people not so rich as to endanger the republic, not so poor as to have no stake in it. Indeed, many progressives felt that the middle class was threatened by both plutocrats from above and the potentially dangerous mob from below.

Thus, virtually all progressives were committed to destroying the immense power of the great corporations and banks or, at least, to control the manner in which that power was used. The progressives intended that the Rockefellers and the Morgans behave in ways that were compatible with the good of society, as the progressives defined it.

While the progressives were concerned with the material and moral welfare of those below them on the social ladder, they also feared the masses. In the cities, progressive reformers often voiced concern that the slums were tinderboxes of anger, ready to explode in destructive anarchy. In the Midwest and West, most progressive leaders had been staunch anti-Populists because they saw the farmers' rebellion as an upheaval of the impoverished, uneducated, and unwashed. William Allen White, a leading progressive journalist, first made his name as the author of a scathing anti-Populist manifesto called "What's the Matter with Kansas?" Years later, a little sheepishly, White explained that he had written the piece not because an idea had occurred to him in his study, but because he had been jostled on a street corner in Emporia, Kansas, by "lazy, greasy fizzles" whose crudeness and vulgarity had offended him.

Many progressives saw clearly the relationship between the power of great wealth and dangerous restiveness among the exploited poor. Early in the century, Woodrow Wilson of New Jersey put the thought in a curious way when he blamed the automobile, then a plaything of the rich, for the spread of socialism.

Driving their cars around recklessly, frightening horses, killing chickens, and scattering ordinary folks, Wilson wrote, the rich were bringing their arrogance to every country road in the nation.

Righteous Optimists

Louis Brandeis, a Louisville, Kentucky, lawyer who helped design the Democratic party's reform program, was Jewish. Alfred E. Smith and Robert F. Wagner, progressive politicians in New York state, were Irish and German, respectively, and Roman Catholic in religion. W. E. B. Du Bois, who helped found the National Association for the Advancement of Colored People, was black. But they were exceptions. Most progressive leaders were "WASPs," White Anglo-Saxon Protestants from "old stock," people whose American roots ran through several generations.

Most were urban in background, brought up in cities or towns. Even those progressive politicians who represented rural states, such as Robert M. La Follette of Wisconsin and George Norris of Nebraska, had grown up in small towns. As boys, they had rubbed elbows

The Progressives came from the new middle class such as the Drummond family, posing on the back porch of their New York home.

with farmers, but they had not walked behind plows or milled about anxiously next to their wagons as agents weighed, graded, and put a price on the year's crop. Indeed, like William Allen White, LaFollette had been an anti-Populist during the 1890s.

Progressive political leaders inclined to be moralistic to the point of self-righteousness, ever searching for the absolute right and absolute wrong in every political disagreement. California's Hiram Johnson irked even his strongest supporters with his clenched-teeth sanctimony. Robert M. La Follette did not know what a sense of humor was. To "Fighting Bob," life was one long crusade for what was right. Theodore Roosevelt described the beginning of an election campaign in biblical terms: "We stand at Armageddon and do battle for the Lord." Woodrow Wilson, stern of visage in wing collar and pince-nez, eventually destroyed himself because he would not compromise with his critics in order to save the most important cause of his life.

And yet, while their noses were ever to the wind for hint of foul odors, the progressives believed that progress was indeed possible because human nature was intrinsically good. "Our shamelessness is superficial," wrote Lincoln Steffens, "beneath it lies a pride which, being real, may save us yet." They were optimists.

A Coat of Many Colors

Almost all progressives believed that a powerful government, active in taking the initiative and holding it, was the key to improving America. In this statism they were rather unlike earlier reformers who were as apt to consider government a part of the problem. Jane Addams, whose main work concerned helping the urban poor, said that private institutions like her Hull House were "today inadequate to deal with the vast numbers of the city's disinherited."

As for the corporations that threatened American ideas, the progressives believed that a powerful state was the only agency that could bring them to heel. The goals were still Jeffersonian, Herbert Croly wrote in *The Promise of American Life* (published in 1909), the welfare of the many determined by the will of the

---

REFORM

What is reform? One dictionary defines it as "to change into a new and improved condition; removal of faults or abuses so as to restore to a former good state, or bring from bad to good." In the context of American history, *reform* has also come to mean peaceful, usually gradual change, as opposed to violent and sudden change, which Americans define as *revolution*.

---

many. But, to Croly, the old Jeffersonian principle of "the less government the better" had been rendered obsolete by the magnitude of social problems and the vast power of the plutocrats. Croly would have "Jeffersonian ends" served by "Hamiltonian means," the power of the state.

Beyond a committment to active government, progressivism was variety, a frame of mind rather than a single coherent movement. There were Democratic progressives and Republican progressives. In 1912, breakaway Republicans formed the Progressive party. Some progressives considered some socialists to be kin.

On specific issues, progressives differed among themselves as radically as they differed from the "Old Guard" against whom they battled. For example, while many progressives believed that labor unions had the right to exist and fight for the betterment of their members, others opposed unions for the same reason that they disliked powerful corporations: organized special-interest groups were at odds with the American ideal of serving the good of the whole. On one occasion, a few leaders of the National American Woman Suffrage Association said that women should work as strikebreakers if by so doing they could win jobs currently held by men.

Some progressives were ultranationalists. Others clung to a humanism that embraced all people of all countries. Some progressives were expansionists. Senator Albert J. Beveridge of Indiana saw no conflict in calling for broadening democracy at home while urging the United States to rule colonies abroad without regard to the will of their inhabitants. Others were anti-imperialists, even isolationists who looked on Europe as a fount of corruption.

Progressives disagreed on the subject of laws regulating child labor. By 1907, about two-thirds of the states that were governed or influenced by progressives forbade the employment of children under 14 years of age. However, when progressives in Congress passed a federal child-labor law in 1916, the progressive President Woodrow Wilson expressed grave doubts before signing it. Wilson worried that to forbid children to

work infringed on their rights as citizens. This was essentially the same reasoning that was offered by the conservative Supreme Court in *Hammer* vs. *Dagenhart* (1918), which struck down the law.

Race

Many, perhaps most, progressives could not imagine blacks as citizens participating fully and actively in American society. Some were frank racists, especially the southern progressives: Governor James K. Vardaman of Mississippi, Governor Jeff Davis of Arkansas, Senator Benjamin "Pitchfork Ben" Tillman of South Carolina. As president of Princeton University, Woodrow Wilson helped to segregate the town of Princeton on racial lines, including even water fountains. As president of the United States, he approved the introduction of "Jim Crow" practices in the federal government. Other progressives tolerated discrimination against blacks out of habit or because they feared the consequences of black equality with 45 percent of the black population being illiterate.

Other progressives regarded racial prejudice and discrimination as among the worst evils afflicting America. Journalist Ray Stannard Baker wrote a scathing and moving exposé of racial segregation in a series of articles entitled "Following the Color Line." In 1910, white progressives, including Jane Addams, joined with the black Niagara Movement to form the National Association for the Advancement of Colored People. Except for his color, W. E. B. Du Bois, the guiding spirit of the Niagara Movement, was the progressive *par excellence*: genteel, middle class, university educated, and devoted to the idea that an elite should govern. Du Bois believed that a "talented tenth" of the black population would lead the race to civil equality in the United States.

Forebears

So diverse a movement had a mixed ancestry. From the Populists' Omaha Platform, the progressives took

---

FILTHY LUCRE

Progressives were morally appalled by money grubbing. When he was president, Theodore Roosevelt expressed this sentiment when he tried to have "In God We Trust" deleted from American coins. "It seems to me," he wrote, "eminently unwise to cheapen such a motto by use on coins, just as it would be to cheapen it by use on postage stamps and advertisements." A few coins were struck without "In God We Trust," but Congress, failing to appreciate T.R.'s point, restored it.

a good deal. Indeed, as William Allen White remarked, the progressives "caught the Populists in swimming and stole all of their clothing except the frayed underdrawers of free silver." They called for the direct election of senators and a graduated income tax that would hit the wealthy harder than the poor and middle classes (both enacted by constitutional amendment in 1913). Progressives also favored the initiative, referendum, and recall. Some, but by no means all, progressives wanted to nationalize the railways and banks. Many more believed that local public utilities such as water, gas, and electric companies, being natural monopolies, should be government-owned.

The progressives also harkened back to the "good government" idealism of the Liberal Republicans and Mugwumps. Indeed, in the progressives' intense moralism, their compulsion to stamp out personal sin as well as social and political evils, they sometimes sounded like the evangelical preachers of the early nineteenth century.

In exalting expertise and efficiency, and in their belief that a new social order must be devised to replace the disorder of the late nineteenth century, the progressives owed a debt to people whom they considered their enemies. Marcus A. Hanna, described as a conservative when he died in 1904, had spent half his life preaching collaboration between capital and labor as an alternative to class conflict.

Frederick W. Taylor, the inventor of "scientific management," was rarely described as a progressive and personally took little interest in politics. Nevertheless, in his conviction that the engineer's approach to solving problems could be fruitfully applied to human behavior, he was a forebear of the progressive movement. The progressives believed that society could be engineered as readily as Taylor engineered machine tools and the way a man wielded a shovel.

PROGRESSIVISM DOWN HOME

Progressivism originated in the cities. In the last years of the nineteenth century, capitalizing on widespread disgust with the corruption that had become endemic to municipal government, a number of reform mayors swept into office and won national notoriety. They were not, as had been their predecessors in the 1870s and 1880s, easily ousted after a year or two.

Good Government

One of the first of the city reformers was Hazen S. Pingree, a shoe manufacturer who was elected mayor of Detroit in 1890. Pingree spent seven years battling the corrupt alliance between the owners of the city's public utilities and Detroit city councilmen. In nearby Toledo, Ohio, another businessman, Samuel M. Jones, ran for mayor as a reformer in 1897. Professional politicians mocked him as an addleheaded eccentric because he plastered the walls of his factory with the golden rule and other homilies. But Jones also treated his employees fairly, including sharing profits with them. As "Golden Rule" Jones, he took control of Toledo and proved to be a no-nonsense administrator. Within two years, he rid Toledo's city hall of graft.

Another progressive mayor from Ohio was Cleveland's Thomas L. Johnson. A former single-taxer, Johnson was elected in 1901. Not only did he clean up a dirty government, but he actively supported woman's suffrage, reformed the juvenile courts, took over public utilities from avaricious owners, and put democracy to work by presiding over open "town meetings" at which citizens could make known their grievances and suggestions.

Lincoln Steffens, a staff writer for *McClure's*, called Cleveland "the best-governed city in the United States." Steffens was the expert; in 1903, he authored a sensational series of articles for *McClure's* called

Journalist Lincoln Steffens, pioneer of investigative journalism, exposed corrupt practices in America's big cities.

"The Shame of the Cities." Researching his subject carefully in the country's major cities, he named grafters, exposed corrupt connections between elected officials and dishonest businessmen, and demonstrated how ordinary people suffered from corrupt government in the quality of their daily lives.

Steffens's exposés hastened the movement for city reform. Joseph W. Folk of St. Louis, whose tips put Steffens on the story, was able to indict more than 30 politicians and prominent Missouri businessmen for bribery and perjury as a result of the outcry that greeted "The Shame of the Cities." Hundreds of reform mayors elected after 1904 owed their success to the solemn, bearded journalist.

The Muckrakers

No single force was more important in spreading the gospel of progressivism than the mass-circulation magazines. Already well established by the turn of the century thanks to their cheap price and lively style, journals such as *McClure's*, the *Arena*, *Collier's*, *Cosmopolitan*, and *Everybody's* became even more successful when their editors discovered the popular appetite for the journalism of exposure.

The discovery was almost accidental. Samuel S. McClure himself had no particular interest in reform.

Progressive journalist Ida Tarbell. Standard Oil executives assumed she was a gullible female reporter, but learned otherwise after she attacked John D. Rockefeller's business practices in McClure's magazine.

Selling magazines and advertising in them was his business, hobby, and obsession. When he hired Ida M. Tarbell and Lincoln Steffens at generous salaries, he did so not because they were reformers, but because they wrote well. Indeed, Tarbell began the "History of the Standard Oil Company," exposing John D. Rockefeller's dubious business practices because of a personal grudge: Rockefeller had ruined her father. Steffens was looking for a story, any story, when he stumbled upon the same of the cities.

But when Tarbell's and Steffens's sensational exposés caused circulation to soar, McClure and other editors were hooked. The mass-circulation magazines soon brimmed with sensational revelations about corruption in government, chicanery in business, social evils like child labor and prostitution, and other subjects that lent themselves to indignant, excited treatment. In addition to his series on racial segregation, Ray Stannard Baker dissected the operations of the great railroads. John Spargo, an English-born socialist, discussed child labor in "The Bitter Cry of the Children." David Graham Phillips, who later succeeded as a novelist dealing with social themes, revealed that the United States Senate, elected by state legislatures, had become a kind of "millionaires' club."

Theodore Roosevelt called the new journalists "muckrakers" after an unattractive character in John Bunyan's religious classic of 1678, *Pilgrim's Progress.* The writers were so busy raking through the muck of American society, he said, that they failed to look up and see its glories in the stars and the crown that could be their own.

He had a point, especially when after a few years the quality of the journalism of exposure deteriorated into sloppy research and wild, ill-founded accusations made for the sake of attracting attention. During the first decade of the century, no fewer than 2,000 articles and books of exposure were published. Inevitably, the conscientious muckrakers ran out of solid material, and muckraking as a profession attracted incompetent hacks and sensation-mongers.

But the dirt could be real enough, and the early reform journalists were as determined to stick to the facts as to arouse their readers' indignation. Their work served to transmit the reform impulse from one end of the country to the other. The ten leading muckraking journals had a combined circulation of 3 million. Because the magazines were also read in public libraries and barbershops, and just passed around, the readership was many times larger.

In the Jungle with Upton Sinclair

Upton Sinclair was probably the most influential muckraker of all. An obscure young socialist, in 1906 he wrote a serialized novel, *The Jungle*, about how ethnic prejudice and economic exploitation in Chicago turned a Lithuanian immigrant into a revolutionary determined to smash the capitalist system. The message did not particularly appeal to the editors of the mass-circulation magazines, and Sinclair turned to a Socialist-party weekly newspaper, the *Appeal to Reason*, to run it. Even the *Appeal* had a big readership; one issue sold over 1 million copies. In its pages, *The Jungle* was a mighty success. As a book, it sold 100,000 copies, even reaching the desk of President Theodore Roosevelt.

Sinclair's book may have converted a few of its readers to socialism (although its literary quality decayed rapidly in the final chapters when the protagonist takes up the red flag). However, the passages that made it a best seller were those that luridly described the conditions under which meat was processed in Chicago slaughterhouses. *The Jungle* publicized well-documented tales of rats ground up into sausage, workers with tuberculosis coughing on the meat they packed, and filth at every point along the disassembly line.

"I aimed at the nation's heart," Sinclair later said, "and hit it in the stomach." He meant that within months of the publication of *The Jungle*, a federal meat-inspection bill that had been languishing in Congress was rushed through under public pressure and promptly signed by President Roosevelt. It and a second Pure Food and Drug Act, which forbade food processors to use dangerous adulterants (the pet project of a chemist in the Agriculture Department, Dr. Harvey W. Wiley), expanded government power in a way that had been inconceivable a few years earlier.

Efficiency and Democracy

In 1908, Staunton, Virginia introduced a favorite progressive municipal reform, the city-manager system of government. The office of mayor was abolished. Instead, voters elected a city council, which then hired a nonpolitical, professionally trained administrator to serve as city manager. Proponents of the city manager system reasoned that democracy was protected by the people's control of the council; and because the daily operations of the city were supervised by an executive who was free of political influence, they would be carried out without regard to special interests. By 1915, over 400 mostly medium-sized cities had followed Staunton's example.

The "Oregon system" was the brainchild of one of the first progressives to make an impact at the state level. William S. U'ren, a former Populist and single-taxer, believed that the remedy for corruption in government was simple: more democracy. The trouble lay in the ability of efficient, well-organized, and wealthy special interests to thwart the good intentions of the people. Time after time, U'ren pointed out, elected officials handily forgot their campaign promises and worked closely with the corporations to pass bad laws or defeat good ones.

In 1902, U'ren persuaded the Oregon legislature to adopt the initiative, recall, and referendum. The Oregon system also included the first primary law. It took the power to nominate candidates for public office away from the bosses and gave it to the voters. Finally, U'ren led the national movement to choose United States senators by popular vote rather than in the state legislatures.

U'ren lived to the ripe old age of 90, long enough to see 20 states adopt the initiative and 30, the referendum. A number of progressive states also instituted primaries of one kind or another, but until the 1970s, the primary was a less popular idea. In the South, the "white primary," by which Democratic party candidates were chosen, was used in the interests of racism: since most whites were Democrats, the primary was the contest that counted; and because the primary was an election within a private organization, blacks could be legally excluded from it.

"Fighting Bob"

The career of Wisconsin's "Fighting Bob" La Follette is almost a history of progressivism in itself. Born in 1855, he studied law and served three terms as a Republican in Congress before 1890. He showed few signs of the crusader's itch until a prominent Republican offered him a bribe to fix the verdict in a trial. La Follette flew into a rage at the shameless audacity of the suggestion, and he never quite calmed down for the rest of his life.

In 1900, he ran for governor in defiance of the Republican organization, attacking the railroad and lumber interests that dominated the state. He promised to devote the resources of the government to the service of the people and his timing was perfect. A state that recently had rebuffed the Populists was ready for reform, and La Follette was elected. As governor, he pushed through a comprehensive system of regulatory laws that required every business that touched the public interest to conform to clear-cut rules and submit to close inspection of its operations.

The "Wisconsin Idea"

La Follette went beyond the negative, or regulatory, powers of government to create agencies that provided positive services for the people. La Follette's "Wisconsin idea" held that in the complex modern world,

Robert La Follette speaking to a crowd in Cumberland, Wisconsin, in 1897.

people and government needed experts to work on their behalf. A railroad baron could not be kept on a leash unless the government had the support of knowledgeable specialists who were as canny as the railroad men. Insurance premiums could not be held at reasonable levels unless the state was able to determine what profit was just and what was rapacious. The government could not intervene to determine what was fair in a labor dispute unless it had the help of the labor experts and economists.

La Follette formed a close and mutually beneficial relationship with the University of Wisconsin. His organization generously supported the institution, making it one of the nation's great universities at a

time when most state-supported schools were little more than poorly funded agricultural colleges. In return, distinguished professors like Richard Ely, Selig Perlman, and John Rogers Commons put their expertise at La Follette's disposal. The law school helped build up the first legislative reference library in the United States so that assemblymen would no longer have to rely on lobbyists to draft their laws.

The university's School of Agriculture not only taught future farmers, but carried out research programs that addressed problems faced daily in Wisconsin's fields and barns. La Follette even made use of the football team. When enemies hinted there would be trouble if he spoke at a political rally, he showed up in the company of Wisconsin's burly linemen, who folded their arms and surrounded the platform. There was no trouble.

Perhaps La Follette's most original contribution to progressivism was his application of machine methods to the cause of reform. He was idealistic. But he was not naive. In order to ensure that his reforms would not be reversed, he built an organization that was more finely integrated than Boss Tweed's. Party workers in every precinct got out the vote, and if they did not violate La Follette's exacting demands for honesty in public office, they were rewarded with government patronage.

In 1906, La Follette took his crusade to Washington as a United States senator. He held that office until his death in 1925, and made several unsuccessful tries at winning the presidency. In Wisconsin and elsewhere he was loved as few politicians have been. He was "Fighting Bob," incorruptible and unyielding in what he regarded as right. La Follette's thick, neatly cropped head of brown hair combed straight back, which turned snow white with years, waved wildly during his passionate speeches. He looked like an Old Testament prophet, and, in a way, La Follette devoted his life to saving the soul of American society, as Jeremiah had done for Israel.

Progressives in Other States

In New York state, Charles Evans Hughes came to prominence as a result of his investigation into public utilities and insurance companies. Tall, erect, dignified, with a smartly trimmed beard such as was going out of fashion at the turn of the century, he lacked the charisma of La Follette and other progressives. If they were humorless in their intensity, Hughes was "a cold-blooded creature" (in the words of the hot-blooded Theodore Roosevelt). But he was unshakably honest as governor of New York between 1906 and 1910.

ATTEMPTED MURDER?

In late May 1908, Robert La Follette led a filibuster against a financial bill of which he disapproved. He spoke for nearly seventeen hours before giving up. Through much of this time, La Follette sipped a tonic of milk and raw eggs prepared in the Senate dining room. After he had been taken violently ill on the floor, it was discovered that there was enough ptomaine in the mixture to kill a man. Because no one else suffered from eating in the Senate dining room that day, many assumed that La Follette's enemies had tried to kill him.

William E. Borah was elected to the Senate from Idaho in 1906, but not as a progressive. On the contrary, his career in politics had been characterized by a close and compliant relationship with the mining and ranching interests that ran the state. Once in the Senate, however, Borah usually voted with the growing progressive bloc. This record and his isolationism—like many westerners, Borah believed that the United States would be corrupted by close association with foreign powers—guaranteed his reelection until he died in office in 1940.

Progressivism in California

Hiram Johnson of California came to progressivism by much the same path as had La Follette. A prim, tight-lipped trial lawyer from Sacramento, Johnson won fame by taking over the prosecution of the corrupt political machine of Boss Abe Ruef in San Francisco.

At first it appeared to be an ordinary graft case. Ruef and his allies, Mayor Eugene E. Schmitz and a majority of the Board of Aldermen won office by appealing to ethnic voters. They collected payoffs from brothels, gambling dens, and thieves in return for running a wide-open city. In the wake of the great San Francisco earthquake and fire of 1906, Ruef set up a system by which those who wished to profit from the rebuilding had to clear their plans with him. Scarcely a street could be paved or a cable-car line laid out until money changed hands. On one occasion, Ruef pocketed $250,000, of which he kept one-quarter, gave one-quarter to Schmitz, and distributed the remainder among the aldermen whose votes were needed to authorize public works. Like other city bosses, Ruef bought and sold judges in lawsuits.

But Johnson discovered that Ruef not only was associated with vice and petty graft, but was intimately allied with the most powerful corporation in the state, the Southern Pacific Railroad. The distinguished and ostensibly upright directors of the Southern Pacific, men whom Johnson had admired, were tangled in a web that stretched to include profiting from the misfortune of the wretched syphilitic whores on the city's notorious Barbary Coast.

The never equanimous Johnson was transformed into "a volcano in perpetual eruption, belching fire and smoke." In 1910, he won the governorship on the slogan, "Kick the Southern Pacific out of politics." Never again would he assume that great wealth and a varnish of propriety indicated a decent man. Indeed, his sense of personal rectitude was so great that it cost him a chance to be president. In 1920, Republican party bosses such as Johnson loathed asked him to run as vice president in order to balance the conservative presidential nominee, Warren G. Harding. Johnson

H   O   W   T   H   E   Y   L   I   V   E   D

THE CASUAL WORKERS

"Home, a permanent place of abode, respect of others, the decencies of right living, have neither meaning nor attraction for them," wrote the editor of the *Record*, a newspaper in the northern California farm town of Chico. He was talking about people who were familiar to everyone who lived west of the Mississippi in 1910—the hobos, otherwise known as migrant workers or casual laborers.

Most of these wandering workers were men who had no homes, families, or ties to the sort of proprieties to which the editor referred. They were essential to the economic life of the western states. They brought in the wheat from the Mississippi to Oregon; picked the fruit in the Pacific states from Washington to the Mexican border; and manned the construction crews on projects far from any town, such as the aqueduct that rerouted the Owens River 300 miles across the Mojave Desert to the thirsty metropolis of Los Angeles in southern California. They worked in canneries and lumber mills, and those with the skills were the lumberjacks in the great redwood, spruce, and Douglas fir forests of the Northwest.

Almost all this work was seasonal or temporary; a mammoth construction job like the aqueduct took years to complete, but the day came when hands were no longer needed. Therefore, the kind of worker who made his way to a job at his own expense and disappeared when the job was done was precisely the kind of worker who was called for.

Of course, the casual worker did not disappear into thin air. When there was no work, as in winter, or when he did not feel like working, the casual laborer headed for a town in which he could expect to find a "main stem" or "skid row" on which were located cheap restaurants, cheap saloons, cheap hotels, pawnshops, second-hand clothing stores, brothels, and "missions" run by evangelical religious groups.

Here was a big part of their problem. On the main stem, the hobos rubbed elbows with derelicts, and it took a practiced eye to distinguish between the two groups. The casual workers knew the difference. Whereas "tramps" wandered but did not work and "bums" did little but drink, hobos were self-sufficient workers. They held tough jobs, albeit only as long as they chose to work, and when they were down on their luck, they chopped wood, hauled water, or mowed a lawn in return for a meal. They did not beg for handouts. Hobos explained to dozens of investigators that they could usually be identified by the bedroll or "bindle" that they carried. Most of the jobs they took required them to furnish their own bedding, whereas tramps and bums had little use for it. One of the terms used to describe casual workers was "bindle-stiff."

Nevertheless, the hobos looked much the same as tramps and bums. When they were traveling by freight train (which was illegal but generally tolerated), they were dirty, in clothing just a few notches above rags, unshaven, and ripe to the nose. And they patently did not live as the "respectable classes" believed people should live. The "hobo jungle" on the outskirts of every railroad town, a camp where casual workers gathered to eat and sleep while waiting for a train, was a dangerous and forbidden place in the imagination of children and many adults as well.

The hobos believed that they were the builders of the West. "It is we," one of their songs had it, who

> Dug the mines and built the workshops, endless miles of railroad laid.
> Now we stand outcast and starving, 'mid the wonders we have made. . . .

A hobo poem caught the same sense of resentment that society should scorn them:

> He built the road,
> With others of his class, he built the road,
> Now o'er it many a mile he packs his load,
> Chasing a job, spurred on by hunger's goad,
> He walks and walks, and wonders why
> In Hell he built the road.

The casual worker considered himself to be the last frontiersman—freewheeling, independent, not "afraid of his job" but quick to quit when something about it displeased him. In other words, he was the kind of American who, already by the turn of the century, was enshrined in nostalgic myth as the best kind of American.

At the very least they were not afraid to stand up for their rights when they believed that those rights were threatened. In 1894, when Jacob Coxey led his march of the unemployed from Ohio to Washington, the "petition in boots" demanding federal action to create jobs during the depression, a contingent of western casual laborers called "Kelley's Army" set off from Oakland, traveling to Washington by freight trains that they virtually commandeered.

After the turn of the century, western migrant workers turned in large numbers to the Industrial Workers of the World to voice their grievances. Between 1909 and 1914, they fought a number of "free-speech fights" in such western towns as Missoula, Spokane, and San Diego. These actions, directed against laws that forbade street speaking on the main stem, anticipated the protest tactic of nonviolent civil disobedience that later was employed by Mohandas Gandhi in India and Martin Luther King, Jr., in the United States. By deliberately disobeying the obnoxious laws but peacefully submitting to arrest, the free speechers put the burden of law enforcement on the shoulders of the authorities.

Seasonal workers and hobos used trains as a free form of transportation.

They were happy to be arrested. As long as they were in jail, the city governments had big bills to feed them, and the judicial calendars were clogged because every free speecher demanded a separate jury trial. Most of the cities in which free-speech fights were joined found it preferable to repeal the ordinances.

What happened to the army of casual workers? The virtual completion of the western railroad system eliminated many jobs. Mechanization of harvesting wheat or even picking fruit destroyed other jobs that had been filled by hobos. So did the practice of sound forestry: by farming trees and harvesting a forest in order to have a steady supply of timber ("sustained yield"), lumbermen could maintain a permanent, more reliable work force rather than send out the call for migrant workers.

Perhaps as important as anything else was the advent of the cheap automobile. By the 1920s, the used Model T Ford, which almost everyone could afford, led to the family's becoming the chief unit of the migrant work force. A family of five or six, including children, was cheaper to hire than were the homeless men who rode the rails. Moreover, with children to feed, the family was more stable as employees than was the vagabond adventurer who was not "afraid of his job."

By the 1930s, when the Great Depression caused a big jump in the number of people who were tramping the country, the working hobo was already a vanishing figure. Indeed, the work of harvesting fruit and vegetables on the west coast was becoming increasingly dependent on Mexicans who, coming from extreme poverty, could be hired even more cheaply than the solitary hobo.

turned them down in a huff. As a result, when Harding died in office in 1923, he was succeeded by the conservative Calvin Coolidge instead of the volcano from California.

ON THE FRINGE

Most progressives advocated municipal ownership of public utilities, but they were staunchly anti-socialist. Indeed, progressive politicians like La Follette and Johnson warned that the reforms they proposed were necessary to preserve the institution of private property from a rising Red tide in American politics.

This message had a special urgency in the early years of the twentieth century because the Socialist party of America, founded in 1900, came very close to establishing itself as a major force in American politics. Pieced together by local Socialist organizations and frustrated former Populists, the Socialist party nominated labor leader Eugene V. Debs for president in 1900, and he won 94,768 votes. In 1904, running again, Debs threw a scare into progressives and conservatives alike by polling 402,460.

Debs and Berger

In many ways, Debs resembled a progressive politician. He was a fiery, flamboyant orator, a master of the theatrical and gymnastic style of public speaking that not only was necessary in an age when sound amplification was primitive, but was favored by Americans in their preachers and politicians. He was more a moralist than either an intellectual or a politician. He freely admitted that he had little patience with the endless ideological hairsplitting of which other Socialists were quite fond. And Debs's followers worshiped him as progressives worshiped La Follette, Borah, and Roosevelt. The adulation and loyalty accorded him made him a presidential candidate five times between 1900 and 1920. In 1912, he won almost 1 million votes, 6 percent of the total.

But Debs differed from the progressives in other ways. He did not seek to smooth over the conflict between classes, but to exhort the working class to take charge. If he was not an ideologue, he nevertheless agreed with the Marxists that the class that produced wealth should decide how that wealth was to be distributed.

Victor Berger of Milwaukee more clearly linked socialism and progressivism. An Austrian immigrant, middle-class in background, Berger forged an alliance among Milwaukee's large German-speaking population, the labor movement, and the city's reform-

American Socialist Eugene V. Debs speaking in Canton, Ohio.

minded middle class. His Social Democratic party (a part of Debs's Socialist party) soft-pedaled revolutionary rhetoric and promised Milwaukee honest government and efficient city-owned public utilities. Once, while he and Debs were being interviewed by a journalist, Debs said that capitalists would not be compensated when their factories were taken from them; their "property" had been stolen from working people, and theft would not be rewarded. Berger interrupted, no, capitalists would be compensated for their losses. Property might well be theft; nevertheless, Berger would not frighten his middle-class supporters with loose talk about confiscation. .

In 1910, Berger was elected to the House of Representatives and Socialist candidates for mayor and city council were swept into power in Milwaukee. To radical members of the party, Berger's "sewer socialism," a reference to his emphasis on city ownership of utilities, was nothing more than progressivism. Berger thought otherwise. He insisted that by demonstrating to the American people the Socialists' ability to govern a large city, the Socialist party would win their attention to the revolutionary part of its program.

Labor's Quest for Respectability

Berger also hoped to advance the fortunes of socialism by capturing the American Federation of Labor. Socialists were a large minority in the union movement, a majority among members who were not Roman Catholic. At the AFL's annual conventions, the Socialists challenged the conservative leadership of Samuel Gompers and several times came close to ousting him from the presidency.

In the end they failed. Presenting a moderate face to the American people was also central to Gompers's strategy for establishing the legitimacy of the labor movement, and his version of moderation included support of progressive capitalism. His glad willingness to cooperate with employers won him many friends among progressives (and some conservatives such as Mark Hanna). In 1905, President Theodore Roosevelt intervened in a coal miners' strike. During the William Howard Taft administration (1909–13), progressives established a Commission on Industrial Violence with a membership that was skewed in a pro-union direction. Progressive Democratic President Woodrow Wilson named Samuel Gompers to several prestigious government posts and appointed a former leader of the AFL's United Mine Workers, William B. Wilson, to be secretary of labor.

The union movement grew in the favorable climate of the Progressive Era, but by no means sensationally. Membership in the AFL rose from about 500,000 in 1900 to 1.5 million in 1910, with some 500,000 workers holding cards in independent organizations. This was a pittance among a nonagricultural labor force of almost 20 million.

The "Wobblies"

The most important unions outside the AFL were the cautious and conservative Railway Brotherhoods (of Locomotive Engineers, Firemen, Brakemen, etc.) and the radical Industrial Workers of the World (IWW), or, as members were called, "the Wobblies." Founded in 1905 by Socialists and other radicals who were disgusted by Gompers' conservatism and his reluctance to organize unskilled workers, the IWW also found friends among progressives, but more often, sent chills racing down their spines.

Progressives supported West Coast and wheatbelt Wobblies when, between 1909 and 1913, the hobo members of the union waged a series of "free speech fights" to protect their right to recruit members by speaking from soapboxes on street corners. Progressive sensitivity to traditions of personal liberty and common decency was agitated when policemen assigned to destroy the union arrested Wobblies for reading publicly from the Declaration of Independence and the Constitution. In 1912, progressive organizations, particularly women's clubs, helped the IWW win its

Strikers—both men and children workers—march in Lawrence, Massachusetts, 1912.

greatest strike victory among immigrant textile mill workers in Lawrence, Massachusetts. They publicized the horrendous living conditions in Lawrence, lobbied congressmen, and took the children of strikers into their homes, a masterful public-relations ploy.

The capacity of middle-class progressives to back the Wobblies could not, however, go much beyond well-wishing. The Wobblies called loudly and gaily for revolution, precisely what progressives were determined to avoid. Although the IWW officially renounced violence, including violent sabotage, individual members spoke of driving spikes into logs bound for sawmills and throwing hammers into the works of harvesters, threshers, and balers. And, although the first blow was more often thrown by employers than workers, fistfights, riots, and even murder characterized enough Wobbly strikes to besmirch the union's reputation.

Nor were middle-class progressives alone in considering the IWW beyond the pale. No one used fiercer language in denouncing the organization than Samuel Gompers. In 1913, Victor Berger and a prominent New York Socialist, Morris Hillquit, led a movement within the Socialist party that successfully expelled the leader of the IWW, William D. "Big Bill" Haywood, from the party's National Executive Committee.

Feminism and Progressivism

Another "-ism" with an ambivalent relationship to the progressive movement was feminism. In 1900, the struggle on behalf of equal rights for women was more than 50 years old. Despite the tireless work of leaders like Elizabeth Cady Stanton and Susan B. Anthony, the victories had been few. In their twilight years at the beginning of the Progressive Era, Stanton and Anthony could look back on liberalized divorce laws, women voters in six western states, a movement unified for the moment in the National American Woman Suffrage Association, and the initiation of a new gen-

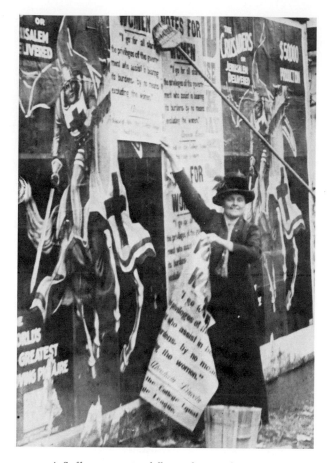

A Suffragette posting bills to advertise their cause.

eration of leaders including Carrie Chapman Catt and Anna Howard Shaw, a British-born physician.

But the coveted prize, a constitutional amendment that would guarantee women the right to vote, seemed as remote as it had at Seneca Falls in 1848. Most articulate Americans, women as well as men, continued to believe that women's delicacy and fine moral sense made it best that they remain in a separate sphere from men. If women participated in public life, they would be sullied as men had been and lose their vital moral influence in the home.

In fact, when Anthony died in 1906, success was fewer than 15 years away. The democratic inclinations of the progressives made it increasingly difficult for them to deny the franchise to half the American people. Even progressive leaders who had little personal enthusiasm for the idea of female voters publicly supported the cause.

Changing Strategies

Much more important in accounting for the victory of the suffrage movement was a fundamental shift in its

---

WOBBLIES

Members of the IWW were called Wobblies by both friends and enemies. There are several explanations of the origin of their name; according to one, they were so strike prone that they were "wobbly" workers. The story the IWW favored told of a Chinese restaurant operator in the Pacific Northwest who would give credit only to Wobblies because they could be depended on. When someone asked for a meal on credit, the restaurant owner, unable to pronounce the name of the letter *W*, asked, "I-Wobbly-Wobbly?"

appeal. Under the leadership of Carrie Chapman Catt, the National American Woman Suffrage Association came to terms with progressive prejudices and quietly shelved the comprehensive critique of women's status in American society that the early feminists had developed, including doubts about the institution of marriage. The suffragists also downplayed the traditional argument that women should have the right to vote because they were equal to men in every way.

A few "social feminists" clung to the old principles. Charlotte Perkins Gilman, an independently minded New Englander, argued in *Women and Economics* (1898) that marriage was itself the cause of women's inequality. Alice Paul, a Quaker like many feminists before her, insisted that the suffrage alone was not enough to solve "the woman question."

But most of the middle-class suffragists argued that women should have the right to vote precisely because they were more moral than men. Their votes would purge society of its evils. Not only did the suffragists ingeniously turn the most compelling antisuffrage argument in their favor, but they told progressives that in allowing women to vote they would be gaining huge numbers of allies. In fact, women were in the forefront of two of the era's most important moral crusades, the struggle against prostitution and the prohibition movement.

White Slavery

To earlier generations, prostitution had been an inevitable evil that could be controlled or ignored by decent people, but not abolished. Most states, counties, and cities had laws against solicitation on the grounds that streetwalking "hookers" were a public nuisance. Somewhat fewer governments declared the quiet sale of sex to be a crime. Even where prostitution was nominally illegal, it was common to tolerate "houses of ill repute" that were discreetly operated (and often made contributions to worthy causes such as the welfare of the police).

Communities in which men vastly outnumbered women—cow towns, mining camps, seaports, migrant farm-worker and logging centers—typically tolerated red-light districts in a corner of town. A stock figure of small-town folklore was the woman on the wrong

Feminist Carrie Chapman Catt, leader of the National American Woman Suffrage Association.

side of the tracks who sold favors to those sly or bold enough to knock on her door.

In the large cities, prostitution ran the gamut from lushly furnished and expensive brothels for high-society swells, such as Sally Stanford's in San Francisco, to "the cribs," tiny cubicles rented by whores who catered to working men. Because their pay was so low, thousands of New York working women moonlighted as prostitutes at least part of the time. Novelists Stephen Crane in *Maggie: A Girl of the Streets* (1892) and Upton Sinclair in *The Jungle* both dealt with the theme of tacitly forced prostitution.

The world's oldest profession had affronted proper people long before the Progressive Era. In most places, the middle class was content to declare the trade illegal and then tolerate it out of their sight. Some cities restricted prostitution to neighborhoods far from middle-class residential areas, such as New Orleans's Storyville, San Francisco's Barbary Coast, and Chicago's South of the Loop.

The progressives, spearheaded by women's organizations, determined to wipe out the institution. During the first decade of the twentieth century, most states and innumerable communities passed strict laws against all prostitution and enforced them rigorously. In 1917, prodded by the army when it established a big training camp nearby, even wide-open Storyville, the birthplace of jazz, was officially closed. By 1920, all but a few states had an antiprostitution law on the books. Within a few more years, only Nevada, with its stubborn mining-frontier outlook, continued to tolerate the institution within the law.

The Limits of Progressive Moralism

Action on the federal level was more complicated. Prostitution was clearly a matter for the police powers of the states and localities. However, progressives were so convinced that government held the key to social reform and must act at every level that, in 1910, they joined with some conservatives to put the interstate commerce clause of the Constitution to work in the cause. Senator James R. Mann of Illinois sponsored a bill that struck against the probably exaggerated practice of procurers luring poor girls from one part of the country to become prostitutes elsewhere. The Mann Act forbade transporting women across state lines "for immoral purposes." It was this law under which the boxer Jack Johnson was prosecuted.

Of course, neither local, state, nor federal law abolished prostitution. The campaign may be the best example of the progressives' excessive faith in the powers of the government. Brothels continued to operate, albeit less openly and probably with more police graft than before. Streetwalkers, previously the most de-

A prostitute poses for the camera. Ending prostitution became a goal of the progressives and members of the women's movement in the early 1900s.

spised and degraded of whores, became the norm because they were less easily arrested. Wealthy men continued to maintain paid mistresses and created the "call girl," a prostitute who stayed at home until "called" by a hotel employee or pimp who worked the streets and hotel lobbies.

Prohibitionism

The nineteenth-century impulse to combat the evils of drink never quite died. Temperance advocates and outright prohibitionists had battled back and forth with the distillers of liquor and with ordinary people who simply enjoyed a cup of good cheer. By 1900, however, anti-alcohol crusaders were emphasizing social arguments over their moral distaste for drunkenness and, in so doing, won widespread progressive support.

The prohibitionists pointed out that the city saloon was often the local headquarters of the corrupt political machines. Close the saloons, the reasoning went, and the bosses would be crippled. Moreover, generally overlooking the fact that poverty caused a widespread drinking problem among the working classes, the prohibitionists argued that the misery of the working classes was the result of husbands and fathers spending their wages on demon rum and John Barleycorn. Because the public bar was then an all-male institution, the temperance movement formed a close alliance with feminists.

Carry Nation of Kansas was one woman who suffered her whole life with a drunken husband and poverty. Beginning in 1900, she launched a campaign of direct action, leading hatchet-wielding women into saloons where, before the bewildered eyes of saloonkeeper and customers, they methodically chopped the place to pieces.

Frances Willard, head of the Woman's Christian Temperance Union, opposed such tactics. She and her followers also entered saloons, but instead of breaking them up, they attempted to shame drinkers by kneeling to pray quietly in their midst. In addition, the WCTU turned to politics, supporting woman suffrage for its own sake as well as for the purpose of winning the final victory over liquor.

Increasing numbers of progressives adopted the reform. Only in the big cities, mostly in the eastern states, did socially minded politicians like Alfred E. Smith and Robert Wagner of New York actively fight the prohibitionists. The large Roman Catholic and Jewish populations of the cities had no religious tradition against alcohol; on the contrary they used wine as a part of religious observance. Elsewhere, libertarian progressives argued that the government had no right to interfere with the individual decision of whether or not to drink.

Nevertheless, the possibilities of moral improvement, of striking a blow against poverty, and of joining battle against the political manipulations of the big distillers and brewers converted many progressives to prohibition, and in the waning days of the movement (though they were not thought to be waning at the time), they had their way.

For Further Reading

Once again, see Vincent P. DeSantis, *The Shaping of Modern America, 1877–1916* (1973), and Robert H. Wiebe, *The Search for Order, 1880–1920* (1967) for context. William L. O'Neill, *The Progressive Years: America Comes of Age* (1975) is perhaps the most readable survey of the era written in recent years. However, the following general interpretations are also quite valuable: Arthur Ekirch, *Progressivism in Practice* (1974); Lewis L. Gould, *Reform and Regulation: American Politics, 1900–1916* (1978); Otis L. Graham, Jr., *The Great Campaigns: Reform and War in America, 1900–1928* (1971); the appropriate chapters of Richard Hofstadter, *The Age of Reform* (1955); Gabriel Kolko, *The Triumph of Conservatism* (1963); Christopher Lasch, *The New Radicalism in America* (1965); and George E. Mowry, *The Era of Theodore Roosevelt* (1958).

More narrowly focused books about progressives with excellent insights are John D. Buenker, *Urban Liberalism and Progressive Reform* (1973); D. M. Chalmers, *The Social and Political Ideas of the Muckrakers* (1964); Carl M. Degler, *At Odds: Women in the Family in America from the Revolution to the Present* (1980); Louis Filler, *Crusaders for American Liberalism* (1939); Samuel T. Hays, *Conservation and the Gospel of Efficiency:* *The Progressive Conservation Movement, 1890–1920* (1959); David M. Kennedy, *Birth Control in America: The Career of Margaret Sanger* (1970); Jack D. Kirby, *Darkness at the Dawning: Race and Reform in the Progressive South* (1972); Roy Lubove, *The Progressives and the Slums* (1962); George E. Mowry, *The California Progressives* (1951); William L. O'Neill, *Everyone Was Brave: The Rise and Fall of Feminism* (1969); J. T. Patterson, *America's Struggle Against Poverty* (1981); Jean Quandt, *From the Small Town to the Great Community: The Social Thought of Progressive Intellectuals* (1970); James H. Timberlake, *Prohibition and the Progressive Movement, 1900–1920* (1963); James Weinstein, *The Corporate Ideal in the Liberal State, 1900–1918* (1968); and Robert H. Wiebe, *Businessmen and Reform* (1962).

Important biographical studies include John M. Blum, *The Republican Roosevelt* (1954); David McCullough, *Mornings on Horseback* (1981); W. H. Harbaugh, *Power and Responsibility: The Life and Times of Theodore Roosevelt* (1961); R. S. Maxwell, *La Follette and the Rise of Progressivism in Wisconsin* (1956); Henry F. Pringle, *Theodore Roosevelt* (1931); David P. Thelen, *Robert M. La Follette and the Insurgent Movement* (1976).

37

VICTORS AT ARMAGEDDON

The Progressives in Power, 1901–1916

By 1904, the progressive movement commanded the allegiance of a large bloc of senators and congressmen from both major parties—and the president himself, Theodore Roosevelt. T.R. was sometimes bemused by the irony that he, the scion of an old and privileged family, should be the titular leader of a popular protest movement. In a letter to his friend Chauncey Depew, a former protégé of Cornelius Vanderbilt and the decidedly non-progressive senator from New York, Roosevelt wrote in mock weariness: "How I wish I wasn't a reformer, Oh Senator! But I suppose I must live up to my part, like the Negro minstrel who blackened himself all over!" But then, it was not so odd that T.R., having had great powers thrust into his hands, was willing to use them to admonish and chastize those industrial capitalists whom he considered to be "malefactors of great wealth." His family's fortune and status were preindustrial; he was a member of an old American elite that, to some degree, had been slighted and shunted aside by the *nouveax riches* of the late nineteenth century. Moreover, despite the sigh of resignation to duty in the letter to Depew, Roosevelt loved to be in the thick of things. During his nearly eight years in the White House, reform was where the action was.

T.R. TAKES OVER

At first, Roosevelt moved cautiously. He was well aware of the fact that the bosses of the Republican party distrusted him as a "damned cowboy," that Mark Hanna was openly discussing his interest in the 1904 Republican presidential nomination with party leaders like Tom Platt of New York and Matthew Quay of Pennsylvania.

But no one was to contest T.R.'s claim on party leadership in 1904. Mark Hanna died suddenly in February of that year, Matt Quay a short time later. Even had they lived and been hale and hearty, they would have had to step aside for the damned cowboy. In a little more than two years, he had left them in the dust, building up an immense personal following and quietly replacing members of the Old Guard in government positions with his own men. Ever graceful in his maneuvers, he eased the McKinley-Hanna men who were mediocrities out of this cabinet, and won the loyalty of those he kept by giving them an authority and autonomy that they had not enjoyed under McKinley.

Among the McKinley appointees whom he kept in office were Secretary of State John Hay, Secretary of War Elihu Root (who succeeded Hay, in the State Department in 1905), Attorney General Philander C. Knox, Secretary of the Interior E. A. Hitchcock, and Secretary of Agriculture James Wilson. All were competent officials, some of them outstanding.

Busting Taboos and Trusts

So overwhelming was Roosevelt's self-confidence that he had no fear of ability in his subordinates. He was happy and able to delegate responsibility because there was no doubt in his or in the public's mind as to who was in charge. He blurted out his opinions on every subject. He gaily lambasted what annoyed him. He

Theodore Roosevelt aggressively enforced antitrust laws. In this cartoon he is depicted as a powerful lion tamer whipping the trusts into shape.

thumbed his nose at the color line by lunching at the White House with the prominent black educator Booker T. Washington. He slapped at anti-Semites by naming a Jew, Secretary of Commerce Oscar S. Straus, to his cabinet.

In April 1902, T.R. conspicuously directed Attorney General Knox, a former corporation lawyer, to have a go at the most powerful corporate organizers in the United States. His target, the Northern Securities Company, had been designed by J. P. Morgan and railroaders Edward H. Harriman and James J. Hill to end struggles for control of the railroads in the northern quarter of the country. Funded by the nation's two richest banks, Northern Securities was a holding company that was patterned after Morgan's United States Steel Corporation.

Morgan was shocked by Roosevelt's prosecution. Under McKinley, the Sherman Antitrust Act had nearly died from disuse. In a pained and revealing moment, the great financier wrote to Roosevelt, "If we have done anything wrong, send your man to my man and we can fix it up." The message was not apt to appeal to the president, who read it as in invitation to sit in Morgan's waiting room.

Roosevelt blithely ignored the invitation and Knox pushed on in the courts. In 1904, they won; the Supreme Court ordered the Northern Securities Company to dissolve, and progressives cheered. When Roosevelt instituted other antitrust suits, 40 in all, of which he won 25, progressives nicknamed him the "trust-buster."

It was an overstatement. Roosevelt did not believe that bigness in business was itself an evil, and he continued to socialize on good terms with the millionaires with whom Knox was contending in the courts. Indeed, in 1907 he allowed Morgan's United States Steel Company to gobble up a major regional competitor, Tennessee Coal and Iron without public statement.

The trust-buster's criteria for determining what made one business combination "good" and another "bad" were rather too vague to be defined. In a way, his suits were drama and symbol, like naming a Jew to his cabinet; Roosevelt wanted to show big business and the American people that he and the United States government were in charge. In the Tennessee Coal and Iron case, J. P. Morgan had to send his man, hat in hand, to see T.R.'s man, and not vice versa.

The Workingman's Friend

Quite as startling as trust-busting was Roosevelt's personal intervention in the autumn of 1902 in a strike by 140,000 anthracite coal miners. The men's demands were moderate. They wanted a 20 percent increase in pay, an eight-hour day, and their employers to recognize and negotiate with their union, the United Mine Workers (UMW). The mine owners refused to yield on a single point. Theirs was a competitive, unstable business; with so many companies engaged in mining coal, the price of the commodity fluctuated radically and unpredictably. Employers traditionally avoided long-term committments to anyone—buyers, shippers, or employees.

Most of the coal operators were entrepreneurs of the old hard-nosed school, easy for muckraking reporters to caricature, which they did. Their property was

Striking miners, members of the United Mine Workers, parade silently in their Sunday best during the 1902 coal strike.

theirs and that was that; they would brook no interference in their use of it, least of all by grimy employees. George F. Baer, the ringleader of the operators
and more pious than prudent, stirred up a furious
public reaction when he told a journalist that he would
never deal with the UMW because God had entrusted
him with his company's mines.

By way of contrast, union leader John Mitchell was
depicted in the progressive press as a moderate, modest, and likable man. T.R., keenly sensitive to public
opinion, knew where the applause was to be had.
Moreover, Mitchell was a conservative union leader,
constantly engaged in a battle with socialists in the
UMW Roosevelt was inclined to help him win his
factional battle by giving him a boost in his fight with
the operators. In October, the president let it be
known that if the strike dragged on through the winter
with no settlement, he might use federal troops to
dispossess the owners and open the mines. Knowing
the Rough Rider was capable of so drastic and dangerous an act, the ubiquitous Morgan stepped in and
pressured the mine owners to go to Washington to
work out a settlement.

The result was a compromise that rather favored the
owners. The miners got a 10 percent raise and a nine-
hour day; the operators were not required to recognize
the UMW as the agent of the workers. (Baer and the
others refused even to meet face to face with Mitchell.) Nonetheless, the miners were elated. So were
people who counted on coal to ward off winter's cold.
But the big winner, as in most of his chosen battles,
was Theodore Roosevelt. He had reversed the tradition of using federal troops to help employers break
strikes and had forced powerful industrialists to bow
to his will on behalf of a "square deal" for workingmen.

Teddy's Great Victory

By 1904, T.R. was basking in the sun of a nation's
adulation. He was unanimously renominated by the
Republicans and presented with a huge campaign
chest. The Democrats, hoping to capitalize on the
grumbling of some conservatives over the president's
actions and remarks about arrogant businessmen, did
a complete about-face from the party's agrarianism of
1896 and 1900. They nominated a Wall Street lawyer
and judge with impeccable social credentials but, also,
a record of sympathy for labor, Alton B. Parker, to
oppose him. The urbane but colorless Parker was the
antithesis of Boy Bryan and, Democratic bosses hoped,
a foil to the histrionic Roosevelt.

Parker was hopelessly stodgy, but even the second
most colorful politician in the country would have
looked like a cardboard cutout next to T.R. Not even
Parker's Wall Street friends voted for him. If they

disliked T.R.'s antitrust adventures, they recognized
that Roosevelt hewed to conservative lines in advocating an anti-inflationary money policy and a high
tariff, which were of far greater importance to business
interests than courtroom spats. J. P. Morgan, recently
stung in the Northern Securities case, donated
$150,000 to Roosevelt's campaign.

The president won a lopsided 57.4 percent of the
vote, more than any candidate since popular totals
had been recorded. His 336 to 140 electoral sweep was
the largest since Grant's in 1872, and he did it without
the help of the southern states. Building on the coalition of money and respectability that had been put
together by McKinley and Hanna in 1896, T.R.
enlarged the Republican majority by appealing to
progressives.

THE PRESIDENT AS REFORMER

The only sour note for the Republicans in a giddy
election week was the remarkable showing of the Socialist party candidate, Eugene V. Debs. His 400,000
votes amounted to only 3 percent of the total, but
represented an astonishing fourfold increase over his
vote in 1900. Roosevelt did not like it either. Increasingly after 1904, he seized every opportunity—and
created more than a few—to denounce anticapitalist
radicals.

Perhaps his most gratuitous attack followed the arrest and illegal extradition late in 1905 of Charles
Moyer and Big Bill Haywood, the leaders of the militant Western Federation of Miners. Charged with
murder in Idaho, the two radicals were, in effect,
kidnapped by authorities in Denver, Colorado. Roosevelt shrugged off the irregularity of the arrest because
the two were "undesirable citizens." Moyer and Haywood's lawyer, Clarence Darrow, justifiably complained that with the president of the United States
making such statements, a fair trial was not likely.
(Nevertheless, both men were acquitted.)

At the same time he assailed the socialists, Roosevelt set out to co-opt them by unleashing a whirlwind
of reform. He was determined to eliminate the abuses
that gave the Socialists their easiest targets.

The Railroads Derailed

As they had been for 30 years, the railroads remained
a focus of popular resentment. The freewheeling arrogance of their directors and the vital role of transportation in the national economy preoccupied progressives at every level of government. Prodded by
regional leaders, most notably Senator Robert La Fol-

lette, Roosevelt plunged into a long, bitter struggle with the railroad companies. In 1906, he won passage of the Hepburn Act. This law authorized the Interstate Commerce Commission to set maximum rates that railroads might charge their customers, and forbade them to pay rebates to big shippers. This prohibition had been enacted before but had not been effectively enforced; the Hepburn Act gave the ICC some teeth. More than any of T.R.'s previous actions, it blasted the railroaders' traditional immunity from government interference.

Also in 1906, Congress passed an act that held railroads liable to employees who suffered injuries on the job. By European standards, it was a mild compensation law, but in the United States, it marked a sharp break with precedent, which held employees responsible for most of their injuries.

Purer Food

Affecting more people, and therefore better headlines, was the Pure Food and Drug Act and the Meat Inspection Act, both signed in 1906, that eliminated adulteration of foods (by large processors), enforced stringent sanitary standards on them, and put the lid on the patent-medicine business, which marketed dangerous and addictive drugs as "feel-good" nostrums.

By requiring food processors to label their products with all ingredients used in making them and providing hefty penalties for violators, the Pure Food and Drug Act eliminated sometimes toxic and often worthless preservatives and fillers from canned, bottled, and sacked foodstuffs. The Meat Inspection Act provided for federal inspection of meat-packing plants to eliminate the abuses that Upton Sinclair had detailed so gruesomely in *The Jungle*.

Big meat packers like Armour, Swift, Wilson, and Cudahy grumbled about the federal inspectors, notebooks in hand, puttering about their abattoirs. But, in time, they learned that meat inspection worked in their favor and to the detriment of smaller regional slaughterhouses. That is, with their greater resources, the big meat packers were able to comply with the federal standards. By way of contrast, smaller companies, able to stay in business only by slashing costs at every turn, found the expense of sanitation in an inherently dirty business to be beyond their means. The big packers actually made advertising hay of the inspection stamps on their products: the government approved of them! Small companies closed their doors or restricted their sales to the states in which they were located. (Like all national reforms, federal meat inspection applied only to firms involved in interstate commerce.) Some progressives were not pleased to be helping big business against small, but T.R. was not one of them. It was not bigness itself to which he objected, but irresponsibility in business.

War on Drugs

Proportionately, there may have been more drug addicts in the United States at the turn of the century than in the 1980s. Some were frankly hooked on opium or morphine and had had minimal difficulty meeting their needs at unregulated pharmacies. Others were addicted to various patent medicines advertising themselves as cure-alls. Even Lydia Pinkham's Vegetable Compound, decorously packaged and aimed in fine print at ladies suffering from female complaints was a rather strong alcoholic elixir laced liberally with opiates.

The Pure Food and Drug Act, which restricted the use of addictive drugs and required labeling of ingredients, undercut the patent medicine business. Soft drink companies were also affected, for some, including the gigantic Coca Cola Company of Atlanta, had used a by-product of cocaine processing in their beverages to give it a "kick." Coca Cola actually introduced caffeine as a stimulant as early as 1903 but, with the passage of federal drug legislation in 1906, was able to advertise its "purity" like the big meat packers.

Resources in Jeopardy

Theodore Roosevelt and his progressive allies were not always far-seeing. Many of their enactments were the fruit of passionate impulse or playing to their constituents. In their campaign to conserve natural resources, however, they looked to the distant future and created monuments for which they are quite rightfully honored.

As a lifelong outdoorsman, T.R. loved camping, riding, hiking, climbing, and hunting. As a historian,

AMERICAN ESSENCE

Coca-Cola, which William Allen White called "the sublimated essence of all that American stands for," had its beginning as a kind of health food. An Atlanta druggist concocted it in 1886 as an alternative to alcohol. Within a year, a pious Methodist named Asa G. Candler purchased all rights to "Coke" for $2,300 and sold it as a "brain tonic," promoting its kick. Indeed, until 1902, Coke was made with coca leaves and may have been addictive; southerners called it "dope." Candler's advertising was certainly addictive. By 1908, the Coca-Cola Company had plastered 2.5 million square feet of billboard and walls with posters. By 1911, more than a million dollars a year was spent on promoting the elixir.

*Theodore Roosevelt and Sierra Club founder John Muir
in Yosemite National Park.*

he was more sensitive than most of his contemporaries to the role of the wilderness in forging the American character. He actively sought and gained the friendship of John Muir, the adopted Californian and Alaskan who had founded the Sierra Club in 1892. Muir's interest in nature was aesthetic, cultural, and spiritual. He wanted to protect from development such magnificent areas of untouched wilderness as Yosemite Valley, which he had helped to establish as a national park in 1890. Roosevelt shared these sentiments.

The motives of progressive conservationists such as T.R.'s tennis partner and America's first trained forester, Gifford Pinchot of Pennsylvania, were somewhat different. While by no means oblivious to the cultural and aesthetic values of wilderness, Pinchot's major concern was protecting forests and other natural resources from rapacious exploiters interested only in short-term profits. He wanted to ensure that future generations of Americans would have their share of nonrenewable natural resources—minerals, coal, and oil—to draw on and the continued enjoyment of renewable resources—forests, grasslands, and water for drinking and generating power.

Roosevelt had good reason to worry about the nation's natural resources. Lumbermen in the Great Lakes states had already mowed down once endless forests, moved on, and left the land behind them to useless scrub and waste. Western ranchers put too many cattle on delicate grasslands, turning them into deserts. Coal and phosphate mining companies and drillers for oil thought in terms of open account books and never of the fact that, in a century, the United States might run out of these vital resources. Virtually no one in extractive industries worried that they were destroying watersheds vital to urban water supplies, polluting rivers, and sending good soil into the sea.

Americans had always been reckless with the land, none more so than the pioneers of legend. But there was a big difference between what a few frontiersmen could do to it with axes and horse-drawn plows and the potential for destruction of irresponsible million-dollar corporations.

Conservation

The National Forest Reserve, today's National Forest System, dates from 1891, when Congress empowered the president to withhold forests in the public domain from private use. Over the first ten years of the law, Presidents Harrison, Cleveland, and McKinley had declared 46 million acres of virgin woodland off limits to loggers without government permission.

Enforcement had been desultory until, prodded by Pinchot, Roosevelt began to prosecute "timber pirates," who raided public lands and cattlemen who abused government-owned grasslands. Within a few years, Roosevelt added 125 million acres to the national forests, as well as reserving 68 million acres of coal deposits, almost 5 million acres of phosphate beds (vital to production of munitions), a number of oil fields, and 2,565 sites suitable for the construction of dams for irrigation and generation of electrical power.

Progressives cheered. Some of the "multiple uses" to which the national forests were dedicated—recreation, preservation—won the plaudits of groups like the Sierra Club. Others—flood control, irrigation, development of hydroelectric power—pleased social planners. The principle of "sustained yield," managing forests to ensure an adequate supply of lumber into the indefinite future, appealed to the big lumber companies with their huge capital investments, and encouraged them to employ foresters on their own lands.

In the West, however, an angry opposition developed. Cattlemen, clear-cut loggers, and private power companies banded together in an anticonservation movement that succeeded, in 1907, in attaching a rider to an agricultural appropriations bill that passed Congress. It forbade the president to create any additional national forests in six western states. Roosevelt had no choice but to sign the bill; the Department of Agriculture could not have functioned otherwise. But he had one last go at what he called the "predatory interests." Before he wrote his name on the bill, he reserved 17 million acres of forest land in the interdicted states.

Concern for the Farm

Theodore Roosevelt's conservation campaign remains one of the single most important contributions of his presidency. Nevertheless, his policies could hurt ordinary people as well as special interests. For example, he and Pinchot helped Los Angeles, the burgeoning metropolis of southern California, to grab the entire Owens River, 300 miles to the north, for its water supply. The president regarded the mammoth construction project, now known as the Los Angeles Aqueduct, as a showpiece of resource development and public control of electrical power. In the process, however, he helped to destroy the fertile Owens Valley. Then a land of prosperous, self-reliant small farmers, it would become by 1930 an arid, desolate region of sagebrush, dust storms, and tarantulas.

Had Roosevelt lived to see its results, he might well have regretted his action. He was a devotee of the family farm as one of the essential American institutions. He established the Country Life Commission, which lamented the steady disappearance of this way of life and submitted to Congress a number of recommendations designed to help family farmers. Conservative congressmen who had soured on their progressive president refused even to publish the report.

The Reformer Retires

In two major speeches in 1908, Roosevelt called for a comprehensive, even radical, program that included federal investigation of major labor disputes and close regulation of both the stock market and businesses that were involved in interstate commerce. But Congress sidestepped virtually all of his proposals because the damned cowboy had become a "lame duck." It was a presidential election year and, four years earlier, celebrating the great victory of 1904, T.R. had impulsively declared that "a wise custom which limits the President to two terms regards the substance and not the form, and under no circumstances will I be a candidate for or accept another nomination." Having served three and a half years of McKinley's term, Roosevelt had defined himself as a two-term president.

In 1908, he almost certainly regretted his vow. Except, perhaps, for Coolidge and Reagan, Theodore Roosevelt relished his job, and flourished in it, as no other twentieth-century president has. Unlike Coolidge and Reagan, who treated the presidency as a personal honor, he was a worker and a marvelous success. He was not yet 50 years of age in 1908 and as popular as ever with the voters. He would undoubtedly have won reelection had he been willing to forget his pledge not to run.

But he kept his word and settled for hand-picking his successor, which no president had been able to do since Andrew Jackson in 1836. That William Howard Taft, then secretary of war, was not the man whom either conservative or progressive Republicans would have chosen indicates just how high Roosevelt was riding.

A CONSERVATIVE PRESIDENT IN A PROGRESSIVE ERA

Taft never would have been nominated without Roosevelt's blessing. He would not have dreamed of running for president. Regularly in his correspondence he dashed off the exclamation "I hate politics!" and he meant it. He was a lifelong functionary, not a politician. His only elective post prior to 1908 was as a judge in Ohio. Taft remembered that job as the most congenial he had ever held, for his temperament was judicial. Slow to think, sober, cautious, reflective, dignified, Taft worked well in a study, but he was no showman.

Amidst a people who savored Roosevelt's gymnastic style, Taft's very body militated against him. He weighed over 300 pounds and was truly at ease only when he settled into a swivel chair behind a desk or sank into an overstuffed couch with other easygoing men. His single form of exercise, golf, did not help his image; batting a little white ball around an oversize lawn was considered a sissy's game in the early twentieth century.

Taft was no reactionary. He had loyally supported Roosevelt's reforms, and T.R. calculated that he, more than anyone else, would carry out the Square Deal. So did other progressives. They supported him, as did the conservative wing of the Republican party. Anyone was preferable to the man whom they had begun to refer to privately as "the mad messiah."

The Election of 1908

The election was an anticlimax. The Democrats returned to William Jennings Bryan as their candidate, but the thrill was gone. The Boy Orator of the Platte, no longer young, was shopworn beyond his years. He had grown jowls and a paunch as penance for his lifelong vulnerability to the deadly sin of gluttony, and he was rapidly losing his hair.

William Howard Taft on a Republican campaign banner of 1908.

Moreover, his loyal supporters, the staple farmers of the Midwest, were no longer struggling to survive. They were beginning to dress like the townsmen they had jostled in 1896 and to build substantial homes. Even the issue of 1900, imperialism, was dead. Taft, who had served as American governor of the Philippines, could claim credit for having transformed the anti-American Filipinos, whom he called his "little brown brothers," into a placid and apparently content colonial population. Puerto Rico was quieter. Hawaiians did the hula for increasing numbers of American tourists. Central America simmered but the spectre of American power kept the lid on. Thousands of men were digging their way across Panama under American direction, thrilling the nation.

The upshot was that a lethargic Bryan won a smaller percentage of the popular vote than in either of his previous tries. The Socialist party was also disappointed in the results. Bubbling with optimism at the start of the campaign, they chartered a private train, the "Red Special," on which candidate Debs crisscrossed the country. The crowds were big and enthu-

siastic. But Debs's vote was only 16,000 higher than in 1904 and represented a smaller percentage of the total. It appeared that Roosevelt's tactic of undercutting the socialist threat with a comprehensive reform program had worked.

Taft Blunders

Taft lacked both the political skills and the zeal to keep the campaign going. For example, even though he initiated 90 antitrust suits during his four years as president, twice as many as Roosevelt had launched in seven and a half years, no one complimented him as a trust-buster. Taft had managed to alienate the progressives immediately after taking office when he stumbled over an obstacle that T.R. had danced around quite nimbly, the tariff.

In 1909, duties on foreign goods were high, set at an average 46.5 percent of the value of imports by the Dingley Tariff of 1897. Republican conservatives insisted that this rate was necessary in order to protect the jobs of American factory workers and to encourage industrial investment by capitalists. Some midwestern progressives disagreed. They believed that American industry was strong enough to stand up to European manufacturers in a fair competition. To maintain the Dingley rates was to subsidize excessive corporate profits by allowing manufacturers to set their prices inordinately high. Farmers were twice stung because the European nations, except Great Britain, retaliated against the Dingley Tariff by levying high duties on American agricultural products. Ominously, in the election of 1908, several western states that had supported Roosevelt returned to the Democratic column.

T.R. had let Republican conservatives have their way on the tariff, placating (or distracting) progressives by pounding the tub on other reforms. By 1909, evasion was no longer possible, and Taft called Congress into special session for the purpose of tariff revision. The House of Representatives drafted a reasonable reduction of rates in the Payne bill. In the Senate, however, Nelson Aldrich of Rhode Island, a trusty ally of industrial capitalists, engineered 800 amendments to what became the Payne-Aldrich Act. On most important commodities, the final rate was higher than under the Dingley Tariff.

Taft was in a bind. Politically, he was committed to lower rates. Personally, however, he was more comfortable with the aristocratic Aldrich and the five corporation lawyers in his cabinet than with low-tariff men in the Senate, who were Democrats or excitable Republican progressives like La Follette and Jonathan Dolliver of Iowa. After equivocating, Taft worked out what he thought was a compromise in the Roosevelt tradition. The conservatives got their high tariff but agreed to a 2 percent corporate income tax and a constitutional amendment that legalized a personal income tax. (It was ratified in 1913 as the Sixteenth Amendment.) Instead of emphasizing the progressive aspects of this arrangement, as T.R. surely would have done, Taft described the Payne-Aldrich Act as "the best tariff that the Republican party ever passed."

The Insurgents

This angered the midwestern Republican progressives, especially after Taft came out in favor of a trade treaty with Canada that threatened to dump Canadian crops on the American market. But they broke with the new president only when he sided with the reactionary Speaker of the House of Representatives, Joseph G. Cannon of Illinois, against them.

"Uncle Joe" Cannon offended the progressive Republicans on several counts. He was so hidebound a conservative as to be a stereotype. As Speaker of the House and chairman of the House Rules Committee, he put progressives on unimportant committees and loaded the meaningful ones with Old Guard friends. Finally, while the progressives inclined to be highly moralistic, even priggish in manner, Uncle Joe was a crusty tobacco chewer, a hard drinker who was not infrequently drunk, and a champion foulmouth.

The proper Taft also found Cannon's company unpleasant. However, the president believed in party loyalty, and when a number of midwestern Republican progressives, calling themselves Insurgents, voted with

Illinois congressman "Uncle Joe" Cannon, a hard-bitten Republican conservative.

Democrats to strip Cannon of his near-dictatorial power, Taft joined with the Speaker to deny the Insurgents access to party money and patronage in the midterm election of 1910. The result was a Democratic victory and Cannon was out of the speakership, never to return.

Pinchot Forces a Break

It is impossible to say how Theodore Roosevelt would have handled the quarrel between Cannon and the Insurgents. But he assuredly would not have done what Taft did in a dispute between Secretary of the Interior Richard A. Ballinger and Chief Forester Gifford Pinchot.

When Ballinger released to private developers a number of hydroelectric sites that Pinchot had persuaded Roosevelt to reserve, Pinchot protested to Taft and won the president's grudging support. However, when Pinchot leaked his evidence against Ballinger to *Collier's* magazine, which was still in the muckraking business, Taft fired him. This may have been exactly what Pinchot wanted. He acted as if he were prepared, almost immediately booking passage to Italy, where his friend and patron, former president Roosevelt, was vacationing. Pinchot brought with him an indictment of Big Bill Taft as a traitor to the cause of reform.

Enter Stage Left the Conquering Hero

Roosevelt was having a bully time on his extended world tour. He had left the country shortly after Taft's inauguration to give his successor an opportunity to function outside his predecessor's aura. First Roosevelt traveled to East Africa, where he shot a bloody swath through the still abundant big game of Kenya and Tanganyika (Tanzania). He bagged over 3,000 animals, a good many of which he had stuffed for the trophy room of his home at Oyster Bay, Long Island.

Then he went to Europe to bask in an adulation that was scarcely less fierce than he enjoyed at home. He hobnobbed with aristocrats and politicians, who thought of him as the ultimate American, much as Benjamin Franklin had been considered in eighteenth-century France. Roosevelt topped off his year-long junket by representing the United States at the funeral of King Edward VII, shining in the greatest collection of royalty ever assembled.

And yet, something was missing. Roosevelt longed for the hurly-burly of politics, and he was all too willing to believe Pinchot's accusations. When he returned to the United States in June 1910, he exchanged only the curtest greetings with the president. He spoke widely on behalf of Republican congressional candidates, at first playing down the split between

The Father of the Amusement Park: George C. Tilyou, 1862–1914

George C. Tilyou was born to Irish-American parents in 1862. When he was three years old, his father leased a lot on the beach in the then independent community of Coney Island for $35 a year. It was a brilliantly timed act. The end of the Civil War was the signal for the runaway growth of resorts in the United States, and Coney Island was strategically located, far from the congestion of New York City but close enough to be convenient for a stay of a few days. The wealthy came first, sometimes by yacht, but also middle-class people to whom Newport, Rhode Island, and Palm Beach, Florida, were just names. Tilyou's hotel, the Surf House, catered to the middling sort. In fact, because Tilyou, Sr., was active in Democratic party politics, at any time his hostelry was likely to be filled with ward heelers and other political bosses from Manhattan and Brooklyn.

So George Cornelius Tilyou grew up, as they said at Coney, with sand in his shoes. Like two generations of Coney natives, he found it difficult to leave the place, and when he did, as on a wedding trip to the Columbian Exposition in Chicago in 1893, it was to pick up ideas for how to develop the Beach as a resort.

It developed as a resort for the middle and working classes, soon abandoned by the yachting and horsey sets, and Tilyou recognized the opportunities in providing mass, cheap entertainment. He was one of the first and by far the most successful operators of amusement parks, as shrewd a psychologist as Phineas T. Barnum and, when he died, a rich man.

Tilyou's first venture into the vacation business came in 1876 when the Centennial Exposition in Philadelphia attracted people from all over the nation to the east coast. Calculating that they had money to throw away, the 14-year-old Tilyou filled old medicine bottles with sea water and cigar boxes with Coney beach sand which he sold for 25 cents each. He made enough from dubious but classic resort "gifts" with which to dabble in beachfront real estate. The township did not sell land on the beach but, instead, leased it to people who were part of the political machine, who then sublet choice business locations to others, sometimes at extraordinary profits. Because of his contacts, Tilyou was able to open a theater that featured some of the leading vaudeville acts of the era.

Then he made what appeared to be a fatal mistake. He broke with the political boss of Coney, John Y. McKane, who protected brothels and illegal gambling dens and organized a party devoted to the policy that Coney's future rested on becoming a wholesome family resort. Tilyou denounced McKane for his grafting and when the boss weathered the attack, Tilyou found himself shut out of the profitable leasing deals.

In 1893, however, McKane was jailed for stuffing ballot boxes and Tilyou was back in business. In that same year he discovered the Ferris wheel at the Chicago World's Fair and the young impresario's career took off.

The Ferris wheel was the hit of the fair. It was 250 feet in diameter, almost as high when it was mounted as a football field is long. Suspended on the gigantic circle were 36 "cars," like railroad carriages, each of which held 60 people. The most nominal admission fee promised tremendous profits.

Although he was on his honeymoon, Tilyou was obsessed with the fantastic toy and only briefly disconcerted when he learned that its inventor had already sold it. He contracted with Ferris to build another for Coney. It was only half the size of the original, 125 feet in diameter with 12 cars holding 36 people each but the sign Tilyou erected back home in Coney Island was: "ON THIS SITE WILL BE ERECTED THE WORLD'S LARGEST FERRIS WHEEL!" Tilyou was making money before it was built. He sold concessions around it to various vendors, including one to a purveyor of a frankfurter sausage on a white milk roll, the first hot dog. Then Tilyou built a number of other "amusements," at first simple gravity devices such as giant sliding boards and seesaws but soon enough the electrically powered forerunners of devices still active on boardwalks and at fairs today. From another Coney entrepreneur, Paul Boyton, Tilyou copied the idea of fencing in a large "amusement park" and charging a single admission fee. Coney's clientele did not have the means for extravagant spending; better to commit them to a whole day at Steeplechase Park where they would have to buy their food and other extras rather than having them wander over to Steeplechase's competitors, Luna Park and Dreamland.

Steeplechase Park opened in 1897. Its centerpiece was a gravity driven "horse race" ride imported from England. People mounted wooden horses—a beau and his belle could ride on the same one—which rolled on tracks over a series of "hills" and entered the central pavillion at the Park where, upon exiting, the customers were mildly abused by a clown and costumed dwarf. The biggest hit of the Steeplechase was the jet of compressed air which shot out of the floor blowing young ladies' skirts into the air amidst great shrieking and guffawing.

Innocent sexual horseplay was the idea in many of the mechanical amusements Tilyou constructed. Airjets were everywhere. Other amusements were designed to throw young ladies in such a position that their ankles were exposed or they landed in the laps of their escorts or, perhaps, someone whom they were interested in meeting. In an age when polite society was warily trying to come to terms with sex, dwelling on it through romantic euphemisms in popular songs, Tilyou's formula worked. For a time after the turn of the century, Steeplechase Park lost ground to newer amuse-

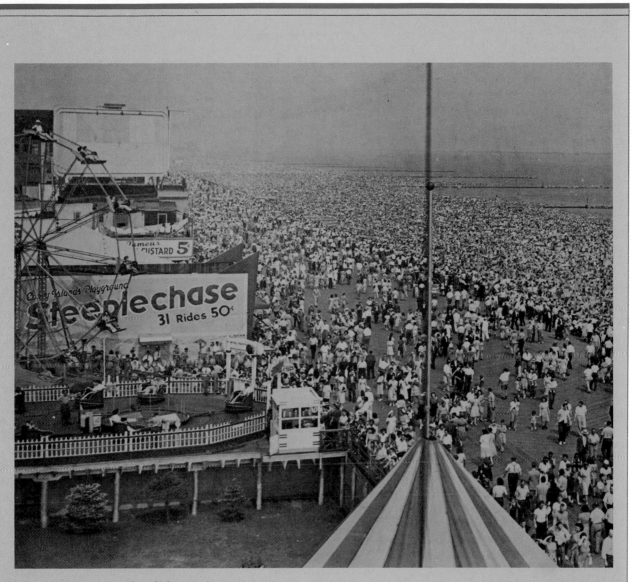

Steeplechase Park on Coney Island provided cheap entertainment for the middle and working classes.

ment parks, Luna Park (featuring "a trip to the moon") and Dreamland, where holiday-makers could stroll through the streets of an Egyptian city, a Somali village, among Philippine headhunters, or see the eruption of Mount Pelee, the Johnstown flood, the Galveston tidal wave, or other natural disasters.

But it was Tilyou who really had the sand in his shoes. When Steeplechase Park burned to the ground in 1907—every wooden Coney Island attraction burned at one time or another—he simply hung up a sign:

I have troubles today that I didn't have yesterday.
I had troubles yesterday that I have not today.
On this site will be erected shortly a better, bigger, greater Steeplechase Park.

Admission to the Burning Ruins—10 cents.

Tilyou also built Steeplechase Pier in Atlantic City, a New Jersey oceanfront town that competed with Coney. He died in 1914, only 52 years of age. Coney's Steeplechase Park closed in 1967.

regulars (conservatives) and insurgents (progressives). Then, at Osawatomie, Kansas, in September 1910, Roosevelt proclaimed what he labeled the "New Nationalism," a comprehensive program for further reform. To Republican conservatives, it was frighteningly radical.

Among other proposals, Roosevelt called for woman suffrage, a federal minimum wage for women workers, abolition of child labor, strict limitations on the power of courts to issue injunctions in labor disputes, and a national social-insurance scheme that resembled present-day Social Security. He struck directly at Taft's policies by demanding a commission that would set tariff rates "scientifically" rather than according to political pressures. He supported the progressive initiative, recall, and referendum, including a new twist, a referendum on judicial decisions. This was enough in itself to aggravate the legalistic Taft, but in demanding a national presidential-primary law under which the people, and not professional politicians, would make party nominations, Roosevelt also hinted that he was interested in running for the presidency again.

Challenging Taft

Taft was not the only politician who worried about Roosevelt's presidential plans. Robert La Follette had been preparing to seek the Republican presidential nomination in 1912, and believed he had a chance to defeat Taft, that is, if Roosevelt did not also run. Little as he liked doing it, he sent mutual friends to ask Roosevelt his intentions, implying that he would drop out if T.R. was running. Roosevelt responded that he was not interested in the White House. In January 1911, LaFollette organized the Progressive Republican League to promote his candidacy.

Most progressive Republicans supported La Follette, including Roosevelt backers who not so secretly hoped that their real hero would change his mind. In fact, Roosevelt was itching to run. In March 1912, when La Follette collapsed from exhaustion during a speech, Roosevelt announced with unseemly haste, "My hat is in the ring."

La Follette was not seriously ill, and he never forgave T.R. for having, as he believed, used him as a stalking-horse. But Fighting Bob was no match for the old master when it came to stirring up party activists, and his campaign fell apart. Roosevelt swept most of the thirteen state primary elections, winning 278 convention delegates to Taft's 48 and La Follette's 36. If La Follette was beaten, however, the suddenly aroused Taft was not, and he had a powerful weapon in his arsenal.

Taft controlled the party organization. As president, he appointed people to thousands of government jobs,

A Harper's Weekly cartoon depicting Theodore Roosevelt as a bull moose that relies on a trust for survival.

wedding their careers to his own success. In the Republican party, this power of the patronage was particularly important in the southern states, where the party consisted of little more than professional office-holders, including many blacks, who made their living as postmasters, customs collectors, agricultural agents, and the like. While the Republicans won few congressional seats and fewer electoral votes in the South, a substantial bloc of delegates to Republican conventions spoke with a Dixie drawl. They were in Taft's pocket and, along with northern and western party regulars, they vastly out-numbered the delegates Roosevelt had won in the primaries.

Consequently, when the convention voted on whether Taft or Roosevelt would be awarded 254 disputed seats, Taft delegates won 235 of them. Roosevelt's supporters shouted "Fraud!" and walked out. They formed the Progressive party, or, as it was nicknamed for the battle with the Republican elephant and the Democratic donkey, the Bull Moose party. (In a backhanded reference to La Follette's allegedly poor health and Taft's obesity, Roosevelt had said that he was "as strong as a bull moose.")

DEMOCRATIC PARTY PROGRESSIVISM

In one piece, the Republican party was unambivalently the nation's majority party, as four successive presidential elections had demonstrated. Split in two, however, the GOP was vulnerable and the Democrats smelled victory. When the convention assembled in Baltimore, there was an abundance of would-be nominees ready to leap into the breach. As at the Republican convention, but for a rather different reason, the key to winning the party's presidential nomination lay in the southern state delegations.

Because the South was "solid" in delivering electoral votes to the Democratic column, it held a virtual veto power over the nomination. The old two-thirds rule, so important in shaping Democratic party policy before the Civil War, had been reinstituted after it. In order to be nominated, a Democrat needed the votes of two-thirds of the delegates and no one could approach that total if the southern delegates opposed him as a group. A candidate with the southern delegates solidly behind him had a handsome head start on the nomination.

Democratic Hopefuls

In 1912, none of the leading candidates was offensive to the South, and each had southern supporters; thus the usual southern bloc was split. William Jennings Bryan was still popular with southerners, and he was interested. As a three-time loser, however, he was not a very attractive candidate. Bryan's only hope was a deadlocked convention when he might be selected as a compromise candidate.

Oscar Underwood of Alabama was another minor hopeful; he commanded the support of the southern "Bourbon" conservatives, but for that reason he was unacceptable to southern progressives, who might more accurately be described as Populists who had learned to preach racism along with attacks on big business. Some progressives supported Judson Harmon of Ohio. Others backed Champ Clark, the "Old Hound Dawg" of Missouri, which was as much a southern as a western state. In fact, Clark went into the convention confident of winning. The man who left it a winner, however, was New Jersey governor Woodrow Wilson, who was nominated on the forty-sixth ballot.

A Moral, Unbending Man

Wilson was a southerner himself; he had been born in Virginia and raised in Georgia. He practiced law, then abandoned it, earned a Ph.D. degree, and ended up as a professor of political science at Princeton University. In 1902, he had been named president of Princeton, the first nonminister to hold that post at the still strongly Presbyterian school.

Wilson had more than a little of the Presbyterian clergyman in him. His father and both grandfathers had been parsons. So was his wife's father. He had been raised to observe an unbending Calvinist morality, and his sensitivity to the struggle between good and evil in the world was reflected in an ascetic, lean figure and a sharply chiseled, thin-lipped face. With his family and a few intimate friends, Wilson was fun-loving and playful, a fan of the cinema, liable to erupt in horseplay with his daughters, who adored him. Publicly, he was formal, sometimes even icy. A less talented man with such a personality would never have risen half so high as Wilson did.

In fact, his meteoric rise in politics was almost accidental. In 1910, he was merely an honored educator,

Woodrow Wilson was the president of Princeton University before entering political life.

the president of an Ivy League university. He had transformed the college from an intellectually lazy finishing school where rich young men made social contacts into a institution that commanded intellectual respect. But Wilson's stubbornness caught up with him in a rather trivial matter. He tried to close down Princeton's "eating clubs," exclusive student associations much like fraternities, and clashed with trustees and alumni dedicated to their preservation.

When he was offered the Democratic nomination for governor of New Jersey, he quit academic life. To everyone's surprise except, perhaps, Wilson's, he won the governorship in the traditionally Republican state and the upset made him a national figure overnight. He was less social reformer than an honest-government progressive and set about cleaning up the state bureaucracy and the Democratic party. Like Teddy Roosevelt in New York a decade before, Wilson was soon at odds with the bosses of his own party in New Jersey.

WILSONIAN HORSEPLAY

Stern and forbidding in person, Woodrow Wilson's private personality was rather the opposite. On the morning after his wedding to his second wife in 1915, he was seen in a White House corridor doing a dance and singing, "Oh, you beautiful doll." His daughters by his first wife, Margaret, Jessie, and Eleanor, certainly showed no signs of moralistic browbeating. One of their amusements in the White House was to join tourists who were being shown around by guides and make loud remarks about the homeliness and vulgarity of the president's daughters.

They were delighted when he decided to seek the presidency. Ironically, in terms of what was to follow, he offered himself to the party as a safe and sane alternative to William Jennings Bryan and Champ Clark, a conservative.

The Campaign of 1912

In fact, Wilson's "New Freedom," as he called his program, was a decidedly less ambitious blueprint for reform than was Roosevelt's "New Nationalism." Wilson emphasized states' rights to the extent that he opposed the Progressive party's comprehensive social program as strongly as Taft did. He considered Roosevelt's proposals to augur a dangerous expansion of government powers.

The two men differed even more sharply on the question of the trusts. Whereas T.R. had concluded that consolidation, even monopoly, was inevitable in a modern industrial society and that the federal government should supervise and even direct the operations of the big corporations in the public interest, Wilson condemned this vision as "a partnership between the government and the trusts." Wilson believed that competition in business was still possible in modern America. In his view, the government's task was to play watchdog over business, ensuring and restoring free competition by breaking up the trusts. In 1912, he opposed the huge, permanent government apparatus that Roosevelt endorsed.

With the Republican organization in tatters and Taft practically dropping out of the race, it would have been difficult for Wilson to have lost the election. Nevertheless, he campaigned tirelessly and skillfully. Articulate, as a college professor is supposed to be, Wilson was also exciting—as few college professors are. Lifelong dreams of winning public office flowered in eloquent speeches that left no doubt that the Presbyterian schoolmaster was a leader.

Wilson won only 41.9 percent of the popular vote but a landslide in the electoral college, 435 votes to Roosevelt's 88 and Taft's 8. Eugene V. Debs, making his fourth race as the Socialist party nominee, won 900,000 votes, 6 percent of the total. The big jump after four years of a conservative president seemed to indicate that it was necessary to reform in order to stifle the socialist challenge. Taft, the only conservative candidate, won but 23.2 percent of the total vote.

Tariffs and Taxes

T.R. had usually gotten his way by outflanking Congress, interpreting the president's constitutional powers in the broadest possible terms. Taft had deferred to congressional leaders, ultimately collapsing before the most persuasive of them. Wilson's style was to act

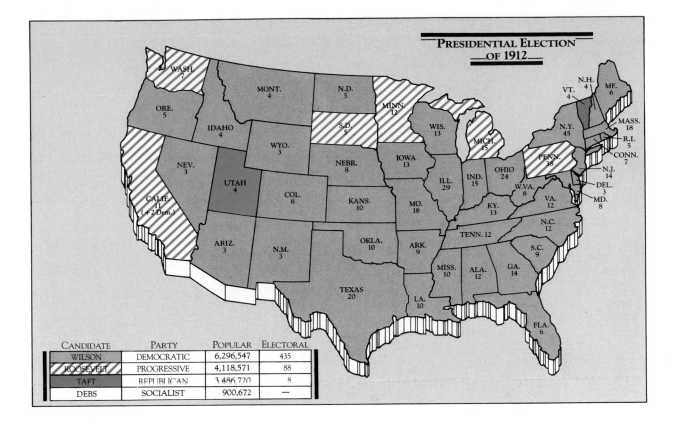

CANDIDATE	PARTY	POPULAR	ELECTORAL
WILSON	DEMOCRATIC	6,296,547	435
ROOSEVELT	PROGRESSIVE	4,118,571	88
TAFT	REPUBLICAN	3,486,720	8
DEBS	SOCIALIST	900,672	—

PRESIDENTIAL ELECTION OF 1912

as a prime minister. He was not a member of Congress, as the British prime minister is a member of the House of Commons, but he could and did address Congress personally as though he were. He was the first president to appear personally before Congress with his program since John Adams. Adams's successor, Thomas Jefferson, had suffered from a stammer and had set the precedent of communicating with Congress only through written messages.

Wilson's brief address was aimed less at persuading congressmen than at inspiring their constituents to put pressure on them, and it worked. A number of Democratic senators who had been dragging their feet on tariff revision fell into line. The Underwood-Simmons Tariff reduced the Payne-Aldrich rates by 15 percent and put on the free list several commodities that were controlled by trusts—iron, steel, woolens, and farm machinery—thus lowering prices on them.

The lower tariff reduced revenue for the government. To make up the losses, Wilson sponsored both a corporate and a personal income tax. It was not high by late twentieth-century standards. People who earned less than $3,000 a year paid no tax. On annual incomes between $3,000 and $20,000, a tidy sum in 1913, the rate was only 1 percent. People in the highest bracket, $500,000 and up, paid only 7 percent,

a fraction of the low brackets today. Nevertheless, by forcing the rich to pay proportionately more toward supporting the government, the tax provisions of the tariff law represented a triumph of progressive principles.

Wilson's Cabinet

Wilson designed his cabinet in order to unite the Democratic party behind him. The president never had liked William Jennings Bryan, but he named him secretary of state because Bryan had helped to nominate him and still owned the affection of many western Democrats.

Most other appointments rewarded key components of the party, especially the South and, through Secretary of Labor William B. Wilson, the labor movement, whose support the president wanted and needed. The most valuable member of the cabinet was Secretary of the Treasury William G. McAdoo. He provided the president with shrewd advice on banking policy. When McAdoo married Wilson's daughter, he became a kind of heir apparent.

Three confidants did not sit in the cabinet. Joseph Tumulty, a canny Irish politician, served as Wilson's private secretary and reminded the president of the

President Woodrow Wilson conferring with aides.

sometimes sordid realities involved in keeping together a political machine. Colonel Edward M. House, a Texas businessman, was a shadowy, but not sinister figure. Self-effacing and utterly devoted to the president, House neither desired nor accepted any official position. Instead, he traveled discreetly throughout the United States and abroad, informally conveying the president's views and wants, to businessmen and heads of state.

Louis D. Brandeis, a corporation lawyer become antitrust progressive, provided Wilson with both economic principles and a social conscience. The father of the New Freedom, Brandeis turned Wilson away from the limitations of the program after 1914 and toward a broader progressivism. In 1916, Wilson rewarded him by naming him to the Supreme Court, on which Brandeis served as one of the most influential liberal justices of the twentieth century. He was the first justice to consider sociological information along with legal precedent in adjudging the constitutionality of laws.

The New Freedom in Action

Two laws that reflected Brandeis's influence were the Federal Reserve Act of 1913 and the Clayton Antitrust Act of 1914. The first was designed both to bring order to the national banking system and to hobble the vast power of Wall Street. The law established twelve regional Federal Reserve Banks, which dealt not directly with people but with other banks. The Federal Reserve System was owned by private bankers who were required to deposit 6 percent of their capital in it. However, the president appointed the majority of the directors, who sat in Washington, theoretically putting the government in control of the money supply.

The greatest power of the Federal Reserve System is its control of the discount rate, the level of interest at which money is lent to other banks for lending to private investors and buyers. By lowering the discount rate, the Federal Reserve could stimulate investment and economic expansion in slow times. By raising the rate, the Federal Reserve could cool down an overactive economy that threatened to blow up in inflation, financial panic, and depression.

The Federal Reserve Act did bring some order to the national banking system. But it did not, as many progressives hoped, tame the great bankers. Indeed, because representatives of the private banks sat on the Federal Reserve Board, the long-term effects of the law were to provide Wall Street with an even more efficient, albeit more accountable, control of national finance.

In 1914, Wilson pushed his antitrust policy through Congress. The Clayton Antitrust Act stipulated that corporations would be fined for unfair practices that threatened competition, forbade interlocking directorates (the same men sitting on the boards of "competing" companies and thereby coordinating policies), and declared that officers of corporations would be held personally responsible for offenses committed by their companies. Another bill that was passed at the same time created the Federal Trade Commission to supervise the activities of the trusts. This agency looked more like T.R.'s New Nationalism than the New Freedom Wilson had plumped for in 1912.

Wilson Changes Direction

After the congressional elections of 1914, Wilson shifted far more sharply toward the reforms that Teddy Roosevelt had promoted. Although the Democrats retained control of both houses, many progressives returned to their Republican voting habits in 1914 and cut the Democratic margin in the House. It was obvious to both the president and Democratic congressmen that if they were to survive the election of 1916 against a reunified Republican party, they would have to woo these progressive voters.

Consequently, Wilson agreed to support social legislation that he had opposed as late as 1914. He did not like laws that favored any special interest, farmers any more than bankers, but in order to shore up support in the West, he agreed to the Federal Farm Loan Act of 1916, which provided low-cost credit to farmers. Early in his administration, Wilson had opposed a child-labor law on constitutional grounds. In 1916, he supported the Keating-Owen Act, which severely restricted the employment of children in most jobs.

The Adamson Act required the interstate railroads to put their workers on an eight-hour day without a reduction in pay. Wilson even moderated his anti-

---

FORM 1040

The income tax, somewhat as it is known today, was first collected in March 1914. The original tax was designed to have well-to-do Americans pay the bulk of the federal government's bills. At a time when the average worker made $800 a year, no person earning less than $3,000 (about $35,000 in today's values) paid the tax. The rate was just 1 percent after deductions, with a surtax of 6 percent on incomes over $500,000 (about $6 million today). In part because the income tax was progressive, hitting the well-to-do harder than the tariff and excise tax did, it was quite popular at first.

During World War I, however, the need for funds lowered the minimum taxable income to $1,000. What had been a tax on the upper classes became a tax on almost all who worked. In 1990, after the tax reforms of the Reagan administration, lower- and middle-income families pay disproportionately more of the government's expenses than they did before the income tax was adopted.

---

black sentiments, although Washington definitely took on the character of a segregated southern city during his tenure. Despite a lifelong opposition to woman's suffrage, the president began to encourage states to enfranchise women and to hint that he supported a constitutional amendment that would guarantee the right nationwide.

By the summer of 1916, Wilson could say with considerable justice that he had pushed progressive reform farther than had any of his predecessors. He enacted or supported much of Theodore Roosevelt's program of 1912, as well as his own. By 1916, however, Americans' votes reflected more than their views on domestic issues. They were troubled about their nation's place in a suddenly complicated world. Simultaneous with the enactment of Wilson's New Freedom and more than a little of T.R.'s New Nationalism, Europe had tumbled into the bloodiest war in history.

For Further Reading

Overviews of the era are Vincent P. DeSantis, *The Shaping of Modern America, 1877–1916* (1973); Arthur S. Link, *Woodrow Wilson and the Progressive Era* (1954); George E. Mowry, *The Era of Theodore Roosevelt* (1958); William L. O'Neill, *The Progressive Years: America Comes of Age* (1975); Robert H. Wiebe, *The Search for Order, 1880–1920* (1967).

Indeed, virtually all the books cited at the conclusion of Chapter 36 are relevant to this chapter as well. In addition, see D. F. Anderson, *William Howard Taft: A Conservative's Conception of the Presidency* (1973);

John M. Blum, *Woodrow Wilson and the Politics of Morality* (1956); P. E. Coletta, *The Presidency of William Howard Taft* (1973); John A. Garraty, *Woodrow Wilson* (1956); Lewis L. Gould, *Reform and Regulation: American Politics, 1900–1916* (1978); Otis L. Graham, Jr., *The Great Campaigns: Reform and War in America, 1900–1928* (1971); Samuel T. Hays, *Conservation and the Gospel of Efficiency: The Progressive Conservation Movement, 1890–1920* (1959); and the multivolume Arthur S. Link, *Woodrow Wilson* (1947–65).

A few days before his inauguration in 1913, Woodrow Wilson was reminded of some difficulties in American relations with Mexico. He thought about the problem for a moment and set it aside, remarking, "It would be the irony of fate if my administration had to deal chiefly with foreign affairs."

Wilson did not fear such a challenge. His self-confidence was as sturdy as Theodore Roosevelt's. But his academic and political careers had been devoted to domestic concerns. He had paid scant attention to the thorny snarls in which relations among nations could be tangled, and he never had been particularly interested in them. When the Wilson of 1913 considered the rest of the world, it was on the basis of assumptions and sentiments rather in terms of a coherent, deliberate policy.

38

AMERICA DISCOVERS EUROPE

The First World War, 1914–1918

Soldiers man the trenches that zigzagged across the French countryside during the First World War.

WILSON, THE WORLD, AND MEXICO

Like most Americans, the president was proud that because of its population and industrial might, the United States ranked with only a handful of nations as a great world power. Also like other Americans, he believed that the United States was unique among great and lesser powers alike. Protected from Europe by a broad ocean, the United States required no huge armies to defend its security but, instead, expended its resources in constructive ways. Founded on the basis of an idea in men's minds rather than on inheritance of a common culture and territory, the American nation should act toward other countries in accordance with principles rather than out of narrow self-interest.

Moral Diplomacy

As a man with a moralistic view of the world, Wilson had roundly criticized Teddy Roosevelt's gunboat diplomacy. To bully small nations was to betray the principle of self-determination on which the United States had been founded. He pointedly announced that his administration would deal with the weak and turbulent Latin American countries "upon terms of equality and honor." As a progressive who was suspicious of Wall Street, Wilson also disapproved of Taft's dollar diplomacy. Shortly after he took office, Wilson canceled federal support of an investment scheme in China because of the implication that the government had an obligation to intervene in the event that the investors' profits were threatened. If Wall Street financiers wanted to risk money in China, they would have to risk it, not expect Uncle Sam to underwrite their profiteering.

Wilson was influenced by the Christian pacifism toward which Secretary of State William Jennings Bryan also leaned. Bryan believed that war was justified only in self-defense. If nations would act cautiously and discuss their problems, they would not have to spill blood. With Wilson's approval, Bryan negotiated conciliation treaties with 30 nations. The signatories pledged that in the event of a dispute, they would wait and talk for one year before declaring war. Bryan believed that during this "cooling-off" period, virtually every dispute between nations could be resolved without the use of force.

The Missionary Position

High ideals, but once in the cockpit, Wilson found that applying them consistently was more difficult than flying the recently invented airplane. In part, this was

Wilson shakes his finger at Mexico in rebuke in this cartoon from Punch.

because of the untidy and unruly characteristics of reality. In part, it was because he was also impelled by assumptions that conflicted with the moral principles by which he had been raised and the progressive principles he had absorbed.

A southerner, Wilson had no doubts about the superiority of the white race. By no means a lynch-mongering redneck, Wilson had the attitudes toward blacks of a southern gentleman, patronizing but also firm. The academy in which he had spent his adult life was permeated with theories and pseudo-sciences assuming the white man's superiority. As president, Wilson found it difficult to act as an equal in dealing with nonwhite nations such as Japan and the racially mixed Latin Americans.

His commitment to diplomacy by good example was complicated by a missionary's impulse to dictate proper behavior. When weaker nations did not freely emulate American ways of doing things, Wilson could wax arrogant, patronizing, and demanding. If other peoples did not realize what was good for them, Wilson would teach them.

So he raised no objections to a California state law that insulted race-sensitive Japan by restricting the right of Japanese immigrants to own land. In 1915, he ordered the marines into black Haiti when chaotic conditions there threatened American investments; the next year, he landed troops in the Dominican Republic under similar circumstances. These actions angered Latin Americans, but they were minor irritants compared with Wilson's prolonged and blundering interference in Mexican affairs.

¡Viva Madero!

In 1911, the Mexican dictator for 35 years, Porfirio Díaz, was overthrown following a revolution supported by practically every Mexican region and social group except the tiny elite that Díaz had favored. Foreign investors, who had reaped rich rewards by cooperating with the dictator, waited and fretted, none more so than the British and Americans. The leader of the revolution spoke of returning control of Mexican wealth to Mexicans, and Americans alone owned $2 billion in property in Mexico, most of the country's railroads, 60 percent of the oil wells, and more mines than Mexicans controlled. About 50,000 Americans lived in Mexico.

Francisco Madero was the reflective idealist who headed the revolution. He and Wilson would have disagreed, but they might also have gotten along. Madero was cultivated, educated, and moderate, not given to acting rashly. Moreover, he shared Wilson's liberal political philosophy and admired American institutions.

They never had to chance to communicate. Quietly encouraged by American diplomats during the Taft administration, a group of Díaz's generals led by Victoriano Huerta staged a coup. Apparently making their plans in the American embassy, the rebels struck shortly before Wilson was inaugurated, murdered Madero, and seized control of the federal government.

¡Viva Carranza!

The murder offended Wilson. He said that he would not deal with "a government of butchers," and he pressured England to withdraw its hasty recognition of the Huerta government. When peasant rebellions broke out in scattered parts of Mexico and a Constitutionalist army took shape behind a somber, long-bearded aristocrat, Venustiano Carranza, Wilson openly approved.

In April 1914, the United States intervened directly in the civil war. Seven American sailors on shore leave in Tampico were arrested by one of Huerta's colonels.

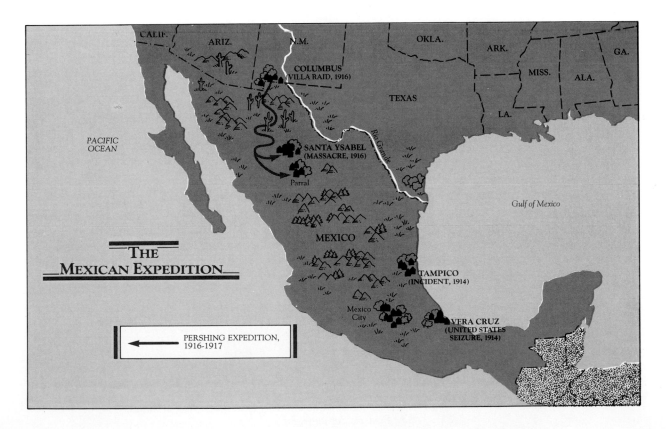

They were freed almost immediately, but Huerta refused the demand of Admiral Henry T. Mayo for a 21 gun salute as the appropriate apology. Claiming that American honor had been insulted (and seeking to head off a German ship that was bringing arms to Huerta), Wilson ordered troops into the important port of Vera Cruz.

To Wilson's surprise, ordinary Mexicans joined the fight against the Americans, and street fighting in Vera Cruz claimed more than 400 lives. Wilson failed to understand that while Huerta was unpopular, the memory of the Mexican War was fresh in the Mexican memory. Rebel groups generally resented gringo interference as much as Huerta did. Even Carranza, in control of the north of Mexico, condemned the American landing. Somewhat alarmed by his fix, Wilson agreed to an offer by Argentina, Brazil, and Chile to mediate the crisis.

¡Viva Villa!

Before anything could be settled, Carranza ousted Huerta. However, he then quarreled with one of his own generals, a bizarre, charismatic character who had been born Doroteo Arango, but was universally known as Pancho Villa. Alternately jovial and peevish, part-time bandit and part-time social revolutionary, Villa

was romanticized by the young American journalist John Reed as "The Robin Hood of Mexico." Villa cleverly played for American approval and, for a time, Wilson was convinced that Villa represented democracy in Mexico.

But Wilson wanted stability most of all. When Carranza took Mexico City in October 1915, Wilson recognized his de facto control of the government. This stung Villa, prompting him to show his seamier side. Calculating that American intervention would destabilize Mexico and create an opportunity for him to seize power, Villa stopped a train carrying American engineers invited by Carranza to reopen mines, and shot all but one. Early in 1916, he sent a raid across the border into the dusty little desert town of Columbus, New Mexico, where his brigands killed 17 people.

Instead of allowing Carranza to root out and punish Villa, as was proper with neighboring nations that were sovereign equals, Wilson ordered General John J. Pershing and 6,000 troops, including the black Tenth Cavalry, to pursue and capture the bandit guerrilla. They were humiliated. In the arid mountainous state of Chihuahua that was his home, Villa easily evaded the American expedition, leading the soldiers on 300 miles of a zigzag route during which time they never gained sight of Villa's main force. Pershing's

Bandit and revolutionary Pancho Villa (center) with the leader of agrarian revolt in Mexico, Emiliano Zapata (right).

men did, however, exchange shots several times with Carranza's troops. In one skirmish, 40 died. While accomplishing nothing, Wilson had succeeded in alienating every political faction in Mexico.

In January 1917, he finally gave up and ordered "Black Jack" Pershing to return home. Only because Americans were faced by a more formidable enemy, the German Kaiser, were they able to make light of their humiliation at the hands of a man whom they considered an illiterate *bandido*.

THE GREAT WAR

By the beginning of 1917, Europe had been at war for two and a half years. In June 1914, a Serbian (Yugoslavian) nationalist, Gavrilo Princip, had assassinated Archduke Franz Ferdinand of the Austro-Hungarian Empire, which included among its provinces two, Bosnia and Herzogovina, that were largely Serbian in population. At first it appeared that the incident would pass; turn-of-the-century Europe had seen an epidemic of sensational assassinations.

But Austro-Hungarian sensitivity to the decline of its once majestic empire, obligations among the great powers of Europe written into secret treaties, the weakness of the Russian czar and the irresponsibility of the German Kaiser, and the reckless arms race in which the European nations had been engaged for a generation, plunged the Continent into war.

Tangled Alliances

Serbia, a slavic nation, was an ally of Russia, which backed the little country in defying Austria. Austria-Hungary looked to powerful Germany for encouragement, and got it. France, sworn to revenge a defeat at the hands of the Germans in 1870, became involved due to French fears of German industrial might, which had led to secret agreements promising mutual support to Russia. England, traditionally aloof from European wrangles, had been frightened by Germany's construction of a worldwide navy (larger than America's and second only to Britain's) and, early in the century, had signed mutual-assistance treaties with both France and Russia.

Many of the smaller nations of Europe were associated with either the Central Powers (Germany, Austria-Hungary, Bulgaria, Turkey) or the Allied Powers (England, France, Russia, eventually Italy). By August 1914, most of Europe was at war. Eventually, 33 nations would be involved.

Americans React

The American people reacted to the explosion with a mixture of disbelief and disgust. For a generation, Eu-

Kaiser Wilhelm's love of militarism bordered on the ludicrous and did nothing to help his image in the United States.

ropean rulers had filled the air with the sounds of saber rattling. Americans were used to that; their own Teddy Roosevelt was a master of bluff and bluster, and he liked the military strut. But T.R., it seemed, had understood the difference between a bully show and a catastrophe. Until 1914, so had the Europeans. Even Kaiser Wilhelm II of Germany, an absurd and broadly ridiculed figure with his extravagant military uniforms, golden spiked helmet, comic-opera waxed moustache, and penchant for bombast, had acted prudently in the crunch. Like most Europeans, Americans concluded that the constant talk about war without going to war would continue indefinitely. They did not really believe that powerful, civilized countries would turn their terrifying technology for killing on one another.

Once European nations had done just that, Americans consoled themselves that their nation, at least, remained above such savagery. Politicians, preachers, and editors quoted and praised the wisdom of George

THE EUROPEAN ALLIANCES

CENTRAL POWERS	BRITISH WAR ZONE
ALLIED POWERS	GERMAN SUBMARINE WAR ZONE
NEUTRAL NATIONS	

Washington's and Thomas Jefferson's warning against "entangling alliances." They blamed Europe's tragedy on Old World corruptions, its kings and princes, religious intolerance, nationalistic hysteria, and insane stockpiling of armaments that were superfluous if they were not used, suicidal if they were.

Never did American political and social institutions look so grandly superior. Never had Americans been more grateful to have turned their backs on Europe's ways. As reports of hideous carnage on the battlefield began to hum over the Atlantic Cable, Americans shuddered and counted their blessings. No prominent person raised an objection when President Wilson proclaimed absolute American neutrality. However, when the president also called on Americans to be "neutral in fact as well as in name, . . . impartial in thought as well as in action," he was, as he was wont to do, demanding too much of human nature.

Sympathy for the Allies

A large proportion of Americans looked to England as their ancestral as well as cultural motherland, and they were naturally sympathetic to Britain's cause. Wilson himself was an unblushing Anglophile. Before becoming president, he had vacationed regularly in Great Britain. He had written a book in which he broadly admired the British parliamentary form of government, and in his first year in office, he had resolved the last

minor points of difference between England and the United States: a border dispute in British Columbia, a quarrel between Canadian and American fishermen off Newfoundland, and British objections to discriminatory tolls on the Panama Canal.

Hardly noted at first, but ominous in the long run, American and British capitalists were closely allied. British investments in the United States were vast, and when the cost of purchasing everything from wheat to munitions required that these holdings be liquidated, they were sold to Americans at bargain rates. Banking houses like the House of Morgan lent money to the English, at first with Wilson's disapproval, and acted as agents for Allied bond sales. By 1917, Great Britain owed American lenders $2.3 billion. It was a strong tie, when compared to the meager $27 million that the Germans managed to borrow in the United States. Wall Street had good reason to favor a British victory or, at least, to pale at the thought of a British defeat.

Many Americans were also sympathetic to France. The land of Lafayette was America's "oldest friend," the indispensable ally of the Revolution. Americans never had formally gone to war with the French. And France was, except for the United States, the only republic among the world's great powers, constitutionally pledged to civil equality and representative institutions.

Sympathy for the Central Powers

But Americans were by no means unanimously favorable to the Allies. One American in three was either foreign-born or a first-generation citizen, many of them with strong Old World sentiments that made them pro-German or unfriendly toward the Allied Powers. Millions of Americans traced their roots to Germany or Austria-Hungary. While they had come to the United States for its economic opportunities, many of them clung to their old culture. Few German-, Austrian-, or Hungarian-Americans seriously believed or suggested that their adopted country take the side of the fatherland. But they did hope for American neutrality, and in heavily German areas like Wisconsin and other parts of the Midwest, they said so loudly. The National German League numbered 3 million members and actively worked against intervention.

German-Americans joined with Irish-Americans in the German-Irish Legislative Committee for the Furtherance of United States Neutrality and the Labor's National Peace Council. Many of the nation's 4.5 million people of Irish descent hated England. When England crushed an Irish rebellion in 1916 (which was backed by Germany), a few prominent Irish-Americans declared for the German cause.

Similarly, many Russian and Polish Jews, who had suffered brutal persecution under the czars, supported Germany. They thought of Germany and Austria as countries where Jews enjoyed civil equality. Socialists, an important minority within both the Jewish and German-American communities, hated Russia above all other countries because of the cruelty of the czar's secret police.

With so diverse a population and such a tangle of conflicting loyalties, Wilson's policy of neutrality not only was idealistic, but was the only practical alternative, especially for a Democratic party politician who depended on ethnic voters. And it might have worked if Europe's "Great War" (as the First World War was called until the Second broke out in 1939)

had been fought for clearly stated and limited goals, and had been concluded with an early victory by one side or the other.

The Deadly Stalemate

A quick victory was what the German General Staff had in mind. Germany's "Schlieffen Plan," which dated back to 1905, was to knock the modern French army out of the war by flanking its defensive line. This meant invading France through neutral Belgium. Once in control of France's Channel coast, German troops would be able to keep the British army from landing in Europe and sweep down on Paris, just as the Germans and done in 1870.

In the meantime, Von Schlieffen had said, weakened German forces on the Eastern Front would take a drubbing from the Russians. However, once France was defeated and Britain neutralized, troops from the western front could be sped to meet the Russians on railroads designed for just that purpose.

The Schlieffen Plan failed because, instead of providing a broad avenue into France, the Belgians resisted heroically. Capturing the single fortress city of Liége took the Germans twelve days, longer than they expected to be in Belgium. Frustrated, the invaders treated the Belgians with a chilling ferocity, earning a reputation as "the savage Hun," which profoundly influenced public opinion in the United States and elsewhere.

During the delay, the Russians advanced deeply into German territory, and the German General Staff lost its nerve. At a critical moment, the high command weakened the army on the western front in order to stop the Russians in the east. They did so, winning a tremendous victory at the Battle of Tannenberg. But the war bogged down into stalemate. Enemy armies dug entrenchments and earthworks and faced one another—along 475 miles in the west—across a "no man's land" of moonscape craters, spools of barbed wire, and the smell of death. For three years men on both sides would hurl themselves "over the top" and die by the tens of thousands for the sake of advancing the trenches a few miles.

The Technology of Killing

A revolution in military technology, and the inability of the generals to comprehend it, made the war unspeakably bloody. Although the airplane, first flown at Kitty Hawk, North Carolina, in December 1903, captured the imagination of romantics, it was of little importance in battle. (Ordinary soldiers considered pilots playboys. They were, but they were not sissies; the life expectancy of British pilots once at the front was two weeks.) Nor was poisonous mustard gas, used

---

WHAT'S IN A NAME?

The British called it the European War, and Americans were inclined to use that term until the United States intervened in April 1917. Then, a few idealistic but awkward tags were tried: War for the Freedom of Europe, War for the Overthrow of Militarism, War for Civilization, and—best known—Woodrow Wilson's War to Make the World Safe for Democracy. Only after 1918 did the Great War and the World War become standard—until 1939 when the outbreak of another great worldwide war made it World War I.

NOTABLE PEOPLE

WILLIAM D. HAYWOOD
1869–1927

Big Bill Haywood was famous during the years before the Great War. As the head of the IWW, the Industrial Workers of the World, he came close to wielding real power as a leader of the unskilled industrial and agricultural working people so vital in the economy. But the war was to destroy Haywood's career and shatter his vision of what America should mean. Within a few years after the guns were stilled, he was a lonely exile who would never come home.

William D. Haywood was born in Salt Lake City in 1869. He became a miner in northern Nevada while still a teenager. Several times he turned to other work, cowboying, prospecting for a mine of his own, homesteading on the site of an abandoned army post. Haywood was a quintessential westerner, looking for the chance to improve himself, an implicit believer in the American gospel of opportunity that said the West was the place a man could best do such a thing.

Bad luck and the attractive wages gold and silver miners took home brought Haywood back to the mines of Silver City, Idaho. There he found his opportunity to rise within the Western Federation of Miners, the militant labor union of the miners, mill, and smelter workers of the region. His forceful personality and aptitude for running an organization brought him to the attention of the WFM's leadership in Denver. At the turn of the century, Haywood moved to the metropolis as the WFM's Secretary-Treasurer.

In Silver City, Haywood had supervised an orderly union local, negotiating wages and conditions across a table from the owners of the mines. Elsewhere in the West, union miners fought violent strikes with their employers, which were increasingly large corporations with headquarters in San Francisco, New York, and London.

The miners resented absentee control of the gold and silver they believed they had found and which they won from the earth. They worked daily with explosives and were apt, when pushed, to fight back with dynamite and guns. The bosses, when they sensed a chance to break the miners' unions and gain uncontested control of labor in the mining camps, were equally quick to use violence in the form of hired thugs and pliant local and state authorities. Bill Haywood found himself one of the leaders of an organization engaged in what was unmistakeably class warfare. He did not disdain the role. During the 1890s, he had concluded that some form of socialism, common rather than private ownership of the means of production, was the only way to achieve social justice in the United States.

The miner owners and their allies in government considered Haywood one of an "Inner Circle" of sinister conspirators whom they held responsible for the disorder. If he could be removed from the scene, they believed they could gain the upper hand in labor rela-

Bill Haywood and Elizabeth Gurley Flynn of the IWW march with striking textile workers in Paterson, New Jersey.

tions. In 1906, when a ne'er-do-well known as Harry Orchard confessed that he had murdered a former governor of Idaho on the orders of the "Inner Circle," Haywood was brought to trial in Boise.

The prosecution's case relied heavily on the testimony of the unsavory Orchard. Haywood's lawyer, Clarence Darrow, seized on this and defended him by prosecuting Orchard's character. Haywood was acquitted.

His career in the WFM was at an end. Other leaders of the union believed Haywood's tough talk was responsible for the trial (and may have believed him guilty of the crime). It mattered little to Haywood. The publicity had made him an eminent man. Intellectuals, particularly in New York's Greenwich Village, lionized him as a primal, exemplar of the working masses. He lectured widely, building his image with a simple, eloquent platform manner. He was elected to the Socialist party's National Executive Committee and twice represented the party at international conferences. He became an organizer for the IWW, the revolutionary union of unskilled workers he had helped found in 1905. He was in the headlines during strikes the IWW led in Lawrence, Massachusetts, in 1912 and Paterson, New Jersey in 1913.

In 1914, Haywood became Secretary-Treasurer of the IWW, in effect its leader. He introduced a degree of order to an organization that had been almost guerrilla-like in its operations. He regularized dues collections, set up an efficient national office in Chicago, and perfected a system for enrolling the dispersed casual workers who brought in the nation's grain harvest, previously a virtually unorganizable workforce.

Haywood's IWW opposed American entrance into World War I. Haywood was, however, very cautious in the issue. He believed that the workers' business lay "at the point of production," in the factory, field, forest, and mine, not in fighting causes that, however noble, were beyond their power to effect. He attempted to soft-pedal the IWW's antiwar line. He dropped bitterly sardonic antiwar lyrics from the IWW's songbook and said that it was a matter of personal choice whether or not members registered for the draft.

To no avail. In the fall of 1917, federal authorities launched nationwide raids of IWW headquarters. Either because they believed that the IWW was really treasonous, because they feared what the union's strength in the critical areas of agriculture, lumber, and copper could mean to the war effort, or simply because they saw a chance to use wartime hysteria as an opportunity to crush the anticapitalist IWW and Big Bill Haywood, the federal prosecutors did just that.

Long trials for sedition drained the IWW's resources and distracted its leaders from the business of running a union. Vigilante action against the IWW in the field reduced its membership. For all his cynical comments about the capitalist enemy, Haywood was shocked that he and more than a hundred other IWW leaders were found guilty of charges that bordered on the absurd.

By 1921 he was stunned by the shattering of the IWW. Like many American socialists, Haywood found consolation only in the success of the Bolsheviks in far-off Russia. Instead of reporting to prison, he slipped aboard a ship and sailed for the Soviet Union.

For a few years, while the Russian Communists deluded themselves that international revolution was just around the corner, Haywood acted like a leader of that campaign, appearing at ceremonies in Moscow. When the capitalist order proved far from dead in Europe and America, and the Soviet leaders engrossed themselves in domestic affairs, Haywood was first put in charge of a factory (he was apparently a failure at the job) and then pensioned off in a small apartment in the Russian capital.

He was delighted to receive American visitors but was miserable as an exile. There was no alternative. To return to the United States meant prison. In 1927, he suffered a stroke and died.

by both sides, very effective. Its results were devastating, but a slight shift in the wind blew the toxic fumes back on the army that had loosed it.

The machine gun, on the other hand, made the old-fashioned mass infantry charge, such as had dominated battle during the American Civil War, an exercise in suicide. When one army charged out of its trenches, enemy machine guns filled the air with a hurricane of lead that mowed down soldiers by the thousands. On the first day of the Battle of the Somme in July 1916, 60,000 young Britons were slaughtered or wounded, the majority of them within the first half hour. By the time the Somme campaign sputtered to a meaningless end, British losses totaled 400,000; French, 200,000; and German, 500,000.

The British developed the tank as a means of neutralizing German machine guns. Armored vehicles could drive unharmed directly into gun emplacements. But the generals never used their edge intelligently. They attached the tanks to infantry units, thus slowing them to a walk, rather than sending groups of the steel monsters in advance of the foot soldiers.

Incompetence at the top of every army contributed substantially to the bloodshed. Petty personal jealousies among generals of the Allies, especially between the English and the French, resulted in decisions that had nothing to do with the welfare of the common soldier or even the winning of the war.

The War at Sea

Americans were sickened by the news from Europe, but it was the war at sea that directly touched American interests. As in the past, naval war was economic war; it was aimed at destroying the enemy's commerce and, therefore, its ability to carry on the fight. Naval superiority allowed Great Britain to strike first, proclaiming a blockade of Germany.

According to the "rules of war," all enemy merchant ships were fair game for seizing or sinking, although tradition required that crews and passengers be rescued. The ships of neutral nations, however, retained the right to trade with any nation as long as they were not carrying contraband (at first defined as war materiel).

The laws of blockade, which had caused friction between the British and the Americans in the past, were more complicated, and in 1914 Great Britain introduced several new wrinkles. The British "blockaded" Germany by mining some parts of the North Sea. Ships, including those of neutrals, would risk being destroyed merely by attempting to trade with Germany. The Royal Navy stopped many American ships on the high seas and took them to British ports for search. Britain also redefined contraband to mean almost all trade goods, including some foodstuffs. When neutral Holland, Denmark, and Sweden began to import goods for secret resale to Germany (pastoral Denmark, which never before purchased American lard, imported 11,000 tons of it in the first months of the war), the British slapped strict regulations on trade with those countries.

American objections were mild. The German market never had been important to American shippers, and wartime sales to England and France rose so dramatically that exporters needed no extra business. Trade with the Allies climbed from $825 million in 1914 to $3.2 billion in 1916, a fourfold increase in two years.

At first the Germans were indifferent to the British blockade. Their plan had been to win a quick victory on land, which rendered economic warfare moot. When the war stalemated, however, the German General Staff recognized the necessity of throttling England's import economy. Germany's tool for doing this was another creation of the new military technology, the *Unterseeboot* (undersea boat, or U-boat), the submarine.

Submarine Warfare

Ironically, the modern submarine was the invention of two Americans, John Holland and Simon Lake. When the navy rejected their device as frivolous, however, they took their plans to Europe. The Germans recognized the submarine's potential and launched a large-scale construction program. By February 1915, Germany had a large enough flotilla of the vessels, each armed with 19 torpedoes, to declare the waters surrounding the British Isles to be a "war zone." All enemy merchant ships within those waters were liable to be sunk, and the safety of neutral ships could not be absolutely guaranteed. Within days, several British vessels went to the bottom, and President Wilson warned the Kaiser of Germany's "strict accountability" for American lives and property lost to U-boats.

Because submarines were so fragile, the kind of warfare in which they engaged appeared to be particularly inhumane. On the surface, the submarine was helpless; a light six-inch gun mounted inconspicuously on the bow of a freighter was enough to blow a U-boat to bits. Because submarines could dive only slowly, British merchant vessels were instructed to ram them. Therefore, German submarines had to strike without warning, giving crew and passengers no opportunity to escape. And since submarines were tiny, their crews were cramped, and there was no room to take aboard those who abandoned ship. Survivors of torpedoed boats were on their own in the midst of the ocean.

Many Americans grumbled that if the British block-

With a large flotilla of submarines, Germany turned British waters into a war zone during World War I.

"All the News That's Fit to Print."

The New York Times.

EXTRA
5:30 A. M.
Weather Today and Sunday. Fair.

VOL. LXIV...NO. 20,923.   •••••   NEW YORK, SATURDAY, MAY 8, 1915.—TWENTY-FOUR PAGES.   ONE CENT   In Greater New York, Jersey City and Newark.   Elsewhere TWO CENTS.

LUSITANIA SUNK BY A SUBMARINE, PROBABLY 1,260 DEAD; TWICE TORPEDOED OFF IRISH COAST; SINKS IN 15 MINUTES; CAPT. TURNER SAVED, FROHMAN AND VANDERBILT MISSING; WASHINGTON BELIEVES THAT A GRAVE CRISIS IS AT HAND

SHOCKS THE PRESIDENT

Washington Deeply Stirred by the Loss of American Lives.

BULLETINS AT WHITE HOUSE

Wilson Reads Them Closely, but Is Silent on the Nation's Course.

HINTS OF CONGRESS CALL

Loss of Lusitania Recalls Firm Tone of Our First Warning to Germany.

CAPITAL FULL OF RUMORS

Reports That Liner Was to be Sunk Were Heard Before Actual News Came.

Special to The New York Times.
WASHINGTON, May 7.—Never since that April day, three years ago, when word came that the Titanic had gone down, has Washington been so stirred as it is tonight over the sinking of the Lusitania. The early reports told that there had been no loss of life, but later reports told of the loss of the Lusitania...

The Lost Cunard Steamship Lusitania
X Where the First Torpedo Struck.   XX Where the Second Torpedo Struck.

Cunard Office Here Besieged for News; Fate of 1,918 on Lusitania Long in Doubt

Nothing Heard from the Well-Known Passengers on Board—Story of Disaster Long Unconfirmed While Anxious Crowds Seek Details.

List of Saved Includes Capt. Turner; Vanderbilt and Frohman Reported Lost

LONDON, Saturday, May 8, 5:30 A. M.—The Press Bureau has received from the British Admiralty at Queenstown a report that all the torpedo boats and tugs and armed trawlers, except the Heron, which went out from Queenstown to the relief of the Lusitania have returned.

Three vessels have landed 595 survivors and forty dead. Fifty-two...

Saw the Submarine 100 Yards Off and Watched Torpedo as It Struck Ship

Ernest Cowper, a Toronto Newspaper Man, Describes Attack, Seen from Ship's Rail—Poison Gas Used in Torpedoes, Say Other Passengers.

SOME DEAD TAKEN ASHORE

Several Hundred Survivors at Queenstown and Kinsale.

STEWARD TELLS OF DISASTER

One Torpedo Crashes Into the Doomed Liner's Bow, Another Into the Engine Room.

SHIP LISTS OVER TO PORT

Makes It Impossible to Lower Many Boats, So Hundreds Must Have Gone Down.

ATTACKED IN BROAD DAY

Passengers at Luncheon—Warning Had Been Given by Germans Before the Ship Left New York.

Only 650 Were Saved, Few Cabin Passengers

QUEENSTOWN, Saturday, May 8, 4:28 A. M.—Survivors of the Lusitania who have arrived here estimate that only about 650 of those aboard the steamer were saved, and say only a small proportion of those rescued were saloon passengers.

Official Confirmation
WASHINGTON, May 8.—A dispatch to the State Department early today...

The front page of the New York Times *on May 8, 1915, announcing the sinking of the* Lusitania, *an English luxury liner.*

ade was illegal, the German submarine campaign was immoral. The British were thieves, but the Germans were murderers, drowning seamen by the score. And more than seamen. The issue came to a head on May 7, 1915, when the English luxury liner *Lusitania* was torpedoed off the coast of Ireland, and 1,198 people of the 1,959 abroad were killed, including 139 Americans. What kind of war was this, Americans asked, that killed innocent travelers? The New York *Times* described the Germans as "savages drenched with blood."

Wilson Wins a Victory

The Germans replied that they had warned Americans against traveling on the *Lusitania* through advertisements in major New York and Washington newspapers. They pointed out that the *Lusitania* had not been merely a passenger ship. It had been carrying 4,200 cases of small arms purchased in the United States and some high explosives. So many people were lost because the *Lusitania* had gone down in only 18 minutes,

blown wide open not by the torpedo but by a secondary explosion. The British had been using innocent passengers as hostages for the safe conduct of war materiel.

Wilson was well aware of this and did not hold the British blameless in the tragedy. Nevertheless, Germany's military right to use the new weapon was less important to him than the principle of freedom of the seas for those not at war. He sent a series of strongly worded notes to Germany. The second was so antagonistic that the pacifistic Bryan feared it meant war. He resigned rather than sign it, and Wilson replaced him in the State Department with Robert Lansing, an international lawyer.

While making no formal promises to Wilson, the Germans stopped attacking passenger vessels, and the uproar faded. Then, early in 1916, the Allies announced that they were arming all merchant ships, and Germany responded that the U-boats would sink all enemy vessels without warning. On March 24, 1916, a sitting duck, a French channel steamer on a scheduled run between Dieppe and Folkestone, the

Sussex, went down with an American among the casualties. Wilson threatened to break diplomatic relations with Germany, the last step before a declaration of war, if "unrestricted submarine warfare" were continued.

The German General Staff did not want the United States to enter the war. Plans for a major offensive on all fronts were afoot, and the German navy did not have enough U-boats to launch a full-scale attack on British shipping. In the Sussex Pledge of May 4, 1916, the German foreign office promised to observe the rules of visit and search before attacking enemy ships. It meant effectively abandoning the use of the submarine, but it kept the United States out of the war.

AMERICA GOES TO WAR

Wilson had won a spectacular diplomatic victory at the beginning of his campaign for reelection. He was enthusiastically renominated at the Democratic convention, and his campaign was given a theme that did not entirely please him. The keynote speaker designed his speech around the slogan "He Kept Us Out of War."

He Kept Us Out of War—While Preparing for It

Wilson did not like the slogan because, as he confided to an aide, "I can't keep the country out of war. Any little German lieutenant can put us into war at any time by some calculated outrage." He meant that a submarine commander, acting on his own, could bark out the order that would torpedo the Sussex Pledge. Like many national leaders before and since, Wilson had trapped himself in a position where control over a momentous decision was out of his hands. He, at least, had the wisdom to know it.

Wilson began to prepare for the possibility of war as early as November 1915, when he asked Congress to beef up the army to 400,000 men and fund a huge expansion of the navy. He was pushed into this "preparedness" campaign by his political enemy Theodore Roosevelt, who jabbed and poked at the fact that American forces totaled fewer than 100,000; that the Quartermaster Corps (entrusted with supply) had only recently begun using trucks; that at one point in 1915 the American artillery had only enough ammunition for two days' fighting with cannon that were a generation obsolete.

Wilson also had to contend with an antipreparedness Congress led by Representative Claude Kitchin of North Carolina. With widespread backing among the western and southern progressives, on whom Wil-

A flag-waving preparedness parade of 1916.

son generally depended for support, the antipreparedness forces pointed out that it had been "preparedness" that had led to war in Europe in the first place. If the United States had the means to fight, they argued, it was all the more likely that the United States would fight. Wilson had to settle for a compromise, less of a military build-up than the Roosevelt forces wanted, more than Kitchin and his supporters liked.

The Election of 1916

While Wilson wrestled with the preparedness issue, the Republicans patched up their split of 1912. Progressives who were able to stomach T.R.'s aggressiveness wanted to maintain the Bull Moose party's independence. They met and nominated the Colonel to run. But Roosevelt wanted to win; he wanted the Republican nomination too. When he could not get it, he favored his friend, Henry Cabot Lodge, who was warlike enough, but no progressive. So easily, in the heat of war, he had lost sight of the ideal of 1912. When the Republicans actually nominated Supreme Court Justice Charles Evans Hughes, progressive in the past but a moderate on the war issue, T.R. lost heart and dropped out of the race. William Allen White wrote that the Progressives were all dressed up with nowhere to go.

Hughes's integrity was unimpeachable. In dignity and presidential bearing, he was Wilson's peer. His distinguished gray beard was a reminder of the simpler days before the Great War. He spoke in high-sounding phrases. But Hughes was also a dull fellow on the speaker's platform, and he lacked Wilson's moral toughness. Nor did his views on the war issue differ much from the president's; he too wanted to avoid war, but knew the United States could be forced into it. Nevertheless, thanks to Theodore Roosevelt, who stormed about the country sounding like the German Kaiser, the Republican choice came to be known as the war candidate.

This undeserved reputation cost Hughes just enough votes to give the election to Wilson. It was very close. Hughes carried every northeastern state but New Hampshire and every midwestern state but Ohio. He went to bed on election night believing that he was president. Then one antiwar western state after another turned in majorities for Wilson. When he carried California by a paper-thin margin, he was elected, 277 electoral votes to 254. The election was on Tuesday. Not until Friday did the American people know for certain who would lead them for the next four years.

Trying and Failing to Keep the Peace

Elated by the surprise but still nervous about the "little German lieutenant" who could plunge the United States into war, Wilson set out to mediate between the Allies and Central Powers. He had concluded that only by ending the war in Europe could he be sure of keeping the United States out of it. During the winter of 1916–17, he believed that he was making progress, at least with the Germans. For a time, the British seemed to be the major obstacle to peace.

On January 22, 1917, Wilson outlined his peace plan to Congress. Only a "peace without victory," a "peace among equals" with neither winners nor losers, could solve the problem. The progressive idealist did not call for a mere cessation of hostilities. He proposed to pledge the warring powers to uphold the principles of national self-determination and absolute freedom of the seas, and to establish some kind of international mechanism for resolving future disputes.

But it was all an illusion. He and the American people were in for a rude awakening. The proposal was not even half-digested when, a week later, the German ambassador informed Wilson that on February 1, German submarines would begin sinking neutral as well as enemy ships in the war zone around Great Britain. With a fleet of 100 submarines, the German military planners believed that they could knock Great Britain out of the war within a few months. They knew that breaking the Sussex Pledge meant almost certain American intervention. But because the United States was far from ready to intervene, the German leaders calculated that the war would be over before more than a token American force could be landed in Europe.

Wilson was crestfallen, then irate. He broke off diplomatic relations with Germany, as he had threatened to do, and asked Congress for authority to arm American merchant ships. When former progressive allies such as La Follette and Borah filibustered to prevent this, he denounced them as "a little group of willful men, representing no opinion but their own." For the first time, the president was the leader of the war party. Nevertheless, Wilson did not abandon all hope of staying out until German submarines sent three American freighters to the bottom. On the evening of April 2, mourning that "it is a fearful thing to lead this great peaceful people into war," a solemn Wilson asked Congress for a formal declaration.

A banner headline on the New York American *reported the beginning of war between the United States and Germany, April 6, 1917.*

For four days a bitter debate shook the Capitol. Six senators and about 50 representatives fought to the end, blaming Wilson for having failed to be truly neutral and claiming that the United States was going to spill its young men's blood in order to bail out Wall Street's loans to England and to enrich the munitions manufacturers, the "merchants of death." In one of the most moving speeches, freshman Senator George Norris of Nebraska said, "We are going into war upon the command of gold. . . . We are about to put the dollar sign on the American flag."

Why America Went to War

In later years, some historians would say that Norris had been right. With varying emphases, they agreed that special interests had methodically maneuvered the United States into a war that did not concern the country. To the extent that Wall Street favored a British victory for the sake of its own profits and that the "merchants of death" fed off the blood of soldiers, they were correct.

But to say that certain interest groups wanted to go to war is not to say that they had their way with Wilson and Congress. Woodrow Wilson was as unlikely to take his cues from Wall Street and the Dupont munitions works as he was to seek advice on a church matter from Theodore Roosevelt. To Wilson, the freedom of the seas was sacred, a right on which Americans had insisted since the 1790s. Moreover, the president shared in the profound shift in public sentiment from 1914 and even 1915, when virtually no American dreamed of declaring war, to the spring of 1917, when the majority favored entering the conflict. The reasons for his about-face lie in the growing belief that Germany represented a force for evil in the world and the skillful propaganda of the British and pro-British Americans in encouraging this perception.

The Hun and His Kultur

The depiction of Germans as barbaric "Huns" practicing a diabolical *Kultur* (merely German for "culture," but having a sinister ring to it in American ears) had its origins in the German violation of Belgian neutrality. Figuratively at first, the British and French called the invasion "the rape of Belgium" and soon discovered the propaganda value of the word. In fact, the German occupation of the little country, while harsh, was generally no more brutal than the wartime controls the British slapped on the ever-rebellious Irish. But wall posters representing the broken body of a young girl being dragged away by a bloated, beast-like German soldier in a spiked helmet elicited all the horrible implications that rape connotes.

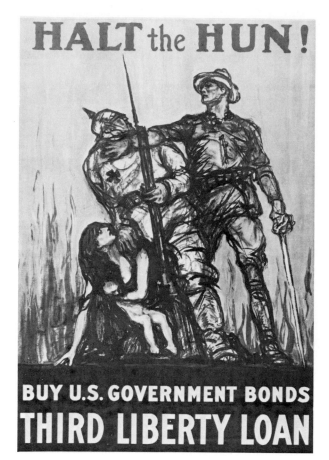

The art of the poster—expressing a thought instantly and forcefully—reached its apogee during World War I.

German insistences that their troops observed all due proprieties toward civilians were undermined in October 1915, when the German army executed Edith Cavell, the British head of the Berkendael Medical Institute in Brussels. Although Cavell was guilty of acts that were considered espionage under international law (she helped a number of British prisoners escape), the execution of a woman for charitable deeds was profoundly stupid in an age when women were only rarely executed for murder.

The submarine war further angered Americans. Not everyone agreed with Wilson that the rights of neutrals during modern war could be absolute. But repeated incidents of unarmed merchant seamen and innocent passengers drowning in the dark, cold waters of the North Atlantic touched a delicate nerve. Artists brilliantly aroused basic human fear in posters that showed seamen fighting vainly to swim while their ship sank in the moonlit background.

German saboteurs were probably not so active in the United States as British and pro-British propagandists claimed. Nevertheless, several German diplomats were caught red-handed in 1915 when a bumbling agent left incriminating papers on a train, and in 1916, the huge Black Tom munitions stores in New Jersey was completely destroyed in a suspicious "accident."

But the real blockbuster was a mere piece of paper. On February 25, 1917, while Wilson was searching for a last chance to avoid war, the British communicated to him a message that the German foreign minister, Arthur Zimmermann, had sent to the Mexican government. In the event that the United States declared war on Germany, Zimmermann had proposed, Germany would finance a Mexican attack on the United States. Assuming Germany won, Mexico would be rewarded after the war with the return of some of the territory that it had given up in the Mexican War 70 years earlier, specifically the "lost provinces" of New Mexico and Arizona.

It was a foolish proposal. Mexico was still wracked by civil turmoil, and was in no condition to make war on Guatemala, let alone the United States. Nevertheless, with the American people already angered, the Zimmermann Telegram persuaded many that the unprincipled Hun must be stopped.

The American Contribution

The Germans provoked the American intervention on a gamble. German leaders bet that their all-out U-boat attack would starve England into surrender before the Americans could contribute to the war effort. For three frightening months, it appeared as though they had guessed right. In February and March 1917, German submarines sank 570,000 tons of shipping bound to and from England. In April, the total ran to almost 900,000 tons. A quarter of the British merchant fleet lay at the bottom of the sea. (All told, 203 U-Boats sank 5,408 ships during the war, some 11 millions tons.) At one point in April 1917, the British had enough food on hand to feed the island nation for only three weeks.

But the worst passed and the Germans lost their wager. At the insistence of American Admiral William S. Sims, merchantmen ceased to travel alone. Guarded by naval vessels, particularly the small, fast, and heavily armed destroyers (the nemesis of the U-boats), merchant ships crossed the Atlantic in huge convoys. Over the objections of the Royal Navy (but with the support of Prime Minister David Lloyd George), Sims succeeded in building his "bridge of ships." As early as May 1917, U-boat kills dropped drastically, far below what the German navy claimed it could do. By July, the American navy took over most defense operations in the Western Hemisphere

and sent 34 destroyers to Queenstown, Ireland (present-day Cobh, Ireland), to assist the British. So successful was the well-guarded convoy system that only 200 out of 2 million American soldiers sent to France in 1917 and 1918 were drowned on the way. In the meantime, by commandeering more than a hundred German ships that were in American ports at the time war was declared (including the behemoth *Vaterland*, renamed the *Leviathan*) and by launching a massive shipbuilding program, the Americans were soon producing two ships for every one that the Germans sank.

The Fighting Over There

Soldiers went too. General John Pershing arrived in Paris in July 1917 with the first units of the American Expeditionary Force, the First Infantry Division. This was primarily a symbolic gesture. Because Pershing refused to send poorly trained men to the front, the Germans were proved right in gambling that American reinforcements could not in themselves turn the tide.

American troops head for the front in 1918.

American soldiers move supplies during the Argonne offensive, the last large battle involving Americans before World War I came to an end.

85,000 Americans helped hurl them back at Belleau Wood.

The Supreme Allied Commander, Field Marshal Ferdinand Foch, wanted to incorporate American troops into exhausted British and French units. Pershing stubbornly insisted that the Yanks fight as a unit. This was important to him not only for reasons of morale, but because Wilson had made it clear that the United States was not an "ally" of Britain and France but merely their "associate." In order to ensure his "peace without victory," Wilson was determined to play an independent role at the peace conference that would follow the war. Foch had no choice but to give in and grumble.

By the summer of 1918, the Americans in France represented the margin of victory over the Germans. In July, the Americans took over the attack on a bulge in the German lines called the St. Mihiel Salient, and succeeded in clearing it out. The final great American battle was along a 24-mile line in the Argonne Forest, a naturally rugged country just short of the border between France and Germany that had been transformed into a ghostly wasteland by four years of digging and shelling. It was in that position that over 1 million "doughboys" were sitting when, on November 11, 1918, the Germans surrendered.

The first Americans to see action, near Verdun in October, were used only to beef up decimated French, British, and Canadian units.

The autumn of 1917 went poorly for the Allies. The Germans and Austrians defeated the Italians in the south and, in November, knocked Russia out of the war. A liberal democratic government that had deposed the czar in March 1917 proved unable to keep a mutinous Russian army supplied, and a group of revolutionary Communists, the Bolsheviks, led by Vladmir Ilyich Lenin, seized power on the basis of promises of "Peace and Bread." The Treaty of Brest-Litovsk, which the Germans forced on the Russians, was vindictive and harsh. News of it convinced many Americans that they had done well in going to war to stop the Hun's hunger for world conquest. By closing down the eastern front, however, the Germans were able to throw a bigger army into France.

In May 1918, Germany launched a do-or-die offensive. The Allies fell back to the Marne River, close enough to Paris that the shelling could be heard on the Champs Elysées. But by this time there were 250,000 fresh American troops in France, including about 27,000 at Chateau-Thierry, near the hottest of the fighting. By the middle of July, when the Germans attempted one last drive toward the capital, about

WORLD WAR I CASUALTIES				
	Total mobilized forces	Killed or died	Wounded	Prisoners & missing	Total casualties
United States	4,791,000	117,000	204,000	5,000	326,000
Russia	12,000,000	1,700,000	4,950,000	2,500,000	9,150,000
France	8,410,000	1,358,000	4,266,000	537,000	6,161,000
British Commonwealth	8,904,000	908,000	2,090,000	192,000	3,190,000
Italy	5,615,000	650,000	947,000	600,000	2,197,000
Germany	11,000,000	1,774,000	4,216,000	1,153,000	7,143,000
Austria-Hungary	7,800,000	1,200,000	3,620,000	2,220,000	7,020,000
TOTAL	58,520,000	7,707,000	20,293,000	7,187,000	35,187,000

Armistice

In the trenches and back home, Americans celebrated deliriously. Millions of people gathered in city centers throughout the country, dancing and whooping. They believed that the Yanks had won the war. After all, the Germans had stalemated the French and British until the boys had gone "over there," in the words of a popular song of the time. Then, just a year after the Americans had begun to fight, it was over.

The American intervention was invaluable to the Allied victory, but the unmitigated joy in the United States was possible only because the American sacrifice was a comparatively minor one. Over 100,000 Americans were dead, more than half of them from disease (particularly the influenza that swept the world in 1918) rather than from bullets. By comparison, 1.4 million French and almost 1 million British soldiers died. Three-quarters of all the Frenchmen who served in the armed forces were casualties. Both France and Britain were badly maimed. Germany and Russia were defeated. If it was not true that the United States had "won the war," it was certainly true that the United States was the only nation whose people could feel like victors.

For Further Reading

Still within the momentous and exhaustively studied Progressive Era, books several times cited above remain basic, particularly Vincent P. DeSantis, *The Shaping of Modern America, 1877–1916* (1973); Arthur S. Link, *Woodrow Wilson and the Progressive Era* (1954); George E. Mowry, *The Era of Theodore Roosevelt* (1958); William L. O'Neill, *The Progressive Years: America Comes of Age* (1975); Robert H. Wiebe, *The Search for Order, 1880–1920* (1967).

Somewhat more narrowly focused on dealing with this era in part are E. H. Buehrig, *Woodrow Wilson and the Balance of Power* (1955); Foster R. Dulles, *America's Rise to World Power, 1898–1954* (1955); Lewis L. Gould, *Reform and Regulation: American Politics, 1900–1916* (1978); Otis L. Graham, Jr., *The Great Campaigns: Reform and War in America, 1900–1928* (1971); P. Edward Haley, *Revolution and Intervention: The Diplomacy of Taft and Wilson with Mexico, 1910–1917* (1970); George F. Kennan, *American Diplomacy, 1900–1950* (1951); David Kennedy, *Over Here: The First World War and American Society* (1980); N. G. Levin, Jr., *Woodrow Wilson and World Politics: America's Response to War and Revolution* (1968); A. S. Link, *Wilson the Diplomatist* (1957) and *Woodrow Wilson: War, Revolution, and Peace* (1979).

Also see Ernest R. May, *The World War and American Isolation, 1914–1917* (1959); Walter Millis, *The Road to War* (1935); R. E. Quirk, *An Affair of Honor: Woodrow Wilson and the Occupation of Vera Cruz* (1962); Lawrence Stallings, *The Doughboys* (1963); Charles C. Tansill, *America Goes to War* (1938); and William A. Williams, *The Tragedy of American Diplomacy* (1959).

For military history, an excellent source is Russell Weigley, *The American Way of War: History of United States Military Policy and Strategy* (1973). See also A. E. Barbeau and F. Henri, *The Unknown Soldiers* (1974); and Lawrence Stallings, *The Doughboys* (1963).

Woodrow Wilson called the Great War "a war to make the world safe for democracy." He sent the doughboys to Europe, and threw the industrial might of the United States behind the Allies on the understanding that there would be no victors in the traditional sense of the word, but, instead, a new world order dedicated to settling disputes between nations justly and peacefully. He also called the First World War "a war to end wars." And yet, while sincerely impelled by these high ideals, Wilson was also apprehensive. In April 1917, when the crusade had just begun, Wilson told a newspaper reporter, "Once lead this people into war, and they'll forget there ever was such a thing as tolerance. To fight you must be ruthless and brutal,

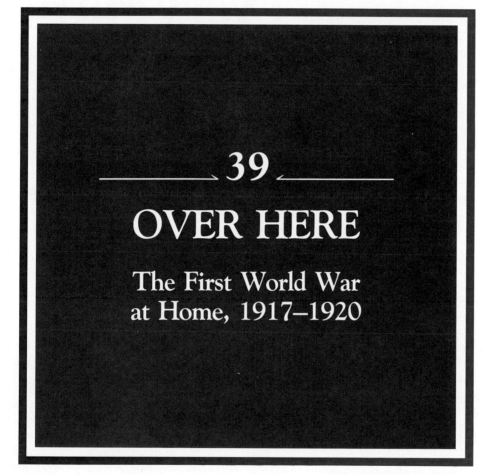

39
OVER HERE
The First World War at Home, 1917–1920

Jubilant American soldiers prepare to depart for Europe, "over there."

and the spirit of ruthless brutality will enter into the very fiber of our national life." It was to be one of the tragic ironies of Wilson's career that he was to initiate many of the policies that made his prophecy come true.

THE PROGRESSIVE WAR

The First World War was simultaneously the apogee of progressivism, when reformers had a free hand in turning their beliefs into policy, and the undoing of the progressive movement. For two years, progressive moralists and social planners of the New Nationalist stripe had their way in Washington. Within two years of the conclusion of the war, there was no progressive *movement*, only a few isolated voices crying in the wilderness of a hostile congressional minority and getting no replies but echoes from the past.

The Movement Splits

The conflict in Europe split the progressives. A few of them itched to fight. The most famous was Theodore Roosevelt, a pathetic shrill figure in his waning years. When the United States finally intervened, T.R. asked for a command in Europe. Prudently, for this was no splendid little war, Wilson ignored him, and in doing so permanently embittered many of Roosevelt's devotees.

Other Republican progressives, mostly westerners such as La Follette, Norris, Borah, and Hiram Johnson, held out to the bitter end for American neutrality. After the declaration of war, they toned down their rhetoric in the interests of national unity. (And in order to save their careers: some newspaper cartoonists depicted them accepting medals from the German Kaiser.) But they never changed their opinion that going to war was a tragic blunder that had been foisted on the country by munitions makers and bankers. They prolonged the debate on the Conscription Act of 1917 for six weeks, finally forcing Congress to exempt men under 21 from the draft. Any warmth they felt toward Wilson before April 1917 quickly dissipated thereafter.

Not so with other progressives. In Congress and out, the majority of them wholeheartedly supported the war. Like Wilson, they had come to believe that imperial Germany represented a deadly threat to free institutions all over the world. Moreover, in the task of mobilizing resources in order to fight the war, and in the wave of patriotic commitment that swept the country, the progressives saw a golden opportunity to put their ideas for economic and social reform to work.

This poster reminded men to register for the draft.

They were right on one count. It was impossible to wage modern total war and cling to the nineteenth-century vision of a free, unregulated economy. Armies that numbered millions of men could not be supplied with food, clothing, shelter, medicine, and arms by companies that were free to do as their owners chose. France and England had clamped tight controls on their factories and farms. American progressives believed that the United States would have to do the same.

The progressives were not disappointed. Suggestions for regulation of business that had been rejected in peacetime as too radical proved, in the emergency of wartime, to be less than was necessary. The federal government virtually took over the direction of the economy.

The Planned Economy

Some 5,000 government agencies were set up during the 20 months that the United States was at war, a statistical average of more than eight new agencies a day! Some were useless, wasteful bureaucracies that were established without careful thought and served little purpose save to provide desks, chairs, paper clips, and salaries for the functionaries who ran them. A few were failures. The Aircraft Production Board was commissioned to construct 22,000 airplanes in a year. That figure was unrealistic. But the 1,200 craft and 5,400 replacement motors that the board actually delivered to France were far fewer than a hustler with a bank loan could have supplied.

Other agencies were more successful. The Shipping Board, actually founded in 1916 before the declaration of war, produced vessels twice as fast as the Germans could sink them. Privately run shipbuilding companies, loaded with deadwood in management, were not up to that herculean task.

The United States Railway Administration, headed by Wilson's son-in-law and secretary of the Treasury, William G. McAdoo, was created early in 1918 when the owners of the nation's railroads proved incapable of moving the volume of freight the war created. The government paid the stockholders a rent equal to their earnings in the prosperous prewar years and simply took over. McAdoo untangled a colossal snafu in management within a few weeks, and reorganized the railroads into an efficient system such as the nation had never known. About 150,000 freight cars short of what was needed to do the job in 1917, American railroads enjoyed a surplus of 300,000 by the end of the war.

The various war production boards were coordinated by a superagency, the War Industries Board, which was headed by a Wall Street millionaire, Bernard Baruch. His presence at the top of the planning pyramid indicated that the progressives had not won their campaign for a directed economy without paying a price. American industry and agriculture were regulated, indeed regimented, as never before. But democratically elected officials and public-spirited experts with no stake in the profits were not in the driver's seat. Businessmen were.

Herbert Hoover: The Administrator as War Hero

The task given to Food Administrator Herbert C. Hoover was even more difficult than McAdoo's, and his achievement was daily in the public eye. Hoover's job was to organize food production, distribution, and consumption so that America's farms could feed the United States, supply the huge Allied armies, and help maintain many European civilians.

Only 43 years old when he took the job, Hoover already was known as a "boy wonder." An orphan when still a boy in Iowa, Hoover moved to California and worked his way through Stanford University. A mining engineer, he decided to work abroad on new strikes rather than for established mining companies at home. He had his adventures; he and his wife were besieged in China during the Boxer Rebellion. Mostly, however, Hoover made shrewd investments and was soon a millionaire. He also grew bored with making money when he was still young and pointed his ambitions toward public service. Like Andrew Carnegie, Hoover believed that able, wealthy men had special responsibilities to society. Unlike Carnegie, who gave money away, Hoover meant to devote his talents for administration and organization to public service.

He got his chance when he happened to be in London when the Great War began. He was asked to take over the problem of getting food to devastated Belgium and jumped at the challenge. He liquidated his business, quickly mastered the complex and ticklish task of feeding people in a war zone, and undoubtedly saved tens of thousands, if not hundreds of thousands, of lives.

Hoover did it without charm or personal flash. He was an intense, outwardly humorless person—all business. His method was to apply engineering principles to the solution of human problems. Progressives admired just such expertise, and the cool, methodical Hoover was a refreshing contrast to other humanitarians who moved about in a cloud of pious self-congratulation. It is an insight into the spirit of the times that he became a war hero comparable to Black Jack Pershing and America's dashing ace pilot, Eddie Rickenbacker.

Hooverizing America

Hoover preferred voluntary programs to coercion, and food was not rationed in the United States as it was in Europe. Instead, Hoover sponsored colorful publicity campaigns that urged American families to observe Wheatless Mondays, Meatless Tuesdays, Porkless Thursdays, and so on. The program worked because compliance was easy, yet psychologically gratifying. Making do without a vital commodity one day a week was no real sacrifice, but doing so made civilians feel as though they were part of the fighting machine. And when a Meatless Tuesday was observed by millions, the savings were enormous.

Hoover also encouraged city dwellers to plant "Victory gardens" in their tiny yards. Every tomato that was raised at home freed commercially produced food for the front. His agency promoted classes in economizing in the kitchen and distributed cookbooks on how to prepare leftovers. The impact was so great that, half-seriously, Americans began to use the word hooverize to mean "economize." Chicago proudly reported that the housewives in that city had hooverized the monthly production of garbage down by a third.

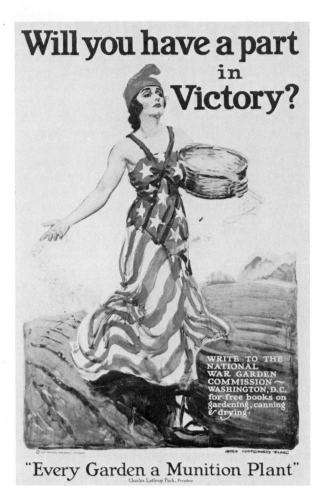

Will you have a part in Victory?

WRITE TO THE
NATIONAL
WAR GARDEN
COMMISSION ~
WASHINGTON, D.C.
for free books on
gardening, canning
& drying

"Every Garden a Munition Plant"

Charles Lathrop Pack, President

A National War Gardens Commission poster encouraged citizens to plant home vegetable gardens, thus freeing commercial producers to concentrate on providing goods for the war effort.

Hoover increased farm production through a combination of patriotic boosting and cash incentives. He helped increase wheat acreage from 45 million in 1917 to 75 million in 1919. American exports of foodstuffs to the Allies tripled over already high prewar levels. Hoover was called "the Miracle Man," and another young Washington administrator, Undersecretary of the Navy Franklin D. Roosevelt, wanted the Democratic party to nominate him for president in 1920.

Managing People

People were mobilized too: workers and ordinary citizens as well as soldiers. In May 1917, Congress passed the Selective Service Act, the first draft law since the Civil War. Registration was compulsory for all men between the ages of 21 and 45. (In 1918, the minimum age was lowered to 18.) From the 10 million who registered within a month of passage (24 million by the end of the war), local draft boards selected able-bodied recruits according to quotas assigned them. Some occupational groups were deferred, but no one was allowed to buy his way out, as had been done during the Civil War. Indeed, authority to make final selections was given to local draft boards in order to silence critics who said that conscription had no place in a democracy. The draft contributed about 3 million young men in addition to the 2 million who volunteered.

About 21,000 draftees claimed to be conscientious objectors on religious grounds, although, in the end, only 4,000 insisted on being assigned to noncombatant duty, as medics or in the Quartermaster Corps. Approximately 500 men refused to cooperate with the military in any way, some for political rather than religious reasons. Under the terms of the Selective Service Act, they were imprisoned and, generally, treated poorly. Camp Leonard Wood in Missouri had an especially bad reputation. In Washington state, a man who claimed that Jesus had forbidden him to take up arms was sentenced to death. He was not executed, but the last conscientious objector was not freed from prison until 1933, long after most Americans had come to agree with him that the war had been a mistake.

SOCIAL CHANGES

War is a revolutionary or, at least, an agitator. The changes impressed on American society from the top in the interests of victory inevitably affected social relationships. Some groups consciously took advantage of the government's wants, needs, and preoccupations to achieve old goals. Others were merely caught up by the different rhythms of a society at war.

Labor Takes a Seat

In order to keep the factories humming, Wilson made concessions to the labor movement that would have been unthinkable a few years earlier. He appointed Samuel Gompers, the patriotic president of the American Federation of Labor, to sit on Baruch's War Industries Board. In return for this recognition, Gompers pledged the AFL unions to a no-strike policy for the duration of the conflict.

Because wages rose during the war, there were comparatively few work stoppages. Business boomed, and employers dizzy with bonanza profits did not care to jeopardize them by resisting moderate demands by their employees. Most important, the National War Labor Board, on which five AFL nominees sat, mediated industrial disputes before they disrupted production and, in many cases, found in favor of the workers.

The quiet incorporation of organized labor into the decision-making process made the AFL "respectable," as it never had been before. From 2.7 million members in 1914, the union movement (including independent unions) grew to 4.2 million in 1919.

Blacks in Wartime

Like Gompers, leaders of black organizations hoped that by proving their patriotism in time of crisis, blacks would win an improved status. About 400,000 young black men enlisted or responded to the draft; proportionately, more blacks than whites donned khaki.

It was difficult to ignore the contradiction between Wilson's ringing declaration that the purpose of the war was to defend democracy and liberty and the second-class citizenship suffered by black people. W. E. B. Du Bois, the leader of the NAACP, pointedly reminded the president of the dichotomy, and Wilson did go so far as to issue a strong condemnation of lynching. Nevertheless, mere war could not destroy deeply rooted racist sentiments. Black soldiers were assigned to segregated units and usually put to menial tasks such as digging trenches and loading trucks behind the lines. Only a few black units saw combat, although one regiment that did was awarded the Croix de Guerre for gallantry in battle by the French government.

Members of the 369th Infantry, a black regiment, returned to the United States in 1919 wearing medals given to them by the French government commending them for gallantry in battle.

Military segregation had its advantages for some blacks. To command black units, the army trained and commissioned more than 1,200 black officers. This was particularly gratifying to Du Bois, who staked his hopes for the future on the creation of a black elite.

Race Riot at Home

More important in the long run than service in the army was the massive movement of blacks from the rural and strictly segregated South to the industrial centers of the North. Before 1914, only about 10,000 blacks a year drifted from the South to cities like New York, Philadelphia, Detroit, and Chicago. After 1914, when the risks of ocean travel choked off immigration from abroad while factories filling war orders needed workers, 100,000 blacks made the trek each year. It was not so great a leap in miles as the European immigration, but it was just as wrenching socially. From a Mississippi delta cabin to a Detroit factory and slum was a big change in way of life.

Those who served in the army, and most of those who moved north, were young people. They were less inclined to accept the daily humiliations that accompanied being black in white America. This was particularly true of the men in uniform, who believed that their service entitled them to respect.

The result was that 1917 was a year of racial conflict, with a frightening race riot in industrial East St. Louis, Illinois. In Houston, white civilians fought a pitched battle with black soldiers, and twelve people were killed. Although both sides shared the blame for the riot, thirteen black soldiers were hanged and fourteen were imprisoned for life. Du Bois and the NAACP were only partly correct in their analysis of how the war would affect blacks. Society made economic concessions to blacks in the interests of winning the war, but it did not grant civil equality.

It's a Woman's War

The woman's suffrage movement, on the contrary, skillfully parlayed wartime idealism and fears into final victory for the long-fought cause. Imitating British and French examples, the armed forces inducted female volunteers, mostly as nurses and clerical workers. More important was the same labor shortage that created opportunities in industry for blacks. Working-class women began doing factory work and other jobs that had been closed to them. Women operated trolley cars, drove delivery trucks, cleaned streets, directed traffic, and filled jobs in every industry from aircraft construction to zinc galvanization.

Middle-class women took the lead in organizing support groups. They rolled bandages, held patriotic rallies, and filled the holds of ships with knitted sweaters

Women riveters in a Puget Sound shipyard in 1918.

and socks and home-baked cookies for the boys in France. With women's contributions to waging the war so obvious, it was increasingly difficult for patriotic politicians to oppose suffrage with the argument that women belonged in the nursery minding infants.

Voting at Last

By 1917, the feminist movement was split once again into radical and conservative wings. Curiously, while the "radicals" and "conservatives" often had harsh words for one another, their different approaches both contributed to the victory of the suffrage movement. Thus, when the aggressive Women's Party led by Alice Paul demonstrated noisily in Washington, burning a copy of Wilson's idealistic Fourteen Points and chaining themselves to the fence in front of the White House, many politicians went scurrying for reassurance to the more polite National American Woman Suffrage Association.

Led by Carrie Chapman Catt, the association shrewdly obliged them. Not only did most American women oppose such irresponsible behavior, Catt argued, but social stability and conservative government could be ensured only by granting women the vote. Their numbers would counterbalance the increasing influence of radicals and foreigners at the polls, not to mention the blacks who were demanding their rights.

The suffrage movement was too long in the field and too large to be denied. Even Wilson, who instinctively disliked the idea of women voting, announced his support. On June 4, 1919, a few months after the Armistice, Congress sent the Nineteenth Amendment to the states. On August 18, 1920, ratification by Tennessee put it into the Constitution. "The right of citizens . . . to vote," it read, "shall not be denied or abridged by the United States or by any State on account of sex." Carrie Chapman Catt had no doubt about what had put it over. It was the war, the former pacifist said, that liberated American women.

The Moral War

Another long progressive campaign already had been brought to a victorious end. Like the suffragists, the prohibitionists appeared to be stalled permanently on the eve of the war. In 1914, only one-quarter of the states had prohibition laws on the books, and many of those were casually enforced. With American intervention in the war, however, the antidrinking forces added a new and decisive argument to their armory: the distilling of liquor consumed vast quantities of grain that were needed as food. Shortly after the declaration of war, Congress passed the Lever Act, a section of which forbade the sale of grain to distilleries.

Because many breweries were run by German-Americans, with their teutonic names emblazoned proudly on bottle and barrel, they were doubly handicapped in fighting the prohibitionists. Although Americans had developed a taste for cold lager beer, the beverage was still associated with Germans. Moralism, hooverizing, and the popular insistence on 100 percent Americanism all combined to bring about, in December 1917, the passage of the Eighteenth Amendment, which prohibited "the manufacture, sale, or transportation of intoxicating liquors" in the United States. It was ratified in 1919 and put into effect by the Volstead Act.

War usually leads to relaxation of sexual morality, as young men are removed from the social restraints of family and custom. The First World War proved to be no exception. However, well-meaning moralists in Wilson's administration hoped to take advantage of the mobilization of millions in order to instill high moral standards in the young men under their control. Josephus Daniels, the deeply religious secretary of the navy, thought of his ships as "floating universities" of moral reform. He gave orders to clear out the red-light districts that were a fixture in every naval port, and the army did the same in cities near its bases.

Prostitution was not eliminated by these orders any more than whiskey and beer drinking were abolished by the Eighteenth Amendment. But the short-term victories encouraged reformers in their belief that, among the horrors, the First World War was a blessing on reformers.

In 1920, for the first time, women in every state were eligible to vote.

CONFORMITY AND REPRESSION

It was not a blessing on civil liberties. As Wilson had predicted, white-hot patriotism scorched the traditions of free political expression and tolerance of disparate ways of life. Of course, free speech, religious expression, and ethnic variety had been violated before the First World War. But never had violation of the Bill of Rights been so widespread as during the war, and never had the federal government so stridently supported, even initiated, repression.

The Campaign against the Socialists

The Socialist party of America was the only important national political institution to oppose American intervention. In April 1917, just as war was being declared in Washington, the party met in an emergency convention in St. Louis and proclaimed "unalterable opposition" to a conflict that killed workingpeople and paid dividends to capitalists. Rather than hurting the party at the polls, this stance earned the party an increase in votes as many non-Socialists cast ballots for Socialists as the only way short of soap-boxing, a dangerous idea, to express their dissent.

Government moved quickly to head off the possibility of an antiwar bandwagon. The state legislature of New York expelled seven Socialist assemblymen simply because they objected to the war. Not until after the war did courts overrule the unconstitutional action. Victor Berger was elected to Congress from Milwaukee, but denied his seat by the House. When he then defeated the candidate supported by both the Democratic and Republican parties in the special election to fill the vacancy, Congress again refused to seat him. Berger's seat remained empty until 1923 when he was allowed to fill it. In the meantime, the Milwaukee Socialists' *Social Democratic Herald* and many other Socialist papers were denied cheap mailing privileges by Postmaster General Albert S. Burleson. Most of them never recovered from the blow.

The most celebrated attack on the Socialists was the indictment and trial of the party's longtime leader Eugene V. Debs for a speech opposing conscription. In sending Debs to prison, the Wilson administration was taking a chance. The four-time presidential candidate was loved and respected by many non-Socialists. At his trial in September 1918, Debs's eloquence lived up to its reputation. "While there is a lower class I am in it; while there is a criminal element I am of it; while there is a soul in prison, I am not free," he told the jury. But in prosecuting and jailing him and other prominent Socialists such as Kate Richards O'Hare, the government also made it clear that dissent on the war issue would not be tolerated.

The Destruction of the IWW

The suppression of the IWW was more violent. There was an irony in this because, while the radical union officially opposed the war, Secretary-Treasurer "Big Bill" Haywood tried to play down the issue. For the first time since its founding in 1905, the IWW was enrolling members by the thousands every month. Haywood hoped to ride out the patriotic hysteria of wartime and emerge from the war with a powerful economic organization.

But the government did not decide to move against the IWW because of its paper position on the war. Unlike the Socialists, who numbered many articulate and politically active middle-class people among their supporters, the IWW worked among the lowest ranks of the working class, people with little influence on public opinion. By 1917, however, most of these "Wobblies" were concentrated in three sectors of the economy that were vital to the war effort: among the migrant harvest workers who brought in the nation's wheat; among loggers in the Pacific Northwest; and among copper miners in western towns like Globe and Bisbee in Arizona and Butte in Montana. And these "Wobblies" refused to abide by the no-strike pledge that Samuel Gompers had made on behalf of the American Federation of Labor.

The IWW was crushed by a combination of vigilante terrorism and government action. In July 1917, a thousand "deputies" wearing white armbands in order to identify one another rounded up 1,200 strikers in Bisbee, loaded them on a specially chartered train, and dumped them in the Hermanas desert of New Mexico, where they were without food for 36 hours. The next month, IWW organizer Frank Little was lynched in Butte, possibly by police officers in disguise. In neither case was any attempt made to bring the vigilantes to justice. President Wilson pointedly ignored Haywood's protest of the Bisbee deportation and his demand for action in the case of Little's murder.

In the grain belt, sheriffs and farmers had a free hand in dealing with suspected Wobblies. In the Sitka spruce forests of Washington and Oregon (Sitka spruce was the principal wood used in aircraft construction), the army organized the Loyal Legion of Loggers and Lumbermen to counter the popularity of the IWW. There, at least, conditions were improved as the union was repressed, but attacks on the IWW were consistently vicious. Local police and federal agents winked at and even participated in everyday violations of civil rights and violence against Wobblies and their sympathizers.

Civil Liberties Suspended

The fatal blow fell in the autumn of 1917, when the Justice Department raided IWW headquarters in several cities, rounded up the union's leaders, and indicted about 200 under the Espionage Act of 1917. Along with the Sedition Act of 1918, the Espionage Act outlawed not only overt treasonable acts, but made it a crime to "utter, print, write, or publish any disloyal, profane, scurrilous, or abusive language" about the government, the flag, or the uniform of a soldier or sailor. A casual snide remark was enough to warrant bringing charges, and a few cases were based on little more than that.

In *Schenck* vs. *the United States* (1919), the Supreme Court unanimously upheld this broad, vague law. Oliver Wendell Holmes, Jr., the most liberal-minded and humane justice on the Court, wrote the opinion which established the principle that when "a clear and present danger" existed, such as the war, Congress had the power to pass laws that would not be acceptable in normal times.

Even at that, the government did not prove that the IWW was guilty of sedition. In effect, the individuals who were sentenced to up to 20 years in prison were punished because of their membership in an unpopular organization. Many liberals who had no taste for IWW doctrine but who were shocked at the government's cynical policy of repression fought the cases. In 1920, led by Roger Baldwin, they organized the American Civil Liberties Union to guard against a repetition of a shameful chapter in American judicial history.

Manipulating Public Opinion

The attack on the Socialists and the Wobblies was only one fulfillment of Wilson's prediction that a spirit of ruthless brutality would enter the fiber of American life. Americans in general were stirred to believe that they were engaged in a holy crusade, "a war to end war" against a diabolical foe. Violent acts against German-Americans and the very idea of German culture were commonplace.

Some of the innumerable incidents of intolerance that marred the wartime years were spontaneous; for example, a midwestern mob dragged a German-American shopkeeper from his home, threw him to his knees, forced him to kiss the American flag, and made him spend his life savings on war bonds. But the fire of intolerance that burned from coast to coast was also instigated and abetted by the national government.

The agency that was entrusted with mobilizing public opinion was the Committee on Public Information (CPI). Ironically, it was headed by George Creel, a progressive newspaperman who had devoted his career to fighting the very sort of intolerance and social injustice he now found himself encouraging. Creel faced a twofold task. First, to avoid demoralization, the CPI censored the news from Europe. The CPI dispatches emphasized victories and suppressed or played down stories of setbacks and the misery of life in the trenches between battles. With most editors and publishers solidly behind the war, Creel had little difficulty in convincing them to censor their own correspondents.

Crushing Kultur

Second, and far more ominously, the CPI took up the task of molding public opinion so that slight deviations

A wartime poster that was one of many used to encourage Americans to support their government's involvement in World War I.

"THEY DROPPED LIKE FLIES": THE GREAT FLU EPIDEMIC OF 1918

About 10 million people died as a result of battle during the four years of the First World War. Small wonder that the event staggered the confidence and morale of the European nations.

But the war was a modest killer compared with the "Spanish flu." During only *four months* late in 1918 and early in 1919, a worldwide flu epidemic, or pandemic, killed 21 million people. The American army in Europe lost 49,000 men in battle and 64,000 to disease, the majority of them to the flu. At home, fully 548,452 American civilians died, 10 times as many as soldiers felled in battle.

In the United States, the yet unnamed disease first appeared in March 1918, at Fort Riley, Kansas. After a dust storm, 107 soldiers checked into the infirmary complaining of headaches, fever and chills, difficulty in breathing, and miscellaneous aches and pains. Most curious to them, the illness had befallen them in an instant; one moment they were feeling fit, the next they could barely stand. Within a week, Fort Riley had 522 cases, and in a little more than a month, when the affliction abruptly disappeared, 8,000 cases. Almost 50 of the sick men died, not too disturbing a rate in an age when any number of contagious diseases forgotten today were considered deadly. Some doctors noted that these flu victims were in the prime of life and, presumably after basic training, in excellent condition. Moreover, most of them were strapping farm boys, who usually shook off such ailments as though they were colds.

It was wartime, however, and the soldiers from Fort Riley were shipped to Europe in May. The flu made a brief appearance in the cities of the eastern seaboard, but did not rival any of a number of epidemics, including a serious one in the United States in 1889 and 1890.

In Europe, the disease was far more deadly. In neutral Switzerland alone, 58,000 died of it in July. The deaths in the trenches on both sides of the line were enough, according to the German general Erich von Ludendorff, to curtail a major campaign. By June, the flu was sweeping Africa and India, where the mortality was "without parallel in the history of disease." That could be attributed to the wretched poverty of the subcontinent. But what of Western Samoa, where 7,500 of the island's 38,000 people died?

The total figures had not been calculated when the flu began a second and even more destructive tour of the world. The war had created ideal conditions for such a pandemic. People moved about in unprecedented numbers; 200,000 to 300,000 crossed the Atlantic to Europe each month, and many were carrying the unidentifiable germ. Moreover, war crowded people together so that conditions were also perfect for the successful mutation of viruses. With so many handy hosts to support propagation, the emergence of new strains was all the more likely.

That is apparently what happened in August, in western Africa, France, or Spain, which got the blame. A much deadlier variation of the original swept over the world, and this time the effects in the United States were cataclysmic.

In Boston, where it struck first, doubtless carried in by returning soldiers, 202 people died on October 1. New York City reported 3,100 cases in one day; 300 victims died. Later in the month, 851 New Yorkers died in one day, far and away the record. Philadelphia, which was particularly hard hit, lost 289 people on October 6; within one week, 5,270 were reported dead. The death rate for the month was 700 times its usual rate. Similar figures came in from every large city in the country. Just as worrisome, the disease found its way to the most obscure corners of the country. A winter logging camp in Michigan, cut off from the rest of humanity, was afflicted. Oregon officials reported finding sheepherders dead by their flocks.

Most public officials responded about as well as could be expected during a catastrophe that no one understood. Congress, many of its members laid low, appropriated money to hire physicians and nurses and set up clinics. Many cities closed theaters, bars, schools, and churches, and prohibited public gatherings such as parades and sporting events. Others, notably Kansas City, where the political boss frankly said that the economy was more important, carried on as usual. Mystifying moralists, Kansas City was no harder hit than were cities that took extreme precautions. (Nationwide and worldwide, about one-fifth of the population caught the Spanish flu, and the death rate was 3 percent.)

Several city governments required the wearing of gauze masks and punished violators with fines of up to $100. Many photographs that were taken during the autumn of 1918 have a surreal quality because of the masks. San Franciscans, their epidemic at a peak on Armistice Day, November 11, celebrated wearing gauze. Some wretched poet wrote the lines:

> Obey the laws
> And wear the gauze
> Protect your jaws
> From septic paws

Philadelphia gathered its dead in carts, as had been done during the bubonic plague epidemics of the Middle Ages. The city's A. F. Brill Company, a maker of trolley cars, turned over its woodshop to coffinmakers. The city of Buffalo set up its own coffin factory. Authorities in Washington, D.C., seized a trainload of coffins headed for Pittsburgh.

*An office worker wears a facemask to protect herself
during the deadly flu epidemic of 1918.*

Then, once again, the disease disappeared. There was a less lethal wave (perhaps another mutation) in the spring of 1919, with President Wilson one of the victims; and a leading historian of the phenomenon, Alfred W. Crosby, suggests that another minor epidemic in 1920 may have been a fourth wave. But the worst was over by about the time that the First World War ended, leaving physicians to reflect on the character of the disease and to wonder what they could do if it recurred.

There were some things to reflect on. The first has already been noted: the Spanish flu struck very suddenly, offering individuals no way to fight it except to lie down and wait.

Second, the disease went fairly easy on those people who are usually most vulnerable to respiratory diseases, the elderly; and it was hardest on those who usually shake off such afflictions, young people. In the United States, the death rate for white males between the ages of 25 and 34 was, during the 1910s, about 80 per 100,000. During the flu epidemic it was 2,000 per 100,000. In a San Francisco maternity ward in October, 19 out of 42 women died. In Washington, a college student telephoned a clinic to report that 2 of her 3 roommates were dead in bed and the third was seri-

ously ill. The report of the police officer who was sent to investigate was "Four girls dead in apartment." Old people died of the flu, of course, but the death rate among the elderly did not rise a point during the epidemic!

Third, people who had grown up in tough, poor, big-city neighborhoods were less likely to get the disease and, if they got it, less likely to die of it than were people who had grown up in healthier environments.

These facts eventually led scientists to conclude that the Spanish flu was a mutation of a common virus that caused a flu that was nothing more than an inconvenience. It was postulated, although never proved, that the deadly germ was the issue of an unholy liaison between a virus that affected humans and another that affected hogs. Spanish flu became "swine flu."

Thus, poor city people, who were more likely to suffer a plethora of minor diseases, had developed an immunity to the virus that farm people had not. Because old people were spared in 1918 and 1919, it has been said that the Spanish or swine flu was related to the less fatal virus that had caused the epidemic of 1889 to 1890. Having been affected by it, the elderly were relatively immune to its descendant.

Anti-German sentiment became part of Hollywood movies after the United States entered World War I. In the film Stake Uncle Sam to Play Your Hand, *actress Mae Marsh was shown under the threatening grasp of an evil German soldier, played by A. C. Gibbons.*

from full support of the war were branded as disloyal. Obviously, all German-Americans could not be imprisoned. (Only 6,300 were actually interned compared with 45,000 of Great Britain's much smaller German community.) However, the CPI could and did launch a massive propaganda campaign that depicted German *Kultur* as intrinsically vile.

The CPI issued 60 million pamphlets, sent prewritten editorials to pliant (or merely lazy) newspaper editors, and subsidized the design and printing of posters conveying the impression that a sinister and ubiquitous network of German spies was operating in the United States. With money to be made in exploiting the theme, the infant film industry centered in Hollywood, California, rushed to oblige. A typical title of 1917 was *The Barbarous Hun*. (Another film company was prosecuted in 1917 for releasing a film about the American Revolution that depicted British troops in an unfavorable light.)

At movie theaters before shows and during intermissions, a corps of 75,000 "Four-Minute Men," volunteers, delivered patriotic speeches of that length, 7.5 million such messages in all. Film stars such as Douglas Fairbanks, Charlie Chaplin, and Mary Pickford ("America's Sweetheart") appeared at Liberty Bond rallies and spoke anti-German lines written by the CPI.

Liberty Hounds and Boy Spies

The anti-German hysteria could take laughable form. Restaurants revised their menus so that sauerkraut became "liberty cabbage," hamburgers became "Salisbury steak" (after a liberal British lord), and frankfurters and wiener sausages, named after German and Austrian cities, became widely known as "hot dogs."

The real dog, the dachshund, had to be transformed into a "liberty hound." Towns with names of German origin chose more patriotic designations. German measles, then a common childhood disease, became "patriotic measles." Hundreds of schools and some colleges dropped the German language from their course offerings. Dozens of symphony orchestras refused to play the works of German composers, leaving noticeable holes in the repertoire. Prominent German-Americans who wished to save their careers found it advisable to imitate the opera singer Ernestine Schumann-Heinck. She was a fixture at patriotic rallies, her ample figure draped with a large American flag and her magnificent voice singing "The Star-Spangled Banner" and "America the Beautiful."

But the firing of Germans from their jobs, discriminating against German farmers, burning of German books, and beating and occasional lynching of German-Americans were not so humorous. Nor was the treatment of conscientious objectors by organizations of self-appointed guardians of the national interest with names like "Sedition Slammers," "Terrible Threateners," and even "Boy Spies of America." The members of such organizations stopped young men on the streets and demanded to see their draft cards. The largest of these groups, which were responsible for hundreds of illegal acts, was the American Protective League. At one time it numbered 250,000 members, many of whom probably had signed up simply to avoid having their loyalty questioned.

WILSON AND THE LEAGUE OF NATIONS

Why did Woodrow Wilson, a Jeffersonian liberal before the war, tolerate and even encourage such government-abetted behavior? The answer lies in the fact that the president's dream of building a new and just world order became an obsession with him. Like no president before him (but like several since), he lost interest in domestic affairs except insofar as they affected his all-consuming foreign policy concerns. The one-time enemy of big government presided over its extraordinary expansion. Repression of dissenters, even unjust and illegal repression, appeared to hasten the defeat of the Kaiser, so Wilson abandoned values that had guided his life.

The President's Obsession

In January 1918, Wilson presented to Congress his blueprint for the postwar world. It consisted of "Fourteen Points," which, Wilson insisted, were to be incorporated into the treaty that would eventually be found. Mostly, Wilson's points dealt with specific European territorial problems to be resolved, but several general principles were woven through the plan.

First, Germany must be treated fairly and generously in order to avoid the festering resentments that could lead to another war. Wilson was well aware that, for more than 40 years before the war, French politicians had called for revenge for Germany's defeat of France in 1870. In practical terms, Wilson meant that Germany must not lose territory occupied by German-speaking people and must not be saddled with huge reparations payments—"fines" as punishment for the war—such as British and French leaders were at that very time telling their people would be paid.

Second, the boundaries of all European countries must conform to nationality as defined by language. Like many others, Wilson believed that the aspirations of people to govern themselves had been a major cause of the war. No such concessions were to be made to the nonwhite peoples in Europe's colonies, however, although Wilson called for Germany's colonies to be disposed of on some basis other than as spoils of war divided among the victors.

Third, Wilson demanded "absolute freedom upon the seas, . . . alike in peace and in war." This was a reference to the German submarine campaign that Wilson blamed for American intervention, but it also hearkened to Britain's historical inclination to use British primacy on the waves to interfere with neutral shipping.

Fourth, Wilson demanded disarmament. It was obvious to all parties that the arms race of the two decades preceding the war had not been a deterrent but a major cause of the tragedy.

Finally and most important toward avoiding another Great War, Wilson called for the establishment of "a general assembly of nations," a kind of congress of countries, to replace the alliances and secret treaties that, he believed, had contributed to the tragedy of 1914. More than any other aspect of his program, the dream of a League of Nations came to obsess the president.

Wilson Fools Himself

As ultimate victory was ensured by an Allied breakthrough during the summer of 1918, Wilson turned virtually all his energies to planning for the peace conference to be held in Paris. He announced that he would personally head the American delegation, the first president to take so active a part in diplomatic negotiations.

The enormity of the First World War justified such an innovation, but Wilson somewhat mistook his enthusiasm for remaking the world as reflecting the mood of the American people. In the congressional elections of 1918, held just a week before the armistice, the voters returned Republican majorities of 240 to 190 to the House of Representatives and of 49 to 47 to the Senate. The new Congress not only was Republican, but had a decidedly unidealistic tinge. Old bosses and professional politicians who had struggled against the reformers for a decade were coming back to Washington.

They were not all hidebound reactionaries, nor Wilson-haters, by any means. They were the kind of men who were willing to make deals. But Wilson did not try to cultivate their good will by including a prominent Republican among the delegates with whom he

*None of his three fellow heads of government at the Versailles Conference shared Wilson's
ideals or hopes for the future.*

sailed to Europe on December 4. Nor did he recognize that, in choosing so many Republican regulars, the American people were reflecting a weariness with the idealism and rigorously active government of the Wilson administration.

Wilson also misinterpreted his reception in England, France, and Italy. Everywhere he went he was greeted with roaring cheers and blizzards of flowers thrown by adoring crowds. With a new democratic government in Germany surrendering on the basis of the Fourteen Points, Wilson believed that the people of Europe had risen to greatness, expressing their support for a peace without victors and a postwar world organized on principles of justice.

The Peace Conference

He could not have been more mistaken. The cheering crowds were welcoming not a visionary leader, but a conqueror, the man who, they believed, had tilted the stalemated war in their favor, enabling their countries to win it. Their leaders, the men with whom Wilson sat down in Paris, understood this. They had a much more realistic view than the American president of what the four years of terribly destructive war had meant to Europe. The peoples of the Allied nations wanted to avenge the bitterness of their sacrifices by tasting the sweet fruits of victory. For four years, the other three members of the "Big Four" had promised

them those fruits. Now, in 1919, they paid lip service to Wilson's ideals, but once behind the closed doors of the conference room, they put their national interests first.

Indeed, Georges Clemenceau, the prime minister of France, commented wryly, "God gave us the Ten Commandments and we broke them. Wilson gives us the Fourteen Points. We shall see." Clemenceau was a cagey, tough, and bitter infighter whom a lifetime in politics, mostly in opposition, had turned into a cynic. He was determined to hang the blame for the war on Germany and to ensure that France would never again be attacked. Clemenceau wanted to strip Germany of valuable territory and saddle the German people with huge reparations payments that, on top of their massive war debt, would hobble Germany for a generation.

David Lloyd George of Great Britain was personally more cordial to Wilson. But he was a habitual backroom manipulator given to inconstancy and outright deceit; and he too had political demands to meet. His country had suffered dreadfully from the bloodletting and wanted reparations. Moreover, the Royal Navy had no intention of giving up its dominance on the high seas.

Vittorio Orlando of Italy was only casually interested in the larger questions. He went to Versailles to make sure that Italy was rewarded with Austrian territory, including several regions of the Alps that were home to 200,000 German-speaking people, and the port of Fiume on the Adriatic, a city that was largely Serbian in population. His goals directly contradicted Wilson's Point Nine. The Japanese delegate, Count Nobuaki Makino, not a member of the Big Four, was determined to retain the German colonies in the Pacific that Japan had seized. So much for Point Five.

Bit by bit the Allies drew new lines on Wilson's blueprint. When the president revealed how all-important the League was to him by insisting that its Covenant (constitution) be acted on early in the proceedings, they calculated that he would give in on other questions in order to save it. He did. The terms of the Treaty of Versailles, which Wilson brought home in July 1919, bore only a passing resemblance to the Fourteen Points he took to Europe eight months earlier.

Article 10

Europe's rejection of Wilson's call for national self-determination in Europe and just treatment of Germany did not much concern the senators who had the constitutional responsibility to approve or reject the treaty. On the contrary, only 12 of the 49 Republican senators, mostly the western progressives who had opposed going to war in 1917, announced themselves to be "irreconcilable" in their opposition to the pact. Still fuming because the United States went to war in the first place, they meant to isolate the United States from corrupt Europe once again.

In March 1919, before Wilson returned from Versailles, the other 37 Republican senators signed a round robin declaring themselves to be "reservationists" on the issue. That is, while they considered the Treaty of Versailles as it stood to be unacceptable, they let the president know that they would vote to ratify if Wilson made some changes in it or accepted their reservations. What worried them most was Article 10 of the League Covenant, which pledged all member states to "preserve against external aggression the territorial integrity and . . . political independence

PRESTIGE

John Maynard Keynes, a member of the British delegation at the Versailles Peace Conference, wrote that Woodrow Wilson enjoyed a prestige and a moral influence throughout the world unequaled in history. His bold and measured words carried to the peoples of Europe above and beyond the voices of their own politicians. The enemy peoples trusted him to carry out the compact he had made with them; and the Allied peoples acknowledged him not as a victor only but almost as a prophet.

ROUND ROBIN

A round robin is a petition or statement that is signed by several people with no one of them identified as the leader or instigator. All sign around the text of the document in order to disguise the order of signing. The intent of the round robin is precisely the opposite of that of John Hancock in signing his name so prominently to the Declaration of Independence.

of all members." Article 10 seemed to commit the United States to go to war if any other member of the League were attacked.

Wilson replied that Article 10 was merely a moral obligation on the part of members, and, long after his day, he would be proved correct; throughout its history, the League was unable to enforce its decisions. Nevertheless, having said that the article had little concrete meaning, Wilson refused to make a single concession to the worried senators. In his stubbornness, he created an opportunity for the chairman of the Senate Foreign Relations Committee, an old friend of Theodore Roosevelt who despised everything about the president, to destroy his dream.

The Fight for the League

Henry Cabot Lodge was a dapper, ill-tempered senator from Massachusetts who was not very popular with his colleagues. As stubborn and demanding as Wilson, he lacked a shred of Wilson's greatness. Nevertheless, Lodge proved in the battle over the League to be a much shrewder politician than the president. Perceiving that Wilson was growing less flexible, Lodge became open and cooperative with senators who disliked the League less avidly than he did. Understanding that the longer the debate dragged on, the less the American people would be interested in the League, Lodge played for time and welcomed every one of Wilson's refusals to compromise. He read the entire 264 pages of the treaty into the record of his committee's hearings, even though it already had been published and placed on every senator's desk.

Lodge guessed right, and Wilson, less reasonable with every day, guessed wrong. Whereas the majority of Americans doubtless favored the League in the first months of 1919, their interest waned slowly but perceptibly as the months passed.

The climax came in September. With the treaty about to come before the Senate, Wilson undertook an exhausting 8,000-mile speaking tour. He believed that by rallying the people behind him, he could pressure the reservationist senators to vote for the treaty. By September 25, when he moved into Colorado, the crowds seemed to be with him. At Pueblo, however,

A weakened Woodrow Wilson relied on a cane and the aid of an escort following a massive stroke.

his speech was slurred, and he openly wept. Wilson either suffered a mild stroke at that time or was on the verge of a nervous breakdown. His physician hastily canceled the remainder of the tour and rushed him back to Washington. A few days later he crumpled to the floor of his bedroom, felled by a cerebral thrombosis, a blood clot in the brain.

The Invisible President

No one really knows just how seriously Wilson was disabled over the next several months. His protective and strong-willed wife isolated him for six weeks from everyone but his physicians. She screened every document brought to him and returned them with shaky signatures at the bottom. When suspicious advisers insisted on seeing him, they discovered that his left side was paralyzed and his speech was halting. However, he appeared to be in complete control of his wits. To a group of senators who told him, "We've all been praying for you," he replied, "Which way, Senator?"

Wilson did not meet officially with his cabinet for six months, and photographs of that occasion show a haggard old man with an anxiety in his eyes that cannot be found in any earlier picture. The clarity of his thinking undoubtedly was affected. But since Wilson in the best of health had refused to consider compromising with Lodge, the president's removal from the scene probably had little effect on the final outcome of the battle.

That outcome was defeat. In November, on Wilson's instructions, the Democratic senators voted with the irreconcilables to kill the treaty with the Lodge reservations by a vote of 55 to 39. When the treaty was introduced without the reservations, the reservationists and the irreconcilables defeated it against the Democrats. In March, over Wilson's protest, 21 Democrats worked out a compromise with the reservationist Republicans and again voted on the treaty. The 23 Democrats who went along with Wilson's insistence that he get the original treaty or no treaty at all made the difference. They and the irreconcilables defeated it.

The Election of 1920

Wilson believed that he could win the Treaty of Versailles and the League of Nations in the presidential election of 1920. Incredibly, given his shaky health and the tradition against a third term, he wanted to be the Democratic party's nominee. That was too much for even the most faithful Democrats to swallow. They chose Governor James M. Cox of Ohio, a lackluster party regular who looked like a traveling salesman. For vice president the Democrats nominated a staunch but slight young Wilsonian with a magical name, Undersecretary of the Navy Franklin D. Roosevelt. The Democrats were pessimistic. But perhaps the Roosevelt name on the Democratic ticket would win enough progressive votes to put the party across.

The Republicans expected to win. The congressional elections of 1918 had seemed to show that despite six years of Democratic government, the Republicans remained the majority party. As is common when parties are optimistic, there was a fight for the nomination between General Leonard Wood, an old comrade of Theodore Roosevelt (but no progressive) and Illinois governor Frank O. Lowden, who had a reputation as an innovative scientific farmer. Both arrived in Chicago with large blocs of votes, but neither had a majority.

Early in the proceedings, a group of reporters cornered a political wheeler-dealer from Ohio named Harry M. Daugherty and asked him who he thought would be nominated. Daugherty replied genially: "Well boys, I'll tell you what I think. The convention will be deadlocked. After the other candidates have failed, we'll get together in some hotel room, oh, about 2:11 in the morning, and some 15 men, bleary-eyed with lack of sleep, will sit down around a big table and when that time comes Senator Harding will be selected."

Senator Harding was Warren G. Harding. A Daugherty crony, Harding was a handsome, likable man who was considered one of the least competent figures in Congress. Perhaps because of that, he was acceptable to almost everyone. Because Harding had been a "mild reservationist" on the treaty issue, as usual taking an innocuous stand, Henry Cabot Lodge (in whose "smoke-filled room" at the Blackstone Hotel the nomination took place) undoubtedly believed that he could control him.

The Great Bloviator

During the campaign, Harding waffled on the treaty, sometimes appearing to favor it with reservations and at other times hinting that he would let the issue quietly die. If there was a theme to his campaign, it was the need for the country to cool off after almost two decades of experimental reform and white-hot wartime crusading. This circumstance allowed Harding to implement his technique of "bloviation." Bloviating, as Harding was happy to define it, was "the art of speaking for as long as the occasion warrants, and saying nothing." In Boston, in September, Harding said that "America's need is not heroism but healing, not nostrums but normalcy, not agitation but adjustment, not surgery but serenity, not the dramatic but the dispassionate, not experiment but equipoise, not submergence in internationality but sustainment in triumphant nationality."

The acerbic journalist H. L. Mencken said that Harding's speech reminded him of "stale bean soup, of college yells, of dogs barking idiotically through endless nights." But he added that "it is so bad that a sort of grandeur creeps through it." A Democratic politician remarked that the normalcy speech "left the impression of an army of pompous phrases moving over the landscape in search of an idea."

But Harding did have an idea. The great bloviater had sensed that no specific issue, including the League of Nations, was as important to the American people in 1920 as "a return to normalcy," and he was right. He won 61 percent of the vote, more than any candidate who preceded him in the White House since popular votes were recorded and the landslide record until 1964.

Wilson lived on quietly in Washington until 1924, a semi-invalid specter out of the past, frustrated and bitter. Unlike the pedestrian Harding, he was a giant who loomed over an age. His intelligence, dignity, steadfastness, and sense of rectitude overshadowed even Theodore Roosevelt, something T.R. himself must have sensed in his final, pathetic years. Wilson's end was therefore more tragic than that of any other president, including those who were assassinated. For Wilson, like the tragic heroes of great drama, was murdered by his own virtues.

For Further Reading

The regnant study of the American homefront during the First World War is David Kennedy, *Over Here: The First World War and American Society* (1980). See also Ellis W. Hawley, *The Great War and the Search for a Modern Order: A History of the American People and their Institutions, 1914–1920* (1979); the early chapters of William E. Leuchtenburg, *The Perils of Prosperity, 1914–1932* (1958); Arthur S. Link, *Woodrow Wilson: War, Revolution, and Peace* (1979); Preston Slosson, *The Great Crusade and After* (1930); Daniel M. Smith, *The Great Departure: The United States in World War I, 1914–1920* (1965); and the later chapters of Robert H. Wiebe, *The Search for Order, 1880–1920* (1967).

Worthwhile diplomatic studies include Thomas A. Bailey, *Woodrow Wilson and the Lost Peace* (1944) and *Woodrow Wilson and the Great Betrayal* (1945); John M. Blum, *Woodrow Wilson and the Politics of Morality* (1956); John A. Garraty, *Henry Cabot Lodge* (1953); N. G. Levin, Jr., *Woodrow Wilson and World Politics: America's Response to War and Revolution* (1968); the classic Harold Nicholson, *Peacemaking: 1919* (1939); and Ralph Stone, *The Irreconcilables: The Fight Against the League of Nations* (1970).

On economic mobilization, see Robert Cuff, *The War-Industries Board: Business-Government Relations During World War I* (1973). On social aspects of the wartime experience, see Maurine W. Greenwald, *Women, War, and Work: The Impact of World War I on Women Workers in the United States* (1980); Frederick C. Luebke, *Bonds of Loyalty: German Americans and World War I* (1974); Frederick L. Paxson, *American Democracy and the World War* (1948); William Preston, Jr., *Aliens and Dissenters: Federal Suppression of Radicals, 1903–1933* (1953).

The 1920s have come down to us with a ready-made personality, a nickname that supposes to capture the flavor of the decade. In the popular imagination, in novels and films and in television shows, the 1920s are the "Roaring Twenties." The picture is familiar: exhausted by the prolonged fervor of the progressive era, unsettled and then disillusioned by a righteous war that failed to save humanity from itself, the American people set out to have a little fun, and ended up by having a lot.

Images of the Roaring Twenties readily flood the mind: speakeasies, college boys and flapper girls defying traditional morality during breaks between dancing to the exciting new jazz music played by happy blacks; bootleggers and gangsters, somehow menacing and

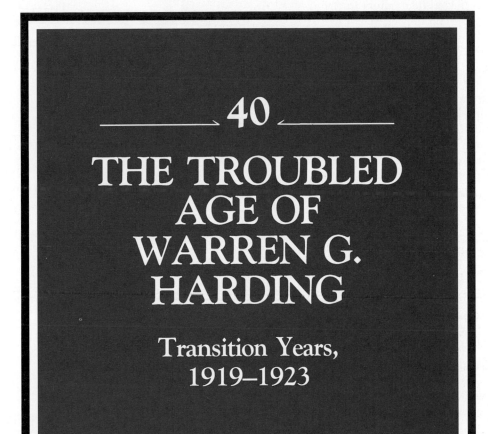

40

THE TROUBLED AGE OF WARREN G. HARDING

Transition Years, 1919–1923

Bound to uphold Prohibition, federal agents smash 749 cases of bottled beer.

engaging at the same time. The 1920s were the golden age of sport: Babe Ruth's Yankees and John McGraw's Giants were the superteams of baseball; Harold "Red" Grange was the saint of the regional religion of football; Jack Dempsey and Gene Tunney were prizefighters as mythic as Odysseus and Hercules. Robert T. "Bobby" Jones of Georgia made golf a popular sport for both participants and spectators. Bill Tilden did the same for tennis.

Radio made its debut: the first commercial broadcast told of Warren G. Harding's landslide victory in the presidential election of 1920. The movies were a fixture of everyday life in the cities and towns, and in their golden age what with Charlie Chaplin, Rudolph Valentino, and Clara Bow, the "It" girl. The automobile, the modern world's amulet of personal freedom, was everywhere, from the homely, accessible Model T Ford to the Stutz Bearcat, Dusenberg, and Cord, still among the most glorious creations of the auto maker's technology and craft.

The list can go on, but at any length it will be a distortion. Only a small proportion of the American population—the wealthy and the comfortably fixed middle classes who lived in cities and sizable towns—enjoyed even a semblance of the legend's roaring good times. And the gravy years were not ten, but five or six in number, beginning only after Calvin Coolidge became president in 1923.

THE WORST PRESIDENT

During the four years that preceded the reign of "Silent Cal" Coolidge, from 1919 to 1923, American life was beset more by contradictions, uncertainties, and fears than by diverting good times. In fact, during the two years immediately before and the two immediately after the inauguration of President Harding in March 1921, American society was on edge, and so was the man whom many historians consider to have been the worst president.

Gamaliel

A newspaperman, Warren Gamaliel Harding worked his way up in politics on the basis of a friendly smile, a firm handshake, the reliable support of the Republican party line in his newspaper, the Marion *Star*, and the happy discovery by Ohio's political bosses that whenever they asked favors, and whatever favors they asked, Warren G. Harding said yes.

He loved the Senate, where voters sent him in 1914; the job suited his temperament. Being a senator called for making the occasional speech—Harding was good

"He looked like a president." Warren G. Harding won the election with his impressive appearance and likeable manner.

at that—but as only one senator among 96, he was not expected to take the lead in anything. The Senate was a club in which members watched out for one another, across party lines as well as within the parties. No one objected that Harding helped old cronies find government jobs that they were unfit to perform, and the affable Ohioan had plenty of time to enjoy the all-night poker and bourbon parties with his pals that were his second most favorite recreation.

Because newspaper reporters were rather more restrained in dealing with the private lives of public officials than they are today, Harding got only slightly censorious treatment in the press. He was widely thought to be among the least effective of senators, but his adulterous relationships with several women, while no secret, were never publicized. Only after his death did one of Harding's ladies, Nan Britton, go to the newspapers with the story that Harding had fathered her illegitimate daughter.

A Decent Man

It is easy to look back and feel sympathy for this weak man because Harding himself had no illusions about his intelligence or his moral capacity for leadership. He freely and openly admitted that he could not hope to be "the best president," and said he would try to be "the best-liked."

Such a man did not belong in public life, but Harding was personally kind and decent. After the sour experience with the brilliant and imperious Wilson, the American people did not regard an ordinary mind and a self-effacing personality as handicaps.

Harding displayed his humanity when, at Christmas 1921, he pardoned Eugene V. Debs and other Socialists who had opposed the war. (Vindictive toward the end, Wilson had refused to do so.) Harding personally put pressure on the directors of the United States Steel Corporation to reduce the workday in their mills to eight hours, not because he challenged their asserted "right" to do with their property as they chose, but because he was appalled at the idea of a twelve-hour day for anyone.

Most striking was Harding's reaction when political enemies whispered that he was part black. In an era when most white people thought in at least mildly racist terms, that kind of talk could ruin a career. Other politicians would have responded with a lawsuit or an indignant racist diatribe that outdid their accusers for spleen. But Harding merely shrugged, an extraordinary response in that era. How did he know whether or not one of his forebears "had jumped the fence."

PRESIDENTS AND BASEBALL

In 1910, William Howard Taft instituted the custom that the president throw out the first ball of the baseball season in Washington, D.C. Perhaps the most avid presidential baseball fan was his successor, Woodrow Wilson, who drove often to Griffith Stadium where he watched the Washington Senators play from his limousine in foul territory beyond the right-field flagpole. (A spare player stood nearby to shield Wilson from errant foul balls.)

Warren G. Harding, Herbert Hoover, Franklin D. Roosevelt, and Harry S Truman were also fans, and Jimmy Carter was a pretty good softball player. Ronald Reagan had been a baseball announcer as a young man, and had portrayed the great pitcher, Grover Cleveland Alexander, in a film of 1952. As president, however, he rarely remained at a game longer than ceremony required. In April 1989, by way of contrast, newly elected George Bush took Egyptian President Hosni Mubarak to a game and both stayed to the end.

Smart Geeks

Harding made some excellent appointments to his cabinet, or had them pushed on him by political expedience. As secretary of commerce, he picked Herbert Hoover, whom Franklin D. Roosevelt had wanted to oppose Harding in the election of 1920. In fact, Hoover was a Republican by inheritance, temperament, and philosophy and, while he must have been slightly appalled by Harding, he accepted. Harding was ill at ease with the prissy, all-business Hoover, but knew that he needed the advice of men like him. He called Hoover (not to his face) "the smartest geek I know."

As he had done during the First World War, Hoover worked quietly. He mollified conservative Republicans by encouraging the formation of private trade associations in industry and agriculture rather than, in the manner of the progressives, putting the government in the driver's seat. Hoover's hope was that these organizations would eliminate waste, develop uniform standards of production, and end "destructive competition."

As secretary of state, Harding named Charles Evans Hughes, a gesture to the progressive wing of the Republican party, with which Hughes had been associated. A man of moderate temperament, an able if unimaginative Supreme Court justice between 1910 and 1916, Hughes had waffled on the issue of the League of Nations, just as Harding had done.

By 1921, that issue was dead but, because the Senate had not ratified the Treaty of Versailles, the United States was still officially at war with Germany. Hughes ironed out that diplomatic difficulty by prevailing on Congress to pass a simple resolution that the war was over and by extending recognition to the new German republic.

The Treaty of Washington

Hughes then presented his alternative to the League of Nations as a means of keeping the peace. He called on the world's nine most important naval powers to an international conference in Washington to discuss naval disarmament. The delegates, who expected the usual round of receptions and meaningless platitudes that most such conferences entailed, followed by backroom horsetrading, were shocked when Hughes opened the conference by proposing a detailed plan for disarmament. All the naval powers were to scrap many of their capital ships (battleships and battle cruisers) and cancel plans for future naval construction.

Every diplomat agreed that the arms race had been instrumental in bringing on the First World War. Therefore, the delegates in Washington had little choice but to listen, particularly when Hughes reminded them that by limiting the size of their navies, their governments could save millions of dollars: the construction of even a single capital ship was a major line item in a national budget.

In the Treaty of Washington of 1921, the five major naval powers agreed to limit their fleets according to a ratio that reflected their interests and defensive needs. For each five tons that Great Britain and the United States floated in capital ships, Japan would have three, and France and Italy somewhat smaller fleets.

Each nation gave up ships, but each benefited too. Great Britain maintained naval equality with the United States, a primacy that American plans for ship construction would have destroyed. (The United States scrapped 30 battleships and cruisers that were under construction or on the drawing boards.) The American government slashed its expenditures, a high Republican party priority. Japan, which needed only a one-ocean navy whereas Britain and the United States had worldwide interests, got parity (or even superiority) in the Pacific. Italy and France, still reeling from the war, were spared the strain of an arms race, but retained naval strength in the Mediterranean.

The Harding Scandals

Unfortunately, the work of Hoover and Hughes just about sums up the accomplishments of the Harding administration. The president's other appointees were either servants of narrow special interests or outright crooks. Secretary of the Treasury Andrew Mellon pursued tax policies that extravagantly favored the rich and helped bring on the disastrous depression that would end the Roaring Twenties. More dismaying in the short run were those old cronies whom Harding favored with government jobs. No sooner were they settled in their Washington offices than they set about filling their pockets and ruining their generous friend.

Attorney General Harry Daugherty winked at violations of the law by political allies. Probably with Daugherty's connivance, Jesse L. Smith, a close friend of the president, sold favorable decisions and public offices for cold cash. Charles R. Forbes, the head of the Veterans Administration, pocketed money intended for hospital construction. The grandest thief of all, Secretary of the Interior Albert B. Fall leased the navy's petroleum reserves at Teapot Dome, Wyoming, and Elk Hills, California, to two freewheeling oilmen, Harry Sinclair and Edward L. Doheny. In return, Fall accepted "loans" of about $300,000 from the two. Fall also tarred Harding with his corruption because, some time earlier, he had persuaded the president to transfer the oil reserves from the navy's authority to that of the Interior Department.

By the summer of 1923, Harding realized that his administration was shot through with corruption. When he set out on a vacation trip to Alaska, he knew that it was only a matter of time before the scandals hit the newspapers and destroyed his name. His health was already suffering; the famous handsome face is haggard and gray in the last photographs.

Nevertheless, weak and obliging to the end, Harding allowed his friend Forbes to flee abroad, and he took no action against the others. Jesse Smith killed himself. Mercifully, perhaps, Harding died too, before he got back to Washington. Only later did Americans learn of the secrets that plagued him, from the corruption in his administration to the irregularities in his personal life. So tangled were the affairs of the Harding administration that scandalmongers suggested that Harding's wife had poisoned him, and they were widely believed. Actually, the president suffered a massive heart attack, possibly brought on by the realization that he had failed on so colossal a scale.

A cartoon showing a teapot that looks suspiciously like an embarrassed elephant illustrated the Republican party's uncomfortable involvement in the Teapot Dome scandal.

SOCIAL TENSIONS: LABOR, RADICALS, IMMIGRANTS

If Harding's poignant tale is symbolic of his time, the social tensions that strained and snapped while he was in the White House ran far deeper than the personality of an unhappy man from Marion, Ohio. Had Harding been a pillar of moral strength and probity, the years he presided over would have been much as troubled as they were. Indeed, the tensions of the early 1920s began two years before Harding was inaugurated. As far as most Americans were concerned, the social conflicts that first broke into the open then were quite closely related: labor, political radicalism, and the presence of so many immigrants in an idyllic America that had never really existed.

1919: A Year of Strikes

During the First World War, the conservative trade unions of the American Federation of Labor seemed to become part of the federal power structure. In return for recognition of their respectability, most unions agreed not to strike for the duration of hostilities. Unfortunately, while wages rose slowly during 1917 and 1918, the prices of consumer goods, including necessities, increased quickly and then soared during a runaway postwar inflation. The end of the war also led to the cancellation of government contracts; tens of thousands doing war-related work lost their jobs, and the inevitable occurred: 3,600 strikes during 1919 involving 4 million workers.

Striker grievances were generally valid, but, to the surprise of many workers, few Americans outside the labor movement were sympathetic. When employers described the strikes of 1919 as the handiwork of revolutionaries, aimed at destroying middle-class decency, much of America agreed. In Seattle, a dispute that began on the docks of the busy Pacific port turned into a general strike involving almost all the city's 60,000 workers. Most of them were interested in nothing more than better pay. However, the concept of the general strike was associated in the popular mind with class war and revolution. Mayor Ole Hanson was able to depict the dispute as an uprising that had been inspired by dangerous foreign "Bolsheviks" like those who had taken over Russia during the war. With the help of the marines, he crushed the strike.

Steelworkers Walk Out

The magnates of the steel industry employed similar methods to fight a walkout in September by 350,000 workers, largely in the Great Lakes region. The men had good reason to strike. Many of them worked a twelve-hour day and a seven-day week. It was not unusual for individuals to put in 36 hours at a stretch. That is, if a man's relief failed to show up, he was told to stay on the job or lose it. When the extra shift ended, his own began again.

For this kind of life, steelworkers took home subsistence wages. For some Slavic immigrants in the industry, that home was not even a bed to themselves.

They contracted with a landlord to rent half a bed. After their wearying shift and a quick, cheap meal, they rolled under blankets still warm and damp from the body of a fellow worker who had just trudged off to the mill.

These wretched conditions were well known. And yet, the heads of the industry, Elbert Gary of United States Steel and Charles Schwab of Bethlehem Steel, easily persuaded the public that the strike was the work of revolutionary agitators like William Z. Foster. Because Foster had a radical past (and future as the leader of the American Communist party) and because many steelworkers had ethnic roots in Eastern Europe, the nursery of Bolshevism, the strikers were almost universally condemned. The strike ended in failure although, under pressure from the president, working conditions were somewhat improved.

The Boston Police Strike

The Boston police strike of 1919 frightened Americans more than any other. While the shutdown of even a basic industry like steel did not immediately affect daily life, the absence of police officers from the streets caused a jump in crime as professional hoodlums and desperately poor people took advantage of the situation.

Boston's policemen, mostly Irish-Americans, were underpaid. They earned prewar wages, not enough to support their families decently in a city where many prices had tripled. Nevertheless, they too commanded little public support. When Massachusetts governor Calvin Coolidge ordered the National Guard into Boston to break the strike, the public applauded. When Samuel Gompers asked Coolidge to restore the beaten workers to their jobs, the governor replied that "there is no right to strike against the public safety by anybody, anywhere, anytime," and he became a national hero. His hard-line policy won him the Republican vice-presidential nomination in 1920 when the California progressive, Hiram Johnson, refused to balance the ticket by running with the conservative Harding.

Some of the strikes of 1919 ended in victory. Most failed and the debacle ushered in a decade of decline for the labor movement. The membership of unions stood at over 5 million in 1919, but at only 3.6 million in 1929, despite the expansion of the nonagricultural working class during the same years.

Red Scare

Public reaction to the strikes of 1919 revealed widespread hostility toward recent immigrants and second generation Americans. This xenophobia took more virulent form in the Red scare of 1919. Even before the Armistice was signed, a new stereotype had replaced the "bloodthirsty Hun" as the villain whom Americans had most reason to fear: the seedy, bearded, and wild-eyed Bolshevik. American newspapers exaggerated the many real atrocities that took place during the civil war that followed the Russian Revolution and invented tales of mass executions, torture, children turned against their parents, and women proclaimed the common property of all men. Already in an uneasy mood, Americans were prepared to believe the worst about a part of the world from which so many immigrants recently had come.

Many Americans believed that foreign-born Communists were a threat to the United States. In March 1919, the Soviets organized the Third International, or "Comintern," an organization explicitly dedicated to fomenting revolution around the world. So it seemed to be no accident when, in April, the Post Office discovered 38 bombs in the mail addressed to prominent capitalists and government officials. In June, several bombs reached their targets. One bomber who was identified—he blew himself up—was a foreigner, an Italian. And in Chicago in September 1919, two American Communist parties were founded with the press emphasizing the immigrant element in the membership. Many Americans concluded that the Red threat was closely related to the large number of immigrants and their children within the United States.

In reality, a small minority of ethnic Americans were radicals, and many of the prominent Socialists and Communists boasted impeccable WASP origins. Max Eastman, the editor of the radical wartime magazine *The Masses*, was of old New England stock. John Reed, whose *Ten Days That Shook the World* remained for many years the classic English-language account of the Russian Revolution, was a Harvard boy from Portland, Oregon. Debs and William Z. Foster had no ethnic ties. William D. Haywood observed that he could trace his ancestry "to the Puritan bigots." Moreover, neither they nor the foreign-born radicals posed a real threat to established institutions. Within a few years, the combined membership of the two Communist parties and the Socialist party numbered only in the thousands.

The Palmer Raids

But popular dread of Communists was real enough, and the temptation to exploit it for political gain was overwhelming. Wilson's attorney general, A. Mitchell Palmer, tried to ride the Red scare into a presidential nomination by ordering a series of well-publicized raids on Communist headquarters.

Although an investigation found that only 39 of those he had arrested could be deported under the law, Palmer nonetheless put 249 people on a steamship

dubbed "the Soviet Ark" and sent them to Russia via Finland. On New Year's Day 1920, Palmer's agents again swooped down on hundreds of locations, arresting 6,000 people. Some of them, such as a Western Union delivery boy, merely had the bad luck to be in the wrong place at the wrong time. Others were arrested while merely peering into the windows of Communist storefront offices. Nevertheless, all were imprisoned for at least a short time.

Palmer's popularity fizzled in the spring of 1920. He predicted that there would be mass demonstrations on May Day, the international socialist and communist holiday, and nothing happened. By midsummer, the great scare was over, but antiforeign feeling continued to affect both government policy and popular attitudes throughout the 1920s.

Sacco and Vanzetti

The two most celebrated victims of the wedding of antiradicalism to xenophobia were Nicola Sacco and Bartolomeo Vanzetti. In 1920, the two Italian immigrants were arrested for an armed robbery in South Braintree, Massachusetts, in which a guard and a paymaster were killed. They were found guilty of murder, and sentenced to die in the electric chair.

Before they could be executed, the American Civil Liberties Union, Italian-American groups, and labor organizations publicized the fact that the hard evidence against Sacco and Vanzetti was scanty and, at least in part, invented by the prosecution. The presiding judge, Webster Thayer, had been openly prejudiced against the defendants because they were anarchists and Italians; Thayer was overheard speaking of them as "damned dagos."

At the same time, Sacco and Vanzetti won admiration by acting with dignity during their trial, steadfastly maintaining their innocence but refusing to compromise their political beliefs. "I am suffering," Vanzetti said in court, "because I am a radical and indeed I am a radical; I have suffered because I was an Italian, and indeed I am an Italian . . . but I am so convinced to be right that if you could execute me two times, and if I could be reborn two other times, I would live again to do what I have done already."

Despite a movement to save them that reached international proportions, Sacco and Vanzetti were finally executed in 1927. Although recent research has indicated that at least Sacco was almost certainly guilty of the Braintree murder, that question lost its relevance to both sides during the 1920s.

The Passing of the Great Race

In 1883, the American poet Emma Lazarus had written, "Send these, the homeless, tempest-tost to me, I

Nicola Sacco and Bartolomeo Vanzetti, immigrants and anarchists whose case became an international cause in the 1920s.

lift my lamp beside the golden door." As if they had heard her, European immigrants continued to pour into the United States at high levels until 1915, when all-out naval war made the Atlantic too dangerous for large numbers of people to cross. In 1918, immigration into the United States declined to 110,000.

Even before the war, many Americans of WASP and "Old Immigrant" stock had become nervous about the large numbers of eastern and southern Europeans among them—or rather, about the immigrants who clustered in ethnic ghettos in the larger cities. Unlike earlier arrivals, including the once-despised Irish, the "New Immigrants" seemed determined not to become Americans.

Around the turn of the century, this essentially cultural and social anxiety took on racist overtones as respected anthropologists began to describe significant genetic distinctions among the European peoples. The most important of these writers was William Z. Ripley, whose *Races of Europe* was published in 1899. Ripley divided Caucasians into the Teutonic, Alpine, and Mediterranean races. While all three had their re-

deeming traits (the Mediterranean Italians, for example, were credited with a finely developed artistic sense), there was no question that Teutons—Britons, Germans, northern Europeans generally—were the ones who were committed to liberty and to the American way of life. Slavic peoples got very bad reviews.

In 1916, a lawyer and natural scientist of some repute, Madison Grant, took up where Ripley left off. In *The Passing of the Great Race*, Grant maintained that, through intermarriage with old-stock Americans, the New Immigrants were literally destroying, through dilution, the nation's prized genetic heritage. The book was immensely successful, running through several editions. (During the war, Grant demoted the Germans out of the Great Race.) After the war, when immigration soared again—to 805,000 in 1921—the time for action seemed to have come.

Immigration Restriction

There was a precedent for restricting immigration on the basis of race. In 1882, Congress had excluded the Chinese from the United States. In that same year,

Congress determined that criminals, idiots, lunatics, and those likely to become a public charge (people with glaucoma, tuberculosis, and venereal disease were the chief targets) could no longer immigrate. By 1900, pressure groups such as the Immigration Restriction League began to call for an immigration law that would discriminate against other genetic inferiors—southern and eastern Europeans, in brief, the New Immigrants.

Four times between 1897 and 1917, Congress tried to discriminate against the New Immigrants by enacting bills requiring all newcomers to pass a literacy test. Few peasants from southern and eastern Europe could read and write. Four times, however, three times by Woodrow Wilson alone, the bills were vetoed. The importance of ethnic voters to the Democratic party, and the demand of a still expanding industry for cheap labor, stymied the restrictionists.

Then the election of 1920 brought the Republicans to power. In 1921, Congress enacted and President Harding signed a law limiting annual immigration to 350,000 people. Each European nation was entitled to send 3 percent of the number of its nationals who had been residents of the United States in the base year of 1910. In 1924, an amendment reduced the number of immigrants from outside the Americas to 150,000, the quota to 2 percent, and changed the base year to 1890. Because most southern and eastern Europeans had begun to emigrate to the United States after 1890, the quotas of such poor countries as Poland, Czechoslovakia, Hungary, Rumania, Yugoslavia, Bulgaria,

Greece, and Italy were very low. For example, the annual quota for Italy was a minuscule 6,000, and was inevitably filled within the first few months of each year.

By way of contrast, the quotas for the comparatively prosperous countries of northern and Western Europe, the nations of the Old Immigration, were generous and rarely filled. The annual quota for Great Britain under the 1921 law was 65,000, one-fifth of the total. During the 1930s, an average of only 2,500 Britons emigrated to the United States each year.

SOCIAL TENSIONS: RACE, MORAL CODES, RELIGION

The 1920s were also a time of anxiety and tension in relations between the two major American races, between people who held fast to traditional moral codes and those who rejected them, and (closely allied to the moral issue) between rural people and urban people.

Black Scare

Having supported the war effort with extraordinary enthusiasm, blacks looked forward to a greater measure of equality after the Armistice. The 200,000 young black men who had served in the army in Europe had been exposed to a white society in which their color was not a major handicap. Although they had been segregated within the armed forces, they had found that the French people looked on them as Yanks of a different color, nothing more or less, and had been grateful for their help against Germany. At home, blacks who moved to northern cities experienced a less repressive life than they had known in the rural South and felt freer to express themselves.

But white America had not changed its mind about race. In 1919, of the 78 blacks who were lynched, 10 were veterans; several were hanged while dressed in their uniforms. Race riots broke out in 25 cities with a death toll of more than a hundred. The worst of the year was in Chicago, where a petty argument on a Lake Michigan beach in July mushroomed into vicious racial war. White and black gangs with guns roamed the streets shooting at anyone of the wrong color whom they stumbled across. In all, 38 people were killed and more than 500 were injured.

Black Nationalism

In this charged and disillusioning atmosphere emerged a remarkable leader. Born in the British colony of

---

ANTI-SEMITISM

The hatred of Jews that was to acquire nightmarish proportions in Germany had its counterpart in the United States, albeit never so vicious or significant as it was under Adolf Hitler. For a time during the 1920s, automobile millionaire Henry Ford sponsored a newspaper, the *Dearborn Independent*, that insisted, as Hitler did, that Jews in general were party to an "international conspiracy" to destroy Western Christian civilization. The most astonishing aspect of this kind of anti-Semitism was that it posited an alliance between wealthy, conservative Jewish bankers like the Rothschild family of Europe and their worst enemies, Jewish Socialists and Communists.

These allegations never were taken very seriously in the United States. However, anti-Semitism was acceptable and even respectable when it took the form of keeping Jews out of some businesses (banking, ironically) and social clubs. Moreover, a number of universities applied Jewish "quotas" when they admitted students. Jews were admitted, but only up to a certain percentage of each class.

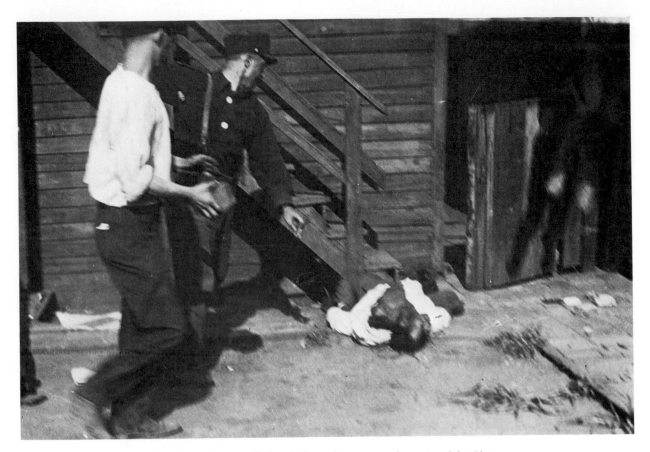

A black man lies wounded at the base of a staircase, the victim of the Chicago race riot of 1919.

Jamaica, Marcus Garvey came to the United States in 1916. He concluded that whites would never accept blacks as equals, and, filled with a glowing pride in his own race, he rejected integration. Garvey's alternative to the violent racial conflicts of the postwar years was the joining together of blacks throughout the world to organize a powerful black nation in Africa.

Garvey's Universal Negro Improvement Association (UNIA) was based on pride in race, the strong organizing point of all racial-separatist movements. "When Europe was inhabited by a race of cannibals, a race of savages, naked men, heathens, and pagans," Garvey told cheering throngs in New York's Harlem, turning white stereotypes of blacks upside down, "Africa was peopled by a race of cultured black men who were masters in art, science, and literature."

He made little headway in the South, but in the North, urban blacks who already were uprooted found his call for a return to Africa appealing, at least in the abstract. Estimates of UNIA membership as high as 4 million were probably exaggerated, but many more blacks than that listened to Garvey's message with open minds and enjoyed the pageantry of nationhood with which he surrounded himself.

Garvey bedecked himself in ornate, regal uniforms and commissioned paramilitary orders with exotic names such as "The Dukes of the Niger" and the "Black Eagle Flying Corps." Even veterans in the fight for racial equality were influenced by Garvey's magic. W. E. B. Du Bois wrote, "The spell of Africa is upon me. The ancient witchery of her medicine is burning in my drowsy, dreamy blood."

The popularity of black nationalism unnerved whites who were accustomed to a passive black population. When Garvey ran afoul of the law with one of the dozens of his business enterprises, the authorities moved against him with an enthusiasm that bore little relation to the seriousness of his offense. Whether because of mismanagement or fraud, Garvey's Black Star Line, a steamship company, had sold worthless shares through the mails at $5 a share. Some 35,000

HOW THEY PLAYED THE GAME

Originally, baseball was a gentleman's game, played by wealthy amateurs for the pleasure of competition. By the turn of the twentieth century, this had changed. Baseball became a business, potentially very lucrative. The players were paid for their skills by teams organized into two major leagues, the National and the American. The profits to the owners, who called themselves "sportsmen" and their properties "clubs," lay in paid admissions to games. Because the better the team, the more people willing to pay to attend, it stood to reason that clubowners would seek to build winning teams. However, it did not always work that way. While the players indeed competed with one another to win games, the sportsmen did not compete with one another to win the best players.

In order to avoid bidding wars among themselves for the services of star pitchers, hitters, and fielders, the clubowners devised the "reserve clause," an agreement that every player was required to sign. The reserve clause was based on the dubious assumption that a baseball player was a professional like a physician or lawyer and not a lowly employee. Unlike a machinist or miner who, of course, as industrial employers never tired of saying, were free at all times to quit their job and find another, the professional baseball player was not free to do so. In signing the reserve clause, he agreed that he could not leave to play with another team without the owner's consent. His services were reserved unless the clubowner "sold" or "traded" him to another owner with whom the player then had no choice but to come to terms—if he wanted to stay in baseball.

As in other businesses, practices varied from team to team, but perhaps the most frankly businesslike of the owners was Cornelius "Connie Mack" McGillicuddy, who also managed his Philadelphia Athletics of the American League. The dominant team in baseball in the years before the First World War, the A's won six league pennants and three world series. Mack twice built up powerhouse teams in that era and then broke them up, selling his star players off for a cash profit. And again by the end of the 1920s he created a team that was better than the New York Yankees of the era. Once again Mack cashed in, selling off his players.

There was no reconciling the concept of sportsmanship or a sense of civic responsibility with Mack's policies, and yet, simply because he continued to manage the A's into his 90s, he was touted as one of the grand old men of the "game."

Charles A. Comiskey, owner of the Chicago White Sox, was another kind of businessman. Until the First World War he was content with mediocre players to whom he paid the lowest salaries in either major league. Then, during the war, while attendance in all cities declined, the White Sox jelled behind such stars as hard-hitting outfielder Joseph "Shoeless Joe" Jackson

Chicago White Sox outfielder "Shoeless Joe" Jackson.

and third baseman George "Buck" Weaver. After finishing high in the standings in 1917 and 1918, the White Sox won the American League pennant in 1919 and were regarded by most sports journalists as unbeatable in the World Series, particularly because the National League champion was an old team but an upstart champion, the Cincinnati Red Stockings.

There was trouble in the White Sox team, however. While their sterling play had caused attendance and profits to soar, Comiskey had actually taken the lead in calling for a league-wide paycut. At a time when wages in almost every job were rising, the two leading White Sox pitchers, who won 50 games between them, were paid a combined salary of only $8,600. Adding insult to exploitation, Comiskey allowed his champion players considerably lower expenses when they were on the road than any other team in either league.

The White Sox lost the World Series to the Red Stockings 5 games to 3. (Only in 1922 was the Series reduced to 7 games.) An investigation during the winter and spring revealed that it was no mere upset. Eight White Sox players, including stars Weaver and Jackson, had conspired with gamblers to throw the match and make a killing on longshot bets.

It was rumored that Comiskey had been aware of the fix all along but was willing to sacrifice the Series for the chance to intimidate future players. Indeed, although the eight accused "Black Sox" were acquitted in criminal court for lack of hard evidence, they were banned from playing professional ball for life by a newly installed Commissioner with broad powers to regulate the business, Judge Kenesaw Mountain Landis. Like the head of a government commission, Landis showed no reluctance to discipline owners whose actions threatened the good of the whole, but he backed up the owners in disputes with players.

Not every club ownership was so cash-oriented as Mack or so exploitative as Comiskey. Indeed, during the same years that Landis was brushing up baseball's reputation for honesty at the top, an ugly, pot-bellied, spindly legged, and atrociously vulgar orphan from Baltimore was revolutionizing the game and winning huge salaries from ungrudging employers, the New York Yankees.

George Herman "Babe" Ruth started in baseball as a pitcher—quite a good one—for the Boston Red Sox. In 1919, the year of the Black Sox Scandal, while playing the outfield on days he did not pitch, Ruth hit 29 home runs, double that of any previous player. In fact, the major leagues did not even keep official home run statistics until 1921; baseball B. R.—before Ruth—was a game of tactics played by lithe, swift men who eked out runs one at a time with scratch hits off over-powering pitchers, and gritty base running. Tyrus J. "Ty" Cobb of the Detroit Tigers, a genuinely mean-spirited man whose specialty was sliding into second with file-sharpened cleats slicing the air, was the most respected player of the 1910s.

Now, with a single swing, the "Sultan of Swat" could put up to four runs on the scoreboard and the fans loved it. Purchased from the Red Sox by the Yankees for $100,000—itself an unprecedented windfall under the reserve clause—Ruth hit 59 home runs in 1921, the record until his own 60 in 1927. Rather than haggle with their godsend, the Yankee ownership paid him annually higher salaries. By the end of the decade when his pay was higher than that of the president of the United States, Ruth shrugged nonchalantly, "I had a better year than he did."

Not only did he make the Yankees the best team in baseball, Babe Ruth made them the richest. In 1923, New York opened the largest baseball stadium of the era, Yankee Stadium, which was properly nicknamed, "the house that Ruth built." Other owners and Commissioner Landis took notice too. If home runs sold tickets, they would have more home runs. The baseball itself was redesigned into a livelier "rabbit ball" and the slugger became the mythic figure in the game. Hack Wilson of the Chicago Cubs hit 56 home runs in 1930, setting the National League's record, and Jimmy Foxx of the Philadelphia Athletics was eclipsing Ruth himself by 1932 when he hit 58 (and was promptly sold by Connie Mack). The New York Yankees remained the team that most totally staked its fortunes on men who swung the heavy bat and the "club" that was the most liberal with a paycheck. It would not have much mattered to Connie Mack and Charles Comiskey, perhaps, but the Yankees were also, of course, the most successful team in the history of both the sport and the business.

Babe Ruth as a pitcher for the Boston Red Sox.

blacks lost $750,000, a comparatively minor take during the 1920s. Nevertheless, the government pressed its case for five years, draining the resources of the UNIA.

The Ku Klux Klan

Marcus Garvey's ritual, costume, and ceremony was paralleled in a white racist organization of the same era, the Ku Klux Klan. The twentieth-century KKK was founded in 1915 by William Simmons, a Methodist minister. After viewing *The Birth of a Nation*, a film that glorified the antiblack movement of the post-Civil War period, Simmons began organizing, first in the South but, by 1919, in the North and West as well.

Under Hiram Wesley Evans, the KKK gave local units and officials exotic names such as Klavern, Kleagle, Grand Dragon, and Exalted Cyclops. Evans was a shrewder businessman than Garvey. The Klan's central office retained a monopoly of "official" bedsheet uniforms that all members were required to buy. The Klan provided a cash incentive for local organizers by giving them a percentage of all money that they collected, a kind of franchised bigotry. By the mid-1920s, membership may have risen as high as 4.5 million.

In the South, the KKK was primarily an antiblack organization. Elsewhere, KKK leaders exploited whatever hatreds, fears, and resentments were most likely to keep the bedsheet orders rolling in. In the Northeast, where Catholics and Jews were numerous, Klan leaders inveighed against them. Immigrants generally were a handy target. In the Owens Valley of California, a region of small farmers whose water was drained southward to feed the growth of Los Angeles, the big city was the enemy. In the Midwest, some Klaverns concentrated their attacks on saloonkeepers who ignored Prohibition and "lovers' lanes" where teenagers flaunted traditional morality on weekend nights.

Setting aside the hocus-pocus and the mercenary motives of the central office, the Klan represented the belief of generally poor, Protestant, and small-town people that the America they knew was under attack by immigrants, cities, and modern immorality. Nevertheless, the Klan prospered in cities too. The twentieth-century metropolis was an unsettling phenomenon, but it continued to attract people of every kind.

Klan power peaked in 1924. In that year, the organization boasted numerous state legislators, congressmen, senators, and even governors in Oregon, Ohio, Tennessee, and Texas. In Indiana, state Klan leader David Stephenson was a virtual dictator. At the Democratic national convention of 1924, the Klan was strong enough to prevent the party from adopting a plank that was critical of its bigotry.

The KKK declined as rapidly as the UNIA. In 1925, Grand Dragon Stephenson was found guilty of second-degree murder in the death of a young woman whom he had kidnapped and taken to Chicago. In an attempt to win a light sentence, he turned over evidence showing that virtually the whole administration of the KKK was involved in thievery and that Indiana Klan politicians were thoroughly corrupt. By 1930, the KKK had dwindled to 10,000 members.

Wets and Drys

To some extent, the Klan was a manifestation of hostility between cities and country and small towns. This social conflict was also evident in the split that developed after the Eighteenth Amendment went into effect in 1920. Violation of the Prohibition law was widespread. While some bootleggers smuggled liquor into the country from Mexico, the West Indies, and Canada, individual liquor distillers in isolated corners of rural America continued to practice their ancient crafts, distilling "white lightning" and "moonshine"

Wearing ornate uniforms and commissioning paramilitary orders, Marcus Garvey led a large black nationalist movement that was born in response to the violent racial conflict that scarred America in 1919.

Ku Klux Klan members march in Washington, D.C., in August 1925, without the masks that concealed their identities.

and battling government agents with guns as well as stealth.

Nevertheless, there was a clear geographical and social dimension to the political battle between "drys," people who supported Prohibition, and "wets," those who opposed it. The drys were strongest in the South and in rural areas generally, where the population was largely composed of old-stock Americans who clung to fundamentalist Protestant religions. The wets drew their support from the big cities, where Roman Catholics and Jews, who generally had little understanding of or sympathy for Prohibition, were numerous.

Wet mayors and city councils often refused to help federal officials enforce Prohibition. Democratic Mayor James J. Walker of New York openly frequented fashionable speakeasies, illegal saloons. Republican "Big Bill" Thompson of Chicago ran for office on a "wide-open-town" platform and won. As a result, smuggling, illegal distilleries and breweries, and theft of industrial and medicinal alcohol were commonplace and provided the basis for an extremely lucrative, if illegal, business. In Chicago by 1927, the Alphonse "Al" Capone bootleg ring grossed $60 million by sup-

plying liquor and beer to the Windy City's speakeasies. (Capone also made $25 million that year from gambling and $10 million from prostitution.)

Gangsters as Symbols

As far as Al Capone was concerned, he was a businessman. He supplied 10,000 drinking houses and employed 700 people. He and other gangsters needed the administrative acumen of a corporation executive to run their affairs and the same kind of political influence that conventional businessmen courted. "What's Al Capone done?" he told a reporter. "He's supplied a legitimate demand. . . . Some call it racketeering. I call it a business. They say I violate the prohibition law. Who doesn't?"

With incredible profits at stake, rival gangs engaged in open, bloody warfare for control of the trade. More than 400 "gangland slayings" made the name of Chicago synonymous with mob violence, although other cities had only slightly better records.

Very few innocent bystanders were killed in these affrays. As conscious of public relations as other businessmen of the era, Capone and his ilk tried to keep

Renowned Federal agents, Izzy Einstein and Moe Smith (flanking an illegal still) became national celebrities by using comical tactics to trap bootleggers.

education, and, to get started, little money. With less to lose than the respectable established people who patronized the speakeasies, ethnics had fewer compunctions about the high risks involved. But the majority of Americans were not inclined to take a sociological view of the matter. To them, organized crime was violent, and "foreigners" were the source of it.

Hollywood as Symbol

Show business was also a low-status enterprise that presented few competitive advantages to wealthy and established groups. The film industry, which was booming by 1919, had been largely dominated from the beginning by Jewish studio bosses such as Samuel Goldwyn and Louis B. Mayer, graduates of the Yiddish-language theater tradition of New York City. Consequently, when protest against nudity and loose moral standards in Hollywood films boiled over, it too took on an ethnic flavor. Preachers who demanded that controls be slapped on filmmakers were not above attri-

their violence on a professional level. But Americans were appalled by the carnage, and they did not overlook the fact that most prominent gangsters were "foreigners." Capone and his predecessors in Chicago, Johnny Torrio and Big Jim Colosimo, were Italians. Dion O'Bannion (Capone's rival), "Bugsy" Moran, and Owney Madden were Irish. Arthur "Dutch Schultz" Flegensheimer of New York was of German background. "Polack Joe" Saltis came from Chicago's Polish West Side. Maxie Hoff of Philadelphia, Solly Weissman of Kansas City, and "Little Hymie" Weiss of Chicago were Jews.

"Illegal business" attracted members of groups on the bottom of the social ladder because success in it required no social status or family connections, no

HOORAY FOR HOLLYWOOD

The first filmmakers set up shop wherever they happened to be. By the 1920s, however, the movie industry had become concentrated in Hollywood, one of the myriad communities that grew together to form greater Los Angeles. The official explanation of the choice of location was the weather; southern California is one of the sunniest parts of the nation, and early filmmakers depended on natural light. But there was another reason for choosing Hollywood. Like the organizers of many infant industries, filmmakers took considerable liberties with business law, particularly copyright and contract law. Everyone, it seemed, was engaged in a dozen lawsuits at all times. Hollywood was only a hundred miles from the Mexican border. If a case seemed to be getting serious, the filmmakers could make a quick dash out to Tijuana.

Al Capone, a gangster who supplied thousands of drinking houses with illegal liquor, regarded himself as a businessman fulfilling a public demand.

*Exotic themes and lavish sets characterized the escapist
films of the 1920s. Americans were hooked.*

buting immorality on the screen to "non-Christian" influences aimed at subverting Protestant America.

By 1922, Hollywood's nabobs feared that city and state governments were on the verge of banning the showing of their films. They headed off the movement to do so by joining together to censor themselves. Sensitive to the ethnic angle in the anti-Hollywood campaign, they hired a man who was the epitome of the small-town midwestern Protestant to be chief censor and film-industry spokesman. Will H. Hays of Indiana, Postmaster General under Harding, supervised the drafting of a code that forbade movies that allowed adultery to go unpunished or that depicted divorced people in a sympathetic light. The Hays Code went so far as to prohibit showing a married couple in bed together or, indeed, a double bed in the background of bedroom scenes. In the movies, couples slept in twin beds, and so powerful was the medium that separate beds became fashionable in three-dimensional society too.

The Evolution Controversy

The clash between traditional values and the worldly outlook of the twentieth century was clearest cut in the controversy that surrounded the theory of the evolution of species as propounded half a century earlier by the English biologist Charles Darwin. Although many scientists insisted that there was no contradiction between the biblical account of the creation of the world (if interpreted as literary) and Darwin's contention that species emerged and changed character over the eons, fundamentalist Protestants who insisted on the literal truth of every word of the Bible disagreed. Feeling threatened by fast-changing times and urged on by such influential leaders as William Jennings Bryan, the fundamentalists tried to prohibit the teaching of evolution in the public schools; in Tennessee, they succeeded in passing a law to that effect.

In the little Appalachian town of Dayton in the spring of 1925, a group of friends who had been arguing

Clarence Darrow for the defense and William Jennings Bryan for the prosecution at the Scopes "Monkey Trial," which addressed the question of evolution and its instruction in classrooms.

about evolution decided to test the new law in the courts. One of their number, a high school biology teacher named John Scopes, would deliberately break it. In front of adult witnesses, Scopes would explain Darwin's theory, submit to arrest, and stand trial. The motives of the men were mixed. The earnest young Scopes hoped that the law would be struck from the books. Some of his friends wanted to see it confirmed. Yet others, Dayton businessmen, could not have cared either way. They looked on a celebrated trial as a way to put their town on the map and to make money when curiosity-seekers, sensation-mongers, cause-pleaders and reporters—the more the merrier—flocked to Dayton in search of lodgings, meals, and other services.

The "Monkey Trial"

Dayton's boosters succeeded beyond their dreams. The "Monkey Trial," so called because evolution was popularly interpreted as meaning that human beings were "descended" from apes, attracted broadcasters and reporters by the hundreds; among them was the nation's

leading iconoclast, Henry L. Mencken, who came to poke fun at the "rubes" of the Bible belt.

Number-one rube in Mencken's book was William Jennings Bryan, quite aged now—he died shortly after the trial ended—who agreed to go to Dayton to advise the prosecution. Bryan wanted to fight the case on the strictly legal principle that, in a democracy, the people of a community had the right to dictate what might and what might not be taught in tax-supported schools. His advice was ignored. Their heads spinning from the hullabaloo and carnival atmosphere of the town, even the prosecuting attorneys wanted to debate religion versus science.

The defense, which had been put together and funded by the American Civil Liberties Union, also intended to fight the case on the basis of two significant principles. Led by the distinguished lawyer and libertarian Arthur Garfield Hays, the attorneys planned to argue that the biblical account of creation was a religious doctrine and therefore could not take precedence over science (evolution) because of the constitutional separation of church and state. The defense also insisted that freedom of intellectual inquiry, including a teacher's right to speak his or her mind in the classroom, was essential to the health of a democracy.

Hays was assisted by the era's leading criminal lawyer, Clarence Darrow, who loved publicity and the drama of courtroom confrontation more than legal niceties. Darrow regarded the trial as an opportunity to discredit fundamentalists by making their leader, Bryan, look like a superstitious old fool. Against his better judgment, Bryan allowed Darrow to put him on the stand as an expert witness on the Bible. Under the trees—the judge feared that the tiny courthouse would collapse under the crowd—Darrow and Bryan talked religion and science. Was the world created in six days of 24 hours each? Was Jonah literally swallowed by a whale?

Supporters of Darrow rested content that Bryan himself turned out looking like a monkey, but they lost the case; Scopes was found guilty and given a nominal penalty. It was a small consolation to the anti-evolutionists, who were crestfallen when Bryan admitted that some parts of the Bible may have been meant figuratively. In fact, the only winners in the Monkey Trial were Dayton's businessmen, who raked in outside dollars for almost a month, and the masters of ballyhoo. This was appropriate in itself, for by 1925, the second full year of Calvin Coolidge's "New Era," raking in money and ballyhoo were what America seemed to be all about.

For Further Reading

It is not the definitive history of the 1920s, but still the most enjoyable to read: Frederick Lewis Allen, *Only Yesterday* (1931). Also eminently readable and less subjective are William E. Leuchtenburg, *The Perils of Prosperity, 1914–1932* (1958); Robert K. Murray, *The Harding Era* (1967); and George Soule, *Prosperity Decade: From War to Depression, 1917–1929* (1947).

On the crisis of labor in 1919 and after, see Irving Bernstein, *The Lean Years* (1960); David Brody, *Labor in Crisis: The Steel Strike of 1919* (1965); Robert L. Friedheim, *The Seattle General Strike* (1965); and Francis Russell, *A City in Terror: 1919, the Boston Police Strike* (1975). On the xenophobia that was closely related to fears of a social rising, see John Higham, *Strangers in the Land* (1955); Robert K. Murray, *Red Scare* (1955); and William Preston, Jr., *Aliens and Dissenters: Federal Suppression of Radicals, 1903–1933* (1963).

The history of American blacks during the 1920s has been the subject of several excellent books in recent decades. See Nathan J. Huggins, *Harlem Renaissance* (1972); Gilbert Osofsky, *Harlem: The Making of a Ghetto, 1890–1930* (1966); William Tuttle, Jr., *Race Riot: Chicago and the Red Summer of 1919* (1970); and Theodore G. Vincent, *Black Power and the Garvey Movement* (1971).

The response of white America to rapidly changing times is the subject of D. M. Chalmers, *Hooded Americanism* (1965); N. H. Clark, *Deliver Us From Evil* (1976); Ray Ginger, *Six Days or Forever* (1958); Kenneth T. Jackson, *The Ku Klux Klan in the Cities, 1915–1930* (1967); Don S. Kirschner, *City and Country: Rural Responses to Urbanization in the 1920s* (1970); Lawrence Levine, *Defender of the Faith: William Jennings Bryan, The Last Decade* (1965); and George M. Marsden, *Fundamentalism and American Culture* (1980).

Other social and cultural themes are treated in Loren Baritz, *The Culture of the Twenties* (1969); Isabel Leighton, *The Aspirin Age* (1949); Larry May, *Screening Out the Past* (1980); Humbert S. Nelli, *The Business of Crime* (1976); John Roe, *The Road and the Car in American Life* (1971); Andrew Sinclair, *Prohibition: The Era of Excess* (1962); and Robert Sklar, *Movie-Made America* (1975).

On the politics of the Harding era, see Wesley Bagby, *The Road to Normalcy* (1962); Stanley Cohen, *A. Mitchell Palmer: Politician* (1963); Robert K. Murray, *The Politics of Normalcy* (1973); Burt Noggle, *Teapot Dome: Oil and Politics in the 1920s* (1962); J. W. Prothro, *Dollar Decade: Business Ideas in the 1920s* (1954); Francis Russell, *The Shadow of Blooming Grove: Warren G. Harding in His Times* (1968); and Andrew Sinclair, *The Available Man* (1965).

Vice President Calvin Coolidge was visiting his father in rural Vermont when the news of President Harding's death arrived. He might have rushed to Washington to be sworn in by the Chief Justice of the Supreme Court. Instead, Coolidge walked downstairs to the darkened farmhouse parlor, where his father, a justice of the peace, administered the presidential oath by the light of a kerosene lantern. At the very pinnacle of his political career, Coolidge remained the epitome of unpretentious simplicity and rectitude. Or, as some have suggested, he was, even in this grave moment, the epitome of sloth and showmanship.

41

CALVIN COOLIDGE AND THE NEW ERA

When the Business of America Was Business, 1923–1929

Members of an organization of "boosters," the Minneapolis Commercial Club, gather for a meeting.

THE COOLIDGE YEARS

Coolidge was not a bit like his predecessor. Far from strapping and handsome, he was thin with a pinched face that, even when he smiled, seemed to say that he wished he were somewhere else. Alice Roosevelt Longworth, the acidulous daughter of Theodore Roosevelt, said that Coolidge looked as if he had been weaned on a pickle.

Whereas Harding's private life was suspect, even tawdry, Coolidge was a man of impeccably proper, even dreary personal habits. His idea of a good time was a good nap. As president, he spent 12 to 14 hours out of 24 in bed except on slow days, when he was able to sneak in a few extra winks. When in 1933 writer Dorothy Parker heard that Coolidge had died, she asked, "How could they tell?"

A Quiet Clever Man

Coolidge might have appreciated that. He may have been known as "Silent Cal," hesitant to say much of anything, but when he spoke he was often witty. In an attempt to break the ice at a banquet, a woman seated next to Coolidge told the president of a friend who had bet her that untalkative Cal would not say three words all evening. "You lose," Coolidge replied, and returned to his appetizer, resuming the bland, non-committed gaze that was his trademark. "I found out early in life," this fabulously successful politician once noted, "that you don't have to explain something you haven't said."

And he was clever. At a meeting of American heads of state in the West Indies, Coolidge was sitting in a semicircle with his colleagues when a waiter began to walk down the line serving drinks. It was the Prohibition Era; if Coolidge took a drink while out of the country, it would make juicy front-page news, and American reporters and photographers (who were undoubtedly enjoying their West Indian daiquiris) waited on tenterhooks for the waiter to reach Coolidge with his tray. If, on the other hand, Coolidge doughtily turned the waiter away, it would be a mild but stereotypically American insult of his hosts. Coolidge fooled everyone. The instant before the waiter tried to serve him, he bent down to tie his shoe, and remained hunched over until the waiter moved on.

Coolidge took a curious pleasure in posing for photographers in costumes that looked ludicrous on him: wearing a ten-gallon hat or a Sioux Indian war bonnet; strapping himself into skis on the White House lawn; dressing as a hard-working farmer at the haying; in patent leather shoes with a Pierce Arrow in the back-

An old hand at grabbing publicity, Calvin Coolidge posed in an Indian headdress for photographers.

ground. Perhaps the photos were Coolidge's quiet way of saying that he was at one with the American people of the 1920s in enjoying novelties and pranks. On being asked about the costuming, he said that he calculated that "the American public wants a solemn ass as President and I think I'll go along with them."

He was assuredly at one with the majority of the American people in abdicating political and cultural leadership to the business community. Coolidge worshiped financial success and believed without reservation that millionaires knew what was best for the country. "The man who builds a factory builds a temple," he said. On another occasion, he put his faith with sublime simplicity: "The business of America is business."

"Keeping Cool With Coolidge"

And so, while Coolidge quickly rid the cabinet of the racketeers and hacks whom he had inherited from Harding, he retained Harding's appointees from the business world, most notably Herbert Hoover (with whom he was as uncomfortable as Harding was) and Secretary of the Treasury Andrew Mellon. He then sat back to preside over the most business-minded administration to his time, and, in return, business praised his administration higher than they built skyscrapers in New York and Chicago. The Republicans crowed about "Coolidge prosperity," the recovery from the erratic postwar economy that began in 1923, and, thanks to the president's unblemished record for honesty, the GOP never suffered a voter backlash as a result of the Harding scandals.

On the contrary, the biggest of the scandals, Teapot Dome, hurt progressive Democrats, for the Wilsonian, William G. McAdoo, a leading contender for the Democratic nomination in 1924, had been an attorney for the oilman Edward L. Doheny. Although McAdoo knew no more of the crooked transaction than did Coolidge, people associated him more closely with the thieves than they did the Republicans. When Montana Senators Thomas J. Walsh and Burton Wheeler, who led the investigation into the oil leases, attacked the Republicans, they were squelched by the slogan "Keep Cool With Coolidge." The president's supporters chastised them for ranting and raving about past crimes that Coolidge had remedied in his quiet way. By the summer of the election year of 1924, it was clear that Coolidge had the confidence of the country.

The Election of 1924

Then the Democrats obliged by tearing themselves apart. The convention, held in New York, pitted the Empire State's favorite son, Alfred E. Smith, against William G. McAdoo, whose support came mostly from the South and the West. Smith was a Roman Catholic and had the backing of ethnics in the Northeast and urban Midwest as a symbol of their arrival in American politics. McAdoo, although no bigot himself, drew support from southerners and westerners who regarded Catholicism with at best distaste, and virulently anti-Catholic Ku Kluxers. So bitter was the split and so vicious the whisper campaign that neither candidate would yield for more than a hundred ballots, long after it was obvious neither could win the nomination.

Finally, the weary delegates settled on a compromise candidate, Wall Street lawyer John W. Davis. He was not absent from his lucrative practice for long. Davis won a mere 29 percent of the vote to Coolidge's 54 percent. Aged Robert La Follette, trying to revive the Progressive party in 1924, captured 17 percent of the popular vote and carried his native Wisconsin.

For four more years, Calvin Coolidge napped through good times. It was eight months after he left office, in October 1929, that what businessmen called the "New Era" came crashing to an end. Ironically, in view of the impending Great Depression, Coolidge retired from office with great reluctance. It was whispered that when the Republican convention of 1928 took his coy statement, "I do not choose to run for president in 1928," as a refusal to run, and nominated Herbert Hoover to succeed him, Coolidge threw himself on his familiar bed and wept.

Mellon's Tax Policies

The keystone of New Era government was the tax policy sponsored by Secretary of the Treasury Andrew Mellon from Pittsburgh. Mellon looked less like the political cartoonist's stereotype of a big businessman—a bloated, fleshy moneybags—than like a sporting duke, but a moneybags he was. Trim, with chiseled aristocratic features, and dressed in deftly tailored suits and tiny pointed shoes that shone like newly minted coins, Mellon was one of the three or four richest men in the world, a banker with close ties to the steel industry.

Believing that economic prosperity depended on the extent to which capitalists reinvested their profits in

Andrew Mellon, a powerful businessman and a member of the Coolidge cabinet.

economic growth, Mellon favored the rich by slashing taxes that fell most heavily on them. He reduced the personal income tax for people who made more than $60,000 a year, and by 1929, the Treasury was actually shoveling taxes back to large corporations. United States Steel received a nice refund of $15 million. Other big corporations were comparably blessed.

To compensate for the loss in government revenues, Mellon cut government expenditures. The costs of government that he conceded were indispensable were to be paid for in two ways. First, Mellon raised the tariff on imported products, a double benefit for industrial capitalists. In the Fordney-McCumber Tariff of 1922, import duties reached levels that had been unheard of for a generation.

Second, Mellon sponsored modest increases in regressive taxes, that is, taxes that fell disproportionately on the middle and lower class. The costs of some kinds of postal services increased. The excise tax was raised and a new federal tax was imposed on automobiles. Both were paid by consumers. To those who complained that these measures penalized the middle classes and to some extent the poor, Mellon replied that the burden on each individual was small, and that his overall scheme helped ordinary people as well as the rich.

He contended that when businessmen reinvested their government-sponsored windfalls, they created jobs and, therefore, the means of a better standard of living for all. The share of the middle and lower classes in Coolidge prosperity would "trickle down" to them. Moreover, the inducement to get rich, encouraged by government policy, would reinvigorate the spirit of enterprise among all Americans.

For six years, from late 1923 to late 1929, it appeared as though Mellon was right. His friends toasted him as "the greatest Secretary of the Treasury since Alexander Hamilton." Just how much damage his policies did to the national economy would not be known until after the collapse of the New Era in 1929. As early as 1924, however, the policy of subordinating federal policy to the short-term interests of big business and banking was helping to make a shambles of the international economy.

The Legacy of the Treaty of Versailles

The fundamental weakness of the international economy during the 1920s owed to the fabulous costs of World War I. The war had pushed every participant nation except the United States to the brink of bankruptcy (and Russia over the cliff). Germany, for example, spent more during four years of war than during the previous four decades of the nation's existence. Britain and France were also deeply in debt—$10 bil-

RACY READING

In 1919, publisher Emanuel Haldeman-Julius sensed that there was a mass market for books if they could be priced cheaply and marketed correctly. His "Little Blue Books" were printed in a small, uniform format on cheap paper and were immensely successful. By 1951, Haldeman-Julius had published more than 2,000 titles and sold more than 500 million "Little Blue Books." Many were racy for the times or, at least, had racy come-ons. Haldeman-Julius liked to publish classics on which no royalties had to be paid, but he retitled the minor ones in order to boost sales. Thus, when he renamed Théophile Gautier's *Golden Fleece* as *The Quest for A Blond Mistress*, annual sales jumped from 600 to 50,000. Haldeman-Julius had similar results when he retitled Victor Hugo's *The King Amuses Himself* to read *The Lustful King Enjoys Himself*.

lion to the United States alone—and France bore the additional burden of having been the battlefield. Both countries demanded that Germany pay them $13 billion in reparations. In addition to fixing guilt for causing the war on the Germans, the money was earmarked for repaying the debts owed to Americans.

The result was a flow of international payments from Germany to Britain and France (and other smaller countries), and from there to the United States. The trouble was that too much wealth was drained from Germany for the economy of that important industrial nation to remain healthy. The gold went abroad. At home, paper German marks inflated crazily; in time it took bundles, even wheelbarrows full of paper money to buy food. Economists warned that to continue to bleed Germany was to promote political extremism (including Adolf Hitler's Nazi party) and to threaten the economies of all the European nations.

Some British and French statesmen acknowledged the point but insisted that as long as they were obligated to make huge debt payments to the United States, they had no choice but to insist on German payments to them. The burden of finding a remedy was on Americans.

A Foreign Policy for Bankers

There were several ways out of the morass. First, the United States, the world's wealthiest nation, could invigorate European industry by importing more European products. The Fordney-McCumber Tariff, a vital part of Mellon's fiscal policy, shut the door on that idea. Alternatively, the United States could forgive Britain and France all or most of their debts, in return for which they would cancel reparations pay-

Transportation

Transportation—the movement of people, goods, and ideas—has played a major role in shaping the United States. Here Irish immigrants disembark in New York City.

The Erie Canal, 364 miles long and originally four feet deep, took eight years to complete and connected the frontier to New York City.

This view of Lockport, New York, shows 10 of the 83 locks on the Erie Canal.

Where there were no waterways, the trip west was made by Conestoga wagon or prairie schooner.

Chinese laborers cheer for the first passenger train through the Sierra Nevada on the western end of the transcontinental railroad.

Railroads quickly replaced canals and stagecoaches for transporting goods and passengers between cities.

Passengers and train crew shoot buffalo along the Kansas Pacific Railroad.

*In 1903 Wilbur and Orville Wright successfully completed
the first controlled, engine-powered flight with their
homemade airplane.*

*With assembly-line production, Henry Ford transformed the automobile from a toy for the rich to
an inexpensive transportation necessity. The Model T was first marketed in 1908.*

Boomtown *by Thomas Hart Benton (1928) depicts life in the oil fields.*

Robots weld truck chassis in a modern assembly plant.

Beginning with the Interstate Highway Act of 1956, billions of dollars each year were used for highway construction, resulting in the grandiose Interstate freeway system.

Project Mercury, *the first U.S. manned space program of the early 1960s, led to the first moon landing by Apollo 11 astronauts on July 20, 1969.*

ments from Germany. The international economy would, so to speak, have a fresh start.

Unfortunately, an administration that was closely allied with banking interests would not do that. "They hired the money, didn't they?" Coolidge said of the French and British war debts, as though he were talking about a grocer having trouble paying for his automobile. Indeed, American bankers were profiting doubly from the European financial mess by loaning money to the Germans to, in part, subsidize their reparations payments. Interest, and a little bit of principal, was coming in from everywhere.

And that fact, bank profiteering, was good enough for the Republican administrations of the 1920s. In the Dawes Plan of 1924 (named for Budget Director Charles G. Dawes) and the Young Plan of 1929 (named for Owen D. Young), the United States agreed to a rescheduling of reparations payments, but not to a reduction of the total burden.

The circular flow of payments continued. American bankers loaned money to Germany; Germany paid about $2.5 billion in reparations to Britain and France between 1923 and 1929; Britain and France paid $2.6 billion to American creditors. The European economy was steadily, if slowly, sapped, and the American economy was indirectly damaged: capital that was supposed to be reinvested at home to "trickle down" was devoted to a nonproductive balancing of international books that did little to benefit American workers.

Isolationism?

After the Treaty of Washington, the Harding and Coolidge administrations resisted meaningful cooperative agreements with other nations. There was no question of joining the League as more and more Americans became convinced that it had been a mistake to intervene in the war that had produced it. America's international efforts on behalf of maintaining the peace were restricted to proclamations of goodwill much like William Jennings Bryan's "cooling off" treaties. In 1928, Secretary of State Frank B. Kellogg joined with French Foreign Minister Aristide Briand to write a treaty that "outlawed" war as an instrument of national policy. Eventually, 62 nations signed the Kellogg-Briand Pact, a clear indication that, as a broad and pious statement of unenforceable sentiment, the pact was meaningless.

Because the United States refused to cooperate internationally in any meaningful way, the foreign policy of the 1920s is usually described as "isolationist." This is, however, something of a misnomer. Towards Latin America, the Harding and Coolidge administrations were active and aggressive on behalf of the interests of American investors.

American investments in Latin America climbed from about $800 million in 1914 to $5.4 billion in 1929. The United States replaced Great Britain as the chief economic power in Latin America, particularly in the nations of the Caribbean.

The poorer Latin American nations sorely needed capital, and to that extent every dollar invested there was potentially a boon—if the population of the host countries as a whole benefited from it. Unfortunately, American businessmen had little interest in how the Latin American countries were governed until their profits were threatened by political instability. They ignored the depredations of predatory elites until they were in trouble.

When dictators in the "banana republics" were unable to contain popular resentments, American investors turned to Washington for protection of their profits. By 1924, American officials directly or indirectly administered the finances of ten Latin American nations. For at least part of the decade, the marines occupied Nicaragua, Honduras, Cuba, Haiti, and the Dominican Republic. The business of the entire Western Hemisphere was the business of Coolidge's America too.

PROSPERITY AND BUSINESS CULTURE

In the late twentieth century, it is easy to see the damage wreaked by the Coolidge administration. But the voters of the 1920s supported Silent Cal and his policies with unmistakeable enthusiasm. The Republican party held comfortable majorities in every Congress between 1920 and 1930. Only in the South and some thinly populated western states, and in a few big cities, could the Democrats count on winning elections.

The Anticlimactic Election of 1928

In 1928, the 54 percent of the vote that Coolidge had won in 1924 rose to 58 percent. The victorious Republican candidate was Herbert Hoover, who was, in his energy and rather opaque written celebrations of business, even better an exemplar of the New Era than Silent Cal.

Hoover's opponent, Alfred E. Smith of New York, had spent four years mending fences with southern and western Protestants who had supported McAdoo in 1924. Smith was unable to win over the bigots, however. For the first time since Reconstruction, a number of prominent southerners, including Methodist bishop James Cannon, urged voters to support the Republican

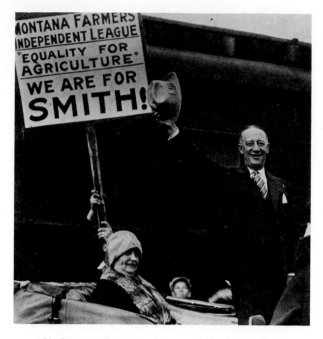

Alfred E. Smith was popular among Montana farmers, but, being Catholic, he could not win support in the "Bible Belt."

party. Their reason was partly Smith's Roman Catholic religion. But they also drummed on Smith's opposition to Prohibition. Like many urban politicos, Smith not only urged repeal, he openly flaunted the law. Herbert Hoover probably disapproved of Prohibition personally, but in 1928 he called it "a great social and economic experiment, noble in motive and far-reaching in purpose." He was the "dry" candidate, Smith the "wet."

Smith also invited hostility from southern, western, and rural voters with his rasping, nasal New York accent. Heard over the radio—or "raddio" as Smith called it—his voice conjured up all the unsavory images associated with New York City for half a century.

Still, had he been a Kansas Presbyterian who never drank even patent medicines, Smith would have lost in 1928. Business and the Republican party reigned supreme because of the general prosperity of the New Era, and because a great many Americans were sincerely convinced that businessmen were the new messiahs that Woodrow Wilson had tried so hard to be.

The Shape of Prosperity

Industrial and agricultural productivity soared during the 1920s, even though there was not much increase in the size of the industrial work force, and the number of agricultural workers actually declined. Wages did not keep up with the contribution that the more effi-

cient workers were making to the economy, however. While dividends on stock rose 65 percent between 1920 and 1929, wages increased only 24 percent.

Nevertheless, the increase in wages was quite enough to satisfy the workingpeople who enjoyed them, particularly because consumer goods were relatively cheap and business promoted an alluring new way for a family to live beyond their means—consumer credit.

Buy Now, Pay Later

Before the 1920s, borrowing was something one did in order to build a business, to get crops in the ground, or to save or improve an enterprise. In theory, borrowed money was invested in productivity, thus providing the means to retire the debt. Or, people borrowed in order to build or buy a home, in which case their debt was secured by real property. During the 1920s, for the first time, large numbers of Americans began to borrow simply in order to live more pleasingly. They went into debt not to produce but to consume and enjoy.

The chief agency of consumer borrowing during the 1920s was the installment plan. A refrigerator that sold for $87.50 could be ensconced in a corner of the kitchen for a down payment of merely $5 and monthly payments of $10. Even a comparatively low-cost item like a vacuum cleaner ($28.95) could be had for $2 down and "E-Z payments" of $4 a month. During the New Era, 60 percent of all automobiles were bought on time; 70 percent of furniture; 80 percent of refrigerators, radios, and vacuum cleaners; and 90 percent of pianos, sewing machines, and washing machines. With 13.8 million people owning radios by 1930 (up from virtually none in 1920), the Americans who basked in the glow of Coolidge prosperity were also up to their necks in hock.

THE TIN LIZZIE

Although Americans did not invent the automobile, they democratized it by putting cars within the reach of almost everyone. But striving for simplicity (shunning all "extras," including a choice of color), by adapting the assembly line to the manufacture of cars, and by refusing to change his design, Henry Ford managed to whittle the price of a brand-new Model T to $260 in 1925. that is more than $2,000 in today's dollars, but still considerably less than the cheapest new car on the market. By 1927, Ford had sold 15 million tin lizzies, as Model T Fords were affectionately known, more than all other auto makers combined.

1855 · SEVENTY-FIFTH ANNIVERSARY · 1930

Defining the true meaning of the word "chic"

Coined in Paris to express originality plus taste, the word "chic" has come to mean many things to many people. In London, swagger; in America, pertness; in Japan, genuineness. The original and last meanings are the ones contained in the undoubted chic of Crane bathrooms. Always originality and taste are found in Crane fixture designs and decorative suggestions; genuineness in the service given. At Crane Exhibit Rooms, you will find ideas for rooms as elaborate as the one above and others for the simplest cottage. Complete installation can be on monthly payments under the Crane Budget Plan. Let your architect help you plan. Buy from a Crane Qualified Contractor-Dealer, always a highly skilled registered or licensed master plumber or heating contractor.

Valves **CRANE** *Fittings*

FIXTURES, VALVES, FITTINGS, AND PIPING FOR DOMESTIC AND INDUSTRIAL USE

Crane Co., General Offices: 836 S. Michigan Ave., Chicago · 23 W. 44th St., New York · Branches and sales offices in one hundred and ninety-six cities
October 1930 Good Housekeeping

An advertisement for Crane bathroom fixtures encouraged consumers to buy on credit, a new marketing concept in the 1920s.

Moralists pointed out that borrowing in order to consume marked a sharp break with American ideals of frugality—the axioms of Benjamin Franklin—but others spoke louder and in more dulcet tones. They were the advertisers, members of a new profession dedicated to creating wants in people's minds—the advertising men called them needs—which people had never particularly noticed before.

Buy, Buy, Buy

The earliest advertisements, dating to antiquity, were announcements. In the eighteenth and nineteenth centuries, a merchant placed a tiny notice in a newspaper describing goods, perhaps unusual ones, available for purchase, or special "sale" prices on common products.

During the 1870s, Robert Bonner, the editor of a literary magazine, the New York *Ledger*, learned by accident the curious effectiveness of repeating a mes-

sage over and over. He intended to place a conventional one-line ad in a newspaper—"Read Mrs. Southworth's New Story in the Ledger"—and the compositor misread his specification of "one line" as "one page." The line ran over and over, down every column. To Bonner's surprise, the blunder did not bankrupt him; his magazine sold out in one afternoon.

The lesson was unmistakable. During the 1890s, C. W. Post, without a cent to his name, borrowed enough money to plaster an entire city with the name of his new breakfast cereal, Post Toasties, and was a millionaire within a month. Bombarded by the name in newspapers, on billboards, painted on the sides of buildings, slipped under doors on leaflets, people bought. By the 1920s, advertisers had moved on to making the extravagant claims of the snake oil salesman, telling outright lies, and bringing sexual titillation into the game: suggestive young ladies in advertisements for such products as soda pop and tickets on railroads.

Advertising became a profession, and the pros styled themselves as practical psychologists. They sold goods by exploiting anxieties and, in the words of Thorstein Veblen, "administering shock effects" and "trading on

LET'S HAVE A LOOK UNDER THE HOOD

Americans and Britons speak a different language when they talk about their cars. What Americans call the hood, the British call the bonnet. Some other differences:

American English	British English
clunker or junker	banger
gas	petrol
generator	dynamo
headlight	headlamp
muffler	silencer
station wagon	estate wagon
trunk	boot
windshield	windscreen

The different vocabularies provide a little case study in how languages develop. The automobile roared into history long after the United States and Great Britain had gone their separate political and cultural ways, but before instantaneous electronic communication allowed words coined on one side of the Atlantic to become immediately familiar on the other.

Because the early automobile was largely a French development, many American automotive terms were taken from the French language: *automobile* itself, *cabriolet* (later shortened to *cab*), *chassis, chauffeur, coupe, garage, limousine,* and *sedan.*

ANXIETY ADVERTISING

The text that follows was taken from a magazine advertisement of the 1920s for Listerine Antiseptic, a mouthwash. The illustration that accompanied it showed an elderly, attractive, poignantly sad woman sitting in a darkened parlor (with a photograph of Calvin Coolidge on the wall) pouring over old letters and a photograph album.

"Sometimes, when lights are low, they come back to comfort and at the same time sadden her—those memories of long ago, when she was a slip of a girl in love with a dark-eyed Nashville boy. They were the happiest moments of her life—those days of courtship. Though she had never married, no one could take from her the knowledge that she had been loved passionately, devotedly; those frayed and yellowed letters of his still told her so. How happy and ambitious they had been for their future together. And then, like a stab, came their parting . . . the broken engagement . . . the sorrow and the shock of it. She could find no explanation for it then, and now, in the soft twilight of life when she can think calmly, it is still a mystery to her."

The advertiser then went on so as to leave no doubt that "halitosis"—bad breath—was the source of the woman's tragedy.

the range of human infirmities which blossom in devout observances, and bear fruit in the psychopathic wards." In the age of Coolidge, the makers of Listerine Antiseptic, a mouthwash, invented a disease, "halitosis," of which the symptoms included nothing more than a curter greeting than usual from a friend: "Even your best friend won't tell you." Listerine made millions. Fleischmann's yeast, losing its market as people began buying instead of baking their bread, advertised their product as excellent for curing constipation and adolescent pimples. The success of anxiety advertising resulted in the creation of underarm deodorants, a nicety without which humanity had functioned for millennia.

Chain Stores

With manufacturers of "small-ticket" items like toothpaste and mouthwash spending millions to create a demand for their products, it became advantageous to retail advertised goods on a nationwide basis too. Individual "Mom and Pop" grocery stores and locally owned and managed haberdasheries and sundries shops sold comparatively few cans of Chef Boy-Ar-Dee Spaghetti, Arrow shirts, and tubes of Ipana each month. Therefore, they paid the regional wholesaler a premium price. A centrally managed chain or franchise company, on the contrary, could buy the same goods for hundreds of stores at once, secure a better wholesale price, and keep shipping charges down through "vertical integration." The result was they sharply undersold "Mom and Pop," and their retail chains spread rapidly throughout the country.

By 1928, 860 grocery chains competed for the dollars of a population that was eating better. Among the biggest success stories between 1920 and 1929 were Piggly-Wiggly (from 515 to 2,500 stores), Safeway (from 766 to 2,660 stores), and A & P (Atlantic and Pacific Tea Company, from 4,621 to 15,418 stores). Chains also came to dominate the sundries trade (F. W. Woolworth and J. C. Penney), auto parts (Western Auto), and, of course, the retailing of gasoline.

Image Advertising

"Image" advertising—associating a product with values or a certain attractive kind of person—characterized the selling of automobiles at a time when dozens of manufacturers competed for a share of the market. Pierce Arrows and Lincolns implied, none too subtly, that possession of one of these automobiles indicated a person of high social standing. Stutz Bearcat was the car of the sport and the swell. Dodge affected a stodgy and stolid comfortable "old shoe" family image. Henry Ford insisted that his car be presented as common and democratic.

In 1925 Sears, Roebuck opened its first retail store while continuing its catalogue sales.

During the 1920s, Americans became accustomed to advertisements like this one appealing to middle-class America to follow the lead of "many people who can afford to pay far more."

By the end of the decade, there were 27 million cars registered by state departments of motor vehicles. Indeed, everything related to automobiles, from publicly financed highway construction to those new features of the American landscape, service stations and the roadside motor hotel or "motel," flourished during the New Era.

The Limits of Prosperity

A few economists joined the moralistic critics of runaway consumption, pointing out that the time would come when everyone who could afford a car, a washing machine, and other consumer durables would have them. They would no longer be buying, and the consumer industries would be in trouble.

Another major weakness of the Coolidge economy was that significant numbers of Americans did not share in the good times and were, therefore, shut out completely from the buying spree. The 700,000 to 800,000 coal miners and 400,000 textile workers and their dependents suffered depressed conditions and wages throughout the decade; they were not buying many cars and radios. Staple farmers were once again struggling to stave off bankruptcy. Even those who did well often lived in places where there was no electricity; they were buying no appliances that had to be plugged in.

The southern states generally lagged far behind the rest of the country in income and standard of living. Blacks, Indians, Hispanics, and other minority groups tasted Coolidge prosperity only in odd bites.

Business Culture

But economically deprived groups are rarely politically articulate when the mainstream society is at ease in its world, and in the 1920s, mainstream America was quite at ease. Business leaders hastened to take the credit for good times, and they got it.

On a local level, businessmen's clubs such as the Rotary, Kiwanis, Lions, and Junior Chambers of Commerce seized community leadership and preached *boosterism:* "If you can't boost, don't knock." Successful manufacturers like Henry Ford were looked to for wisdom on every imaginable question. Any man who made $25,000 a day, as Ford did during most of the 1920s, must be an oracle on whatever subject he chose to speak about. Even that once most hated man in America, John D. Rockefeller, now in his eighties and retired to Florida, became a figure of respect and affection, thanks to Coolidge prosperity and the skillful image building of the Rockefeller family's public relations expert, Ivy Lee.

A BUSINESSMAN'S PRAYER

The following is not a parody, but a "prayer" that was quite seriously recommended to those in business during the 1920s:

God of business men, I thank Thee for the fellowship of red-blooded men with songs in their hearts and handclasps that are sincere;

I thank thee for telephones and telegrams that link me with home and office, no matter where I am.

I thank thee for the joy of battle in the business arena, the thrill of victory and the courage to take defeat like a good sport.

I thank thee for children, friendships, books, fishing, the game of golf, my pipe, and the open fire on a chilly evening.

AMEN.

Rows of parked automobiles lining a main street became a common sight in American cities in the 1920s.

The career of an advertising man, Bruce Barton, showed just how thoroughly the business culture dominated the way Americans thought. In 1925, Barton published a book called *The Man Nobody Knows*. It depicted Jesus as a businessman, a hail-fellow-well-met, a sport, an entrepreneur, and an advertising genius whose religion was like a successful company. Instead of finding Barton's vision blasphemous or laughable, Americans bought *The Man Nobody Knows* by the hundres of thousands. It was a best seller for two years!

John Jacob Raskob of General Motors promoted the worship of business in popular magazines such as *The Saturday Evening Post*. Because the value of many kinds of property was rising throughout the 1920s under the stewardship of business, Raskob said that it was a simple matter for workingmen to save a little money and invest it, thus becoming capitalists themselves. To an astonishing degree, middle-class Americans who had a small nest egg in the bank believed him. They plunged their savings into one get-rich-quick scheme after another, feeding but at the same time dooming, the speculative economy.

GET RICH QUICK

The most colorful get-rich-quick craze of the decade centered on Florida, previously a backward and isolated agricultural state. Improved train connections with eastern and midwestern population centers, retirement to Florida by such celebrities as Rockefeller and William Jennings Bryan, and the lively nationwide ballyhoo of ingenious promoters such as Wilson Mizner put people on notice of the Sunshine State's possibilities as a vacation and retirement paradise.

The Florida Land Boom

The development of places like Orlando, Fort Lauderdale, and Miami Beach would take time, of course, no one denied that. The way to make money from their growth, therefore, was to buy orange groves and sandy wasteland at bargain prices and hold the land for resale to the actual builders of vacation hotels and retirement homes. The number of people rich enough to make such a long-term commitment was small. In 1925, however, Florida's boosters attracted more modestly fixed people to send their money south by promoting a get-rich-quick speculative fever that fed on itself.

As had happened repeatedly in the American West, the price of Florida land rose not because development was underway and residents were pouring in by the hundreds of thousands, but because speculator bought from speculator, each planning to sell to another as quickly as possible at an even higher price. Some lots in Miami Beach on which no one dreamed of building changed hands dozens of times within a few months, the price climbing with every sale. At the height of the craze, one issue of a Miami newspaper ran more than 500 pages of advertisements of land for sale. There were over 2,000 real-estate offices in the little city.

Since the price of every acre in Florida seemed to be skyrocketing, many northerners were willing to buy sight unseen, and frauds were inevitable. More than a few snowbound dreamers in Chicago and Minneapolis purchased tracts of alligator-infested swampland from fast-talking salesmen who assured them that they were purchasing a site that Piggly-Wiggly or Woolworth's would find highly desirable. Others bought "beach-

MANUFACTURED HEROES

"Shakespeare, in the familiar lines, divided great men into three classes: those born great, those who achieve greatness, and those who have greatness thrust upon them. It never occurred to him to mention those who hire public relations experts and press secretaries to make themselves look great."

Daniel Boorstin, *The Image* (1962)

JESUS AS ADVERTISING MAN

He would be a national advertiser today, I am sure, as he was the greatest advertiser of his own day. Take any one of the parables, no matter which—you will find that it exemplifies all the principles on which advertising textbooks are written.

1. First of all they are marvellously condensed, as all good advertising must be. Jesus hated prosy dullness.

2. His language was marvellously simple—a second great essential. All the greatest things in human life are one-syllable things—love, joy, hope, child, wife, trust, faith, God.

3. Sincerity glistened like sunshine through every sentence he uttered. The advertisements which persuade people to act are written by men who have an abiding respect for the intelligence of their readers, and a deep sincerity regarding the merits of the goods they have to sell.

4. Finally he knew the necessity for repetition and practiced it. No important truth can be impressed upon the minds of any large number of people by being said only once.

Bruce Barton, *The Man Nobody Knows* (1925)

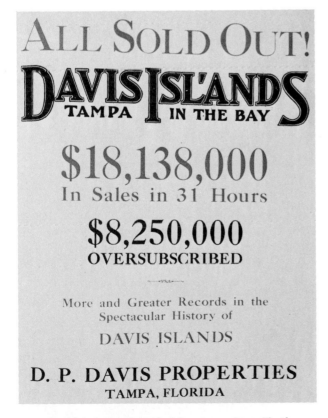

An advertisement typical of those prompting a Florida land boom among real-estate speculators in the 1920s.

front lots" that were closer to the ocean than they counted on—underneath six feet of salt water at high tide. But the major fuel of the mania was not fraud. It was a foolishness born of a culture that exalted business and money-making above all else.

Bust

As with all speculative crazes, the day inevitably arrived when there were no more buyers, no one willing to bet on higher prices in the future. After a few months of making mortgage payments on land that was not moving, would-be land barons decided, as herd-like as they had bought, to get out of Florida real estate with their winnings, to break even, or just to cut their losses. The market was flooded with offerings at ever lower prices. The speculators who were caught holding overpriced property there saw paper fortunes evaporate; the banks that had lent them money to speculate failed; people who had trusted those banks to invest their savings sensibly lost their accounts.

N O T A B L E   P E O P L E

AIMEE SEMPLE MCPHERSON (1890–1944)

Aimee Elizabeth Kennedy was born in a small town in Ontario, Canada, in 1890. Little is known of her youth except that she underwent an intense religious experience and was "born again" while a young woman after hearing an impassioned sermon by an illiterate but eloquent preacher named Robert Semple. She married Semple—the dates are uncertain—and went with him to China where they intended to devote their lives to missionary work. In less than a year, however, Aimee's husband died, and she returned home.

She married again, to Harold McPherson, but the marriage appears to have been unhappy from the start; Aimee was an ambitious person with an effervescent personality, and McPherson was shy, perhaps dull. After separating from her husband, she was apparently destitute except in ideas. A handsome woman, extroverted with a theatrical bent at a time when women were leading more public lives, Aimee's religiosity made her a natural as a preacher. Her model was Billy Sunday, a major-league baseball player turned revivalist who combined an appeal for simple, emotional fundamentalism with vaudeville entertainment. Sunday leaped around the speaker's platform, used colorful, sometimes almost salacious illustrations for his lessons, and condemned cities, Roman Catholics, Jews, alcohol, smoking, and dancing—save for that done in the pulpit in the name of Jesus. He also knew how to fill a collection basket. More than a few theatrical producers gladly would have exchanged their receipts for Billy's offerings.

Aimee never quite outdid him, but she came close. With her practical-minded mother acting as business manager, she started out on the "sawdust trail," traveling up and down the east coast in what she called her "gospel automobile." It was a difficult life with modest returns. Aimee preached to whatever congregation would allow her in the pulpit in exchange for a share of the collection. Her audiences were poor, rural people or recent emigrants to the cities. They could not afford to contribute much to what, for them, was religion, fellowship, relief from hardship, and entertainment combined.

In 1918, Aimee made the same decision that a great many people were making at that time—she decided to move to southern California—and it changed her life.

Los Angeles, just a dusty pueblo a generation earlier, had boomed and boomed again as the city fathers had brought water into what was a natural desert and successfully touted the pleasures of the southern California climate to people who were tired of struggling "back East" but who had enough money to put a down payment on a home lot. Everyone in Los Angeles had arrived only recently. No one had roots there, and the extraordinary growth of the city (the population doubled every few years) made for a sense of insecurity that

Evangelist Aimee Semple McPherson.

sent people searching desperately for something unchanging to grab. "Old-time religion" was a perfect response, as Aimee Semple McPherson understood before anyone else.

Aimee and Los Angeles suited each other. She was as good a showman, alternately poignant and clownish, as Charlie Chaplin and Buster Keaton. She dressed in flowing, low-cut white robes, surrounded herself with choirs of angels, dropped rose petals from the ceiling of her Angelus Temple (which seated more than five thousand people), released balloons and pigeons at climactic moments in her sermons, pounded the Bible, broke down in tears, exploded in ecstatic exultation, and dependably healed several people of fatal diseases and impairments at every meeting. On one occasion she set the congregation to cheering by entering the temple on a motorcycle, roaring up the aisle. Before another meeting in San Diego, she bombarded the city with tracts from an airplane.

The anomaly of Aimee Semple McPherson and her less successful imitators was the fact that they exploited the technology, novelties, and social trends of the New Era at the same time that they inveighed against the evils of them. Aimee condemned sinful radio, but she owned a station. She railed against the immorality of Hollywood movies, but missed no opportunity to be filmed in her highly sexual and suggestive act. "To visit Angelus Temple," one cynic wrote, "is to go on a sensuous debauch served up in the name of religion." She called herself "Everybody's Sister," but encouraged the racism and violence of the Ku Klux Klan.

And the formula worked. Not only did she fill the Angelus Temple, but on a month-long visit to Denver, she spoke to twelve thousand people nightly. She founded a college, owned a publishing house, opened branch churches of her "Foursquare Gospel Religion" every month during the 1920s, and sent money to overseas missions (or at least she said she did).

But it would be presumptuous to say that she and other revivalists were simply cynics, parting generally poor people from their money. Novelist Sinclair Lewis recognized the difficulty of sorting out sincere religious commitment and humbug for profit in his book about fundamentalism during the 1920s, *Elmer Gantry* (in which a major character is patterned on Aimee).

A pall was thrown over Aimee's reputation in the summer of 1926. On May 18, after an excursion to the beach, Aimee failed to show up for a meeting at the Angelus Temple. For weeks the papers were filled with sensational speculations about what had happened to her. On June 24, just when the press was losing interest in the case, Aimee stumbled into a desert town in Arizona. From a hospital bed in Douglas, she told of having been kidnapped, tortured by men who burned her with cigars, and held in an isolated desert dwelling.

Skeptical reporters noted that Aimee's wrists were bruised, but there were no other signs of mistreatment. A physician who examined her noted wryly that she was neither sunburned, dehydrated, nor especially dirty, which was remarkable considering that she had fled across a parched wasteland in order to get to Douglas.

Rumors flew furiously. Aimee had been enjoying a month-long tryst with a radio operator from the Angelus Temple who also had been missing (and showed up in Los Angeles about the same time that Aimee stumbled into Douglas). Others said that there had been a Mexican abortion. Yet others wrote off the incident as a plain and simple publicity stunt to distract people from dissension within Aimee's organization and to fill those five thousand seats at the temple. Sister Aimee did not quell that tale when she reenacted the kidnapping for photographers from the Los Angeles *Examiner*, a newspaper that fully exploited the event and indignantly defended the evangelist. (Publisher William Randolph Hearst, who knew how to put on a show, also appreciated one.) In any case, while there never was any positive evidence that an abduction had taken place, Aimee was quickly acquitted when she stood trial for fraud.

Aimee lost her celebrity status in the years that followed the abduction and had to fight a series of civil suits to protect her share in the property of the Foursquare Gospel Church. But the organization survived her, and today has more than two hundred thousand members in almost one thousand congregations.

The Florida crash was triggered by a hurricane that hit Miami and showed, as Frederick Lewis Allen put it, what a soothing tropical wind could do to a vacation paradise when it got a running start from the West Indies. The price of land plunged within weeks to dollars per acre. Citrus farmers who had cursed themselves a thousand times for having sold their groves so cheaply at the beginning of the boom discovered that, thanks to a chain of defaults, they were back in possession of their orchards only a little worse for the wear of speculators tromping through them imagining hotels and happy beach loungers. Wilson Mizner, one of the architects of the boom and a big loser in the bust, was good humored about the debacle. "Always be pleasant to the people you meet on the way up," he said, "because they are always the very same people you meet on the way down." He moved on to Hollywood.

Buying on Margin

Middle-class America was almost as nonchalant as Mizner. Even before Florida busted, they began to fuel another speculative mania, driving up the prices of shares on the New York Stock Exchange.

Speculation in stocks had always been a game for a few very rich people. However, the prosperity of the 1920s created savings accounts for middle-class Americans, even after their consumption spree. In order to tap their capital, stockbrokers offered the possibility of purchasing stock on an installment plan in which, so it seemed, there were no installments to pay.

That is, investors with just a few hundred or thousands of dollars to risk in the market could buy stocks "on margin." They bought shares of RCA-Victor, the New York Central, or Illinois Gadget by paying out as little as 10 percent of the quoted price of those companies' shares. In this way, they were able to hold title to ten times as many shares as they could afford to buy with cash. A bank or broker loaned the speculator the balance of the stocks' actual price with the stocks themselves serving as collateral. This—the money the speculator owed—was "the margin." When the shares were sold, presumably at a big profit—the loan was paid off and the shrewd speculators pocketed the difference, also ten times what they would have made if they had bought with cash. At least that was how the 1.5 million Americans "playing the market" in 1926 understood the margin to work.

The Bull Market

Beginning in 1927, that was how it did work for hundreds of thousands of people. Prices of shares began to soar as more and more people rushed to buy. During

Businessmen crowd Wall Street on October 24, 1929, the day the stock market began to crash, sending America into economic depression.

the summer of 1929, values went crazy. American Telephone and Telegraph climbed from $209 a share to $303; General Motors went from $268 to $391, hitting $452 on September 3. Some obscure issues enjoyed even more dizzying rises. And with each tale of a fortune made overnight, related breathlessly or with smug self-congratulation at the country club, lodge hall, community dance, or, indeed, on the porch of the church on Sunday, more people were hooked, encouraged to carry their savings to stockbrokers, whose offices were as easy to find as auto parts stores.

Historically and ideally, the value of a share in a corporation represented the earning capacity of the company. The money that a corporation realized by selling shares was to be expended, theoretically, to improve the company's plant, equipment and marketing capacity, and to be used in other productive ways. Thus, when the price of stock in General Motors or Radio Corporation of America rose during the late

1920s, it represented to some extent the extraordinary expansion of the automobile and radio industries.

During the speculative Coolidge Bull Market, however, the prices of shares also reflected nothing more than the willingness of people to pay those prices because, as in Florida, they expected someone else to buy from them at yet higher prices. It was immaterial to such speculators that the companies in which they had put their money did not pay dividends or even use their capital to improve productive capacity. The rising prices of stocks fed on themselves. It became more profitable for companies to put their capital into speculation—making loans to margin buyers, for example—than into production. The face value of shares in the Coolidge Bull Market bore little relationship to the health of the American economy.

Politicians, either unable to understand what was happening or afraid to appear pessimistic in a time of buoyant optimism, reassured their constituents that there was nothing wrong. When a few concerned economists warned that the bull market was a bubble that had to burst, with calamitous consequences, others scolded them. President Coolidge told people that he thought stock prices were cheap, in effect encouraging others to rush to the broker.

The Inevitable

Joseph P. Kennedy, a Boston millionaire (and father of President John F. Kennedy), said in later years that he had sold all of his stocks during the summer of 1929 after the man who shined his shoes had mentioned that he was playing the market. Kennedy reasoned that if such a poorly paid person was buying stock, there was no one left out there to bid prices higher. The inevitable crash was coming soon.

Kennedy was right. On September 3, 1929, the average price of shares on the New York Stock Exchange peaked and then dipped sharply. For a month, prices spurted up and down. Then on "Black Thursday," October 24, a record 13 million shares changed hands, and values collapsed. General Electric fell 47½ points on that one day; other major issues dropped almost as much.

On Tuesday, October 29, the wreckage was worse. In a panic now, speculators dumped 16 million shares on the market. Clerical workers on Wall Street had to work through the night just to sort out the avalanche of paperwork. When the dust settled early the next morning, more than $30 billion in paper value had been wiped out.

It was phony value, representing little more than the irrational belief that prices could rise indefinitely. Nevertheless, the eradication of so many dollars profoundly shattered the confidence of businessmen and belief in the business culture of the 1920s. The Great Crash eventually contributed to the hardship of millions of people who did not even know what a share in a company looked like.

Crash and Depression

The Great Crash of 1929 did not cause the Great Depression of the 1930s. That was the result of fundamental weaknesses in the economy that had little to do with the mania for speculation. But the crash helped to trigger the decline in the American economy that was well under way by New Year's Day 1930.

Middle-class families who had played the market lost their savings. Banks that had recklessly lent money to speculators went broke. When they closed their doors, they wiped out the savings accounts of frugal people who looked on a bank as a vault to protect their money from robbers.

Corporations whose cash assets were decimated shut down operations or curtailed production, thus throwing people out of work or cutting their wages. Those who had taken mortgages during the heady high interest days of 1928 and 1929 were unable to meet payments and lost their homes; farmers lost the means by which they made a living. This contributed to additional bank failures.

Virtually everyone had to cut consumption, thus reducing the sales of manufacturers and farmers and stimulating another turn in the downward spiral: curtailed production meant layoff; increased unemployment meant another reduction in consumption by those newly thrown out of work. And so it went, from buy, buy, buy to down, down, down.

For Further Reading

See these several general histories of the 1920s: Frederick Lewis Allen, *Only Yesterday* (1931); Loren Baritz, *The Culture of the Twenties* (1969); Paul A. Carter, *The Twenties in America* (1968); Ellis W. Hawley, *The Great War and the Search for a Modern Order: A History of the American People and Their Institutions, 1917–1933* (1979); William E. Leuchtenburg, *The Perils of Prosperity, 1914–1932* (1958); George Soule, *Prosperity Decade: From War to Depression, 1917–1929* (1947).

Focusing on politics are David Bumer, *The Politics of Provincialism: The Democratic Party in Transition* (1968); Otis L. Graham, Jr., *The Great Campaigns: War and Reform in America, 1900–1928* (1971); Oscar Handlin, *Al Smith and His America* (1958); John D. Hicks, *Republican Ascendancy, 1921–1933* (1960);

Donald Lisio, *The President and Protest* (1974); E. A. Moore, *A Catholic Runs for President* (1956); Theodore D. Saloutos and John D. Hicks, *Twentieth Century Populism: Agricultural Discontent in the Middle West, 1900–1939* (1951); D. R. McCoy, *Calvin Coolidge: The Quiet President* (1967); Arthur M. Schlesinger, Jr., *The Crisis of the Old Order* (1957); William Allen White, *A Puritan in Babylon* (1938); Joan Hoff Wilson, *Herbert Hoover: Forgotten Progressive* (1975).

On economic and financial questions, see Irving Bernstein, *The Lean Years* (1960); C. P. Kinderberger, *The World in Depression* (1973); J. W. Prothro, *Dollar Decade: Business Ideas in the 1920s* (1954); and the incomparable John K. Galbraith, *The Great Crash* (1955).

The stock market crash of late 1929 was a headline story day after day. The depression that began in 1930 made its impact less dramatically at first, but by the end of the year it engulfed the nation. The bad times did not really lift until 1940, after the economy had been jolted into full activity by the outbreak of war in Europe.

The Great Depression was not only the most serious economic crisis in American history, it was a more jarring psychological and moral experience for the American people than any other event in their past except the Civil War. The Great Depression was a national trauma that left lifelong scars. Americans who had lived through the First World War and the Roaring

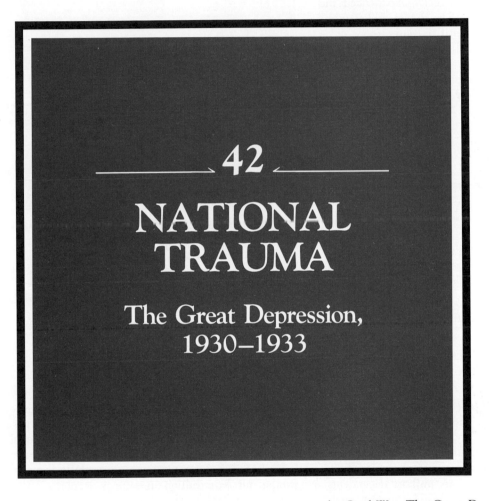

42

NATIONAL TRAUMA

The Great Depression, 1930–1933

A mother and her children, victims of the Great Depression, in front of their makeshift home. This photograph, entitled "Children in a Democracy," was taken by Dorothea Lange as part of her work for the Farm Securities Administration.

Twenties found their recollections of those periods vague and inconsequential after 1930. People who came of age during the 1930s would remember the deprivation, anxieties, and struggles of the decade more vividly than they would remember the Second World War, the return of prosperity, and the beginning of the nuclear age in the 1940s. So large did the memory of hard times loom in their minds that they passed on to their children, who were born in the 1930s and 1940s and never really experienced the depression, a sense that it was the most important event in their lives. Not until the later 1960s did a generation come of age for which the Great Depression was irrelevant "ancient history." Not until 1980, half a century after the depression began, did voters in a national election decisively repudiate the political "liberals" whom the Great Depression brought to the fore.

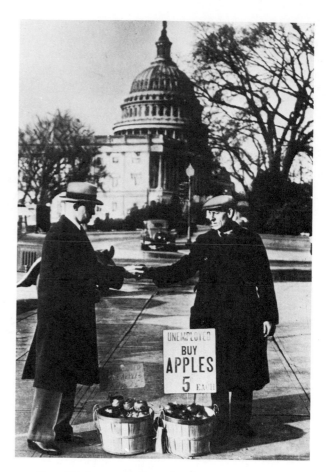

On a Washington, D.C., sidewalk, a man sells apples to support himself while unemployed.

THE FACE OF CATASTROPHE

Not every memory of the 1930s was a bad one. On the contrary, many people were proud that when times had been worst, they nevertheless had survived and, what is more, had carried on vital cultural, social, and personal lives. Negative or positive, however, the depression generation was the last American generation to date whose character and values were forged in an era of economic decline, denial, and insecurity.

The Depression in Numbers

During the first year after the crash of the stock market, 4 million workers lost their jobs. By 1931, 100,000 people were being fired each week. By 1932, 25 percent of the work force was unemployed, 13 million people with about 30 million dependents. Black workers, "the last hired and the first fired," suffered a higher unemployment rate than whites, 35 percent. In Chicago, 40 percent of those people who wanted work could not find it. In Toledo, 80 percent were unemployed. In some coal-mining towns like Donora, Pennsylvania, virtually no one had a job.

Employees who held on to their jobs took cuts in pay. Between 1929 and 1933, the average weekly earnings of manufacturing workers fell from $25 to less than $17. The income of farmers plummeted from a low starting point. By the winter of 1933, some corn growers were burning their crop for heat—shades of the 1890s—because they could not sell it at a profit. Growers of wheat estimated that it took five bushels to earn the price of a cheap pair of shoes. The wholesale price of cotton dropped to 5 cents a pound, laughably low if the consequences were not so tragic.

Banks failed at a rate of 200 a month during 1932, wiping out $3.2 billion in savings accounts. When New York's Bank of the United States went under in December 1930, 400,000 people lost their deposits. Much of the money was in small accounts that had been squirreled away by workingpeople as a hedge against economic misfortune. When, understandably frightened, they withdrew their emergency funds, the downward spiral continued.

Hundreds of thousands of people lost their homes between 1929 and 1933 because they could not meet mortgage payments. One farm family in four had been pushed off the land by 1933, mainly in the cotton, grain, and pork belts of the South and Midwest. With their customers unable to buy, more than 100,000 small businesses went bankrupt, 32,000 in 1932 alone (88 per day). Doctors, lawyers, and other professionals reported huge drops in income. Some schools closed for lack of money; in others, teachers took sharp cuts or worked without pay as the only means of keeping them open. Some teachers in Chicago were not compensated for ten years. Others never were.

What Depression Looked Like

Even people who did not personally suffer were reminded of the depression at every turn. More than 5,000 people lined up outside a New York employment agency each week to apply for 500 menial jobs. When the city government of Birmingham, Alabama, called for about 800 workers to put in an eleven-hour day for $2, 12,000 applicants showed up. In 1931, a Soviet agency, Amtorg, announced openings for 6,000 skilled technicians who were willing to move to Russia; 100,000 Americans said they would go. Once-prosperous workers and small businessmen sold apples or set up shoeshine stands on street corners, claiming that they preferred any kind of work to accepting charity.

Charitable organizations were not up to the flood of impoverished people. Philadelphia's social workers managed to reach only one-fifth of the city's unemployed in order to provide $4.23 to a family for a week, not enough to buy food, let alone pay for clothing, rent, and fuel. Soup kitchens set up by both religious and secular groups offered little more than a crust of bread and a bowl of thin stew, but for three years, they were regularly mobbed by people who waited in lines that strung out for blocks.

On the outskirts of most large cities (and right in the middle of New York's Central Park), homeless men and women built shantytowns out of scavenged lumber, scraps of sheet metal, flimsy packing crates, and cardboard boxes. The number of people who simply wandered the land brought the face of catastrophe to rural America. Because it was impossible to stay the flood, railroads gave up trying to keep people off the freight trains. Detectives for the Missouri Pacific Rail-

road counted 14,000 people hopping its freights in 1928; in 1931, 186,000 rode the same rails. Rough estimates indicate that 1.5 million people were moving about in search of casual work, and others were simply moving about; railroad officials noted ever increasing numbers of children in the trek.

This revelation plus increased desertion of their families by unemployed men, a rise in the divorce rate, and a decline in the birth rate—from more than 3 million births in 1921 to 2.4 million in 1932—convinced some moralists and sociologists that the depression was destroying the American family. Others responded that hardship was causing families to pull together.

This was true of the tragic odyssey of the "Okies" and "Arkies." In 1936 and 1937, the hardships of depression were compounded by a natural disaster in the arid regions of Oklahoma, Texas, Kansas, and Arkansas: dust storms literally stripped the topsoil from

---

SOUP LINE

A reporter for *The New Republic* described the soup line at the Municipal Lodging House in New York City in 1930:

There is a line of men, three or sometimes four abreast, a block long, and wedged tightly together—so tightly that no passer-by can break through. For this compactness there is a reason: those at the head of the grey-black human snake will eat tonight; those farther back probably won't.

A CHICKEN IN EVERY POT

The Republican party slogan in the election campaign of 1928 had been "A Chicken in Every Pot and Two Cars in Every Garage." In 1932, the advertising man who had coined it was out of work and reduced to begging in order to support his family.

NO ONE HAS STARVED

At the worst of times early in the Great Depression, it was common to say that "no one has starved." But some came close, as these two excerpts from the *New York Times* indicate:

MIDDLETOWN, N.Y., December 24, 1931.—Attracted by smoke from the chimney of a supposedly abandoned summer cottage near Anwana Lake in Sullivan County, Constable Simon Glaser found a young couple starving. Three days without food, the wife, who is 23 years old, was hardly able to walk.
DANBURY, Connecticut, September 6, 1932.—Found starving under a rude canvas shelter in a patch of woods on Flatboard Ridge, where they had lived for five days on wild berries and apples, a woman and her 16-year old daughter were fed and clothed today by the police and placed in the city almshouse.

Although the heart of the "Dust Bowl" was Oklahoma, dust storms suffocated places like Baca County, Colorado, too.

the land and blacked out the sun. Whole counties lost half their population as people fled across the desert to California, typically in decrepit Model T Fords piled with ragged possessions. Novelist John Steinbeck captured their desperation, and their plucky inner resourcefulness in *The Grapes of Wrath*, a popular novel published in 1939.

THE FAILURE OF THE OLD ORDER

Will Rogers, himself an "Okie" and the nation's most popular humorist, quipped that the United States would be the first country to go to the poorhouse in an automobile. He was trying to restore a sense of proportion to the way people thought about the Great Depression. No one was starving, President Hoover added in one of his many ham-handed attempts to ease tension.

In the broadest sense, both men were right. There was no plague or famine. Indeed, to many people the troubling paradox of America's greatest depression was that deprivation was widespread in a country that was blessed with plenty. American factories remained as capable as ever of producing goods, but they stood silent or working at a fraction of capacity because no one could afford to buy their wares. Farms were pouring forth food in cornucopian abundance, but hungry people could not afford to consume it. One of the most striking images of the early 1930s transformed a mild, white-haired California physician into an angry crusader. Early one Saturday morning, Dr. Francis E. Townsend looked out his window to see old women picking through the garbage pails of a store that was heaped high with foodstuffs.

The Tragedy of Herbert Hoover

Business and the Republican party had reaped credit for the soothing breezes of prosperity. Now they took the blame for the whirlwind of depression, and the recriminations were aimed particularly at the titular head of the party, Herbert Clark Hoover. The shantytowns where homeless thousands dwelled were called

Hoovervilles; newspapers used as blankets by men who were forced to sleep on park benches were Hoover blankets; a pocket turned inside out was a Hoover flag; a boxcar on the railroad was a Hoover Pullman.

Still remembered as a great humanitarian when he entered the White House in 1929, Hoover was the callous torturer of the people a year later. Celebrated for his energy and efficiency as secretary of commerce, Hoover as president was perceived to be incompetent, paralyzed by the economic crisis. When Hoover made one of his rare public appearances, a motorcade through the hard-hit industrial city of Detroit, sidewalk crowds greeted him with dead silence and sullen stares. The president could not even take a brief vacation without arousing scorn. "Look here, Mr. Hoover, see what you've done," an Appalachian song had it. "You went a-fishing, let the country go to ruin."

In truth, Hoover's self-confidence decayed rapidly during his four years in the presidency. If never a warm man, Hoover had always exuded confidence, beaming smugly for photographers. Now he sat subdued, withdrawn, and embittered in the White House. Sitting down to talk with him, an adviser remembered, was like sitting in a bath of ink.

Hoover was unjustly accused when critics called him uncaring, a do-nothing president, a stooge for the Mellons and other big businessmen. The president was moved by the suffering in the country. He gave much of his income to charity and urged others to do the same. Far from paralyzed, he worked as hard at his job as Woodrow Wilson and James K. Polk. Nor was he a Coolidge, letting business do as it pleased; Hoover led government to greater intervention in the economy than had any preceding president except Wilson. It would soon be forgotten, but the man who replaced Hoover in the White House, Franklin D. Roosevelt,

Suffering from unemployment and poverty, these men constructed homes from scrap lumber at West Houston and Mercer Streets in New York. They were photographed by Berenice Abbott on October 25, 1935.

Herbert Hoover entered the presidency with a reputation for humanitarianism. He left it unmourned and despised.

several times criticized Hoover for improperly expanding the powers of government. It would be forgotten because Roosevelt would recognize, as Hoover never did, that the Republican administration had not done enough.

Hoover's Program: Not Enough

Something had to be done. A good many Americans personally recollected that the somewhat less severe economic crisis of the 1890s had led to a briefly terrifying social unrest among dispossessed farmers. Now, in the 1930s, urban industrial workers—and the middle class—were suffering as they had not suffered in the depression of the 1890s.

The progressives (of whom Hoover might be considered one) had established the precedent that government was responsible for guiding the economy. Only in flush times like the Coolidge era could an administration abdicate its obligations and remain popular. Indeed, Hoover promptly broke with the immediate past by cutting Mellon's regressive consumer taxes in order to encourage purchasing and, therefore, production.

Hoover also broke with the Coolidge-Mellon policies of withdrawing the government from active intervention in the economy. He spent $500 million a year on public works, government programs to build or improve government properties. These projects created some jobs that would otherwise not have existed.

The most famous of them was the great Boulder Dam, now called Hoover Dam, on the Colorado River southeast of Las Vegas. The great wall of concrete was the single most massive example of government economic planning and construction to its time and provided work and relief for thousands. But, of course, the Boulder Dam project did nothing in the short run for those who were not involved in building it. (In the long term, the most conspicuous consequence of this water-conservation and power-generation project was to transform Las Vegas into a pleasure dome of casinos.)

In the Reconstruction Finance Corporation (RFC), established by Congress in 1932, Hoover created an agency to help banks, railroads, and other key economic institutions stay in business. The RFC lent money to companies that were basically sound but were hamstrung by the shortage of operating capital.

The trouble was that cutting consumer taxes did nothing for those who were unemployed and paying few taxes. Those who still had jobs inclined not to spend what little windfalls came their way but to squirrel them away against the day when they might be out of work. Moreover, there was a glut in the urban middle class of the "big ticket" consumer durables like appliances and automobiles, the sale of which might have put people to work.

The RFC was a positively unpopular program. People in trouble saw it not as a recovery policy but as relief for big business while individuals were told to shift for themselves. The RFC alone looked very much like an extension of Andrew Mellon's "trickle-down" economics; except in the arid early years of the Great Depression, little seemed to trickle down.

The Blindness of the Rugged Individual

More was needed—massive relief to get the poor, who were growing in numbers, over the worst of the crisis. This Hoover would not authorize. A self-made man himself, he had forgotten the role of talent and good luck in getting ahead. He believed that "rugged individuals"—his very phrase—who looked to no one but themselves were the secret of American cultural vitality. For the federal government to encourage that trait of the national character was one thing; for the government to sponsor huge handouts was quite another. Federal relief measures were not, in Hoover's opinion, the first step in defeating the depression, but were the first step in emasculating the American spirit. There was a difference between helping Belgians devastated by war and helping Americans deprived by economic dislocations.

Hoover also clung to certain assumptions that prevented him from realizing just how much federal guid-

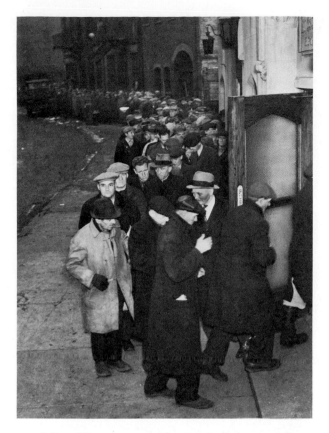

*A line of hungry men stretches into the darkness outside
a soup kitchen in New York City.*

coming true. Most economic indicators made modest gains. Then the entire industrialized world followed the United States into the economic pit. In May, a major European bank, the Kreditanstalt of Vienna, went bankrupt, badly shaking other European banks that had supported it, and toppling many. In September, Great Britain abandoned the gold standard; that is, the Bank of England ceased to redeem its paper money in gold bullion or coin. Worried that all paper money would lose its value, international investors withdrew $1.5 billion in gold from American banks, further weakening the financial structure and launching a new wave of local failures.

But the worst consequence of the European collapse was what it did to Hoover's state of mind. It persuaded him that America's depression was not the fault of domestic problems that he might help remedy, but of foreigners over whom he had no power. The most cosmopolitan president since John Quincy Adams had sunk to the ignorant provincial's easy inclination to blame others—foreigners. The result was that by 1932 his administration was paralyzed. The country was drifting as Hoover tacitly admitted that he was helpless and could only wait. And conditions worsened by the month.

AMERICANS REACT TO THE CRISIS

If Hoover's failure represented the inability of the New Era Republicans to cope with the depression, radicals were unable to offer a plausible alternative. Critics of capitalism believed that the crisis represented the death throes of the system and that they would soon be in power. To an extent, they, like Hoover, waited for inevitable forces beyond their control to summon them to the helm.

The Not-So-Red Decade

After polling only 267,000 votes in prosperous 1928, Socialist party presidential candidate Norman Thomas won 882,000 in 1932. Communist candidate William Z. Foster doubled his vote in those four years, from 49,000 to 103,000. But the combined anticapitalist vote of less than a million was minuscule compared with the 23 million cast for the Democrats in that year and even the 16 million won by the discredited Hoover. Thomas's total in 1932 was less than the Socialists had won 20 years before, when the electorate was much smaller and the economy was in much better health.

Later in the 1930s, American Communists made some gains among intellectuals and in the leadership

ance was needed. Failing to recognize that state boundaries had no economic significance, he wanted the states to take the lead in fighting the depression. Viewing government as much like a business, he was particularly inflexible when it came to the ideal of a balanced budget and the government's power to manipulate the value of the currency.

Government, Hoover insisted, must spend no more money than it collected; the books must balance. As for money questions, Hoover knew that during every depression since the Civil War, only Greenbackers, Populists, and others regarded as radicals had proposed increasing the supply of money (deliberately inflating prices) in order to stimulate the economy. Each time they had been defeated, and each time the country had emerged from hard times more prosperous than before. Hoover was positive that this cycle would be repeated if the old faith were kept: if the budget were balanced and the dollar remained rooted in gold.

The Depression Goes International

For a few months, in 1931, Hoover's prediction that "prosperity was just around the corner" seemed to be

H O W   T H E Y   L I V E D

WEEKNIGHTS AT EIGHT

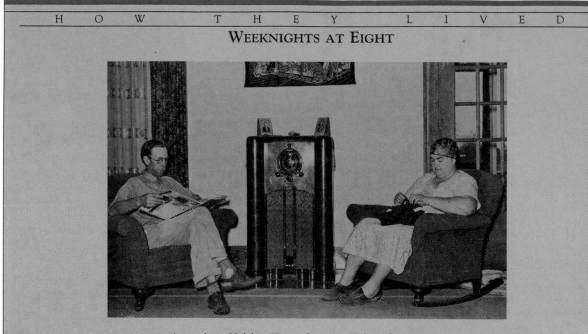

A couple in Hidalgo, Texas, listening to the radio in 1939.

Although commercial radio broadcasting began in 1920 and the first radio network, the National Broadcasting Company, was founded in 1926, it was during the Great Depression of the 1930s that the new medium of communication and entertainment found a place in the lives of almost all Americans. Radio receivers were ensconced in about 12 million American households in 1930. By 1940, they were in 28 million. Fully 86 percent of the American people had easy daily access to radio sets. They were designed not to look like electronic equipment but as a prized piece of furniture, the twentieth-century equivalent of the wardrobe. Some were sleekly modern "art deco," others gothic with the pointed, vertical arches of a medieval cathedral.

Hard times themselves were a big reason for the dramatic expansion of radio. During the 1920s, the average price of a receiver was $75, far out of reach of most families. During the 1930s, a serviceable set could be bought for $10 or $20, an amount that, with sacrifices, all but the utterly destitute could scrape up.

The New Deal also played a part in the radio boom. While most cities and towns were electrified before 1933, very little of the countryside was. Private power companies were not interested in the small return to be had from stringing wire into the hinterlands. By putting the advantages of electrification for country people above profits, Roosevelt's Rural Electrification Administration brought isolated farm families into the mainstream of society. With more than 57 million people defined as living in "rural territory" in 1940, the significance of radio to American culture may be said to have owed largely to New Deal reforms. Indeed, country people depended more on the crackling broadcasts of news, music, and dramatic programs for brightening their lives than did city dwellers.

Manufacturers that produced consumer goods rushed to advertise on the three networks: the Columbia Broadcasting System; the Mutual; and the National Broadcasting Company with its two chains, the red and the blue networks. (When antitrust proceedings forced NBC to dispose of one of its networks, the American Broadcasting Company was born.) In 1935, the first year for which there are reliable statistics, networks and local stations raked in $113 million from advertisers with operating expenses at an estimated $80 million. In 1940, expenses were up to $114 million, but advertising revenues had almost doubled to $216 million.

The manufacturers of Pepsodent toothpaste got the best bargain of all. In 1928, they contracted with two white minstrel-show performers who had a program in black dialect on Chicago station WGN. "Sam 'n' Henry" agreed to pick two new names and do their show nationally on the NBC network. The new show was called "Amos 'n' Andy," and from the start it won a popularity that, comparatively speaking, has probably never been duplicated in the history of the entertainment industry.

Basically, "Amos 'n' Andy" was a blackface minstrel show set in Harlem instead of on a southern plantation. One of the two performers, Freeman Gosden of Richmond, said that he based the character of Amos Jones on a black boyhood friend. Amos was the honest, hard-working proprietor and sole driver of the Fresh Air Taxi Company—his cab had no windshield. Neither during the program's 32 years on radio nor after it had moved to television was Gosden's character offensive. However, Amos came to play a comparatively small part in the series as the program evolved. The chief protagonist was George (Kingfish) Stevens, a fast-talking con man who usually bungled his stings and ended up outsmarting himself. During the 1950s, black groups began to protest that the Kingfish, who was rather stupid underneath his pretensions and self-estimation, was an insulting stereotype.

The character of the Kingfish's usual mark, Andrew "Andy" H. Brown, also caused trouble. Andy was infinitely gullible, a character whom even the Kingfish easily swindled. He depended for survival on the con man's own ineptitude or on Amos's intervention.

Everyone in America, it sometimes seemed, listened to the program, which ran on weeknights at eight o'clock. Particularly interesting plots were discussed each day. Few needed to be told what Amos, Andy, and the Kingfish were like, or even the minor characters (also played by Gosden and his partner, Charles Correll): Lightnin', who swept up the hall of the Mystic Knights of the Sea; the shyster lawyer Algonquin J. Calhoun; Ruby Jones; and Sapphire Stevens, who made life as miserable for George as he made it for Andy.

In November 1960, "Amos 'n' Andy" went from radio to television in a weekly half-hour format featuring black actors who mimicked the voices that had been created by Gosden and Correll. Already, however, the program was an anachronism. The civil-rights movement was in full swing by 1960, pushing toward victory in the long campaign to establish full equality for blacks. The National Association for the Advancement of Colored People denounced "Amos 'n' Andy" as "a gross libel on the Negro."

The show's sponsors believed that blacks enjoyed the program as much as whites (which appears to have been so until the 1960s), and Gosden insisted that "both Charlie and I have deep respect for black men"; he felt that the show "helped characterize Negroes as interesting and dignified human beings." Today, it is easy to see the point. Even the most ridiculous characters on "Amos 'n' Andy" were stock comic figures in traditional comedy, and there was nothing derogatory in the depiction of Amos and Ruby Jones. Nevertheless, the NAACP had a point too. The social effects of ridiculing members of an oppressed group are mischievous at best. It is easy to shrug off ridicule when it does not relate to reality or ignore stereotypes when the stereotyped group is well established. But in the fight in which blacks were engaged in the early 1960s, such ridicule and stereotypes stood in the way of justice. After 100 episodes, "Amos 'n' Andy" went off the air.

of the labor movement. Distinguished writers such as Mary McCarthy, Edmund Wilson, and Granville Hicks joined the Communist party. Even F. Scott Fitzgerald, the chronicler of "flaming youth" during the 1920s, flirted with Marxist ideas that he did not really understand. Theodore Dreiser, the dean of American novelists, wanted to join the Communist party but was told by party leaders that he could do more good for the cause outside the organization than in. Perhaps they thought that if he wrote calls for revolution in his tortured version of the English language that it would all sound quite dull.

The Communist love of conspiracy and manipulation drove intellectuals out of the party as quickly as they joined. It also prevented the Communists from establishing a base in the labor movement despite making contributions to its growth that, in retrospect, can be seen to have been invaluable. Wyndham Mortimer of the United Automobile Workers, labor journalist Len De Caux, lawyer Lee Pressman, and many other Communists and "fellow travelers" (sympathizers who were not members of the party) devoted their lives to building up the union movement. However, most Communist organizers either denied or thickly camouflaged their affiliation with the party and their anticapitalist ideology. The result was that few rank-and-file union members were exposed to, let alone converted to, Communist ideas. When anti-Communist labor leaders took the offensive against the reds in the 1940s, they found it easy to oust party members from the unions.

A Curious Response

But Americans simply did not interpret the Great Depression as evidence that capitalism had failed. During prosperous times, Americans had believed that individual success was primarily due to individual initiative, and not to general social conditions. So their initial response to the depression was to blame themselves for the hardships that beset them. Sociologists and journalists reported on homeless hitchhikers who apologized for their shabby clothing. A walk through any big-city park revealed unsuccessful job seekers slumped on benches, heads in hands, elbows on knees, collars drawn up, wondering where they, not the system, had failed.

The Gillette Company, a manufacturer of razor blades, exploited the feeling of personal failure by running an advertisement that showed a husband reporting shamefully to his wife that he still had not found a job. The message was that employers had turned him down not because there were no jobs available but because he cut a poor appearance with his badly shaved whiskers. A maker of underwear put the responsibility for the unemployment of a bedridden man squarely on his own shoulders. He was out of work not because 13 million others were, but because he wore an inferior brand of undershirt and so caught a cold that he well deserved.

Long after the depression ended, it was the proud boast of many families that however bad things had gotten, they never had gone "on the county," never had taken handouts from public-welfare agencies. The unmistakable message was that coping with hard times was a personal responsibility. The implication for radicals who sought to direct anger and frustration against the system was not encouraging.

Episodes of Violence

There was violence. Hungry, angry people rioted in St. Paul and other cities, storming food markets and clearing the shelves. Wisconsin dairy farmers stopped milk trucks and dumped the milk into ditches, partly in rage at the low prices paid by processors, partly to dramatize their need for help. In Iowa, the National Farmers' Holiday Association told hog raisers to withhold their products from the market—to take a holiday—and attracted attention by blockading highways. Eat your own products, Holiday Association leader Milo Reno told the Iowans, and let the money men eat their gold.

But these incidents were isolated and exceptional. For the most part, Americans coped with the depression peacefully and without a thought for revolution. In fact, the most violent episode of the early depression was launched not by stricken people but by the authorities. This was the demonstration and destruction of the "Bonus Expeditionary Force" in Washington during the summer of 1932.

The Bonus Boys were 20,000 veterans of the First World War and their wives who massed in Washington to demand that Congress immediately, as a relief measure, vote them a bonus for their wartime service that had been scheduled for their old age. When Congress

The Bonus Marchers' encampment on Anacostia Flats was destroyed by troops led by Douglas MacArthur and sent by a frustrated President Hoover.

"Machine Gun" Kelly under arrest in 1933.

adjourned in July 1932 without having done so, all but about 2,000 of the demonstrators left the capital. Those who remained set up a Hooverville on Anacostia Flats on the outskirts of the city, policed themselves, cooperated with authorities, and were generally peaceful.

Hoover, thoroughly frustrated by the stubborness of the depression and his own abysmal unpopularity, persuaded himself that the Bonus Boys were led by Communist agitators. (Actually, the most influential organization among the Bonus Boys was the right-wing and militantly anti-Communist American Legion.) The president sent General Douglas MacArthur to disperse them. MacArthur, a talented commander but a ludicrous coxcomb, arrayed himself in his best dress uniform and ceremonial sword and actually delayed the raid on Anacostia Flats until his photogenic ensemble was complete. Using armored vehicles and tear gas, MacArthur made short work of the protesters. However, when an infant died from asphyxiation and Americans mulled over the spectacle of young soldiers attacking old soldiers on presidential orders, Hoover's reputation sank even lower.

Midwestern Robin Hoods

Americans displayed their disenchantment with traditional sources of leadership in other, less direct ways. Businessmen, who had been almost universally lion-ized just a few years before, became objects of ridicule in films, on radio programs, and in the columns and comic strips of daily newspapers.

Perhaps the most curious example of cynicism toward traditional values was the admiration lavished on a new kind of criminal, the midwestern bank robber who exploited automobiles and the wide-open highways of the Midwest to flee the scene of his dirty work. A sensationalist press transformed John Dillinger, "Pretty Boy" Floyd, "Machine Gun" Kelly, Bonnie Parker and Clyde Barrow, and "Ma" Barker and her family-centered gang into Robin Hoods.

Unlike the businessmen-gangsters of Prohibition, the depression bank robbers were small-time, guerrilla operators who botched as many holdups as they pulled off. They were also reckless with their guns, killing bank guards and even innocent bystanders in their attempt to create an atmosphere of terror to cover their escape. But because they robbed the banks whose irresponsibility had ruined many poor people and because they came from poor rural (and WASP) backgrounds themselves, the outlaws aroused a kind of admiration among midwesterners down on their luck.

Some of the gangsters themselves cultivated the image of Robin Hood. John Dillinger (who killed ten men) made it a point to be personally generous. "Pretty Boy" Floyd, who operated chiefly in Oklahoma, never had trouble finding people who would hide him from the authorities. Bonnie Parker actually sent doggerel epics that celebrated the exploits of "Bonnie and Clyde," to newspapers, which greedily published them.

The Movies: The Depression-Proof Business

The film industry exploited this envy of a few who "beat the system" by making movies that slyly glamorized lawbreakers. Still fearful of censorship, the studios always wrote a moral end to their gangster films: the wrongdoer paid for his crimes in a hail of bullets or seated in the electric chair. But the message was clear: criminals played by George Raft, Edward G. Robinson, and James Cagney were pushed into their careers by poverty and often had redeeming qualities.

The film industry did not suffer during the depression. Movies flourished during the worst years, occupying the central position in American entertainment that they would hold until the perfection of television. Admission prices were cheap. Each week, 85 million people paid an average of 25 cents (10 cents for children) to see Marie Dressler, Janet Gaynor, Shirley Temple, Mickey Rooney, Jean Harlow, and Clark Gable in a dizzying array of adventures and fantasies.

The favorite themes were escapist. During the mid-1930s, Shirley Temple, an angelic if chillingly saccharine little blonde girl who sang and danced, led the list of moneymakers. Her annual salary was $300,000, and her films made $5 million a year for Fox Pictures. Royalties from Shirley Temple dolls and other paraphernalia made her a millionaire. Director Cecil B. DeMille specialized in costume epics, especially those that transported viewers into Biblical times.

Choreographer Busby Berkeley made millions for Warner Brothers by staging dance tableaux featuring dozens of beautiful starlets (transformed by mirrors and trick photography into hundreds). People bought tickets to Berkeley films to escape the gray rigors of depression life. For the same reason, they supported the production of hundreds of low-budget Westerns each year. The cowboy was still a figure of individual freedom in a world in which public events and private lives had become all too complexly interrelated.

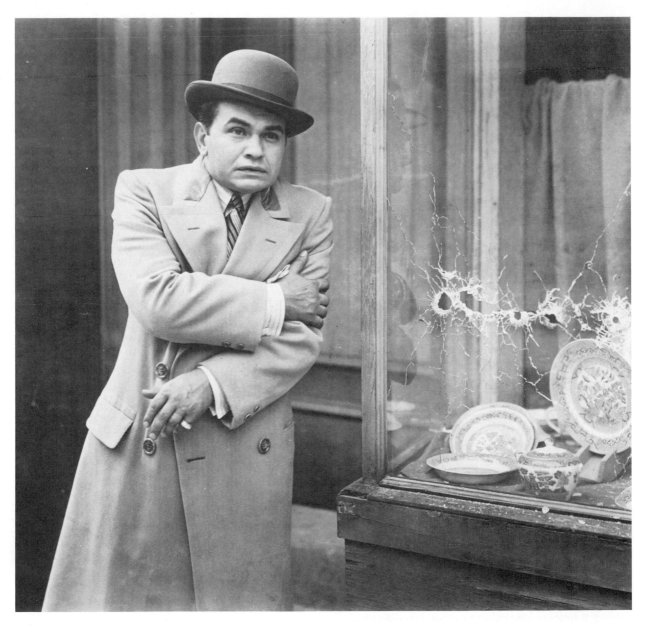

Edward G. Robinson as the gangster "Little Caesar."

In Dinner at Eight, *glamorous Jean Harlow made movie-goers forget the Depression—at least for a few hours.*

nickel, slowly revived the business. By 1939, there were 225,000 jukeboxes in the United States scratching up 13 million records a year. Sales of records increased from 10 million in 1933 to 33 million in 1938 (and then soared, with the return of prosperity, to 127 million in 1941).

The chief beneficiaries were the "big bands," which played "swing," an intricately harmonized orchestral jazz music intended for dancing. For 50 cents (and even less), a young "jitterbugger" could dance for three or four hours to the music of Benny Goodman, Harry James, or dozens of other groups. It was not an every-evening diversion. The 50 cents needed for admission was precious enough that the big bands had to rush from city to city and to towns too, on a series of one-night stands. Even the most popular orchestras might find themselves appearing in 30 different ballrooms in as many nights.

Nevertheless, they were lionized when they came to town. In the Palladium Ballroom in Hollywood, California, Harry James once drew 8,000 dancers in a single night, 35,000 in a week. At other capitals of swing music, like the Glen Island Casino in New Rochelle, New York, big bands earned extra revenue by playing for a radio audience. Because a good radio could be ensconced in the parlor for $10 or $20, and operated for the cost of electricity, it was far and

By way of contrast, some directors specialized in didactic films on social themes that were often hard-hitting. Frank Capra's métier was films that lovingly celebrated old American values and threats to them. Typically, they pitted decent ordinary men and women against indolent, parasitical, and usually crooked businessmen and politicians.

Music, Music, Music

At first almost destroyed by the depression, the popular music business rebounded quickly to rank a close second behind the movies as the ordinary American's entertainment outside the home. Sales of records, about $50 million a year during the 1920s, collapsed in 1932 to $2.5 million. The chief casualties were the "hillbilly" and traditional black "blues" singers whose audiences were among the hardest hit social groups in the country. Companies like Columbia, Decca, and RCA discontinued their "race record" lines and only a few black and Appalachian artists, like Bessie Smith and the Carter Family, continued to make money.

The advent of the 78 rpm record, which cost only 35 cents, and the jukebox, that provided a play for a

Benny Goodman was the "King of Swing" during the big band era.

away most depression-era Americans' favorite form of entertainment.

THE ELECTION OF 1932

The nostalgic glow that could come to surround listening to a favorite radio program, or going to a ballroom or a movie palace decorated like a Turkish harem, meant that many people would think back about the Great Depression as quite a good time. In the summer of 1932, however, when the economy hit bottom, few people took the situation with a light heart. The country's mood during the presidential election campaign of that year was somber and anxious.

A Roosevelt for the Democrats

A Democratic victory was a foregone conclusion, and the Republicans resignedly renominated Herbert Hoover to bear the brunt of the reaction against the New Era. Democratic hopefuls, by way of contrast, fought a hair-pulling fight to win a ticket to the White House. The chief candidates at the Chicago convention were John Nance Garner of Texas, who had inherited the McAdoo Democrats from the South and West; Al Smith, the party's standard-bearer in 1928 who believed he deserved a second chance; and Governor Franklin D. Roosevelt of New York, once Smith's protégé but now a national figure in his own right.

When the beginnings of a convention deadlock brought back memories of 1924 and a bitterly divided party, a large number of Garner supporters switched to Roosevelt and gave him the nomination. With a nose for the dramatic, Roosevelt broke with tradition, according to which a nominee waited at his home to be informed of the convention's decision. He flew to Chicago (conveying a sense of urgency) and told the cheering Democrats that he meant to provide a "New Deal" for the American people. In so saying, Roosevelt simultaneously slapped at Republican policies during the 1920s (the New Era) and reminded people of both major parties that he was a distant cousin of the energetic president of the Square Deal, Theodore Roosevelt.

The Campaign

Hoover's campaign was dispirited. He was in the impossible position of having to defend policies that had failed. Roosevelt, on the contrary, like any candidate who expects to win, avoided taking controversial stands. Any strong position on any specific question could only cost him votes. At times, indeed, Roosevelt seemed to be calling for the same conservative approach to the economic crisis that Hoover already had tested; he warned against an unbalanced budget and reassured voters that he was no radical.

The most obvious difference between the president and his challenger was Hoover's gloomy personality and Roosevelt's buoyant charm. Roosevelt smiled constantly. He impressed everyone who saw him as he was whisked around the country as a man who knew how to take charge, liked to take charge, and was perfectly confident in his ability to lead the country out of its crisis. The theme song of Roosevelt's campaign, which was blared by brass bands or played over loudspeakers at every whistle stop and rally, was the cheery "Happy Days Are Here Again."

Only after his lopsided victory—472 electoral votes to Hoover's 59—did it become clear that Roosevelt had spelled out no program for recovery. Because Inauguration Day came a full four months after the election, there was one more long winter of depression under Herbert Hoover. The repudiated president, now practically a recluse in the White House, recognized that a void existed and attempted to persuade Roosevelt to endorse the actions he had taken.

Roosevelt nimbly avoided making any commitments either in favor of or opposed to Hoover's policies. He took a quiet working vacation. He issued no statements of substance, but he was not idle. During the interregnum, Roosevelt met for long hours with experts on agriculture, industry, finance, and relief. Organized by Raymond Moley, a professor at Columbia University, this "brains trust," as reporters called it, marked a rather significant shift in the personnel of people who ran Washington. During the 1920s, the capital had been a businessman's town. Now they were turning over their apartments and selling their homes to intellectuals, men (and a few women) from universities who hungered to have a go at making policy.

For Further Reading

Arthur M. Schlesinger, Jr., *The Crisis of the Old Order* (1957) and *The Coming of the New Deal* (1959) provide a superb overview of the critical years of the early

1930s. See also Irving Bernstein, *The Lean Years* (1960); C. Bird, *The Invisible Scar* (1965); Albert Romesco, *The Poverty of Abundance: Hoover, the Nation, and the Great Depression* (1965); Jordan A. Schwarz, *The Inter-regnum of Despair: Hoover, Congress, and the Depression* (1970); and Studs Terkel, *Hard Times* (1970). For background, refer once again to Ellis W. Hawley, *The Great War and the Search for a Modern Order: A History of the American People and Their Institutions, 1917–1933* (1979); John D. Hicks, *Republican Ascendancy, 1921–1933* (1960); and William E. Leuchtenburg, *The Perils of Prosperity, 1914–1932* (1958). Frederick Lewis Allen's sequel to *Only Yesterday, Since Yesterday* (1940) provides the same highly individual insights as his better-known book.

Valuable more broadly or more narrowly focused books include Roger Daniels, *The Bonus March* (1971); John K. Galbraith, *The Great Crash* (1955); John A. Garraty, *Unemployment in History: Economic Thought and Public Policy* (1979); Susan Estabrook Kennedy, *The Banking Crisis of 1933* (1973); C. P. Kinderberger,

The World in Depression (1973); Donald Lisio, *The President and Protest* (1974); Van L. Perkins, *Crisis in Agriculture* (1969); Theodore Saloutos and John D. Hicks, *Twentieth Century Populism: Agricultural Discontent in the Middle West, 1900–1939* (1951); Robert Sklar, *Movie-Made America* (1975); Peter Temin, *Did Monetary Forces Cause the Great Depression?* (1976); Raymond Walters, *Negroes and the Great Depression* (1970).

Franklin D. Roosevelt has been the subject of numerous biographies both political and personal. Among the most rewarding are James MacGregor Burns, *Roosevelt: The Lion and the Fox* (1956); Frank Freidel, *Franklin D. Roosevelt* (1952–73); Joseph P. Lash, *Eleanor and Franklin* (1971). Also see H. G. Warren, *Herbert Hoover and the Great Depression* (1956).

43

REARRANGING AMERICA

Franklin D. Roosevelt and the New Deal, 1933–1938

A few days before his inauguration, Franklin D. Roosevelt visited Miami. From the crowd that surged around him, a jobless worker named Joe Zangara, later found to be unbalanced, stepped up and emptied a revolver at him. Anton Cermak, the mayor of Chicago who was accompanying Roosevelt, died from his wounds. The president-elect escaped without a scratch. The American people learned from the episode that they had chosen a leader who was cool in a crisis: Roosevelt barely flinched during the chaos of the shooting. But what else did they know about him? Not a great deal on March 4, 1933, and that little was not altogether reassuring.

Franklin Roosevelt is sworn into office as president, March 4, 1933.

THE PLEASANT MAN WHO CHANGED AMERICA

Walter Lippmann, a political columnist of liberal leanings, called Roosevelt "a pleasant man who, without any important qualifications, would very much like to be president." Many others wondered if a person who had enjoyed so pampered and sheltered a life as Roosevelt had was capable of appreciating the difficulties and suffering that had befallen millions of Americans.

Silver Spoon

The new president had been born into an old, rich, privileged, and rather idle New York family. Boyhood vacations were spent in Europe and at elegant yachting resorts in Maine and Nova Scotia. He attended the most exclusive private schools and was sheltered to the point of suffocation by an adoring mother. When Roosevelt matriculated at Harvard, Mother Sara Roosevelt packed up, followed him, and rented a house near the university so that she could keep an eye on her boy. F.D.R.'s wife, Eleanor Roosevelt, was from the same tiny and exclusive social set. Indeed, she was the president's distant cousin.

Franklin Roosevelt's cheery grin and ever-present cigarette holder became his trademarks.

Even the charm with which Roosevelt ran his campaign—the jaunty air, the toothy smile a bit too quick to take shape, an effortless knack of putting people at their ease with cheery small talk—was very much a quality of the socialite who, in the 1930s, was a popular satirical target of filmmakers. Roosevelt was the real life incarnation of a genial but fluffy character Cary Grant was to play in half a dozen movies: "Tennis, anyone?"

And yet, from the moment F.D.R. delivered his ringing inaugural address—"the only thing we have to fear is fear itself!"—the clouds over Washington parting on cue to let the March sun through, it was obvious that he was a natural leader. From the first day, Roosevelt dominated center stage as cousin Theodore had done 30 years earlier, and without the tiresome bluster and bullying. Where Teddy had been liked, F.D.R. was loved. Poor sharecroppers and blacks living in big-city slums tacked his photograph on the walls of their homes next to prints of Christ in Gethsemane, and named their children for him.

Conversely, he was hated, as T.R. never was. It was said that some of the nation's wealthiest people despised him so much that they could not bear to pronounce his name. Much to the amused satisfaction of Roosevelt's supporters, they referred to him through clenched teeth as "that man in the White House," and as a "traitor to his class."

Long before F.D.R. died in office in 1945, after winning four times, he was ranked by historians as among the greatest of the chief executives along with Washington, Lincoln, and Wilson (his one-time political idol). No succeeding generation of judges has demoted him.

Roosevelt's Contribution

Roosevelt's unbounded self-confidence was a major contribution to the battle against the Great Depression. His optimism was infectious. The change of mood he brought to Washington and the country was astonishing, and shortly after assuming office he exploited his charisma by launching a series of "Fireside Chats" on the ubiquitous radio. In an informal living-room manner, he explained to the American people what he was trying to accomplish and what he expected of them. Millions listened avidly and trustfully.

But Roosevelt was much more than a charmer. He was not afraid to make decisions or to accept responsibility. He acted. One day after he was sworn in, he called Congress into special session for the purpose of enacting crisis legislation, and he declared a "bank holiday." Calling on emergency presidential powers that are rarely used, he ordered all banks to close their doors temporarily in order to forestall additional failures. Although the immediate effect of the bank holiday was to tie up people's savings, the drama and decisiveness of his action won wide approval.

Roosevelt was by no means brilliant. He never fully understood the complex economic and social processes with which his administration had to grapple, and did not think it was necessary that he should. If an indifferent student, he had the professors at his command. He sought the advice of experts, his "brains trust," and was open to suggestions from all quarters. But because he never doubted his responsibilities as the nation's elected "chief," he maintained complete authority over his stable of headstrong intellectuals, many of them prima donnas. He stroked their vanities when it suited his purposes, played one brains truster against another, and retained the personal loyalty of some of those whose advice he rejected. Faces changed in the White House anterooms. Friends became critics. But Roosevelt never lacked talented advisers.

In the end, Roosevelt's greatest strength was his flexibility. "The country needs bold, persistent experimentation," he said. "It is common sense to take a method and try it. If it fails, admit it frankly and try another." Roosevelt's pragmatic approach to problems not only suited the American temperament, but contrasted boldly with Hoover's insistence on making policies conform to a badly rotted ideology.

A Real First Lady

Not the least of F.D.R.'s assets was his remarkable wife, Eleanor. Only much later, in the age of anything-goes journalism, did Americans learn that their marriage had been shattered by an affair between Franklin

Although she grew up privileged and sheltered, Eleanor Roosevelt developed a genuine compassion for the disadvantaged.

and Eleanor's one-time personal secretary, Lucy Mercer. Eleanor offered a divorce; Franklin begged off; Eleanor said that Lucy had to go, and she did, or so it seemed.

Not only would a scandal and a divorce have killed Roosevelt's political career far short of the presidency, it would have denied him the services of his one aide who may be called indispensable. During the New Deal years, the homely, shrill-voiced Eleanor was thought of by friend and foe alike as the alter ego of the president. She was his legs and eyes, for F.D.R. was a cripple, paralyzed from the waist down by polio in 1921 and unable to walk more than a few steps in heavy, painful steel leg braces, while Eleanor Roosevelt was a locomotive. With no taste for serving tea and honoring Boy Scouts, she raced about the country,

F.D.R. THE PRAGMATIST

In a conversation with Secretary of Commerce Daniel Roper, Roosevelt made clear his practical policy-making: "Let's concentrate upon one thing. Save the people and the nation and if we have to change our minds twice a day to accomplish that end, we should do it."

picking through squalid tenements, wading in mud in Appalachian hollows, and descending into murky coal mines to see how the other half made do. Whereas F.D.R. was cool, detached, and calculating, Eleanor was compassionate, deeply moved by the misery and injustices suffered by the "forgotten" people on the bottom of society.

She interceded with her husband to appoint women to high government positions. She supported organized labor when F.D.R. tried to straddle a difficult question. She made the grievances of black Americans a particular interest. Much of the affection that redounded to F.D.R.'s benefit in the form of votes was earned by "that woman in the White House."

THE HUNDRED DAYS

Never before or since has the United States experienced such an avalanche of laws as Congress passed and the president signed during the spring of 1933. By nature a cautious and deliberate body, Congress was jolted by the crisis and by Roosevelt's forceful demands to enact most of his proposals without serious debate, a few without even reading the bills through. During what came to be known as the Hundred Days, Franklin D. Roosevelt and his brains trusters were virtually unopposed. Conservative congressmen simply shut up, cowed by their own failure and the decisiveness of the New Dealers.

Saving Banks and Farms

The most pressing problems were the imminent collapse of the nation's financial system, the massive foreclosures on farm and home mortgages that were throwing people out on the streets and roads, and the distress of the millions of unemployed.

The Emergency Banking Act eliminated weak banks merely by identifying them. Well-managed banks in danger of folding were saved when the Federal Reserve System was empowered to issue loans to them. Just as important, when the government permitted banks to reopen, people concluded that they were safe. They ceased to withdraw their deposits and returned funds that they had already taken home and out of circulation. Roosevelt also halted the drain on the nation's gold reserve by forbidding its export and, in April, by taking the nation off the gold standard. No longer could paper money be redeemed in gold coin that was hoarded. Instead, the value of money was based on the government's word, and the price of gold was frozen by law at $35 an ounce. ("Well, that's the end of western civilization," a Wall Street financier was quoted as saying.)

The New Deal attempted to halt the dispossession of farmers through the establishment of the Farm Credit Administration. This agency refinanced mortgages for farmers who had missed payments. Another agency, the Home Owners' Loan Corporation, provided money for town and city dwellers who were in danger of losing their homes.

Helping the Helpless

Nothing better illustrated the contrast between Hoover's hidebound inaction and Roosevelt's flexibility than the establishment of the Federal Emergency Relief Administration (FERA). Whereas Hoover had resisted federal relief measures on ideological grounds, the FERA quickly distributed $500 million to states so that they could save or revive their exhausted programs for relieving the desperate plight of the poor. The agency was headed by Harry Hopkins, an Iowa boy become New York sidewalk social worker with a cigarette dangling from his lip and a fedora pushed back on his head.

Actually, Hopkins disliked the idea of handouts. He believed that people who were able to work should be required to do so in return for help. It did not matter to him that the jobs they did were not particularly useful. His point was that government-paid jobs should not only get money into the hands of those who needed it, but give relief workers a sense of personal worth.

Nevertheless, Hopkins recognized that the crisis of 1933 was so severe that money had to be gotten out into the country quick. Setting aside his insistence on work for pay in administering FERA, he won F.D.R.'s confidence with his able and energetic direction of the

---

NEW HOUSEHOLD ECONOMY FOR MILLIONAIRES

Eleanor Roosevelt is generally attributed with being her husband's eyes and ears among ordinary people. However, when she was complimented by the *New York Times* during World War II for insisting that the ten servants in her household economize for the sake of the war effort, it was F.D.R. who indicated that he was the one who realized that his and Eleanor's privileged past had little to do with the lives of most Americans. In a note to her, he teased: "All I can say is that your latest newspaper campaign is a corker and I am proud to be the husband of the Originator, Discoverer and Inventor of the New Household Economy for Millionaires! Please have a photo taken showing the family, the ten cooperating servants, the scraps saved from the table. . . . I will have it published in the Sunday *Times*."

In an effort to stave off panicky customers, President Roosevelt ordered banks to close their doors for emergency "holidays."

program. There was waste and bureaucratic boondoggling, but FERA worked, creating hope where there had been ennui and despair.

Alphabet Soup: CCC, CWA, WPA

New bureaucracies, with and without boondoggling, were the order of the day in 1933. With an initial appropriation of $500 million, the Civilian Conservation Corps (CCC) employed 250,000 young men between the ages of 18 and 25 and about 50,000 First World War veterans. Organized into crews, they reforested land that had been raped by cut-and-run lumbermen and undertook other conservation projects in national parks and forests.

Ultimately, 500,000 people worked for the CCC, and it became one of the New Dealers' favorite programs. The CCC not only relieved distress (employees were obligated to send part of their ' paychecks to their families), but accomplished many needed conservation measures, and got city boys into the fresh air of the woods and mountains, a moral tonic in which Americans place great faith.

Critics of the CCC fastened on the quasi-military discipline with which the army ran the program, but the idea of relief through jobs rather than through charity remained a mainstay of the New Deal. The Civil Works Administration (CWA), which Harry Hopkins headed after November 1933, put 4 million unemployed people to work within a few months. They built roads, constructed public buildings—post offices, city halls, recreational facilities—and taught in bankrupt school systems.

The Civilian Conservation Corps was one of the New Deal's most popular relief programs, in part because it allowed city boys to work in national parks and forests.

When the CWA spent more than $1 billion in five months, F.D.R. shuddered and called a halt to the program. But private investors would not or could not take up the slack, and unemployment threatened to soar once again. In May 1935, the president turned back to Hopkins and Congress to establish the Works Progress Administration (WPA).

The WPA broadened the CWA approach. In addition to basic construction, the agency hired artists to paint murals in public buildings, and writers to prepare state guidebooks that remain models of their kind. In the South, the WPA sent out workers to collect reminiscences of old people who remembered having been slaves. The WPA even organized actors into troupes that brought theater to people who never had seen a play. By 1943, when the agency was liquidated, it had spent more than $11 billion and had employed 8.5 million people. The National Youth Administration, part of the WPA, provided jobs for 2 million high school and college students.

Repeal

Roosevelt's support of the Twenty-first Amendment, the repeal of Prohibition, might be listed as one of the New Deal's relief measures. On March 13, 1933,

F.D.R. called for the legalization of weak beer, and when the amendment was ratified in December, most states quickly legalized more potent waters. Certainly many people looked on the possibility of buying a legal drink as relief. An Appalachian song praising Roosevelt pointed to repeal of Prohibition as his most important act: "Since Roosevelt's been elected Moonshine liquor's been corrected. We've got legal wine, whiskey, beer, and gin."

The NRA

The New Deal's relief programs were a great success. Although direct benefits reached only a fraction of the people who were hurt by the depression, they were the worst off who were helped, and the government's willingness to act in the crisis encouraged millions of other people. Still, relief was just a stopgap. F.D.R. and the New Dealers were also concerned with the problem of actual economic recovery, and in this area their accomplishments were less effective.

The National Industrial Recovery Act, which created the National Recovery Administration (NRA), was a bold and controversial attempt to bring order and prosperity to the shattered economy. The NRA was headed by General Hugh Johnson, something of a blowhard but also a peerless, inexhaustible organizer and cheerleader, and a zealous believer in economic planning. Johnson supervised the drafting of codes for each basic industry and, before long, some less than basic industries, too.

The codes set minimum standards of quality for products and services, fair prices for which they were to be sold, and the wages, hours, and conditions under which employees in various industries would work. Section 7(a) of the National Industrial Recovery Act was path-breaking in the area of labor relations; it required companies that signed the codes to bargain collectively with their workers through labor unions that had the backing of a majority of the company's employees.

The NRA was designed to eliminate waste, inefficiency, and destructive competition—the goal of industrial consolidators since Vanderbilt and Rockefeller. In making the federal government the referee among companies and between employers and employees, the NRA was the legatee of Theodore Roosevelt's New Nationalism of 1912 (Johnson was an old Bull Mooser), the mobilization of the economy during the First World War, and even Herbert Hoover's trade associations. The difference was that the NRA codes were compulsory. A business was bound to its industry's code not by the moral suasion that Hoover had preferred, but by the force of law. Noncompliance led to prosecution by the government.

Blue Eagle Mania

Critics of the NRA, including some within the New Deal administration, likened it to the Fascist system that had been set up in Italy in 1922 by Benito Mussolini, and to the Nazi economy that was being instituted in Germany at the same time under Adolf Hitler. This was unfair. Mussolini and Hitler suppressed free labor unions; the NRA promised them a part in making industrial policy.

More to the point was the criticism that NRA functionaries went ridiculously far. Johnson was indeed

Eight thousand children form an eagle at a National Recovery Administration rally in San Francisco.

How the Wealthy Coped

The Union Cigar Company was by no means an industrial giant, but the collapse of its stock in the Great Crash of 1929 nevertheless made history. When the price of Union shares plummeted from $113.50 to $4 in one day's trading, the president of the company jumped to his death from a hotel room that he had rented for that purpose. The incident helped fuel a legend that rich men shouting "Ruined!" were hurling themselves wholesale from high buildings during late 1929 and early 1930. Cartoonists in newspapers and magazines had a field day with the theme. But it was only wishful thinking. When a historian researched the matter, he discovered that the suicide rate was higher in the months just preceding the crash than it was thereafter.

While many, perhaps most, middle-class investors and speculators were "ruined" in the collapse, the very rich suffered little more than a loss in paper wealth (relative richness) and not poverty. Still, the moneyed classes, which had been so at home during the age of Coolidge, very confident of their right and duty to govern the country, were stunned and even paralyzed by their failure. "I'm afraid," said Charles Schwab, chairman of the United States Steel Corporation, "that every man is afraid." Franklin D. Roosevelt, celestially noncommittal during his campaign for the presidency, may have had as much support from the nation's financial elite as did Hoover. Certainly the attitude of Wall Street and corporate boardroom alike was to give him a chance.

It did not last. By 1936, Roosevelt was being called "a traitor to his class" in society circles. Some of the jokes told about him and his wife, Eleanor, were vicious and ugly. Others were simply lame, as was this attack on Roosevelt's programs for putting people to work as welfare in disguise:

Q. Why is a WPA worker like King Solomon?
A. Because he takes his pick and goes to bed.

By 1937, when most people were wrestling with the recession of that year, the very wealthy were living comfortably again. Stock prices were up—although far below 1929 levels—and a new kind of social whirl made its appearance. Unlike the society of Mrs. Astor, J. P. Morgan, and Bradley Martin, with its regal ballrooms, private railroad cars, club parlors, and yachts, the café society of the late 1930s centered in Prohibition era speakeasies that had come above ground with repeal as restaurants and as clubs in which to sit and to dance all night, to see and to be seen. In New York City, the undisputed capital of café society, the chief seats were El Morocco, the Stork Club, and the "21" Club, which reveled in its cryptic speakeasy designation.

The young always had played an important part in the social whirl. Marrying daughters to European noblemen had been a way to display wealth during the late nineteenth century; youth had set the pace of fashion during the 1920s. In café society, however, the "rich, young, and beautiful" became the center of the piece.

What was more remarkable about café society was the interest that ordinary Americans took in its doings. Whom Alfred Gwynne Vanderbilt was dating was

Wealthy customers lounge at a cafe.

breathlessly reported in syndicated "society columns" by hangers-on such as Walter Winchell and "Cholly Knickerbocker." It was a news item if the heiress of an industrial fortune dropped in at El Morocco several times a week in order to dance the rhumba with her "agile husband." Naughtier gossip made reference to blond hubbies dancing the rhumba with willowy debutantes.

Debutantes (or debs), young women who were "coming out" into society, when in fact they had been lounging around night clubs since they were fifteen or sixteen, were the queens of café society. The leading deb of 1937 was Gloria "Mimi" Baker, whose mother replied to someone who called her a decadent aristocrat: "Why Mimi is the most democratic person, bar none, I've ever known." Indeed, café society was "democratic" in ways that earlier high societies had not been. Because status depended on beauty, on what passed for wit and talent, and on simply being well known and rich, the café set admitted movie stars, athletes, and even impoverished but slickly mannered nobles from Europe. They, in turn, were delighted to rub shoulders and dance the rhumba with the very rich.

Indeed, international "playboys" jumped at the opportunity to do more than be photographed at night clubs and race tracks they could not afford, and therein lay the great morality play of the 1930s and, possibly, part of the explanation for the fascination of many Americans with the doings of café society. Like people who attend high-speed automobile races, they were interested in the collisions as much as in the running.

Barbara Hutton, who had to stick to spartan diets in order to keep her weight down, was sole heiress to $45 million made in the five-and-tens of F. W. Woolworth. In 1933, she married Alexis Mdivani, who claimed to be a dispossessed Russian prince. Almost immediately after the marriage, the debonair Mdivani began to make her miserable, railing particularly at her weight problem. Drawing on the $1 million that Barbara's father had given him as a wedding present, the prince spent much of his time in the company of other women. In 1935, Barbara won Mdivani's consent for a divorce by giving him $2 million.

Almost immediately, she married a Danish count, Kurt von Haugwitz-Reventlow. Hutton showered him with gifts, including a $4.5 million mansion in London, but divorced him in 1937. The same photographers who snapped pictures of laughing, dancing debutantes at the Stork Club rushed about to get shots of tearful Barbara Hutton, the "poor little rich girl."

Some of the people who pored over them were sympathetic. "She's made mistakes," wrote columnist Adela Rogers St. Johns, "been a silly, wild, foolish girl, given in to temptations—but she's still our own . . . an American girl fighting alone across the sea." Others took pleasure in her repeated comeuppances. "Why do they hate me?" Barbara asked. "There are other girls as rich, richer, almost as rich."

code-crazy, wanting to regiment the most peripheral and even trivial businesses. There was a code for the burlesque "industry" that specified how many strippers were to undress per performance, what vestments they were to discard, and the quality of tassels and G-strings in NRA houses. Had prostitution been legal in the United States, Johnson would have risen to even more ludicrous heights.

Such extremes were possible in part because of the enthusiasm with which Americans initially took to the NRA. Rooted on by the bombastic Johnson, 200,000 people marched in an NRA parade in New York, carrying banners emblazoned with the NRA motto, "We Do Our Part." The symbol of the NRA, a stylized blue eagle clutching industrial machinery and thunderbolts, was painted on factory walls, pasted on shop windows, and adopted as a motif by university marching bands.

For a brief time, Hugh Johnson seemed as popular as Roosevelt himself. He was certainly more conspicuous. Johnson stormed noisily about the country, publicly castigating as "chiselers" those businessmen who did not fall into line. He apparently inherited his bullying personality from his mother, who at an NRA rally in Tulsa said that "people had better obey the NRA because my son will enforce it like lightning, and you can never tell when lightning will strike."

THE NEW DEAL THREATENED; THE NEW DEAL SUSTAINED

The New Deal suffered its first setback not in Congress but at the Supreme Court. It was a conservative body in 1933, with six Harding, Coolidge, and Hoover appointees and one dating back to the presidency of William Howard Taft. Out of synchronization with the revolution in government, the "nine old men," as F.D.R. was to denounce them, declared two major piece of New Deal legislation unconstitutional, and threatened others.

Death of the Blue Eagle

The NRA met its death because of a suit brought by a small poultry company specializing in slaughtering chickens for use in the kosher kitchens of religious Jews. The Schechter brothers, owners of the company, found the sanitary standards required by the NRA code for their industry incompatible with the ritual requirements of kosher slaughter. They claimed that NRA regulations represented unjustifiable federal interference in intrastate commerce. (Their business was carried out almost entirely within New York state.) In

THE REGULATED SOCIETY

Regulatory agencies are established by Congress and given authority to act as watchdogs over specific aspects of American life. For example, the Interstate Commerce Commission (ICC) regulates the movement of goods and people across state lines, assigning rights over certain routes to trucking companies, setting rates, settling disputes, and so on. The Federal Communications Commission (FCC) keeps an eye on the practices of radio and television broadcasters. Today, 55 major regulatory commissions in the United States government turn out 77,000 pages of decisions and rules each year.

1935, the Supreme Court ruled unanimously that the Schechter Brothers were right, declaring that the National Industrial Recovery Act was unconstitutional.

The fuss was minimal. Both Roosevelt's and the people's enthusiasm for the NRA had waned since 1933. Many codes were indeed so picayune as to seem impediments to economic recovery. Moreover, Congress moved promptly to salvage the one provision of the NRA codes that had widespread support, Section 7(a). In the Wagner Labor Relations Act or National Labor Relations Act of 1935, the New Dealers reinstated the requirement that employers recognize and negotiate with labor unions that claimed the support of a majority of a company's employees.

In fact, the Wagner Act went further than Section 7(a) by setting up the National Labor Relations Board (NLRB) to investigate unfair labor practices and to issue "cease and desist" orders to employers found responsible for them. Most important, the law guaranteed the right of unions to represent those workers who voted for those unions in NLRB-supervised elections.

Farm Policy

A similar salvage operation preserved parts of the Agricultural Adjustment Act that the Supreme Court negated in 1936. Also enacted during the Hundred Days, the Agricultural Adjustment Act established yet another agency, the Agricultural Adjustment Administration (AAA), which was to enforce the principle of "parity," for which farmers' organizations had fought throughout the 1920s.

"Parity" meant increasing farm income from the depths it plumbed in 1933 to the ratio that it had borne to the prices of nonfarm products during the prosperous years of 1909 to 1914, a kind of golden age of agriculture as farmers looked back on it. The AAA accomplished this by restricting farm production.

Growers of wheat, corn, cotton, tobacco, rice, and hogs were paid subsidies to keep some of their land out of production. The costs of this expensive program ($100 million was paid to cotton farmers alone in one year) was borne by a tax on processors—millers, refiners, butchers, packagers—which was then passed on to consumers in higher food, clothing, and tobacco prices.

Because the crops of 1933 were already in the ground when the AAA was established in May, it was necessary to destroy some of them. "Kill every third pig and plow every third row under," Secretary of Agriculture Henry A. Wallace said. The results were mixed. Many people were repelled by the slaughter of 6 million small pigs and 220,000 pregnant sows. Others not so sensitive wondered why food was being destroyed when millions were hungry. (In fact, 100 million pounds of the prematurely harvested pork was diverted to relief agencies and inedible waste was used as fertilizer.) Nevertheless, the AAA worked; the income of hog growers began to rise immediately.

Fully a quarter of the 1933 cotton crop was plowed under, the fields left fallow. Unfortunately, because cotton farmers tended those fields still under cultivation more intensely, production actually rose in 1933. Within two years, however, cotton (and wheat and corn) prices rose by over 50 percent.

A less desirable side effect of AAA restrictions on production was the throwing of people off the land. Landowners dispossessed tenant farmers in order to get the subsidies that fallow land would earn. Between 1932 and 1935, 3 million American farmers lost their livelihood. Most of them were very poor black and white tenants who already were struggling to survive.

Anxious Days

Despite its negative effects, the New Dealers were devoted to the principles of the AAA. Its rejection by the Supreme Court was a far more serious blow than the loss of the Blue Eagle. Again, they salvaged what they could. In the Soil Conservation and Domestic Allotment Act, parity and the limitation of production were saved under the guise of conserving soil.

Much more worrisome was the fear that, piece by piece, the conservative Supreme Court would dismantle the entire New Deal. Roosevelt's supporters were particularly worried about the Rural Electrification Act and the law that had set up the Tennessee Valley Authority (TVA).

The Rural Electrification Administration (REA) brought electricity to isolated farm regions that had been of no interest to private utility companies. It was vulnerable to Court action because it put the government into the business of distributing power, indirectly competing with private enterprise. The TVA was farther reaching yet. It was a massive government construction, flood control, and electrification project that shaped an entire region, a model of government economic and social planning.

TVA

The TVA was the brainchild and lifelong darling of Senator George Norris, a Republican progressive who advocated economic planning and regional development engineered by the government. Although he was from Nebraska, Norris had fastened on the valley of the Tennessee River, in the southern Appalachians, as the place to put his ideas to work.

Almost every year, the wild Tennessee River flooded its banks and brought additional hardship to southern Appalachia, one of the nation's poorest areas. Norris's idea was to use the stricken region as a laboratory. The government would construct a system of dams both to control the raging floods and to generate electricity. In homes, the cheap power would bring the people of Appalachia into the twentieth century. The government-generated electricity would also make possible the construction of factories, especially for the manufacture of fertilizers, which would invigorate the economy of a chronically depressed region.

Norris also pointed out that by generating electricity itself, the government would be able to determine the fairness of the prices of power demanded by other companies elsewhere in the country. Until the 1930s, the actual cost of generating electrical power was something of a mystery outside of the business.

During the 1920s, Henry Ford had tried to buy key sites on the Tennessee River from the government, notably Muscle Shoals, a tumultuous rapids, in order to build a privately owned power plant. Norris had fought Ford off in Congress, arguing that the Tennessee Valley provided an ideal laboratory for the testing of theories of regional planning. Fortunately for Norris, scandalous government giveaways of valuable property to profiteers, notably the oil reserves at Teapot Dome, were still alive in the public memory. However, while he had been able to keep Muscle Shoals and other sites in federal hands, Norris was unable to push through his plan for government development of the Tennessee Valley until the election of F.D.R.

Creeping Socialism

Predictably, the TVA and REA were attacked as socialistic. Big business, which had approved F.D.R.'s banking reforms and, for a time, the NRA, launched a political offensive against programs that put the government into the production and distribution of electrical power. As early as 1934, having recovered from the demoralization of 1929, some bankers and big businessmen founded the American Liberty League, which accused Roosevelt of trying to destroy free enterprise and set up a dictatorship.

Most Liberty Leaguers were Coolidge-Mellon Republicans, but they were joined by some prominent Democrats, including the party's presidential nominees of 1924 and 1928, John W. Davis and Alfred E. Smith. Davis was a corporation lawyer and found his role familiar. Smith turned against Roosevelt in part because of his peeve over losing his chance to be president to a man whose rise in politics he had helped to advance. Abandoning the sidewalks of New York for seats on a number of corporate boards, the once progressive Smith took increasingly reactionary positions on public questions.

Combating such critics was like swatting mosquitoes for the able Roosevelt. A majority of Americans remained distrustful of big businessmen, even still bitter towards them. F.D.R. labeled the Liberty Leaguers "economic royalists" and they never did have a large following.

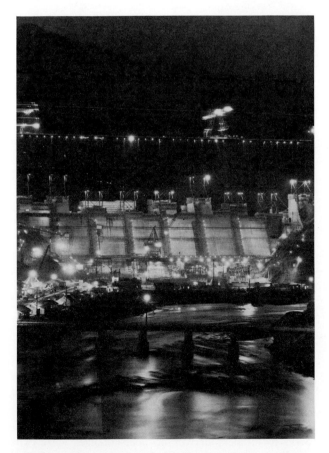

A dam under construction by the Tennessee Valley Authority.

The Supreme Court was another matter, a major threat to the New Deal. Making one of his rare political miscalculations, Roosevelt proposed a scheme to save his reforms by packing the Court with additional justices who would endorse them.

Reaction in both Congress and the nation at large was hostile. The New Deal was popular but Roosevelt's court-packing scheme did indeed look like tampering with the Constitution. Roosevelt quietly retreated and the crisis passed when the Court, perhaps alarmed, approved several key New Deal enactments. Then Father Time lent a hand; beginning in 1937, a series of retirements and deaths allowed Roosevelt to appoint a New Deal majority to the bench without tampering with the traditional size of the Court. When F.D.R. died in 1945, eight of the nine justices were his appointees.

THE SPELLBINDERS

F.D.R. made his court-packing proposal in 1937, at the beginning of his second term. For a while, however, it appeared that he might not win reelection. The threat came not from the American Liberty League or even the Republican party but from three popular demagogues whom Roosevelt and his chief political strategist, Postmaster General James A. Farley genuinely feared.

Father Coughlin

With the coming of depression, Charles E. Coughlin, a Canadian-born Roman Catholic priest, had transformed a religious radio program into a platform for his political beliefs. At first, Coughlin enlisted his mellow, baritone voice and Irish genius with the spoken word in support of Roosevelt. He was not a man

Father Charles Coughlin and Dr. Francis Townsend each commanded broad support but never transformed it into a political movement.

to mince. "The New Deal is Christ's Deal," he said in 1933.

A year later, however, Coughlin became convinced that the key to solving the depression was a complete overhaul of the national monetary system, including the abolition of the Federal Reserve System. Despite Roosevelt's reputation among the "economic royalists" as a radical, the president had no patience for such extreme proposals. But because Coughlin had a huge and devoted following—perhaps 10 million listeners to some programs—his scathing attacks were a source of worry to F.D.R., Farley, and other tacticians.

Dr. Townsend

Dr. Francis E. Townsend, a California physician, rather a different sort than the high-voltage Coughlin, was at least equally a threat to Roosevelt's majority. Himself 66 years old in 1933, Townsend was appalled by the plight of the nation's aged citizens. He proposed that the federal government pay a monthly pension of $200 to all people over 60 years of age, with two conditions attached.

A WELL-FUNDED CAMPAIGN

In 1934, radical novelist Upton Sinclair won the Democratic party's nomination for governor by proposing a comprehensive social welfare program known as EPIC, "End Poverty in California." President Roosevelt was less than delighted by the emergence of another spellbinder within his own party, and pretty much sat out the campaign. The Republican party spent $4 million in the successful effort to defeat Sinclair. By way of contrast, in 1932, the Republicans had spent only $3 million nationally in the campaign to reelect President Hoover.

First, federal pensioners would be forbidden to work. Second, they would spend every cent of their pension within the month. His "Townsend Plan" not only would provide security for the nation's elderly, the kindly doctor told audiences all over the country, but would reinvigorate the economy by creating jobs for young men and women.

By 1936, 7,000 Townsend Clubs claimed a membership of 1.5 million. When Roosevelt rejected the plan as unworkable, Townsend went into the opposition and laid tentative plans to join his movement with those of Father Coughlin and of Roosevelt's most serious political rival, Senator Huey P. Long of Louisiana.

The Kingfish

Huey Long remains one of the most fascinating figures of the depression decade. He rose from among the poor white farm folk of northern Louisiana to educate himself as a lawyer. He never forgot the poor. He built a successful political career as a colorful and often profane orator who baited the railroad and oil industry elite that ran the state. Unlike most southern demagogues, however, Long did not resort to race-baiting

Louisiana politician Huey Long demonstrates his flair for theatrical oratory.

to win votes. He supported segregation, but he also won the support of many of those Louisiana blacks, mostly in New Orleans, who had held on to their right to vote, by providing services for them, too.

As governor of Louisiana between 1928 and 1932, Long built roads and hospitals, provided inexpensive or free textbooks and lunches for schoolchildren, social benefits that were almost unknown in the South and were far from universal in the North and West. Long was an ambitious and egotistic showman. He called himself "the Kingfish" after a clownish (and devious) character on the popular radio program "Amos 'n' Andy." He was the Kingfish, and all the other politicians were little fishes. He made Louisiana State University the best public university in the South and led cheers when LSU played its great rival, the University of Alabama. Once, when a circus announced that it would open in Baton Rouge on the date of an important LSU game, Long killed the competition by closing down the show on the grounds that lion tamers were cruel to animals.

The New Deal Supreme

People loved Huey Long, not only in Louisiana, which he continued to run even after entering the Senate in 1933, but all over the South and Midwest. He based his national ambitions on a plan called "Share the Wealth," which called for a heavy tax on big incomes and no personal incomes of more than $1 million a year. To people struggling for the necessities, it was an appealing program.

Because Long was the virtual dictator of the Pelican State ("I'm the Constitution around here," he said with a puckish smile), Roosevelt considered him a threat to democracy as well as to his own reelection in 1936. In the end, however, the president overcame him and Townsend and Coughlin by a combination of cooptation and good luck.

Roosevelt undercut Coughlin's financial program through his own moderate monetary reforms. To steal Townsend's thunder, he supported the Social Security Act of 1935. Its pensions were tiny compared with the $200 a month for which Townsend called. Nevertheless, it was a revolutionary law; for the first time, the United States government assumed responsibility for the welfare of people who were disabled or too old to work. Also in 1935, Roosevelt supported a revision of the income tax law that did not abolish huge incomes, as Long demanded, but taxed people in the upper brackets much more heavily than those in the lower.

In every case, the New Deal reforms were half a loaf. In no case was the program of the critics adopted. But so great was Roosevelt's personal popularity that

AS MAINE GOES

In the nineteenth century, the people of Maine elected their governor in September, almost two months before the national presidential election. The saying "As Maine goes, so goes the nation" reflected the significance that was attributed to the results there. In the 28 presidential elections in which Maine voters participated, the state's record in picking the winner was 22 to 6, good but not foolproof, as Herbert Hoover learned in 1932: he won Maine, but few other states.

In 1936, Maine again looked to vote Republican. Democratic party campaign manager James Farley quipped, "As Maine goes, so goes Vermont." He was right on the button. F.D.R. won every state that year except Maine and Vermont!

his would-be rivals lost support and, eventually, lost heart. Townsend's clubs declined slowly, as did Coughlin's radio audience. In the end, the "radio priest" discredited himself by turning to a Nazi-like anti-Semitism and praising Adolf Hitler. Long was removed from the scene by fate; in 1935, he was assassinated by a young man whose family Long had injured in his recklessness.

Thus in the election of 1936, Roosevelt had to face only the congenial and moderate Republican governor of Kansas, Alfred M. Landon. Offering no real alternative to the New Deal, Landon was swamped, winning majorities only in Maine and Vermont.

THE LEGACY OF THE NEW DEAL

Even before the election of 1936, Roosevelt had shifted the direction of his reforms. At first, he had viewed the New Deal as very much a new deal for everyone. With some reason, he believed he had saved the capitalist system from the kind of political extremism that the depression was nurturing elsewhere in the world. He felt betrayed when big business, instead of recognizing and rewarding his moderation, vilified him.

In 1935, threatened by the spellbinders and encouraged by his wife, with her ties to disadvantaged groups, F.D.R. became, in varying degrees, the president of the people on the bottom of society. Their response in the election of 1936 only heartened him to push on. It was in this break with "the classes" and partisanship on behalf of "the masses" that the legacy of the New Deal lies. Such phenomena have occurred without revolution only rarely in history.

Blacks Become Democrats

Roosevelt emphasized the economic problems of disadvantaged groups almost to the exclusion of other problems. On the question of civil rights for blacks, for example, F.D.R. was nearly silent. The Democratic party depended heavily on its southern bloc for support, and southern politicians were committed to white supremacy and Jim Crow segregation. As a concession to them, Roosevelt refused even to support a federal antilynching bill, and he tolerated the racial segregation of work gangs on government-supported building projects such as the TVA.

Under constant pressure from the NAACP (National Association for the Advancement of Colored People), from Eleanor Roosevelt, and from such individual black leaders as Mary McLeod Bethune, the New Dealers made sure that blacks shared in relief programs. Black people moved into more than a third of new housing units constructed by the federal government. As a result, the 1930s saw a revolution in black voting patterns. In 1932, about 75 percent of American black voters were Republicans. They still thought of the GOP as the party of Lincoln and emancipation. For example, the only black congressman in 1932 was Oscar De Priest of Chicago, a Republican.

By 1936, more than 75 percent of registered blacks were voting Democratic—even De Priest was defeated

United Mine Workers Union president John L. Lewis.

UNION MEMBERSHIP (Includes Canadian members of U.S. unions)	
1900	791,000
1905	1,918,000
1910	2,116,000
1915	2,560,000
1920	5,034,000
1925	3,566,000
1930	3,632,000
1935	3,728,000
1940	8,944,000
1945	14,796,000

by a black New Dealer—and the trend continued for 30 years. The Democratic party might not have been the friend of the blacks, but it was the friend of the poor, and most blacks were just that.

The Growth of the Unions

Roosevelt also won the organized-labor movement to the Democratic party. Left to his own prejudices, he would have remained neutral in disputes between unions and employers. However, when militant unionists such as John L. Lewis of the coal miners (a lifelong Republican) and Sidney Hillman and David Dubinsky of the large needle-trades unions made it clear that they would throw their influence behind the president only in return for administration support, Roosevelt gave in. Lewis raised a donation of $1 million to the president's campaign for reelection in 1936. In return, Roosevelt had to be photographed accepting the check, smiling with approval on the burly, bushy-browed Lewis.

"The President wants you to join the union," the Committee on Industrial Organization told workers in basic industries after F.D.R. signed the Wagner Act. At first a faction within the American Federation of Labor, the Committee left the AFL in 1937 to form an entirely new association of unions, the Congress of Industrial Organizations (CIO). Massive, colorful campaigns won recruits in unprecedented numbers.

The Steel Workers' Organizing Committee, parent organization of the United Steel Workers, was founded in 1936. By May 1937, it had 325,000 members. The United States Steel Corporation, the nerve center of anti-unionism in the industry, recognized the union as bargaining agent without a strike.

The United Automobile Workers enlisted 370,000 members in a little more than a year. The story was similar among workers in other basic industries: rubber, glass, lumber, aluminum, electrical products, coal mining, the needle trades, even textiles. "The Union" came to have a mystical significance in the lives of many workers. Workers fought for the right to wear union buttons on the job. The union card became a certificate of honor. Old hymns were reworded to promote the cause. Professional singers like Woody Guthrie, Pete Seeger, and Burl Ives lent their talents to organizing campaigns.

Employer Violence

The sit-down strike was one of the most dramatic manifestations of worker militance. Beginning with automobile workers in the Fisher Body Plant of Flint, Michigan, in early 1937, workers shut down factories not by picketing outside the gates, but by occupying the premises and refusing to leave.

Not every employer responded so sensibly as United States Steel. Tom Girdler of Republic Steel called the CIO "irresponsible, racketeering, violent, communistic" and threatened to fight the union with armed force. In this heated atmosphere occurred the "Memorial Day Massacre" of 1937, so called because Chicago police attacked a crowd of union members, killing ten and seriously injuring about a hundred.

Although he eventually came to terms with the United Automobile Workers, Henry Ford at first responded to the new unionism as did Girdler. He employed an army of toughs from the underworld and fortified his factories with tear gas, machine guns, and

Police attack a crowd of union members during the "Memorial Day Massacre" in Chicago, 1937.

grenades. At the "Battle of the Overpass" in Detroit, Ford "goons" (as antiunion strong-arm forces were called) beat organizer Walter Reuther and other UAW officials until they were insensible. Violence was so common in the coal fields of Harlan County, Kentucky, that the area became known in the press as "Bloody Harlan."

But such incidents, well documented in photographs and newsreel films, redounded to the benefit of the union movement, and by the end of the depression decade, organized labor was a major force in American life. In 1932, there were 3.2 million union members. In 1940, there were 9 million, and by 1944, more than 13 million.

The Bottom Line

The greatest positive accomplishment of the New Deal was to ease the economic hardships suffered by millions of Americans and, in so doing, to preserve their confidence in American institutions. In its relief measures, particularly those agencies that put jobless people to work, Roosevelt's administration was a resounding success.

As a formula for economic recovery, however, the New Deal failed. When unemployment dropped to 7.5 million early in 1937 and other economic indicators brightened, Roosevelt began to dismantle many expensive government programs. The result was renewed collapse, a depression within a depression. The recession of 1937 was not so serious as that of 1930 to 1933. But it provided painful evidence that for all their flexibility and willingness to experiment and spend, the New Dealers had not unlocked the secrets of maintaining prosperity during peacetime. Only when preparations for another world war led to massive purchases of American goods from abroad (and to rearmament at home) did the Great Depression end. By 1939, the economy was clearly on the upswing. By 1940, with Europe already at war, the Great Depression was history.

Through such programs as support for agricultural prices, rural electrification, Social Security, insurance of bank deposits, protection of labor unions, and strict controls over the economy, the federal government came to play a part in people's daily lives such as had been inconceivable before 1933. In the TVA, the government became an actual producer of electrical power and commodities such as fertilizers. It was not "socialism," as conservative critics of the New Deal cried, but in an American context it was something of a revolution.

Perhaps the most dubious side effect of the new system was the extraordinary growth in the size of

---

CHRISTMAS SEASON

In 1939, in order to give retailers an extra week of Christmas shopping season, President Roosevelt moved Thanksgiving Day from the last Thursday in November to the next to last. (Some Republican states refused to observe the change for ten years.)

---

government. Extensive government programs required huge bureaucracies to carry them out. The number of federal employees rose from 600,000 in 1930 to 1 million in 1940, a total that would rise more radically during the Second World War. To the extent that bureaucracies are concerned above all with their own survival and expansion, leading to the squandering of tax moneys and to aggravations in dealing with government, the New Deal contributed to American life, with its many blessings, a phenomenon that has, at one time or another, vexed every citizen to near distraction.

A Political Revolution

Between 1896 and 1933, the Republican party had been the nation's majority party. The only Democratic president during that era, Woodrow Wilson, won election only when the Republicans split and the Great War in Europe unsettled American politics at the bottom. During the 36 years before Roosevelt's election, the Democrats controlled the House of Representatives for only ten years, the Senate for just six.

The Great Depression and the New Deal changed everything. F.D.R. and Jim Farley forged a new majority of the solidly Democratic South, northern and western liberals, blue-collar workers (particularly urban white ethnics), and blacks, with substantial support among western farmers and ranchers. The New Deal alliance was not without problems. Beginning in 1937, old fashioned small-government southern Democrats who disapproved of even the New Deal's minimal gestures toward blacks and the prominence in Washington of "Yankee" liberals, sometimes voted with Republicans against New Deal measures.

Roosevelt's charm and his refusal to push civil rights for blacks, plus grass-roots support for the New Deal among southern whites, prevented the crack from widening into a real split during his presidency. The Democratic majority forged during the 1930s lasted for half a century. During the 50 years between 1930 and 1980, Republicans occupied the White House for 16 years, but those presidents (Eisenhower, Nixon, and Ford) were moderates who had made their peace with New Deal institutions.

In Congress, the Democratic majority was even more striking. During the same 50 years between 1930 and 1980, Republicans held majorities in the Senate for only six years and in the House of Representatives for only four. The Republican party simultaneously controlled presidency, Senate, and House for a mere two years (1953 to 1955).

For Further Reading

First of all, see the biographical studies and general works listed at the conclusion of Chapter 43. Other basic studies of the New Deal are Paul Conkin, *The New Deal* (1975); William E. Leuchtenburg, *Franklin D. Roosevelt and the New Deal, 1932–1940* (1963); Arthur M. Schlesinger, Jr., *The Coming of the New Deal* (1959) and *The Politics of Upheaval* (1960). Frederick Lewis Allen, *Since Yesterday* (1940) is an enjoyable popular history.

On the several immediate crises faced by F.D.R. and the New Dealers, see Susan Estabrook Kennedy, *The Banking Crisis of 1933* (1973); C. P. Kinderberger, *The World in Depression* (1973); Roy Lubove, *The Struggle for Social Security, 1900–1935* (1968); Thomas K. McCraw, *T.V.A. and the Power Fight, 1933–1939* (1971); Michael Parrish, *Security Regulation and the New Deal* (1970); E. E. Robinson, *The Roosevelt Leadership* (1955); Elliott Rosen, *Hoover, Roosevelt, and the Brains Trust* (1977); Theodore D. Saloutos and John D. Hicks, *Twentieth Century Populism: Agricultural Discontent in the Middle West, 1900–1939* (1951); Studs Terkel, *Hard Times* (1970).

On Roosevelt's critics: Allan Brinkley, *Voices of Protest: Huey Long, Father Coughlin, and the Great Depression* (1982); Abraham Holtzman, *The Townsend Movement* (1963); Irving Howe and Lewis Coser, *The American Communist Party* (1957); D. R. McCoy, *Angry Voices: Left of Center Politics in the New Deal Era* (1958); David A. Shannon, *The American Socialist Party* (1955); C. J. Tull, *Father Coughlin and the New Deal* (1965); T. Harry Williams, *Huey Long* (1969).

On the labor movement, see Irving Bernstein, *Turbulent Years: A History of the American Worker, 1933–1941* (1970); Sidney Fine, *Sit-Down: The General Motors Strike of 1936–1937* (1969). Other insightful monographs include Frank Freidel, *F.D.R. and the South* (1965); Paul A. Kurzman, *Harry Hopkins and the New Deal* (1974); Richard D. McKinzie, *The New Deal for Artists* (1973); Richard Polenberg, *Reorganizing Roosevelt's Government: The Controversy over Executive Reorganization, 1936–1939* (1966); Harvard Sitkoff, *A New Deal for Blacks* (1978); George Tindall, *The Emergence of the New South, 1914–1945* (1967).

In 1933, the year Franklin D. Roosevelt became president, Germany also got a new leader. Adolf Hitler, the head of the extreme right-wing National Socialist, or "Nazi" party, was named chancellor, or prime minister, of the Weimar Republic's parliamentary government by its elderly war-hero president Paul von Hindenburg. Roosevelt and Hitler paid little attention to each other during their first years in office. F.D.R. had his hands full fighting the Great Depression. Hitler was also preoccupied with the home front, working from the first day he took office to destroy the Weimar constitution and seize absolute power.

The values of the two men could hardly have been more different. The patrician Roosevelt was

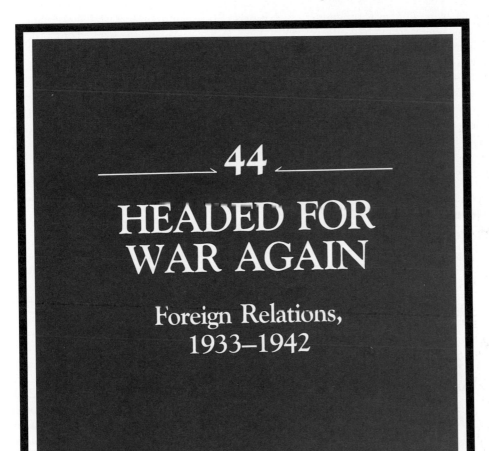

44

HEADED FOR WAR AGAIN

Foreign Relations, 1933–1942

Thousands of German soldiers listen to Adolf Hitler speak at the Nuremberg Rally, 1936.

dedicated to democratic principles and a liberal. The middle-class and rather vulgar Hitler despised democracy and was contemptuous of individual freedoms. Nevertheless, comparisons were inevitable. Pundits noted that both men were virtuosos in using the radio and other modern forms of communication as a means to persuade. Roosevelt was at his best as a soothing voice in his Fireside Chats, quietly reassuring Americans that through reform they could preserve what was of value in their way of life. Hitler was at his best ranting through loudspeakers, whipping up frustrated Germans to a hatred of the Weimar Republic, the foreigners who had humiliated Germany in the Versailles Treaty, and people whom he defined as enemies within: Socialists, Communists, and Jews.

Roosevelt and Hitler would eventually confront each other and clash, but only after Americans had experimented with a foreign policy designed to avoid entanglement in another foreign war, and watched it fail.

NEW DEAL FOREIGN POLICY

When he first took office, Roosevelt seemed to be as casual as Woodrow Wilson about foreign policy. Like Wilson, who chose William Jennings Bryan, he passed over professional diplomats in naming his secretary of state and made a political appointment, the courtly senator from Tennessee, Cordell Hull, whose elegant bearing belied his log-cabin origins.

Hull and Roosevelt were generally content to follow the guidelines that had been charted by Hoover and Secretary of State Henry L. Stimson. Where they departed from blueprint, their purpose was to reinforce the New Deal program for economic recovery at home.

The Good Neighbor

Roosevelt and Hull even embraced Hoover's phrase "good neighbor" to describe the role that they meant the United States to play in Central and South America. Following through on Hoover's announced intentions when he left office, Roosevelt withdrew the marines from Nicaragua, the Dominican Republic, and Haiti, where they had been keeping order. Like Hoover, he refused to intervene in Cuba despite the chronic civil conflicts that plagued the island republic and America's legal entitlement, under the Platt Amendment, to send in troops in times of trouble.

In 1934, when peace returned to Cuba under a pro-American president who later became dictator, Cordell Hull formally renounced the Platt Amendment. No longer would the "Colossus of the North" be a bully, using its overwhelming power to force its way in the Caribbean. As a result of the about-face, no United States president was ever so well liked in Central and South America as was Roosevelt. Even when, in 1938, Mexico seized the properties of American oil companies and offered little compensation to the former owners, Roosevelt kept cool and took a conciliatory stand. A few years later, he worked out a friendly settlement.

By then, the Good Neighbor Policy was reaping concrete benefits for the United States. The Second World War had begun, but despite German efforts to win a foothold in the Western Hemisphere, most Latin American nations backed the United States, and the few neutrals that cozied up to Hitler were very cautious. Had even a single South American country permitted Nazi Germany to establish bases on its soil, it would have seriously inhibited the American contribution to the war in Europe and Asia.

The Stimson Doctrine

Toward Asia, New Deal diplomacy also moved along paths that had been staked out during the Hoover administration. The problem in the East, as policymakers saw it, was to maintain Chinese independence and American trading rights in China—the Open Door Policy—in the face of a very ambitious and expansion-minded Japan.

The trouble was, China's government, headed by Generalissimo Chiang Kai-shek, was disorganized, inefficient, and increasingly corrupt. Late in 1931, taking advantage of the chaos, Japanese military officers detached the province of Manchuria from China and set up a puppet state that they called Manchukuo. Hoover considered but rejected Stimson's proposal that the United States retaliate against Japan by imposing severe economic sanctions, denying Japan the American products that were vital to its industry and navy, particularly oil. Instead, Hoover announced that the United States would not recognize the legality of any territorial changes resulting from the use of force. Curiously, this policy became known as the Stimson Doctrine.

The Stimson Doctrine was little more than a rap on the knuckles, rather more like one of those inexpensive and painless statements of moralistic disapproval that come from critics of foreign policy, rather than from those responsible for making it. Japanese militarists, driven by a compelling sense of national destiny,

A young Chinese survivor of the Japanese air attack on Shanghai, 1937.

shrugged it off. In 1932, they launched an attack on Shanghai and casually tyrannized the population. In 1937, the Japanese bombed the city, one of the first massive bombings of a civilian population. Nevertheless, Roosevelt went no further than Hoover had in 1932. He (and the League of Nations) responded to Japanese aggression with words alone. With economic problems so serious at home, no Western country would risk war with Japan for the sake of a China so dubiously governed and divided.

Recognition of the Soviet Union

Where Roosevelt and Hull parted ways with Hoover and Stimson, the cause was that all-pervasive reality, the depression at home. For example, in May 1933, Roosevelt scuttled an international conference that was meeting in London for the purpose of stabilizing world currencies. Delegates of 64 nations had gathered with Hoover's approval and, so they assumed, with Roosevelt's as well. Before discussions actually began, however, Roosevelt announced that he would not agree to any decisions that ran contrary to his domestic

recovery program, specifically his decision to take the United States off the gold standard. The conference collapsed.

In November 1933, Roosevelt formally recognized the Soviet government, which four presidents had refused to do. In part this was a realistic decision that was long overdue. For good or ill, the party dictatorship headed by Joseph Stalin was firmly in control of the Soviet Union and its traditional territories. But Roosevelt was also swayed by the argument that the Soviet Union would provide a large and profitable market for ailing American manufacturers. This proved to be an illusion. Soviet Russia was too poor to buy much of anything from anyone. Nevertheless, it was the hope of stimulating economic recovery at home that made possible the end of a pointless 16-year policy of nonrecognition.

New Directions, Old Strictures

Increased trade was also the motive behind Secretary of State Cordell Hull's strategy of reducing tariff barriers through reciprocity. With the traditional distaste for high tariffs of a southern Democrat, Hull negotiated reciprocal-trade agreements with 29 countries. The high Republican rates of the 1920s were slashed by as much as half in return for other nations' agreements to lower their barriers against American exports.

Roosevelt probably would have liked his administration to take a more active part in the affairs of nations than the United States did. He admired his cousin Theodore Roosevelt's forcefulness, and he was an old Wilsonian, as was Hull. He had enthusiastically supported the League of Nations when it was first proposed and, while recovering from his polio attack during the early 1920s, had studied and written about foreign policy.

But F.D.R. was first and foremost a politician who thought about voters at every turn. He knew that it was political suicide for an elected official to wander too far from popular prejudices in any matter, and according to an authoritative public-opinion poll of 1935, 95 percent of all Americans were isolationists. They believed that the United States had no vital interests to protect in either Europe or Asia and wanted their government to act accordingly.

EXAMINATION QUESTION

Between 1931 and 1941, every student at the Japanese Naval Academy was required to write an essay on the question: "How would you carry out a surprise attack on Pearl Harbor?"

Suspicion of Europe was reinforced by the theory that the economic collapse of the Old World was responsible for the American depression. This feeling intensified between 1934 and 1936, when Senator Gerald Nye of North Dakota began a series of investigations into the political machinations of the munitions industry. Nye insisted that the United States had been maneuvered into the First World War by "merchants of death," such as the giant Du Pont Corporation and other companies, that had been only too willing to see young men slaughtered for the sake of bigger sales. This belief was popularized in a bestselling book of 1935, *The Road to War* by Walter Millis, and many academic historians took a similarly jaundiced view of the reasons why, in 1917, Americans had gone "over there."

Neutrality Policy

In a series of Neutrality Acts passed between 1935 and 1937, Congress said "never again" with an exclamation point. Taken together, the three laws warned American citizens against traveling on ships flying the flags of nations at war (no *Lusitanias* this time) and required belligerent nations to pay cash for all American goods they purchased and to carry them in their own ships. There would be no United States flagships sunk even by accident, and no American property lost because of a war among Europeans. Finally, belligerent nations were forbidden to buy arms in the United States and to borrow money from American banks. This law was designed to prevent the emergence of an active lobby of munitions makers and bankers with a vested interest in the victory of one side in any conflict.

Critics of the Neutrality Acts argued that they worked to the disadvantage of countries that were the innocent victims of aggression. Such nations would be unprepared for war, whereas aggressor nations would equip themselves in advance. This was certainly the message of Fascist Italy's invasion of Ethiopia in 1935 and of Japan's huge purchases of American scrap iron. But until 1938, Americans were interested only in avoiding a repetition of the events that had taken them into war in 1917. The majority wanted no part of trying to influence international behavior if it meant American involvement.

THE WORLD GOES TO WAR

Each year brought new evidence that the world was drifting into another bloodbath. In 1934, the Nazi government of Adolf Hitler began rearming Germany.

In 1935, Hitler introduced universal military training and Italy invaded Ethiopia, one of but two independent nations in Africa. In 1936, Francisco Franco, a reactionary Spanish general, started a rebellion against the unstable democratic government of Spain and received massive support from both Italy and Germany, including combat troops who treated the Spanish Civil War as a rehearsal for a bigger show.

In July 1937, Japan sent land forces into China and quickly took the northern capital, then called Peiping, and most of the coastal provinces. In March 1938, Hitler forced the political union of Austria to Germany in the *Anschluss* (union), increasing the resources of what Hitler called the Third Reich, or empire. In September, claiming that he wanted only to unite all Germans under one flag, Hitler demanded that Czechoslovakia surrender the Sudetenland to him.

The Sudetenland was largely populated by people who spoke German. But it was also the mountainous natural defense line for Czechoslovakia, the only democratic state in central Europe. Nevertheless, in the hope that they could win peace by appeasing Hitler, England and France agreed to the takeover; Hitler mocked their misplaced goodwill within months. In March 1939, he seized the rest of Czechoslovakia, where the people were Slavic in language and culture and were generally fearful of or hostile to Germans.

GERMAN AND ITALIAN AGGRESSION 1934–1939

Adolf Hitler and Francisco Franco giving the fascist salute.

weak a country could have fallen to Italy's poorly trained and equipped army. Mussolini's tanks were designed for parades rather than for war. Some were actually made of sheet metal that could be dented with a swift kick. By itself, Mussolini's Italy represented no real threat to world peace, and Americans either applauded what progress the Italian economy made under Fascist rule or laughed at newsreel films of Mussolini's slapstick antics.

Beyond his Charlie Chaplin moustache, there was nothing comical about the Nazi dictator of Germany. Adolf Hitler's strutting was all too serious because his theater was a potentially rich and powerful nation. Moreover, Hitler was far more cunning and deliberate than Mussolini. He knew what he wanted and had said as much in an autobiography entitled *Mein Kampf*, or *My Struggle*, German domination of the continent of Europe. While his strategy was not without flaws, Hitler seemed brilliantly to grasp just how much he could get away with in dealing with the other European powers and the United States. Or, as some have suggested, he was very lucky.

The Aggressor Nations

In some respects, the three aggressor nations of the 1930s were very different. Japan was motivated to expand into China primarily for economic reasons. A modern industrial nation, Japan was poor in basic natural resources like coal and iron. China was rich in these raw materials, and Japanese leaders hoped to displace the United States and Great Britain as the dominant imperial power on the Asian mainland.

Until the summer of 1941, Japanese policymakers were split between fanatical militarists who believed they must have war with the United States (and looked forward to it) and moderates who believed they could best serve their country's purposes by coming to an understanding with the United States. American trade was important to Japan; indeed, the Asian nation was the third largest customer of the United States, importing vast quantities of American cotton, copper, scrap iron, and oil.

Italy under the Fascists seemed locked into chronic poverty. Dictator Benito Mussolini, a strutting buffoon in his public posing but ruthless in his use of power, made do with the appearance of wealth and might. Ethiopia was an easy touch, a destitute and backward country that had to send men with antiquated muskets and even spears to combat Mussolini's tanks. Only so

Benito Mussolini loved military displays, but most of the Italian army was in fact poorly trained and armed.

Perverted Nationalism

In other ways, the three aggressor nations were much alike. Japanese militarists, Italian Fascists, and German Nazis were all stridently antidemocratic. They sneered at the ideals of popular rule and individual liberties, regarding them as the sources of the world's economic and social problems. In the place of traditional principles of democratic humanism, they exalted the totalitarian state as mystically personified in a single person: Hirohito, the divine emperor of Japan; Mussolini, the Italian *Duce*; and Hitler, the German *Führer*.

The aggressor nations were militaristic. They worshiped armed force as the best means of serving their national purposes. If militarism could be less than ominous when practiced by a poor country like Italy, it was frightening when combined with fanatical Japanese nationalism or Nazi racism. The Japanese considered Asia to be their garden, off limits to westerners who had dominated the Eastern Hemisphere for a century. Japanese soldiers were sworn to solemn oaths to die serving emperor and homeland.

Nazi racism was criminal from its inception. Calling on ancient Germanic mythology, nineteenth-century pseudoscience, and populist anti-Semitism, it taught that "non-Aryans" were subhuman degenerates who had no claims on the master race save to serve it. After disposing of, exiling, or silencing the German Communists, Socialists, and Democrats, Nazi paramilitary organizations routinely brutalized German Jews. Hitler's government stripped Jews of civil rights and eventually, during the war, murdered those who remained in extermination camps along with millions of Jews from conquered lands, gypsies, congenitally handicapped people, political dissidents, homosexuals, and those bold or foolish enough to resist Nazi tyranny.

And the War Came

Hitler had repeatedly pushed the Western democracies and gotten his way. In September 1939, when he invaded Poland, ostensibly to secure a German-

Japanese soldiers believed that Emperor Hirohito was divine and swore to fight to the death serving him.

speaking part of the country, as he had done in the Sudetenland, Britain and France draw the line, declaring war. However, neither nation had prepared adequately to help Poland, and Hitler had neutralized the Soviet Union by signing a "nonaggression" pact with Communist dictator Joseph Stalin. Stalin knew that Russia was on Hitler's list but he distrusted England and France and needed time to prepare. And territory for a buffer: while Hitler's legions invaded Poland from the west, Russian soldiers streamed into eastern Poland, and the tiny Baltic Sea states of Latvia, Lithuania, and Estonia.

An uneasy quiet fell on Europe during the winter of 1939–40. Journalists spoke of a "phony war" in which neither side attacked the other with force. In fact, the French and British were committed to defensive war, remembering the terrible loss of life in World War I when the men went over the top. They huddled behind the Maginot Line, a system of fortifications to which the French had dedicated vast resources throughout the 1930s.

The Germans had other plans. Appreciating better than the British and French what the motor vehicle

---

TWO DIFFERENT WORLDS

In December 1940, Adolf Hitler told Germans that there could be no reconciliation between Germany, on the one hand, and Great Britain *and the United States*, on the other. They were "different worlds."

The next month, President Roosevelt accepted Hitler's dichotomy and said that his world was devoted to the Four Freedoms, "freedom of speech and expression, freedom of worship, freedom from want, freedom from fear."

meant to armed conflict, they were preparing for *Blitz-krieg* (lightning war): massive land, sea, and air attacks with which, in the spring, the crack German armed forces overran Denmark, Norway, Luxembourg, Belgium, and the Netherlands. In June 1940, France collapsed, and the British managed to evacuate their troops and some French units from the little port of Dunkirk only by mobilizing virtually every ship and boat that was capable of crossing the English Channel. The motley fleet returned 300,000 demoralized men to England to await a German invasion.

The Invasion of Russia

"We shall fight on the beaches, we shall fight on the landing grounds, we shall fight in the fields and in the streets, we shall fight in the hills; we shall never surrender," said Winston Churchill, the new British prime minister, and his eloquence inspired Americans as well as Britons. But few were truly confident that the British alone could withstand a German onslaught.

Instead of invading Great Britain with land forces, Hitler ordered relentless aerial bombardment of the country while Germany expanded its power to the south. Mussolini's Italy had joined the war against France (forming with Germany the Rome-Berlin Axis) and faced British and Anzac (Australian and New

Zealand Army Corps) troops in Libya in North Africa. Then in June 1941, the Führer made what is widely regarded as his greatest strategic blunder: he invaded the Soviet Union.

Stalin, who would later depict himself as the savior of Russia, was oddly unprepared for the onslaught. Soviet armies disintegrated before the German *Wehrmacht* until the fall when, miraculously, the Red Army held. The fighting was barbaric on both sides. Hitler lost 750,000 men in the first year in Russia, more than in the entire war to that point. Nevertheless, the *Wehrmacht* nearly surrounded Leningrad in the north and threatened Moscow. The next year, 1942, the Germans advanced farther, with Stalingrad in the south the chief objective. There the campaign stalled.

THE UNITED STATES AND THE WAR IN EUROPE

The fall of France, the heroic resistance of Britain, and to a lesser extent the invasion of Russia changed American attitudes toward neutrality. With the exception of neutral Sweden, Switzerland, and Eire, Britain and France were the last democracies in Europe. France was "America's oldest friend," and Britain, if

Nazi repression included destroyng ideas as well as people. Here, students burn "subversive" books in front of the Berlin Opera House, May 10, 1933.

the nation's oldest enemy, was nevertheless the cultural motherland with whom its daughter had largely reconciled.

Moreover, ugly pro-Axis and racist rhetoric in the United States by small but noisy Nazi organizations such as William Dudley Pelley's Silver Shirts and Fritz Kuhn's German-American Bund, as well as German machinations in Latin America, persuaded Americans that Hitler had no intention of stopping in Europe. During the "phony war" in March 1940, only 43 percent of Americans thought that a German victory in Europe would threaten them in any way. By July, almost 80 percent thought so. They viewed Hitler as a madman who wanted to conquer the world.

Roosevelt Leads the Way

Franklin D. Roosevelt played no small part in shaping this change of opinion. As early as 1938, when few Americans could conceive of getting involved in a foreign war, and the French and British governments were appeasing Hitler in the belief that he wanted peace, Roosevelt concluded that only a show of force—or the use of it—would stop the Führer. In this

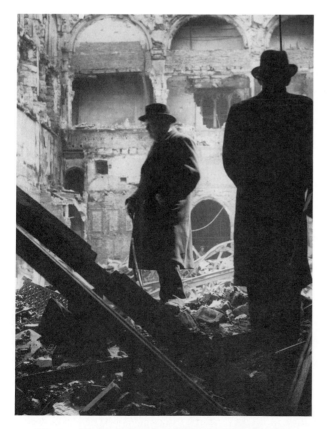

Winston Churchill stands amid the ruins of the bombed-out House of Commons, 1940.

opinion he was one with Winston Churchill, then a bellicose gadfly in Parliament, later the wartime prime minister and F.D.R.'s close personal friend.

But whereas Churchill was in opposition and could snipe at Britain's policy of appeasement, waiting for events to rally public opinion behind him, Roosevelt was president. He could not afford to get too far ahead of the country, least of all in calling for preparation for war. His technique was to float trial balloons by delivering militant anti-Nazi speeches. If the reaction was hostile, he backed down; if friendly, he moved ahead.

In 1939, at F.D.R.'s behest, Congress amended neutrality policy so that war materials could be sold on a cash-and-carry basis. (That is, American ships were still banned from the trade.) In 1940, with a large majority of Americans worried about how a Nazi victory would affect them, he announced that he was trading 50 old destroyers the British needed to counter German submarines for eight naval bases in Bermuda, Newfoundland, and British colonies in the Caribbean. Roosevelt described the deal as a defensive measure and not involvement in the war, which, strictly speaking, was so. Preparedness was also the justification for the Burke-Wadsworth Act of September 1940, which instituted the first peacetime draft law in American history (the term of service was one year) and appropriated $37 billion to build up the navy and army air corps.

It was comparatively easy to win support for these measures. Nevertheless, when Roosevelt decided to break with tradition in 1940 and run for a third term as president, he felt it necessary to assure the American people that "your boys are not going to be sent into any foreign wars."

The Third Term

Despite the shift in public opinion in favor of fighting Hitler, Roosevelt feared that an antiwar Republican candidate might eke out a victory against another less eminent Democrat. (The alternatives to F.D.R. were uninspiring: the tobacco-spitting vice president, John Nance Garner; Jim Farley, a political manager without a vision in his history; Joseph P. Kennedy, a playboy who thought prejudices were principles.) Indeed, F.D.R. remembered very well that Woodrow Wilson had won reelection in 1916 only by claiming the antiwar position for himself.

Therefore, he blithely ignored the two-term tradition, and the Democrats were delighted with his decision. However, the war versus peace debate never materialized. The Republicans chose a man who did not disagree with Roosevelt on any essentials. Indeed, utilities magnate Wendell Willkie had been a Democrat most of his life. An attractive and personable Indianian who had relocated to Wall Street, Willkie made it clear that he differed only in degree from the popular incumbent.

Thus, Willkie criticized the undeniable waste of many New Deal programs without calling for their abolition. He assailed the vast presidential powers that Roosevelt had assumed as bordering on dictatorship, but he did not propose to dismantle the huge executive apparatus that the New Deal had created. Willkie claimed that he was the better bet to keep the United States out of war, but he did not oppose either arming for defense or aiding Great Britain. In short, he offered Americans the kind of choice that was better resolved by sticking to the leader who was already tested.

Still, Willkie ran a strong race. He captured Maine, Vermont, and eight midwestern states and more popular votes than any losing candidate to that time, 45 percent of the total. But Roosevelt's popularity was too great to overcome. The president ran an incumbent's campaign. He did his job while the exuberant challenger barnstormed the country. His landmark third-term reelection, which broke the tradition established by Washington and Jefferson and challenged by only Grant and Theodore Roosevelt, was an anticlimax, and it did not interrupt the nation's drift toward war.

Undeclared War on Germany

A few weeks after the election, Roosevelt responded to Winston Churchill's plea for additional aid by sending the Lend-Lease bill to Congress. As enacted, the bill provided that the United States would serve as the "arsenal of democracy," turning out arms of all sorts to

Winston Churchill welcomes Franklin Roosevelt to the Atlantic Charter Conference, which took place off the Newfoundland coast, August 1941.

be "loaned" to Britain. Eventually, with lend-lease extended to the Soviet Union, such aid totaled $54 billion.

Because no amount of aid in materiel could help the British defend their shipping against "wolf packs" of German submarines, Roosevelt proclaimed a neutral zone that extended from North American waters to Iceland. He sent troops to Greenland, a possession of conquered Denmark, and ordered American destroyers to patrol the sea lanes, warning British ships of enemies beneath the waves. This permitted the British to concentrate their navy in the waters around their home islands.

The United States was at war in everything but name. Indeed, in August 1941, Roosevelt met with Churchill on two ships, the British *Prince of Wales* and the American *Augusta*, a cruiser, off the coast of Newfoundland. There they adopted what amounted to mutual war aims patterned after Wilson's Fourteen Points. The Atlantic Charter called for self-determination of nations after the war; free trade and freedom of the seas; the disarmament of aggressor nations; and some new means of collective world security, a provision that would evolve into the United Nations.

It was only a matter of time before guns were fired. After a few ambivalent incidents involving German submarines and American destroyers, the U.S.S. *Reuben James* was sunk in October 1941 with a loss of 100 sailors. Prowar sentiment flamed higher.

LEND-LEASE

Britain could not afford to pay for the destroyers that Winston Churchill requested at the end of 1940. Britain had spent $4.5 billion in the United States for arms, and in December 1940 had only $2 billion in reserve. Roosevelt explained the "loan" of the ships to Britain with the following parable:

Suppose my neighbor's house catches fire, and I have a length of garden hose. If he can take my garden hose and connect it up with his hydrant, I may help him to put out the fire.

Now what do I do? I don't say to him before that operation, "Neighbor, my garden hose cost me $15; you have to pay me $15 for it." What is the transaction that goes on? I don't want $15—I want my garden hose back after the fire is over.

H   O   W   T   H   E   Y   L   I   V   E   D

RATIONING AND SCRAP DRIVES

German submarines set a pair of four-man saboteur teams ashore in Florida and on Long Island. (They were immediately captured.) Japanese subs ran a few torpedoes up on California beaches,
and several paper bombs, explosives held aloft and
pushed by winds, detonated over Texas. Otherwise, the
continental United States was physically untouched by
the war that devastated most of Europe, half of China,
and the cities of Japan. Considering the colossal scale
of the American material contribution to the war, it is
a remarkable testament to the nation's wealth that people on the home front experienced the war only in the
form of shortages in consumer commodities and then
not to a degree that could be called sacrifice.

Because the Japanese quickly gained control of 97
percent of the world's rubber-tree plantations in Malaya, automobile tires were the first consumer goods to
be taken off the market. Washington froze the sale of
new tires and forbade recapping early in 1942; the
armed forces badly needed tires, and the national stock-
pile of rubber was only 660,000 tons, or just about
what civilians consumed in a year. Huge quantities
were collected in a scrap drive. One Seattle shoemaker
contributed 6 tons of worn rubber heels that he had
saved, and a Los Angeles tire dealer provided 5,000
tons of trade-ins. People cleared closets of old over-
shoes, and the Secretary of the Interior took to picking
up rubber doormats in federal office buildings. Unfortunately, reclaimed rubber was not suitable to tire manufacture, and doormats were usually made of previously
reclaimed rubber, so they were not particularly suitable
for new doormats.

It was fear of a rubber rather than a gasoline shortage
that accounted for the first controls on driving, although, on the east coast, which was dependent on
tanker imports, gasoline was also short by the summer
of 1942. The president proclaimed a nationwide speed
limit of 35 miles per hour, and pleasure driving was
banned. (Zealous officials of the Office of Price Administration jotted down license numbers at picnics, race
tracks, concert halls, and athletic events.) In addition,
the total miles a car could be driven was limited by the
category of sticker issued to each owner. Ordinary mo-
torists received "A" cards, entitling them to four gallons of gasoline a week, later three, and for a short
time only two. A "B" card added a few gallons; these
were issued to workers in defense plants for whom driving to work was necessary. Physicians and others whose
driving was essential got "C" cards, a few more gallons.
Truckers ("T") got unlimited gas, as did some others,
including political bigwigs who got "X" cards (a source
of resentment). Counterfeiting and selling of gas cards
(usually "C" category) was common, as was theft from
government warehouses. The OPA discovered that 20
million gallons' worth of cards were stolen in Washington alone.

*A group of children, signaling a "V" for victory, display
a pile of scrap metal collected for the war effort.*

Surplus gasoline could not be collected, but just
about every other commodity that was vital to the war
effort could be and was. Community organizations like
the Boy Scouts sponsored scrap drives through 1942
and 1943, collecting iron, steel, brass, bronze, tin, nylon stockings (for powder bags), bacon grease (for munitions manufacture), and waste paper. Many of these
campaigns were more trouble than they were worth, but
not those that collected iron, steel, tin, and paper.
Scrap iron and steel made a significant contribution to
the national output, and about half of the tin and paper products came not from mines and forests but from
neighborhood drives. So assiduous were the Boy Scouts
in their scrap-paper drive of 1942 that in June the government had to call a halt to it; the nation's paper
mills simply could not keep up with the supply of "raw
materials."

The tin shortage was responsible for the rationing of
canned goods. In order to buy a can of corn or sar-
dines, as well as coffee, butter, cheese, meat, and many
other food items, a consumer had to hand the grocer
ration stamps as well as money. These stamps were issued regularly in books and served as a second, parallel
currency. In order to buy a pound of hamburger, a
shopper needed stamps worth 7 "points" as well as the
purchase price. A pound of butter cost 16 points; a
pound of cheese, 8 points; and so on. The tiny

stamps—which were color-coded red (meat, butter), blue (processed food), green, and brown—were a tremendous bother. More than 3.5 billion of them changed hands every month. In order to restock shelves, a grocer had to turn in the stamps to a wholesaler, who, in turn, had to deposit them with a bank in order to make additional purchases.

Everyone had a complaint of one sort or another, although, except for butter, the allotments were not stringent. For example, the weekly sugar ration was 8 ounces a person, about as much as a dentist would wish on a patient in the best of times. In 1943, the standard of living was 16 percent higher than it had been in 1939, and by 1945, despite rationing, Americans were eating more food and spending more money on it than ever before. Among the major foods, only butter consumption dropped appreciably, from seventeen to eleven pounds per capita per year, and some home economists believed that because of butter rationing, a larger proportion of the population was eating it.

In fact, the OPA noticed a curious fact about consumer habits in the cases of coffee and cigarettes. Coffee was rationed because of the shortage of ships available to carry it from South America. When rationing began in November 1942 (one pound a person per five weeks), people began to hoard it. At restaurants, some diners would trade their dessert for an extra cup. When rationing of coffee was dropped in July 1943, sales of coffee dropped! Then, in the autumn of 1943, when a coffee stamp was inadvertently included in ration books, Americans anticipated that coffee would be rationed again and stripped the market shelves bare. When the OPA announced that there would be no coffee ration, sales dropped again.

Cigarettes were rationed because 30 percent of the industry's production was reserved for the armed forces, which comprised only 10 percent of the population. The government was, in effect, subsidizing the smoking habit among the men and women in the service. At home, the operation of the principle that scarcity equals status may also have caused an increase in the incidence of the bad habit.

A much more salutary consequence of wartime shortages was the popularity of gardening. There was no shortage of fresh vegetables, and they were never rationed. But because canned vegetables were and because truck and train space was invaluable, the government encouraged the planting of Victory gardens. Some 20.5 million individuals and families planted them, and by 1945, consumers were raising between 30 and 40 percent of all the vegetables grown in the United States. Nutritionists recognized that this was paying dividends in the national diet, but when the war was over, Americans quickly shed their good taste. By 1950, they had returned to canned vegetables and to the frozen products of Clarence Birdseye.

A Nasty Debate

Roosevelt still did not ask Congress for a formal declaration of war. He hoped that Britain and the Soviet Union could defeat Germany without the expenditure of American lives, a commodity with which every wartime American president since Lincoln had been cautious. More important, Roosevelt did not want to go to war without a unified nation behind him. By the autumn of 1941, he had his majority. Most Americans had concluded, without enthusiasm but with resolve, that Hitler must be stopped at any cost. Even the Communist party, which had opposed American intervention until Hitler invaded the Soviet Union, was now in the prowar camp, and much of the eastern big-business establishment had concluded that Hitler represented a threat to American commercial primacy in the world.

There was, however, an opposition. Roosevelt did not worry about the antiwar agitation of extremist Hitler supporters such as Father Coughlin and members of the Bund and Silver Shirts. But he was concerned about the old-fashioned isolationists who formed the well-financed and active America First Committee. Former president Herbert Hoover, ex-New Dealer Hugh Johnson, and progressive intellectuals such as Charles A. Beard despised Hitlerism. Whatever hostility toward Great Britain they harbored was aimed at British imperialism; they feared that the United States would go to war to protect the British Empire, an unworthy goal in their eyes. Their priority in supporting the America First Committee was to avoid making the mistake of 1917 as they saw it—pulling British chestnuts out of the fire.

The America First Committee's case was weakened because most of its members agreed that the United States should arm for defense. Roosevelt and the rival Committee to Defend America by Aiding the Allies described every contribution to the British cause in just such terms, and this justification confounded the isolationists. Nevertheless, Roosevelt hesitated. He confided to Winston Churchill that he would not ask for war until some dramatic incident—in other words, a direct attack on the United States—rallied the America Firsters to his cause.

As it turned out, the bitter debate over intervention missed the point. Both sides in the argument trained their eyes on Europe and the Atlantic as the crisis area. The dramatic incident was to occur in the Pacific, where Japan moved into the former French colonies of Indochina and continued its war against the indecisive government of Chiang Kai-shek. War in Asia was an old story. It seemed reasonable to conclude that it would go on indefinitely without a decisive turn

Destruction of the American fleet at Pearl Harbor, December 7, 1941.

in either direction. If Roosevelt took a tougher line toward Japan after the occupation of Indochina, negotiations with Tokyo continued too, into the summer and autumn of 1941.

AMERICA GOES TO WAR

All the while the Japanese "peace party," headed by Prince Fumimaro Konoye, continued to negotiate during the summer of 1941, the prowar faction of the imperial government, headed by General Hideki Tojo, increased its influence. When he was named premier in October 1941, Tojo gave the negotiators until early November to come up with a formula for peace that the United States would accept. But the minimum Japanese demand that Japan be recognized as the dom-

inant economic power in China could not be reconciled with the Open Door Policy, to which the United States was committed.

Pearl Harbor

Curiously, the Japanese and American governments concluded on the same day that they were unlikely to resolve their differences peacefully. Talks continued, as they always do, but Secretary of State Hull told the War Department that it should take over responsibility for Japanese-American relations, and military commanders in the Pacific were warned that hostilities could begin at any minute. In fact, the Japanese had initiated preparations for an attack that could not easily be reversed.

On December 7, 1941, it was launched. Admiral Isoroku Yamamoto, a tragic figure who admired the

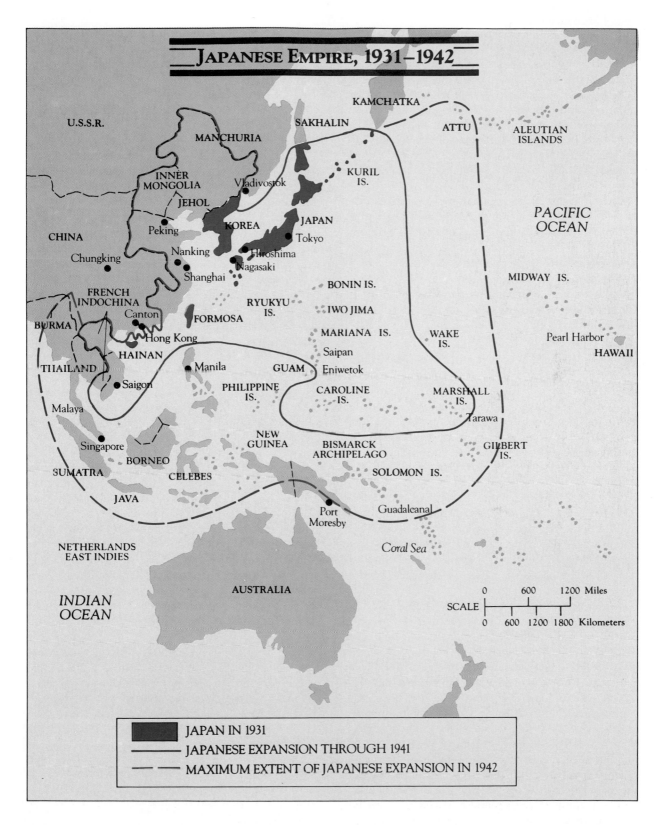

JAPANESE EMPIRE, 1931–1942

U.S.S.R.

MANCHURIA

KAMCHATKA

SAKHALIN

ATTU

ALEUTIAN
ISLANDS

INNER
MONGOLIA

Vladivostok

KURIL
IS.

JEHOL

CHINA

Peking

KOREA

JAPAN

Tokyo

PACIFIC
OCEAN

Chungking

Nanking

Hiroshima
Nagasaki

Shanghai

MIDWAY IS.

BONIN IS.

FRENCH
INDOCHINA

RYUKYU
IS.

IWO JIMA

BURMA

Canton

FORMOSA

MARIANA IS.

WAKE
IS.

Pearl Harbor

Hong Kong

Saipan

HAWAII

HAINAN

THAILAND

Saigon

Manila

GUAM

Eniwetok

PHILIPPINE
IS.

CAROLINE
IS.

MARSHALL
IS.

Malaya

Tarawa

Singapore

NEW
GUINEA

BISMARCK
ARCHIPELAGO

GILBERT
IS.

BORNEO

SUMATRA

CELEBES

SOLOMON IS.

JAVA

Port
Moresby

Guadalcanal

NETHERLANDS
EAST INDIES

Coral Sea

INDIAN
OCEAN

AUSTRALIA

SCALE

0   600   1200 Miles

0   600 1200 1800 Kilometers

JAPAN IN 1931

JAPANESE EXPANSION THROUGH 1941

MAXIMUM EXTENT OF JAPANESE EXPANSION IN 1942

United States and feared the result of a war he did not want, engineered a tactically brilliant aerial attack on Pearl Harbor, the huge American naval base on Oahu in the Hawaiian Islands. His planes sank or badly damaged 8 battleships, 7 other vessels, and 188 airplanes, and killed or wounded 3,435 servicemen. Yamamoto did not fully join in the celebrations that swept over his fleet and the people of Japan. The three American aircraft carriers that he believed would be at Pearl Harbor were at sea when the assault force arrived and thus escaped unscathed.

Yamamoto understood that air power was the key to war in the broad Pacific, and, in this area, the United States retained superiority over Japan. As a one-time resident of the United States, he also appreciated better than did the Tojo group how great American industrial might was compared with Japan's.

"I fear we have only awakened a sleeping giant," he told his officers, "and his reaction will be terrible."

The Reaction

The wounded giant awakened with a start. Pearl Harbor was attacked on Sunday. The next day, Roosevelt went before Congress and described December 7, 1941, as "a day that will live in infamy." He got his unanimous vote, or very nearly so. In both houses of Congress, only Representative Jeannette Rankin of Montana, a pacifist who had voted against entry into the First World War, refused to endorse the declaration of war.

In every city in the nation during the next several weeks, the army and navy's enlistment offices were jammed with stunned and angry young men. Pearl Harbor was so traumatic an event in the lives of Americans that practically every individual remembered exactly what he or she had been doing when news of the attack was announced.

Quietly at the time, more publicly later, Roosevelt's critics accused him and other top officials of having plotted to keep Pearl Harbor and nearby Hickham Field, an air base, completely unprepared for the attack. It was said that Washington knew the assault was coming but withheld vital intelligence from Hawaii, sacrificing thousands of American lives for the political purpose of getting the United States into the war.

In truth, the lack of preparation at Pearl Harbor was stupid and shameful. As early as 1924, air-power advocate Billy Mitchell had said that Pearl was vulnerable to air attack. In 1932, Admiral Harry Yarnell had snuck two aircraft carriers and four cruisers to within bombing range of Oahu before he was detected. Had his force been hostile, an attack comparable to that of December 7, 1941, would have ensued. In early

December 1941, numerous indications that something was brewing either were ignored or reached the appropriate commanders after unjustifiable delays. At Hickham Field, fighter planes were drawn up wing tip to wing tip so that they could be protected against sabotage on the ground. This made destruction from the air all the simpler, and, even after the attack began, it was difficult to get the fighters into the air.

But to say that there was a deliberate conspiracy among the highest ranking officials in the United States government was absurd, an example of the paranoia that periodically taints American politics. The blunders of the military in Hawaii were just another example of the chronic incompetence inherent in all large organizations, and the key to the stunning Japanese victory was the brilliant planning behind it.

Nevertheless, there is no doubt that Roosevelt was relieved to get officially into the conflict with a united people behind him. He was totally convinced by December 1941 that the survival of democracy, freedom, and American influence in the world depended on the total defeat of the aggressor nations, which only American might could ensure.

Getting the Job Done

Of all the nations that went to war, only Japan, whose participation in the First World War had been nominal, celebrated at the start of it. In Europe and the United States, there was very little of the exuberance with which people had greeted the first days of the fighting in World War I. Among Americans, the attitude was that there was a job to be done.

The popular songs of the period were concerned with getting home again. There was a melancholy tenor to "I'll Be Seeing You" and "I'll Never Smile Again." The lyrics told of the sadness of separation, however necessary it might be. Few people were attracted by the foot-stomping patriotism of George M. Cohan's "Over There," the American anthem during the First World War.

Once in the service, soldiers and sailors referred to the conflict as "W-W-2," a sardonically mechanical description of a war that was reminiscent of the name

OLD PERSONAL FRIENDS

Kichisaburo Nomura, the Japanese ambassador to the United States during 1941, had known President Roosevelt personally for 25 years. Nomura had been naval attaché at the Japanese embassy during the First World War, when Roosevelt had been Undersecretary of the Navy.

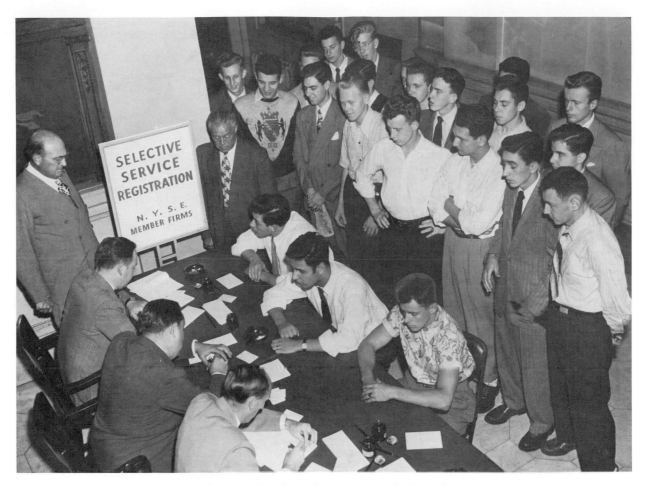

Page boys of the New York Stock Exchange register for the draft in 1942.

of a New Deal public works project. Indeed, because the country had been through it before, and because the New Deal reforms had introduced the idea of government-supervised order to the national economy, mobilization of resources and people was far more orderly and effective than it had been 25 years earlier.

Organizing for Victory

The mobilization of fighting capacity began before Pearl Harbor. By December 1941, more than 1.5 million men were in uniform, most of them well trained. By the end of the war, the total number of soldiers, sailors, and airmen, and women in auxiliary corps in every service climbed to 15 million.

The draft accounted for the majority of these "GI's," a name that referred to the "government issued" designation of uniforms and other equipage. Boards made up of local civic leaders worked efficiently and with comparatively few irregularities to fill the armed forces. The "Friends and Neighbors" who informed young men of their fate with the salutation "Greetings" ex-

empted only the physically disabled and those with work skills designated as essential to the war effort, including farmers and agricultural workers. As time passed, another sad category of those exempted was adopted: "sole surviving sons," men of draft age all of whose brothers had been killed in action. In the windows of homes which lost a soldier, small red, white, and blue banners, with stars enumerating the loss, were sometimes hung. The lady of the house was called a "Gold Star Mother."

Money was mobilized too. When the war began, the government was spending $2 billion a month on the military. During the first half of 1942, the expenditure rose to $15 billion a month. By the time Japan surrendered in August 1945, the costs of the war totaled more than $300 billion. In less than four years, the American government spent more money than it had spent during the previous 150 years of national existence. The national debt, already considered high in 1941 at $48 billion, doubled and redoubled to $247 billion in 1945.

Instead of building automobiles, this Chrysler assembly line turned out tanks for the war effort.

A few businessmen continued to oppose government policy, particularly the wartime labor laws. One of the most graceless was Sewell L. Avery, head of the huge Montgomery Ward retail chain. Roosevelt's policies had saved his company from bankruptcy, and during the war, full employment in the work force resulted in bonanza profits for retailers like him. But Avery had to be carried bodily to jail for refusing to obey a law that guaranteed his employees the right to join a union.

He was not typical. Most big businessmen, including former opponents of the administration, accepted unionization and rushed to Washington to assist the government. They were responding in part to the need for national unity. Corporation executives also recognized that wartime expenditures meant prosperity. General Motors, for example, received 8 percent of all federal expenditures between 1941 and 1945, $1 of every $12.50 that the government spent. Few criticisms came from the General Motors boardroom. Indeed, General Motors president William S. Knudsen was one of the most prominent "dollar-a-year men,"

business executives who worked for Roosevelt in effect without pay. He headed the War Resources Board (WRB), which had been established in August 1939 to plan for the conversion of factories for military production in the event of war. There was a bit of cynical palaver about the patriotic sacrifice dollar-a-year men were making but the country did need their organizational skills.

New Alphabet Agencies

After the congressional elections of 1942, which brought many conservative Republicans to Washington, Roosevelt announced that "Dr. New Deal" had been dismissed from the country's case and "Dr. Win-the-War" had been engaged. He explained that since there was now full employment, social programs were no longer necessary.

However, the New Dealers' practice of establishing government agencies to oversee public affairs was vastly expanded. In addition to Knudsen's WRB, the Supplies Priorities and Allocation Board (SPAB), under Donald M. Nelson of Sears Roebuck and Company, was commissioned to ensure that raw materials, particularly the scarce and critical ones, were diverted to military industries. The Office of Price Administration (OPA) had the task of controlling consumer prices so that the combination of high wages and scarce goods did not lead to runaway inflation.

After Pearl Harbor, a National War Labor Board (NWLB) was set up to mediate industrial disputes. Its principal purposes were to guarantee that production was not interrupted and that wage increases were kept within government-set limits. This offended many of Roosevelt's former supporters in the labor movement, none of them more important than John L. Lewis of the United Mine Workers, who returned to the Republican party. But the NWLB also worked to ensure that employees were not gouged by avaricious employers. The board was reasonably successful. There were strikes, including a serious one led by Lewis in 1943. But labor relations were generally good, and union membership continued to rise.

The Office of War Mobilization (OWM) was the most important of the new alphabet agencies. Theoretically, it oversaw all aspects of the mobilized economy, as Bernard Baruch had done during the First World War. It was considered to be sufficiently important that James F. Byrnes of South Carolina resigned from the Supreme Court to head it as a kind of "assistant president." Many believed that Byrnes's contribution to the war effort earned him the right to a presidential nomination.

Success

In essentials, Dr. Win-the-War's treatment was an overwhelming success. The size of the federal government swelled at a dizzying rate, from 1.1 million civilian employees in 1940 to 3.3 million in 1945. (State governments grew at almost the same rate.) Inevitably there was waste (agencies doing the same thing), inefficiency (agencies fighting at cross-purposes with one another), and corruption (many unessential jobs). But with national unity and military victory constantly touted as essential, the few critics of wartime problems, such as Senator Robert A. Taft of Ohio, sounded petty and were unable to carry the day. Taft was a carper. The most effective check on waste, inefficiency, and corruption, the Senate War Investigating Committee, was headed by a Democratic New Dealer, Senator Harry S Truman of Missouri.

The lessons learned during the First World War and the administrative skills of dollar-a-year businessmen and bureaucrats trained in the New Deal worked wonders on production. New factories and those formerly given to the manufacture of America's automobiles canceled civilian production and churned out trucks, tanks, the versatile jeeps, and amphibious vehicles in

incredible numbers. In 1944 alone, 96,000 airplanes (260 per day) rolled out of American factories. Industrialist Henry J. Kaiser perfected an assembly line for producing simple but serviceable freighters, the so-called Liberty ships. By 1943, his mammoth yards were christening a new one every day. Altogether, American shipbuilders sent 10 million tons of shipping down the ways between 1941 and 1945.

Such statistics would have been regarded as pipe dreams before the war. But they were duplicated in every basic industry, including steel, rubber, glass, aluminum, and electronics.

The Workers

Unemployment vanished as a social problem. Instead, factories running at capacity had difficulty finding people to fill jobs. There was a significant shift of population to the West Coast as the demands of the Pacific war led to the concentration of defense industries in such ports as Seattle, Oakland, San Diego, and Long Beach. Among the new Californians (the population of the Golden State rose from 6.9 million in 1940 to 10.5 million in 1950) were hundreds of thousands of blacks. Finding well-paid factory jobs that previously

LIBERTY SHIPS

Mass production means making something no better than it has to be in order to function. The idea is to turn the product out in vast numbers, quickly and cheaply. Mass production is, obviously, the basis of the high standard of living enjoyed by the masses of people of the United States and other advanced nations. However, one of the most amazing applications of the principle was not in the manufacture of consumer goods, but of the "liberty ship," a freighter built to carry the goods of war.

Liberty ships were "no frills" boxcars of the seas, 441 feet long, 57 feet across the beam, with a rudimentary steam engine. Some 800 of them were lost during the war, most to enemy action, but more than a few as the victims of storms. Because they were welded rather than riveted together, liberty ships were not the sturdiest of vessels.

But welding was what made it possible for American shipyards employing men and women who had never before built ships to float a liberty ship in as few as 40 days after the keel was laid. Some 2,700 were built between 1941 and 1944. Toward the end of the war, several rolled down the ways each day. Liberty ships were so cheap that if one completed a single voyage (carrying freight enough to fill 300 railroad cars), it paid for itself. Their design was such a masterpiece of simplicity that, with just a few old salts aboard, inexperienced crews of 45 (plus 35 navy gunners) could sail them.

*Henry J. Kaiser mass-produced cheap Liberty ships that permitted the United States to fight
a two-theater war.*

had been closed to them, blacks also won a sense of security, which had been unknown to earlier generations, because of the generally antiracist policies of the young CIO unions and F.D.R.'s executive order in 1941 that war contractors observe fair practices in employing blacks.

Economic equality for blacks remained a long way in the future. Everywhere they went they found resentments and discrimination, and serious race riots in 1943. Nevertheless, prodded by Eleanor Roosevelt and pressured by influential black leaders such as A. Philip Randolph of the Brotherhood of Sleeping Car Porters, F.D.R. issued an executive order forbidding racial discrimination in companies that benefited from government contracts.

Women, including many of middle age who never had worked for wages, entered the work force in large numbers. The symbol of the woman performing "unwomanly" work was "Rosie the Riveter," assembling airplanes and tanks with heavy riveting guns. Indeed, women did perform just about every kind of job in the industrial economy. Rosie dressed in slacks, tied up her hair in a bandanna, and left her children with her mother. But off the job, she remained reassuringly feminine by the standards of the time.

Curiously, these genuinely independent women did not turn to traditional feminism. Comparatively little was heard of demands for equality during the war. On the contrary, woman after woman told newspaper reporters that she looked forward to the end of the war, when she could quit her job to return home as wife and mother within the traditional family system. There were exceptions, of course. Many women enjoyed the economic and social freedom. For the most part, however, the female wartime workers were an ideal wartime work force: intelligent, educated, energetic, impelled by patriotism, and generally uninterested in competing with the soldiers who eventually would come back and take their jobs.

Prosperity at a Price

Labor shortages inevitably produced a demand for higher wages. The unions grew stronger; membership rose from 10.5 million to 14.7 million. With a few exceptions, however, strikes were short and did not disrupt production. The NWLB mediated disputes generally keeping raises within the limit of 15 percent over prewar levels that the government had set as an acceptable standard. This made the task of the OPA all the easier.

The success of the OPA was remarkable. Coveted consumer goods—coffee, butter, sugar, some canned foods, meat, shoes, liquor, silk, rayon, and nylon were scarce because of rationing, but high wages gave workers the money to spend on what there was. (Real wages rose 50 percent during the war.) There was a black market, or illegal sale of rationed goods, but it never got out of control, and prices rose only moderately between 1942 and 1945. Instead of consuming wholesale, Americans pumped their wages into savings accounts, including $15 billion in loans to the government in the form of war bonds. It became a point of patriotic pride with some women to paint the seam of a nylon stocking on the calf of a naked leg (although a pair of stockings remained a treasure).

There was a kind of good-humored innocence about the way Americans fought the Second World War. If they did not believe that a world free of problems would follow victory, which few doubted lay ahead, Americans were confident that they and their allies were in the right. By the time the fighting was over, 290,000 Americans were dead. But shocking as that figure is at first glance, and bloody as some individual battles were, American suffering was insignificant compared with that of other nations. Indeed, keeping the casualty list short was one of Roosevelt's priorities throughout the conflict, and he succeeded. If Winston Churchill was right in describing the year 1940, when the British stood alone against Nazism, as "their finest hour," the Second World War was an hour of confidence and pride for Americans too, particularly in view of the difficult depression era that had preceded the war and the age of anxiety that was to follow.

For Further Reading

General studies of foreign policy during the 1930s are numerous. The following are among the most useful: Selig Adler, *Uncertain Giant: American Foreign Policy Between the Wars* (1966); Charles A. Beard, *American Foreign Policy in the Making, 1932–1940* (1946); Paul Conkin, *The New Deal* (1975); Robert Dallek, *Franklin D. Roosevelt and American Foreign Policy, 1932–1945* (1979); R. H. Ferrell, *American Diplomacy in the Great Depression: Hoover-Stimson Foreign Policy, 1929–1933* (1957); William E. Leuchtenburg, *Franklin D. Roosevelt and the New Deal, 1932–1940* (1963); and John E. Wiltz, *From Isolationism to War, 1931–1941* (1968). A book that has profoundly influenced the writing of diplomatic history in the United States in our time is William A. Williams, *The Tragedy of American Diplomacy* (1962).

More intensively focused are W. S. Cole, *America First: The Battle Against Intervention* (1953); Robert A. Divine, *The Illusion of Neutrality* (1962); Lloyd C. Gardner, *Economic Aspects of New Deal Diplomacy* (1964); Walter Johnson, *The Battle Against Isolationism* (1944); Manfred Jonas, *Isolationism in America, 1935–1941* (1966); Warren F. Kimball, *The Most Unsordid Act: Lend Lease, 1939–1941* (1969); Basil Rauch, *Roosevelt: From Munich to Pearl Harbor* (1950); E. E. Robinson, *The Roosevelt Leadership* (1955); and Bryce Wood, *The Making of the Good Neighbor Policy* (1961).

Unsurprisingly, American-Japanese relations in the years leading up to Pearl Harbor have been extensively studied and yet remain a highly controversial subject. Just a few of the many books on the subject are Robert J. Burtow, *Tojo and the Coming of War* (1961); Herbert Feis, *The Road to Pearl Harbor* (1950); Akira Iriye, *After Imperialism: The Search for a New Order in the Far East, 1921–1933* (1965); Gordon W. Prange, *At Dawn We Slept: The Untold Story of Pearl Harbor* (1981); Robert Wohlsetter, *Pearl Harbor: Warning and Decision* (1962).

Biographical studies of key players in making foreign policy in this era are James MacGregor Burns, *Roosevelt: The Soldier of Freedom* (1970); Wayne S. Cole, *Gerald P. Nye and American Foreign Relations* (1962); Richard N. Current, *Secretary Stimson: A Study in Statecraft* (1954); Elting E. Morison, *Turmoil and Tradition: A Study of the Life and Times of Henry L. Stimson* (1960); J. W. Pratt, *Cordell Hull* (1964).

Nazi Germany was defeated by British pluck, Russian blood, and American industrial might. By holding out alone against Hitler in 1940 and 1941, Britain prevented him from establishing an impregnable Nazi "Fortress Europe" in the West. The British saved the foothold that made an invasion of Europe possible. In surviving a terrible onslaught and by sustaining sickening casualties—26 million citizens dead—the Soviet Union slowly sapped the might of the German *Wehrmacht*. The contribution of the United States was to keep both Britain and Russia afloat with Lend-lease and, beginning in 1942, to turn the tide with the full force of the world's most powerful nation. The Pacific war

45

AMERICA'S GREAT WAR

The United States at the Pinnacle of Power, 1942–1945

American troops on a Pacific beachhead during the Second World War.

against Imperial Japan was almost entirely an American show.

American strategists designed the formula that won World War II. American military administrators oversaw the huge and intricate apparatus of two military operations of unprecedented scale. Without the full participation of the United States, Germany and Japan might have been fought to a standstill. But they could not have been totally defeated. The Second World War was America's "Great War," the victory perhaps the chief contribution of the United States to western civilization.

STOPPING JAPAN

As in the First World War, the United States itself was not a battlefield in the Second World War, but Americans knew that they were in a fight between December 1941 and August 1945. Adults of the era were to remember—were to mark passages in their lives—by the dramatic events of the conflict: the day Pearl Harbor was attacked, D-Day when the invasion of Nazi-dominated Europe began, the day Franklin D. Roosevelt died, V-E Day and V-J Day, when Germany and Japan finally surrendered. The memories ended up sweet, to sustain a generation that their lives had meaning; but the memories began with defeat.

Humiliation and Anger

The first months after Pearl Harbor brought nothing but bad news to the United States. Immediately after Admiral Yamamoto paralyzed the American Pacific Fleet, the Japanese army advanced easily into Malaya, Hong Kong, the Philippines, Java, Guam, and even the two most distant islands of the American Aleutians. Within a few weeks, the dramatic Japanese battle flag, rays emanating from the rising sun, snapped in the breezes of British Singapore and Burma, and the Dutch East Indies, present-day Indonesia.

There was heroism in the disaster. On the principal island of the Philippines, Luzon, 20,000 crusty GI's under General Douglas MacArthur and a larger force of Filipinos fought valiantly on the Bataan Peninsula and the rocky island of Corregidor in Manila Bay. At first the men, most of them professional soldiers, thought they would be relieved or evacuated. Slowly the sickening truth sank in: they were quite alone, isolated by an ocean from a helpless navy, the doomed "battling bastards of Bataan." Nevertheless, they

grimly accepted the thankless, hopeless task of delaying the Japanese.

General MacArthur did not stay. Once President Roosevelt realized that the Philippines must fall, he ordered the nation's best-known general to flee to Australia. F.D.R. must have been tempted to let MacArthur fall into Japanese hands. He disliked and distrusted the general; as early as 1934 the president named MacArthur as one of the two most dangerous men in the United States, a threat to constitutional government. Indeed, outside a coterie of doggedly devoted aides, MacArthur riled much of the American military establishment. He was an egomaniac and a posturer, carefully cultivating an image complete with props—sunglasses, corncob pipe—a cooler "WASP" version of Benito Mussolini. "I studied dramatics under MacArthur," General Dwight D. Eisenhower wryly remarked.

Nevertheless, MacArthur was one of the army's senior professionals and F.D.R. believed him essential to winning the war against Japan. His connection with the Philippines was lifelong, intimate, and genuinely affectionate; his father had been military governor of the colony. When MacArthur fled the islands, he promoted his mystique and inspired the Philippine resistance, which proved to be heroic, with a radio message that concluded, "I shall return."

American soldiers surrender to the Japanese on the Philippine island of Corregidor in one of the bitterest military defeats in U.S. history.

On May 6, the last ragged defenders of Corregidor surrendered. Humiliation in the worst military defeat in the nation's history gave way to furious anger when reports trickled into the United States of Japanese cruelty toward the prisoners on the infamous Bataan Death March. Of 10,000 men forced to walk to a prison camp in the interior, 1,000 died on the way. (Another 5,000 of the captives died in the camps before the war was over.)

Japanese Strategy

While the siege of Corregidor dragged on, the Japanese piled up victories elsewhere in South Asia and Oceania. Under the command of Admiral Yamamoto, Japanese strategy was to establish a defense perimeter of fortified islands distant enough from Japan that the Americans, upon recuperating from Pearl Harbor, could not bomb Japan's home islands or force a battle in which the Japanese could be decisively defeated. Then, Japanese policymakers believed, they could negotiate a peace that left Japan in control of the resources of China and South Asia.

By early May 1942, the first phase of the plan—establishment of a distant perimeter—seemed near completion. Japanese soldiers occupied the Solomon Islands and conquered most of New Guinea. At Port Moresby, however, Australian and American forces halted the advance, preventing for the time being any serious assault on Australia. Yamamoto then moved his fleet, as yet unscarred, to the Coral Sea off Australia's northeastern coast. His object was to cut supply lines between Hawaii and Australia, thus choking off the resistance in New Guinea.

The Coral Sea and Midway

On May 6 and 7, 1942, the Japanese and American fleets fought a stand-off battle. The battle of the Coral Sea was a unique naval encounter in that the ships of the opposing forces never steamed within sight of one another. Carrier-based aircraft did the fighting, against one another and against enemy vessels. The Japanese lost fewer ships and planes than the Americans, but the battle was no Japanese victory. Yamamoto was forced to abandon his plan to cut the southern shipping lanes between Hawaii and Australia and, instead, to look to the central Pacific where Japanese supply lines were more secure. His object in the central Pacific was the American naval and air base on the island of Midway, about a thousand miles northwest of Hawaii.

There, between June 3 and 6, 1942, the Japanese suffered a critical defeat. The American fleet under Admirals Raymond A. Spruance and Frank J. Fletcher lost the carrier *Yorktown* to the excellent Japanese

Admiral Baron Isoroku Yamamoto (left) opposed war with the United States.

fighter planes, the "Zeroes," named for the Japanese insignia, a red sun. However, American planes destroyed four Japanese carriers.

It was far more than a one-for-four trade. Unlike the United States, Japan lacked the wealth and industrial capacity to replace so fabulously expensive a vessel as an aircraft carrier. Japan's offensive capacity was smashed just seven months after Pearl Harbor. Moreover, by holding Midway, the Americans controlled the central Pacific. Much earlier than he had planned, and closer to Japan than he had hoped, Yamamoto had to shift to defending what the Japanese had won.

The great commander did not live to see the disastrous end of the war that he had, in effect, predicted. In 1943, the Americans cracked the Japanese navy's communications code and learned that Yamamoto would be flying over Bougainville in the Solomon Islands. They shot down his plane, and Yamamoto was killed. Japan never produced another naval commander of his sagacity nor, during the war, another statesman of his moderation and good sense.

Anti-Japanese Hysteria

Not even the megalomaniacs among Japan's military rulers seriously entertained the possibility of invading the United States. Nevertheless, the stunning Japanese victories of early 1942 and the success of a few submarines in torpedoing ships off the beaches of Oregon and California caused ripples of invasion hysteria to wash over the Hawaiian Islands and the Pacific states. Newspaper magnate William Randolph Hearst, who had baited the Japanese with racial insults for 50

This girl was one of thousands of Japanese-Americans who were forced into concentration camps in 1942 without trial or substantial evidence of their danger to national security.

years, deluded himself into believing that his person was a prime Japanese target. He hurriedly moved out of San Simeon, his fantastic castle on an isolated stretch of the central California coast, for safer haunts inland. Humbler but equally nervous citizens organized patrols to keep an eye on the surf from the Canadian border to San Diego. For a few days, much of Los Angeles was in a panic.

In many California, Oregon, and Washington communities, anger over Pearl Harbor coalesced with long-standing racial hostility toward Japanese-Americans to result in spontaneous outbreaks of violence. Gangs of teenage toughs (and grown men) beat up Japanese and other Asians. People of Chinese and Korean descent took to wearing buttons identifying their origins in order to avoid problems.

West Coast politicians called for the imprisonment of Japanese-born noncitizens (known as *Issei*) and even their native-born children, the *Nisei*. At first, officials of the Justice Department resisted them. Various investigations before the war had revealed that only a few Japanese-Americans, most of whom were known to the Federal Bureau of Investigation, were disloyal and might represent a threat of sabotage. Even the Japanese consul in Los Angeles had advised Tokyo that no help would be forthcoming from the Japanese-American community.

But when the generally moderate governor of California, Earl Warren, and the commanding general at San Francisco's Presidio joined the anti-Japanese

clamor, Roosevelt gave in. Executive Order 9066 defined coastal areas as forbidden to "Japanese" residence, including American citizens. About 9,000 Nisei tried to leave the zone but many were thwarted by prejudice, turned back at the Nevada line or prevented from buying gasoline. In the first months of 1942, the federal government forcibly removed 110,000 Japanese-Americans from their homes, interning them in camps in seven states, from inland California to Arkansas.

Many liberals and more than a few government officials were appalled by the idea of American concentration camps. Because the criteria for relocation were ancestry and race, the federal government seemed clearly to be in violation of the Fourteenth Amendment to the Constitution. But feelings were too high for constitutional niceties. "If the Japs are released," Earl Warren said in June 1943 when there was talk of closing the camps, "no one will be able to tell a saboteur from any other Jap." In the case of *Korematsu* vs. *the United States* in 1944, a Supreme Court dominated by New Deal liberals voted 6 to 3 to uphold an action that cost 110,000 people their freedom for several years and about $350 million in property.

A Better Record

In Hawaii, ironically, where about one-third of the population was of Japanese ancestry, the Nisei were treated brusquely but not grossly abused. A few thousand known sympathizers with Japan were arrested, but, as a vital part of the islands' work force, Hawaiian-Japanese had to cope with only informal prejudice and the inconvenience of martial law. After repeated requests for a chance to prove their loyalty, 17,000 Hawaiian Nisei and some from the mainland fought against the Germans in Italy, turning in one of the war's best unit records for bravery. Others acted as interpreters in the Pacific theater.

Treatment of conscientious objectors and the few individuals who opposed the war on political grounds

SABOTEURS

The Germans attempted to put several teams of saboteurs in the United States from submarines, and there may have been some successful attempts at sabotage at defense plants. However, of 19,649 reported cases, the FBI was unable to trace a single one to enemy action. Between 1938 and 1945, the FBI arrested about 4,000 people, mostly German aliens, who were accused of espionage activities. Only 94 were convicted.

was exemplary in comparison with the treatment of Japanese-Americans. Never did government action approach the ugliness of the First World War period. While some 1,700 known Nazis and Fascists were arrested, German-Americans and Italian-Americans were not persecuted as a people. In retrospect, this might appear to be surprising since the war against Japan was essentially a war for economic domination of Asia, whereas Nazi Germany was palpably a criminal state that—it was clear by 1943—was practicing genocide against Europe's Jews.

But the Japanese were of a different race from most Americans and had a vastly different cultural attitude toward war. Americans found it easier to hate the enemy in Asia and to shrug off or support mistreatment of their distant cousins in the United States.

DEFEATING GERMANY FIRST

Even before the Japanese were stopped at the Battle of Midway, President Roosevelt and his advisers had concluded that they must defeat Germany first, directing the preponderance of American power to the European theater. Their reason was sound. Japan did not threaten the Western Hemisphere, but Germany did. The Nazis had ideological bed-mates in power in several South American republics and there were large German populations in Brazil, Uruguay, and Argentina.

More important, American strategists understood that, in time, Japan must inevitably buckle under superior American power; there was no need to rush in the Pacific. By way of contrast, if either Russia or England collapsed, or if Hitler were allowed too much time to entrench his regime on the continent of Europe, it might be impossible to defeat him. Already in 1942, the Germans were so firmly entrenched in western Europe that Allied leaders could not agree on how best to challenge them.

Friction among the Allies

Roosevelt and British Prime Minister Winston Churchill sometimes disagreed, but the two men were bound together by sincere mutual admiration and trust. Their relations with Soviet Premier Stalin, by way of contrast, was marred by suspicion that, on Stalin's part, bordered in paranoia. Churchill had been a staunch anti-Communist before the war and made no bones about the fact that the Russian alliance was a marriage of convenience. Roosevelt actually liked Stalin personally, and believed he could allay the Russian's suspicions that he and Churchill wanted to sit

the ground war out while Germany and the Soviet Union bled each other to exhaustion.

To weaken the German onslaught in Russia, the United States Army Air Corps (later the independent Air Force) joined the British in nearly constant day and night bombing raids over Germany. Eventually, 2.7 million tons of bombs would level German cities. Roosevelt also dispatched massive shipments of arms and other supplies to Russia and, on an impulse, told Stalin that, before 1942 was out, the British and Americans would open a second front on the ground in Europe, easing the horrendous pressure on the Soviets.

But a second front was out of the question in 1942. American industry was only in the process of converting to wartime production. The best the two western Allies could muster was an attack on German and Italian forces in North Africa.

The African Campaign and Stalingrad

The British and Anzacs (Australians and New Zealanders) had fought a see-saw stalemate in Libya and Egypt with German Field Marshal Erwin Rommel's *Afrika Korps* since the beginning of the war. In mid-1942, the Germans and some Italian desert forces held the forward line not far from Alexandria, threatening the Suez Canal, Britain's link with India. In June, under the command of British Marshal Bernard Montgomery, their arsenal beefed up by Sherman tanks from the United States, the British launched a counterattack at El Alamein. Montgomery sent the Germans reeling and, in November 1942, as he advanced from the east, Americans commanded by General Dwight D. Eisenhower landed far to the west in French North Africa.

Making a deal with French forces, which had been under the thumb of the Germans, Eisenhower moved eastward and, at Kasserine Pass in February 1943, American tank forces fought the first major American battle in the European theater. The confrontation appeared to be a draw when Hitler recalled Rommel, "the desert fox," to Germany. Without him at the helm, the *Afrika Korps* collapsed.

Almost simultaneously, deep within the Soviet Union, the Russians won a far more important victory, surrounding and capturing 250,000 seasoned German soldiers at Stalingrad. There seemed little doubt in any Allied capital that the course of the war had been turned against the Germans. However, the German defeat in North Africa, instead of resulting in relief for the Soviets, enabled Hitler to send even more troops into Russia. Roosevelt told Churchill that "Uncle Joe," as he called Stalin, "is killing more Germans and destroying more equipment than you and I put together."

The Invasion of Italy

In July 1943, an American, British, and Anzac force opened what they believed would be a second front by invading Sicily. After initial reverses, they conquered the island in six weeks and Americans got a colorful hero to crow about: the eccentric General George Patton, who rallied his troops in coarse "blood and guts" language and was a personally brave, even reckless commander of tanks, a cavalry officer from out of the past. (In fact, Patton believed in reincarnation and thought he had lived as any number of fabled soldiers in past lives.)

Patton and General Omar Bradley promptly moved into Italy proper and knocked the Italian army out of the war. Already beset by guerrilla action behind the lines by Italian partisans, mostly Socialists and Communists, Mussolini was ousted by the conservative Field Marshal Pietro Badoglio who believed, quite correctly, that his country had become Hitler's pawn.

Nevertheless, the victories in Italy soon soured. Hitler rescued Mussolini from his captors and established him as the puppet head of the "Republic of Salo" in northern Italy. To take the place of the Italian troops who had gone over to the Allies, he withdrew German units to easily defend strongholds south of Rome. It was ruggedly mountainous country, and only after eight months of bloody, almost constant battle did the Americans reach the capital.

Then, once again, the Germans held. Despite massive bombardment that plunged Italian cities into famine, Hitler was able to establish a defensive line across the Italian boot with very few troops. Germany itself would fall to the Allies before they made much headway against the *Wehrmacht*'s positions in the South. Italy was not the second front that Stalin wanted and Churchill and Roosevelt wanted to give him.

Ike

Churchill wanted to invade through the Balkans, which he called "the soft underbelly of Europe." Roo-

General Dwight D. Eisenhower briefs a group of paratroopers about to leave for the coast of France where they would be among 1 million Allied troops who began liberating that country from Nazi control, June 6, 1944.

THE
EUROPEAN THEATER

SCALE

ALLIED OFFENSIVES
FARTHEST GERMAN
PENETRATION, NOVEMBER 1942

sevelt and his advisors disagreed, believing that the mountains of Greece and Yugoslavia would provide the Germans with the same protections they found in Italy. Moreover, they regarded the problem of supplying an army in the Eastern Mediterranean as unnecessarily difficult. Their plan, slated for 1944, was to attack Hitler's Fortress Europe from Britain, across the English Channel into France.

"Operation Overlord" was to be the largest amphibious invasion in history. To direct it, Roosevelt called on Chief of Staff George C. Marshall, who made a choice of commander that was surprising to many. Marshall chose General Dwight D. Eisenhower, known universally as "Ike." Eisenhower had had a respectable but far from brilliant career in the peacetime army. He had been able enough a field com-

mander in North Africa but by no means an outstanding one. He was not a colorful figure like MacArthur, nor particularly popular with the troops like his friend Omar Bradley. Eisenhower was a desk general, an executive, but such a man, an organizer, was precisely what was called for by an enterprise of the scale of Operation Overlord.

Eisenhower had another indispensable talent. He was a natural diplomat. He had a temper; close aides were terrified by his tirades in private. But when the doors opened and colleagues entered, he was supremely affable, smiling, conciliatory, willing to bend on nonessentials, pleasantly firm in pushing through plans on which his superiors had agreed. Eisenhower had a genius for smoothing over differences among headstrong associates, with whom he was surrounded. Churchill was a great man and aware of it. Field Marshall Montgomery was hideously vain and peevish, the very opposite of Eisenhower. The leader of the Free French in England, Charles DeGaulle, would not accept the fact that he was a principal in making plans more out of courtesy than because of the forces at his disposal. Eisenhower even forged a friendly working relationship with Soviet Marshal Georgi Zhukov.

D-Day

Most important, Eisenhower was cautious and thorough, knowing that if the invasion of France failed, the war in Europe might well be lost. His task was immense beyond imagining. He had to find and mobilize 4,000 vessels, 11,000 aircraft, tens of thousands of motor vehicles and weapons of various sorts, as well as billeting and training more than 2 million soldiers. Such a massive operation could not go unnoticed by the Germans, of course, but the British and Americans successfully kept secret the date of "D-Day" and, rather more remarkably, the place of the invasion.

The date was June 6, 1944, and the place was Normandy in northwestern France. Eisenhower's caution and meticulous planning of every detail paid off. The

Allied troops—1 million men—marched across France and into Paris on August 25. Immediately thereafter they entered Belgium. By September, they were across the German border, farther than the Allies had penetrated by the end of the First World War.

Politics and Strategy

The British and Americans disagreed about how to finish off Germany. Montgomery wanted to concentrate all Allied forces into one thrust into the heart of Germany, a traditional strategy that had much to recommend it. Tactfully, Eisenhower overruled him. In part his decision was military, reflecting his innate cautiousness and perhaps his study of the American Civil War, in which such concentrated assaults were repeatedly stymied. Eisenhower feared that extending supply lines too quickly would tempt the Germans into a massive counterattack that might lead to disaster, a much longer war, even the necessity of negotiating a peace. He preferred to exploit the overwhelming Allied superiority in arms and men by advancing slowly on a broad front that extended from the North Sea to the border of Switzerland, strangling Germany as Grant had strangled the Confederacy.

The ruins of Dresden, Germany, following British and American bombing raids during February 1945.

Diplomatic considerations entered into Eisenhower's decision too. Still absorbing tremendous casualties as they slowly pushed the Germans westward, the Russians remained suspicious of American and British motives. Stalin jumped at every rumor that his allies were considering a separate peace. Some American diplomats feared that too rapid an American and British thrust would only arouse Stalin's suspicions that, when Germany was finished off, the Allies would turn on Russia. On an earthier level, Eisenhower worried about spontaneous trouble between his soldiers and the Red Army if an orderly rendezvous were not arranged in advance.

The Bulge and the End

For a while in 1944, it appeared that Eisenhower's strategy of advancing slowly was a mistake. In the summer, V-2 rockets from sanctuaries inside Germany began to rain down on London, killing 8,000 people. The V-2's were not decisive weapons from a military point of view, but with the end of the war apparently in sight, their psychological effect was disheartening to civilians. There was no warning from a V-2, as there was in conventional aerial attack—only a whine high in the air, a few seconds of silence, and an explosion.

Much more demoralizing was a German military counteroffensive in Belgium in the bitter cold and snowy December of 1944. In the Battle of the Bulge, German troops pushed the Americans and British back, creating a "bulge" in the lines and threatening to split the Allied forces in two. But an army under General Anthony McAuliffe that was isolated at Bastogne refused to surrender ("Nuts!" McAuliffe replied to the German commander), weakening the German offensive as the Belgians had done at Li'ege in 1914.

Then, a break in the weather allowed the Allies to exploit their air superiority and, after two weeks, they advanced again. One by one German defenses collapsed.

Along with his oldest and closest Nazi party associates, a Hitler close to breakdown withdrew to a bunker under the streets of Berlin where he presided over the premature disintegration of his "Thousand-Year Empire." To the end, he thought in terms of the perverted romanticism of his ideology. It was *Götterdämmerung*, the mythical final battle of the Norse gods. On April 30, 1945, Hitler committed suicide after having named Admiral Karl Doenitz his successor as *Führer*. A few days later, Doenitz surrendered.

Wartime Diplomacy

Eisenhower's sensitivity to Russian suspicions reflected President Roosevelt's policy. At a personal meeting with Stalin at Teheran in Iran late in 1943, and again at Yalta in the Crimea in February 1945, F.D.R. did his best to assuage the Russian's fears by acquiescing or, at least, by not strenuously resisting Stalin's proposals for the organization of postwar Europe.

In after years, when the Soviet Union was the Cold War enemy and Americans had come to lament Russian domination of Eastern Europe, Yalta became a

General Anthony McAuliffe (left) and General George Patton inspect Bastogne during the Battle of the Bulge.

Winston Churchill, Franklin D. Roosevelt, and Joseph Stalin pose for photographers at Yalta,
February 1945.

byword for diplomatic blunder and even, to a few extremists, for treasonous "sellout" to Communism. It was at Yalta that Roosevelt and Churchill tacitly consented to Stalin's insistence that the Soviet Union had "special interests" in Eastern Europe, that is, governments friendly to the Soviet Union.

Right-wing extremists were later to say that F.D.R. betrayed the Poles, Czechs, Hungarians, Rumanians, and Bulgarians because he was himself sympathetic to Communism. Other less hysterical analysts suspected that the president's weariness and illness, obvious in the haggard face and sagging jaw of the official photographs, caused him to reason poorly in dealing with the calculating Stalin.

Whatever effect Roosevelt's failing health had on his mental processes, there was nothing irrational about his concessions to Russia. Roosevelt and Churchill did not give Stalin anything that he did not already have. In February 1945, the Red Army was racing over and occupying the very countries that Stalin envisioned as buffer states against renewed German aggression or other threats from the West. No doubt Churchill and F.D.R. expected the postwar states of Eastern Europe to have greater independence than Stalin was willing to allow. Historians disagree as to whether Stalin intended to enforce an iron grip on the region in 1945 or altered his policy later, when the Cold War was underway.

THE TWILIGHT OF JAPAN, THE NUCLEAR DAWN

Also influencing Roosevelt at Yalta was his desire to enlist the Soviet Union in the war against Japan in order to save American lives in the final battles. While agreeing that the Red Army would attack Japanese forces in China, Stalin insisted on delaying action until the Soviet Union felt secure in Europe.

Pacific Strategy

After Midway in June 1942, American strategy in the war against Japan involved three distinct campaigns. First, just as the United States pumped material into Russia, supplies were flown into China from India, "over the hump" of the Himalayas, in order to keep the Chinese in the war. Unfortunately, Chiang Kai-shek was no Stalin, and his Guomindang troops were no Red Army.

Chiang hated and feared his Chinese Communist allies as much as he hated the Japanese. He diverted hundreds of thousands of troops to battling them, and never forced the kind of battle on the Japanese that the Americans needed in order to weaken Japanese defenses in the Pacific. Inefficiency and corruption in Chiang's government resulted in gross misuse of American supplies.

General Joseph W. "Vinegar Joe" Stilwell, the gritty American commander in China, despised Chiang. He poured out an avalanche of warnings to Washington about the incompetence of "the monkey," as he called the Generalissimo, and the corruption of his political allies. But when Stilwell tried to get command of the Chinese army for himself, Roosevelt recalled him. Somewhat to Churchill's amazement, Roosevelt was convinced that Chiang was a valuable ally.

The second and third prongs of the attack on Japan were more successful, but extremely bloody. After driving the Japanese out of the Solomons in order to ensure Australia's security, one force under MacArthur began to push toward the Japanese homeland via New Guinea and the Philippines. Another, commanded by Admiral Chester W. Nimitz, struck through the central Pacific, capturing islands from which aircraft could reach and bomb Japan.

Island Warfare

To soldiers slogging through the mud and frigid cold of Italy and France, the troops in the Pacific were on

An apprehensive Marine photographed during battle against the Japanese on Peleliu Island, Palau, May 1945.

a picnic, basking in a lovely climate and only periodically meeting the enemy in battle. Ernie Pyle, considered the best newspaper correspondent of the war, made this comparison in his celebration of the American fighting man in Europe. (Ironically, Pyle survived Europe and was killed by Japanese machine-gun fire on Ie Shima in the closing months of the war.)

Life behind the lines in the Pacific was pleasant, if not quite idyllic. But capturing islands that were specks on the map meant battles more vicious than those in Europe. The Japanese soldier was a formidable fighter. He was indoctrinated with a fanatical sense of duty and taught that it was a betrayal of national and personal honor to surrender, even when his army was obviously defeated. Japanese soldiers were sworn to fight to the death, taking down as many of the enemy as they could.

To an astonishing degree, this was how they fought. It took the Americans six months to win control of microscopic Guadalcanal in the Solomons beginning in August 1942, even though the defenders had not had time to complete their fortifications.

In New Guinea and along the route through the Gilbert, Marshall, and Mariana islands that Nimitz was to follow, the concrete bunkers and gun emplacements were stronger than in the Solomons, and the resistance of the Japanese was chillingly effective. Marines discovered at places like Tarawa in the Gilberts in November 1943 that when a battle was over, they

WORLD WAR II CASUALTIES			
	Total mobilized	Killed or died	Wounded
United States	16,113,000	407,000	672,000
China	17,251,000	1,325,000	1,762,000
Germany	20,000,000	3,250,000	7,250,000
Italy	3,100,000	136,000	225,000
Japan	9,700,000	1,270,000	140,000
U.S.S.R.	—	6,115,000	14,012,000
United Kingdom	5,896,000	357,000	369,000
TOTAL	72,060,000	12,860,000	24,430,000

STUDYING A NEW KIND OF WAR

"Tarawa was not a very big battle, as battles go," wrote G. D. Lillibridge, the historian who was a second lieutenant there in November 1943, "and it was all over in seventy-two hours." The casualties totaled only 3,300 U.S. Marines, about the same number of elite Japanese Special Naval Landing Forces, and 2,000 Japanese and Korean laborers who doubled as soldiers. A few months earlier, by comparison, half a world away in the Stalingrad campaign, the German *Wehrmacht* lost 500,000 men.

And yet, like Stalingrad, "Bloody Tarawa" was a landmark, even a turning point, of the Second World War. If the numbers were trivial, the incidence of the casualties was appalling, especially for a nation whose wartime leaders, since Lincoln and Grant, have thought of minimizing losses in battle as a major determinant of strategy. Lillibridge's 39-man platoon lost 26; 323 of 500 drivers of landing craft died; overall, more than one-third of the American attackers were killed or wounded. The figures stunned the admirals who planned the battle and the people at home who read about it.

So did the fanaticism of the Japanese defenders. Americans had heard that the Japanese fighting man considered surrender under any circumstances to be shameful. That was in the abstract. Few were prepared to learn that only 17 of 5,000 Japanese on the tiny atoll of Betio were captured, most of them because they were too seriously wounded to commit suicide.

This willingness to die for nothing but a code of honor incomprehensible to Americans was not something that could be taught in a training film. It was bred into Japan's young men from infancy. In his reflections on the battle, something of an attempt to exorcise demons that had haunted him for 25 years, Lillibridge remembered a Japanese man his platoon had trapped during the mopping-up operation. Another Japanese Marine was moaning in agony from his wounds. The defender would reassure his dying friend, then hurl challenges and insults at Lillibridge's platoon,

his voice raised against us in the raging pitch that comes from fear and anger and then lowered to a soothing tone as he sought to comfort his mortally wounded companion. . . . Doomed and knowing he was doomed, he never lost control of himself and remained in command of the situation until the end.

Betio, only two miles long and 800 yards wide—half the size of New York's Central Park—was the largest of the 25 islands of the Tarawa atoll, a coral formation in the sprawling Gilbert Islands. The Japanese airstrip there was the chief strategic objective of the American assault. Japanese planes based in Tarawa could worry American supply lines between Hawaii and Australia.

"Bloody Tarawa" the day after the battle, November 22, 1943.

In a way, by November 1943, Tarawa represented the final fragment of Japanese offensive capability.

It was a tiny fragment. Just as important as the airstrip to Admirals Chester W. Nimitz and Raymond Spruance was to use Tarawa to test their theories of amphibious assault before what was anticipated to be far more difficult fighting in the Marshall Islands early in 1944 and, after that, an island by island advance toward Japan.

"There had to be a Tarawa, a first assault on a strongly defended coral atoll," an American officer explained. An amphibious assault against an entrenched, waiting enemy was a new kind of war for the American military, or at least an untried technique. Ironically, the Americans thought that Tarawa would be easy, more training-exercise than battle. They had no illusions about the fierceness of Japanese troops. However, Betio was small; the Japanese had been digging in there a comparatively short time; the American assault force was huge, covering eight square miles of Pacific; and officers awed by the destructiveness of naval bombardment were sure they would "obliterate the defenses on Betio." Taking his cue from his superiors, Lieutenant Lillibridge told his platoon that "there was no need to worry, no necessity for anyone to get killed, although possibly someone might get slightly wounded."

In fact, the pre-dawn bombardment did destroy Rear Admiral Keiji Shibasaki's communications with most of his troops. However, the network of concrete blockhouses, coconut-log pillboxes, and underwater barricades he had built in just a few months, what one analyst called a "complete defensive system," was substantially untouched by the big guns and aerial bombs. The willingness of the Japanese marines and even common laborers to die more than compensated for their isolation from Shibasaki's bunker.

Nature more than compensated for the massiveness of the American attack. The tide was lower than hoped and the larger American landing crafts could not clear the reef that fringed Betio. This meant that all but the first wave of marines had to wade, breast deep, 800 yards to shore.

This was the element of amphibious attack in the Pacific that was really tested at Tarawa. Could men with no more armor than "a khaki shirt," no way to defend themselves, and in effect no support while they were slogging half a mile in water, even get to the beach, let alone establish enough of a base from which to displace enemies who, during this same critical time, were free to wreak havoc with them?

Getting to the beach was the first horror that would haunt the survivors of Tarawa and subsequent Pacific landings for the rest of their lives. Men remembered it as a "nightmarish turtle race," run in slow-motion. It was "like being completely suspended, like being under a strong anesthetic." "I could have sworn that I could have reached out and touched a hundred bullets." "The water never seemed clear of tiny men."

It was their tininess, perhaps, that enabled the Americans to reach the beach through a storm of machine-gun and cannon fire. They had to push through the floating corpses of their comrades, hundreds of thousands of fish killed by the bombardment, stepping on other dead marines. The lagoon was literally red with blood for hours.

The second nightmare waited on the beach. Shibasaki had constructed a sea wall of coconut logs, three to five feet high. At first it seemed to be a shelter. The exhausted marines threw themselves under it. In fact, Japanese mortars had been meticulously registered to batter the long thin line, while to peek above the palisade meant to draw the fire of 200 perfectly positioned Japanese machines guns. More than one marine remembered that he was capable of moving beyond the sea wall only because to remain there meant certain death. About half the American casualties were suffered in the water, most of the rest on the beach. The carnage was condensed in such a way as to leave lifelong psychological scars.

One by one, almost always at close quarters, the blockhouses and pillboxes were wiped out. Betio was taken in three days, only one more than called-for by commanders who thought it would be a "walkover." The aftermath was as morally devastating as the battle. Like at the Wilderness and the Marne, the vegetation that had covered the island was literally destroyed.

Hundreds of bodies floating in the surf and festering in the blockhouses bloated and rotted in the tropical heat. The triumphant marines looked like anything but victors. They sat staring, exhausted, just beginning to comprehend what they had been through, as if they had been captured by their enemies. "I passed boys who . . . looked older than their fathers," General Holland Smith said, "it had chilled their souls. They found it hard to believe they were actually alive."

Smith and the other commanders learned a great deal from the "training exercise" at Tarawa, not the least of which lessons was not to gamble on tides over coral reefs. Not until the last months of the Pacific War, when the close approach to the Japanese homeland made larger forces of Japanese defenders even fiercer in their resistance, would the extremity of Tarawa's terror be repeated.

The Pacific commanders also learned that while the vast American superiority of armament and firepower was essential and telling, taking the Pacific island was much more personal and human an effort than twentieth century military men had come to assume. With a grace rare in a modern officer, General Julian Smith frankly asserted,

There was one thing that won this battle . . . and that was the supreme courage of the Marines. The prisoners tell us that what broke their morale was not the bombing, not the naval gunfire, but the sight of Marines who kept coming ashore.

Soldiers in the European theater, Americans at home, and more than a few troops in the Pacific Campaign, looked on the Pacific war as a picnic. G. D. Lillibridge and others remembered the idyllic holiday quality, however involuntary the vacation was, of the long months between battles spent in Hawaii, Australia, or New Zealand. Correspondent Robert Sherrod, who lived through Tarawa, wrote of "the brilliant sunlight, the far-reaching, incredibly blue Pacific, the soft breezes at evening and the Southern Cross in the sky." The idyll became a part of American popular culture with the publication of James Michener's *Tales of the South Pacific*, and the musical comedy, *South Pacific*, that was based on it. Hawaii enjoyed a second great tourist boom (the first followed annexation) as a result of the Americans' rediscovery of the islands during the war.

But if life between battles was idyllic—and the whole Pacific war a pleasure to noncombat troops—the ferocity of battle was, as Lillibridge writes in another place, perhaps the greatest in the conflict.

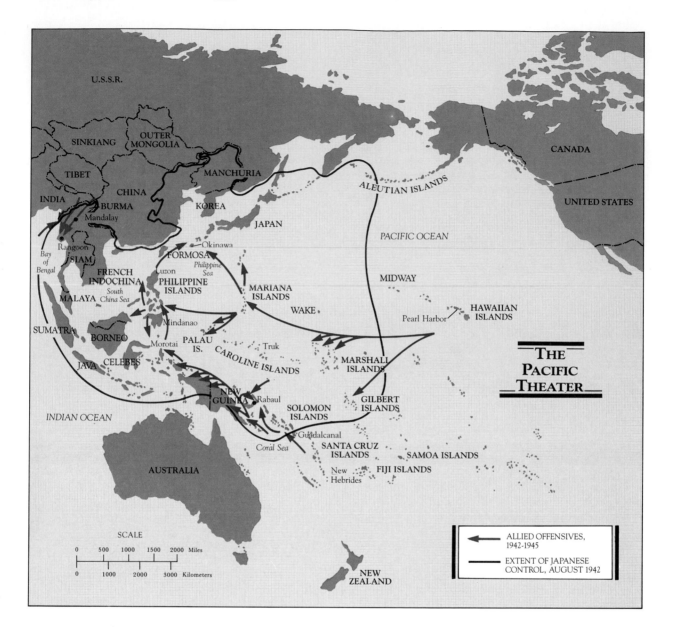

had few prisoners. They had to kill almost every Japanese on the island at high cost to themselves.

As MacArthur and Nimitz moved closer to Japan, the fighting grew tougher. Attacking the Marianas and the Philippines in 1944, both American forces were hit hard. But MacArthur's dramatic return to Luzon boosted morale, and Nimitz's capture of the Marianas enabled larger land-based American planes to bomb the Japanese homeland at will. The wooden cities of Japan went up like tinder when hit by incendiary devices. A single raid on Tokyo on March 9, 1945, killed 85,000 people and destroyed 250,000 buildings.

By no means were all the Japanese-occupied islands retaken. Both MacArthur and Nimitz advocated "island hopping," leaving less-important Japanese hold-

ings alone, to wither as they were cut off from supplies. When the war finally ended, there were still some Japanese units operating in New Guinea, the point of farthest Japanese advance.

Fighting to the Last Man

By the spring of 1945, Japan's situation was hopeless. Germany was defeated, thus freeing hundreds of thousands of battle-hardened soldiers for combat in the Pacific. Japan's leaders correctly calculated that the Soviet Union was on the verge of declaring war on them. After the huge Battle of Leyte Gulf in October 1944, the Japanese navy ceased to exist as a fighting force, while the Americans cruised the seas with 4,000 ships, shelling the Japanese coast at will. United States submarines, which were more effective than German U-boats ever had been, destroyed half of the island nation's vital merchant fleet within a few months.

Some Japanese leaders put out peace feelers via the Russians, with whom Japan was not yet at war. But the high command was divided. Fanatics high in the government prevented an open appeal for peace. They were themselves victims of the extreme nationalistic fervor they instilled in their men, and they had 5 million soldiers in uniform. There were 2 million in Japan itself, and about the same number in China, where Chiang's half-hearted warmaking had been just enough to forge them into first-rate soldiers without inflicting heavy casualties.

With so many soldiers fighting to the death, the taking of islands close to Japan resulted in hundreds of thousands of casualties. Iwo Jima, a desolate tiny volcano needed for a landing strip, cost 4,000 American lives. Saipan was even bloodier and the invasion of Okinawa, considered part of Japan, killed or wounded 80,000 Americans. In the same fighting, more than 100,000 Japanese died, and only 8,000 surrendered. Planners guessed that the invasion of Japan itself, scheduled for November 1, 1945, would cost 1 million casualties, as many as the United States had suffered in over three years of fighting in both Europe and the Pacific.

A Birth and a Death

This chilling prediction helped to make the atomic bomb so appealing to policymakers. The Manhattan Project, code name of the group that built the bomb, dated from 1939, when the German Jewish physicist Albert Einstein wrote to President Roosevelt that it was possible to unleash inconceivable amounts of energy by nuclear fission, splitting an atom. Einstein was a pacifist, but he was also a refugee from Nazism who believed that German science was capable of producing a nuclear bomb. Such a device in Hitler's hands was an appalling prospect.

Einstein was too prestigious to ignore, and the government secretly allotted $2 billion to the Manhattan Project. Under the direction of J. Robert Oppenheimer, scientists working on Long Island, underneath a football stadium in Chicago, and at isolated Los Alamos in New Mexico progressed steadily and, by April 1945, told Washington that they were four months away from testing a bomb.

A view of Hiroshima after it was flattened by an atomic bomb, August 6, 1945.

THE COSTS OF WAR

The Second World War was the most expensive war that the United States ever fought:

Revolutionary War	$149	million
War of 1812	124	million
Mexican War	107	million
Civil War (Union only)	8	billion
Spanish-American War	2.5	billion
First World War	66	billion
Second World War	560	billion
Korean War	70	billion
Vietnam War	121.5	billion

The decision whether or not to use it did not fall to President Roosevelt. Reelected to a fourth term in 1944 over Thomas E. Dewey, the governor of New York, Roosevelt died of a massive stroke on April 12, 1945. He was at Warm Springs, Georgia, sitting for a portrait painter when he said, "I have a terrific headache," slumped in his chair, and died.

The outpouring of grief that swept the nation at the loss of the man who had been in office longer than any other president was real and profound. Silent crowds lined the tracks to watch the train that brought F.D.R. back to Washington for the last time. People wept in the streets of every city. But in Washington, the sorrow was overshadowed by apprehensions that his successor, Harry S Truman, was not up to being president.

Truman, Little Boy, and Fat Man

Truman was an honest politico who had risen as a dependable and hard worker for the Kansas City machine of Boss Thomas J. Pendergast. He proved his abilities as chairman of an important Senate committee during the war, but impressed few as the caliber of person to head a nation. Unprepossessing in appearance and manner, bespectacled, something of a midwestern dandy (he once operated a haberdashery), and given to salty language, Truman had been nominated as vice president in 1944 as a compromise candidate. Democratic conservatives wanted the left-liberal vice president elected in 1940, Henry A. Wallace, out of the number two spot, but they could not force conservative James J. Byrnes on the liberals. The two wings of the party settled on Truman.

Truman was as shocked by his accession as anyone else. "I don't know whether you fellows ever had a load of hay or a bull fall on you," he told reporters on his first full day in office, "but last night the moon, the stars, and all the planets fell on me." If he joined others in being unsure of his abilities, Truman knew how to make difficult decisions and never doubted his responsibility to lead. A plaque on his desk read "The Buck Stops Here"; as the president of the United States, he could not "pass the buck" to anyone else.

Truman met with Churchill and Stalin at Potsdam in July 1945, but to Stalin only alluded to the existence of the bomb. When some—not all—of his advisors informed him that the alternative to using it was a conventional invasion of Japan and 1 million casualties, he opted as Roosevelt always had, to avoid massive carnage. On August 6, an atomic bomb nicknamed "Little Boy" was dropped on Hiroshima, killing 100,000 people in an instant and dooming another 100,000 to death from injury and radiation poisoning. Two days later, "Fat Man" was exploded over Nagasaki.

Incredibly, the Japanese high command still wanted to fight on. Had they known that the Americans had no more atomic bombs in their arsenal, they might have carried the debate. But Emperor Hirohito stepped in and agreed to surrender on August 15, 1945, if he were allowed to keep his throne. Because the Ameri-

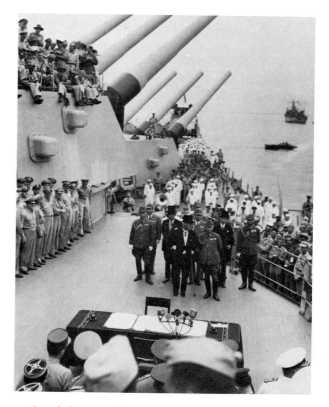

It took the personal intervention of Emperor Hirohito to persuade the Japanese military to surrender to the United States. The official surrender took place aboard the battleship Missouri *on September 2, 1945.*

cans valued him as a symbol of social stability in Japan, they agreed. The war ended officially on the decks of the battleship *Missouri* on September 2.

Was the Bomb Necessary?

At first there was only wonder at a weapon that could destroy a whole city, and joy that the war was over. Within a few years, however, many Americans began to debate the wisdom and morality of having used the atomic bomb. When novelist John Hersey's *Hiroshima* detailed the destruction of that ancient city in vivid, human terms, some of Truman's critics stated that he was guilty of a war crime worse than any the Japanese had perpetrated, and exceeded only by the Nazi murder of 6 million European Jews. Truman and his defenders replied that the nuclear assaults on Hiroshima and Nagasaki were humane acts since millions of Japanese as well as Americans would have been killed had Japan been invaded.

When other critics said that the Japanese surrender could have been forced by a demonstration of the bomb on an uninhabited island, as Secretary of War Stimson had suggested, defenders pointed out that no one was positive that the device would actually work. An announced demonstration that fizzled would have encouraged the Japanese die-hards to fight all the harder.

Much later, a group of historians known as "revisionists" suggested that Little Boy and Fat Man were dropped not so much to end the war with Japan but to inaugurate the Cold War with the Soviet Union. In bombing Japan, the revisionist argument went, Truman was showing the Russians that the United States held the trump card in any postwar dispute. Because history is not a science, capable of absolute proof, the debate over the use of the bomb will continue indefinitely. Only two things are certain: the atomic bomb ended the Second World War decisively and ahead of schedule, and it ushered in a new and dangerous epoch in world affairs, the nuclear age.

For Further Reading

The standard history of America's Great War is Albert R. Buchanan, *The United States and World War II* (1962). More comprehensive studies include Martha Hoyle, *A World in Flames: A History of World War II* (1970) and Fletcher Pratt, *War for the World* (1950) but, of course, the literature is exhaustive, with a great number of excellent popular histories. Although hardly a study in objectivity, Winston Churchill, *The Second World War* (1948–53) will be rewarding to every student.

On diplomatic and political issues, see Robert Beitzell, *The Uneasy Alliance: America, Britain, and Russia, 1941–1943* (1972); John M. Blum, *V Was for Victory: Politics and American Culture During World War II* (1976); Robert Dallek, *Franklin D. Roosevelt and American Foreign Policy, 1932–1945* (1979); Robert A. Divine, *Roosevelt and World War II* (1969); Norman A. Graebner, *The Age of Global Power: The United States Since 1938* (1979); Gabriel Kolko, *The Politics of War: The World and United States Foreign Policy, 1943–1945* (1968); Joseph P. Lash, *Roosevelt and Churchill* (1976); and Gaddis Smith, *American Diplomacy During the Second World War, 1940–1945* (1965).

Military history is the major focus of Stephen Ambrose, *The Supreme Commander: The War Years of General Dwight D. Eisenhower* (1970); William Manches-

ter, *American Caesar: Douglas MacArthur, 1880–1960* (1978); Charles B. McDonald, *The Mighty Endeavor: American Armed Forces in the European Theater in World War II* (1969); Samuel Eliot Morison, *The Two-Ocean War: A Short History of the United States Navy in the Second World War* (1963); Cornelius Ryan, *The Longest Day* (1959); John Toland, *The Last Hundred Days* (1966) and *The Rising Sun: The Decline and Fall of the Japanese Empire* (1970); Russell F. Weigley, *The American Way of War: A History of United States Military Strategy and Policy* (1973).

Books on the home front include Roger Daniels, *Concentration Camps USA* (1971); some chapters of Carl M. Degler, *At Odds: Women and the Family in America from the Revolution to the Present* (1980); Jack Goodman, *While You Were Gone: A Report on Wartime Life in the United States* (1946); Richard Lingeman, *Don't You Know There's a War On* (1970); Richard Polenberg, *War and Society: The United States, 1941–1945* (1972); Michi Weglyn, *Years of Infamy: The Untold Story of America's Concentration Camps* (1976).

The reasons for the dropping of the atomic bomb on Japan in 1945 are hotly argued in Gar Alperovitz, *Atomic Diplomacy: Hiroshima and Potsdam* (1965); Herbert Feis, *The Atomic Bomb and World War II* (1966); and Greg Herken, *The Winning Weapon* (1980).

Rarely has a war ended so abruptly as the atomic bomb ended the Pacific theater of the Second World War. Divided and deliberating one week, the Japanese government collapsed the next.

Never had a new historical era been so unmistakably proclaimed as by the fireballs over Hiroshima and Nagasaki. Slowly during the final months of 1945, it dawned on Americans and other peoples that the world had undergone a major passage, that old rules and guidelines would not necessarily help them to negotiate the future.

But they had not left the past behind. History is legacy. The consequences of past actions live on whether or not people choose to understand them. Three great legacies of the Second World War were so profound that they fostered

46

A TIME OF ANXIETIES

The United States in the Early Nuclear Age, 1946–1952

A radioactive mushroom cloud covers Bikini Atoll following a test of the atomic bomb, July 25, 1946.

anxieties that loom menacingly over the United States and the world to this day.

THE SHADOW OF COLD WAR

The first legacy of the Second World War was, of course, the powerful weaponry that had ended it. Nuclear bombs meant that it was technologically possible for humanity to destroy civilization, perhaps even the natural world as we have known it. Such a circumstance was novel in history.

A second legacy of the war was the realization that human beings were morally quite capable of using such a technology in monstrous ways. It was not so much President Truman's decision to use the atomic bomb. However justified or cynical that decision may have been, neither Truman nor his advisors quite understood how terrible a weapon nuclear fission was. (No one predicted the thousands of maimings and lingering deaths from radiation poisoning in Hiroshima and Nagasaki.)

However, in the spring of 1945, Allied troops discovered that reports of genocide in Nazi Europe had not been exaggerated. The Nazis had systematically exterminated 6 million Jews and probably 1 million other people in factories called "camps" that were specifically designed for killing people and disposing of their bodies on a mass scale. The photographs and films of the walking skeletons of Dachau, Belsen, Auschwitz, and Buchenwald; the "shower baths" where the victims were gassed; the cremation ovens; the human garbage dumps, arms and legs protruding obscenely from heaps of corpses like discarded furniture: these shocking spectacles mocked human pretensions to enlightenment and decency such as not even

Prisoners in a Nazi concentration camp await their release in this 1945 photo by Margaret Bourke-White.

the slaughter of the First World War had done. That, at least, had been mindless. Nazi genocide was deliberate, calculated, and methodical. Never again would it be possible to assume, as most of Western civilization had assumed for more than a century, that reason, science, technology, and efficiency were moving the human race toward an ever better future.

The third legacy of the war was that only two nations emerged from it as genuine victors—the United States and the Soviet Union—and that, once the Nazis were defeated, they had little in common. For about two years after the war, Russian and American leaders tried to preserve the wartime alliance or, at least, to maintain the pretense of friendship. By 1947, however, the two great powers were in a state of "cold war," belligerence without violent confrontation.

At first, Americans were more annoyed than frightened by what they believed was Soviet ingratitude and treachery. Their nation held the trump card, the atomic bomb. Then, in September 1949, the Soviets successfully tested a nuclear device. The holocaust of which the race had proved itself nimbly capable seemed likely to be ignited sooner or later.

Roots of Soviet-American Animosity

The origins of the Russo-American Cold War lay in irreconcilable values and 30 years of history. The American commitment to democratic government and maximum liberty for individuals was incompatible with the conviction of the Bolsheviks of 1917 that they could overcome the "sluggishness of history" and achieve their revolution by the creation, at least temporarily, of a dictatorial, repressive, and ruthless state power.

Obnoxious as Soviet tyranny was to Americans, however, it cannot in itself explain American hostility to the Soviets. (The United States has often found it convenient to come to terms with non-Communist dictators.) Also important was the American commitment to maintaining an "open door" for trade and investment everywhere in the world. This principle was incompatible with Soviet determination to prevent capitalist economic penetration in those parts of the world they controlled, and the apparent Soviet determination to export Communist revolution and expand the U.S.S.R.'s political sway.

With such contradictory values, the Soviet Union and the United States could marry only when there was a shotgun at their backs, which Nazi Germany provided between 1941 and 1945. Even then, despite cordial personal relations between Roosevelt and Stalin, neither American nor Russian policymakers deluded themselves that the conflict of interests had disappeared. People high in the American government, such as James Byrnes and Harry S Truman continued to find Russian Communism intolerably noxious. The Russians, Stalin foremost among them, remained suspicious of the intentions of the United States and Great Britain. For a decade and more after 1917, the Western nations had isolated and threatened to destroy the revolution that the Bolsheviks had made. Stalin fidgeted and seethed when Roosevelt and Churchill were slow to establish a second front in Europe. The Americans and the British worried that, after the war, Communist Russia would be a great power for the first time, in a position to dominate its neighbors.

An Insoluble Problem

Roosevelt apparently believed that he could handle Stalin's repeatedly expressed insistence that the nations bordering Russia be "friendly," while ensuring that they were not Soviet satellites. Although it is difficult to imagine what specifics he had in mind, Roosevelt apparently thought that he could ensure that Poland, Czechoslovakia, and the Balkan countries would be democratic, open to American cooperation and trade while posing no threat to Soviet security.

At best, this was naive. Political democracy, as it was defined in Roosevelt's and Churchill's Atlantic Charter, was alien to Eastern European history and culture. Moreover, some Eastern European countries, particularly Poland, were historically hostile toward Russia. If the Western Allies had suppressed the memory that the Soviet Union had joined Nazi Germany in invading Poland in 1939, the Poles did not. Indeed, Polish hatred for the Russians was given new life in 1943, when the Germans released persuasive evidence that the Red Army had secretly massacred 5,000 captured Polish officers at Katyn in 1939.

Then, late in the war, with Russian troops advancing rapidly toward Warsaw, the Polish government-in-exile in London called for an uprising behind the German lines. At this point, Stalin abruptly halted the Russian advance, and the relieved Germans were able to butcher the poorly armed Polish partisans. Red Army soldiers were as brutal toward Polish civilians as they were toward Germans. A democratic Poland could not be subordinate to Russia in the sense that Stalin demanded Poland be. A Poland friendly to Russia could not be democratically governed.

Roosevelt's confidence that he could iron out these wrinkles on the basis of his personal cordiality toward Stalin also required that he defy his own mortality, to which he should have been very sensitive in early 1945, for his health deteriorated rapidly. Nevertheless, he continued to treat diplomacy as a personal responsibility. When he died before the war was over, he left an inexperienced and uninformed Harry S Truman to make a settlement with Stalin.

Truman Draws a Line

Truman was not the sly manipulator Roosevelt had been. His virtues as a man and as president were his frankness, bluntness, and willingness to make and stick by a decision. On the subject of the Soviet Union he had made a decision decades earlier. Like many Americans he did not like the Russians. Even before he first met Stalin at Potsdam, he summoned Soviet Ambassador V. M. Molotov to the White House and scolded him so harshly for several apparent Russian policy turns that Molotov exclaimed, "I have never been talked to like that in my life!"

By 1946, it was obvious that the Russians were not going to permit free elections in Poland. While Truman remained cautious in his official pronouncements on the subject, he gave full approval to Winston Churchill's speech in Fulton, Missouri, in March 1946. An "iron curtain" had descended across Europe, the former prime minister said, and it was time for the Western democracies to call a halt to the expansion of atheistic Communism.

In September 1946, Truman again signaled the confrontational turn of his Soviet policy. He fired Secretary of Commerce (and former vice president) Henry A. Wallace, the one member of his cabinet who called openly for accommodating the anxieties of the Soviet Union.

Containment and the Truman Doctrine

By 1947, Truman had a policy that went beyond merely "getting tough with the Russians." First in a series of confidential memoranda, and then in an article signed by "Mister X" in the influential journal *Foreign Affairs*, a Soviet expert in the State Department, George F. Kennan, argued that because of the ancient Russian compulsion to expand to the west and the virtually pathological Soviet fear of the Western nations, it would be impossible to come to a quick, amicable settlement with Stalin. American policy must therefore be to contain Russian expansionism by drawing clear limits as to where the United States would tolerate Russian domination, namely, those parts of Europe that already were under Russian control, and no more.

In Kennan's view, the Soviets would test American resolve but, Russian history seemed to show, very carefully. While the Soviets wanted to extend their sway to the west as far as possible, they did not want war any more than did the United States. If American policymakers made it unmistakeably clear that they would tolerate no more Russian gains, the Soviets

would stop. Kennan envisioned a long period of tense, suspicious relations. In time, however, when the Russians felt secure, it would become possible to deal diplomatically with them and establish a genuine peace. In the meantime, Cold War was preferable to bloodletting and the possibility of world destruction.

At the same time "containment policy" was being "leaked" to the public, Truman was presented with an opportunity to put it into practice. In early 1947, the Soviets seemed to be stepping up their support of Communist guerrillas in Greece and Communist parties in Italy and France. On March 12, Truman asked Congress to appropriate $400 million in military assistance to the pro-Western governments of Greece and Turkey. This principle of decisively supporting anti-Communist regimes with massive aid came to be known as the Truman Doctrine.

The Marshall Plan

On June 5, 1947, Secretary of State George C. Marshall proposed a much more ambitious program, soon dubbed the Marshall Plan. The United States would invest vast sums of money in the economic reconstruction of Europe. Not only would the former Western European Allies be invited to apply for American assistance, but defeated Germany (then divided into British, French, American, and Soviet zones of occupation) would receive aid. Indeed, Marshall invited the Soviet Union and the nations behind Churchill's Iron Curtain to participate.

Marshall and Truman calculated that Russia and its satellite states would reject the offer. By late 1947, Stalin's troops were firmly in control of the countries

AN UNSORDID ACT

Winston Churchill called the Marshall Plan "the most unsordid act in history." In a speech at Harvard University in 1947, George Marshall explained his intentions:

The truth of the matter is that Europe's requirements for the next 3 or 4 years of foreign food and other essential products—principally from America—are so much greater than her present ability to pay that she must have substantial additional help, or face economic, social, and political deterioration of a very grave character.

The remedy lies in breaking the vicious circle and restoring the confidence of the European people in the economic future of their own countries and of Europe as a whole. The manufacturer and the farmer throughout wide areas must be able and willing to exchange their products for currencies the continuing value of which is not open to question.

A plane carrying supplies flies into West Berlin following a move by Joseph Stalin in June 1948 to block overland routes to that city from West Germany.

of Eastern Europe, including the one nation there with a strong democratic tradition, Czechoslovakia. Already in June 1946, Stalin had made it clear that he would brook no Western interference in these countries. He turned down a proposal by elder statesman Bernard Baruch to outlaw nuclear weapons because the plan involved enforcement on the scene by the United Nations, which had been formed in 1945 under a charter that had evolved from the agreements of the various wartime Allied conferences.

The Americans had calculated correctly: the Soviets condemned the Marshall Plan. Massive American aid was pumped only into those countries where a political purpose could be served by overcoming the economic and social chaos in which Communism flourished.

Freezing the Lines

Containment policy worked. Neither Greece and Turkey fell to pro-Russian guerrillas nor Italy and France to Communist parties. The policy received its most severe test in June 1948, when Stalin blockaded West Berlin, deep within Communist East Germany. Unable to provision the city of 2 million by overland routes, the United States could have given up Berlin or invaded East Germany. Instead, a massive airlift was

organized. For a year, huge C-47's and C-54's flew in the necessities and a few of the luxuries that the West Berliners needed in order to hold out. By this action, the Truman administration made it clear that the United States did not want war, but neither would it tolerate further Soviet expansion.

The Soviets responded quite as George Kennan had predicted. Instead of invading West Berlin or shooting down the airlift planes, they watched. In May 1949, having determined that the United States would not give in, the Soviets lifted the blockade.

By that time, the Cold War had entered a new phase. In April 1949, with Canada and nine European nations, the United States signed a treaty that established the North Atlantic Treaty Organization (NATO), the first peacetime military alliance in American history since the 1790s. The NATO countries promised to consider an attack against any of them as grounds for going to war together.

The Soviets responded by writing the Warsaw Pact, an alliance of the nations of Eastern Europe. In September 1949, the Soviet Union exploded its first atomic bomb, and soon thereafter the United States perfected the hydrogen bomb, a much more destructive weapon. The nuclear-arms race was under way.

LEARNING FROM PAST MISTAKES

In a number of ways, F.D.R. and Harry S Truman pointedly departed from American policy toward Europe after the First World War. In sponsoring the United Nations, the United States departed radically from the American boycott of the League of Nations. Unlike Woodrow Wilson, who named no prominent Republican to his peace commission at Versailles, thus contributing to American opposition to the League, Roosevelt made Republican Senator Arthur H. Vandenberg, a former isolationist, a member of the American delegation that wrote the Charter of the United Nations.

With the Marshall Plan, President Truman recognized the folly of the Coolidge administration of the 1920s in refusing to help Europe economically by arranging for a significant modification of the flow of reparations from Germany and debt payments by Britain and France.

DOMESTIC POLITICS UNDER TRUMAN

All the while Harry S Truman was designing and effecting a decisive and articulate foreign policy, he was struggling to cope with postwar domestic problems. These were considerable: rapid inflation, a serious shortage of housing, and a series of bitter industrial disputes. At first Truman seemed to founder. Professional politicians and ordinary voters alike began to suspect his competence. In his predecessor's regal shadow, Truman cut a second-rate figure. Compared with dynamic Eleanor Roosevelt, who was even more active in liberal causes after her husband's death, Bess Truman was a plain, frumpy homebody. The deadly serious nuclear age seemed to have caught the United States without a leader up to its challenges.

The Republican Comeback of 1946

Capitalizing on anxieties of this sort, the Republicans ran their congressional election campaign of 1946 on a simple but effective two-word slogan, "Had Enough?" Apparently the voters had. They elected Republican majorities in both houses of Congress for the first time since 1930. One freshman Democratic senator who bucked the landslide, J. William Fulbright of Arkansas, suggested that Truman resign in favor of a Republican president. The Republicans did not take this proposal seriously, but, positive that they would elect their nominee in 1948, they set out to prepare their still-undesignated candidate's way by dismantling as many New Deal reforms as they could.

One of their most striking successes was the Taft-Hartley Labor-Management Relations Act of 1947. This law, enacted over Truman's veto, reversed the New Deal's active support of the union movement that had been enshrined in the Wagner Act of 1935. Taft-Hartley emphasized the rights of workers not to join labor organizations, most notably by abolishing the closed shop. That is, under the New Deal, employees of a company that recognized a union as the workers' bargaining agent—the body that negotiated wages and hours with the company—were required to belong to that union as a condition of employment; employment was closed to all but union members. Taft-Hartley guaranteed the right of individuals not to join a union.

The Taft-Hartley Act was not a "slave labor" law, as Truman called it in his veto message; nor did not cripple the movement. Indeed, its chief effect was to arouse organized labor, now more than 10 million strong, to rally behind Truman. This unexpected support (for Truman had not been considered especially friendly to organized labor) showed the president a way to fight the Republican Eightieth Congress. He vetoed 80 of its anti-New Deal enactments, thus converting himself into a crusading liberal. When Republican critics mocked his homey manners and common appearance, he turned the tables on them by becoming the common man, denouncing his enemies in Congress as stooges of the rich and privileged. Coining his own slogan, the Fair Deal, he sent to Capitol Hill proposal after proposal that expanded social services. Among his programs was a national health-insurance plan such as most European nations had adopted.

Civil Rights

The Truman health plan failed, as did the president's demand that Congress act to mitigate discrimination against blacks. In 1947, the Presidential Committee on Civil Rights reported to Truman on racial discrimination in the United States, particularly as it related to employment practices and the continued condoning of the lynching of blacks in the South. Truman sent its far-reaching recommendations to Congress, where an alliance of complacent Republicans and southern

THE 52-20 CLUB

Members of the 52-20 Club of 1945 and 1946 were demobilized soldiers and sailors who were allowed $20 a week for 52 weeks or until such time as they found a job. Although many were accused of avoiding work because of this payment, the average length of membership in the club was only three months.

Democrats killed them. Truman responded with an executive order that banned racial discrimination in the army and navy, in the civil service, and in companies that did business with the federal government.

Truman's civil-rights program was quite moderate. He did not attempt to touch "Jim Crow," the system of strict social segregation that provided for separate public facilities for the white and black races in the southern and border states, including Truman's home state of Missouri. But he went further than Roosevelt had dared, and his program was politically very shrewd. Hundreds of thousands of blacks had moved out of the South, where they were politically powerless, into big cities in northern and midwestern states with large electoral votes. For a Democratic president to continue to support segregation was to risk throwing these big states to the Republicans, especially because the leading contenders for the Republican presidential nomination, Robert Taft and New York Governor Thomas E. Dewey, had been friendly to black aspirations.

Four Candidates

By the spring of 1948, Truman's popularity was on the upswing. Americans were getting accustomed to, even fond of, the president's hard-hitting style. Nevertheless, no political expert gave Truman a chance to survive the presidential election in November. The Democrats had been in power 16 years, longer than any party since the Virginia Dynasty of Jefferson, Madison, and Monroe. The inefficiency of many New Deal bureaucracies was undeniable, and rumors of corruption were persistent.

Then, to turn worse into impossible, the party split three ways. Henry A. Wallace led left-wing liberals into the newly formed Progressive party. He claimed to be the true heir of New Deal liberalism and insisted

that there was no reason to abandon the nation's wartime friendship with the Soviet Union. Democrats from the Deep South, angry at Truman's civil-rights reforms and a strong plank condemning racial discrimination in the party platform written by the young liberal mayor of Minneapolis, Hubert H. Humphrey, formed the States' Rights, or "Dixiecrat," party. They named Strom Thurmond of South Carolina as their candidate.

Thurmond had fewer illusions of winning the election than did Wallace, who had a mystical streak. Thurmond's purpose was to take credit for denying Truman the election, thus impressing on northern liberal Democrats the necessity of sticking with their traditional support of southern segregationists.

Presented with what looked like a gift victory, the Republicans passed over their leading conservative, Senator Robert A. Taft of Ohio, the son of President William Howard Taft. Robert Taft had led the onslaught on the New Deal and Truman, but he was rather too nasty and peevish, driven as much by hate as principle, to be likeable. Republican moderates calculated that if any candidate would send voters who had "had enough" back to the Democrats for more, it was Taft. Instead, they chose the safe Thomas E. Dewey, their candidate in 1944, to take on Truman.

Give 'Em Hell, Harry

Dewey adopted an election strategy that was tried and true. Every poll showed him winning with ease. Therefore, as F.D.R. had done when a sure victor in 1932, Dewey ran a low-key, noncommittal campaign. He would not jeopardize his lead by saying anything that might alienate any group of voters.

Truman, faced with certain defeat, had nothing to lose by speaking out. "Give'em hell, Harry," a supporter shouted at a rally, and Truman did. During the summer of 1948, he called Congress into special session and a corps of assistants led by Clark Clifford sent bill after bill to the Republican Congress. As the Republicans voted down his proposals, Truman toured the country, blaming the nation's problems on the "no-good, do-nothing Eightieth Congress." Did Americans

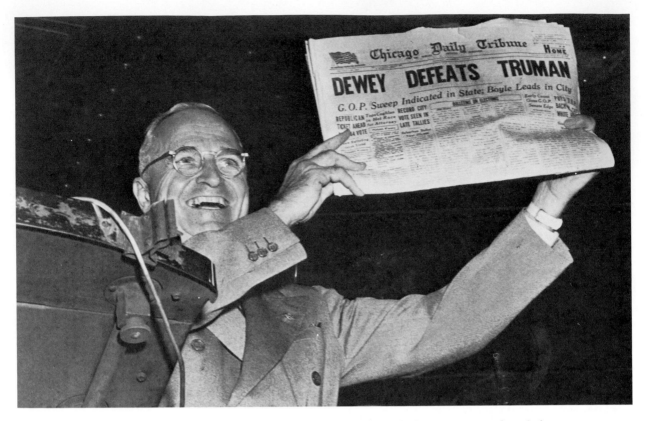

Following his narrow victory in 1948, Harry Truman gleefully displays a newspaper that relied on early returns to predict his defeat to Republican presidential candidate Thomas Dewey.

want four more years of that sort of thing under a lackluster Thomas E. Dewey?

On election night, the editors of the Republican Chicago *Tribune* glanced at the early returns, which favored Dewey, and decided to scoop the competition by publishing an edition declaring the New Yorker to be the new president. The next day, Harry Truman took great pleasure in posing for photographs while pointing to the *Tribune*'s headline, for Dewey had not won. Truman narrowly squeaked out victories in almost all the large industrial states and the majority of farm states. His popular vote was under 50 percent, and he lost a few Gulf states to Thurmond. But he was president and by a whopping 303 to 189 electoral votes.

CONTAINMENT IN ASIA

The Fair Deal did not fare so well as its author did. Like many presidents who had other things in mind, Truman found himself preoccupied with such serious problems abroad that domestic reforms seemed insig-

nificant by comparison. Also like other presidents who had to become diplomats, Truman discovered that he was not chief executive in world affairs, but only one player in a game in which the rules defied the power at his disposal and even his own understanding of them.

In Asia, only the Philippines and Japan were firm American allies. Given independence in 1946, the Philippines remained beholden to American financial aid and responded with friendship. In Japan, a capitalist democracy was slowly emerging as a consequence of massive Marshall Plan-type assistance and the enlightened military occupation of the country under Douglas MacArthur. Understanding Japanese traditions better than he understood American, MacArthur established himself as a shogun, or a dictator who ruled while the emperor reigned. The shogun was a familiar figure in Japanese history, and the Japanese were comfortable with MacArthur's role.

Rejected Option

In China, however, the Truman administration failed because the president ignored the advice of his best advisers and tried to adapt to the Asian mainland the policy of containment that was working in Europe. The trouble was that the Soviet expansionism responsible in part for the Cold War in Europe did not lie at the bottom of Communist successes in China. Nor were, at least until after the Second World War, the Chinese Communists necessarily opposed to an understanding with the United States. Kennan understood the difference between Europe and China and tried to point it out. Truman, the State Department, and the American public did not listen.

During and after the Second World War, two governments claimed to represent the will of the Chinese people: the Guomindang, or Nationalist, regime of Chiang Kai-shek, and the powerful Communist party and military force behind Mao Zedong. Some Americans who were familiar with China urged Washington not to oppose Mao but to come to terms with him during the war. General Joseph W. Stilwell repeatedly warned Roosevelt that the people around Chiang were hopelessly corrupt and unpopular, while Mao commanded the loyalty of China's largest social class, the peasantry.

After the war, acting as a special envoy to China, George C. Marshall suggested that the Chinese Communists were not necessarily tools of the Soviets but could be encouraged to chart an independent course through cooperation and friendship. Mao was bent on revolutionary change at home, particularly in regard to land, which was in the hands of an elite allied to Chiang. Marshall, like many others who were familiar with the Nationalists, did not find Mao's program unattractive since the Guomindang party included butchers of peasants and thieves who misappropriated American material aid for their own profit.

The China Lobby

But Chiang had an active, articulate, and very well-connected American "China Lobby" organized and headed by his brilliant wife, Madame Chiang, who spent much of her time in the United States. This group drew support from conservative congressmen; influential church leaders such as the Catholic archbishop of New York, Francis Cardinal Spellman; and much of the press, most importantly Henry L. Luce, the publisher of *Time* magazine, and Clare Boothe Luce, a Republican congresswoman and eloquent speaker.

Through 1949, the China Lobby bombarded Americans with false information: most Chinese supported Chiang; Chiang was defeating Mao's forces on the battlefield; Mao was a Soviet stooge like the puppet leaders of Eastern Europe. So effective was the campaign that Americans were shocked at the end of 1949 when Chiang suddenly fled the mainland for the island province of Taiwan (then better known by its Japanese name of Formosa). They thought that Chiang had been winning the war. Instead of admitting that they had been wrong, at least in regard to the power of the Nationalists, the China Lobby insisted that Chiang had not been repudiated but merely betrayed by inadequate American support. They urged that aid be increased and that Chiang be "unleashed" for an assault on the mainland.

Truman and new Secretary of State Dean Acheson knew better than to "unleash" Chiang Kai-shek. To have done so would have meant either humiliation when he was defeated or involvement in a war on the mainland of Asia, which every military strategist, from Douglas MacArthur on down, warned against. Whether Truman and Acheson ever rued the fact that they had ignored the advice of Stilwell, Marshall, and others to come to terms with Mao Zedong's Communists is not clear. Whether American friendship would have significantly changed the course of Chinese history under Mao is also beyond certain knowledge. What is known is that China as a foe was dangerous and unpredictable precisely because China was not, as Americans continued to believe, a Soviet satellite.

Containment Policy Falters

Truman and Acheson were applying the principle of containment to East Asia when events left them behind. No one, including themselves, was quite certain

Zhou Enlai, Mao Zedong, and Chu Teh in Yenan province during the final days of the civil war in 1946.

about where the United States would accept Communist control and where the line of containment was to be drawn. Japan was off limits, of course, but what of Quemoy and Matsu, tiny islands off the coast of China that, like Taiwan, were occupied by Chiang's Nationalists? And what of the Republic of Korea, set up by the United States in the southern half of the former Japanese colony of Chosen? Was the little country, bordered on the north by the thirty-eighth parallel (38° north latitude), to be protected like the nations of Western Europe?

Feeling the sting of the China Lobby's attacks, Truman's Secretary of State Dean Acheson was vague, and the president was indecisive. In a similar situation in 1914, the mischievousness of two weak countries started a war, and that was what happened in 1950. The Communist government of North Korea and the pro-American government of Syngman Rhee in South Korea exchanged ever more serious threats. In June, ostensibly responding to South Korean troop movements, the North Korean army swept across the thirty-eighth parallel and quickly drove Rhee's ROK (Republic of Korea) troops to the toe of the peninsula.

The Korean Conflict

Truman already had stationed an American fleet in Korean waters, and he responded immediately and forcibly. Thanks to the absence of the Soviet delegation to the United Nations, he was able to win the vote necessary to make the UN the sponsor of a "police action" on the peninsula. With the United States providing almost all the "police," General MacArthur took command of the expedition.

In a daring maneuver that might have served as the capstone of a brilliant military career, MacArthur engineered an amphibious landing at Inchon, deep be-

"Police action" in Korea: U.S. Infantry troops return from the front, June 1951.

Chinese. Both sides sustained high casualties for the sake of capturing forlorn hills and ridges that did not even have names, only numbers. Even after armistice talks began, first at Kaesong and then in a truce zone at Panmunjom, the war dragged on. The Chinese had won their goal, which was to protect their borders, and the Americans had ensured the independence of the Republic of Korea. In the days when the objects of war were clear and concrete, that was the point at which wars were ended. But in the Cold War, with ideological rivalry taking on a religious significance on both sides, neither side knew quite what to do. Some days at Panmunjom, the negotiators simply sat at the table facing one another and saying nothing.

MacArthur's Debacle

With good reason, the American people were frustrated. Not five years after the Second World War, the Korean Conflict put 5.7 million young men in uniform, killed 54,000 of them, and wounded 100,000. Defense expenditures soared from $40 billion in 1950 to $71 billion in 1952. Truman and Acheson had said that the goal was containment, but having "contained," they were unable to conclude hostilities. What was wrong?

hind North Korean lines, cutting off and capturing 100,000 enemy troops. The Americans and ROKs then surged rapidly northward, crossing the thirty-eighth parallel in September 1950. By October 26, they had occupied virtually the whole peninsula. At one point, American soldiers stood on the banks of the Yalu River, which divides Korea from Chinese Manchuria.

The headiness of winning so quickly prevented Truman and the UN from reflecting on MacArthur's assurances that the Chinese would not intervene in the war. He was wrong. With its coal and iron deposits, Manchuria was vital to Mao's plans to industrialize China. Furthermore, the northeastern province had, twice before, been the avenue through which the Middle Kingdom had been invaded. Mao threw 200,000 Chinese "volunteers" at the Americans. By the end of 1950, these veterans, still hardened by the wars with Chiang, drove MacArthur back to a line that zigzagged across the thirty-eighth parallel.

There, whether because the Chinese were willing to settle for a "draw" or because American troops found their footing and dug in, stalemate ensued. For two years, the Americans, ROKs, and token delegations of troops from other United Nations countries slugged it out to little effect with the North Koreans and

General Douglas MacArthur giving orders at the battle of Inchon, South Korea, in 1950.

AWAKE!

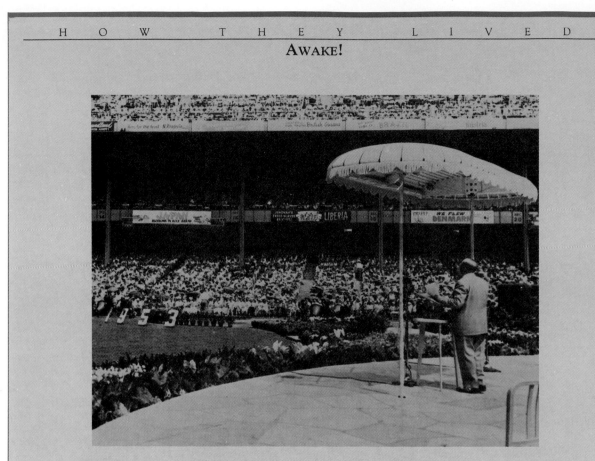

*Jehovah's Witnesses from all over the world meet in
Yankee Stadium in 1953.*

During the Truman years, millions of Americans were introduced to the Jehovah's Witnesses for the first time. Rather than preaching from streetcorner soapboxes, as the sects they seemed to resemble did, the Witnesses showed up on the thresholds of grand homes, middle-class tract houses, and declining urban apartments and row houses alike. Always neatly dressed, always in pairs, often racially mixed, they clutched briefcases or handbags stuffed with their books, tracts, and copies of two monthly magazines, *The Watchtower* and *Awake!*. The Witnesses were never jolly nor backslapping in one well-known American evangelical tradition. Their manner was solemn, grim, thin-lipped. Their ice-breaking question was blunt and cheerless: did the householder (usually a housewife during the daytime hours) think that all was well with the world?

The Second World War left in its wake the lingering smell of the extermination camps and Hiroshima, the shock of the lowering of the Iron Curtain and the Communist triumph in China, news of cold war spies and the cries of subversion in Washington. In the vague but general sense that the war had created a more threatening world than it destroyed, the Jehovah's Witnesses won many invitations to come in and talk. The sect that was 70 years old in 1949, but still tiny, began to grow, and the numbers of its fulltime walkers of streets and ringers of doorbells (24,000 in 1984) became more conspicuous. In 1978, the Witnesses numbered more than 600,000 in the United States, two million worldwide. Their Watchtower Tract Society was one of the largest publishing houses in the world. *Awake!* alone had a circulation of eight million in 34 languages.

The Witnesses took shape during the 1870s in Allegheny City, Pennsylvania, in the midst of the iron and steel belt that epitomized industrial progress to some, a hell of soot, smoke, sparkling flame, and social insecurity to others. The founder, Charles Taze Russell, was a Presbyterian who, like many troubled believers before him, found grievous flaws in the traditional faiths, and styled himself "God's Mouthpiece."

At first, the Witnesses seemed like just another variant on the fundamentalist, millenarian, catastrophe-minded groups that have sprung up in times of trying social ferment. They taught that the Bible was "inspired and historically acccurate," a single, reassuring absolute in a world of whirling flux and instability. In 1987, the American Witnesses' street ministers were probably nimbler in finding the apt Biblical citation for an occasion than the deans and doyennes of America's most prestigious divinity schools.

Like the Millerites of the 1840s, the Witnesses said that "the end of the world" was nigh. In 1876, Russell predicted that Armageddon—the final battle between good and evil—would occur in 1914. When the First World War, with its unprecedented horrors, erupted in that year, Witness membership jumped. Russell's successor named 1918, the end of the Great War. Others have set the date at 1925, 1941, 1975, and 1984. In times of anxiety like the late 1940s and early 1950s, the perception that the state of the world incontrovertibly precludes an indefinite future is a common historical response, particularly by those whom society has rejected, despised, or merely left behind. Like other fundamentalist groups, the Witnesses were most successful among the poor, downtrodden, and ignorant.

However, the Witnesses were unique fundamentalists and millenarians in several ways. Hardly inclined to be "right-wingers" preaching antisemitism and antiblack racism, the Witnesses totally rejected racial discrimination of any kind. As a consequence, they have been immensely successful proselytizers among American blacks.

Hardly uncritical super-patriots, the Witnesses considered all governments—America's included—as evil. Their meeting houses, called "Kingdom Halls," indicate that they consider themselves subjects of God's (Jehovah's) realm. They merely submit to those powers of the state that do not conflict with Jehovah's law. They do not participate in government or politics.

As a result of their refusal to serve in the armed forces, thousands of Witnesses were imprisoned during World War II. They puzzled authorities by their passivity and self-enforced order in prison, and also by their disdain for other political and conscientious objectors to military service. In fact, the Witnesses considered their fellow prisoners as misguided "instruments of satan," too. The Witnesses were not pacifists in any but the functional sense of the word. They looked forward with zest to Armageddon when they will themselves take up arms for Jehovah and exterminate those who have rejected their message and witness.

The Jehovah's Witnesses are also peculiar in that they do not believe in hell. When Jehovah's reign begins, the "instruments of satan" will simply cease to exist. A material universe will be ruled by 144,000 Witnesses who alone, with Jesus, will reside in heaven.

In their vision of the post-Armageddon earth, the importance of the Truman years in the development of the organization can be seen in a most curious way. Pictorial depictions of Jehovah's kingdom in *Awake!* and *Watchtower* show lions laying down with lambs (the ancient biblical image), but the restored Eden is a broad, weedless lawn mowed as closely as a golfing green surrounding a sprawling "ranch-type" house such as was the beau-ideal, the "good life," for millions of Americans in the late 1940s and early 1950s. Smiling, loving, neatly and conventionally dressed and barbered suburbanites (no wings and halos), albeit of all races, populate this paradise. Often, guests are arriving for a backyard barbecue.

The Witnesses' paradise bears a close resemblance to the consumer paradise that advertisers of automobiles, television sets, furniture, and carpets pictured during the postwar years; even the style of the artwork is similar. Such aspirations in a time of increasing affluance allowed most Americans to cope with the anxieties of the Truman Era. To the Witnesses, such things represented the post-millenial universe.

In the late 1980s, when much of society has questioned the suburban ideal of the 1950s, the Witnesses are still loyal to it, perhaps because so few of them have achieved it. The organization also shows signs of evolving into a large, wealthy, well-established, and increasingly bureaucratized body headquartered in Brooklyn, New York. Its chief official, William Van De Wall, said in 1984 that "we do not know the day or the hour, but we do feel that we are in the time of the end. We are living in the general time period." It was such an accommodation—a dodging of specific predictions that lead to crises—that in the nineteenth century transformed disreputable Millerites into acceptable Seventh Day Adventists.

FLYING SAUCER SCARE

In 1947, a commercial pilot over the state of Washington sighted a cluster of "saucer-like things" and reported them to the federal government. By 1950, 600 Americans a year were seeing flying saucers. No one ever proved if the sightings were frauds, the fruit of mass hysteria, evidence of visitors from outer space, or of some new top-secret air force plane. The movie industry, looking for a kind of film with which to combat television, had no trouble making a choice. The early 1950s were years of dozens of movies about creatures—usually, but not always, bent on destruction—who visited earth.

In the spring of 1951, General MacArthur offered an answer. Forgetting his own warning against a war with the Chinese on the Asian mainland, and perhaps bruised in the ego by the stalemate, he complained to reporters that the only reason he had not won the war was that Truman would not permit him to bomb the enemy's supply depots in Manchuria. In April, MacArthur went further; he sent a letter to Republican congressman Joseph W. Martin in which he wrote that "there is no substitute for victory" and directly assailed the commander-in-chief for accepting a stalemate.

This attack on civilian command of the armed forces, a constitutional principle, appalled Truman's military advisers, and on April 11, with their support, the president fired MacArthur. The American people, remembering the general's accomplishments in the Second World War and reckoning that he knew better how to fight than Truman did, cheered the old warrior upon his return to the United States. He was feted with ticker-tape parades in every city he visited, and addressed Congress in a broadcast speech that was listened to by more people than had tuned in to Truman's inaugural address in 1949.

MacArthur concluded his congressional appearance by quoting a line from an old barracks song, "old soldiers never die; they just fade away," but he had no intention of fading anywhere. Establishing residence and a kind of command headquarters at New York's Waldorf-Astoria Hotel, he continued to issue political proclamations. He wanted the Republican nomination for the presidency in 1952; then he would battle Truman's containment policy with his promises of victory in the Cold War.

But the good general was a poor politician. He had spent most of his life outside the country, and he was handicapped by a messianic vision of himself: the people would come to him. They did not. As the very clever politician Harry S Truman had calculated when

he had dismissed the general, enthusiasm for MacArthur faded within a few months. MacArthur was left to spend his final years in obscurity. In the meantime, the Korean War dragged on, chewing up lives like a machine.

YEARS OF TENSION

Periodically in American history, during times of great political or social stress, many people have turned to "conspiracy theories" to account for their anxieties. The era of the Korean War was just such a time. Substantial numbers of Americans came to believe that the failure to achieve a sense of security after the glorious total victory in the Second World War must be the result of sinister forces working quietly but effectively within the United States.

"Twenty Years of Treason"

The view that at Yalta, President Roosevelt had sold out Eastern Europe to Stalin was an early expression of this "paranoid streak," belief in a sinister conspiracy at work to destroy America from within. Then, in March 1947, President Truman inadvertently fueled anxieties by ordering all government employees to sign loyalty oaths, statements that they did not belong to the Communist party or to other groups suspected of disloyalty. Eventually, 30 states followed this example, requiring an oath even of people who waxed the floors of state university basketball courts.

Truman also promoted the belief that there was treason in government by allowing his supporters to "red bait" Henry Wallace in the 1948 presidential campaign. Wallace was an eccentric (he played with all sorts of bizarre religious ideas), and he may well have been mistaken in his analysis of Soviet intentions in 1948. But he was no Communist party stooge. In calling him one, as many Democratic speechmakers did, they created a political tactic that, in the end, could only work against them. If there were traitors in high places, the Democratic party was responsible, for, as of 1952, they had been running the country for 20 years.

Long before 1952, frustrated right-wing Republicans such as John Bricker of Ohio, William F. Knowland of California, and Karl Mundt of North Dakota raised the specter of "twenty years of treason." The two chief beneficiaries of the scare were Richard M. Nixon, a young first-term congressman from southern California, and Joseph McCarthy, the junior senator from Wisconsin.

Alger Hiss and Richard Nixon

Richard M. Nixon built the beginnings of his career on the ashes of the less illustrious but still distinguished career of a former New Dealer named Alger Hiss. A bright young Ivy Leaguer during the 1930s when he had gone to Washington to work in the Department of Agriculture, Hiss had risen to be a middle level aide to Roosevelt at the time of the Yalta Conference. He was aloof and fastidious in his manner, rather a snob, and he was a militant liberal.

In 1948, a journalist named Whittaker Chambers, who confessed to having been a Communist during the 1930s, accused Hiss of having helped him funnel classified American documents to the Soviets. At first his testimony aroused little fuss. Chambers had a reputation for erratic behavior and, indeed, making things up. From a legal point of view, there seemed scant reason to pursue the matter; all the acts of which Hiss was accused had transpired too long in the past to be prosecuted, and he was no longer in government service in 1948. It was Hiss who forced the issue to a reckoning. He indignantly swore under oath that everything Chambers said was false. Indeed, Hiss insisted, he did not even know Chambers.

To liberals, the well-spoken Hiss, with his exemplary record in public service, was obviously telling the truth. The seedy Chambers, with his background in Henry L. Luce's *Time* magazine, was a liar. But many ordinary Americans, especially working-class ethnics and citizens of western farming states, were not so sure. With his nasal aristocratic accent and expensive tailored clothing, Hiss represented the Eastern Establishment, traditionally an object of suspicion, and the long-entrenched New Deal bureaucracy, of which they had grown weary.

Congressman Nixon shared these feelings and, following a hunch, pursued the Hiss case when other Republicans lost interest. Nixon persuaded Chambers to produce microfilms that seemed to show that Hiss had indeed retyped classified documents for some reason, and, in cross-examination at congressional hearings, poked hole after hole in Hiss's defense.

Largely because of Nixon's efforts, Hiss was convicted of perjury. Additional thousands of Americans wondered how many other bright New Dealers were spies. More than one Republican pointed out that Hiss had been a friend of none other than the "no-win" Secretary of State Dean Acheson and that the men resembled each other in their manners and appearance. Indeed, Acheson's style grated even more harshly than Hiss's. He favored London-made tweeds and sported a bristling waxed moustache. Richard Nixon, whose social awkwardness and furtiveness at work might otherwise have obscured him for life, looked good by comparison.

Senator Joe McCarthy

Senator Joseph McCarthy of Wisconsin was another unlikely character to play a major role in the government of a nation. Not only awkward and furtive, he was a crude, bullying man who seems to have been less cruel than uncomprehending of what cruelty was. He was also facing an election in 1950 in which he seemed sure to be defeated, so lackluster had been his record in the Senate. Groping for an issue, he rejected friends' suggestions that he focus on the advantages the proposed St. Lawrence Seaway would bestow on Wisconsin, a Great Lakes state, and instead, almost by accident, discovered that anxiety about Communist subversion was his ticket to a kind of political stardom.

In 1950, McCarthy told a Republican audience at Wheeling, West Virginia, that he possessed a list of 205 Communists who were working in the State Department with the full knowledge of Secretary of State Acheson. In other words, Acheson himself, as well as other high-ranking government officials, actively abetted Communist subversion.

McCarthy had no such list, of course. Only two days later, he could not remember if he had said the names totaled 205 or 57. He never released a single name, and never fingered a single Communist in government. Because he was so reckless, interested in nothing but publicity, McCarthy probably was headed for a fall from the moment he stepped into the limelight. But the tumultuous response that met his use of the "big lie"—making a complete falsehood so fabulous, and retelling it so often that people believe that "it must be true"—was an alarming symptom of just how anxious American society had become.

When a few senators publicly denounced his irresponsibility, McCarthy showed just how sensitive was the nerve he had touched. Senator Millard Tydings of Maryland was a conservative whose family name gave him practically a proprietary interest in a Senate seat in his state. In 1950, McCarthy threw his support behind Tydings's unknown opponent, fabricated a photograph showing Tydings shaking hands with American Communist party leader Earl Browder, and the senator went down to defeat.

McCarthyism

Following Tydings's defeat, civil libertarians outside politics worried because senators who opposed McCarthy's smear tactics were afraid to speak up lest they suffer the same fate. By 1952, McCarthy was so powerful that Republican presidential candidate Dwight

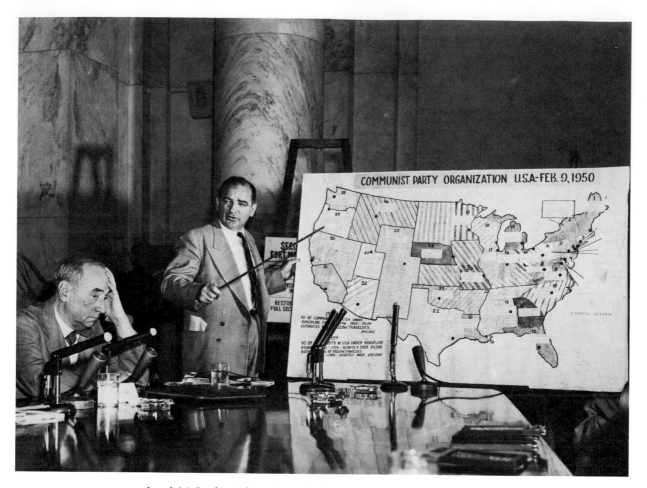

Joseph McCarthy (right) and Joseph Welsh at the Army-McCarthy hearings.

D. Eisenhower, whose military career had been sponsored by George C. Marshall, and who detested the vulgar McCarthy, refrained from praising Marshall in Wisconsin because the former secretary of state was one of McCarthy's "traitors."

In the meantime, liberal Democrats in Congress rushed to prove their loyalty by voting for dubious laws such as the McCarran Internal Security Act, which effectively outlawed the Communist party, by defining dozens of liberal lobby groups as "Communist fronts," and even by providing for the establishment of concentration camps in the event of a national emergency. The Supreme Court fell into line with its decision in *Dennis et al. versus United States* (1951). By a vote of 6 to 2, the Court agreed that it was a crime to advocate the forcible overthrow of the government, a position that Communists were defined as holding by virtue of their membership in the party.

At the peak of McCarthy's power, only a very few

opinion makers outside politics, such as cartoonist Herbert Block and television commentator Edward R. Murrow, and a few universities, including the University of Wisconsin in McCarthy's home state, refused to be intimidated by the senator's bullying. Not until 1954, however, did McCarthy's career come to an end. Failing to get preferential treatment for an intimate draftee friend of his chief aide, Roy Cohn, McCarthy accused the United States Army of being infiltrated by Communists. This recklessness emboldened the Senate to move against him. He was censured in December 1954 by a vote of 72 to 22. It was only the third time in American history that the nation's most exclusive club had turned on one of its own members. McCarthy died two years later.

The Making of a Politician

Nixon and McCarthy built their careers on exploiting and aggravating anxieties. Less directly, the leader of the conservative wing of the Republican party, Senator Robert A. Taft of Ohio, did the same. Although personally less than electrifying, and cultivating an image of rectitude, Taft encouraged his party's hell-raisers as a way of chipping at the Democrats.

But the American people turned to no mover and shaker to guide them through the 1950s. Instead, they chose a man with no background in politics, whose strength was a warm personality and whose talent was a knack for smoothing over conflict.

After the Second World War, General Dwight David Eisenhower wrote his memoirs of the war, *Crusade in Europe*, and, early in 1948, he accepted the presidency of Columbia University. Leaders of both parties approached him in his uptown New York office with offers to nominate him as president. Truman himself told Ike that if he would accept the Democratic nomination, Truman would gladly step aside.

Eisenhower was not interested. He was a career military man who, unlike MacArthur, believed that soldiers should stay out of politics. It is not certain that Eisenhower ever bothered to vote before 1948, and he identified with neither party. But he did not identify with university life either. Ike's intellectual interests ran to pulp western novels and, after a lifetime accustomed to military order and expecting instructions to be carried out, he found the chaos of shepherding anarchic academics intolerable.

As one of New York's most eminent citizens, however, Eisenhower drifted into close professional and personal association with the wealthy eastern businessmen who dominated the moderate wing of the Republican party. They showered him with gifts such as had turned General Grant's head, and financial advice that, uncannily, was inevitably sound. As an administrator himself, something of a businessman in uniform, Eisenhower found it easy to assimilate their politics.

In 1950, Ike took a leave of absence from Columbia to take command of NATO troops in Europe. There, with the Korean Conflict dragging on to no conceivable end, MacArthur's insubordination (which shocked him), and the rise of demagogues like McCarthy, he grew increasingly receptive to the pleas of his moderate Republican friends that he run for president. Like them, Eisenhower felt no obsession to return the United States to the pre-New Deal free-enterprise idyll that Taft fantasized. He and they had come to terms with the basic reforms of the Roosevelt era. What disturbed Ike and the moderates was corruption in the Truman administration, excessive government expenditures, and bureaucratic waste. Gradually, Eisenhower came to concede that he could defeat any Democrat by virtue of his tremendous personal popularity while, with Senator Taft as the party's nominee, the Republicans might well go down to defeat.

The Campaign of 1952

Indeed, many conservative Republicans who admired Taft also wanted Eisenhower to run. They were more interested in victory at the polls than in honoring their veteran leader. They agreed with the Eisenhower moderates that Taft's uncompromising conservative stands would alienate voters who had benefited from the New Deal, but who were otherwise weary of the long Democratic era. Eisenhower's lack of a political record was a positive advantage. Eisenhower did not excite people; he reassured them. But that was precisely what, the majority of the Republican party guessed, the nation craved in 1952.

Eisenhower's Democratic opponent was the governor of Illinois, Adlai E. Stevenson. He was a liberal, but he had taken no part in the increasingly unpopular Truman administration. Stevenson was also a superb campaigner, personable, witty, and as attractively modest in manner as Eisenhower. For a few weeks late in the summer of 1952, it appeared as though Stevenson were catching up. He enchanted reporters covering the election with his eloquence while Eisenhower, who functioned best in small groups, seemed to bumble on the podium.

But Stevenson labored under too many handicaps, and Eisenhower's shrewd campaign managers made the most of them. They actually turned Stevenson's intelligence and glibness on the rostrum against him, pointing out that "eggheads" (intellectuals) were responsible for "the mess in Washington." In October, Eisenhower administered the *coup de grace*. While Stevenson defended the policy on which the limited war in Korea was based, Eisenhower promised that, if he were elected, he would "go to Korea" and end the aimless war. Nothing could have better reminded voters that Eisenhower had been the director of the successful war in Europe.

Landslide

Stevenson won nine southern states. Although a supporter of civil rights for blacks, he brought the Dixiecrats back into the Democratic party by naming a southern moderate who supported segregation quietly, John Sparkman of Alabama, as his running mate. Otherwise, Eisenhower swept the nation, winning 55 percent of the popular vote and 442 electoral votes to Stevenson's 89.

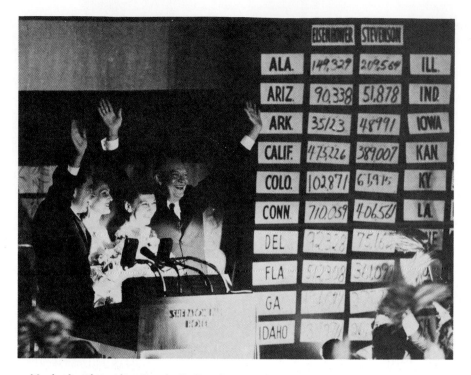

Newly elected president Dwight D. Eisenhower and Vice President Richard Nixon wave to their supporters on election night, 1952.

In December, before he was innaugurated, Eisenhower kept his promise to go to Korea. He donned military gear, and was filmed talking and sipping coffee with soldiers on the front lines. He had long recognized that an all-out conventional offensive was foolish. Now, by threatening to use the atomic bomb to end the stalemate—probably a bluff he had no intention of following through on—he dragooned the Chinese and North Koreans to agree to an end to hostilities in July 1953.

It was an auspicious beginning. Indeed, in March 1953, the *bête-noire* of postwar American frustrations, Soviet dictator Joseph Stalin, had died. The first summer of the Eisenhower presidency was scarcely underway when Americans could feel with reason that they were embarked on a new age of normalcy.

For Further Reading

There are a surprising number of good general histories treating the immediate postwar era. The most recent are William L. O'Neill, *American High: The Years of Confidence, 1945–1960* (1987), and James Gilbert, *Another Chance* (1984), but see also Eric Goldman, *The Crucial Decade and After* (1961); Godfrey Hodgson, *America in Our Time: From World War II to Nixon* (1976); and William E. Leuchtenburg, *A Troubled Feast: American Society Since 1945* (1979). Also consult the introductory sections of C. C. Alexander, *Holding the Line: The Eisenhower Era, 1952–1961* (1975).

On Truman and his administration, see that articulate president's own *Memoirs* (1955–56), and a remembrance by his daughter, Margaret Truman, *Harry S Truman* (1973); William C. Berman, *The Politics of Civil Rights in the Truman Administration* (1970); Bert Cochran, *Truman and the Crisis Presidency* (1973); Susan Hartmann, *Truman and the Eightieth Congress* (1971); R. F. Haynes, *The Awesome Power: Harry S Truman as Commander in Chief* (1973); James T. Paterson, *Mr. Republican: A Biography of Robert A. Taft* (1975); and Allan Yarnell, *Democrats and Progressives: The 1948 Election as a Test of Postwar Liberalism* (1974).

The trying diplomatic problems of the times are treated in Herbert Feis, *Between War and Peace: The Potsdam Conference* (1960) and *From Trust to Terror: The Onset of the Cold War, 1945–1950* (1970); John L. Gaddis, *The United States and the Origins of the Cold*

War, 1941–1947 (1972); Norman A. Graebner, The Age of Global Power: The United States Since 1938 (1979); Gabriel Kolko, The Limits of Power: The World and United States Foreign Policy, 1945–1954 (1972); Walter LaFeber, America, Russia, and the Cold War, 1945–1980 (1981); Thomas G. Paterson, Cold War Critics: Alternatives to American Foreign Policy in the Truman Years (1972); J. L. Snell, Illusion and Necessity: The Diplomacy of Global War (1963); and again William Appleman Williams, The Tragedy of American Diplomacy (1962).

On Korea see Carl Berger, The Korea Knot: A Military-Political History (1957); R. F. Haynes, The Awesome Power: Harry S Truman as Commander in Chief (1973); William Manchester, American Caesar: Douglas MacArthur (1978); G. D. Paige, The Korean Deci-sion (1968); David Rees, Korea: The Limited War (1964); and John W. Spanier, The Truman-MacArthur Controversy (1965). McCarthyism and other manifestations of the red scare of the early 1950s are treated in David Caute, The Great Fear: The Anti-Communist Purge Under Truman and Eisenhower (1978); Stanley Kutler, The American Inquisition (1982); Norman D. Markowitz, Rise and Fall of the People's Century: Henry A. Wallace and American Liberalism, 1941–1948 (1974); Victor Navasky, Naming Names (1980); William L. O'Neill, A Better World (1982); Thomas C. Reeves, The Life and Times of Joe McCarthy (1982); Walter and Miriam Schneir, Invitation to an Inquest (1972); and Allen Weinstein, Perjury! The Hiss-Chambers Conflict (1978).

The voters of 1952 wanted no upheaval. They wanted a change of pace. Virtually all Americans accepted the inevitability of the ongoing Cold War with Communism, but they wanted an end to the stalemate in Korea. Most Americans approved of the basic reforms that the Roosevelt and Truman administrations had carried out; they did not want to return to the days of Coolidge and Hoover. But after a generation of government by the Democratic party, they were ready for new faces in Washington.

Most of all, Americans wanted to cool off. They were weary of crusades, the intense moral demands of reform and war. There was a sense of 1920 about the election of 1952, voters opting for a calmer, reassuring America

47

EISENHOWER COUNTRY

Life in the 1950s

The suburban communities that sprung up across the United States during the 1950s were characterized by rows of nearly identical single-family houses.

in which they could enjoy the rewards of living in the world's richest nation.

Dwight D. Eisenhower, "Ike," personified America in the 1950s.

LEADERSHIP

Reassurance is what Dwight D. Eisenhower gave them. The grinning, amiable Ike was the perfect regent for the times. He kept the peace through two full terms in office. He replaced the jaded political pros, earnest intellectuals, and liberal reformers of the Roosevelt-Truman era with administrators like himself, and with the wealthy businessmen who had become his friends.

They were neither colorful nor exciting. "Eight millionaires and a plumber," a scornful Democrat sniffed about Eisenhower's cabinet, and Secretary of Labor Martin Durkin, the leader of the AFL plumbers union, resigned within a year of his appointment to be replaced by another rich businessman. When Congress created the cabinet-level Department of Health, Education, and Welfare, Eisenhower's choice to head it was not a social worker with a cause to serve, but Oveta Culp Hobby, head of the Women's Army Corps during the Second World War, a military bureaucrat like himself.

Ike's Style and Its Critics

Eisenhower's style was calculated to soothe. Rather than leaping into political cat fights with claws flashing, which had been Truman's way, Ike sidled away from disputes and left the shouting to subordinates. His special assistant, Sherman Adams of New Hampshire, screened every person who applied to see the president. Adams turned away anyone who might involve Ike in a controversy, or trick him into making an embarrassing statement, to which Eisenhower was prone. Adams also studied every document that was to cross the president's desk, weeding out those he thought trivial and summarizing the rest. Eisenhower disliked reading more than a page or so on any subject, a "brief" such as he had dealt with in the army.

Critics claimed that Adams was more powerful than an appointed official should be. They said that he made many presidential-level decisions himself, and he probably did. But there was never any doubt that the thin-lipped New Englander had Eisenhower's complete confidence. In 1958, when it was learned that Adams had rigged some government decisions to favor a long-time friend, businessman Bernard Goldfine, and

had accepted at least an expensive coat from Goldfine in return, he was forced to resign his post. Eisenhower let him go, but he bitterly resented the loss of an aide who had served his purposes so well.

The president delegated considerable power to the members of his cabinet. They were expected to study the details of issues, report to him, and, if they disagreed among themselves, to debate the question. Ike, the commander with ultimate responsibility, listened and handed down the decision. Whenever possible, he preferred compromise to backing one adviser against another. That was how he had worked during the Second World War.

Liberal Democrats and intellectuals, outsiders in Washington during the 1950s, poked fun at Eisenhower's losing battle with the English language at press conferences. Not a reflective man and never quite comfortable before a large audience, Eisenhower lapsed into gobbledygook under pressure: he spoke in disjointed phrases or his sentences meandered endlessly, finally trailing off in a scratch of the head without quite touching on the question he had been asked. Some of Eisenhower's aides suggested that Ike knew exactly what he was doing at all times: "confusing" his interrogators when it did not suit him to answer them.

Eisenhower's apparent lethargy also aroused critics. The nation was drifting, they said, while Ike relaxed on his gentleman's farm on the battlefield at Gettysburg, and took too many vacations in climes where the golf courses were always green and the clubhouses air-conditioned.

We're in the Money

But the critics never got through to the majority of Americans. They did not object to a president who took it easy. In 1956, when Ike ran for reelection against Adlai Stevenson, a year after suffering a serious heart attack and just a few months after undergoing major abdominal surgery, the voters reelected him by an even larger margin than in 1952. Better easy-going Ike in questionable health than a healthy Stevenson forever calling on them to roll up their sleeves again, right wrongs, and finish up the New Deal.

For a majority of Americans, the 1950s were good times, an age of unprecedented prosperity. There had not been a shift in the distribution of wealth. The poor remained about as numerous as they had been for decades. The lowest-paid 20 percent of the population earned the same 3 to 4 percent of the national income that they had earned during the 1920s. The very rich held on to their big slice of the economic pie: the wealthiest 20 percent of the population continued to enjoy 44 to 45 percent of the national income. Proportionately, therefore, the middle 60 percent of the population were no better off than before.

What made the difference in the 1950s was the size of the pie from which all were taking their allotted slices. America was vastly richer as a result of the extraordinary economic growth of the Second World War decade. Thanks to New Deal tax reforms and the powerful labor unions that protected one worker in three, indirectly helping another third, Americans in the middle found themselves with a great deal of "discretionary income," money that was not needed to provide the immediate necessities of life. In 1950, discretionary income totaled $100 billion compared with $40 billion in 1940. This sum increased steadily throughout the decade.

Traditional values of thrift and frugality dictated that such extra money be saved or invested. However, with a generation of daily denial behind them—the hard times of the Great Depression and the sacrifices demanded by the Second World War—newly affluent Americans itched to spend their riches on goods and services that made life more comfortable, varied, and stimulating. A host of new consumer-oriented industries cropped up to urge them on.

Enjoy Yourself

"Enjoy yourself," a popular song went. "It's later than you think." Americans did. They lavished their extra money on a cornucopia of goods and services—some trivial, some momentous in their cultural consequences, and most designed to amuse and entertain economically secure people in their spare time. The middle classes upgraded their diets, eating more meat and vegetables and fewer of the bulky, starchy bread and potatoes that had sustained their parents. Mass-produced convenience foods such as frozen vegetables became staples of middle-class diet. If July in January came with a sacrifice of quality, frozen vegetables could be cooked in five or ten minutes, freeing people to enjoy additional leisure time.

Fashion in dress, buying clothes in order to be "in style," became a diversion in which tens of millions rather than just a handful of very rich people could indulge. Mass-producers of clothing imitated the creations of Paris couturiers with affordable department store versions of "the latest." The designers encouraged the impulse to be a step ahead of neighbors by changing styles annually. In 1953, more people could identify and more or less explain the significance of Christian Dior (a French clothing designer) than the plumber in Eisenhower's cabinet.

Faddism

The 1950s were a time of fads, frivolous behavior in which people participated for no better reason than they could afford to do so and others already were. In late 1954, a Walt Disney television program about the nineteenth-century frontiersman and politician Davy Crockett inspired a mania for coonskin caps (usually made from rabbit or synthetic fur), lunch boxes decorated with pictures of Davy shooting bears, and plastic "long rifles" and bowie knives reasonably safe for use in backyard Alamos. Virtually any homely object with the magic name of Crockett printed on it became a best seller. Within six months, Americans spent more than $100 million in memory of the Tennessee adventurer and Whig who never quite made it big himself.

In 1958, a toy manufacturer brought out a plastic version of an Australian exercise device, a hoop that was twirled about the hips by means of hula-like gyrations. Almost overnight, 30 million "hula hoops" were sold for $1.98 (and, after the fad declined, for as little as 50 cents).

To some extent, the numerous manias of the 1950s were instigated and promoted by the advertising industry. For example, a chemical compound, chlorophyll, became the rage of the early 1950s when manufacturers of more than 90 products, ranging from chewing gum through dog food, said that the green stuff improved the odor of the breath and body of those who ate it, chewed it, shampooed or bathed with it, or rubbed it into the armpits. Americans responded by spending $135 million on chlorophyll products. The boom may have busted when the American Medical Association pointed out that goats, notoriously hard on the nose, consumed chlorophyll all day, every day. More likely, like all fads, chlorophyll simply ran its course.

Other fads profited no one but the newspapers and magazines that reported them. College students competed to see how many of them could squeeze into a telephone booth or a minuscule Volkswagen automobile, challenging others to top their record. Such behavior worried social critics. They concluded that inane faddism revealed the emptiness of lives based on material consumption: people defined themselves in terms of what they could buy. Others were distressed by the conformism of which fads were only the most bizarre example. The American people, it seemed, would do anything and think anything that they were told to do and think, or that others were doing and thinking. But they were afraid of the eccentric, the unpopular, and the adventurous.

The Boob Tube

The most significant new consumer bauble of the 1950s, to become a major force for conformism, was the home television receiver. Developed in workable form as early as 1927, "radio with a picture" had

Children born in the late 1940s and 1950s were the first generation of Americans to grow up with television.

"MAD MAN" MUNTZ

Just as has happened when other completely new consumer goods attracted the fancy of Americans—automobiles, radio receivers, miniaturized calculators, computers—the early television industry was a competitive free-for-all, with dozens of manufacturers hoping to establish themselves as giants of the industry. One of the most intriguing companies was Muntz TV, which promoted its inexpensive sets as if the item were a dubious gadget being hawked at a county fair. "Mad Man" Muntz said that he got his name—he said it on TV as well as on billboards and in magazine advertisements—because he wanted to give his sets away but his wife wouldn't let him. "She says I'm crazy." Also, as in the cases of radios, calculators, computers, the era of all-out competition passed. After the "shakeout," a comparatively few TV set manufacturers remained, mostly old, large electronics makers. In their turn they were displaced by Japanese imports in the 1970s.

remained a toy of electronics hobbyists and the very wealthy until after the Second World War. In 1946, there were only 8,000 privately owned "TV sets" in the United States, about one for every 18,000 people.

Then, gambling that Americans were ready to spend their extra money on a new kind of entertainment, the radio networks plunged into television, making more extensive programming available. By 1950, almost 4 million sets had been sold, one for every 32 people in the country. By 1960, the skeletons of obsolete small-screen receivers were conspicuous in dumps even in rural states. By 1970, more American households were equipped with a television set than had refrigerators, bathtubs, or indoor toilets. Never in history did a whole society fall so suddenly and hopelessly in love with a device.

At first, high-minded network executives and retooled radio reporters such as Edward R. Murrow hoped that television would be an agent of education and uplift. Corporations making consumer products agreed, and sponsored programs bringing serious plays, both classics and dramas written especially for television, to the small screen. Playwrights such as Paddy Chayefsky and Rod Serling got their start writing for shows such as *Playhouse Ninety* and *Studio One*.

But American television, like American radio, was a private enterprise that depended on advertisers for its profits, and advertisers soon learned that a mass audience wanted light entertainment. Americans made a multi-millionaire of "Mr. Television," Milton Berle, who had been only a fair to middling burlesque

comic. Rather more remarkable, a New York gossip columnist utterly lacking in a stage personality, Ed Sullivan, became a national celebrity by hosting a variety show that surrounded one celebrity singer or comedian with trained dog acts, trained bird acts, trained seal acts, and ventriloquists.

Cowboys and Quiz Shows

Beginning in 1955, Americans watched westerns. The networks launched about 40 different dramas set in an imaginary Wild West and, by 1957, one-third of television "prime time," the evening hours between suppertime and bed time, was devoted to horses, sheriffs, badmen, and saloon girls with hearts of gold. In New York City, with seven channels, it was possible to watch 51 western shows a week, in Los Angeles 64 hours of westerns each week.

One of the first, *Gunsmoke*, ran through 635 half-hour episodes; it was estimated that one-quarter of the world's population saw at least one program in which Marshall Matt Dillon made Dodge City, Kansas, safe for decent law-abiding citizens. A somewhat less popular show, "Death Valley Days," revived the career of Ronald Reagan, and set him off on a trail that led to the White House.

Late in the decade, quiz shows offering huge prizes—$64,000 and up—caught the popular imagination. Millions watched avidly as intense intellectuals and idiot-savants rattled off the names of opera characters and kings of Poland. Then, in 1959, it was revealed that Charles Van Doren, a Columbia University professor and scion of a distinguished academic family, had been fed the correct answers before the show, then agonized on camera as he retrieved some obscure morsel of knowledge from deep within his brain. Intellectuals said they were shocked by Van Doren's betrayal of academic integrity. The quiz shows went off the air. Ordinary folks just changed the channel. *Gunsmoke* was still going strong, although its writers admitted some strain in coming up with plots. "We've used up de Maupassant," said one, "and we're halfway through Maugham."

Social and Cultural Consequences

The social and cultural consequences of America's marriage to "the tube" are still not fully appreciated. In the short run, television seemed to kill off other kinds of popular entertainment such as the movies, social dancing, and radio. Hollywood studios that specialized in churning out low-budget films went bankrupt when empty neighborhood theaters closed their doors. However, prestigious movie companies such as

TELEVISION AND THE MOVIES

In 1946, 82 million Americans went to the movies each week. Ten years later, only about half that many did. The others were at home watching television.

Metro-Goldwyn-Mayer, Columbia Pictures, and Warner Brothers survived and prospered by concentrating on expensive, grandiose epics that could not be duplicated on the small black-and-white home screen; by experimenting with themes that were thought unsuitable for showing in homes; and, in the 1960s, by producing shows for home television.

The "big bands" that had toured the country playing for local dances since the 1930s broke up when deserted dance halls closed. But the recorded music industry survived in the age of television by emphasizing individual ballad singers, such as Perry Como, Jo Stafford, Patti Page, and Frankie Laine, who promoted sales of their recordings on television. Radio stations adapted to the big change by scrapping the dramatic and comedy shows that television could do with pictures, and offering instead a format of music, news, and weather aimed at people who were driving their cars or working and could not, during those hours, watch television.

Curiously, the "one-eyed monster" did not much change the reading habits of older Americans. Americans were soon staring into the flickering blue light for three hours a day. However, the time they devoted to magazines and newspapers declined very little, and purchases of books, particularly cheap paperback editions, rose 53 percent over what they had been during the 1940s.

What older Americans cut out in order to watch TV was socializing with one another. Instead of chatting with neighbors or with other members of their families, instead of meeting at dances, clubs, even outside the movie theater, Americans barricaded themselves in their homes, hushing up or resenting all interruptions. The frozen food industry invented the "TV dinner," a complete meal that could be put in and taken out of the oven during commercials or station breaks and eaten in silence in front of the set on a "TV table," a metal tray on folding legs, one for each member of the nuclear family, perhaps an extra one or two for when grandparents, equally agog before the tube, paid a visit.

Fears for the Future

Rather more worrisome was the passive enthusiasm with which children born in the television age were enslaved to the tube. Networks and local stations filled late-afternoon hours and much of Saturday and Sunday mornings with programs that were aimed at children and avidly sponsored by toy makers and manufacturers of breakfast cereals and sweets. If adults who had grown up before the advent of television continued to read, children did not. In 1955, a book by Rudolf Fleisch called *Why Johnny Can't Read* presented Americans with disturbing evidence that they were raising a generation of functional illiterates.

Nevertheless, and regardless of class, race, occupation, or region, Americans took television to their hearts. For good or ill, they were exposed at the same moment to the same entertainment, commercials, and even speech patterns. National businesses discovered that they could compete with local merchants thanks to the hypnotic influence of television advertising.

Because the network and even local news programs preferred announcers who spoke "standard American English," regional variations in speech declined. City people and country people, who had been sharply divided by hostile world views in the previous generation, came to look, speak, and think alike. However, neither country folk nor city folk set the cultural tone of the age of Eisenhower. The people who did were pioneers of a new kind of American community, the middle-class suburb.

SUBURBIA AND ITS VALUES

The essence of the good life, to Americans of the 1950s, was to escape from the cities (and the country) and set up housekeeping in single-home dwellings in the suburbs. In part, this massive movement of population in the late 1940s and 1950s was an expression of an anti-urban bias that dates back to the nation's

TELEVISION IN AMERICA

	Number of TV Households	Percentage of American Homes with TV
1945	5,000	—
1950	3,880,000	9.0
1955	30,700,000	64.5
1960	45,750,000	87.1
1970	59,550,000	95.2
1978	72,900,000	98.0

rural beginnings. As a people, Americans never have been quite at ease with city life.

Flight from the Cities

In part, young couples of the postwar period had little choice as to where they would live. The Second World War had forced millions of them to delay marrying and starting a family for up to four years. In 1945 and 1946, they rushed into marriage, childbearing, and searching for a place to live. But because of the stagnation of the domestic construction industry during the depression and the war, when young couples looked for housing in the cities, they found impossibly high rents and real-estate prices.

To demolish old neighborhoods as the first step of new construction meant temporarily worsening an already critical housing shortage. The solution was the rapid development of entirely new "tracts" or "subdivisions" on the outskirts of cities, far enough from the centers that the price of land was cheap, but close enough that breadwinners could get to their jobs. Of the 1 million housing starts in 1946 and the 2 million in 1950 (compared with 142,000 in 1944), the vast majority was in the suburbs.

The first of the great suburban developments was Levittown, New York, the brainchild of a family company that adapted the assembly line to home building. In order to keep selling prices low, the Levitt brothers used cheap materials and only a few different blueprints. The houses of suburbia were identical, constructed all at once and very quickly. Armies of workers swarmed over the tract, grading thousands of acres at a sweep, and laying out miles of gently curving streets within a few days. Practically before they were done, battalions of men laid down water, gas, sewer, and electrical lines, while teams of carpenters erected hundreds of simple, identical shells.

Then came waves of roofers, plumbers, electricians, carpet layers, painters, decorators, and other craftsmen, each finishing their specialized task on a given house within hours or even minutes. Buyers were so anxious to move in that they were happy to take care of the cleaning up and landscaping themselves. Within four years, Levittown, New York, was transformed from a potato farm into a city of 17,000 homes. On the outskirts of most large cities, developers who imitated the Levitts worked similar miracles. The population of suburbs, never more than a small fraction of the whole, soared. By 1960, as many Americans lived in suburbs as in large cities.

Conformists . . . ?

No sooner did suburbia take shape than it attracted social and cultural criticism. Novelists and sociologists pointed out that the population of the new communities was distressingly homogeneous: 95 percent white, young (20 to 35 years old), married couples with infant children, all of whom made roughly the same income from similar skilled and white-collar jobs.

Not only did the flight from the center cities leave urban centers to the elderly, the poor, and the racial minorities—an implausible tax base—but it segregated the suburbanites too, cutting them off from interaction with other ages, classes, and races of people. Homogeneous communities were narrow-minded communities, critics said; suburbia's values were timid, bland, and superficial.

In politics, people whose comforts and security were made possible by New Deal reforms were afraid to experiment. The suburbanites were staunch supporters of the Eisenhower equilibrium. They swelled the membership lists of churches and synagogues, but insisted on easy, undisturbing beliefs. Rabbi Joshua Liebman, Catholic Bishop Fulton J. Sheen, and the Reverend Norman Vincent Peale told the people of the three major faiths that the purpose of religion was to make them feel good: they, in effect, were at the center of the universe. The Reverend Billy Graham established himself as the country's leading revivalist by shunning the fire and brimstone of earlier evangelists and promoting his transparent blue eyes, wavy hair, and beautiful smile. A survey of Christians showed that while 80 percent believed that the Bible was the revealed word of God, only 35 percent could name the authors of the four gospels and 50 percent could not name one. Among Jews, highly secular and social Reform Judaism displaced Conservative Judaism. Outside of the insular urban communities of Jews who clung to Polish and Russian pasts, Orthodox synagogues were hard to find.

Suburban life was isolated and fragmented, in part because of television, in part because the new communities were built with little thought for social services—schools, shops, parks, professional offices.

INTEGRATED NEIGHBORHOODS

Independent political organizer Saul Alinsky described the pattern of racial segregation in American cities in *Reveille for Radicals* in 1946: "A racially integrated community is a chronological term timed from the entrance of the first black family to the exit of the last white family."

When such traditional social centers were constructed, they were miles from residences; thus suburbanites had to drive some distance even to buy a quart of milk. As a result, the suburban single-family dwelling became a kind of fortress that residents left only to hop into a car and drive somewhere else and back again. The supermarkets encouraged weekly rather than daily shopping expeditions, thus eliminating another traditional occasion of social life.

. . . Or Social Pioneers?

Such criticisms made little impression on the people at whom they were aimed. Suburbanites wanted homes they could afford, and they found the physical roominess of life outside the cities well worth the social isolation and cultural blandness. If the houses were cheaply constructed and identical, they were far better than no houses.

Moreover, the new suburbanites, thrown into brand new towns with no roots and traditions, were great creators of institutions. Lacking established social services and governments, they formed an intricate network of voluntary associations that were entirely supported by private funds and energies. There were the churches and synagogues built from scratch, thousands of new chapters of political parties, garden clubs, literary societies, and bowling leagues. Most important of all were programs that revolved around their children: dancing schools, Cub Scouts and Brownies, Little Leagues, community swimming pools.

Since everyone was a stranger in town, the informal cocktail party became an efficient means by which to introduce people to one another. Because guests milled around the stand-up parties at will, it was not awkward to invite the most casual supermarket or Little League grandstand acquaintances to come on over. Alcohol lubricated easy conversation among strangers, and statisticians noticed a change in American drinking habits toward the consumption of neutral spirits such as gin and vodka, which could be disguised in sweet soda pop or fruit juices. The conclusion was that people who did not like to drink were drinking to make themselves more comfortable and because it was the thing to do.

Insolent Chariots

The suburb could not have developed without the readily available family automobile. In turn, the growth of suburbia made the automobile king, a necessity of life and in some ways a tyrant. Each family needed a car because suburbanites worked at some distance from their homes and public transportation to many of the new communities did not exist. Because

it was necessary for a suburban housewife and mother to cover considerable distances each day, the two-car family became a common phenomenon: one suburban family in five owned two vehicles.

Sales of new cars rose from none during the Second World War to 6.7 million in 1950, and continued to maintain high levels throughout the 1950s. In 1945, there were 25.8 million automobiles registered in the United States. By 1960, with the population increased by 35 percent, car ownership more than doubled, to 61.7 million vehicles.

The automobile was the most important means by which people displayed their status. Unlike the size of paychecks and bank accounts, the family car showed; it sat in the driveway for all to see. Automobile manufacturers devised and encouraged finely honed images for their chariots. The family that was "moving up" was expected to "trade up" from a low-priced Ford, Plymouth, or "Chevy" to a Dodge, Pontiac, or Mercury, and aspire to eventual ownership of a Chrysler, Lincoln, or Cadillac. Indeed, the easy availability of credit made it possible for people to "keep up with the Joneses" by buying beyond their means, going deeply into debt for the sake of appearances. From 1946 through 1970, short-term loans—money borrowed in order to buy consumer goods—increased from $8 billion to $127 billion!

The Automobile Economy

Virtually universal car ownership among the middle classes fueled the growth of businesses that were devoted to cars or dependent on them. Service stations (gasoline consumption doubled during the 1950s), parts stores, car washes, motels, drive-in restaurants, and drive-in movie theaters blossomed on the outskirts of residential suburbs. The suburban shopping mall rivaled city and town centers as the middle-class American marketplace. In 1945, there were eight automobile-oriented shopping centers in the United States. In 1960, there were almost 4,000.

Automobiles demanded roads for use. In 1956, Washington responded with the Interstate Highway Act, under which the government began pumping a total of $1 billion a year into road construction. (By 1960, this expenditure rose to $2.9 billion a year.) Over 41,000 miles of new roads ran crosscountry, but 5,000 miles of freeway were urban, connecting suburbs to big cities.

Not only did this road network encourage further urban sprawl, but it made the cities less livable. Already sapped of their middle classes, once lively urban neighborhoods were carved into isolated residential islands that were walled off from one another by the massive concrete abutments of the freeways. Suburbanite cars roared in on them daily, clogging the streets, raising noise to unprecedented levels, and fouling the air for those who could not afford to move out. Progressively poorer without a middle-class tax base, cities deteriorated physically and suffered from neglected schools and hospitals and rising crime rates. During the 1960s, faced with these problems, the center-city department stores and light industries joined the suburban movement, relocating in shopping centers or on empty tracts near the residential suburbs. When they left, they took not only their tax contributions, but jobs previously available to city dwellers.

Baby Boom

During and immediately after the Second World War, the number of births in the United States took a gigantic leap. While about 2.5 million babies were born in each year of the 1930s, 3.4 million saw the light of day in 1946 and 3.8 million in 1947. Population experts expected this. The depression and war had forced young couples to put off starting families. After a few years of catching up, demographers said, the low birth rate typical of the first half of the century would reassert itself.

They were wrong. The annual number of births continued to increase until 1961 (4.2 million) and did not drop to low levels until the 1970s. The same young couples who were buying unprecedented numbers of new homes and automobiles were having larger families than their parents.

Although all social groups participated in the "baby boom," children were most noticeable in suburbia, where, because most adults were young, children were proportionately more important. Beginning about 1952, when the first boom babies started school, massive efforts were required to provide educational and recreational facilities for them. Businesses oriented toward children, from toymakers to diaper services, sprouted and bloomed.

As the boom babies matured, they attracted attention to the needs and demands of each age group they swelled. By the end of the 1950s, economists observed that middle-class teenagers were a significant consumer group in their own right. They had $10 billion of their own to spend each year. All of it was discretionary! Their necessities were provided by their doting parents.

Magazines that appealed to young people prospered, including *Seventeen* (clothing and cosmetics for girls) and *Hot Rod* (automobiles for boys). Film studios made movies about adolescents and their problems. Beginning in the early 1950s, a new kind of popular music

Hip-swinging, guitar-strumming Elvis Presley popularized rock-'n'-roll during the 1950s.

swept the country. Rock-'n'-roll was based on the rhythms of black music as it had evolved in the mid-twentieth century, but was usually performed by whites, often teenagers themselves. On the one hand, it was rebellious. Elvis Presley, a truck driver from Memphis, scandalized the country with an act that included suggestive hip movements which he said (probably truthfully) he was helpless to control. On the other hand, it was juvenile. Whereas popular songs had previously dealt with themes that were more or less adult, the new music's subjects were high school senior proms, double-dating, teenage lovers lost tragically while racing to beat the Twentieth Century Limited to the crossing. A new kind of record, the compact and nearly unbreakable 45 rpm disk that sold for only 89 cents, became the medium of competition for teenage dollars.

What worried social critics was that older people, seemingly outnumbered by the young, often adopted adolescent ideals and role models. By the end of the decade, one of television's most popular programs was *American Bandstand*, an afternoon show on which teenagers rock-'n'-rolled to recorded music and discussed adolescent problems. Adolescents watched it, of course, but so did housewives at their irons and kitchen sinks. Adults discussed the relative merits of their favorite pubescent dancers. Never before had adult society taken much notice of teenage culture. The baby-boom generation seemed to be proclaiming the society's cultural standards.

H   O   W   T   H   E   Y   L   I   V   E   D

FASHION AND THE FIFTIES

In 1840, the British consul in Boston noted with distaste that Americans did not observe social propriety in the way they dressed. Instead of wearing clothes that were appropriate to their station in life, as an English gentleman thought should be done, Americans dressed more or less the same, and the democracy of dress did not mean a drabbest common denominator. On the contrary, servant girls were "strongly infected with the national bad taste for being over-dressed; they are, when walking the streets, scarcely to be distinguished from their employers." In other words, they were *fashionable*.

By the twentieth century, the democratization of fashion in the United States was complete. The wealthy had a monopoly of the latest from Paris for only as long as it took the American garment industry to copy designs and mass-produce cheap versions of expensive "originals." Indeed, the insistence of American women of almost every social class on their right to dress as the arbiters of fashion pleased accelerated the natural life cycle of a style. The only way the wealthy woman could conspicuously display her capability to spend freely was to move rapidly from one new look to another, always one frantic step ahead of the power shears and sewing machines of the New York garment district.

In 1940, very soon after the Great Depression, the American clothing industry was doing $3 billion in business annually. By the end of the 1950s, it was by some criteria the third largest industry in the United States. Also during those two decades, American dress designers established partial independence from Paris, the capital of fashion, but not from the social preoccupations and values that were neatly reflected in the garments they produced.

The fashions of the years of the Second World War were a product of four forces: the effective shutdown of the design business in occupied Paris; the rationing of materials; the unprecedented prominence of the military in daily life; and the entry of women into the professions and jobs previously held by men.

Because they had been so dependent on Paris for ideas, American fashion designers were disoriented by the fall of France and able on their own to come up with only a variant on 1930s styles. One of the factors that forced some change was the government's restrictions on the amount of fabric that might go into clothing. Skirts could be no larger than 72 inches around. Belts more than two inches wide, more than one patch pocket on blouses, and generous hems were forbidden, as were frills, fringes, and flounces. The result was a severe look in women's dress, accentuated by the fact that with so many uniforms on the streets, civilian clothing took on a military look. It also took on a "masculine look," according to fashion historians; the silhouette of women's clothing was straight and angular,

Full skirts and ponytails were a popular fashion during the 1950s for teenage girls and adult women alike.

with padded shoulders that emulated the male physique.

In 1947, Christian Dior, a Paris designer, reestablished French primacy in the fashion world. His "New Look" celebrated the end of wartime shortages with long, full, and flowing skirts. More interesting, Dior proclaimed a new femininity in fashion. "Your bosoms, your shoulders and hips are round, your waist is tiny, your skirt's bulk suggests fragile feminine legs," an American fashion editor wrote. Dior blouses were left unbuttoned at the top, and more formal bodices were cut in a deep V or cut low to expose shoulders.

The Frenchman either was very lucky or was a very shrewd psychologist. In the United States, the chief market for fashion in the postwar years, women were opting in droves for the home over the office, factory, and public life. As Betty Friedan would later explain, the new domesticity of the 1950s led to a halt and even a drop in the numbers of women entering the professions and other spheres that were traditionally the preserve of men.

But the domesticity of the 1950s was not the domesticity of a hundred years earlier. Thanks to labor-saving home appliances and the money to buy them, a yen for recreation after the austere years of rationing, and the steady relaxation of moral codes, the 1950s housewife was able to be "fashionable" to a degree previously open only to the doyennes of high society.

Another consequence of the new domesticity of the postwar years was the great baby boom, which in turn affected women's fashion. Just as the numerical dominance of young people led to the prominence of juvenile themes in films and popular music, the two-thirds of the female population that was under 30 years of age affected the way women dressed. "For the first time in fashion," wrote Jane Dormer, the British student of the subject, "clothes that had originally been intended for children climbed up the ladder into the adult wardrobe." While Dior and the Parisian couturiers continued to decree what was worn on formal occasions, American teenagers set the standards for casual wear, not only for themselves but for women of all but advanced age. The most conspicuous of these styles was that of the ingénue: "childlike circular skirts," crinolines, hoop skirts, frilled petticoats that were seen not only at junior high school dances but at cocktail parties on mothers of five. Girls and women began to wear their hair loose and flowing or in ponytails, both styles then closely associated with juveniles.

Hollywood both responded to and fed this kind of fashion by coming up with actresses such as Audrey Hepburn, Debbie Reynolds, and Sandra Dee, who specialized in innocent, naïve, little-girlish parts. Well into their thirties, these women clung to what clothing historian Anne Fogarty has called the "paper doll look." Not until the 1960s, when women adopted new values, would this fashion, like all fashions to a later age, look ridiculous.

Christian Dior's "New Look" offered a femininity to contrast with the "severe" fashions of the war years.

Middle-class America's vision of the perfect woman of the 1950s was of a wife and mother with no interest in having a career outside the home.

A New Role for Women

Middle-class America's twin obsessions with enjoying life and catering to its children caused a significant, if temporary, shift in the status of women. Since the beginning of the century, women of all social classes had been moving into occupations and professions that previously had been considered masculine monopolies. Throughout the 1940s, increasing numbers of women finished high school, attended college, studied medicine, the law, and other professions, and took jobs that would have been unthinkable for women before 1900. The Second World War seemed to hasten this blurring of the lines between what the two sexes could do as women took the place of men in heavy and dirty industrial jobs.

When the war ended, however, women willingly left those jobs and enthusiastically embraced the traditional roles of wife, homemaker, and mother. By the 1950s, middle America once more assumed that woman's place was in the home. However, the new woman was not the shrinking violet of the nineteenth century. If she was not employed, the woman of the 1950s was constantly out and about, the backbone of an active social whirl. Because the moral code that had required that women be sequestered had long since withered, the modern American girl, wife, and mother were expected to be active and attractive.

Wives were considered partners in furthering their husbands' careers as sociable hostesses and companions. Women's magazines such as *Cosmopolitan* and *Redbook* first hinted, then shouted that wives should be "sexy."

Sexiness also got a boost from two books published by University of Indiana Professor Alfred Kinsey, *Sexual Behavior in the Human Male* (1948) and *Sexual Behavior in the Human Female* (1953). Although Kinsey studiously versed the conclusions of some 18,000 interviews in scientific language, his revelation that premarital and extramarital sexual intercourse, unorthodox sexual practices, and even homosexual episodes were rather common made for sensational reading and discussion.

Kinsey was condemned as a promoter of immoral and unnatural practices and unspeakable acts, which of course he was not, and even of encouraging communism, a ubiquitous accusation during the 1950s. His methods also came under attack from fellow researchers, and the fact that he described as "human" behavior findings based on a rather narrow segment of humanity: white, generally middle-class America. But that was humanity in suburbia, and white middle-class Americans were the people who bought and read books and, no doubt, were often inspired by them.

AGAINST THE GRAIN

There would be no significant challenge to the new sexy domesticity until 1963, when Betty Friedan published *The Feminine Mystique*. In this best seller, Friedan pointed out that American women had lost ground in their fight for emancipation since 1945. She defined the home as a prison, woman as a sex object, as demeaned, and said that women should move out into the world of jobs, politics, and other realms that she defined as productive. Criticism of other aspects of the culture of the 1950s, however, was widespread even during the age of Eisenhower.

Dissenters

As early as 1942, Philip Wylie's *Generation of Vipers* told the country that indulgence of children, particularly by their mothers ("Momism"), was creating tyrannical monsters. When juvenile-delinquency rates soared during the 1950s, even in the well-to-do suburbs, other writers elaborated on Wylie. John Keats attacked the sterility of suburban life, especially the social irresponsibility of the developers that left new developments without vital social centers. Later, in *Insolent Chariots*, he turned his attention to the automobile as an economic tyrant and a socially destructive force.

In *The Organization Man* (1956), William H. Whyte, Jr., fastened on the work place, arguing that jobs in the huge corporations and government bureaucracies that dominated the American economy placed the highest premium on anonymity, lack of imagination and enterprise, and generally just fitting in. Sociologist David Riesman suggested in *The Lonely Crowd* (1950) that Americans were becoming "other-directed." They no longer took their values from their heritage or their parents, least of all from within themselves, but thought and acted according to what was acceptable to those around them.

Sloan Wilson fictionalized the conformism and cultural aridity of suburban life in *The Man in the Gray Flannel Suit* (1955), a novel about a suburban commuter who works in the advertising industry. In *The Hidden Persuaders* (1957), Vance Packard reinforced the assault on advertising by pointing out that all Americans were manipulated by advertisements that played not on the virtues of the product for sale but on people's feelings and insecurities.

Beatniks and Squares

The beat generation, or "beatniks" as people called its exemplars, offered a less articulate critique of Eisenhower tranquility. Originally a literary school centered around novelist Jack Kerouac and poet Allen Ginsberg, "beat" evolved into a bohemian lifestyle with capitals in New York's Greenwich Village, San Francisco's North Beach, and Venice, California, near Los Angeles.

ELEVATOR MUSIC

"Elevator music," deliberately bland background music played at low volume in restaurants, hotels, offices, shops—and elevators—is heard by 80 million Americans a day. It was originally called "furniture music" by its creator, a composer named Eric Satie, who said in 1920 that it would "fill the same role as light and heat—as *comfort*." Satie urged Americans, "Don't enter a house which does not have furniture music," but the concept caught on only after 1934, when the name "Muzak" was coined.

Muzak is played in the Pentagon and in the White House. President Lyndon Johnson pumped Muzak all over his ranch in Texas by mounting speakers on trees.

Beatniks rebelled against what they considered to be the intellectually and socially stultifying aspects of 1950s America. They shunned regular employment. They took no interest in politics and public life. They mocked the American enchantment with consumer goods by dressing in T-shirts and rumpled khaki trousers, the women innocent of cosmetics and the intricate hairstyles of suburbia. They made a great deal of the lack of furniture in their cheap walk-up apartments, calling their homes "pads" after the mattress on the floor.

The beatniks were highly intellectual. They prided themselves on discovering and discussing obscure writers and philosophers, particularly exponents of an abstruse form of Buddhism called Zen. They rejected the ostensibly strict sexual morality of the "squares" and lived together without benefit of marriage; a few were homosexual or dabbled in homosexual practices. Their music was jazz as played by blacks, whom they regarded as free of the corruptions of white America.

Beatniks simultaneously repelled, amused, and fascinated conventional American society. Traditional moralists demanded that police raid beatnik coffee houses in search of marijuana (which beatniks introduced to white America) and amateur poets reading sexually explicit verse. Preachers in the traditional churches inveighed against the moral decay that the beatniks represented.

But sexual mores were changing in suburbia, too. To be divorced was no longer to be shunned as a moral pariah. The courts approved the publication of books formerly banned as obscene, with celebrated cases revolving around D. H. Lawrence's *Lady Chatterley's Lover* and Henry Miller's *Tropic of Cancer*. The furor over Ginsberg's long poem *Howl* (1955), which included a few racy lines, made it a best seller. Suburbanites, the favorite targets of beat mockery, flocked to Greenwich Village and North Beach on weekends to dabble in beatnik fashions. Like most cultural rebels, the beatniks did not really challenge society's basic assumptions. They merely provided another form of entertainment.

The Awakening of Black America

The protest against racial discrimination was an altogether different matter. Rather than sniping at trivialities such as lifestyle, America's blacks during the 1950s demonstrated to whites that their prosperous society was built in part on the systematic denial of civil rights to 15 million people.

For more than half a century, black leaders such as W. E. B. Du Bois, Mary McLeod Bethune, A. Philip Randolph, and Bayard Rustin had fought a frustrating

Throughout much of the United States, and particularly in the South, racial discrimination was evident in the segregation of schools, neighborhoods, bathroom facilities, and drinking fountains.

battle against racial prejudice. Their most important organization, the National Association for the Advancement of Colored People (NAACP), had won some significant victories in the courts. Lynching, formerly a weekly occurrence in the South and rarely punished, had become rare by the 1950s. Under Truman, the armed forces were desegregated (black recruits were no longer placed in all-black units), and the Supreme Court ordered several southern states to admit blacks to state-supported professional schools because the segregated medical and legal training they offered blacks was not equal in quality to that provided for whites.

Nevertheless, when Eisenhower moved into the White House, all the former slave states plus Oklahoma retained laws on the books that segregated parks, movie theaters, waiting rooms, trains, buses, and schools. Four more states legally permitted one form or another of racial segregation. (Fifteen states explicitly prohibited it.)

In the Deep South, public drinking fountains were labeled "white" and "colored," and some states actually provided different Bibles in court for the swearing in of witnesses. This strict color line had been legal since 1896, when, in the case of *Plessy* vs. *Ferguson*, the Supreme Court had declared that racially separate public facilities were constitutional as long as they were equal in quality.

The Brown Case

In 1954, Thurgood Marshall, the NAACP's legal strategist, argued before the Supreme Court that racially separate educational facilities were intrinsically unequal because segregation burdened blacks with a constant reminder of their inequality. In *Brown* vs. *Board of Education of Topeka* (1954), the Court unanimously agreed.

In some parts of the South, school administrators complied quickly and without incident. However, in Little Rock, Arkansas, in September 1957, an angry mob of white adults greeted the first black pupils to enroll in Central High School with shouts, curses, and rocks. Claiming that he was protecting the peace, but actually currying the favor of white racists, Governor Orval Faubus called out the Arkansas National Guard to prevent the black children from enrolling.

Eisenhower blamed the turmoil on both Earl Warren, the new Chief Justice, and Orval Faubus. Sharing the belief of many Americans that there was no great harm done by segregation, Eisenhower regarded the Brown decision as a mistake. If nothing else, by arousing black Americans to protest, it disturbed the tranquility that Ike treasured, and he did not believe that laws could change people's feelings. He later said that his appointment of Earl Warren to the Supreme Court was the worst decision that he had ever made.

Nevertheless, the Supreme Court had spoken and Ike was a constitutionalist. To him, the Court's ruling had the force of federal law, and Faubus was defying it. Eisenhower superseded the governor's command of the National Guard and ordered the troops to enforce the integration of Central High. Overnight, the mission of the Arkansas National Guard was reversed.

From the Courts to the Streets

The battle to integrate the schools continued for a decade. Beginning in 1955, however, the civil-rights movement ceased to be a protest of lawyers and lawsuits and became a peaceful revolution by hundreds of thousands of blacks who were no longer willing to be second-class citizens.

The leader of the upheaval was Martin Luther King, Jr., a young preacher in Montgomery, Alabama. In

A black airman contemplates the sign indicating the colored waiting room in a southern railroad station.

December 1955, Rosa Parks, a black secretary, refused to give up her seat on a bus to a white man, as city law required, and King became the spokesman for a black boycott of the Montgomery buses. When the city tried to defend the color line, the dispute attracted journalists and television reporters from all over the country.

King's house was bombed, and he explained his strategy for ending racial discrimination from the wreckage of his front porch. Nonviolent civil disobedience, King said, meant refusing to obey morally reprehensible laws such as those that sustained segregation, but without violence. When arrested, protestors should not resist. Not only was this the moral course of action—King hated violence of all kinds—but it was politically effective. When decent people were confronted with the sight of southern police officers brutalizing peaceful blacks and their white supporters simply because they demanded their rights as citizens, they would, King believed, force politicians to support civil rights.

Although it led to considerable suffering by demonstrators and to several deaths, King's strategy worked. A few important labor leaders such as Walter Reuther of the United Automobile Workers marched with the young minister and helped finance the Southern Christian Leadership Conference (SCLC), which

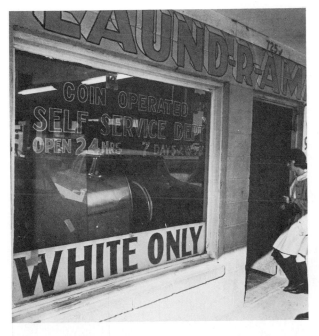

A self-service laundry for white patrons only in New Orleans.

Black students, escorted and protected by the National Guard, enter the all-white Central High School in Little Rock, Arkansas, in 1957.

King founded to spearhead the fight for equality. After 1960, when SCLC's youth organization, the Student Nonviolent Coordinating Committee (SNCC), peacefully violated laws that prohibited blacks from eating at lunch counters in the South, white university students in the North picketed branches of the offending chain stores in their hometowns. When white mobs burned a bus on which white and black "freedom riders" were defying segregation, the federal government sent marshals south to investigate and prosecute violent white racists.

Although King fell out of favor with some younger blacks in the late 1960s, he loomed over his era as only President Eisenhower did, and with far greater historical consequence. After his assassination in 1968, under circumstances that remain somewhat mysterious, several states made his birthday a holiday, and in 1986 it became an official federal holiday. But King and black Americans only began their fight for equality during the age of Eisenhower. It was the next decade, the troubled 1960s, which saw the end of civil discrimination on the basis of race.

For Further Reading

See these solid general histories: C. C. Alexander, *Holding the Line: The Eisenhower Era, 1952–1961* (1975); James Gilbert, *Another Chance: America Since 1945* (1984); Eric Goldman, *The Crucial Decade and After* (1961); Godfrey Hodgson, *America in Our Time: From World War II to Nixon* (1976); William E. Leuchtenburg, *A Troubled Feast: American Society Since 1945* (1979); and William L. O'Neill, *American High: The Years of Confidence, 1945–1960* (1987).

In addition to O'Neill, the following books are good on American society in the 1950s: Daniel Boorstin, *The Image* (1962); John Kenneth Galbraith, *The Af-*

fluent Society (1958); Paul Goodman, *Growing Up Absurd* (1960); E. Larrabee, *The Self-Conscious Society* (1960); David Riesman, *The Lonely Crowd: A Study of the Changing American Character* (1950); the appropriate chapters of Sheila M. Rothman, *Woman's Proper Place: Λ History of Changing Ideas and Practices, 1870 to the Present* (1978); C. Taeuber, *The Changing Population of the United States* (1958); William H. Whyte, *The Organization Man* (1956); and Robert C. Woods, *Suburbia* (1959). The bohemian dissenters of the era are treated in Bruce Cook, *The Beat Generation* (1971).

Racial segregation and its crumbling have been extensively studied. See James Baldwin, *The Fire Next Time* (1963), and Martin Luther King, Jr., *Stride Toward Freedom* (1958) for profound insights into black resentments and aspirations. Also see Archibald Cox, *The Warren Court: Constitutional Decision as an Instrument of Reform* (1968); Richard Kluger, *Simple Justice: The History of Brown versus Brown of Education and Black America's Struggle for Equality* (1975); Philip B. Kurland, *Politics, the Constitution, and the Warren Court* (1970); Louis E. Lomax, *The Negro Revolt* (1963);

Benjamin Muse, *Ten Years of Prelude: The Story of Integration Since the Supreme Court's 1954 Decision* (1964); and C. E. Silberman, *Crisis in Black and White* (1964).

President Eisenhower's reputation among historians has generally risen in recent years, although it is still hotly argued. The standard biography is Stephen Ambrose, *Eisenhower* (1983–84), but also see Marquis Childs, *Eisenhower: Captive Hero* (1958); Dwight D. Eisenhower, *The White House Years* (1965); Peter Lyon, *Eisenhower: Portrait of a Hero* (1974); and F. M. Shattuck, *The 1956 Presidential Election* (1956). Biographical studies of other notables of the 1950s include Townshend Hoopes, *The Devil and John Foster Dulles* (1973); John Bartlow Martin, *The Life of Adlai E. Stevenson* (1976–77); Stephen B. Oates, *Let the Trumpet Sound: The Life of Martin Luther King, Jr.* (1982); James T. Paterson, *Mr. Republican: A Biography of Robert A. Taft* (1975); Thomas C. Reeves, *The Life and Times of Joe McCarthy* (1982); John D. Weaver, *Warren* (1967); and G. Edward White, *Earl Warren: A Public Life* (1982).

48

CONSENSUS AND CAMELOT

Policies of the Eisenhower and Kennedy Administrations, 1953–1963

More than a generation has elapsed since Dwight D. Eisenhower became president in 1953. Most of the leaders of that era are dead. Many of the issues over which they quarreled have long since been resolved; others seem trivial now. Those times are remote to a people who were, overwhelmingly, only children during the 1950s and early 1960s, or not yet born. With our sophisticated electronic means of recording and communicating, the preservation of the events of the 1950s and 1960s in grainy black-and-white film enhances the sense that this is the stuff of "ancient history."

In fact, the age of Eisenhower and Kennedy is recent, almost contemporary history, "only yesterday."

Supreme Court Chief Justice Earl Warren swears in John F. Kennedy as president in 1961. Outgoing president Dwight Eisenhower stands solemnly on the far left, while future presidents, Lyndon Johnson and Richard Nixon, stand on the far right.

Its affairs still register vividly in the memories of the elderly and the middle-aged. The historian who tries to sift out the meaning of a time on which the perspective of remoteness is lacking must be content with a sieve of dubious quality—and be aware of the fact. The many strands of continuity between those times and our own preclude detachment and make objectivity difficult. What was important? What was not? Who can say for sure? Here and there a few fools can.

One characteristic of the decade of Dwight D. Eisenhower and John F. Kennedy does stand out in high relief. Both presidents enjoyed something that none of their successors have, something like an optimistic consensus, the general accord of the people—including political opponents of Eisenhower and Kennedy—that almost all was well in the American corner of the world. There were dissidents and malcontents, as there must be in an open society. But most Americans of the 1950s and early 1960s felt that however serious the problems facing the nation, they were in the hands of leaders who were both capable and well intentioned.

Still, it would be an error to describe the age of Eisenhower and Kennedy as golden, the "Camelot" that Kennedy's devoted aides called his short administration. Many of the domestic tensions and foreign concerns that have unsettled and fragmented Americans since 1963 began to simmer when Eisenhower sat in the White House. Decisions that were taken by both his administration and Kennedy's contributed to their gravity. Nevertheless, because most Americans grew conscious of most of these troubles only after Kennedy's assassination in 1963, the decade that preceded it appears to have been an easier time in which to live.

Although conservative, even Secretary of Agriculture Ezra Taft Benson reflected Ike's flexibility in his policies.

IKE'S DOMESTIC COMPROMISE

In his heart and soul, Dwight D. Eisenhower was an old-fashioned conservative. As a career soldier, he was isolated from the mainstream of political development, and he thought of government in terms of his small-town childhood in Kansas and Texas at the turn of the century, and the gruff platitudes about free enterprise he swapped with the rich businessmen who befriended him after the Second World War.

The tremendous expansion of federal power during the New Deal and the Second World War disturbed him. Perhaps because the peacetime army in which he had served was so stingily financed, he shuddered at the size of the government's budget and at the very notion of annual deficits piling up into a mountain of national debt. He believed that businessmen in the private sector were better qualified to manage the economy than were the bureaucratic agencies that had been created under Roosevelt and Truman. He criticized the Tennessee Valley Authority, the liberal model of regional economic and social planning, as "creeping socialism" and suggested that its facilities be sold off to private power companies.

The Best Laid Schemes o' Mice an' Men . . .

Some of Ike's advisers, such as Secretary of Agriculture Erza Taft Benson of Utah, were downright reactionary in their hostility to government regulation, social-welfare programs, and the big bureaucracies that implemented them. Given his head, Benson would have rampaged through the office buildings of Washington like an avenging angel.

Secretary of Defense Charles Wilson sounded like a ghost of the Coolidge era when he gave his opinion

THE COLD WAR CONTINUES   835

of the role that corporations should play in framing national policy. In what was only in part a slip of the tongue, Wilson told a Senate committee that "what was good for the country was good for General Motors and vice versa." (Wilson came to government from the General Motors board of directors.)

When Jonas Salk, a research physician, perfected a vaccine that promised to wipe out polio, then a scourge of children, Secretary of Health, Education, and Welfare Oveta Culp Hobby warned that even though an immunization program might well eradicate the disease, for the government to sponsor the program would be socialistic.

. . . Gang Aft Agley

That was how Ike's advisers spoke and, no doubt, truly felt. When it came time to take action, however, the president was moderate, pragmatic, and realistic. He was able to face up to the fact that the America of his Kansas boyhood was gone forever and that the federal government had to take some responsibility for economic and social welfare in the complicated world of the mid-twentieth century. His administration did sponsor a polio immunization program.

Eisenhower also discovered the risks in trusting too closely to his businessmen friends when he supported a private company, Dixon-Yates, in a dispute with the TVA over which of them would construct a new generating facility for the Atomic Energy Commission. Rather than the contest between "free enterprise" and "creeping socialism" that had been described to him, Ike discovered that Dixon-Yates executives were mired deeply in collusion with friendly AEC officials in what amounted to a raid on the Treasury—"socialism for the rich." He withdrew his support of Dixon-Yates and accepted a face-saving compromise in which the city of Memphis, in the public sector but not federal, built the plant.

Even troglodytic Ezra T. Benson had to swallow his distaste for the agricultural-subsidy programs that he wanted to abolish. The 1950s were years of distress in the farm belt, and the application of free-market principles would have transformed them into years of catastrophe. As agricultural productivity continued to increase but neither domestic consumption nor foreign demand kept pace, grain piled up in volcano-shaped cones in the streets of farm towns throughout the Midwest. Farm income dipped, and farm families left the land for city and town jobs in numbers not seen since the 1920s. Food production never lagged; big agri-business corporations gobbled up and consolidated family farms, operating them like any other industry. They were able to profit where farm families could not because the Eisenhower administration quietly expanded the subsidy programs against which Benson had railed.

The Soil Bank Act of 1956 authorized the payment of money to landowners for every acre they took out of cultivation in order to reduce production. Within ten years, $1 of every $6 that farmers and agricultural corporations pocketed at harvest time came not from sales but from the federal government—for crops that were never planted. Eisenhower also adopted New Deal-like policies when he introduced programs under which the federal government purchased surplus crops for school lunches and foreign-aid programs.

Dynamic Conservatism

The clearest indication that "dynamic conservatism" (as Eisenhower called his political compromise) included taking responsibility for the health of the economy came when the sharp reduction of military expenditures after the Korean War threatened to drop the country into a depression. Eisenhower responded by asking Congress to lower taxes, and he persuaded the Federal Reserve Board to loosen credit restrictions so as to put more money into the hands of consumers, that is, to make it easier for them to borrow and spend.

In 1957 and 1958, a worse recession threw 7 percent of the work force out of jobs. Ike responded with several large public-works projects like the New Deal programs that he earlier had condemned. In the area of social welfare, over 10 million names were added to the lists of people who received Social Security payments during Eisenhower's presidency.

THE COLD WAR CONTINUES

The Cold War continued under Eisenhower. Indeed, every president after Harry S Truman had to design foreign policy around the overwhelming fact that the United States was locked into a competition with the Soviet Union that left very little room for maneuver. Or, at least, all so believed.

The Nature of the Beast

Because the United States and the U.S.S.R. were nuclear superpowers, the contest between them could not rationally be resolved by the timeless test of decisive war. Already by the age of Eisenhower, it was obvious that armed conflict between the United States and the Soviet Union would lead to vast physical devastation in both countries and the death of tens of millions of people. By 1961, when Ike retired, nuclear technology was advanced to the point that world war could readily lead to the destruction of civilization and, conceivably, the earth's capacity to support human life. Every president from Ike to Jimmy Carter has understood and clearly stated that there would be no winners in a nuclear war.

Therefore, until the United States and the Soviet Union trusted each other enough to agree on disarmament, policymakers had to live with the balance of terror and compete with their rivals under the threat of it. The history of American foreign relations after 1953 is the story of how a succession of presidents and secretaries of state coped with these restraints.

More Bang for a Buck

Although Dwight D. Eisenhower spent much of his life in an army uniform, he wanted to be remembered as a man of peace. "I have seen enough war," he said, and as president he acted with moderation in crisis situations. By the time he left office, Eisenhower appeared to distrust the motives of his generals and the business leaders who supported him. In his farewell address of 1961, Ike told Americans to beware of the "military-industrial complex," the intimate and self-serving alliance of the Pentagon (the Department of Defense), and the big corporations that made their money by selling weapons to the government. Along with like-minded intellectuals in the universities and "think tanks," with their ivory-tower theories of how to fight the Cold War, Ike said, the military establishment and arms industry were apt to be reckless in the use of armed force.

Eisenhower's fiscal conservatism also played a role in his defense policy. If he were to balance the federal budget—to spend no more money in a year than the Treasury collected in taxes—he had to cut military expenditures, the biggest single item in the budget. Because complete disarmament was out of the question, Eisenhower adopted a comparatively inexpensive plan for maintaining national security, the "more bang for a buck" policy. Encouraged by penny-pinching Secretary of the Treasury George Humphrey, the president cut spending on the conventional army and navy and concentrated on building up America's nuclear deterrent: atomic and hydrogen bombs and the sophisticated ships, planes, and missiles capable of delivering them to Soviet targets. This purely defensive policy threatened no one, Ike told the world. The United States would never start a nuclear war, but the Soviet Union, unless it were deterred by the threat of "massive retaliation," might very well do so.

Critics claimed that the policy meant all or nothing. The United States could destroy the world, but could the nation respond in proportion to minor Soviet provocations? Secretary Humphrey was not impressed.

U.S. Army Airborne troops occupy the Beirut, Lebanon, airport in 1958.

With the frustrations of the limited war in Korea fresh in his mind, he growled that the United States had "no business getting into little wars . . . . Let's intervene decisively with all we have got or stay out."

Other Eisenhower supporters said that the reduced army and navy were more than adequate to act in minor crises. In 1958, when Eisenhower suspected that Communists intended to take over Lebanon, he was able to send marines into the Middle Eastern nation to stabilize a government friendly to the United States. It was only a long, expensive, and demoralizing conventional war like Korea for which he did not choose to prepare.

Peaceful Coexistence

The United States was directly involved in no wars of note during Eisenhower's eight years in office. In part this may have been due to a significant change in Soviet leadership. Joseph Stalin, suspicious to the point of mental imbalance late in life, died in 1953. After a few years of figurehead leaders and murky maneuvering in the Kremlin, he was succeeded by an altogether different kind of strong man, a rotund, homely, and quite clever Ukrainian named Nikita Khrushchev.

Khrushchev confused American "Kremlinologists," as Soviet experts came to call themselves. And that may have been one of his purposes. At times he seemed to be a coarse buffoon who habitually drank too much vodka and showed it. Visiting the United Nations, he stunned the assembly of dignitaries by taking off his shoe and banging it on the desk in front of him to protest a speaker of whom he disapproved. At other times Khruschev was witty and charming, almost slick.

The new premier could issue frightening warlike challenges to the United States. But he was also the man who denounced Stalinist totalitarianism at home in 1956 and called for peaceful coexistence with American capitalism. Khrushchev claimed that the Cold War would be resolved by historical forces rather than by armed conflict. "We will bury you," he told American capitalists; the world would peacefully choose the Soviet way of life. (Anti-Communist extremists in the United States quoted the quotable phrase as an example of Khruscehv's bellicosity.)

Kitchen Debates

A comparison of American and Soviet societies in the 1950s and 1960s mocked Khrushchev's boast, and helped to explain his interest in slowing down the arms race. Despite his reforms, Soviet citizens remained under tight political controls; the secret police was not dissolved. The Soviet economy was sluggish. Because a country inestimably poorer than the United States had to match American spending on armaments, daily life in Russia was drab. Long lines of people at shops waiting not only for the most modest of luxuries but for basic foodstuffs was hardly preferable to the American consumer cornucopia.

Vice President Richard Nixon debates with Russian premier Nikita Khrushchev in front of a mock-up of a typical American kitchen in Moscow, 1959.

Vice President Richard M. Nixon understood the impact of the contrast on both Americans and people in other countries when he visited Moscow in 1959. He engaged Khrushchev in a debate in front of a mock-up of an appliance-filled American kitchen, pointing out that there was nothing like it in Russia.

Khruschev was annoyed at being sandbagged by Nixon on his own ground—American photographers were carefully placed for the "kitchen debate"—but the yawning gulf between daily life in the two superpowers was a major reason he wanted some sort of rapprochement with the United States. Only by cutting the cost of the arms race could Soviet agriculture and consumer industries be built up.

Khrushchev had one big edge in the salesmanship contest with American spokesmen. He was flexible and opportunistic, even cynical, while the chief foreign representative of the United States under Eisenhower, Secretary of State John Foster Dulles, was a man of antique principle, petrified mind, and the charm of the bullfrog he resembled.

John Foster Dulles, secretary of state under Eisenhower, was a staunch supporter of the Cold War.

Dull, Duller, Dulles

On the basis of his credentials, Dulles should have been a grand success. He was related to two previous secretaries of state, and he had begun his diplomatic career half a century earlier. During the years he was out of government, Dulles practiced international law with a firm that was considered the best in the business. At the top of that business in 1953 when Eisenhower named him secretary of state, Dulles turned out to be handicapped by an impossible personality for a diplomat and a simplistic view of the world. He was a pious Presbyterian of a discredited old school, as self-righteous, intolerant, and humorless as any Puritan of old New England. "Dull, Duller, Dulles," the Democrats intoned.

He believed that Communists were evil incarnate, veritable agents of Satan. He was unable to respond when Khrushchev hinted that he wanted to ease tensions, and he found it difficult to deal with neutral nations that maintained friendly relations with the Soviets. Photographs of Dulles with neutral national leaders like Jawaharlal Nehru of India reveal a man who fears he will be defiled if he sits too closely.

Such undiplomatic manners made him unpopular not only in the Third World (countries aligned with neither the United States nor the Soviet Union), but among the diplomats who represented America's allies. To make matters worse, Dulles insisted on representing his policies in person. He flew 500,000 miles on the job, demoralizing American ambassadors by converting them into mere ceremonial figures who greeted his plane and then disappeared.

In his conception of the emerging nations of the Third World and of revolutionary movements in the republics of Latin America, Dulles's limitations were even more damaging. The old colonial empires of the European nations were falling apart during the 1950s as new Asian and African countries were founded

AMERICA UNDERGROUND

For a time in the 1950s, fear of Soviet nuclear attack spawned a minor building boom in "fallout shelters," covered pits in backyards to which, upon hearing the sirens, families would repair and thus survive the atomic bomb. Although magazines such as *Popular Science* and *Popular Mechanics* suggested fairly cheap do-it-yourself models, a professionally built shelter, carpeted and painted beige, cost $3,000, the price of a decent house. Even if her family never used their shelter, a suburban Los Angeles woman said, it "will make a wonderful place for the children to play in." Other people pointed out that shelters were useful storage areas. In the theological journals, ministers and priests argued about a person's moral justification in shooting neighbors and relatives who had not been so prudent in building their own shelters and, in the moment of crisis, were trying to horn in.

almost annually. Often committed at least in word to radical social reform, including socialist institutions, the leaders of these countries were rarely pro-Soviet. They needed American friendship and, most of all, American financial aid. In many parts of Latin America, revolutionaries determined to oust reactionary and repressive dictatorships had, by necessity and principle, to reduce American economic power in their countries. But all but the infantile ideologues among them recognized the advantage of having good relations with the nation that had sponsored the Marshall Plan.

Picking the Wrong Friends

Instead of exploiting the widespread good will toward the United States or, at least, the cordiality of necessity, Dulles divided the world into "us" and "them," with "us" defined as those nations that lined up behind the United States in every particular. He wrote off all independently minded national leaders and all revolutionary movements as Communist inspired. Along with his brother, Allen Dulles, who headed the semisecret Central Intelligence Agency (CIA), he threw American influence behind reactionary regimes, including repressive and often brutal dictatorships in Portugal, Nicaragua, the Dominican Republic, and Cuba, simply because they were pro-American, "us."

Dulles wasted no time in implementing his simplistic views. In 1953, the United States helped the unpopular Shah of Iran overthrow a reform-minded prime minister, Mohammed Mossadegh, despite the fact that, with its border on the Soviet Union and long fear of Russian domination, Iran could not afford to cozy up to Russia no matter who was in power. In 1954, the CIA took the lead in overthrowing a democratically chosen prime minister in Guatemala, Jacobo Arbenz, because he expropriated American-owned banana plantations.

Also in 1954, Dulles refused to sign the Geneva Accords, which ended a long and tragic war in Vietnam between France and a Communist-led independence movement that, because of the historical Vietnamese hostility toward China, was probably open to cooperation with the United States.

Dulles's actions in Iran, Latin America, and Southeast Asia were to redound in setbacks to American foreign policy for four decades. Dulles said, in effect, that the United States opposed social progress in those parts of the world where change was most sorely needed. His blindness provided Khrushchev with the opportunity to play the friend of anticolonialism, freedom, and reform. The pretense ill-suited the imperialist, dictatorial, and ideologically hidebound Soviet Union, but Khrushchev and Dulles worked together to make it look plausible.

Brinkmanship and Massive Retaliation

Eisenhower, by conviction or default, backed up Dulles's policies in the Third World. He balked, however, at the secretary's advocacy of "brinkmanship" and "massive retaliation" in relations with the Soviet Union and, because the Chinese Communists were defined as Soviet flunkeys, the People's Republic of China.

Dulles rejected containment as immoral because George Kennan and the Truman administration had called for merely holding the line against the spread of Communism in the hopes that, in the future, the Soviets would prove amenable to a settlement based on trust and goodwill. Dulles could not imagine accepting Communist states as part of the world community and said that it was not necessary that the United States do so. America would win the Cold War by going to the brink of hot war, threatening "massive retaliation," nuclear attack, in disputes with the Soviets.

Indeed, Dulles meant to provoke disputes that would enable him to put brinkmanship into action. In 1953, the Korean War just concluded, Dulles hinted that he would support Chiang Kai-shek if the exiled Nationalist Chinese leader invaded the People's Republic. In the same year, with the Soviet leadership in a state of flux following Stalin's death, Dulles led the peoples of the satellite states of Eastern Europe to believe that Americans would come to their aid if they rebelled against Russian domination.

Moderation in Practice

However, when the Chinese Communists began to shell two tiny islands controlled by Chiang, Quemoy and Matsu, Ike backed off, forcing Dulles to do the same. Eisenhower stated clearly for the first time that it was only Taiwan the United States would defend. The artillery exchanges between the two Chinas soon developed into a ritual worthy of the Mandarins, a far more "limited war" than Korea. At one point, the Communists insisted only on the right to shell Quemoy and Matsu on alternate days of the month.

In Hungary in 1956, Dulles's talk of rolling back the iron curtain contributed to a more tragic event. Anti-Soviet Hungarians rebelled and took control of Budapest. The Soviets hesitated, as though waiting to see what the Americans would do. They regarded Hungary as vital to their security, but feared all-out war on the issue. When Eisenhower did nothing,

Soviet tanks and infantry rolled into Budapest, easily quashing the revolution. The net effect of the episode was to undercut confidence in Dulles's bold words throughout the world.

Also in 1956, Eisenhower and Dulles angered three important allies by first appearing to encourage them to take action against increasingly pro-Soviet Egypt, and then refusing to back them. Britain, France, and Israel invaded Egypt to prevent the government of President Gamal Abdel Nasser from taking control of the Suez Canal. When Khrushchev threatened to send Russian "volunteers" to Egypt's aid, Eisenhower announced his opposition to the allied assault. Humiliated, the British, French, and Israelis withdrew. They could not carry on without American support.

Summitry and the U-2

When Dulles resigned a month before he died of cancer in 1959, Eisenhower took personal charge of for-

eign policy. Oddly, having allowed so much rein to Dulles for six years, he was rather well equipped to administer foreign relations. Of all American presidents, only Hoover and John Quincy Adams had spent more of their lives abroad than he. Eisenhower had lived for long periods in France, England, the Philippines, Panama, and Algeria. His experience in dealing with American allies during the Second World War had demanded the utmost in diplomatic tact.

For a time, Ike seemed to be easing Soviet-American tensions. With Dulles out of the way, he and Khrushchev outdid one another with statements of good will, and they agreed to exchange friendly visits. Khrushchev made his tour of the United States in 1959 and scored a rousing personal success. In the flesh and on his best behaviour, he captivated many Americans with his unpretentious manner and interest in everyday things. Khrushchev even drew laughter when, having been refused admission to Disneyland for se-

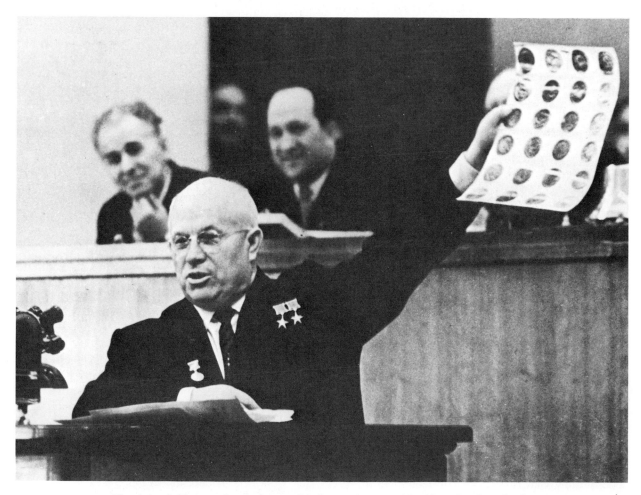

Khrushchev holds up evidence of spying found in an American U-2 plane shot down by the Russians on May 1, 1960.

curity reasons, he explained that the real reason was that the amusement park was a disguise for rocket installations.

Eisenhower's visit to Russia was scheduled for May 1960. Because Eisenhower had been a hero in the Soviet Union during the Second World War, there was every reason to expect another amicable tour. Then, on May 5, Khrushchev announced that the Russians had shot down an American plane in their air space. It was a U-2, a top-secret high-altitude craft designed for spying. Assuming that the pilot had been killed in the crash (or had committed suicide, as U-2 pilots were provided the means to do), Eisenhower said that it was a weather-monitoring plane that had flown off course.

Khrushchev pounced. He revealed that the U-2 pilot, Francis Gary Powers, was alive and had confessed to being a spy. Possibly because he hoped to salvage Eisenhower's forthcoming trip to Russia, Khrushchev hinted in the wording of his announcement that Ike should lay the blame on subordinates.

Ike refused to do so. Smarting under Democratic party attacks that he had never been in charge of foreign policy, he acknowledged his personal approval of all U-2 flights. Khrushchev attacked Eisenhower as a warmonger and canceled his invitation to tour Russia. The Cold War was suddenly chillier than at any time since the truce in Korea.

1960: A CHANGING OF THE GUARD

The chill in Soviet-American relations perfectly suited the strategy of the Democratic presidential nominee in 1960, John Fitzgerald Kennedy. A 42-year-old senator from Massachusetts, Kennedy's chief criticism of the Eisenhower administration was his contention that Ike had, with his stingy spending policies, let American defenses and the power to deter Soviet aggression slip dangerously low. Kennedy hammered on about a dangerous "missile gap," a gross disparity between the rockets the Soviets had available to assault the United States, and those in the American arsenal. This was colossal nonsense but, such matters as numbers of missiles being secret, neither Eisenhower nor the Republican candidate for president, Richard M. Nixon, could convincingly respond.

Times Change

Eisenhower was still very popular in 1960. Had the Twenty-second Amendment to the Constitution, adopted by Republicans in 1951 as a posthumous slap at F.D.R., not forbidden a third term, the 70-year-old

president would likely have been reelected. Americans still liked Ike.

And yet the country was a little tired of the 1950s. The American population was younger than at any time in the twentieth century and restless under the cautious style of the dead decade. As prosperous as the age of Eisenhower was, it was a stale and boring time in the opinion of an increasing number of Americans. The books of social critics such as Whyte and Packard had been best sellers. Although they were out of power, the Democratic liberals had loudly and relentlessly criticized Eisenhower lethargy in journals like *The Nation* and the *New Republic*. Liberal university professors were effective propagandists, spreading their views among young people. Although it was not a liberal majority, the Democrats had controlled both houses of Congress for six of Eisenhower's eight years in office.

As 1960 approached, the feeling that it was time "to get the country moving again" was in the air. In 1959, *Life*, the favorite magazine of the middle classes, published a series of articles by prominent Americans ranging from Adlai Stevenson to Billy Graham on the subject "the national purpose." Almost all the contributors expressed an uneasiness that a sense of purpose was just not there.

John F. Kennedy

Kennedy was a politician who knew how to exploit this apprehension of drift. As Eisenhower was tailor-made for the 1950s, Kennedy seemed to fit the spirit of the emerging new decade. He was rich and attractive, breezy and witty. He had distinguished himself for bravery (although not the best of sense) during the Second World War; he had an attractive young wife, and was ambitious.

Kennedy had weaknesses that would have destroyed a political career 20 years later. He was something of

---

THE KENNEDY WIT

When we got into office, the thing that surprised me most was to find that things were just as bad as we'd been saying they were.

Washington is a city of southern efficiency and northern charm.

It has recently been observed that whether I serve one or two terms in the presidency, I will find myself at the end of that period at what might be called an awkward age—too old to begin a new career and too young to write my memoirs.

a satyr who boasted to friends of the number of his one-night conquests, and he maintained relationships with several mistresses, including actress Marilyn Monroe and one Judith Flexner, who had personal connections with organized crime.

But he was generally discreet and journalists were more restrained in the 1960s, regarding such matters as sexual habits a man's or woman's own business. Kennedy was unbeatable in Massachusetts politics. He had won election to the House and the Senate in years that had not been kind to Democrats, and in 1956, he had made a bid for the Democratic party's vice-presidential nomination. He lost, but that turned out to be a blessing. Kennedy had not shared in the humiliation of the party's defeat that year, but by putting up an exciting fight on national television (the only contest in a dull political year), he had made his name known in every corner of the country.

The avalanche of publicity in 1956 had done another favor for Kennedy by initiating discussion of his religion. The senator was a Roman Catholic, and it was thought that too many people would vote against any Catholic for a member of that church to be elected to national office. The longer the question was examined, however, the less attractive the anti-Catholic position looked. When Martin Luther King, Sr. (a Baptist minister) expressed his old-fashioned prejudices on the score, Martin Luther King, Jr., as a civil-rights leader, so hastily dissociated himself from the anti-Catholics that he became, in the process, virtually committed to the Democratic nominee.

Kennedy and his team of advisers, which he started to assemble in 1957, understood the importance of manipulating the mass media, especially television, in creating a favorable image of their candidate. The campaign that he launched was calculated to convince younger Americans that he was more flexible, more open to change, than any of his rivals.

The Democratic Campaign

Kennedy's competition for the nomination included Adlai Stevenson, badly shopworn in an age that craved novelty, but still hoping to be drafted; Lyndon B. Johnson of Texas, the efficient leader of the Senate Democrats; Hubert H. Humphrey of Minnesota, a leading liberal; and several minor candidates who prayed for a deadlocked convention.

Humphrey was the only one to challenge Kennedy head-on in the primary elections, and he was quickly eliminated. By edging him in Wisconsin, which neighbors Minnesota, Kennedy established himself as a national figure. Kennedy then won in West Virginia, a heavily Protestant "Bible belt" state where, experts said, anti-Catholic feeling would wipe Kennedy out. Humphrey dropped out, and Kennedy's forces talked old-time political bosses like Governor Mike Di Salle of Ohio and Mayor Richard E. Daley of Chicago, who had been sitting the fence as bosses do, into supporting him as the most likely to win in November. By the time of the convention, Lyndon Johnson had been outraced, and Kennedy won on the first ballot.

Kennedy then chose Johnson as his vice-presidential running mate. He expected and wanted to be turned down, but knew he needed Johnson's goodwill to win votes in the South. When Johnson shocked him by accepting, Kennedy's good manners turned out to be the shrewdest move of a brilliantly played game. Although Johnson's syrupy Texas drawl occasioned ridicule in the Northeast, he was popular in the southern states where Kennedy was weak. Single-handedly,

John F. Kennedy and Richard Nixon grimly face each other in a television studio during the presidential campaign debates of 1960.

*Aided by a handsome family that included photogenic toddler John-John, John Kennedy
increased his popularity among the public as his term in office progressed.*

Johnson won Texas for the Democrats, a key to a close election. In the North, Kennedy's religion actually helped him by winning back many upwardly mobile Catholics who had been drifting toward the Republicans as the party of respectability.

A Modern Election

The Republican standard-bearer was Vice President Richard M. Nixon, who easily fought off a challenge by New York governor Nelson Rockefeller. Nixon had a difficult assignment. In order to keep the Republican organization behind him, he had to defend Eisenhower's policies. But he also had to appeal to the new spirit of youth and change.

Nixon handled this juggling act remarkably well, but not without cost. Emphasizing his experience in the executive branch, he created an image of the responsible diplomat that did not mesh with his past reputation for free-swinging smears and dirty tricks. Reporters revived the nickname "Tricky Dicky" and the line, "Would you buy a used car from this man?" Kennedy wisecracked that Nixon played so many parts

that no one knew who the real Nixon was, including the vice president himself.

Mistrust would dog Richard Nixon to the end of his career. Nevertheless, in 1960 he almost won the election. The totals gave Kennedy a wafer-thin margin of 118,574 votes out of the almost 70 million cast. His 303 to 219 electoral vote margin, apparently more comfortable, concealed narrow scrapes in several large states. Many analysts believed that Illinois went Democratic only because of fraudulent vote counts in Richard E. Daley's Chicago.

Other commentators said that Kennedy won because his wife was more glamorous than Pat Nixon, who abhorred public life, or because the Massachusetts senator looked better in the first of four nationally televised debates with Nixon. Kennedy was tan, healthy, confident, and assertive, while Nixon was visibly nervous, and an inept make-up job failed to cover his five-o'clock shadow.

It is impossible to know how much the appearances of the candidates affected the decisions of 70 million people. After 1960, however, many politicians and

SUBURBAN LANDSCAPE

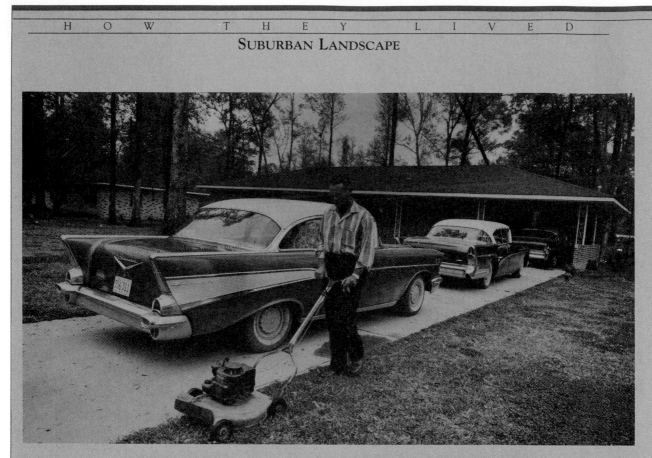

*With their move to suburbia, Americans needed automobiles to commute to their jobs in the
city. Cars were also a means to display status.*

Until the 1950s, most American cities were
densely populated and quite compact. Crowded
urban neighborhoods of tenements and row
homes abutted directly on farmland or other open
country. Indeed, as late as 1940, there were 10,000
acres of cultivated land *within* the city limits of Philadelphia.

There were suburbs, but they did not much resemble
the classic American suburban community of today. Before the Second World War, suburbs radiated out from
city centers in ribbons, along the commuter train lines
that made them possible. Prewar suburbs were themselves rather compact villages of two- and three-storey
homes and even apartment blocks of five and six sto-
reys. Suburbanites may have fled the dirt, noise, traffic,
and crowding of city life, but they had no choice but to
live near the railway station that was the lifeline of
their community. The typical breadwinner's work remained in the city, and all but the wealthiest commut-

ers had to walk from their homes to the train. Shops,
markets, banks, public buildings, movie theaters, and
other commercial services clustered conveniently near
"the station."

This suburban landscape was reshaped beyond recognition during the late 1940s and 1950s. The architect
of the change was the automobile in the possession of
millions of modestly fixed people who formerly had only
dreamed of owning one. In the age of mass automobile
ownership, getting to work and just getting around the
suburbs no longer depended on a combination of shoe-
leather and the commuter railway. Instead of radiating
out from cities in ribbons of population, postwar suburbs sprawled over what had been farmland or wasteland without reference to traditional transportation networks.

Even the least pretentious of the new communities,
such as the several Levittowns, were spacious tracts,
with modest blue-collar homes built on lots of a quarter-

acre. To young couples accustomed to three-room apartments or a bedroom in the home of a parent, they were veritable greenswards. To celebrate their liberation from urban congestion, many of the new suburbanites demanded a kind of domestic architecture they had learned from Hollywood films to associate with the wide open spaces of the Far West and the glamor of southern California.

The ranch house was the brainchild of architect Clifford May of San Diego. A designer of grand homes for well-to-do clients during the 1930s, May was inspired by the traditional single-storey dwellings of the Hispanic Southwest, where the weather was mild (or hot), where acreage had always been plentiful, and where adobe construction discouraged building walls too high. During the depression, May designed some 50 homes in southern California that were, in his words, "about sunshine and informal outdoor living." His ranch houses featured courtyards and rooms that opened wide to the clement outdoors.

Such a lifestyle was impossible in the Northeast and Midwest, where winters were long and cold. However, single-storey construction came to be a status symbol by the end of the Second World War. May himself built tracts of "Yankee Version" ranch houses with board and batten or clapboard siding instead of stucco, and a roof of shingles instead of tile. There were no courtyards in ranch houses built "back East," but picture windows let the sight of the outdoors in without its weather. Much of Levittown, Pennsylvania, was built in ranch houses costing between $9,900 and $15,500.

Such suburbs had no focal point like the prewar suburb's railroad station. However, new landmarks of the good life, once exotic curiosities like the ranch house, became commonplace in postwar suburbia. The supermarket, a huge self-service grocery store providing just about everything needed to keep a house, dated from 1930 when Michael Cullen opened a "warehouse grocery" on Long Island, New York. Cullen patented a shopping cart that could hold a week's worth of groceries and touted himself "The World's Greatest Price Wrecker." He kept costs down by locating his supermarkets in factories and warehouses that had been closed by the depression. Landlords were delighted to sign long leases with him at minimal rents. Cullen lured shoppers to his stores by offering about 300 of the 1,000 items he stocked at his own cost.

Still, in order to exploit the supermarket's bargains, a shopper needed a car. Although more costly, the long-established and conveniently located "Mom and Pop" grocery, to which marketers could walk daily, remained the norm of food retailing in suburb as well as in the cities during the 1930s. By 1940, there were only 6,000 supermarkets in the United States, about one for every 22,000 people.

By 1950, however, with automobile suburbs sprawling on the outskirts of every large city, there were 14,000 supermarkets nationwide, one for each 11,000 people. Throughout 1951, new ones opened at the rate of three each day. By 1960, the supermarket was by far the chief source of the American family's daily bread—purchased weekly. In 33,000 markets (one per 5,400 people, just about the saturation point), Americans purchased 70 percent of the foods they consumed at home. Car-owning suburbanites had transformed the American means of food distribution as well as the very landscape through which they drove daily.

The first drive-in theater opened on June 6, 1933, in Camden, New Jersey, on a busy highway leading from Philadelphia to the seashore. Richard Hollingshead had had the idea while showing home movies in his backyard during hot summer evenings. He laid out a tract of wasteland into 50-foot-wide aisles, built ramps so that viewers could see over the cars in front of them, sunk the projection pit, and charged 25 cents a person, a maximum of $1 per car, to watch old movies (the only ones distributors would rent to him or other drive-in operators). Originally, Hollingshead used a few huge speakers to bring the soundtrack to his customers. However, this system meant he had to shut during cold weather, when customers could not be expected to leave their car windows open. In the 1940s, operators of drive-ins solved the problem of seasonal closings by developing the individual in-car speaker.

The drive-in theater was ready-made for the suburbs. It could be profitable only where land was cheap and the population of the postwar suburbs was comprised largely of young couples with small children, for whom going to a traditional movie theater was inconvenient. Early drive-ins were advertised as family centers where people bored with the film could chat, kids could frolic safely in playgrounds built directly under the towering screens, and "inveterate smokers could smoke without offending others." There were only 10 drive-in theaters in the United States in 1939. Between 1945 and 1950, as the suburbs mushroomed, 5,000 were built.

The drive-in soon lost its image as a family center. Indeed, a writer for Motion Picture Daily commented when Hollingshead opened the first, "the Romeos who lost out in the back seats of picture houses when West Point ushers . . . came into deluxe houses are waking up in a new world." As the "passion pit," however, the drive-in theater continued to prosper in suburbia, for the tots in the playground in the 1940s became the lusty teenagers of the 1950s.

political scientists came to believe that in the age of television a candidate's image, rather than issues, was the key to winning elections. By 1990, no major politician would dream of running a campaign without the advice—even the control—of a high-priced advertising firm.

CAMELOT

As president, Kennedy remained a master at projecting an attractive image. Although no more an intellectual than Eisenhower (his favorite writer was Ian Fleming, creator of British superspy James Bond), the new president won the hearts and talents of the intelligentsia that had attacked Ike to his cause with friendly gestures. He invited the venerable poet Robert Frost to read his verses at the inauguration, and cellist Pablo Casals to perform at the White House. Genuinely athletic and competitive, Kennedy appealed to young suburbanites by releasing photographs of his large family playing rough-and-tumble touch football at their Cape Cod vacation home.

There were plenty of Kennedy haters, but the vigor of his administration (vigor was a favorite Kennedy word) and his undeniable charm, wit, and self-deprecating humor captivated a good many Americans. Inspired by the blockbuster musical of the early 1960s *Camelot*, they spoke of the Kennedy White House as though it were an idyll, like King Arthur's reign in the mythical past.

Like Eisenhower, Kennedy seemed to be assembling a consensus that excluded only groups of the lunatic fringe and, much to Kennedy's dismay, southern segregationist Democrats. But just as in the Arthurian legend, the Kennedy Camelot was short lived. One Mordred outside the house of the Round Table was quite enough to bring him down.

The New Frontier

Historically, John F. Kennedy is more important as an inspiration for the reforms (and tragedies) of the 1960s than for what he actually accomplished. His inaugural address was eloquent and moving. "The torch has been passed to a new generation of Americans," he warned the world, and to Americans he said, "Ask not what your country can do for you; ask what you can do for your country." He sent Congress a pile of legislation that was more innovative than any presidential program between the time of F.D.R.'s Hundred Days and Ronald Reagan's conservative agenda of 1981.

The New Frontier, as Kennedy called his program, included federal aid to education (both to institutions and in the form of low-interest student loans), assistance to chronically depressed Appalachia and the nation's decaying center cities, and help for the poor, the ill, and the aged. In 1962, Kennedy proposed a massive space research and development program that set the goal of overtaking the Soviet Union, which had beaten the United States in orbiting: the first artificial satellite in 1957 and the first human space traveler in 1961. Kennedy meant to send an American to the moon by 1970.

In Congress, however, despite comfortable Democratic majorities, the president was frustrated. Not only did most Republicans oppose the New Frontier, but Kennedy was unable to swing the powerful bloc of southern Democrats behind his program. The southerners traditionally opposed big government spending on anything but defense and public-works projects located in the South, and they were angered when the president and his brother, Attorney General Robert F. Kennedy, made friendly overtures to the growing civil-rights movement. Consequently, Kennedy was able to push through only a few of his proposals, such as the Peace Corps (volunteers working in underdeveloped

A Peace Corps volunteer helps a girl learn to read in Chimbote, Peru.

Police dogs attack a civil-rights demonstrator in Birmingham, Alabama, 1963.

countries in Latin America, Asia, and Africa) and the space program (which brought money to the South).

We Shall Overcome

Kennedy wanted southern congressmen on his side and was willing to go slow in accommodating the growing civil-rights movement. But blacks and increasing numbers of white allies would not be put off for the sake of Kennedy's legislative program. Martin Luther King, Jr.'s, Southern Christian Leadership Conference, its offshoot, the Student Non-violent Coordinating Committee (SNCC), and other older groups like the Congress of Racial Equality (CORE) were energized by the election of 1960. They struck out at racial discrimination on a dozen fronts, sponsoring demonstrations, protests, and nonviolent civil disobedience throughout the South.

White mobs pummeled black and white demonstrators and law officers turned high-pressure fire hoses on them, unleashed vicious attack dogs, and tortured demonstrators with electric cattle prods. Black churches, the typical meeting place of civil-rights workers, were firebombed and several children were killed. A bus carrying CORE "freedom riders" was burned to the ground. In April 1963, Medgar Evers, the moderate leader of the NAACP in Mississippi, was shot to death in the driveway of his home.

Kennedy and his brother, Attorney General Robert F. Kennedy, could not ignore such violence. However, they were forced to take decisive and dramatic federal action only when two southern governors, Ross Barnett of Mississippi and George Wallace of Alabama, said that they would personally prevent the integration of their state universities and tacitly encouraged mobs

TO REACH THE MOON

In his address to Congress on May 25, 1961, President Kennedy said: "I believe that this nation should commit itself to achieving the goal, before this decade is out, of landing a man on the Moon and returning him safely to earth." Although Kennedy did not live to see it, his commitment—seemingly farfetched in 1961—was fulfilled. Astronaut Neil Armstrong set foot on the moon in 1969, more than a year ahead of schedule.

American astronaut Buzz Aldrin on the moon, July 1969.

to riot. Unable to reason with the governors by phone, the Kennedy's sent 400 marshalls, 300 soldiers, and spent $4 million to ensure that one black man, James Meredith, be admitted to the University of Mississippi. George Wallace of Alabama, after making a show to appeal to segregationists in his state, stepped aside without violence.

The March on Washington

What wedded the Kennedys to the civil-rights movement, however, was a massive demonstration, the March on Washington of August 1963, which was organized and led by Martin Luther King, Jr. Believing that the time had come for decisive federal action, King led 200,000 supporters to the Lincoln Memorial in Washington, where he delivered the greatest sermon of his life. "I have a dream today," he began.

I have a dream today that one day . . . little black boys and black girls will be able to join hands with little white boys

and white girls and walk together as sisters and brothers. . . . When we let freedom ring, when we let it ring from every village and every hamlet, from every state and every city, we will be able to speed up that day when all of God's children, black men and white men, Jews and Gentiles, Protestants and Catholics, will be able to join hands and sing, in the words of that old Negro spiritual, "Free at last! Free at last! Thank God Almighty, we are free at last!:"

Concluding that he had no choice but to choose between racist Democrats in the South (who were not supporting him on much of anything) and the large black vote in the North, which was strategically located in the cities of the states with the most electoral votes, Kennedy announced his support of a sweeping civil-rights bill to be debated in Congress in 1964.

KENNEDY'S FOREIGN POLICY

Kennedy was committed to fighting the Cold War with the Soviet Union and he could sound like a young John Foster Dulles in saying so: "Freedom and communism are in deadly embrace; the world cannot exist half slave and half free." Acting on his campaign claim that a missile gap between the Soviet Union and the United States threatened American security, he lavished money on research programs designed to improve the rockets with which, in case of war with Russia, nuclear weapons would be delivered.

Flexible Response

However, Kennedy's foreign policy advisors, mostly intellectuals from universities and "think tanks" such as Walt W. Rostow and McGeorge Bundy, were critics of Dulles "brinkmanship," threatening massive retaliation with nuclear weapons at every Soviet provocation. Instead, updating containment policy to apply to a world theater, they advocated a policy of "flexible response." The United States would respond to Soviet actions in proportion to their seriousness.

PREJUDICE

Marian Anderson (black operatic soprano): "Sometimes, it's like a hair across your cheek. You can't see it, you can't find it with your fingers, but you keep brushing at it because the feel of it is irritating."

James Baldwin: "It is a great shock at the age of five or six to find that in a world of Gary Coopers you are the Indian."

For example—what was to prove a fatal example—if the Soviets were suspected of funding or actively aiding guerrilla movements against regimes that were friendly to the United States or sought American aid, the United States would fund the military forces of those regimes and offer expert advisors to help them. If the Soviets were suspected of subverting elections in the Third World, the United States would launch its own covert operations to manipulate events on disputed turf. Toward these ends, Kennedy sponsored the development of elite antiguerrilla units in the army, most notably the Special Forces or Green Berets, and he increased funding of the spy network maintained by the Central Intelligence Agency.

Into the Third World

Unlike Eisenhower, who thought in traditional terms that wealthy Europe and Japan were the areas that counted in the Cold War competition, Kennedy stated that "the great battleground for the defense and expansion of freedom today is the whole southern half of the globe—Asia, Latin America, Africa, and the Middle East—the lands of the rising peoples."

He preferred to back democratic reform movements in the developing countries. Kennedy took the lead in organizing the Alliance for Progress in the Western Hemisphere, a program that offered economic aid to friendly Latin American nations in the hope that they would adopt free institutions.

However, the choice in the volatile Third World was rarely between liberal-minded reform movements and pro-Communist dictatorships. Envy of American riches, a legacy of American support for repressive and exploitative dictators, the flexibility and opportunism of the Soviets, and the romantic zaniness common in revolutionary movements meant that most "liberation movements" were at best suspicious of American intentions and willing to overlook the Russian record because of Soviet revolutionary rhetoric. Consequently, Kennedy and his successors often found their only friends among reactionaries hostile to reform.

The Bay of Pigs

Cuba was the first Third World battleground to come to Kennedy's attention, and his "flexible response" proved to be a disaster. Since 1959, Cuba had been under the control of a revolutionary regime headed by Fidel Castro. Constantly baiting the United States in interminable but impassioned speeches, Castro began, during 1960, to expropriate American property before negotiating compensation. He had riled Eisenhower, who approved a CIA project to arm and train 2,000 anti-Castro Cubans in Florida and Central America.

They were ready to invade Cuba when Kennedy took over and, despite misgivings, Kennedy decided to go ahead. The Central Intelligence Agency assured him that Castro was unpopular with the Cuban people. At the sound of the first shot, anti-Castro rebellions would break out all over the island.

On April 17, 1961, the anti-Castro forces waded ashore at the Bahia de Cochinas, the Bay of Pigs, on Cuba's southern coast. The invasion was a disaster from the start. There was no uprising. Castro's troops, seasoned by three years of revolution, made short work of the battle and Castro's popularity soared at home for having resisted what he called imperialist aggression.

Kennedy, instead of ousting an anti-American but still flexible revolutionary leader, pushed Castro into the arms of the Soviets for fear of another assault. Indeed, Kennedy was denounced all over Latin America, and, on national television, he assumed full responsibility for the fiasco.

The Vienna Summit

The Bay of Pigs disaster heartened Soviet leader Nikita Khrushchev to take a harder line toward the United States than he had through most of the 1950s. Perhaps he sensed that the youth and inexperience of the new president provided rare opportunities for easy limited victories in the game of maneuver at which Khrushchev was so deft.

At a summit meeting in Vienna in June, Kennedy found himself outwitted and upstaged by Khrushchev. The Russian tongue-tied him in private and, when they were before reporters, treated him like a nice boy who only needed teaching. A man of perhaps too much self-confidence, Kennedy returned home seething with anger, and Khrushchev was encouraged to act more recklessly. The Soviets resumed nuclear testing in the atmosphere and ordered the sealing of the border between East and West Berlin.

The Berlin Wall

The Communist regime of East Germany had been plagued by the defection of their citizens, particularly highly trained technologists who could double and triple their incomes in West Germany's booming economy. This "brain drain" threatened to cripple East German industry, and the Communists winced at each defection as a Western propaganda victory, people "voting with their feet." To put an end to it, Khrushchev built a wall through the city that was as ugly in reality as it was symbolically.

Kennedy allowed the Berlin Wall to stand, and he was immediately attacked by critics who said that he

John Kennedy peers over the Berlin Wall into East Berlin during a Cold War era visit to West Berlin, June 26, 1963.

could have bulldozed it without interference from the Russians. The proposition was arguable but Kennedy was no brinkman—until October 1962.

The Big Crunch

In October 1962, a U-2 flight over Cuba revealed that the Soviets were constructing installations for nuclear missiles aimed at the United States. Such a threat based but a hundred miles from the United States was, Kennedy knew, something the American people would not tolerate. Before revealing his discovery, he met with a committee specially constituted to analyze the crisis.

Quickly, Kennedy rejected a proposal by Dean Acheson and others that bombers be dispatched to destroy the missile sites. He also rejected a proposal for an American invasion of the island. Although the president did not know it at the time, this was a wise decision. While the CIA had reported (blundering again) that there was only a handful of Soviets on the island, in fact there were 40,000 Russian troops. The CIA also grossly underestimated the size of the Cuban Army, which numbered 270,000 men and women.

Instead, President Kennedy adopted his brother's more moderate and flexible approach. Announcing the discovery of the missiles to the American people, he simultaneously proclaimed a naval blockade of Cuba and demanded that the sites be dismantled and any nuclear weapons on the island be removed.

Castro panicked (it was learned in 1989), fleeing to a bunker beneath the Soviet Embassy and demanding a Russian nuclear strike on the United States. No doubt, the Cuban's rashness gave Khrushchev pause but, for four days, he refused to budge. Work on the sites continued, and Soviet ships loaded with 20 missiles continued on their way to Cuba to be added to the 20 already there (fully a third of the Russian arsenal!). Americans gathered solemnly around their television sets, apprehensive that the nuclear holocaust would begin any hour. Secretary of State Dean Rusk revealed that the White House was nervous too. "We're eyeball to eyeball," he said.

Rusk added, "I think the other fellow just blinked." The Cuba-bound freighters first stopped in mid-ocean and then turned around. On October 26, Khrushchev sent a long conciliatory letter to Kennedy in which he agreed to remove the missiles if the United States pledged never to invade Cuba. The next day, a second letter said that the Soviets would withdraw their nuclear weapons if the United States would remove its missiles from Turkey, which bordered the Soviet Union.

Before the Cuban missile crisis began, Kennedy had been considering dismantling the Turkish missile sites as a gesture of friendship. Calculating that the difference in the two Soviet offers indicated indecision in the Kremlin, he saw a chance for a prestigious victory. Kennedy ignored Khruschev's second note and accepted the terms of the first. On October 28, Khrushchev accepted.

Relations Improve

The president thought that the Cuban missile crisis was the turning point of his presidency. He made commemorative gifts to everyone who had advised or merely stood by him during that tense October. In fact, both Kennedy and the Soviets were shaken by their flirtation with catastrophe and acted more responsibly after 1962. A "hot line" was installed in both the White House and the Kremlin so that, in future crises, Russian and American leaders could communicate instantly with one another. Then, following a Kennedy speech, the Soviet Union joined the United States and the United Kingdom in signing a treaty that banned nuclear testing in the atmosphere. (France and China, the only other nuclear powers, did not sign.)

The Assassination

By the fall of 1963, Kennedy had regained the confidence he had exuded in the campaign of 1960. He had scored a major diplomatic victory in the Cuban Missile Crisis and was no longer uneasy about his decision to embrace the civil-rights movement and write off southern white extremists. He believed that the Civil Rights Act he proposed for 1964 would ensure the electoral votes of the populous northeastern states in the presidential election that year, and began to make plans to convince southern moderates that they should accept the civil-rights revolution.

Toward this end, he agreed to accompany Vice President Johnson on a major political tour in Texas. It began with cheering crowds, and Kennedy was reassured. Then, as the long motorcade passed through Dealey Plaza in downtown Dallas, the president's head was literally blown to bits by rifle fire from at least a

As a grief-stricken America watched on television, Lyndon B. Johnson, his wife to his right and Jacqueline Kennedy to his left, takes the oath of office aboard Air Force I, *November 22, 1963.*

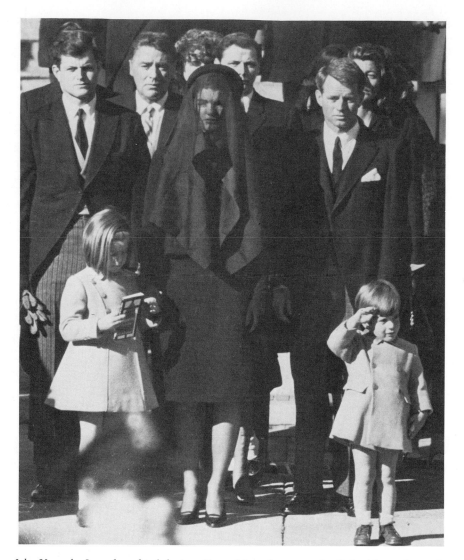

John Kennedy, Jr., salutes his father's coffin on November 25, 1963. Behind him is his uncle, Robert Kennedy, who was assassinated during his own presidential campaign in 1968.

Mannlicher carbine in the hands of Lee Harvey Oswald, a ne'er-do-well ex-marine, and worker in a textbook clearing house that overlooked the plaza.

The murder unleashed a raft of pent-up anxieties and conspiracy theories. Because Dallas, where Kennedy was killed, was a hotbed of often paranoiac rightwing political organizations, including the John Birch Society, which believed that Dwight D. Eisenhower was a conscious agent of international Communism, liberals were inclined to blame Kennedy's loss on such unhealthy extremism. Stories circulated of Dallas schoolchildren cheering when they heard the news.

But Oswald's own political associations seemed to have been entirely with leftwing organizations. In-deed, he had lived for a time in the Soviet Union and tried to renounce his American citizenship. Right-wingers were confirmed in their theories that Communist agents were everywhere. Others posited a "Mafia Connection," yet others attributed the murder to the Central Intelligence Agency.

Lee Harvey Oswald was not able to clear (or further muddy) things up. Two days after the assassination, he was murdered in the basement of the Dallas police headquarters by a night-club operator named Jack Ruby, who claimed to have been distracted by the death of a president he idolized.

A blue-ribbon investigating commission headed by Chief Justice Earl Warren found that Oswald had acted alone; he was neither associated with any political tendency nor assisted in his act. Simply put, he was a misfit. However, sloppy evidence gathering and soft spots in one or another of the Warren Commission's conclusions continued to serve as grist for literally hundreds of articles and books that espoused theories about how the murder had taken place. In 1988, on the twenty-fifth anniversary of the Kennedy assassination, a large majority of Americans stated that they did not accept the official account of the murder as the true story.

Beginning of an Era

John F. Kennedy was not a great president. He accomplished little at home and his policy of intervening directly in what was, in 1961, a minor war in Southeast Asia, was to poison American life and squander the international goodwill the United States had banked in the Second World War and its aftermath.

But his assassination was a great tragedy, far more momentous in its consequences than even the murder of Abraham Lincoln nearly a hundred years earlier. For Lincoln's work was largely done when he died; Kennedy, if not particularly successful in pushing through the legislation his administration sponsored during the "Thousand Days" of his presidency, had just begun. He was building a basis of political support such as had allowed Dwight D. Eisenhower to govern with authority, and doing so by appealing to the better instincts of the American people. His untimely death not only created a climate in which conspiracy theories about it flourished, it left a void of idealism, confidence, and goodwill that has not yet been filled.

For Further Reading

Overviews of the 1950s and 1960s include James Gilbert, *Another Chance: America Since 1945* (1984); Eric Goldman, *The Crucial Decade and After* (1961); Godfrey Hodgson, *America in Our Time: From World War II to Nixon* (1976); William E. Leuchtenburg, *A Troubled Feast: American Society Since 1945* (1979); and James L. Sundquist, *Politics and Policy: The Eisenhower, Kennedy, and Johnson Years* (1968).

On the Eisenhower years, see C. C. Alexander, *Holding the Line: The Eisenhower Era, 1952–1961* (1975); See also Eisenhower's own *The White House Years* (1965); P. A. Carter, *Another Part of the Fifties* (1983); B. W. Cook, *The Declassified Eisenhower* (1981); Robert A. Divine, *Eisenhower and the Cold War* (1981); T. Hoopes, *The Devil and John Foster Dulles* (1973); Peter Lyon, *Eisenhower: Portrait of a Hero* (1974); Richard M. Nixon, *Six Crises* (1962); William L. O'Neill, *American High: The Years of Confidence, 1945–1960* (1987); and H. G. Vatter, *The U.S. Economy in the 1950s* (1963).

The brief era of John F. Kennedy's presidency has been, if anything, studied more intensively than Eisenhower's. See Ronald Berman, *America in the Sixties* (1968); Bruce Miroff, *Pragmatic Illusions: The Presidential Politics of John F. Kennedy* (1976); William L. O'Neill, *Coming Apart: An Informal History of the 1960s* (1971); L. G. Paper, *The Promise and the Performance: The Leadership of John F. Kennedy* (1975); Herbert Parmet, *Jack: The Struggle of John Fitzgerald Kennedy* (1980) and *JFK: The Presidency of John Fitzgerald Kennedy* (1983); and Arthur M. Schlesinger, Jr., *A Thousand Days* (1965). On Kennedy's election, see the first in a series of such studies by Theodore H. White, *The Making of the President 1960* (1961). The president's assassination has been the subject of so many books, some crackbrained, many insightful, that it is impossible to be representative and name but a few. Perhaps the one with which to begin a study of that tragic event is William Manchester, *Death of a President* (1967).

The decisions of Chief Justice Earl Warren's Supreme Court were as important in shaping the American politics of the future as presidental and congressional policies. See Archibald Cox, *The Warren Court: Constitutional Decision as an Instrument of Reform* (1968), and Philip B. Kurland, *Politics, the Constitution, and the Warren Court* (1970).

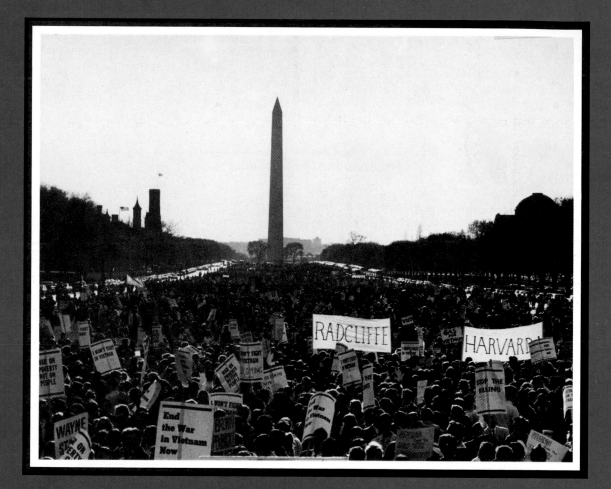

In classical drama, the tragic hero overcomes great obstacles to rise to lofty heights, not always by the most delicate of means. Then, at the pinnacle of attainment and glory, he is destroyed, not so much by enemies (although they are glad to be present to pick up the pieces), as by flaws in the hero's own character. Lyndon Baines Johnson and Richard M. Nixon were tragic figures in this mold. In the face of formidable personal and social handicaps, both rose to the presidency of the United States, and both were confirmed in their eminence by huge majorities at the polls. Both were able men and both savored the exercise of power. Both were successful in the spheres in which they preferred to labor: Johnson as a domestic reformer in the footsteps

49

YEARS OF TURBULENCE

Conflict at Home and Abroad, 1961–1968

Marchers protest the Vietnam War in Washington, D.C., 1965.

of his idol, Franklin D. Roosevelt; Nixon as a diplomat, an arranger of affairs among nations, which he regarded as the twentieth-century president's principal responsibility.

And both were cast down in disgrace, Johnson because he clung stubbornly to a cause both lost and discredited, and Nixon because of behavior that was not only unworthy of a national leader, but explicable only as a reflection of a severely flawed character. Johnson's undoing came about in foreign policy, which had never particularly interested him before he became president, and Nixon's on the domestic front, which he believed could take care of itself.

LYNDON BAINES JOHNSON

Lyndon Johnson—L.B.J.—came out of what people call "the sticks," the Pedernales River country of rural Texas. His family's means were ordinary, Johnson's father uninspiring or simply not much interested in his son. Although the distinguished University of Texas was nearby, Johnson was able to attend only a small teacher's college. He taught school for a year, but the life seemed dull compared to the hubbub, machinations, and possibilities of Texas politics. In 1931, he went to Washington as a congressman's aide, became a devotee of the New Deal, and returned to Texas to win a special election to Congress in 1937.

In 1948, Johnson won the Democratic nomination to the Senate in a controversial primary. Because his margin was a handful of somewhat dubious votes, Texans called him "Landslide Lyndon," but in the Lone Star State in the 1940s, the Democratic nomination, however secured, was tantamount to election and the voters did their duty. Back in Washington as a Senator in 1949, Johnson's rise was meteoric. Sponsored by Sam Rayburn, the Speaker of the House of Representatives who looked on Johnson as a son, he was named party whip in 1951 and majority leader of the Senate in 1955.

The Wheeler-Dealer

Johnson owed his speedy rise to power to Rayburn, but he held fast to it because he was very good at what he did. He was the master assembler of Senate majorities, by turns administering large doses of folksy charm, bargaining with senators who were pursuing pet projects, arm-twisting, and, so it was said, a little blackmail. Rumor was that Johnson "had something"

on every Democrat and most of the Republicans in the Senate; he was not a man to be crossed when he was after something.

These political skills enabled President Lyndon B. Johnson to push through Kennedy's New Frontier and much more, a comprehensive program of national reform that he called the Great Society. Oddly, except in political terms, this very expensive program began with a tax cut. By reducing Kennedy's budget for 1964 by a mere $3.6 billion, Johnson was able to win congressional support for a $10 billion tax cut, always a crowd pleaser. After so popular a start, Johnson moved on to what was to be the greatest of his monuments, a veritable revolution in the civil status of black Americans and the beginnings of a social revolution in relations between the races. In the Civil Rights Act of 1964, Johnson put the Fourteenth Amendment to the Constitution, in abeyance for a century, to work.

A Southerner Ends Segregation

Between 1955 and 1965, when civil-rights activists were fighting to end racial segregation in the South, a few faint voices suggested that when the Jim Crow laws were gone, as they must go, white and black southerners would enjoy better, more human relations than black and white northerners would. Such observers reasoned that while legal segregation was a southern institution, interaction between blacks and whites in the South was personal and even intimate; in the North, by way of contrast, while blacks suffered few legal disabilities, comprehensive residential segregation in the big cities isolated the two races as if they were two nations.

With southern police forces routinely brutalizing black protesters during those years, and high-ranking southern white politicians huffing and puffing that they would fight to the death to save white supremacy, it was difficult to take such notions seriously. But it was a southerner, himself a nominal exponent of segregation as late as 1960, who wrote an end to Jim Crow. In fact, Johnson had long found segregation distasteful and reactionary while, for the sake of election, he accepted it in Texas. "I'll tell you what's at the bottom of it," he said to an aide in 1960, echoing the Georgia Populist Tom Watson, "If you can convince the lowest white man he's better than the best colored man, he won't notice you're picking his pocket. Hell, give him somebody to look down on, and he'll empty his pockets for you."

By 1964, like the Kennedys, Johnson was convinced that the days of Jim Crow were gone and that the future of the Democratic party might depend on black votes in large northern cities—and in the South. By means of shrewd bargaining and "the Johnson treat-

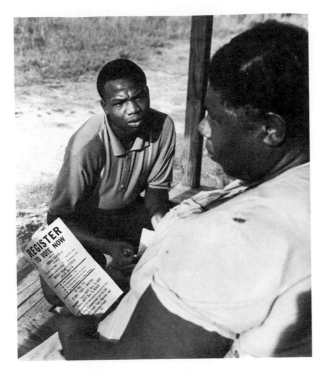

A young black man urges an elder to register to vote in Edwards, Mississippi.

ment," he pushed through the Civil Rights Act of 1964, effectively outlawing school segregation and the "white" and "colored" signs on public accommodations that had marked everyday life in the South for half a century. The Act also created a Fair Employment Practices Commission to work towards ending a yawning "unemployment gap" between the white and black work forces.

Nor was Johnson done. When Mississippi extremists took irregular and violent action against a civil-rights campaign in that state in 1964—the Mississippi Freedom Summer—Johnson responded with another civil-rights bill that ensured the right of black people to vote.

The Mississippi Freedom Summer

White Mississippians may well have been the most stubborn of segregationists. The symbol of the Mississippi Democratic party was a white cock and the words "white supremacy." Because the state was perceived as the sturdiest redoubt of Jim Crow, the Student Nonviolent Coordinating Committee, an alliance of black and white university students, chose Mississippi as the focus of a campaign in the summer of 1964 to register blacks to vote. If Mississippi could be cracked, they reasoned, racial discrimination would crumble all over the South.

The Freedom Summer was a disillusioning experience to many of the idealistic young white liberals who descended on Mississippi from northern states. Instead of finding a black population as articulate, idealistic, and militant as their black colleagues back home, they found a people as wary of outsiders as "the rednecks" around them were, and cautious to the marrow after more than a half century of witnessing unpunished lynchings and suffering daily humiliation. Poor Mississippi blacks resented their oppression, but they knew that when the bright-faced northern white students went back to school in September and the newspaper reporters were gone, they would still be there, vulnerable to economic manipulation and violence. Many blacks did register to vote—or tried to do so; others sat on the porches of their shacks rocking, gave the SNCC militants a glass of ice water, and sent them on their way.

Indeed, the presence of northern civil-rights workers and dozens of reporters did not stay violence even during the summer of 1964. SNCC workers were harassed as a matter of daily routine, tailed by cars full of men wherever they drove, and regularly terrorized. The most celebrated case of violence occured near Philadelphia, Mississippi, when one black SNCC worker and two whites were kidnapped and murdered, almost certainly with the connivance of law enforcement officials.

Amidst these atrocities and fear, some Mississippi blacks and a few white allies, led by the forceful and articulate Fannie Lou Hamer, organized the Mississippi Freedom Democratic party and sent a delegation to the 1964 Democratic party convention in Atlantic City, New Jersey. The Freedom Democrats, supported by most northern state delegates, demanded that they, and not the segregationist regular Democrats, be recognized by the national party.

Working through longtime liberal Hubert Humphrey, whom he had selected to be his vice-presidential running mate, Johnson tried to work out a compromise, dividing Mississippi's convention votes between the rival groups. The Freedom Democrats were not happy with "half a loaf," but the segregationists were furious and walked out of the convention, announcing that they would vote Republican in November.

THE GREAT SOCIETY

The Atlantic City convention was a turning point for the Democratic party. It marked the party's transformation into an unequivocally liberal party and, for a time, a triumphant one. Johnson and the Democratic

"Ten, nine, eight, seven . . .

six, five, four, three . . .

two, one . . .

These are the stakes. To make a world in which all of God's children can live . . .

or to go into the dark. We must either love each other or we must die . . .

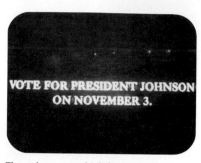

The stakes are too high for you to stay home."

One of the most powerful political messages ever seen on television, this commercial for Lyndon Johnson intimated that, if elected, Barry Goldwater would plunge the nation into nuclear war.

leadership had no choice but to let the die-hard southern segregationists go. In shedding them, they not only lost the faction of the party that had stood in the way of wooing black voters, they discarded southern Democrats who had traditionally opposed liberal legislation of all kinds.

The Election of 1964

The election of 1964 seemed to prove the political wisdom of Johnson's "black strategy." The president's Republican challenger, Senator Barry Goldwater of Arizona was personally a tolerant man, but racists and other extremists of the far right had made him their hero. Their fanaticism helped transform his conservatism into a carping, vindictive negativism based on hatred, fear, and frighteningly simple solutions to problems that seemed to threaten democracy and the rights of the weak.

Republican moderates cringed when Goldwater, accepting the party's nomination, said that "extremism in the pursuit of liberty is no vice." Worst of all in an age of a nuclear balance of terror, the grandson of a gun-toting frontier merchant sounded like a lover of war when he spoke on foreign policy. He seemed to say that the Cold War with the Soviet Union was a matter of which country was "tougher." Democratic strategists were able to depict Goldwater as a man who

would rush for the red button in times of crisis. One Democratic television commercial depicted a little girl playing in a field of wildflowers and dissolved into a film of a nuclear blast.

The Democrats won in a landslide. Johnson won 61 percent of the popular vote and majorities in all but six states, five states of the Deep South plus Goldwater's native Arizona. As important as the prestige the big victory meant, Johnson's coattails pulled in 70 first-term Democratic congressmen from normally Republican districts. The party's edge in the House was 295 to 140, in the Senate 68 to 32. The congressional logjam that stymied Kennedy had been blown into toothpicks, and Johnson did not hesitate to act. He sent waves of legislation rolling down Pennsylvania Avenue to the Capitol, not only rounding out the civil-rights revolution, but enacting his "Great Society," the creation of a government that assumed responsibility for social welfare on a massive scale.

The Voting Rights Act of 1965

The Voting Rights Act of 1965 put the federal power of law enforcement behind the rights of blacks to vote. Secure in this right for the first time in almost a century, southern blacks rushed to register. In only ten years after Martin Luther King, Jr., had led his boycott against segregation on buses in Montgomery, the legal obstacles to black equality fell. Before long, southern white politicians who had built their careers on race-baiting were showing up at black gatherings, beaming, shaking hands, kissing babies, and talking about unfortunate misunderstandings.

A former SNCC worker named Julian Bond was elected to the Georgia state assembly. He was amused that businessmen who once called him a dangerous incendiary now wanted to take him out to lunch. By the early 1970s, all southern Democrats were courting black votes, however awkward it was for some. In Alabama's gubernatorial election of 1982, George Wallace, the southern symbol of resistance to integration in the early 1960s, not only courted black votes, but owed his election to them: Alabama blacks found his Republican opponent by far a worse choice.

Even southern Republicans stopped expressing the sentiments that had originally taken them into the GOP. Strom Thurmond of South Carolina, a deft practititioner of the "nigger-baiting" school of southern politics who became a Republican in part because of liberal Democratic policies on race, was addressing black audiences by 1982.

The Voting Rights Act of 1965 also prompted an increase in black voting in the northern and western states. Not only Atlanta and New Orleans, but Newark, Gary, and Detroit elected black mayors during the 1970s. By 1984, the nation's second and third largest cities, Chicago and Los Angeles, plus Philadelphia, had black mayors. Tom Bradley of Los Angeles, a former policeman, just missed winning the governorship of California in 1982.

The Great Society

If L.B.J.'s sponsorship of full civil rights for blacks was partly forced on him by political realities, his concern for the poor and disadvantaged of all races was sincere and deeply felt. He had had to struggle himself and, in Texas politics, had been regarded as a friend of Mexican-Americans, most of whom were poor and treated scarcely better than blacks. Johnson worshiped Franklin D. Roosevelt and wanted to be remembered

A VISTA volunteer, one of thousands of recruits in the war on poverty, talks to a child in Alabama.

in history as the president who completed what the New Deal had started. He envisioned an America

where no child will go unfed and no youngster will go unschooled; where every child has a good teacher and every teacher has good pay, and both have good classrooms; where every human being has dignity and every worker has a job; where education is blind to color and employment is unaware of race: where decency appeals and courage abounds.

Johnson's "War on Poverty," which was directed by the new Office of Economic Opportunity (OEO), funded a Job Corps that retrained unemployed people for the new kinds of jobs available in high-technology industries. The OEO recruited boys and girls from impoverished families for catch-up education in special Head Start schools and young men and women for placement in universities. Other programs provided financial help and tutoring in order to compensate for the economic and cultural handicaps of growing up in poverty. Volunteers in Service to America (VISTA) was a domestic Peace Corps, sending social workers and teachers into decaying inner cities and poor rural areas. Medicare provided government-funded health insurance for the elderly, chronically ill, and very poor.

Nor did the Great Society neglect the middle and working classes. Generous funding of schools, colleges, and universities and extremely cheap student loans made it possible for hundreds of thousands of young people to secure an education otherwise closed to them. Some of these acts were legislated before the lopsided election of 1964. But it was after his great victory, thanks to the hordes of freshman Democratic congressmen beholden entirely to Johnson's landslide for their seats, that the program was completed.

VIETNAM! VIETNAM!

"Were there no outside world," the political journalist Theodore H. White wrote in 1969, just five years after Lyndon Johnson's great electoral triumph, "Lyndon Johnson might conceivable have gone down as the greatest of twentieth-century presidents." Obviously, White had written off the possibility of such an honor.

So had all but a few Americans. By 1969—by 1967!—virtually no one was saying as, just a few years earlier, L.B.J.'s aide Jack Valenti did without embarrassment, "I sleep each night a little better, a little more confidently because Lyndon Johnson is my president." More typical in 1967 was the statement of Senator Eugene McCarthy, a member of Johnson's own party: "We've got a wild man in the White House, and we are going to have to treat him as such."

What happened? A war happened. The builder of the Great Society at home mired the United States in a war in a Southeast Asian country of which, before 1964, few Americans had even heard. Johnson inherited the American presence in Vietnam from Kennedy—and from Eisenhower and Dulles. But it was he who made the decisions that transformed a minor foreign policy problem, and apparently one that could have been easily resolved, into an insidious cancer that spread into every organ of the American body politic.

A Long Way from the Pedernales

During the nineteenth century, the French had established firm imperial control over most of Indo-China, the peninsula that pendles from the Asian mainland east of India and includes the present-day nations of Vietnam, Laos, and Cambodia. As elsewhere in their empire, the French fostered the growth of a native elite dedicated to French culture and often Roman Catholic in religion. This Indochinese elite prospered and was favored by the French both economically and with a share in governing the colony.

However, the majority of Vietnamese, Cambodians, and Laotians remained peasants or menial laborers, perhaps treated the worse because their rulers were foreign, perhaps not, but in any case resenting the French presence and wanting them out. One such nationalist was Ho Chi Minh, who went to Paris as a seaman and, in 1920, was a founding member of the

Ho Chi Minh founded the Viet Minh to fight for an independent Vietnam.

French Communist Party. Ho lived in Russia and China until the Second World War when he returned to Vietnam to organize a guerrilla movement, the Viet Minh, to fight the Japanese who had occupied the country after the defeat of France in Europe.

Partly because of Ho Chi Minh's contribution to the war effort in harassing the Japanese, President Roosevelt favored setting up an independent Vietnam after the war. Ho, with support from many non-Communists, proclaimed the republic of Vietnam in 1945. Later, when French forces returned, he agreed to keep Vietnam within the French imperial community so long as the nation was a self-governing commonwealth.

The French, their pride wounded by their ignominious collapse during the Second World War, refused to cooperate with Ho. Instead, they set up a puppet regime and the Viet Minh took once again to the jungles and rice paddies where they launched a guerrilla war that lasted eight years. Finally, after a decisive defeat in the battle of Dien Bien Phu in 1954, the French gave up and left. According to the Geneva Accord signed that same year, Vietnam was to be temporarily divided at the seventeenth parallel into two zones. Ho's Viet Minh would govern the northern half of the country from Hanoi; a non-Communist government would administer the southern part of the country from Saigon. After two years, when the bitterness and tumult of the long war had moderated, democratic elections would be held to determine the nation's future.

It was all a long way from the Pedernales River. What did the United States have to do with a war between Indochinese demanding independence and a weak and divided France trying to salvage an obsolete empire?

The Beginnings of American Involvement

The Cold War and John Foster Dulles's obsessive crusade against Communism involved the United States in Vietnamese affairs. As he was elsewhere in the world, Dulles was blind to the fact that, although a Communist, Ho Chi Minh had initially been cordial to the United States. Ho was aware that F.D.R. had favored an independent Vietnam and patterned Vietnam's Declaration of Independence on the American document of 1776. Although it is impossible to know Ho's long-term intentions during the long war with the French, his Viet Minh included substantial non-Communist elements and some evidence indicates that Ho counted on American economic aid to build up the Vietnamese nation.

Instead of feeling Ho out, Dulles pumped millions of dollars into the French war effort and even considered using nuclear weapons to lift the Viet Minh's siege of the French at Dien Bien Phu. Eisenhower vetoed that proposal, as he usually did when Dulles began to tremble with fervor, and the United States attended the Geneva conference that ended French rule. Dulles refused to sign the Geneva Accord, but the United States announced that it would do nothing to interfere with its provisions, including the election to be held in 1956.

Events and propaganda by the Chinese Lobby altered American policy. About a million anti-Communist North Vietnamese fled below the seventeenth parallel between 1954 and 1956, and there were several instances of mistreatment of Roman Catholics in the North. A Vietnamese nationalist who had lived in exile in the United States, Ngo Dinh Diem, returned to the South and was portrayed in the United States as his nation's George Washington. The Eisenhower administration gave Diem $320 million in aid in 1955 and supported his refusal to hold elections in 1956. Instead, he proclaimed the Republic of Vietnam in the South.

For several years, Diem appeared to succeed. Then, in 1960, opposition groups, including South Vietnamese Communists, formed the National Liberation Front (NLF) and launched, yet again, a guerrilla war aimed at unifying the country. The NLF attacked isolated patrols of Diem's soldiers, killed village officials loyal to the regime, and actually set up local governments in many parts of South Vietnam, collecting taxes and administering justice, not always gently or fairly.

Diem described his enemies as "Viet Cong," Vietnamese Communists, although many non-Communists also belonged to the NLF. He claimed that the guerrilla movement was inspired, aided, and abetted by North Vietnam, which was quite true, but obscured the fact that virtually all of the Viet Cong's 15,000 soldiers in 1960 were South Vietnamese peasants. Both the Eisenhower and Kennedy administrations pumped millions into his regime.

Kennedy's Uncertainty

Kennedy's military advisors urged him to send 10,000 American troops to help Diem, telling him that "the essence of the problem in Vietnam is military." Kennedy was unconvinced. He had just been stung by CIA advice at the Bay of Pigs and wondered why Diem's ARVN (Army of the Republic of Vietnam), which numbered 250,000, could not handle a few thousand part-time guerrillas. He compromised by sending 3,000 "Green Berets," U.S. Army Special Forces expert in counter-insurgency, fighting guerrillas, to advise the ARVN. Slowly, the American presence

Buddhist monk Quang Duc immolates himself to protest the anti-Buddhist policies of South Vietnamese president Ngo Dinh Diem. The photo was taken by Malcolm Brown and was among the most shocking to come out of the Vietnam War.

increased. By the end of 1962, there were 11,000 American military advisors in South Vietnam.

By mid-1963, however, Kennedy had soured on Diem. Isolated from the people of the country as he shambled around the presidential palace day and night, surrounded and dominated by corrupt relatives, Diem approved of repressive policies, high taxes, and favoritism toward Roman Catholic Vietnamese. In a few short years, the George Washington of Vietnam had become a peevish, unpopular dictator. Buddhist monks led protests in Saigon, Hue, and other cities, some setting themselves aflame in intersections. Capitalizing on the unrest, the NLF stepped up its campaign in the countryside. During the day, Diem's regime more or less governed South Vietnam. Once the sun had set, the Saigon government controlled little more than the capital, other major towns, and part of the fertile rice-growing Mekong River delta. Elsewhere, NLF guerrillas moved freely.

Kennedy seems to have given up on the possibility of military victory. At least, he ordered a reduction in the American contingent in the country, 16,000 strong by the fall of 1963. When some advisers protested, insisting that another increase in American manpower would win the war, he replied that to get involved more deeply was like "taking a drink. The effect wears off, and you have to take another."

Perhaps hoping to arrange a political settlement—like much recent history, the story is muddled and

hotly argued—Kennedy agreed to tolerate a coup d'etat by high-ranking ARVN officers that would remove Diem from the scene. An American plane was reserved to take Diem and his family out of the country but, in October 1963, when the ARVN struck, Diem was assassinated. A month later, Kennedy was dead. While the United States was undergoing a period of mourning and transition, South Vietnam was plunged into comic-opera political instability as one general toppled another and the NLF increased its power in the countryside.

MR. JOHNSON'S WAR

In his last days, Kennedy seemed determined to wind down the war in Vietnam. Although President Johnson ordered modest increases in the number of American military "advisors" in early 1964, he too seemed, at first, to want to get out. Through intermediaries, he offered economic aid to North Vietnam in return for peace talks. The North Vietnamese replied that they could not speak for the NLF. The NLF, to which Johnson also refered as the Viet Cong, refused to negotiate until all American soldiers were withdrawn from the country.

The President's Vision

This Johnson refused to do. Although he was no John Foster Dulles, L.B.J.'s view of the Cold War had been shaped in the 1950s by the belief that Communism was monolithic, an international movement directed ultimately from the Kremlin. Just enough men and supplies reached the NLF from the North to convince him that the war in Vietnam was not civil, but a war of subversion dependent on outside interference. He vowed that he was "not going to be the President who saw Southeast Asia go the way China went."

Johnson subscribed to the "domino theory" of Communist expansion propounded none too gracefully by President Eisenhower several years earlier: "You knock over the first one, and what will happen to the last one is the certainty that it will go over very quickly." When Johnson looked at Southeast Asia, he saw a line of fallen dominos stretching from Russia through China to North Vietnam, and a line of standing dominos beginning in South Vietnam, Laos, and Cambodia and extending to the Philippines and even Japan. As early as 1961, he had said, "We must decide whether to help these countries to the best of our ability or throw in the towel in the area and pull back our defenses to San Francisco."

U.S. Marines prepare to advance on North Vietnamese positions around Hue during the Tet Offensive.

The Tonkin Gulf Resolution

As late as October 1964 (shortly before Johnson faced the saber-rattling Goldwater in the presidential election), the president assured Americans that "we are not about to send American boys nine or ten thousand miles away from home to do what Asian boys ought to be doing for themselves." In reality, he was thinking about widening the war by means of a massive American military effort as early as the summer of 1964. In August, he was informed that North Vietnamese patrol boats had attacked American destroyers in the Gulf of Tonkin. He then asked Congress for authority "to take all necessary measures to repel any armed attack against the forces of the United States and to prevent future aggression."

Only two senators voted against the Gulf of Tonkin Resolution. One of them, Ernest Gruening of Alaska, said that he would not vote for "a predated declaration of war." In fact, whatever Johnson's motives at the time, he was to use the Gulf of Tonkin Resolution to turn the Vietnam conflict into a major war. By the end of 1964, the American military contingent in South Vietnam had been increased to 23,000, all, however, still described as advisors.

Escalation

Then, in February 1965, the Vietcong attacked an American military base near Pleiku. Citing the Tonkin Gulf Resolution, Johnson sent in 3,500 U.S. Marines, the first official combat troops, to South Vietnam. In April, 20,000 more troops arrived. By the end of 1965 there were 200,000 American troops in South Vietnam. This number doubled by the end of 1966 and reached 500,000 by the end of 1967. Between 1965 and 1968, the U.S. Air Force carried out heavy bombing of North Vietnam. To deprive the Viet Cong of shelter in the South Vietnam jungle, planes sprayed defoliants over tens of thousands of acres, killing trees, underbrush, and crops. American soldiers then moved in on "search and destroy" missions.

Johnson's policy of step by step increases in the intensity of the war was known as "escalation." His object was to prove to the enemy that fighting the American military machine was a hopeless cause. Briefly in 1965 and 1967, he stopped bombing and offered peace terms to North Vietnam. Both proposals were rejected. Instead, North Vietnam matched each American escalation with an escalation of its own. Beginning in 1966, North Vietnam sent its own soldiers into the war to replace dead Viet Cong. Within two years, 100,000 North Vietnamese were in the South. Step by step, a civil war between two groups of South Vietnamese had become very largely a war between Americans and North Vietnamese.

China and the Soviet Union also escalated their contribution to the war. Both countries supplied North Vietnam with ground-to-air missiles and other sophisticated weapons as well as economic aid.

The Tet Offensive

Nevertheless, at the beginning of 1968, the American commander, General William Westmoreland, told L.B.J. that victory was within reach. His words had scarcely been reported in the newspapers when, in the midst of the celebrations of Tet, Vietnam's traditional lunar New Year, 70,000 Viet Cong and North Vietnamese launched attacks on 30 South Vietnamese cities. For several days they controlled much of the city of Hue. In Saigon, enemy commandos attacked the American embassy itself. The Viet Cong took back jungle areas the "search and destroy" missions had cleared.

The Americans regrouped and, when the Tet Offensive was over, the Viet Cong and North Vietnamese had suffered horrendous casualties. In May, they agreed to begin peace talks in Paris. However, the American people's confidence in the war had also been severely shaken. The number of American boys dead, reported each evening on television, had soared from an average 26 a week in 1965 to 96 a week in 1966 and 180 a week in 1967. In 1968, more than 280 Americans were killed in Vietnam each week. The cost of the war had risen to $25 billion a year, nearly $70,000,000 a day!

Despite this tremendous effort and loss of life, victory seemed as distant as ever. In just a few weeks after the Tet Offensive, public approval of Johnson's handling of the war dropped from 40 percent to 26 percent. L.B.J. was badly shaken. Years later, two top aides reported they were so worried about his judgment that they secretly consulted psychiatrists.

TROUBLED YEARS

Johnson craved consensus, a word he used as often as Kennedy had called for vigor. In making his plea for civil-rights legislation, he adopted the slogan of the movement, "We Shall Overcome." He meant that all Americans would rise above the blight of racial hatred and discrimination. Another favorite presidential saying was a quotation from the biblical book of Isaiah, "Let us come together." The old manipulator of votes was not, as president, content with a majority, not

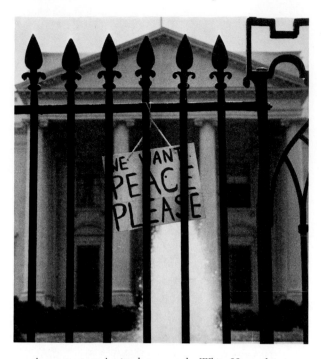

A war protestor's sign hangs on the White House fence.

even so large a one as he won in 1964. He wanted a unity of Americans behind him and his vision of a Great Society. The practical politician was a dreamer.

What L.B.J. got was a people divided more bitterly, perhaps, than at any time since the Civil War. The major cause of the social divisions of the 1960s was the war in Vietnam.

Hawks and Doves

Until 1965, the chief criticism of Johnson's Vietnam policy came from conservative Republicans like Barry Goldwater, some retired military men, and extremists like members of the John Birch Society. They said that in moving so cautiously, Johnson was making the same mistake President Truman had made in Korea. He was fighting for a limited purpose, a negotiated peace, rather than for total victory. Known as "Hawks," these critics wanted to use American military might to crush the Viet Cong and North Vietnamese. Former Air Force Commander Curtis LeMay called for bombing North Vietnam "into the Stone Age."

After L.B.J. escalated the war, becoming a Hawk himself, his chief critics were the "Doves," people who called for an end to the fighting or, at least, more serious efforts to negotiate a peace. As the war dragged on and the casualty lists mounted, this antiwar movement grew in size and militance.

Most Doves were liberal Democrats, members of L.B.J.'s own party. Doves included members of Congress, university professors and school teachers, ministers, priests, and nuns, some working people, many middle-class professionals, and even several retired generals. College students, although deferred from the draft that sent young men to Vietnam, were attracted to the antiwar movement in great numbers.

Mass demonstrations made for good television news features and put the antiwar movement at the center of public attention. In October 1965, 100,000 people attended demonstrations in 90 cities. In April 1967, about 300,000 Americans marched in opposition to the war in New York and San Francisco. Some young men burned their draft cards and went to jail rather than into the army. Some 40,000 went into exile, especially Canada and Sweden. More than 500,000 soldiers deserted during the Vietnam years and there were some 250,000 "bad discharges." Draft dodgers with influential social and political connections could join the National Guard in order to avoid combat service.

Antiwar Arguments

Doves opposed the war for many different reasons, some contradictory. A few were members of radical groups such as the Progressive Labor party, which ad-

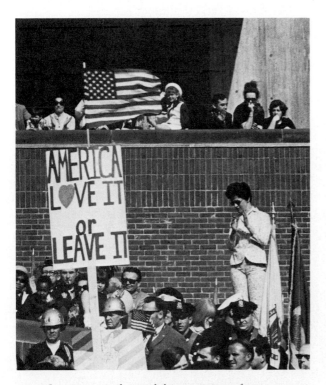

In response to the vocal demonstrations of antiwar activists, supporters of the Vietnam War organized rallies at which they displayed their sentiment with slogans such as "America, Love It or Leave It."

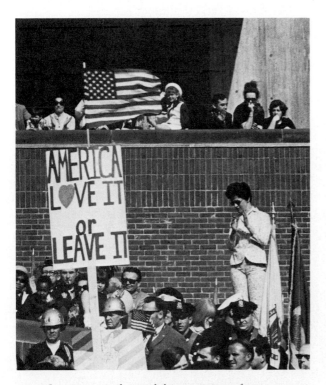

> ## Demonstration Decade
>
> Between 1963 and 1968, according to the National Commission on the Causes and Prevention of Violence, there were
>
> 369 civil-rights demonstrations
> 239 black riots and disturbances
> 213 white terrorist attacks against civil-rights workers
> 104 antiwar demonstrations
> 91 student protests on campus
> 54 segregationist clashes with counter-demonstrators
> 24 anti-integration demonstrations

mired Mao Zedong. They openly hoped that Ho Chi Minh would defeat the "imperialist capitalist" United States. Many youthful romantics, who knew little about Communism, were enchanted by the spectacle of the outnumbered, poorly equipped Viet Cong resisting American power. Other Doves like the famous pediatrician, Dr. Benjamin Spock, were anti-Communists. However, they believed that the United States was fighting against the wishes of a majority of Vietnamese and, therefore, was in the wrong. They disapproved of the fact that their powerful nation was showering terrible destruction on a small, poor country.

Religious pacifists like the Quakers opposed the war because they opposed all wars. Other morally concerned people, who agreed that some wars were justified, felt that the war in Vietnam was not one of them. They objected to the fact that, with no clear battle lines, American troops were making war on civilians as well as on enemy soldiers.

Bombs and defoliants took many innocent lives. In addition, a few American soldiers were guilty of deliberate atrocities. The worst occured at the village of My Lai in March 1968 when American troops killed 347 unarmed men, women, and children. The Viet Cong were guilty of similar crimes but that, Doves said, did not justify Americans in stooping to the same level.

Some critics of the war emphasized politics and diplomacy. They pointed out that the United States was exhausting itself fighting in a small, unimportant country while the power of China and the Soviet Union was untouched. Diplomat George Kennan and Senator William Fulbright of Arkansas argued that the United States was neglecting its committments elsewhere in the world. Senators Gaylord Nelson of Wisconsin and Wayne Morse of Oregon pointed out that the American war effort was alienating other Third World nations and even America's most trusted allies.

Black Separatism

The antiwar movement was not the only expression of discontent in the Great Society. What is most remarkable about the troubles of the 1960s is that anti-Johnson protest was noisiest among the very groups that most benefited from L.B.J.'s reforms. Some of the fiercest anti-Johnson rhetoric came from blacks, for whom the president believed he did so much. While the majority of black people supported the Great Society, many younger militants, particularly in the North, attacked the president's integrationist policies in the name of the "black-power" movement.

Black power meant many things. To sensible black leaders such as the Reverend Jesse Jackson, and to intellectuals such as sociologist Charles Hamilton, it meant pressure politics in the time-honored tradition of American ethnic groups: blacks demanding concessions for people of their race on the basis of the votes they could either deliver to or withhold from a political candidate. To a tiny group of black nationalists, it meant demanding a part of the United States for the formation of a separate nation for blacks only. To the great majority of advocates of black power, the slogan was reduced to nothing more than fad and fashion, dressing up in dashikis, wearing hair styles called "Afros," and cutting off friendships and casual social relationships with whites.

Black power was not a political program, but a cry of anguish and anger against the discrimination of the past and the discovery that civil equality of itself did little to remedy the social and psychological burdens from which American blacks suffered: poverty, high unemployment, inferior educational opportunities, severe health problems unknown to whites, high crime rates in black neighborhoods, a sense of inadequacy bred over three centuries of oppression.

Malcolm X and Violence

The most formidable spokesman for black separatism was Malcolm Little, a Detroiter and ex-petty criminal who styled himself Malcolm X, stating that a slave-

Malcolm X was a founder of the black-power movement of the 1960s.

owner had stolen his real African name. An adherent of a religious sect known as the Nation of Islam, or Black Muslims (for Christianity was said to be a white man's religion), Malcolm was a spellbinding preacher, although perhaps more popular with romantic white university students than among blacks.

Malcolm said that black people should reject Martin Luther King, Jr.'s, call to integrate into American society and, instead, separate from whites and glory in their blackness. Many young blacks, particularly in the North, were captivated by this message of defiance. One convert was a West Indian immigrant, Stokely Carmichael, who expelled all whites from SNCC in 1966, effectively taking that group out of the civil-rights movement.

Malcolm X's admonition to meet white racist violence with black violence appealed to former civil-rights workers who had been beaten by police and to teenage blacks in the urban ghettos. Carmichael's successor as the head of SNCC, Hubert Geroid "H. Rap" Brown, proclaimed as his motto, "Burn, Baby, Burn." In Oakland, California, two college students, Huey P. Newton and Bobby Seale, formed the Black Panther Party for Self-Defense. They were immediately in-

---

BLACK POWER

The most conspicuous individual in the emergence of the black-power movement was West Indian-born Stokely Carmichael. In 1966, he explained what he meant by black power: "If we are to proceed toward true liberation, we must cut ourselves off from white people. We must form our own institutions, credit unions, co-ops, political parties, write our own histories. . . ."

volved in violent confrontations with police because of their insistence that they be allowed to patrol black neighborhoods with firearms.

Violence haunted black America during the 1960s. Malcolm X fell out of favor with the Black Muslims and was gunned down by assassins in 1965. Also in 1965, a riot in the Watts district of Los Angeles resulted in 34 deaths and $35 million in property damages. In 1966 and 1967, black riots raged in the ghettos of many cities. When Martin Luther King, Jr., was killed by a white racist, James Earl Ray, in 1968, the smoke from buildings set afire by rioters in Washington wafted into the White House itself.

The Student Movement

Just as troubling was discontent among another group that was favored by Johnson's Great Society reforms, university students. By 1963, it already was clear that the baby-boom generation was not so passive in its politics as the youth of the 1950s had been. Students demonstrated against capital punishment, protested against the violations of civil liberties by groups like

A mule-drawn cart carries the body of civil-rights leader Martin Luther King, Jr., at his funeral in Atlanta, Georgia.

PROTEST IN AMERICA

Saul Alinsky, a well-known radical organizer, had little but contempt for the "New Left" of the 1960s. He regarded university student rebels as dilettantes and chided them for their claims that the United States was a repressive nation: "True, there is government harassment, but there still is that relative freedom to fight. I can attack my government, try to organize to change it. That's more than I can do in Moscow, Peking, or Havana."

the House Un-American Activities Committee, and worked in the civil-rights movement. In 1963, a new national youth organization, Students for a Democratic Society (SDS), issued the "Port Huron statement," a comprehensive critique of American society written by a graduate of the University of Michigan, Tom Hayden. The SDS called for young people to take the lead in drafting a program by which the United States could be made genuinely democratic and a force for peace and justice.

Like the advocates of black power, the New Left, as SDS and other organizations came to be called, was not so much a political movement as an explosion of anger and frustration. Hayden and a few other youth leaders tried to channel student energies into concrete concerns like civil rights for blacks, the problems of the poor, and the power of large corporations in American society. But most of the campus riots of the late 1960s were unfocused, aimed at local grievances such as student participation in setting university rules, or directed against the war in Vietnam, a matter beyond the competence of university presidents and local merchants (major targets of student rebellion) to solve.

Massive protest on campuses began at the University of California at Berkeley with the founding of the Free Speech Movement in 1964. By 1968, protest took a violent turn with students at Columbia University seizing several buildings and refusing to budge until they were forcibly removed by police.

The Counterculture

By 1966, many young people, high school as well as college students, were dropping out of politics to pursue a personal rebellion. In the Haight-Ashbury district of San Francisco and in the East Village of New York, thousands of teenagers gathered to establish what they called a "counterculture," a new way of living based on promiscuous sex, drugs (particularly marijuana and a synthetic hallucinogen, LSD), and extravagant colorful clothing. They called themselves

N O T A B L E P E O P L E

BOB DYLAN (b. 1941)

Minstrel of the 1960s, Bob Dylan.

Bob Dylan is the stage name of Robert Zimmerman, who was born on May 24, 1941, in Duluth, Minnesota, and grew up in Hibbing, a drab hard-working industrial town in the Mesabi Range, America's principal source of iron ore. Hibbing was a working-class town; the majority of its people were immigrants or the children or grandchildren of immigrants, particularly from Finland and the Slavic nations of Eastern Europe. This made Bob Zimmerman twice alienated, not quite at home. His family was Jewish, albeit not religious, and was middle class; the proprietors of a furniture store.

The Zimmermans' fortunes were closely tied to employment in the iron mines. Later, as Bob Dylan, Zimmerman said that his least favorite job at the store was repossessing furniture on which the purchasers could not make payments. It is possible that he was assigned that unpleasant task, although the repossession of sofas and chairs from frustrated, burly miners was not the kind of job on which one sent a skinny teenager. Indeed, much of what Bob Dylan said about himself as one of the most successful entertainers of the troubled 1960s was romantic contrivance. He told of living a vagabond's life and of struggling to make his voice heard. But his story was much more that of an instant sensation. He enjoyed an ordinary middle-class youth, and it was perhaps for that reason that he was so important to the discontented middle-class youth of the 1960s who demonstrated their anger by protesting noisily and buying his recordings.

By 1965, half the American population was under the age of 25 and, as marketing experts had calculated before the decade began, they were extremely affluent. Because they could spend their money on things that amused them, teenagers were responsible for 75 percent of the phonograph records sold in the United States.

Bob Dylan was one of the major beneficiaries of this phenomenon. Already as a teenager in Hibbing, he was rebelling. He adopted the styles of 1950s beatniks and took an interest in both past and contemporary critics of comfortable, materialistic, security-conscious, and conformist middle-class America.

He expressed his own criticisms through a guitar and harmonica bought for him when he was a teenager, learning to play both instruments simultaneously in the manner of the old "one-man band" comedy acts.

The songs that he wrote were far from comic. On the contrary, they were serious, if maudlin, romanticizations of the "common people" and sarcastic assaults on the America of the corporations, racial prejudice, war, and the timid middle classes. He disdained the slick, professional groups that were recording folk songs in the late 1950s, such as the Weavers, the Kingston Trio, and the Limeliters, and searched in the past for their predecessors. His hero was the Oklahoma balladeer Woody Guthrie, who had been a genuine vagabond and the author of perhaps hundreds of songs that celebrated the common people and condemned wealth and power.

Not only did Bob Dylan visit Guthrie, who was dying in a New Jersey hospital of a rare hereditary disease, but he updated the flavor of Guthrie's protest and imitated his rough-edged, grating singing style. Dylan could not sing very well; there must have been many better guitarists in the country; and the lyrics he wrote were trite. But he struck a chord in young people. He arrived in New York at the beginning of 1961, was a sensation in the coffeehouses of Greenwich Village within months, and had a contract with Columbia Records by fall.

His first album, released in February 1962, was an immediate hit. The curly-headed kid from Minnesota was the heir to such singing sensations of the 1950s as Bill Haley and the Comets, the first white musical group to record rock-'n'-roll, and Elvis Presley, the entertainment king of the decade. During the first half of the 1960s, only the Beatles, a quartet from England, made more money than Dylan in the recorded-music business.

With the exception of the Beach Boys, who marketed a cheery romanticization of Southern California teenage indolence, there was something new about the entertainers of the 1960s. Bill Haley and Elvis Presley had been content to be show people, and troubadors such as Woody Guthrie and Pete Seeger, who sang about social issues, had only small followings. But songs of protest were at the center of the popular culture marketplace in the 1960s, and the stars of the decade were considered teachers and moral leaders by their fans.

They reacted in different ways to this beatification. John Lennon, the most articulate of the Beatles, commented on the absurd implications of the mass worship of his group that the Beatles were better known than Jesus. (Instead of recognizing Lennon's barbed criticism of Beatlemania, religious leaders attacked *him* for being blasphemous.) Joan Baez, the leading woman protest singer, took her messianic role very seriously, solemnly divulging intimate details of her life to "good friends" gathered in groups of 10,000 and 20,000. Dylan, however, was overwhelmed and angered by it.

He refused to play the moral spokesman and, after a near-fatal automobile accident, retired to his country home in Woodstock, New York. Even when the central event of the counterculture of the 1960s was held within a few miles of his farm, Dylan refused to appear. He was, however, still taken very seriously. Professors of psychology, sociology, history, and political science wrote serious studies of his songs. In 1970, Princeton University awarded Dylan an honorary doctorate, which he accepted.

"flower children," free of the pressures and preoccupations of American materialism. Other Americans called them "hippies" and were alternately amused by them, or condemned them as lazy, immoral "long-haired kids." In both New York and San Francisco, tour buses took curiosity seekers through hippie neighborhoods as though they were exotic foreign countries. When tourists from small towns snapped shots of counterculture fauna, some hippies whipped out cameras and took pictures of them.

When commercialization seemed to be destroying the vitality of the counterculture, numerous flower children retreated to communes in the California mountains and New Mexico desert. But because the self-fulfillment of individuals was the principal goal of the phenomenon, and because drugs played a large part in the culture, the communes were doomed from the start. The most fundamental matters of procuring the necessities of health and sanitation were neglected.

THE ELECTION OF 1968

No president can survive a serious economic depression in a year that he must stand for reelection. Lyndon Johnson, able to shout gleefully while striding through an airplane in 1964, "I am the king! I am the king!" discovered in 1968 that a reigning monarch cannot survive a serious social, cultural, and moral depression. He did not even try. Early in 1968, the Great Society in tatters, he announced that he would not run for reelection.

Eugene McCarthy, Regicide

In 1967, Eugene McCarthy was in his second term as senator from Minnesota. He was a tall man with a gray solemnity about him that bordered on glumness. His record as a liberal workhorse was solid, but no one thought of him as a mover and shaker. Minnesota already had its walking earthquake of energy and exuberance in Vice President Hubert Humphrey. McCarthy seemed just right to stay at home, anchoring Minnesota's long liberal tradition in midwestern bedrock. But McCarthy was anguished by the issue that the vice president had to dodge, the war in Vietnam. Late in 1967, he announced that he would stand as a candidate for the Democratic presidential nomination, challenging Lyndon B. Johnson on that issue.

Political pundits admired McCarthy's principle and pluck. A few were enchanted by his diffidence: with plenty of mediocrities lusting unashamedly after public office, he seemed genuinely to believe that a public

Eugene McCarthy campaigns during the 1968 primaries.

servant should serve a cause. But the experts gave him little chance. McCarthy's only base of support was within the largely middle-class antiwar movement. The labor unions, vital to Democratic party success at the polls, begrudged him several votes against their legislative programs; he struck no chord among either black or ethnic minorities (despite his somewhat mystical Roman Catholic religion); and he positively disdained big city mayors like Chicago's Richard E. Daley. A portion of the educated, cultured, affluent liberal middle class was not, the professionals said, a foundation on which to build an electoral majority.

Johnson's Resignation

Time was to prove them right. But in 1968, antiwar activists were so aroused that, like Barry Goldwater's right-wing shock troops in the Republican party in 1964, they were able to turn the Democratic party upside down. At McCarthy's call, thousands of university students dropped their studies and rushed to New Hampshire, scene of the first presidential primary. They agreed to get "clean for Gene," shearing their long "hippie" hair, shaving their beards, and donning neckties, brassieres, and proper dresses so as not to alienate the people of the conservative state from the issue at hand—the war. Sleeping on the floors of McCarthy storefront headquarters, they rang door bells, handed out pamphlets at supermarkets, and stuffed envelopes.

President Johnson knew enough of the country's anxiety over the war to be concerned. He kept his name off the ballot. Instead, the governor of New Hampshire ran as his proxy. The vote was evenly split, but such a rebuke of an incumbent president in a traditionally cautious and conservative state promised bigger McCarthy victories elsewhere. Johnson knew it. On national television, he announced that he would retire when his term expired.

The Democrats: Who Will End the War?

Johnson's announcement caught everyone by surprise. Vice President Humphrey, in Mexico on a good-will tour, rushed back to Washington to throw his hat in the ring. He had an immediate edge on McCarthy because of long-standing ties with labor, blacks, big city Democratic machines, the party's professionals, and contributors generous with a dollar.

The McCarthy backers expected Humphrey to run and welcomed the contest. What they could not foresee was that in the wake of Johnson's withdrawal, Robert F. Kennedy also rushed to enter the race. Kennedy was a real threat to both McCarthy and Humphrey. Johnson had eased him out of his cabinet as soon after John Kennedy's death as it was seemly to do so. L.B.J. did not like "Bobby," whose presence kept him in the Kennedy shadow. In fact, R.F.K.

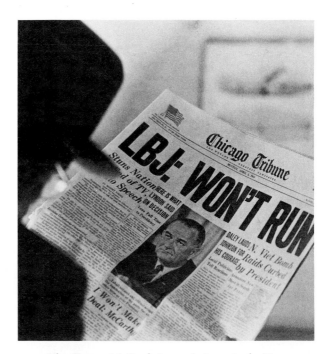

After Eugene McCarthy's moral victory in the New Hampshire primary in March 1968, President Johnson announced his retirement.

Minutes before he was assassinated, Senator Robert F. Kennedy celebrates his victory in the California Democratic primary

looked on Johnson almost as a usurper of a Kennedy birthright. After methodical public opinion polls typical of the Kennedy clan showed that he could win a Senate seat in New York despite his lack of association with the state, Robert Kennedy ran, won, and became a critic of the war and a leading liberal spokesman.

His connections with minorities were as strong as Humphrey's. He was a close personal friend of Cesar Chavez, leader of the mostly Hispanic farmworkers' union in California and the Southwest. Even with blacks, on whose behalf Humphrey had labored since the 1940s, Kennedy was popular. When Martin Luther King, Jr., was assassinated on April 4, 1968, Bobby's response seemed more sincere and was better received than the respects of any other Democrat. He had maintained his connections with the old-line party professionals and the labor movement. Indeed, within the Democratic party, his political realism and opportunism made him anathema only to the group that continued to support McCarthy. They attacked him as avidly as they attacked Johnson and Humphrey as an exemplar of the "old politics."

Kennedy ran strong although not without setbacks. For example, McCarthy won the next-to-last primary, in Oregon. Then, on the very night he won the last of the primaries in California, Robert Kennedy was assassinated, shot point-blank in the head by Sirhan

B. Sirhan, a Jordanian who disliked Kennedy's support for the Jewish state of Israel.

The tragedy demoralized the antiwar Democrats and undoubtedly contributed to the week-long riots in Chicago that made a mockery of the Democratic national convention. Many Kennedy supporters found it impossible to swing behind McCarthy and backed Senator George McGovern of South Dakota instead. With a divided opposition, Humphrey was able to win the Democratic nomination on the first ballot. As a gesture toward blue-collar ethnics whose aspirations had been aroused by John F. Kennedy, and who seemed to be supporting Bobby, Humphrey chose a Roman Catholic running mate, Senator Edmund B. Muskie of Maine.

Nixon and Wallace

Richard M. Nixon easily won the Republican nomination at a placid convention in Miami Beach. Although the former vice president had retired from politics in 1962, after failing in an attempt to become governor of California, he had doggedly rebuilt his position in the GOP. He firmed up his support among eastern moderate Republicans and won over Republican conservatives by working hard for Goldwater in 1964. After 1964, Nixon attended every local Republican function to which he was invited, no matter how

Hubert Humphrey with running mate Edmund B. Muskie.

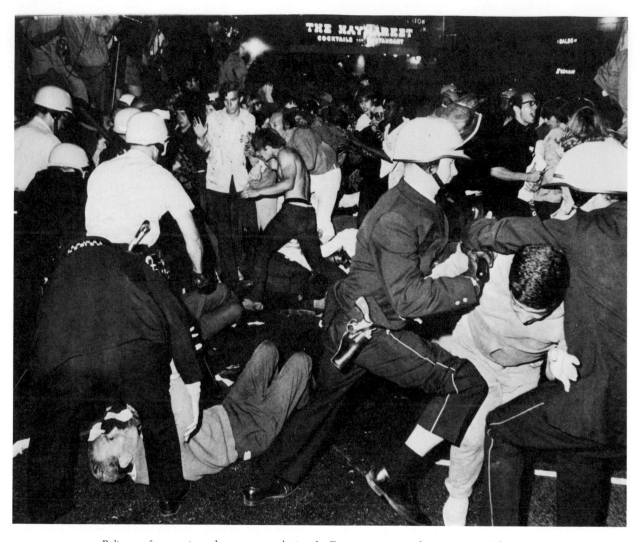

Police confront antiwar demonstrators during the Democratic national convention in Chicago,
August 28, 1968.

small the town, insignificant the occasion, or tawdry the candidate he was to endorse. By making himself so available to the party's grass-roots workers, the far from charismatic Nixon built up energetic, active cadres of supporters.

The Democrats were badly split; many in the antiwar wing of the party announced that they would vote for the pacifist pediatrician Benjamin Spock. Humphrey tried to woo them back by hinting that he would end the war but, as Johnson's vice president, he could not repudiate L.B.J.'s policy. The Democratic split and Humphrey's ambiguity enabled Nixon to waffle on the war issue. He espoused a hawkish military policy at the same time that he reminded voters that a Repub-

lican president, Dwight D. Eisenhower, had ended the war in Korea.

The chief threat to a Nixon victory seemed to come from the American Independent party, founded by Governor George Wallace when he calculated that he had no chance to win the Democratic nomination. A diminutive, combative man—reporters called him a bantam fighting cock—Wallace barnstormed the country and attempted to forge an odd alliance of Republican right-wing extremists and blue-collar working-people who felt that the Democratic party had forgotten them in its anxiety to appeal to the blacks. This "white backlash" vote appeared to grow after Robert Kennedy was killed. Already indifferent to the aloof McCarthy, many blue collar white ethnics who had liked Kennedy personally found Wallace much more to their taste than civil-rights pioneer Hubert Humphrey.

A Close Call

It was obvious that Wallace could not win the election. His purpose was to take just enough electoral votes from both Humphrey and Nixon to throw the election into the House of Representatives. Because each state casts one vote when a president is selected in the House, anti-integration southern congressmen under Wallace's leadership, so Wallace imagined, could make a deal with Nixon: a reversal of Democratic party civil-rights policies in return for their support.

Fearing this possibility, Humphrey called on Nixon to pledge with him that neither of them would deal with Wallace and his thinly veiled racism. Instead, Humphrey proposed, he and Nixon should pledge that

in the case that neither won in the electoral college, each would direct his supporters in the House to vote for whomever of the two finished with the most votes.

Nixon evaded the challenge, and in the end it did not matter. Although Wallace did better than any third-party candidate since 1924, winning 13.5 percent of the popular vote and 46 electoral votes, Nixon eked out a plurality of 500,000 votes and an absolute majority in the electoral college. It was close. A rush of blue-collar workers back to Humphrey during the final week of the campaign indicated to some pollsters that he would have won had the election been held a week or two later. Indeed, the Democrats continued to hold a comfortable edge in both houses of Congress. The key to Nixon's victory may well have been those antiwar Democrats who could not bring themselves to vote for Humphrey. In time, their "New Age" politics would transform the great political alliance forged by Franklin D. Roosevelt into the nation's minority party.

For Further Reading

Consult the bibliographies for Chapters 47 and 48 for overviews of the 1960s. In addition, see Ronald Berman, *America in the Sixties* (1968); Robert Caro, *The Years of Lyndon Johnson* (1982); Theodore Draper, *Abuse of Power* (1967); Jim F. Heath, *Decade of Disillusion: The Kennedy-Johnson Years* (1975); Doris Kearns, *Lyndon Johnson and the American Dream* (1976); Merle Miller, *Lyndon: An Oral Biography* (1980); William L. O'Neill, *Coming Apart: An Informal History of the 1960s* (1971); Richard Walton, *The Foreign Policy of John F. Kennedy* (1972); Theodore H. White, *The Making of the President, 1964* (1965) and *The Making of the President, 1968* (1969).

There is a huge literature dealing with the Vietnam War, its causes and consequences. Among the most useful books are Frances Fitzgerald, *Fire in the Lake* (1972); David Halberstam, *The Making of a Quagmire* (1956); G. C. Herring, *America's Longest War* (1986); G. M. Kahn, *Intervention: How America Became Involved in Vietnam* (1986); Gabriel Kolko, *Anatomy of a War* (1985); Marcus G. Raskin and Bernard Fall, *The Vietnam Reader* (1965); and Arthur M. Schlesinger, Jr., *Bitter Heritage: Vietnam and American Democracy* (1967).

On the antiwar and related agitations of what was called "the Movement," see Joseph R. Conlin, *The Troubles: A Jaundiced Glance Back at the Movement of the 1960s* (1982); Morris Dickstein, *Gates of Eden: American Culture in the Sixties* (1977); Todd Gitlin, *The Whole World is Watching* (1981); Kenneth Keniston, *Young Radicals* (1968); Theodore Roszak, *The Making of a Counter-Culture* (1969); Kirkpatrick Sale, *SDS* (1973); and Irwin Unger, *The Movement* (1974).

On the rather more significant civil-rights movement, see D. Garrow, *Bearing of the Cross* (1986); Alex Haley, *The Autobiography of Malcolm X* (1965); Sam A. Levitan et al., *Still a Dream: The Changing Status of Blacks Since 1960* (1975); Anthony Lews, *Portrait of a Decade* (1964); David Lewis, *King: A Critical Biography* (1970); Stephen B. Oates, *Let the Trumpet Sound* (1982); James T. Patterson, *America's Struggle Against Poverty, 1900–1980* (1981); H. Sitkoff, *The Struggle for Black Equality* (1981); and Harold Zinn, *SNCC* (1965).

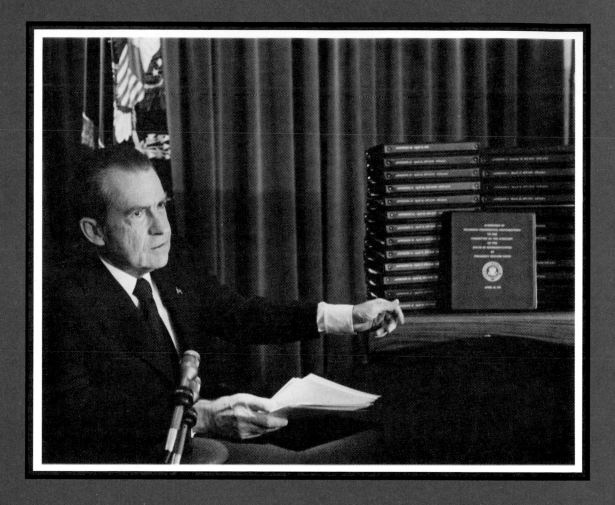

The heroes of Greek myth were constantly pursuing Proteus, the herdsman of the seas, for he could foresee the future and, once captured, he was obligated to reveal what he knew. But Proteus was rarely captured. He also possessed the curious power to assume the shape of any creature or thing, easily wriggling out of a captor's grasp. Richard Milhous Nixon, so his critics and even his backers said, was never captured because he was never in his own shape. John F. Kennedy, who ran against him for the presidency in 1960, said that Dick Nixon had assumed so many shapes that he had forgotten who he was and what he stood for. Liberals called him "Tricky Dicky." At several turns in his career, his Republican partisans felt constrained to assure

—— 50 ——

THE PRESIDENCY IN CRISIS

Policies of the Nixon, Ford, and Carter Administrations, 1968–1980

Richard M. Nixon with transcripts of the Watergate tapes that implicated him in the criminal cover-up of a break-in at the Democratic party headquarters.

Americans that the "Old Nixon" was no more; it was a "New Nixon" who needed their votes.

But the "Real Nixon," like the real Proteus, remained elusive and enigmatic to the end. Senator Barry Goldwater said that Richard M. Nixon was "the most complete loner I've ever known."

THE NIXON PRESIDENCY

Nixon remains a compelling figure. He lacked all the personal qualities the pundits said were keys to success in late twentieth-century politics: physical attractiveness, grace, wit, a camera presence, the aura of "a nice guy." Nixon was shy and furtive in manner. He often exuded discomfort, defensiveness, and insincerity in front of a crowd.

The liberals' hatred for him had the intensity of a diabolical possession, but those who disliked liberals did not love Nixon. Dwight D. Eisenhower came within a hair of dumping him as his vice president in 1952 and considered doing so in 1956. In 1960, Ike humiliated Nixon by saying he was unable to recall a single instance in which Nixon contributed to a presidential decision. The right-wing Republicans whom Nixon served well for more than two decades accepted him without quite trusting him.

Richard Nixon clawed his way from a lower middle-class background in southern California to the top of the heap through hard work and the tenacious bite of a pit bulldog. Although he overstated it in his autobiographical *Six Crises*, he overcame genuine obstacles and repeated humiliation. If the self-made Horatio Alger boy is an American hero, Nixon should be ensconced in a pantheon for, unlike the Alger heroes, Nixon was all pluck and little luck. Whatever else may be said of Richard Nixon, he earned everything he ever got.

Political Savvy

As president, Nixon took little interest in domestic matters. He told advisors that "the country could run itself domestically without a president." He left important decisions and directives to two young White House aides, H. R. Haldeman and John Ehrlichman. Brassy where their boss was secretive, Haldeman and Erlichman insulated Nixon from Congress and even his own cabinet as effectively as Sherman Adams had done for Ike. But they were themselves arrogant, un-

solicitous, and unpopular with Washingtonians; they did nothing to shore up political support for the Nixon administration.

Nixon left politicking to Vice President Spiro T. Agnew, a former governor of Maryland who had been named to the ticket to attract blue-collar and white ethnic voters who were drawn to George Wallace. Agnew was an energetic campaigner and, once elected, cheerleader, storming around the country on speaking tours. He delighted conservatives by flailing student antiwar protestors, permissive educators who tolerated their disruptive activities, liberal Supreme Court justices, and the national news media. Agnew was fond of tongue-twisting alliteration, and his partisan audiences loved it. His masterpiece was "nattering nabobs of negativism," that is, liberal journalists.

Agnew's liberal-baiting provided Nixon with a superb smokescreen for, despite his many denunciations of big-spending liberal government, the president was not interested in dismantling the New Deal or even the Great Society. His only major modification of the liberal welfare state he inherited was "the New Federalism," a policy of turning federal tax monies over to the states to spend on social programs.

On other fronts, Nixon might have been a middle-of-the-road Democrat. He sponsored a scheme for welfare reform, the Family Assistance Plan, that was to provide a flat annual payment to poor families in return for the agreement by heads of household to register with employment agencies. (It failed in Congress.) In 1971, when inflation threatened his reelection campaign, Nixon slapped on wage and price controls, a Republican anathema for half a century.

And yet, few conservatives yelped. Quite shrewdly, Nixon understood that the grassroots conservatives he called the "Silent Majority" had been repelled far less by liberal economic policy than by the myriad non-economic causes that liberals had come to emphasize by the 1970s: what many whites perceived as kid-glove treatment of blacks, the often gamey demands of feminists and advocates of "gay rights," the antiwar movement's antipatriotism, and the decisions of the Warren Court that emphasized the rights of accused criminals and seemed to hobble police in enforcing the law.

Reshaping the Supreme Court

Thanks to a mistake by Lyndon Johnson in the waning days of his administration, Nixon was able to move immediately to reshape the Supreme Court. Elderly Chief Justice Earl Warren (an old Nixon nemesis) had offered to retire while Johnson was still president so that L.B.J. could name another liberal activist in his place. Johnson picked an old Texas crony already on

Richard Nixon in the Oval Office with aides Robert Haldeman (left) and John Erlichman (center, seated).

the Court, Abe Fortas, who was immediately revealed to have accepted payments for public appearances that were, at best, of dubious propriety. Johnson had to back down and Warren retired only after Nixon was sworn in.

Nixon's choice to replace him was Warren Burger of Minnesota. Burger was conservative but, as an advocate of judicial restraint rather than antiliberal activism, he was somewhat disappointing to the right wing of the Republican party. When Fortas himself left the Court in 1970, Nixon tried to mollify the right-wingers by naming Clement Haynsworth of South Carolina to the Court. However, Haynsworth had several pro segregation decisions in his portfolio, and Senate Democrats rejected him.

An angry Nixon then blundered badly. Insisting that the South must have a seat on the Court, he hurriedly named a mediocrity from Florida whose mere knowledge of the law was problematical. When he too was rejected by the Senate, the president had to return to another advocate of judicial restraint, a friend of Burger from Minnesota, Harry A. Blackmun. Nixon's two additional appointments, Lewis F. Powell and William H. Rehnquist (later Chief Justice) were conservatives but also generally temperate and restrained.

Just as Nixon left the basic outlines of the welfare state intact, the Burger Court merely moderated Warren Court rulings. On the domestic front, Nixon seemed to achieve just what he wanted, an equilibrium enabling him to concentrate on what he believed to be the modern president's chief responsibility and his own ticket into the history books: foreign relations.

NIXON'S VIETNAM

No foreign problem was so pressing as the ongoing war in Vietnam. Nixon (and everyone else) knew that Lyndon Johnson's political career had been prematurely snuffed out by the agonizing, endless conflict. "The damned fool" Johnson had, in the words of a protest song of the era, mired himself "hip deep in the Big Muddy," and been helpless to do anything but to tell the nation to "push on." Nixon wanted out of the war. But how to turn the trick?

Vietnamization

Nixon had been vice president when Eisenhower freed the nation from another quagmire in Korea. But Ike's

Children hit by napalm flee in agony in Trangbang, South Vietnam, June 8, 1972.

course of action in 1953 was not available in 1969. Eisenhower had threatened the Chinese and North Koreans with nuclear weapons; that was not an option in the era of the nuclear balance of terror. Ike had settled the Korean Conflict on the basis of an independent South Korea with American troops on the scene to ensure security. In 1969, the Viet Cong and North Vietnamese insisted that they would not conclude hostilities as long as there were American troops in South Vietnam. Finally, Eisenhower had not had to deal with a militant antiwar movement at home.

Nixon's scheme was of necessity more subtle. First, to neutralize antiwar movement, Nixon set out to reduce the sickeningly long casualty lists that weekly provided the movement with new recruits. In July 1969, he promulgated the Nixon Doctrine, stating that while the United States would "participate in the defense and development of allies and friends," Americans would no longer "undertake all the defense of the free nations of the world."

In Vietnam, the Nixon Doctrine translated as the "Vietnamization" of the war. The large but unreliable ARVN was thoroughly retrained to replace American boys on the bloody front lines. As South Vietnamese

units were deemed ready for combat, American troops came home. At about the same speed that L.B.J. had escalated the American presence, Nixon de-escalated it. From a high of 541,000 American soldiers in South Vietnam when Nixon took office, the American force declined to 335,000 in 1970 and 24,000 in 1972.

Nixon had returned the American ground war to where it had been in 1964 and, so it seemed at first, he had reduced the militant antiwar movement to a hard core of pacifists and New Left "anti-imperialists" whom Agnew denounced as traitors and Nixon as "bums." Democrats in Congress who had defended Johnson's war demanded that Nixon make more serious efforts to negotiate an end to it. But the president replied, not implausibly, that a truculent North Vietnam, and not he, was the major obstacle to peace.

Expanding the War

Politically, Nixon could not afford simply to pull out of Vietnam. He was beholden for his election to his own hard core of "Hawks" who believed that Johnson had failed in Vietnam because he had not been "tough" enough. Nixon reassured such supporters:

"We will not be humiliated. We will not be defeated." Much as he and his chief foreign policy advisor, Henry A. Kissinger, wanted the war ended, they had to salvage the independence of South Vietnam in order to save face.

Consequently, all the while he reduced the American presence in Vietnam, Nixon attempted to bludgeon the enemy into meaningful negotiations by expanding the scope of the war. In the spring of 1969, Nixon sent Air Force bombers over neutral Cambodia to destroy sanctuaries where about 50,000 North Vietnamese troops rested up after battles. For a year, the American people knew nothing of these attacks. Then, in 1970, Nixon sent ground forces into Cambodia, an attack that could not be concealed.

The result was a thunderous uproar. Critics condemned the president for attacking a neutral nation. Several hundred university presidents closed their campuses for fear of student violence, and events at two colleges proved their wisdom in doing so. At Kent State University in Ohio, members of the National Guard, many of whom had joined to avoid being drafted and sent to Southeast Asia, opened fire on demonstrators. Four persons were killed and eleven wounded. Ten days later, two students at Jackson State College in Mississippi were killed by police.

Congress reacted to the widening of the war by repealing the Tonkin Gulf Resolution, which had given President Johnson authority to fight it. Nixon responded that the repeal was immaterial. As Commander in Chief, he said, he had the authority to take whatever military action he believed necessary. Nonetheless, when the war was further expanded into Laos in February 1971, ARVN troops carried the burden of the fighting.

Falling Dominos

Vietnamization did not work. Without American troops by their side, the ARVN was humiliated in Laos. The Communist Pathet Lao grew in strength until 1975 when it seized control of the country. Tens of thousands of refugees who feared Communist rule fled.

In Cambodia, the consequences of expanding the war were far worse. Many young Cambodians were so angered by American bombing that they flocked to join the Khmer Rouge, once scarcely large enough to stage a soccer game. The Khmer Rouge increased in size from a mere 3,000 in 1970 to 30,000 in just a few years. In 1976, the head of the force, Pol Pot, came to power and created one of the most criminal regimes of the century. In three years, his fanatical followers murdered as many as 3 million of their own people out of a population of 7.2 million! If Hitler's campaign of genocide against the Jews of Nazi-occupied Europe had been proportional to Pol Pot's, the toll in the Nazi death camps would not have been 6 million, but something on the order of 150 million.

Eisenhower's Asian "dominos" had fallen, but not because the United States had been weak in the face of a military threat. They toppled because the United States had escalated and expanded a war that, in 1963, had been little more than a brawl. In the process, Southeast Asian moderates and neutrals like Cambodia's Prince Sihanouk were destroyed. By the mid-1970s, North Vietnam was dominated by militarists and Cambodia by a monster. Laos was in the hands of a once tiny Communist movement, and South Vietnam had fallen.

President Nixon was fond of historical firsts and absolutes. His speeches sometimes read as if they were entries in the *Guinness Book of World Records*: Nixon was the first president in history to visit such and such a town in Idaho; never before had the American people completed so many dams in one year; and suchlike. One superlative of which the president neglected to apprise the American people was the fact that never, without exception, had the United States pursued any major policy that was so utterly disastrous as the war in Vietnam.

Finis

The fighting dragged on until the fall of 1972 when, after suffering twelve days of earth-shaking bombing, the North Vietnamese finally faced up to the fact that the war was a stalemate. Foreign Minister Le Duc Tho met with Kissinger and arranged a cease-fire. The Paris Accords they signed went into effect in January 1973. The treaty required the United States to withdraw all its troops from Vietnam within 60 days while the North Vietnamese released all prisoners of war. Until free elections were held, North Vietnamese troops could remain in the country.

With good reason, South Vietnamese president Nguyen Van Thieu regarded the settlement as a sellout. It enabled Nixon to save face while Thieu was faced with a massive enemy force within South Vietnamese borders. For two years, the country simmered. Then, in April 1975, the North Vietnamese army attacked Saigon and the ARVN collapsed. A short time later, North and South Vietnam were united and Saigon was renamed Ho Chih Minh City.

Ironically, Cambodia's nightmare was brought to an end only when the North Vietnamese invaded the country and overthrew Pol Pot. Rather more remarkable, as late as 1989, the United States insisted that

Pol Pot was the legitimate ruler of Cambodia. Policymakers of both parties had transferred their obsessive opposition to anything the Soviet Union espoused to unified Vietnam.

The Bottom Line

The long war ravaged a once prosperous corner of the world. Once an exporter of rice, Vietnam was chronically short of food. About 1 million ARVN soldiers lost their lives, the Viet Cong and North Vietnamese about the same number. Estimates of civilian dead ran as high as 3.5 million. About 5.2 million acres of jungle and farmland were ruined by defoliation. American bombing also devastated hundreds of cities, towns, bridges, and highways. The Air Force dropped more bombs on Vietnam than on all of Europe during the Second World War.

The vengefulness of the victors caused a massive flight of refugees. About 10 percent of the people of Southeast Asia fled their homelands after the war. Some spent everything they owned to bribe venal North Vietnamese officials to let them go. Others piled into leaky boats and cast off into open waters, untold numbers to die. To the credit of American policymakers, nearly 600,000 Vietnamese, Laotians, Cambodians, and ethnic minorities (whom every government in Southeast Asia persecuted) were admitted as immigrants.

The war cost the United States something like $150 billion, more than any other American war except the Second World War. Some 2.7 million American men and women served in the conflict; 57,000 of them were killed and 300,000 were wounded. Many men were disabled for life. Some lost limbs; others were poisoned by Agent Orange, the toxic defoliant the army used to clear jungle. Yet others were addicted to drugs or alcohol. Mental disturbances and violent crime were alarmingly common among Vietnam veterans.

And yet, for ten years, Vietnam veterans were ignored, shunned, even discriminated against. Politicians, not only liberals who had opposed the war but the super-patriotic Hawks who had wanted the troops to fight on indefinitely, neglected to vote money for government programs to help them. Only in 1982, almost a decade after the war ended, was a monument to the soldiers erected in Washington, D.C.

The Vietnam War Memorial in Washington, D.C., was erected in November 1982, seven years after the conclusion of the war.

NIXON-KISSINGER FOREIGN POLICY

Nixon called the Vietnam War a "sideshow." Henry A. Kissinger said that it was a mere "footnote" to history. Both men wanted to bring the conflict to an end so that they could bring about what, quite rightly, they regarded as a revolution in world diplomacy, a complete reordering of relations among the world's great powers.

The Long Crusade

It is impossible to say just how much of the Nixon-Kissinger foreign policy was Nixon's and how much was Kissinger's, and apportioning credit (or blame) is not very important. The fact was that both men envisioned a new relationship among the great powers that flew in the face of American assumptions since the dawn of the Cold War.

That is, for more than 20 years before the Nixon presidency, virtually all American policymakers and shapers of public opinion had described the world as divided into two inevitably hostile camps: the United States and its allies, most importantly Western Europe and Japan; and the Soviet Union and its client states, particularly the gigantic People's Republic of China. Few so eagerly looked forward to a showdown between the two camps as John Foster Dulles had done, but diplomats and politicians who favored détente—a relaxation of tensions—had to phrase their views very carefully or have their courage and patriotism questioned.

The pre-presidential Richard M. Nixon had been one of those who had most consistently played on the theme of inevitable superpower hostility and the disloyalty of those who were "soft on Communism." But at some point during Nixon's eight years as a private citizen, he ceased to believe in his rhetoric. Privately, Nixon came to two important conclusions quite at odds with the great anti-Communist crusade.

Premises of Détente

First, Nixon concluded that the nuclear balance of power made a superpower showdown unthinkable. Therefore, to continue to incite high tension between the Soviets and Americans was to waste resources while indefinitely running the risk of accidental world war.

Second, Nixon recognized that the old bipolar view of geopolitics on which the Cold War was predicated was nonsense. Japan, once a docile American client, was now one of the world's economic powers. The nations of Western Europe, groping toward unity, were

openly trying to define an independent economic, political, and military role. The People's Republic of China, if ever subservient to the Soviet Union, was no longer so. Reliable reports reached the West of Sino-Soviet battles on their 2,000-mile-long border.

Nixon thought of himself as a hard-headed realist. He meant to win his place in history by effecting a diplomatic revolution in which the great powers dealt with one another not as Hatfields and McCoys but as "interested parties" rationally making deals for the benefit of each, and ensuring peace. In 1971 he said, "It will be a safer world and a better world, if we have a strong and healthy United States, Europe, Soviet Union, China, Japan—each balancing the other, not playing one against the other, an even balance."

Nixon's views were influenced and reinforced by Henry Kissinger. A witty, urbane, and cheerfully conceited refugee from Nazism, Kissinger never quite lost his German accent nor his taste for *Realpolitik*, the amoral, opportunistic approach to diplomacy of one of his historical idols, Count Otto von Bismarck. Kissinger believed that the leaders of the Soviet Union and China were as little concerned with ideology and crusades as he and Nixon were, and only needed encouragement to launch a new era. His calculation was dramatically confirmed in 1971 at a time when the Vietnam War was raging and, officially, the ripest of denunciations were flying among Chinese, Russians, and Americans.

Rapprochement with China

In 1971, an American table-tennis team on a tour of Japan was startled to receive an invitation from the People's Republic of China to play a series of exhibition games there before they returned home. Sports writers noted wryly that the Chinese had picked a game in which they would trounce the Americans (they did), but diplomats recognized the implications of the apparently trivial event. For more than 20 years,

Nixon and Chinese leader Zhou Enlai toast each other during Nixon's visit to China in 1972.

the United States and China had had no open contact with one another, the leaders of both nations ritually denouncing the other as mortal enemies.

Kissinger virtually commanded the ping-pong players to go to China and shortly thereafter opened talks with Chinese diplomats. He flew secretly to Beijing where he arranged for a good-will tour by Nixon himself in February 1972. Only then was the amazing news announced: the lifelong scourge of Red China would tour the Forbidden City and Great Wall and sit down with chopsticks at a Mandarin banquet with Mao Zedong and Zhou Enlai, drinking toasts to eternal Sino-American amity with fiery Chinese spirits.

Nixon's meeting with Mao was ceremonial; the Chairman was senile and fading. However, discussions with Zhou, who had long advocated better relations with the West and his protégés, Hua Guofeng (who was to succeed Mao in 1976) and Deng Xiaoping, who had done time in prison for advocating "capitalistic"

reforms of China's moribund economy, reassured Nixon that he had calculated correctly.

Almost overnight, Sino-American relations warmed. The United States dropped its opposition to China's demand for a seat in the United Nations and established a legation in Beijing. (In 1979, the two countries established full diplomatic relations.) Chinese students were invited to study in American universities and China opened its doors to American tourists, who came by the tens of thousands. American industrialists involved in everything from oil exploration to the bottling of soft drinks flew to China, anxious to sell American technology and consumer goods in the market that had long symbolized the traveling salesman's ultimate "territory."

Détente with the Soviet Union

China did not turn out to be much of a customer. The Chinese population was huge, but the country was poor and in economic chaos; there was neither money nor goods with which to pay for the expensive high-technology exports in which alone, by the 1970s, American industry was still supreme. Nor were the new leaders of China interested in resuming the status of a colonial market or in embracing wide-open political institutions. Their principal motive in courting American friendship was diplomatic, to win some edge of security in their conflict with the Soviet Union. They were "playing the American card."

That was alright with the realistic Nixon and Kissinger. They were "playing the China card," putting the fear of a closer Sino-American relationship into the Soviets, who represented a genuine threat to American security. Their gambit worked. In June 1972, just months after his China trip, Nixon flew to the Soviet Union and signed a preliminary agreement in the opening series of Strategic Arms Limitation Talks (SALT), the first significant step toward a slowdown of the arms race since the Kennedy administration.

At home, the photos of Nixon clinking champagne glasses with Mao and hugging Brezhnev bewildered his conservative supporters and flummoxed his liberal critics. In fact, as Nixon knew, undoubtedly savoring it, only a Republican with an impeccable Cold-Warrior past could have accomplished what he did. Had a liberal Democratic president shared a Peking Duck with Mao Zedong, Nixon himself would have held the noose at the demonstrations outside the White House.

Shuttle Diplomacy

Nixon was grateful to Kissinger and, in 1973, named him secretary of state. Well into 1974, Kissinger's diplomatic successes piled up. His greatest triumph came in the Middle East after the Yom Kippur War of 1973, in which Egypt and Syria attacked Israel and, for the first time in the long Arab-Israeli conflict, inflicted terrible casualties and fought the Israelis to a draw.

Knowing that the Israelis were not inclined to accept less than victory and fearing what a prolonged war in the oil-rich Middle East would mean for the United States, Kissinger shuttled seemingly without sleep among Damascus, Cairo, and Tel Aviv, carrying proposal and counterproposal for a settlement. Unlike Dulles, who also had represented American interests on the fly, Kissinger was a brilliant diplomat. He ended the war and the terms he prevailed on all the warring powers to accept actually increased American influence in the region. He won the gratitude and friendship of Egyptian President Anwar el-Sadat, while not alienating Israel.

After 1974, however, Kissinger lost his magic touch, in part because of revived world tensions that were not his fault. Soviet Premier Leonid Brezhnev may have wanted to reduce the chance of direct conflict between Russia and the United States. However, he continued to aid guerrilla movements in Africa and Latin America. Cuba's Fidel Castro, with a large army to keep in trim, exported advisors and combat troops to several countries, most notably to Angola in southwestern Africa.

But Nixon and Kissinger were also willing, even anxious to fight the Cold War by proxy in the Third World, competing with the Soviets for spheres of influence. While right-wing Republicans opposed to *détente* stepped up their attacks on Kissinger, he was actually pursuing their kind of confrontational policies in strife-torn countries like Angola.

The most damaging mark on Kissinger's record as the diplomat-in-chief of a democratic country came in 1974. It was revealed that, the previous year, he had been aware of and may have instigated and aided militarists in Chile who overthrew and murdered the president, Salvador Allende. Allende had been a bungler but he was Chile's democratically elected head and his American-backed successor, Agostín Pinochet, instituted a barbaric and brutal regime marked by torture and murder of opponents.

WATERGATE AND GERALD FORD

By 1974, when news of the Pinochet connection broke in the United States, Kissinger was no longer serving Richard Nixon. The crisis of the presidency that had begun when Lyndon Johnson was repudiated took on a new dimension of gravity when Nixon was forced to resign in disgrace. The debacle had its beginnings in the election campaign of 1972 in which, thanks to a transformation of the Democratic party, victory was in Nixon's hip pocket from the start.

Redefining Liberalism

Between 1968 and 1972, activist middle-class liberals won control of several key Democratic party committees and remade party machinery according to their ideals. They enacted new procedures and standards for selecting convention delegates that penalized old party stalwarts: the labor unions, the big city machines, those southern "good old boys" who had not already gone Republican, and other political pros. The McGovern reforms (named for the liberal, antiwar Senator from South Dakota) guaranteed minimum representation of women and minority groups at party

MEXICAN-AMERICANS:
CHANGING TIMES, CHANGING VALUES

In 1971, a Chicano teaching fellow at Harvard Law School told a reporter for the *Boston Sunday Globe* that "my parents pushed me very hard in an Anglo direction. I rejected every Chicano value. For 29 years I have lived a life of total pretension. It has led to horrible complications in myself. I am just now learning who I am." Having expressed a deep-felt wish to be reconciled to Chicano culture, he referred to the handful of Mexican-American students at Harvard and observed, "None of us would be here if we hadn't tried to be Anglo." The implication was that Harvard Law School should also bestow its appointments and generous salaries on people who had clung to Chicano culture.

Agonizing about "identity" was a favorite activity of the "Me Decade" among privileged members of minority groups as well as among affluent members of the majority culture. It was, among other things, a way to get ahead by playing on the sensitivity of the government, business, and academic establishments to their heritage of discrimination against minorities. It was difficult to sympathize with such identity crises when the vast majority of the members of minority groups such as Mexican-Americans struggled daily just to get by.

But such posing helped anthropologists and sociologists to focus on genuine clashes between traditional group values and the values that lead to success in the mainstream society. With Chicanos in the 1970s, as with immigrant groups of the early twentieth century, there was a wrenching cultural adjustment to be made in order to win a decent share of the benefits of American society. Old ways had to be abandoned, new ones adopted, and the process was more difficult for Chicanos because of the closeness of the mother country and the well-meaning but damaging policies of the Anglo establishment. (*Chicano* is a slang contraction of *Mexicano* and connotes political activism; in Chicano usage, *Anglo* refers to all white Americans, not just those of English descent.)

Mexican-Americans were the second largest minority in the United States in the 1970s; only blacks were more numerous. They made up the single largest ethnic group in the southwestern states of California, Arizona, New Mexico, Texas, and Colorado. As recently as the 1950s, they had been a majority in New Mexico.

A word of caution is in order. Sociologically, no other American ethnic group has such a variety of backgrounds as the 7 million people who are lumped together by the Census Bureau as "Spanish surname." Setting aside Puerto Ricans, Cubans, and immigrants from other Spanish-speaking countries, seven categories of Mexican-Americans can be identified, of which four are not immigrants at all: (1) descendants of the *californios*, inhabitants of California before it was seized by the United States, most of whom were Indians or of mixed race; (2) the more quickly assimilated descendants of the upper-class Caucasian *californios*; (3) *tejanos*, descendants of the inhabitants of Texas before it became independent; (4) *nuevo mexicanos*, descendants of pre-Anglo New Mexicans, who were self-consciously more Spanish than Mexican because they were never much under the control of or particularly fond of the government of the Mexican Republic; (5) descendants of the refugees from the Mexican Revolution during the 1910s and 1920s, many of them well educated and affluent; (6) descendants of the *braceros*, imported farm laborers, of the 1930s and 1940s; and (7) immigrants of the 1960s and 1970s, who entered the United States (many illegally) in search of work.

A people of so many origins may be spoken of as an ethnic group only because of the development of the Chicano consciousness movement in the mid-1960s, which led to the first successful expressions of Mexican-American wishes through Cesar Chavez's United Farm Workers; *La Raza Unida*, a political party formed in Texas and similar to the blacks' Mississippi Freedom Democrats; and any number of university campus organizations. It is ironic that, as with those who spoke for other minorities, it was possible to represent Chicano interests effectively only to the extent that spokesmen had transcended the values of Mexican-American subculture.

Sociologist Fernando Peñalosa found examples of Mexican-Americans whose forebears had lived in Texas for 200 years and yet "largely retained the language and culture." Such a phenomenon was possible only as long as Anglo prejudice shut such people out of the mainstream society and forced them to cling to traditional ways as solace. Despite their numbers in Texas, California, and New Mexico, communities of the sort Peñalosa discovered could not produce effective leaders so long as they were despised for being Mexican-Americans.

As a by-product of the black struggle for civil equality in the 1960s, the external, legal obstacles that had prevented Chicanos from winning a place in American society were also struck down. However, long-established cultural habits could not be abolished with the signing of a law, and they continued to impede Mexican-American progress. Studies of Mexican-American social mobility in Albuquerque, Los Angeles, and San Antonio in the 1970s revealed a direct correlation between income and social station, and the degree to which the more successful had broken with old ways and adopted those of Anglo society. For example, in all three cities, Chicanos and Chicanas who had married Anglos already had moved out of the *barrio* and up the economic ladder.

In a 1972 study, B. S. Bradshaw and F. D. Bean divided a sample of 348 Mexican-American couples in Austin, Texas, into two groups according to their socioeconomic status. They found that 74 percent of those in the higher group lived outside the Austin *barrio,* but only 27 percent of the lower group did. The women in the higher group were more likely to work outside the home and to demand of their husbands an equal voice in household decisions. The higher group was more likely to have close Anglo friends, to speak English exclusively or more than they spoke Spanish, and generally to have middle-class values.

"Making good" in the United States by adopting American ways had been the experience of almost all immigrant groups, from the Irish and Germans of the mid-nineteenth century to the Jews, Greeks, Italians, Slavs, and other New Immigrants of the early twentieth century. However, the Mexican-Americans of the 1970s labored under two burdens that these groups had not.

First, the closeness of Mexico and the steady influx of new immigrants from Mexico constantly reinvigorated the traditional values, including some that stood squarely in the way of social and economic advancement: valuing interpersonal relationships over competitiveness and acquisition of material wealth; emphazing family welfare over individual advancement; recognizing male dominance (*machismo*) and female submissiveness; and producing extremely large families. In 1970, the Mexican-American annual fertility rate was higher than that of any other major ethnic group: 42.32 children per 1,000 women compared with 28.91 for Anglos and 34.89 for blacks.

Other ethnic groups had brought similar cultural baggage from Europe. But far from sentimentalizing the old ways and lamenting their loss, the leaders of Jews, Italians, Poles, and others browbeat their communities into recognizing that the United States was not Russia, Italy, or Poland and adjusting to that reality, however painful it might be to do so. Although the southern and Eastern European ethnic groups hardly approved of them, the immigration quota laws of 1921 and 1924 worked to their benefit by preventing the reinforcement of old-country ways by new arrivals.

Second, well-meaning state and federal policymakers in the 1970s did a disservice to Chicanos when they encouraged them to cling to traditional ways and particularly to the Spanish language by making it easy to do so. In California, for example, all state documents were published in Spanish (and Chinese) as well as in English. In many schools, catch-up classes in English for Spanish-speaking children were neglected and even abolished in favor of classes in which the regular curriculum was taught in Spanish.

Unlike the children of other ethnic groups, who were forced to learn English in public schools and therefore were given access to the world beyond their neighborhoods, Mexican-American children were chained to the *barrios,* in other words, to chronic poverty. While it was easy at the end of the 1970s to get along in the *barrios* speaking only Spanish, and to read every California state publication in that language, Harvard Law School, which is in Massachusetts, had not instituted a program for the training of attorneys who remained loyal to this aspect of "Chicano consciousness." Richard Rodriguez, a Chicano writer from Sacramento, California, who is ambivalent about the choices facing Mexican-Americans, summed it up: "Those who have the most to lose in a bi-lingual America are the foreign-speaking poor, who are being lured into a linguistic nursery."

Young Chicanos face a difficult choice between preserving their native language and traditional culture and adopting values that lead to success in American society.

conventions on the basis of their sex and ethnic origins.

The Election of 1972

As an immediate result of the reforms, the Democratic delegates who gathered in Miami in the summer of 1972 formed the youngest convention in political history, counted more women and minorities among the delegates than any other, and was strongly antiwar. They nominated Senator McGovern to head their ticket and adopted a platform calling for a negotiated end to the Southeast Asian war (then Vietnamized but still raging), and supporting the demands of some women's organizations that the decision as to whether or not a fetus should be aborted belonged to the pregnant woman herself, and to no other person or institution.

A sincere and decent man who was deeply grieved by the war, McGovern tried to distance himself from the zanies in his party, particularly "gay rights" advocates who, McGovern understood, were not likely to win the affection of working-class people who traditionally cast Democratic ballots. He emphasized peace in Vietnam, tax reform that would benefit middle- and lower-income people, and his integrity compared with Nixon's longstanding reputation for deviousness.

But virtually no labor unions supported him and many political pros sat on their hands. The Republicans, by way of contrast, ran an effective campaign. They depicted McGovern as a bumbling and indecisive radical. When McGovern first defended his running mate, Senator Thomas Eagleton, who had undergone psychiatric treatment several years earlier, and then forced Eagleton to drop out, his race was doomed.

Nixon won 60.8 percent of the popular vote and carried every state but Massachusetts and the District of Columbia. In only eight years, he had reversed the Republican humiliation of 1964. He had had a lot of help from the Democrats but his achievement was nonetheless remarkable. But Nixon's days of glorious triumph were, like Lyndon Johnson's in 1964, to be few.

Covering up a Burglary

On June 17, 1972, early in the presidential campaign, Washington police had arrested five men who were

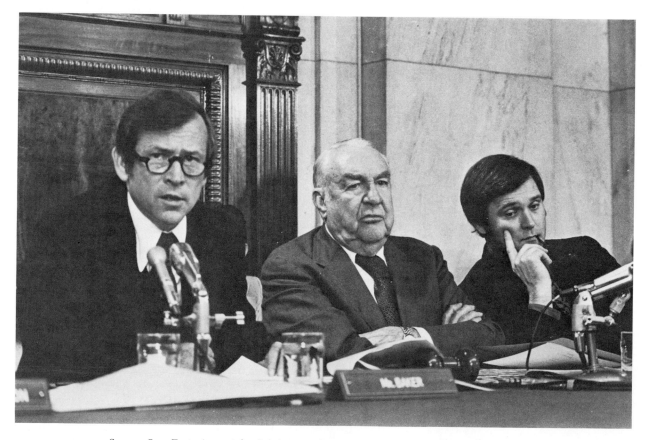

Senator Sam Ervin (center) headed the special committee to inquire into charges of corruption in the 1972 election. The televised hearings reached an enraptured nation.

trying to plant electronic eavesdropping devices in Democratic party headquarters in a Washington apartment and office complex called the Watergate. Three of the suspects were on the payroll of the Committee to Re-elect the President (an unwisely chosen name inasmuch as it abbreviated as CREEP), and McGovern tried to exploit the incident as part of his integrity campaign. But the ploy fizzled when Nixon and his campaign manager, Attorney General John Mitchell, denied any knowledge of the incident and denounced the burglars as common criminals.

In fact, Nixon knew nothing about the break-in in advance, but he soon learned that the burglars had acted on orders from his own aides. He never considered reporting or disciplining his men. Instead, almost nonchalantly, he instructed his staff to find money to hush up the men in jail. However, two of them, James E. McCord and Howard Hunt refused to take the fall and informed Judge John Sirica that they had taken orders from highly placed Nixon administration officials.

Rumors began to fly. Two reporters for the *Washington Post*, Robert Woodward and Carl Bernstein, made contact with an anonymous informant who fed them information. A special Senate investigating committee headed by Sam Ervin of North Carolina picked away at the tangle from yet another direction, slowly tracing not only the Watergate break-in and cover-up but other illegal acts to the White House itself.

The Imperial Presidency

Each month that passed, dramatic insights into the inner workings of the Nixon presidency were revealed. On Nixon's own orders, an "enemies list" had been compiled. On it were journalists, politicians, intellectuals, and even movie stars who had made statements criticizing Nixon. One Donald Segretti was put in charge of a "dirty tricks" campaign, planting half-truths, rumors, and lies to discredit critics of the administration. G. Gordon Liddy, who was involved in the Watergate break-in, had proposed fantastic schemes involving yachts and prostitutes to entrap "enemies." The "dirty tricks" campaign grew so foul that not even J. Edgar Hoover, the none too squeamish head of the FBI, would touch it.

Watergate, it turned out, had been just one of several "surreptitious entries" sponsored by the administration. Nixon's aides also engineered the burglary of a Los Angeles psychiatrist's office to secure information about a Defense Department employee who had published confidential information about the prosecution of the war in Vietnam.

Observers spoke of an "Imperial Presidency." Nixon and his advisors had become so arrogant in their pos-

Nixon announcing on television on August 8, 1974, that he is resigning from the presidency.

session of power that they believed they were above the law. Indeed, several years later, Nixon himself was to tell an interviewer on television, "When the president does it, that means it is not illegal."

If imperial in their pretensions, however, "all the president's men" were singularly lacking in a sense of nobility. One by one, Nixon aides abandoned ship, each convinced that he was being set up as the sole fall-guy for his colleagues. Each deserter named others and described their roles in the cover-up and dirty-tricks campaign. A snarl of half-truths and lies descended on the president himself.

In the midst of the scandal, Vice President Spiro Agnew pleaded no-contest to income-tax evasion and charges that he had accepted bribes when he was governor of Maryland. Agnew was forced to resign from the vice presidency in October 1973. He was replaced under the Twenty-Fifth Amendment by Congressman Gerald Ford of Michigan.

Resignation

Then came Nixon's turn and he was, as the old saw has it, hoist on his own petard. He had kept tape recordings of conversations in his Oval Office that clearly implicated him in the Watergate cover-up (and revealed him as having a rather foul mouth: the transcripts of the tapes were peppered with "expletive deleted"). After long fights in the courts, the president was ordered to surrender the tapes to investigators.

Why Nixon did not destroy the incriminating recordings early in the Watergate crisis remains a mystery. It was suggested that greed—the money that the electronic documents would bring after he left the presidency—accounts for his fatal blunder. Others saw the preservation of the tapes as another manifestation of Nixon's imperial megalomania. He could not conceive of the fact that a court could order the president of the United States to abide by laws that applied to mere citizens.

The House of Representatives Judiciary Committee was on the eve of recommending the impeachment of Nixon when he threw in the towel. On August 9, 1974, on national television, he resigned the presidency and flew to his home in San Clemente, California.

A Ford, Not a Lincoln

Gerald Ford's career had not been distinguished. Holding a safe seat in the House from Michigan, he had risen to be minority leader on the basis of seniority and dutifully toeing the Republican party line. His sole ambition when events made him first vice president and then president, was to be Speaker of the House, but the Republicans never came close to winning a majority of Representatives.

Ford was not a particularly intelligent man. Lyndon Johnson once told reporters that Gerry Ford's trouble was that he had played center on the University of Michigan football team without a helmet. Others quipped that he could not walk and chew gum at the same time. Newspaper photographers fairly laid in wait to ridicule him by snapping shots of him bumping his head on door frames, tumbling down the slopes of the Rockies on everything but his skis, slicing golf balls into crowds of spectators.

Gerald R. Ford apppointed Nelson Rockefeller as his Vice President.

CONSTITUTIONAL CONTRADICTION?

Gerald Ford was appointed to the vice presidency under the provisions of the Twenty-Fifth Amendment, ratified in 1967, which stipulates that "whenever there is a vacancy in the office of the Vice President, the President shall nominate a Vice President. . . ." When he succeeded to the presidency, he appointed Nelson A. Rockefeller to the vice presidency. Neither the president nor the vice president held office by virtue of election. However, as some constitutional experts were quick to point out, Article II, Section 1 of the Constitution provides that the president and vice president are to "be elected."

In fact, the contradiction was always there, if never put to the test. The U.S. Constitution and laws hold that the secretary of state and the Speaker of the House were next in line to the presidency after the vice president. A case could be made that the Speaker was elected, but not the secretary of state.

And yet his simplicity and forthrightness were a relief after Nixon's squirming and deception. He told the American people that fate had given them "a Ford, not a Lincoln," and he had no pretensions. Democrats howled "deal" when Ford pardoned Nixon of all crimes he may have committed, but Ford's explanation, that the American people needed to put Watergate behind them, was plausible and in character. Two very nearly successful attempts to assassinate him by deranged women in California helped to win sympathy for the first president who had not been elected to any national office.

Despite his unusual route to the White House, Gerald Ford had no more intention of being a caretaker president than John Tyler had when he became the first president to succeed to the office by reason of death. But it was Ford's misfortune, as it had been Tyler's, to face serious problems without the confidence and support of an important segment of his party. The Republican party's right wing, led by former California governor Ronald Reagan, did not like détente nor Nixon's, now Ford's refusal to launch a frontal attack on government regulation and the liberal welfare state.

Running on Half-Empty

The most serious of the woes that faced Ford struck at a reflexive assumption of twentieth-century American life: that cheap energy was available in unlimited quantities to fuel the economy and support the free-wheeling lifestyle of the middle-class.

By the mid-1970s, 90 percent of the American economy was generated by the burning of fossil fuels: coal, natural gas, and petroleum. Fossil fuels are nonrenewable sources of energy. Unlike food crops, lumber, and water—or, for that matter, a horse and a pair of sturdy legs—they cannot be called on again once they have been used. The supply of them is finite. While experts disagreed about the extent of the world's reserves of coal, gas, and oil, no one challenged the obvious fact that one day they would be no more.

The United States was by far the biggest user of nonrenewable sources of energy. In 1973, while comprising about 6 percent of the world's population, Americans consumed fully 33 percent of the world's annual production of oil. Much of it was burned to less than basic ends. Americans overheated and overcooled their offices and houses. They pumped gasoline into a dizzying variety of purely recreational vehicles, some of which brought the roar of the freeway to the wilderness and devastated fragile land. Their worship of the wasteful private automobile meant that few taxes were spent on public mass transit systems. They packaged their consumer goods in throwaway containers of glass, metal, paper, and petroleum-based plastics; supermarkets wrapped lemons individually in transparent plastic and fast-food cheeseburgers were

cradled in styrofoam caskets that were discarded within seconds of being handed over the counter. The bill of indictment went on but, resisting criticism and satire alike, American consumption increased.

OPEC and the Energy Crisis

About 61 percent of the oil that Americans consumed in the 1970s was produced at home, and large reserves remained under native ground. But the nation also imported huge quantities of crude, and in October 1973, Americans discovered just how little control they had over the 39 percent of their oil that came from abroad.

In that month, the Organization of Petroleum Exporting Countries (OPEC) temporarily halted oil shipments and announced the first of a series of big jumps in the price of their product. One of their justifications was that the irresponsible consumption habits of the advanced Western nations, particularly the United States, jeopardized their future.

OPEC leaders reasoned that if the oil-exporting nations continued to supply oil cheaply, consuming nations would continue to burn it profligately, thus hastening the day the wells ran dry. On that day, if the

The lines at a Los Angeles gas station stretched for blocks during a gasoline shortage in 1979.

> ### CLEANUP
>
> In 1912 the Chicago Sanitation Department cleared the streets of the carcasses of 10,000 dead horses. In 1968 the Chicago Police Department cleared the streets of 24,500 carcasses of dead automobiles.

oil-exporting nations had not laid the basis for another kind of economy, they would be destitute. Particularly in the oil-rich Middle East, there were few alternative resources to support fast-growing populations. Therefore, by raising prices, the OPEC nations would earn capital with which to build for a future without oil, while simultaneously encouraging the consuming nations to conserve, thus lengthening the era when oil would be available.

From a geopolitical perspective, there was much to be said for the argument, but ordinary Americans (and the people of other consumer nations) rarely thought geopolitically. They were stunned when they had to wait in long lines in order to pay unprecedented prices for gasoline. In some big cities and Hawaii, gasoline for private cars was not to be had for weeks.

The price of gasoline never climbed to Japanese or European levels (as much as $5 a gallon), but it was shock enough for people who were accustomed to buying "two dollars' worth" to discover that $2 bought a little more than enough to drive home. Moreover, the prices of goods that required oil in their production climbed too. Inflation, already a problem under Nixon, worsened from 9 percent a year when Ford became president to 12 percent.

Whip Inflation Now!

Opposed to wage and price controls such as Nixon had employed, Ford launched a campaign called WIN!, for "Whip Inflation Now!" He urged Americans to slow down inflation by refusing to buy exorbitantly priced goods and by ceasing to demand higher wages from their employers. The campaign was ridiculed from the start, and within a few weeks Ford quietly retired the WIN! button that he had been wearing on his lapel. He had seen few others in his travels about the country and began to feel like a man in a funny hat.

Instead, Ford tightened the money supply in order to slow down the economy, which resulted in the most serious recession since 1937, with unemployment climbing to 9 percent. Ford was stymied by the same vicious circle that caught up his predecessor and successor: slowing inflation meant throwing people out of work; fighting unemployment meant inflation; trying to steer a middle course meant "stagflation," mild recession plus inflation.

Image Problems

As a congressman, Ford had been a hawk on Vietnam. When the North Vietnamese launched their attack on Saigon early in 1975, his first impulse was to intervene with American troops. Congress refused to respond and Henry Kissinger, who had stayed on as secretary of state, talked him out of presidential action. Ford tried to display his determination to exercise American armed might in May 1975, when Cambodian Communists seized an American ship, the *Mayaguez*. Ford ordered in the marines, who successfully rescued the captives. But in order to rescue 39 seamen, 38 marines died.

Kissinger savored the reports that the president hung breathlessly on his every word, but such stories only further enraged the Kissinger-hating right wing of the Republican party and made it easier for the Democrats to mock Ford as being not bright enough to handle his job.

Early in 1976, polls showed Ford losing to most of the likely Democratic candidates. Capitalizing on them, Ronald Reagan, the sweetheart of the right-wing Republicans, launched a well-financed campaign to replace him as the party's candidate. Using his control of party organization, Ford beat Reagan at the

President Gerald Ford and Secretary of State Henry Kissinger.

Jimmy Carter walks with his family from the capitol to the White House following his inauguration as president.

convention but the travails of his two years in office took their toll. He could not overcome the image that he was the most accidental of presidents, never elected to national office. His full pardon of Nixon came back to haunt him and, in November, he lost narrowly to a most unlikely Democratic candidate, James Earl Carter of Georgia, who called himself "Jimmy". The Democrats were back, but the decline in the prestige of the presidency continued.

QUIET CRISIS

Since Eisenhower, every president had been identified closely with Congress, the arena of national politics. The day of the governor candidate seemed to be in the past. Then Jimmy Carter came out of nowhere to win the Democratic nomination in 1976. His political career consisted of one term in the Georgia assembly and one term as governor.

Indeed, it was Carter's lack of association with the federal government that helped him win the nomination and, by a slim margin, the presidency. Without

a real animus for Gerald Ford, many Americans were attracted to the idea of an "outsider," which is how Carter presented himself. "Hello, my name is Jimmy Carter and I'm running for president," he told thousands of people face to face in his softly musical Georgia accent. Once he started winning primaries, the media did the rest. When television commentators said that there was a bandwagon rolling, voters dutifully responded by jumping on it.

Inauguration Day, when Carter and his shrewd but uningratiating wife, Rosalyn, walked the length of

JIMMY CARTER AND THE SEGREGATIONISTS

Future president Jimmy Carter had an unusual record for a white southerner of his age on the segregation issue. In the 1950s, as a successful businessman in Plains, Georgia, he had been asked to join the anti-black White Citizens' Councils, whose membership fee was only $5. Carter replied, "I've got $5 but I'd flush it down the toilet before I'd give it to you."

Pennsylvania Avenue, was very nearly the last entirely satisfactory day of the Carter presidency. Whether the perspective of time will attribute his failure as chief executive to his unsuitability to the office or the massiveness of the problems he faced, it is difficult to imagine future historians looking at the Carter era other than it is now remembered, dolefully.

The Panama Treaty

Carter had his successes, especially in foreign relations. Among his achievements was defusing an explosive situation in Central America where Panamanians and others had long protested American sovereignty over the Panama Canal Zone. The narrow strip of U.S. territory bisected the small republic and seemed to be an intolerable insult in an age when nationalist sensibilities in small countries were as touchy as boils.

American diplomats saw no need to hold on to the Canal Zone in the face of Panamanian protests. The United States would be able to occupy the Canal within hours in the case of an international crisis. After several false starts at working out a treaty under

Johnson and Nixon, in 1978 the Senate narrowly ratified an agreement with Panama to guarantee the permanent neutrality of the canal itself while gradually transferring sovereignty over it to Panama, culminating on December 31, 1999.

By signing the treaty, Carter muted Latin American denunciations of "*yanqui imperialismo.*" Nevertheless, right-wing politicians, led by Ronald Reagan, who had begun to campaign for the presidency as soon as Carter was inaugurated, denounced the treaty. In the tradition of Joseph McCarthy, Reagan called it yet another retreat from national pride and greatness by a weak president.

Peacemaking

Carter's greatest achievement was to save the rapprochement between Israel and Egypt that began to take shape in November 1977, when Egyptian President Anwar Sadat, risking the enmity of the entire Arab world, addressed the Israeli Knesset, or parliament, calling for a permanent peace in the Middle East. Rather than cooperate with Sadat, Israeli Prime Minister Menachem Begin, a former terrorist, seemed to sabotage Sadat's peacemaking efforts by refusing to make concessions commensurate with the Egyptian president's high-stakes gamble.

In 1978, Carter brought Sadat and Begin to meet with him at Camp David, the presidential retreat in the Maryland woods outside Washington. There, Sadat grew so angry with Begin's refusal to compromise that he actually packed his suitcases. Although Carter was unable to persuade Begin to agree that the West Bank of the Jordan River, which Israel had occupied in 1967, must eventually be returned to Arab rule, he did bring the two men together. In March 1979, Israel and Egypt signed a treaty.

In the United States, the political effect of this dramatic diplomatic turn was to swing American sympathies in the dispute in the direction of Sadat. Begin was unpopular even among American Jews, who traditionally were staunch supporters of Israel. Jewish contributions to Israeli causes dropped sharply. Carter himself betrayed impatience and annoyance with the Begin government and sympathy for the Palestinian refugees. Carter deserved the Nobel Peace Prize for pulling off the Camp David Accords.

The End of Détente

The Nobel Committee may have snubbed him because, while Carter advanced the cause of peace in the Middle East, he shattered the policy of détente that Nixon, Kissinger, and Ford had nurtured. Like Nixon, Carter virtually ignored his first secretary of

---

MINORITY PRESIDENTS

When Jimmy Carter won the forty-eighth presidential election by just a hair under 50 percent of the popular vote, it was the sixteenth time the victor had the support of less than half the voters:

President	Year	Percent
John Quincy Adams	1824	30.5
James K. Polk	1844	49.6
Zachary Taylor	1848	47.4
James Buchanan	1856	45.3
Abraham Lincoln	1860	39.8
Rutherford B. Hayes	1876	48.0
James A. Garfield	1880	48.5
Grover Cleveland	1884	48.5
Benjamin Harrison	1888	47.9
Grover Cleveland	1892	46.1
Woodrow Wilson	1912	41.9
Woodrow Wilson	1916	49.4
Harry S Truman	1948	49.5
John F. Kennedy	1960	49.9
Richard M. Nixon	1968	43.4
Jimmy Carter	1976	50.0

Lincoln would surely not have won the election of 1864 by an absolute majority (or at all) had the southern states not been in rebellion. Three victorious candidates had fewer popular votes than their opponents who lost: John Quincy Adams in 1824, Rutherford B. Hayes in 1876, and Benjamin Harrison in 1888.

Anwar Sadat, Jimmy Carter, and Menachem Begin shake hands following the signing of the Camp David Accords in 1978.

state, Cyrus Vance, a professional diplomat, and depended on a White House advisor, Zbigniew Brzezinski, for advice.

Unlike the flexible and opportunistic Kissinger, Brzezinski was an anti-Soviet ideologue. Himself a Polish refugee from Communism, Brzezinski's distrust of the Soviet Union blinded him to opportunities to improve relations between the nuclear superpowers, or even prompted him to sabotage Soviet overtures. Moreover, whereas Kissinger had been a charmer, Brzezinski was tactless and crude in a world in which protocol and manners can be as important as substance. The foreign ministers of several of America's allies discreetly informed the State Department that they would not deal with him under any circumstances.

But Carter was as obsessively hostile to the Soviet Union as Brzezinski and pre-Nixon policymakers. He denounced the Soviet Union for trampling on human rights while neglecting to mention the far more brutal policies of American allies such as Iran, Chile, and several Central American states.

In March 1977, Carter interrupted and set back the Strategic Arms Limitation Talks with completely new proposals. Eventually, a new SALT-II treaty was negotiated and signed, but Carter withdrew it from Senate consideration in December 1979 when the Soviet Union invaded Afghanistan to prop up a client government in December 1979. By the end of Carter's term of office, détente was dead.

Plus Ça Même Chose

Inflation reached new heights under Carter, almost 20 percent during 1980. By the end of the year, $1 was worth only 15 cents in 1940 values. That is, on the average, it took $1 in 1980 to purchase what in 1940 cost 15 cents. The dollar had suffered fully half of this loss during the 1970s.

Carter could not be faulted for the energy crisis. After the crunch of 1974, Americans had become energy conscious, replacing their big "gas guzzlers" with more efficient smaller cars. Even this sensible turn contributed to the nation's economic malaise, however. American automobile manufacturers had repeatedly refused to develop small energy-efficient cars. For a while in the 1960s, after the success of the Germans' Volkswagen "Beetle," Ford, General Motors, and Chrysler had made compact cars. But within a few years, "compacts" had miraculously grown to be nearly as large as the traditional "full-sized car." Now, in the crunch of the 1970s, American auto makers had nothing with which to compete with a flood of Japanese imports: Toyotas, Datsuns, Hondas, and myriad others. The autombile buyer's dollars sailed abroad across the Pacific.

Even then, by 1979, oil consumption was higher than ever, and an even higher proportion of it was being imported than in 1976. American oil refiners actually cut back on domestic production, which led many people to wonder if the crisis was genuine or was just a cover while the industry reaped windfall profits—which it did. As prices soared, all the refiners reported dividends of unprecedented size.

The price of electricity also rose, by 200 percent and more, because so much of it was generated by burning fossil fuels. The utility companies called for the construction of more nuclear power plants in anticipation of even higher rate increases. But Americans had become apprehensive about nuclear energy as an alternative to fossil fuels following an accident and near catastrophe at the Three Mile Island nuclear plant near Harrisburg, Pennsylvania; the release, at about the same time, of *The China Syndrome*, a film that portrayed a similar accident; the discovery that a California reactor that was about to open was crisscrossed with flaws, and built astride a major earthquake fault; and the tremendous costs needed to build safe nuclear power plants.

Embarrassment and Drift

Carter was repeatedly embarrassed by his aides and family, and himself had a talent for foolery. Genuinely suspicious of the Washington Establishment, he surrounded himself with cronies from Georgia who did not quite understand the etiquettes and rituals of the capital. Banker Bert Lance, whom Carter wanted as Budget Director, was tainted by petty, unacceptable loan scams. Carter's ambassador to the United Nations, former civil-rights activist, Andrew Young, met secretly with leaders of the Palestine Liberation Organization (PLO), an anti-Israel terrorist organization that the United States did not recognize. Carter had to fire him.

The national press, stimulated by its role in uncovering the Watergate scandal to constant muckraking, leaped on every trivial incident—a Carter aide tipsy in a cocktail lounge; the president's "down-home" brother Billy's outrageous opinions—to embarrass the president. The deeply religious Carter himself frankly but disingenuously told an interviewer for *Playboy* magazine, "I've looked on a lot of women with lust. I've committed adultery in my heart many times," and tittering journalists did not allow him to forget it. In 1980, when Carter's career was on the line, his mother told a reporter, "Sometimes when I look at all my children, I say to myself, 'Lillian, you should have stayed a virgin.' "

A much more serious handicap was the Carter administration's lack of direction. "Carter believes fifty things," one of his advisers said, "but no one thing. He holds explicit, thorough positions on every issue under the sun, but he has no large view of relations between them." In this, Carter was not unlike most Americans. He had the "engineer" mentality that is often described as the American way of thinking: as it arises, face each specific problem and work out a specific solution.

Such pragmatism had worked for Franklin D. Roosevelt. It did not work for Jimmy Carter. With him at the helm, pragmatic government resembled a ship without a rudder, drifting aimlessly. Carter was sensitive to what he called a "national malaise" but only embarassed himself when he tried to address the amorphous problem. He called 130 prominent men and women from every sector of American life to Washington and, having heard from them, he was able to announce only that there was "a crisis of the American spirit," right back where he started from.

For Further Reading

James Gilbert, *Another Chance: America Since 1945* (1984) provides a general overview of this period; Godfrey Hodgson, *America in Our Time* (1976) deals with the first part of it. However, we are too close to the 1970s to expect too dependable a narrative history of the decade. Many contemporary historians were themselves participants and partisans during these years. Many of the major players are still around trying to shape their posterity.

Many have written memoirs, perhaps as much for monstrous advances from publishers, as for self-justification. These accounts can, nevertheless, be useful and are, in any case, valuable sources. See *The Memoirs of Richard Nixon* (1978); George McGovern, *Grassroots* (1977); *A Time to Heal: The Autobiography of Gerald Ford* (1979); Henry A. Kissinger, *White House Years* (1979) and *Years of Upheaval* (1982); Jimmy Carter, *Keeping Faith* (1982); Rosalynn Carter, *First Lady from Plains* (1984). A fascinating study of Nixon written before his fall is Garry Wills, *Nixon Agonistes* (1970). On Kissinger, see Robert Morris, *Uncertain Greatness: Henry Kissinger and American Foreign Policy* (1977).

Carl Bernstein and Robert Woodward, *All the President's Men* (1974) is by the two reporters for the *Washington Post* that doggedly investigated the Watergate affair and helped bring about Nixon's fall. Perhaps the most insightful analysis of what happened is Arthur M. Schlesinger, Jr., *The Imperial Presidency* (1973). See also T. H. White, *Breach of Faith* (1975), Leon Jaworski, *The Right and the Power* (1976), and Sam Ervin, *The Whole Truth: The Watergate Conspiracy* (1980).

On national politics and policy during the 1970s, see David Broder, *The Party's Over* (1972); Samuel Lubell, *The Hidden Crisis in American Politics* (1970); A. J. Reichley, *Conservatives in an Age of Change: The Nixon and Ford Administrations* (1981); Theodore H. White, *The Making of a President 1972* (1973). See Henry Kissinger's memoirs above for foreign policy, and on specific issues see R. L. Garthoff, *Détente and Confrontation* (1985); A. E. Goodman, *The Lost Peace: America's Search for a Negotiated Settlement of the Vietnam War* (1978); on Central America, R. A. Pastor, *Condemned to Repetition* (1987); W. B. Quandt, *Decade of Decision: American Foreign Policy Toward the Arab-Israeli Conflict* (1978); and G. Sick, *All Fall Down: America's Tragic Encounter with Iran* (1985).

In the 1970s and 1980s, so it would seem, Aesop's fable "The Grasshopper and the Ants" lost any fascination that it might once have held for Americans. In the tale, as solemnly read by generations of schoolteachers to their pupils, the grasshopper passes the summer frolicking and chirping gaily in the grain field while the ants rush industriously back and forth storing kernels in their nests. When winter's first frost lays waste to the land, the grasshopper, trembling near death, begs the ants for food. "All the summer long thou didst sing," the ants reply, turning their backs on him, "Now thou canst dance."

In the wake of Vietnam and Watergate, much of America seemed to be frolicking and singing in an

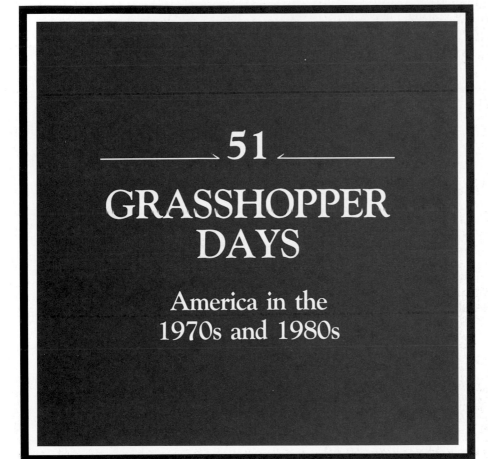

51

GRASSHOPPER DAYS

America in the 1970s and 1980s

orgy of self-indulgence. Cultural critic, Tom Wolfe wrote of the 1970s as the "Me Decade." Jimmy Carter anguished about a crisis of the American spirit.

During the 1980s, national wealth amassed over a century was squandered in consumption and nonproductive financial manipulations so that the United States, the world's largest creditor nation in 1980, was its greatest debtor in 1989. The federal government's debt grew so large as to threaten the American standard of living for generations to come. The Americans of the 1970s and 1980s seemed to value the short-term killing more highly than their children's future: grasshopper days.

THE TEMPER OF AN ERA

B reak out the flag, strike up the band, light up the sky!" In disarming old-fashioned band-concert language, President Gerald Ford proclaimed the bicentennial of the United States on July 4, 1976. The highlight of the celebration was the visit to New York harbor of sailing vessels from all over the world. On July 4, 1986, Americans held another big party, this time to celebrate the hundredth birthday of the Statue of Liberty. Again the "tall ships" came and the night sky over New York harbor was illuminated with a fireworks display said to be the biggest in history.

For those who looked for symbols in the parties, there were plenty. Whereas, in 1876, the centerpiece of the centennial exposition had been the giant Corliss steam engine, a symbol of the future, the sailing ships were a nostalgic look backward, as if Americans saw little advantage in looking ahead. A mammoth exposition had to be called off because the people who lived near the selected site in Philadelphia did not want millions of their countrymen as guests. Have the party somewhere else—anywhere else—they said; but no one else wanted it either. (NIMBY, "Not In My

---

ANCESTORS

In 1982, the Census Bureau reported that 51.6 million Americans traced their ancestry to Germany compared with 43.7 million who claimed an Irish background and 40 million who had English forebears. But if Scots-Americans and Welsh-Americans were added to the English as being of British origin, that would have been the largest group. About 16 million claimed African ancestors; and 2.8 million, Asian.

NATION OF IMMIGRANTS

In early 1989, when the Immigration Service announced that there would be a special issue of 20,000 immigration visas in 1991 and 1992, some 10 million people from Bangladesh, a tenth of the nation's population, were said to have expressed an interest in applying.

Back Yard," was a catch phrase of the era.) The promoters, mourning the profits they would not pocket, gave up.

Money seemed to be the motive force behind the Statue of Liberty celebration, too. Exclusive rights to televise a national patriotic observance were auctioned to the highest bidder, as if the event were a prizefight. The fireworks display was splendid and yet, also an extraordinary expenditure for a few moments of glitter, an encapsulation of the era of Ronald Reagan.

Us

To observers at the time, the mood of the nation appeared to shift radically in the early 1970s. Whereas the young people of the 1960s had been selfless and socially conscious—they said—concerned with racial injustice, poverty, and war, in the 1970s Americans turned inward, obsessed with their personal pleasure and individual potential.

Part of the reason for the shift was the meandering of Father Time. "The Movement" of the 1960s had a motto, "You can't trust anyone over thirty" and, in the 1970s, the baby boomers who were the shock troops of the 1960s agitations began to celebrate their thirtieth birthdays. The baby boomers were still the "do your own thing" generation and, thanks to their numbers, they were still dictating the national style. But their "thing" had changed; they had grown bored with political action and moral outrage as a means of self-gratification and were looking elsewhere.

The ex-New Leftists were generally affluent, as had been observed even during the 1960s. During the 1970s, their self-indulgence took on commercial shape. One boom in consumer goods followed another, with some of the biggest profits made by companies that sold products combining fun and physical exercise. Successively and simultaneously, Americans spent billions of dollars on ski equipment, tennis paraphernalia, ten-speed bicycles, and backpacking gear.

Jogging became a national mania, claiming as devotees one adult in five by 1980. The most primitive form of exercise became the subject of portentous analysis and the basis of a multimillion dollar business in the impedimentia thought essential to running properly and attractively.

A woman works out with weight equipment, a popular form of exercise during the 1970s.

Self-Fulfillment

The Yuppies (young, upwardly mobile professionals) of the 1970s were also preoccupied with psychological self-fulfillment. Indian gurus who had made their appearance in the 1960s survived the dissipation of the "hippie" counterculture and multiplied. The Maharishi Mahesh Yogi, who had earlier sold his Transcendental Meditation as a means of spiritual fulfillment, retooled it in the 1970s as a means to make more money. A guru known as the Bhagwan took over a town in Oregon, encouraged free sexual expression, denounced material values, and accepted two dozen gifts of Rolls Royce automobiles from his disciples.

Some of the cults of the 1970s attracted hostility. Critics of the Hare Krishnas—who shaved their heads, dressed in saffron robes, and marched and chanted picturesquely in city streets—said that they were emotionally disturbed, easily manipulated young people who were, in effect, brainwashed. The same criticism was leveled against the "Moonies," followers of a Korean preacher who claimed to be divine. Few lodged the critique against the well-scrubbed Yuppies crowding the tanning salons.

The Natural History of Swinging

A revolution in sexual morality that was long in the making reached its climax in the 1970s. Widespread acceptance of casual sexual encounters owed first of all to the development of a reliable birth-control device—popularly called "the pill"—which eased the single woman's fear of pregnancy. Control of venereal disease by means of antibiotics eliminated yet another dread that had inhibited previous generations.

A third source of freewheeling sexual attitudes was the decision by the Supreme Court in several cases that graphic depiction of sexual acts were protected by the constitutional right of free speech. While standards of enforcement varied radically from state to state and city to city, sexually explicit books and films were freely available.

"Singles bars," bistros frequented by people quite frankly to meet a sexual partner for a "one night stand," became fixtures in every big city and many towns. "Adult motels" suspended mirrors on ceilings and pumped pornographic movies to TV sets in perfumed rooms. Landlords converted apartment complexes to accommodate "swinging singles" with party rooms, saunas, and hot tubs.

Married people could hardly have been unaffected, and the divorce rate soared, reaching 50 percent of all marriages in most states and exceeding it in fashionable, affluent communities like Marin County, north

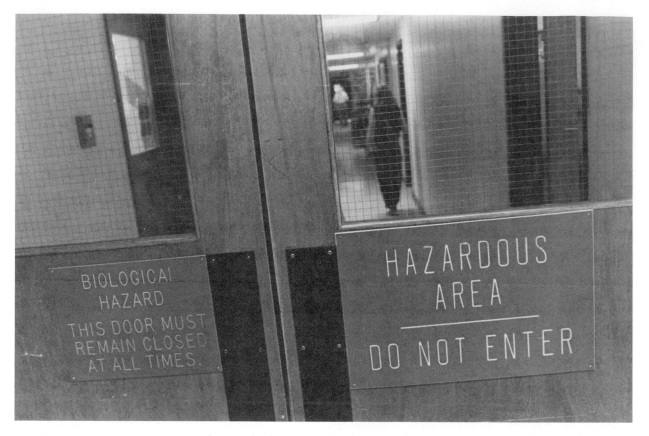

Laboratory for the testing of blood samples of suspected AIDS victims in Denver, Colorado.

of San Francisco, which became a byword for trendiness as Peoria was a byword for conventional midwestern morality.

Homosexuals, previously quietly tolerated in cities such as New York, San Francisco, and New Orleans, "came out of the closet," named themselves "gays," and demanded that their "sexual preference" be recognized as an "alternate lifestyle" at least equal to that of Peoria. Many liberals, carried away by issues of individual liberty and fulfillment promptly obliged.

Flies in the Ointment

Just as medical control of venereal disease helped to launch the sexual revolution, disease played a key part in its leveling off after 1980. A penicillin-resistant strain of gonorrhea made the rounds among swingers, and herpes, an old and minor venereal infection, reached epidemic proportions. Far more serious was an entirely new affliction, Acquired Immunity Deficiency Syndrome—AIDS—which slowly and agonizingly killed its victims.

AIDS, still only partially understood, is transmitted by the direct contact of the blood or other bodily fluid

of an infected person and the bloodstream of another. In impoverished nations such as Uganda and Haiti, plagued by filthy living conditions and chronic public health problems such as open sores, AIDS threatened the general population.

In the United States (and Canada and Western Europe), AIDS was a disease of homosexuals practicing anal intercourse (63 percent of all cases in 1989) and intravenous drug users (27 percent). The remaining 10 percent were hemophiliacs, patients who received a transfusion of infected blood, Haitians or Africans in the United States, and those who had sexual intercourse with a member of the high-risk groups. In 1989, experts estimated that up to 1.5 million Americans were infected with the HIV virus that led to AIDS.

Drugs

In the 1970s, use of recreational drugs spread both in the middle class and among the urban poor. LSD, the hallucinogenic celebrated by the hippies in the 1960s, lost popularity, but marijuana became a staple of Yuppie social life. Cocaine, which had circulated furtively since the nineteenth century, enjoyed a brief reign as a high-status euphoric because it was expensive and thought to be harmless.

When it was revealed to be highly addictive, cocaine lost its appeal to the unaddicted among educated Americans but remained a serious problem among professional athletes paid monstrous salaries. In the 1980s, it was revealed that the use of steroids, which enhanced muscular performance while savaging liver and heart, was widespread even among amateur athletes and bodybuilders.

Much more serious as a social problem was the flood in the nation's big cities of a cheap form of cocaine that was smoked or injected, called "crack." Heroin use also increased among the urban poor, sold openly enough in parks and on streetcorners for transactions to be televised. At the top of a complex international trade were dealers often rich and respected. More than one Latin American strong-man was implicated in the business. At the bottom, where dealing was also lucrative, gangs of teenaged thugs armed sometimes with sophisticated military assault weapons battled for hegemony of slum markets. Drug-related violence was so out of hand in some big cities by the late 1980s that it actually affected the mortality statistics. In 1989,

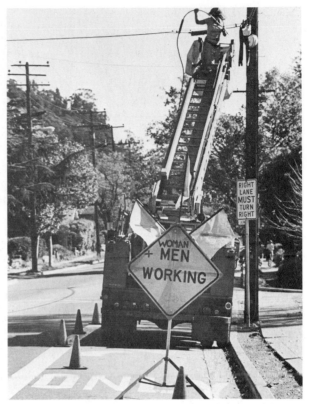

No longer confined to traditional female occupations, women became everything from lawyers to telephone line workers following the women's liberation movement of the late 1960s and early 1970s.

murder, usually gang-related, was the chief cause of death among black males 15 to 34 years of age.

Women's Lib

In the sybaritic 1970s, only one social movement of note achieved a large following, the new feminism. In 1966, after her book *The Feminine Mystique* (1963) received a rousing response, Betty Friedan organized the National Organization for Women (NOW), a pressure group designed to secure legal and social equality for women.

At first, "women's lib" was widely ridiculed because of the antics of fringe elements who held bonfires at which they burned their brassieres and formed groups with names such as SCUM, the "Society for Cutting Up Men." But the essence of the new feminism was too serious to be ignored and the influence of NOW too great to sidestep. NOW attracted women with show-business connections like the attractive journalist, Gloria Steinem, and won the support of first ladies Betty Ford and Rosalyn Carter.

NOW's early victories were deceptively easy. Archaic state laws that prevented married women from

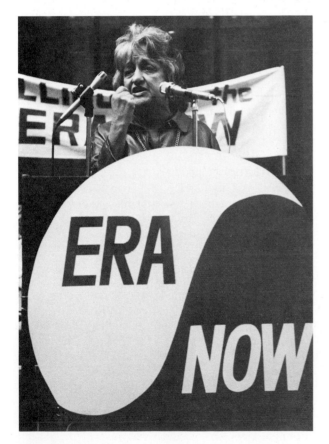

Betty Friedan, feminist author and founder of the National Organization for Women.

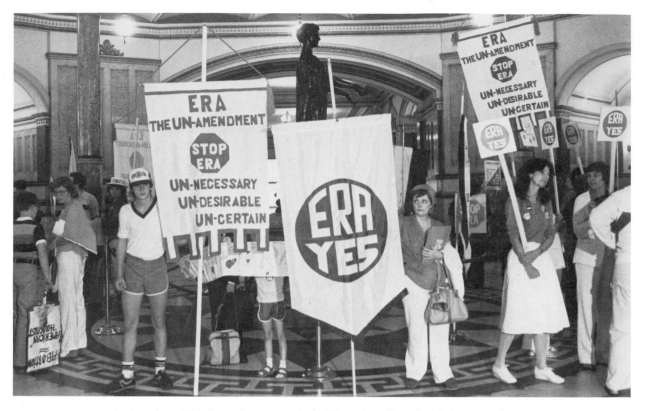

Anti- and pro-ERA forces demonstrate in the Illinois State Capitol while legislators debate.
Illinois never ratified the ERA.

borrowing money without the approval of their husbands were quickly repealed. Divorce laws were changed to provide for equal division of property. Legal action or social pressure forced corporations to pay men and women equally for equal work and women won entrance to jobs that had been restricted to men, particularly in manual and dangerous work such as construction and firefighting.

The women's movement was also successful in replacing "gender specific" words like *fireman, postman,* and *chairman.* Almost instantaneously, businesses and government took to speaking of "mailcarriers" and "chairpersons" (and even "chairs"). On little more than the demand of Gloria Steinem, who founded a magazine of the name, women were addressed as "Ms." rather than "Miss" or "Mrs." To the new feminists, because the ancient titles identified a woman's marital status, they were demeaning.

Professional schools and public and private employers adopted affirmative action programs by which they were obligated to admit or to hire women (and members of designated minority groups) in preference to white males if the applicants were equally qualified. In practice, apparently less-qualified women, blacks,

Hispanics, and others were often given preferential treatment, resulting in quota systems such as liberals had fought against when they had been used to discriminate against minorities. Beginning with the *Bakke* case of 1978, the Supreme Court dealt several major blows to such programs. In 1989, the Court threw out programs in several cities by which a percentage of municipal contracts were reserved for "minority firms" that did not have to bid against firms owned by white males.

ERA

NOW's biggest setback was the failure of the Equal Rights Amendment, which Congress sent to the states for ratification in 1972. First proposed by Alice Paul in the 1920s, the ERA forbade all legal and social discrimination on the basis of sex. During the 1970s, ERA was ratified by all but a handful of the 38 states needed to make it a part of the Constitution.

Then, seemingly from nowhere, emerged a groundswell of opposition led by a longtime right-wing Republican writer, Phyllis Schlafly. Cautioning that ratification of the ERA would lead to the loss of certain privileges that women enjoyed, such as exemption from military conscription, Schlafly's campaign emboldened hundreds of state legislators to fight the women's movement. When the 1979 deadline for ratification was reached, the ERA was still three states short of approval.

Congress promptly extended the deadline to 1982, a dubious changing of the rules in mid-game to which three states responded by reversing their votes for ratification. NOW contested the right of revocation, but the issue was moot; the ERA won ratification in no additional states.

Changing Times

ERA did not augur to accomplish much more for women than had already been enacted by statute, executive order, or voluntary compliance. It was not much more than a statement of what had largely been achieved. And yet, it failed, and its failure presaged the collapse of Democratic party liberalism in the 1980s.

The ERA, like other liberal causes of the 1970s, appealed almost exclusively to educated and affluent middle-class liberals. It never sparked much interest among working-class women (or men), nor even among ethnic minorities. Equal pay for equal work was important to people who struggled to make ends meet, but the "New Age" liberalism of the 1970s (a term coined by a conservative critic)—support for a woman's right to an abortion on demand, tacit acceptance of homosexuality as moral and proper, defense of the rights of accused criminals to the perceived detriment of victims of crime, apparent blanket criticism of American mores, and reflexive support for nearly every foreign critic of the United States—left ordinary Americans cold.

The New Age liberals were articulate and politically active. The McGovern reforms of the Democratic party gave them a voice in making party policy out of all proportion to their numbers. But in their triumph within the party, they alienated important constituents of the Democratic coalition that had governed the country for half a century: southern whites, northern blue-collar workers who valued traditional morality, the labor unions, and patriotic white ethnics.

To capitalize on the unease among traditional Democrats, conservative Republican strategists played down their economic agenda, which favored the well-to-do, and emphasized morality, traditional values, law and order, and patriotism. The Democratic party as a whole was tarred as the source of the apparent decadence in American society. Because of Watergate and the accidental presidency of Gerald Ford, the strategy of the Republican right-wingers did not bear fruit until 1980. But when it did, the vintage was fat and sweet.

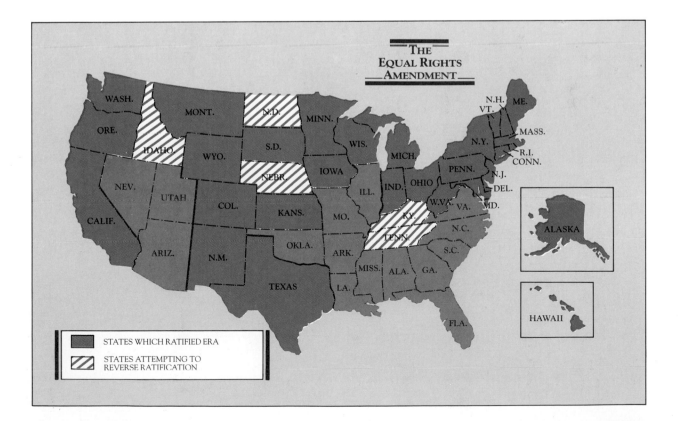

THE EQUAL RIGHTS AMENDMENT

STATES WHICH RATIFIED ERA

STATES ATTEMPTING TO REVERSE RATIFICATION

A CHANGING OF THE GUARD

Republican conservatives grew more sanguine about their prospects in 1980 with each month of the Carter presidency. Carter had won the White House very narrowly in 1976, and "stagflation" steadily eroded his popularity. The Camp David Accords had been a triumph but, in other matters of foreign policy, the president's actions were not especially popular. Then came the disaster.

The Iranian Tragedy

Like Nixon and Ford, Carter believed that Reza Pahlavi, the pro-Western shah of Iran, was a popular ruler at home. Carter described Iran as an "island of stability" in the Middle East.

This was a delusion. The shah had alienated just about everyone in Iran except the westernized middle and upper classes, a tiny part of the whole. Liberal and leftist Iranians suffered brutal tortures at the hands of SAVAK, the shah's secret police. And the deeply religious peasantry, the largest single social group in the country, was under the thumb of reactionary Moslem mullahs who taught that the shah's westernized regime was blasphemous.

In January 1979, after months of rebellion, the shah fled Iran and Moslem fundamentalists, led by the fanatical Ayatollah Ruhollah Khomeini, seized power. In October, when Carter admitted the exiled shah, who was dying of cancer, to the United States for medical treatment, Iranian students seized the United States embassy compound in Teheran and took 50 Americans hostage. For more than a year, they languished in confinement. Not until January 20, 1981, the day Jimmy Carter left the White House, were they to be released.

Political Consequences

A few leftist romantics in American universities celebrated the Ayatollah's rise to power, but the cheers were short-lived. His regime executed political opponents and "moral offenders" on a scale that made the shah look like Good King Wenceslaus. Khomeini prolonged an eight-year war with Iraq that killed 200,000 Iranians, including children sent on suicide attacks.

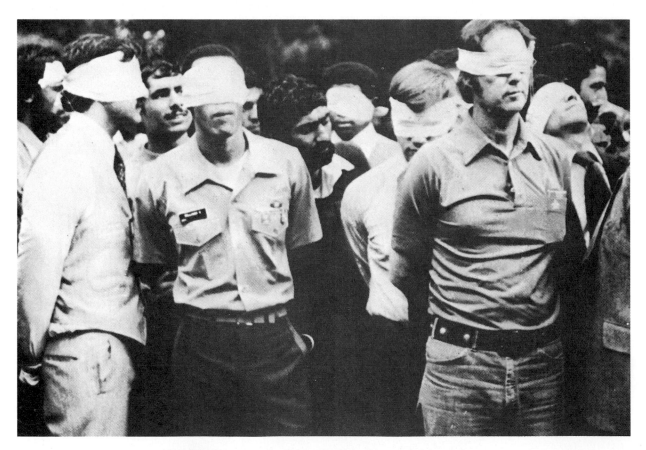

Blindfolded American hostages at the United States embassy in Iran.

CARTER'S BONERS

Jimmy Carter left himself wide open to unnecessary criticism when, running for president, he vowed somewhat sanctimoniously that he would never tell a lie. Again, by claiming that a nation's recognition of human rights would determine how the United States responded to it, and then supporting regimes like that of the Shah in Iran, his moralization caused him serious embarrassment. Perhaps his biggest mistake in this vein was confessing to an interviewer from *Playboy* magazine that he had many times lusted in his heart after women.

In early 1989, shortly before he died, he promised salvation in the Garden of Allah to any Moslem who murdered Salmon Rushdie, a British writer whose book, *Satanic Verses*, was offensive to Islam. Khomeini was an evil madman, an embarrassment to pious Moslems, but his power was immense. In holding the embassy hostages, he wrote an end to the short unhappy political career of James Earl Carter.

Within the Democratic party, sympathy for Carter's attempts to free the hostages helped him. He beat back a challenge for the 1980 presidential nomination by Massachusetts Senator Edward Kennedy largely because of the sentiment that, with American lives at stake, the people should rally around their elected leader. No sooner was Carter renominated, however, than the tide of opinion turned against him.

The Republican party's nominee was the darling of the conservatives, Ronald Reagan. In the Republican primaries, he easily defeated George Bush, who had held a number of high appointed positions in government, and John Anderson, a congressman from Illinois, who sniped at Reagan as a right-wing extremist. Bush called Reagan's economic program "voodoo economics" and Anderson attacked his foreign policy as reckless. But Republican conservatives had worked long and hard to make Ronald Reagan president.

When Anderson left the Republican party to run as an independent, Reagan won moderate support by naming Bush as his vice-presidential nominee.

The Reagan Campaign

Reagan's handlers were masterful campaigners. Rather than attack Carter's handling of the hostage crisis directly, which might have revived sympathy for him, they instructed Reagan to blast Carter's foreign policy in general. Reagan blamed the president for America's low prestige abroad, saying it was due to softness with the Soviets and weakness in backing up foreign friends. Toughness and a massive military buildup, Reagan said, was needed to stop the slide of American influence.

Domestically, Reagan focused on the sorry state of the economy. He promised to reduce regulation of business—which, he said, destroyed initiative—stop inflation, increase employment, cut government spending, and balance the federal budget by 1984.

While Reagan attacked the Democrats of 1980, he flummoxed them by repeatedly quoting Franklin D. Roosevelt, the *bête noire* of conservative Republicans. By this device, he appealed to blue-collar workers who remembered F.D.R. as a hero, but who had lost faith in the Democratic leadership of their own time because of New Age liberalism.

While Reagan courted traditional Democratic voters, his handlers ensured the loyalty of the right-wing Republicans who had won the nomination for him. Fundamentalist preachers such as the Reverend Jerry Falwell organized independent Political Action Committees (PACs) that rallied voters who believed that the Democratic party as a whole was responsible for what they saw as a decline in morality. Falwell's "Moral Majority" blamed the Democrats for everything from the high divorce rate to violent crime in big cities.

The Mandate

On the eve of the election, political experts agreed that the vote would be quite close. Several pollsters

No Olympics

The 1980 Olympic Games were scheduled to be held in Moscow. After the invasion of Afghanistan, President Carter announced that in protest the United States would not send its athletes. Carter apparently assumed that because the Olympics were of great importance to the Soviets as a public-relations gesture, the Soviet Afghan policy might be revised. Although a few other nations followed Carter's example, the Soviet Union did not budge, and the games went on.

Urban Decay

In New York City, every day between 1977 and 1980, 600 to 2,100 subway cars were out of service because of breakdowns due to age or mistreatment and vandalism. Between 80 and 300 trips had to be canceled each day. There were 2,200 to 5,000 fires in the New York subway system each year. In 1980 it took 40 minutes to take a trip that took only 10 minutes in 1910.

Newly inaugurated president Ronald Reagan and his wife Nancy greet a crowd during the inaugural parade.

predicted that the winner might be decided by the outcome in California, the last large state to report. The pollsters had not been so wrong since 1948. The election was over two hours before the polls closed on the West Coast. Reagan won an electoral college landslide, 489 votes to just 49 for Carter. His popular vote edge was 43.9 million to Carter's 35.5 million with 5.7 million votes going to independent John Anderson.

Thanks to the isolation of the New Age liberals and the shrewdness of Reagan's strategists, the old Democratic coalition lay in tatters. The Irish-American and Italian-American vote, always dependably Democratic, went for Reagan. In all but three states, Slavic-Americans voted for him. Jews, who had once been 80 to 90 percent Democratic, split about evenly, as did members of labor unions. Reagan won 60 percent of the elderly vote. "Youth," whom the New Age liberals had lionized as a vanguard, cast 60 percent of its vote for the president.

In state elections, the right-wing PACs defeated half a dozen liberal Democratic senators, including 1972

presidential nominee, George McGovern. For the first time in nearly 30 years, the Republicans had a majority in the Senate. The Democrats still held the House of Representatives but enough conservative Democrats, startled by the results, announced they would support the president that Reagan had a working majority in both houses. A new era had begun.

THE REAGAN REVOLUTION

The election of 1980 changed the nature of American government more than any election since 1932. Ronald Reagan and the people around him were at odds with some basic principles that, since the 1930s, both Democratic and Republican party leaders had accepted. Ronald Reagan was 78 when he left the White House in 1989, the oldest person ever to hold the post. And yet, he stamped his personality and values on the 1980s as indelibly as Franklin D. Roosevelt had stamped his on the 1930s.

Symbol of a Decade

"He has no dark side," one of Reagan's aides said of him. "What you see is what you get." The American people had seen a good deal of Ronald Reagan for more than 40 years. He was a successful film actor in the 1940s and the host of a popular television show in the 1950s. During the 1960s, he was a tireless campaigner for conservative causes. Reagan was governor of California between 1967 and 1975 and almost won the Republican nomination for president in 1976.

Very few people who knew Reagan personally disliked him. In private, he was cheerful, even-tempered, and entertaining with his wealth of show-business stories—a walking *People* magazine. He won the affection of the public when, shortly after his inauguration, he was shot by an emotionally disturbed young man, cracked a joke on the operating table, and recovered as quickly as if he were a teenager.

Reagan remained immensely popular to the end of his term. He was called "the Great Communicator" for his ability to sell himself to the nation. He was also known as "the Teflon president." He was so well liked that nothing messy stuck to him personally, neither his own bad decisions, nor when close associates went to jail, nor when former aides ridiculed him.

The Teflon President

The criticisms that did not stick to Reagan were numerous. After leaving his service, several aides said that Reagan was interested only in the ceremony of being president. He understood few of the complexities of government, they said, and refused to study them. Others were shocked by his habit of sleeping long hours each day. It was said that he dozed off at cabinet meetings and came to life only while watching old movies. Despite his robust constitution, insiders hinted that old age had caught up with him.

Critics charged that Reagan was still an actor reading lines written by others. Always eloquent in his prepared speeches, he often stumbled when asked questions off the cuff. Aides admitted they were elated when he negotiated a press conference without making a major gaffe. He sometimes seemed befuddled. In a debate with Democratic presidential candidate, Walter Mondale in 1984, Reagan did not understand simple questions. In 1985, television news cameras showed his wife, Nancy, whispering that he should say "We're working on that" when a question was asked. Former White House Chief of Staff Donald Regan suspected that Nancy made many of the president's decisions for him after consulting an astrologer.

Nevertheless, even Reagan's fundamentalist supporters, for whom astrology was the teaching of Satan, continued to idolize him. After the Vietnam tragedy, Watergate scandal, and foundering Carter years, Ronald Reagan's breezy cheerfulness and optimism restored popular confidence in the presidency.

Social Policies

Reagan had condemned moral "permissiveness" and leniency in the treatment of accused criminals. Like other conservatives, he held the Supreme Court, dominated by liberals for 50 years, responsible for many of the social ills they saw around them.

The transformation of the high Court had begun under Nixon but Reagan rounded it out. His first appointment was Sandra Day O'Connor of Arizona, a protégée of Nixon's most conservative appointee, William Rehnquist. By naming her, the first woman on the Court, Reagan simultaneously pleased feminists while adding a staunch conservative vote.

When Warren Burger retired in 1986, Reagan made the forceful Rehnquist Chief Justice and added Antonin Scalia, an arch-conservative with a brilliant legal mind. Only in 1988, at the end of his term, did Reagan run into trouble getting his nominees confirmed. Senators found one nominee too political in his judgments and a second, a right-wing Yuppie, proved to have been a marijuana-smoker as a young man.

The episode was particularly embarrassing to Reagan because he had called for an international War on Drugs. Nancy Reagan herself headed a campaign to fight the use of drugs among American teenagers. Stung by criticism that she cared for little but expensive evening gowns, Mrs. Reagan devoted long hours to the antidrug crusade known as "Just Say No!"

"Reaganomics" in Theory

Reagan's immense popularity owed in part to extraordinary good luck. Some of the problems that had damaged Ford and destroyed Carter resolved themselves spontaneously during his presidency. The Iran-Iraq war prevented the Ayatollah from vexing the

---

PRIORITIES IN THE 1980s

In 1983, the United States spent 57 cents *per capita* on public broadcasting, as compared to $10 *per capita* in Japan, $18 in Great Britain, and $22 in Canada. In the private sector, the cost of making one episode of the television program *Miami Vice* was $1.5 million. The annual budget of the vice squad in the city of Miami, Florida, a major clearing house for imported drugs, was just $1.1 million.

The Typical American of the 1980s:
A Statistical Portrait

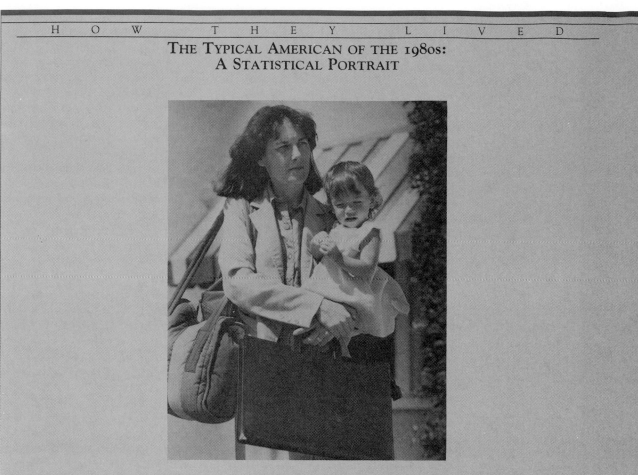

The statistical American of the 1980s was a mother who
very likely had a job. However, because of economic
depression, her employment was precarious.

The statistical American of the year 1980 was a Caucasian female, a little more than 30 years old, married to her first husband, with one child and about to have another. She was a shade over 5 feet 4 inches tall, and weighed 134 pounds. Statisticians are not sure of the color of her hair and eyes, but they were probably on the brownish side. Statisticians are sure that she had tried marijuana when she was younger, but no longer used it in the 1980s (although some of her friends still did). She did not smoke cigarettes, but at least had tried them in the past; she still drank, just this side of moderately.

The statistical American adult female of the 1980s considered herself middle class, and had attended college but had not necessarily graduated. She was likely to work outside the home, but economic conditions during the first half of the decade made her opportunities uncertain. Her household income was about $20,000 a year; she and her husband were watching their budget closely, which they were not accustomed to doing. It is a toss-up whether or not she voted in 1984 (or at all during the 1970s). She was decreasingly interested in feminism as the 1980s progressed and the failure of the ERA faded into memory. She was marginally more likely to be registered as a Democrat than as a Republican, but she was more likely to have voted for Ronald Reagan in 1984 than in 1980.

More than half of the statistical American's female friends were married. Most of her friends who have been divorced have married again within three years. The statistical American of the 1980s attached no stigma to divorce, and experienced only a slight sense of unease with people who lived with members of the opposite sex without benefit of marriage. But she found it difficult to agree that homosexuality is nothing more than an "alternate lifestyle" on a moral parity with heterosexuality. She was both amused and repelled by the culture of the "gay" communities about which she read, but by 1985 was not so indulgent as she had been because of the quantum leap in the spread of deadly AIDS.

She almost certainly had sex with her husband before they married, and almost as likely with at least one other man. There is a fair chance that she had a brief fling since marriage, probably during a "trial separation."

The statistical American was more likely to be Protestant than Catholic. However, she was more likely to be Catholic than a member of any other *individual* denomination. If a Catholic, she practiced birth control, most likely using the pill, in defiance of Church directives. Moreover, Catholic or Protestant, she attended church services far less frequently than had her mother.

The statistical American was in excellent health; she saw a dentist and a doctor more than once a year, and paid a little less than half of the cost of health care (state and federal government picked up about the same, private industry and philanthropy the rest). She had a life expectancy of almost 78 years, and would outlive her husband by eight years, with the prospects that her dotage would be economically trying.

The statistical American lived in a state with a population of about 3 million people—Colorado, Iowa, Oklahoma, Connecticut—and in a city of about 100,000 people—Roanoke, Virginia; Reno, Nevada; Durham, North Carolina.

Or perhaps, she lived at the population center of the United States, which in 1980 was west of the Mississippi River for the first time in American history. It was located "one mile west of the De Soto City Hall, Jefferson County, Missouri." An equal number of people in the continental United States lived east of that point as west, as many north of it as south.

As the question about her state and city of residence indicates, the statistical American is a somewhat absurd contrivance, distilled out of the majorities, means, and medians of the United States Census Bureau; the responses to surveys taken by a number of public-opinion experts; and, simply, the probabilities of the educated guess.

The virtue of the United States remains rooted in its diversity of people as well as of resources and in the survival of those people's right to change their minds as many times as they wish. And, as far as matters of public policy are concerned, to form majorities and effect their wishes. For a nation that has reached its third century, that is not so bad an accomplishment. In the star-crossed history of the human race, it has not been done in many other places.

United States. In the Soviet Union, the senility of Leonid Brezhnev, his death in November 1982, and three years of interim leadership by equally doddering old Bolsheviks meant that the Soviet Union was almost without direction until 1985.

The OPEC nations broke ranks and oil prices collapsed. Indeed, the keystone of Reagan's popularity was the fact that, after two difficult years, his presidency was a time of general prosperity for middle- and upper-class Americans. This prosperity, Reagan believed, was due to his economic policy, known as "Reaganomics."

During the campaign of 1980, Reagan promised to restore prosperity by ending inflation and unemployment, reducing government regulation of business, and balancing the budget. Part of his program was based on "supply-side economics," a theory that emphasized increasing the nation's supply of goods and services while allowing the distribution of wealth—each person's share of prosperity—to take care of itself.

Thus, Reagan called for cutting the taxes of upper- and middle-income Americans. Unlike the poor, who would spend tax savings on consumer goods, supply-siders argued, the affluent already had a comfortable life. Therefore, they would invest tax savings, supplying capital to the economy. Economic growth would create jobs for the unemployed and more people paying taxes. Expensive social welfare programs could be cut back, reducing government expenditures. The budget would be balanced and inflation halted.

Democrats pointed out that the plan resembled the "trickle-down" economics of Calvin Coolidge during the 1920s, policies that, they noted, had led to the Great Depression. Reagan was not impressed. Indeed, he hung the official portrait of Coolidge, which had been gathering dust for 50 years, in a conspicuous spot in the White House.

Prosperity in Practice

At Reagan's behest, Congress reduced taxes by 25 percent over three years. The drop, for those with good incomes, was considerable. A typical family making $75,000 had paid income taxes of 52.9 percent during the 1950s and 39.3 percent during the 1970s. By 1985, after the Reagan tax cut, it paid only 29.6 percent.

With the tax cut, government income dropped $131 billion, which Reagan said he would make up by slashing expenditures on social programs. He cut 37,000 jobs from the federal payroll and reduced expenditures on education, medical research, food stamps, and other programs instituted during the 1960s to aid the

TIME FLIES

A study by a scientific management firm in the late 1980s revealed that the average American living to his or her life expectancy will spend seven years in the bathroom, six years eating, five years waiting in lines, four years cleaning house, three years in meetings, one year "looking for things," eight months opening junk mail, and six months waiting at red lights.

poor. Federal spending on low-income housing dropped from $32 billion in 1980 to $7 billion in 1988. When Reagan left office there were 2.5 million fewer low-income housing units in the United States than in 1980. One child in five had no health insurance, and childhood immunizations declined. Whooping cough, a disease thought conquered, made a comeback among the urban poor.

Reagan did not molest welfare programs that benefitted the middle-class voters who supported him: federal subsidies to agriculture, Medicare, Social Security, and pensions for veterans and other government employees.

For two years, Reagan's program seemed to fail. Inflation slowed but unemployment actually rose to 11 percent in 1982, higher than at any time since the Great Depression. Newspapers reported depression-like scenes such as that at the Sun Oil refinery in Marcus Hook, Pennsylvania, where 35 jobs were advertized and 3,000 applicants showed up. Magazines and television revealed the shocking news that millions of Americans were homeless, living in campgrounds, under freeway overpasses, even in cars parked on city streets. Because of the widespread distress, the Democrats picked up 25 seats in the House of Representatives in 1982.

But Reagan urged America to "stay the course," to give his policies time to work. Then, in the spring of 1983, the economy revived, to remain statistically healthy until the end of Reagan's second term.

CITIZEN CONSUMERS

Immigrants sworn in as United States citizens in Santa Fe in April 1985 received a gift packet including the Preamble to the Constitution, a pamphlet describing etiquette toward the American flag, directories to the Safeway supermarket and Motel 6 chains, discount coupons from local businesses, and membership in the Radio Shack "battery club."

The Deficit Mushrooms

However, the Reagan prosperity had little to do with supply-side economics. Much of the tax savings of upper- and middle-class people went not into investment but into consumption of luxury goods. By 1986, investment in manufacturing was only 1 percent higher than it had been in the recession year of 1982.

By way of contrast, sales of high-priced homes boomed and expensive imports such as Jaguar, Mercedes-Benz, and BMW automobiles soared. Perrier, a French mineral water bottler, found that well-off Americans would pay several dollars for a glass of water because it came from abroad.

The money that fed the Reagan consumption binge came from investors and lenders abroad, especially the West Germans and Japanese. They pumped money into the United States, buying real estate, corporations, banks, stocks, and U.S. Treasury bonds in huge numbers. Then they made their money back as Americans spent it on imported consumer goods. From being the world's largest creditor nation when Reagan became president, the United States became the world's greatest debtor nation. In 1981, foreigners owed Americans $2,500 for each American family of four. By 1989, Americans owed foreigners $7,000 for each family of four.

The federal deficit—the government's debt—was worse than private debt. The costs of Social Security, pensions, and especially Reagan's military buildup were immense and, all the while he called for a constitutional amendment mandating a balanced budget, Reagan spent and borrowed at levels that smashed all records. In 1981, the federal government owed $738 billion, about 26 cents on each dollar produced and earned in the United States that year. In 1989, the debt was $2.1 trillion, about 43 cents on each dollar produced and earned. The president who criticized Jimmy Carter for borrowing borrowed more money in eight years than 39 previous presidents had borrowed in nearly 200 years!

Deregulation

Since the New Deal, the federal government had closely regulated many aspects of economic life, which ideological conservatives like Reagan said discouraged the spirit of enterprise. As president, Reagan weakened the regulatory agencies by cutting their budgets or by abolishing or relaxing restrictions. Some of Reagan's appointees to the agencies simply neglected to do their jobs. Airlines, trucking companies, banks, brokers selling stocks and bonds, and many other businesses found there was no longer a federal watchdog outside their doors.

Profits increased and so did abuses. Airlines closed down routes that did not make enough money and raised fares on well-traveled air lanes. In 1981, a person could fly from San Francisco to Los Angeles on an unrestricted ticket for $36. In 1989, the same ticket cost $148. Consumer advocates claimed that the deregulated airlines sent unsafe planes and unqualified pilots aloft. Similar criticisms were made of the condition of trucks and the qualifications of many truck drivers.

The Environment

Reagan was indifferent to environmental issues. His choice to head the Environmental Protection Agency, Ann Burford, had to resign in 1983 when it was revealed she had actively interfered with the enforcement of agency regulations. The president vetoed a Clean Water Act aimed at stopping the dumping of toxic industrial wastes, and his first secretary of the interior, James Watt of Colorado, tried to open scenic coastline to offshore oil drillers.

Watt was a spokesman for the "sagebrush rebels," western businessmen who wanted the federal government to turn all public lands over to the states that would then open them to private mining, logging, and grazing companies for exploitation. Never popular, he was forced to resign after making a statement that was offensive to blacks, Jews, and the physically handicapped. In the meantime, even after a spurt of growth during the 1970s, environmental groups explosively increased their membership. The Wilderness Society claimed 48,000 members in 1981, 240,000 in 1989. The Sierra Club and Audubon Society had comparable increases.

Financial Fraud

The deregulation of financial institutions led to irresponsible and corrupt practices in banks and savings and loan associations (sometimes called thrift societies). In 1988 alone, 135 thrifts had to be bailed out or closed by the Federal Savings and Loan Insurance Corporation (FSLIC). This agency, like the Federal Deposit Insurance Corporation (FDIC) for banks, guaranteed savings accounts. Before the Reagan deregulation, however, the FSLIC and FDIC had also enforced high management standards on the people who ran the thrifts and banks. During the Reagan years, supervision was virtually nil.

Few savings and loan executives went to jail but corruption was so grand on Wall Street, the nation's financial center, that there were several sensational scandals. Freed of close supervision by the federal Securities and Exchange Commission, respected stock-

brokers turned to fraud. By paying bribes to executives in large corporations, they learned before the general public of important decisions that affected the price of stocks. Using this "insider information," they bought and sold shares at immense profit.

The most celebrated case involved Ivan Boesky, whose frauds were so grand that, in order to avoid prison, he agreed in November 1987 to pay a fine of $100 million and pay back the money he had illegally earned. Just a month before his sentencing, on October 19, the fraud-ridden stock market had crashed, wiping out more than a trillion dollars in investment.

Nevertheless, the Reagan administration continued to approve corporate mergers and takeovers that did little but enrich a few individuals. In 1970, there had been 10 corporate reshufflings paying fees of $1 million or more to those who arranged them. In 1980, there were 94, in 1986, 346. In 1988, the government approved a deal between tobacco giant R. J. Reynolds and Nabisco despite the fact that, even the principals admitted, the only consequences would be higher prices for consumers, fewer jobs in the two companies,

Ivan Boesky leaves federal court after pleading guilty to one count of violating federal securities laws.

and personal profits of $10 million and more for a handful of shareholders.

The Sleaze Factor

Before his fall, Ivan Boesky had been admired as the kind of entrepreneur Reaganism was designed to create. He was applauded when he told graduates of a leading business school that "greed is all right. Greed is healthy. You can be greedy and still feel good about yourself."

Such low moral and ethical standards did not go uncriticized. Reagan's critics said that the president encouraged people like Boesky by his admiration of individual success and disdain for social needs. The administration itself seemed shot through with dishonesty. Several dozen Reagan appointees were prosecuted for corruption or forced to resign because of dubious dealings.

The most important of them was Ed Meese, an old friend of the president who became Attorney General in 1985. Entrusted with enforcing the laws of the nation, Meese spent more time in court or before Congress as a defendant than as a prosecutor. He was accused of doing illegal favors for friends in business and profiting from them.

The Election of 1984

In 1984, Democratic candidate Walter Mondale of Minnesota, vice president under Jimmy Carter, hoped that the "sleaze factor" would be enough to help him overcome the president's personal popularity. Mondale won the Democratic nomination by beating back challenges from Senator Gary Hart of Colorado and the Reverend Jesse Jackson, a civil-rights activist and the first black to be a serious contender for a major party presidential nomination. Jackson was a hypnotic orator in the tradition of the black church from which he had emerged. Hart was the New Age liberal candidate.

But Mondale had the backing of the party's professionals, and he tried to bring the traditional Democratic voters who had gone for Reagan in 1980 back to the party. He was unable to do so, largely because of the perception that he was promising something to every constituent group. Some of Mondale's gestures made little political sense. For example, he named a woman, Geraldine Ferraro, as his running mate despite her slight qualfications and the fact that feminists were not apt to vote Republican under any circumstances.

Reagan's popularity was at its peak in 1984 and he won a massive landslide, carrying every state but Minnesota and the District of Columbia. Almost 59 percent of the voters chose him. He announced that the theme of his second term was "Morning in America."

FOREIGN POLICY IN THE 1980s

Ronald Reagan's domestic program was much the same in 1989 as it had been in 1981, but his foreign policy changed in significant ways. During his first term, Reagan was almost recklessly belligerent towards the Soviet Union. By the time he left office, however, he scored a major breakthrough in nuclear arms reduction.

Cold Warrior

Reagan won fame as a cold warrior. He had criticized his predecessors, including the Republicans Nixon and Ford, for trusting the Soviet Union in negotiations. In 1982, he called Russia an "evil empire . . . the focus of evil in the world" and refused to back down when critics said that, because of the nuclear balance of terror, the United States had no choice but to seek an understanding with the Russians. Reagan also blamed the Soviets for instability throughout the world. He said that "the Soviet Union underlies all the unrest that is going on. If they weren't engaged in this game of dominos, there wouldn't be any hot spots in the world."

His advisors shared his worldview. Foremost among them was his first secretary of state, former general, Alexander Haig and Secretary of Defense Caspar Weinberger. The ambassador to the United Nations, Jeanne Kirkpatrick, frankly advocated supporting dictators abroad who were anti-Communist. The Reagan Doctrine, announced in 1985, held that the United States would support any anti-Communist struggle anywhere in the world.

South Africa and the Middle East

The Reagan Doctrine led the president to support a number of unpopular regimes and movements. While he criticized South Africa's policy of *Apartheid* (strict segregation of races), he resisted calls for economic sanctions designed to force the South African regime to change. Reagan also supported rebels in Angola who were fighting a government backed by the Soviet Union and Cuba.

Reagan continued Jimmy Carter's policy of aiding anti-Russian rebels in Afghanistan many of whom were, ironically, Moslem fundamentalists of the sort who kept Khomeini in power in Iran. In 1983, he sent

Rescuers work to remove the injured from the wreckage of the U.S. Marine command post in Beirut after it was destroyed by terrorists.

marines to Lebanon, which was torn by a multisided war involving religion and foreign intervention. When a suicide bomber driving an explosive-laden truck killed 241 sleeping Marines, he withdrew the force. His "teflon" worked as ever; Reagan was not widely criticized either for sending the Marines in or for withdrawing them in failure.

In 1986, Reagan won applause by bombing Libya. The Libyan dictator, Muammar Qadaffi, had long been suspected of financing terrorists. When American intelligence claimed to have evidence of a direct link between Qadaffi and terrorists in West Germany, American bombers raided several Libyan cities. Even in France, where the government had refused to cooperate with Reagan, public opinion approved the bombing.

Reagan also took action in the long bloody war between Iran and Iraq. In May 1987, to ensure that oil tankers moved safely in the Persian Gulf, he sent American warships to protect the seaways. Although designed to prevent Iranian attacks, the fleet's only serious loss came when an Iraqi plane attacked the U.S.S. *Stark*, killing 37 servicemen. In 1988, the United States was responsible for a tragedy when an Iranian civilian airliner was shot down by accident.

Central America

The president also applied the Reagan Doctrine in the Caribbean and Central America. In October 1983, he ordered a surprise attack on Grenada, a tiny island nation of only 110,000 people. The island was in chaos after the assassination of a Marxist leader. Although critics feared that one such invasion would lead to others, the president's action was popular.

Much more controversial was his policy in Central America. Many liberal critics opposed U.S. support of the repressive government of El Salvador and its opposition to the revolutionary Sandinista government of Nicaragua. In 1983, when El Salvador elected a moderate over an extreme rightist as president, criticism of Reagan's policy in that country faded.

However, many members of Congress continued to oppose American support of the Nicaraguan Contras, guerrillas fighting the leftist Sandinista government of the country. Some said that the United States was causing turmoil and misery in an already wretched and misgoverned country by keeping it at war. Others said that the Contras were reactionary and antidemocratic. Yet others feared that the United States would become involved in another Vietnam quagmire. Reagan replied that the Sandinista government threatened American security.

Between 1984 and 1986, Congress attached the Boland Amendments to a number of bills providing money for foreign aid. The Boland Amendments prohibited the government from giving directly military aid to Nicaragua. Rather than accept this policy, Reagan told a top aide "to figure out a way to take action."

Top Reagan aides then embarked on a bizarre adventure that made a mockery of the president's view of world politics as a competition between good and evil. Two National Security Advisors, Robert McFarlane and John Poindexter, and a marine colonel, Oliver North, secretly sold arms to the Ayatollah Khomeini's Iran. Some of the huge profits from the deal simply disappeared into someone's pocket, adding to the "sleaze factor" attacks on the administration. The remainder was given to the Contras.

This illegal action was taken without the knowledge of either Secretary of Defense Weinberger or Secretary of State Schultz. The role of the president in it was never clearly defined as Reagan changed his story several times. It was clear that he had either supported a violation of the law or that he did not know what was going on in his own administration.

Changing Policies

Even before the Iran-Contra crisis broke, Reagan's foreign policy underwent significant changes. Through 1985, Reagan made it clear that if a dictator was necessary to keep order in a foreign country, his administration would lend support. Then, early in 1986, protests in Haiti against the anti-Communist Jean-Claude Duvalier turned into full-scale revolt. Rather than backing Duvalier, American agents played an important role in persuading him to go into exile.

The United States played a central role in the ouster of the strongly pro-American but hopelessly corrupt president of the Philippines, Ferdinand Marcos. When Marcos declared himself the victor in a disputed election, riots broke out throughout the country. Fearing a civil war, the United States supported his opponent, Corazon Aquino. Marcos was given asylum in Hawaii so as to get him out of the Philippines.

Reagan was unsuccessful in his attempt to topple Manuel Noriega, the military dictator of Panama. Evidence indicated that Noriega was deeply involved in smuggling cocaine and other drugs to the United States. He was indicted in the United States and Reagan cut off the flow of American dollars to Panama. However, Noriega's hold on the Panamanian army was too strong and he rallied public support by attacking the United States, unfailingly a crowd-pleaser in Latin America.

Weapons Buildup

The most important of Reagan's foreign policy shifts was in his view of the Soviet Union. During his first years in office, he destroyed the spirit of détente that had begun under Richard Nixon. He called the SALT-II treaty a "one way street" with Americans making all the concessions to the Soviets, and refused to submit it to the Senate for ratification. In 1986, Reagan announced that the United States would no longer be bound by SALT-I.

In the meantime, the president sponsored the greatest peacetime military buildup in history, spending $2 trillion improving old systems and developing new ones. Battleships were taken out of mothballs and put to sea and he revived the MX missile, which Reagan renamed the Peacekeeper. When it was announced that the Peacekeepers were to be installed in old Minuteman missile silos, critics said that Reagan was plan-

---

CUT-THROAT COMPETITION

In 1984, it was revealed that the Defense Department paid General Dynamics $7,417 for an alignment pin that cost 3 cents at a hardware store, McDonnell-Douglas $2,043 for a nut priced elsewhere at 13 cents, Pratt and Whitney $118 for 22-cent plastic stool leg covers, and Hughes Aircraft $2,543 for a $3.64 circuit-breaker. A Congressman went to a hardware store and purchased 22 tools found in a military repair kit. His price was $92.44; the government's price for the same kit was $10,186.56.

ning a "first strike" against the Soviets. It was well known, they said, that the Russians had the Minuteman sites targeted. Therefore, they were useless unless the missiles in them were to be fired to begin a war.

In 1983, Pershing II missiles were installed in West Germany. These could hit Soviet targets in five minutes and the Russians responded by increasing their striking capacity. A new arms race seemed to be underway. By 1985, the two superpowers had more than 50,000 nuclear warheads between them.

The most controversial of Reagan's weapons proposals was SDI, the Strategic Defense Initiative, known as "Star Wars" after a popular movie. Just a theory, SDI was a system by which satellites orbiting the earth would be equipped with lasers fired at missiles by computer. Reagan claimed that the system would create an umbrella preventing a missile attack on the United States.

Criticism of Star Wars took several forms. Some scientists said that SDI simply would not work. Military experts pointed out that low-flying missiles and planes would not be affected by lasers in space. Financial experts worried that the astronomical costs of the project would bankrupt the United States. Antiwar groups said that SDI was actually an offensive, not a defensive weapon. By making the United States safer from nuclear attack, it would encourage a reckless president to attack the Soviet Union. Yet others said that the Soviets would simply develop countermeasures, which had always been the case in military technology.

Turning toward Disarmament

Still, it was not criticism that led President Reagan to reverse direction on nuclear buildup. During his second term, the hawkish Casper Weinberger resigned as secretary of defense because of the illness of his wife and the statesmanlike Secretary of State George Schultz, the "dove" in the administration, won greater influence over the president.

White House insiders said that Nancy Reagan had great influence in persuading the president to turn toward disarmament. Deeply devoted to her husband, she was concerned about his place in history, something the short-sighted Reagan was incapable of comprehending. She knew that presidents that worked for peace had higher historical reputations than those who seemed to be warmongers.

The concerns of allies in Europe also influenced the president. Antinuclear protesters swarmed around American bases in Germany, Britain, and Spain. Chancellor Helmut Kohl of West Germany, President François Mitterand of France, and Prime Minister

Margaret Thatcher remained loyal to the NATO alliance. However, all made it clear that they were unnerved by Reagan's warlike speeches. Most important, the Soviet Union underwent profound changes during the 1980s.

Mikhail Gorbachev

In 1985, after five years of uncertain leadership in the Soviet Union, Mikhail Gorbachev emerged as head of both the Soviet government and Communist Party. At home, Gorbachev instituted far-reaching economic and political reforms. His policy of *perestroika* (restructuring) was designed to revive the moribund Soviet economy. *Glasnost* (opening) promised political and intellectual freedoms unheard of in the Soviet Union.

Gorbachev's reforms depended on his ability to divert Soviet resources from the military to the domestic economy. Personable and articulate, with a wife as fashionable as Nancy Reagan, Gorbachev soon won confidence in the West, including the United States, that he sincerely meant to wind down the arms race. At first, Reagan resisted Gorbachev's proposals. Then, in Washington in December 1987, the two men, all smiles and cordiality, signed a treaty eliminating many short-range and medium-range missiles. The Soviets destroyed 1,752 missiles and the Americans 867.

These represented only 4 percent of the nuclear missiles in existence. Nevertheless, nuclear power

President-elect George Bush, President Ronald Reagan, and Soviet leader Mikhail Gorbachev pose on Governor's Island, New York, in December 1988.

Jesse Jackson campaigns in New York in 1988.

32,000 times the force of the Hiroshima bomb was wiped out. Reagan's right-wing supporters were furious. Still, he left office with hopes for peace and Soviet-American cooperation higher than at any time since the Nixon administration.

ENTER GEORGE HERBERT BUSH

The Democrats approached the presidential campaign of 1988 with optimism. With some justification, they believed that the Reagan era had been an aberration, the triumph of a fabulously popular individual rather than the first chapter of a Republican party ascendancy. The Democrats had regained control of the Senate in 1986, enjoyed a comfortable grip on the House, and held a majority of the nation's governorships.

The Seven Dwarfs

As always when election victory seems likely, the Democrats were swamped with would-be nominees. The front-runner in the early going was Gary Hart, the former Senator from Colorado had given Mondale a tough race in the 1984 primaries. Then, when Hart was accused of being a womanizer, he angrily dared reporters to dog his steps. They did, tailed him as he left a Georgetown town house late at night with a beautiful young model, and dug up a photo of Hart with the woman in his lap on a vacation yacht, the *Monkey Business*.

Hart withdrew from the race humiliated, leaving candidates who were mocked as "the seven dwarfs" for their lack of presidential stature. In fact, several of the seven dwarfs were able men. Former governor Bruce Babbitt of Arizona overcame national obscurity by speaking with a frankness about issues rare in the age of "image politics." However, he had little money to spend on the television ads that had become the heart of political campaigning, and he dropped out early.

Jesse Jackson of Illinois remained, as he had been in 1984, an electrifying speaker who reached beyond the black community as he tried to form a "rainbow coalition." But Jackson was controversial. Government-funded programs under his supervision were mismanaged; he had made statements that offended some Jewish groups; and he, too, was rumored to be a skirt-chaser.

As the seven dwarfs competed in 35 primary elections, more than ever before, party leaders, pundits, and a good many ordinary voters lamented that the most impressive Democrats were not in the race. Senator Sam Nunn of Georgia was generally described as the nation's leading expert on defense, but he refused to run. Governor Mario Cuomo of New York was an exciting orator whose humanism was tempered by hard-headed political realism. The Democrats were "waiting for Mario," the joke went, as Cuomo apparently waited for a deadlocked convention.

Instead, with a huge campaign chest, Michael Dukakis of Massachusetts won the nomination in the primaries. The son of Greek immigrants, he had been a successful governor, balancing budgets while the Reagan administration spent and borrowed. During his administration, a state with serious economic difficulties became a prosperous center of finance and high-tech industry. For vice president, Dukakis chose Senator Lloyd Bentsen of Texas, a courtly and respected lawmaker.

Bush for the Republicans

George Bush was a wealthy oilman who had held a number of appointive positions in government but who also had a record of losing elections. Running against Reagan as a moderate in 1980, he became the administration's chief cheerleader, thus establishing ties with the conservative wing of the Republican party.

HEAVY BURDEN

During the presidential campaign of 1988, the Bush forces attacked Democratic nominee Michael Dukakis for being a member of the American Civil Liberties Union (ACLU). Dukakis was put immediately on the defensive, claiming that, while indeed a member, he did not agree with all ACLU policies.

Membership in the ACLU was a heavy political burden in the 1980s. Once devoted to defending civil liberties as defined in the Bill of Rights, the ACLU had come to espouse a political agenda that was not too popular in the age of Reagan. The organization opposed all laws regulating the sale and distribution of pornography, opposed imprisonment for any crimes except murder and treason in order to "maximize the liberty of the individual," and defended high school students who had been disciplined for wearing t-shirts emblazoned with the likes of "big pecker" to school on the grounds that they were exercising their right to free speech.

Michael Dukakis answers questions from reporters a week before the 1988 New York primary.

His chief rival for the nomination was Senator Robert Dole of Kansas, an articulate if often nasty political infighter. Like Bush, Dole had ties with both moderate and right-wing Republicans, and tried to create distance between himself and the vice president by hinting that Bush was a "wimp," having led so sheltered a life as to lack the toughness required of a president.

Bush had indeed lived a privileged life and it showed, but he was not lacking in personal courage. He had flown 58 missions as a fighter pilot during the Second World War. Rather more troubling was his reputation as a bumbler. (He had crashed his planes on five of those missions.) After defeating Dole in the primary elections, he made what seemed a fatal political blunder.

As his running mate, Bush chose Senator Dan Quayle of Indiana, all of whose achievements since first tying his shoes seemed to owe to his father's wealth and influence. Quayle admitted he had "majored" in golf at university and dodged military service during the Vietnam War when his father's friends created a place for him in the National Guard. His admission to law school was irregular and he virtually told reporters that he was not very bright. Quayle's political career had been built on his movie-star good looks and careful programming by political handlers. During the campaign of 1988, they made sure that he spoke only to screened groups of party faithful or to high school and elementary school pupils.

Dukakis attacked Bush's judgement in picking Quayle and tried to contrast his proven competence

*The 1988 Republican candidates: Vice President George Bush
and Senator Dan Quayle of Indiana.*

with Bush's reputed bumbling. But the governor's public personality was cold and mechanical: "Zorba the Clerk," a wit nicknamed him. By way of contrast, winning the Republican nomination, his first election victory since 1968, seemed to liberate Bush. He exuded confidence and authority as he promised both to continue the policies of the "Reagan-Bush administration" and to usher in "a kinder, gentler America."

While Bush took the high road, Republican strategists smeared Dukakis by hammering on the fact that a murderer who had been paroled during his tenure as governor of Massachusetts killed again and that Dukakis was a member of the American Civil Liberties Union (ACLU), which had become a a citadel of New Age liberalism. Dukakis took to the defensive, forced to point out that he was not responsible for Massachusetts parole policies and that he disagreed with

many ACLU policies. He never really had the initiative. Bush led throughout the campaign and won 54 percent of the popular vote and 426 electoral votes to 112 for Dukakis.

A Faltering Start

Then, within days of taking the oath of office, Bush faltered. For a moment he seemed a man of action, proposing a plan to bail out the nation's savings and loan associations. Then, however, on the occasion of the funeral of Japanese emperor Hirohito, Bush disappeared on a foreign tour on which he spoke only in platitudes. He announced that he was in no hurry to follow up on the rapprochement with the Soviets instituted during the last months of the Reagan-Bush administration. He seemed paralyzed by the achievement of his lifelong goal.

REAGANISM

Gary Wills, one of the leading political commentators of the 1980s, wrote during the waning months of the Reagan presidency,

Ronald Reagan did not build a structure; he cast a spell. There was no Reagan revolution, just a Reagan bedazzlement. The magic is going off almost as mysteriously as the spell was woven in the first place. There is no edifice of policies solid enough to tumble, piece by piece, its props being knocked out singly or in groups. The whole thing is not falling down; it was never weighty enough for that. It is simply evanescing.

Then, in February and March 1989, Bush entangled himself in a political fight with Senate Democrats that he could not possibly win. Over the protests of many of his own advisors, he named John Tower of Texas to be his secretary of defense. Tower had few friends in the Senate and had a reputation as a heavy drinker and womanizer. Although, ironically, less was made of it than his personal foibles, Tower had taken a sub stantial sum of money from defense contractors as a "consultant."

With Democratic majorities in both houses of Congress, Bush needed bipartisan cooperation, but in the face of the sure defeat of the Tower nomination, he insisted on fighting the battle to the end. The result was bitter acrimony and administrative paralysis. After two months in office, Bush had not made hundreds of top-level appointments in the Departments of Defense, State, and Justice.

It was an inauspicious beginning for a president who had inherited grave problems from his predecessor and patron. Ronald Reagan, as he made plans to sprint back to his home in Santa Barbara, California, may have been thinking about Bush and himself when he told one of his many jokes at the Take Pride in America awards ceremony in July 1988.

Two fellows . . . were out hiking in the woods and suddenly looked up and saw a grizzly bear coming over the hill toward them. One of them immediately reached into his pack, pulled out a pair of sneakers, started removing his boots and putting on the sneakers. And the other one, standing there, said, "You don't think you can outrun that grizzly, do you?" And the first one said, "I don't have to. I just have to be able to outrun you."

For Further Reading

The 1980s are "yesterday" and most historians have long conceded that any attempt to write the history of yesterday is destined to be flawed. Perhaps some of the books listed here will become classics, to be read into the indefinite future because of their extraordinary insights or—in the estimation of the future—their veracity. It is impossible to say of which of these books that will be so, and which will moulder on library shelves.

Surely the most likely candidate as shrewd observer of his times is Garry Wills, whose *Reagan's America: Innocent at Home* (1987) is as provocative as his contemporary study of Nixon. Also useful in understanding the symbol of the 1980s is his *Where's the Rest of Me?* (1965), an account of his conversion from youthful liberalism to the conservative politics for which he will be remembered. Also on this subject, see A. Ed-wards, *Early Reagan: The Rise to Power* (1987). Two of the many books by principals in the Reagan administration are Donald Regan, *For the Record* (1988), and Larry Speakes, *Speaking Out* (1988). See also P. Steinfels, *The Neoconservatives* (1979), and S. Blumenthal, *The Rise of the Counter-Establishment* (1986).

On foreign policy during the 1980s see R. L. Garthoff, *Détente and Confrontation: American Soviet Relations from Nixon to Reagan* (1985), which does not, however, deal with Reagan's turn toward accommodation with the Soviets late in his term. On covert operations, see G. F. Treverton, *Covert Action* (1987), and B. Woodward, *Veil: The Secret Wars of the C.I.A., 1981–1987* (1987). P. Kennedy, *The Rise and Fall of the Great Powers* (1987) may offer an explanation of why contemporary Americans find their nation's place in the world so perplexing.

Appendixes

The Declaration of Independence*

The Unanimous Declaration of the Thirteen United States of America,

When in the Course of human events it becomes necessary for one people to dissolve the political bands which have connected them with another, and to assume among the Powers of the earth, the separate and equal station to which the Laws of Nature and of Nature's God entitle them, a decent respect to the opinions of mankind requires that they should declare the causes which impel them to the separation.

We hold these truths to be self-evident, that all men are created equal, that they are endowed by their Creator with certain unalienable Rights, that among these are Life, Liberty and the pursuit of Happiness. That to secure these rights, Governments are instituted among Men, deriving their just Powers from the consent of the governed. That whenever any Form of Government becomes destructive of these ends, it is the Right of the People to alter or to abolish it, and to institute new Government, laying its foundation on such principles and organizing its Powers in such form, as to them shall seem most likely to effect their Safety and Happiness. Prudence, indeed, will dictate that Governments long established should not be changed for light and transient causes; and accordingly all experience hath shewn, that mankind are more disposed to suffer, while evils are sufferable, than to right themselves by abolishing the forms to which they are accustomed. But when a long train of abuses and usurpations, pursuing invariably the same Object evinces a design to reduce them under absolute Despotism, it is their right, it is their duty to throw off such Government, and to provide new Guards for their future security. Such has been the patient sufferance of these Colonies; and such is now the necessity which constrains them to alter their former Systems of Government. The history of the present King of Great Britain is a history of repeated injuries and usurpations, all having in direct object the establishment of an absolute Tyranny over these States. To prove this, let Facts be submitted to a candid world.

He has refused his Assent to Laws, the most wholesome and necessary for the public good.

He has forbidden his Governors to pass Laws of immediate and pressing importance, unless suspended in their operation till his Assent should be obtained; and when so suspended, he has utterly neglected to attend to them.

He has refused to pass other Laws for the accommodation of large districts of people, unless those people would relinquish the right of Representation in the Legislature, a right inestimable to them and formidable to tyrants only.

He has called together legislative bodies at places unusual, uncomfortable, and distant from the depository of their Public Records, for the sole Purpose of fatiguing them into compliance with his measures.

He has dissolved Representative Houses repeatedly, for opposing with manly firmness his invasions on the rights of the People.

He has refused for a long time, after such dissolutions, to cause others to be elected; whereby the Legislative Powers, incapable of Annihilation, have returned to the People at large for their exercise; the State remaining in the mean time exposed to all the dangers of invasion from without, and convulsions within.

He has endeavoured to prevent the Population of these States; for that purpose obstructing the Laws for Naturalization of Foreigners; refusing to pass others to encourage their migrations hither, and raising the conditions of new Appropriations of Lands.

He has obstructed the Administration of Justice, by refusing his Assent to Laws for establishing Judiciary Powers.

He has made Judges dependent on his Will alone, for the tenure of their offices, and the amount and payment of their salaries.

He has erected a multitude of New Offices, and sent hither swarms of Officers to harass our People, and eat out their substance.

He has kept among us, in times of peace, Standing Armies without the consent of our legislatures.

He has affected to render the Military independent of and superior to the Civil Power.

He has combined with others to subject us to a jurisdiction foreign to our constitution, and unacknowledged by our laws; giving his Assent to their Acts of pretended Legislation:

---

*Reprinted from the facsimile of the engrossed copy in the National Archives. The original spelling, capitalization, and punctuation have been retained. Paragraphing has been added.

For Quartering large bodies of armed troops among us:

For protecting them, by a mock Trial, from Punishment for any Murders which they should commit on the Inhabitants of these States:

For cutting off our Trade with all parts of the world:

For imposing Taxes on us without our Consent:

For depriving us in many cases, of the benefits of Trial by Jury:

For transporting us beyond Seas to be tried for pretended offences:

For abolishing the free System of English Laws in a neighbouring Province, establishing therein an Arbitrary government, and enlarging its Boundaries so as to render it at once an example and fit instrument for introducing the same absolute rule into these Colonies:

For taking away our Charters, abolishing our most valuable Laws, and altering fundamentally the Forms of our Governments:

For suspending our own Legislatures, and declaring themselves invested with Power to legislate for us in all cases whatsoever.

He has abdicated Government here, by declaring us out of his Protection, and waging War against us.

He has plundered our seas, ravaged our Coasts, burnt our towns, and destroyed the lives of our people.

He is at this time transporting large Armies of foreign Mercenaries to compleat the works of death, desolation and tyranny, already begun with circumstances of Cruelty and perfidy scarcely paralleled in the most barbarous ages, and totally unworthy the Head of a civilized nation.

He has constrained our fellow Citizens taken Captive on the high Seas to bear Arms against their Country, to become the executioners of their friends and Brethren, or to fall themselves by their Hands.

He has excited domestic insurrections amongst us, and has endeavoured to bring on the inhabitants of our frontiers, the merciless Indian Savages, whose known rule of warfare, is an undistinguished destruction of all ages, sexes and conditions.

In every stage of these Oppressions We have Petitioned for Redress in the most humble terms: Our repeated Petitions have been answered only by repeated injury. A Prince, whose character is thus marked by every act which may define a Tyrant, is unfit to be the ruler of a free People.

Nor have We been wanting in attentions to our British brethren. We have warned them from time to time of attempts by their legislature to extend an unwarrantable jurisdiction over us. We have reminded them of the circumstances of our emigration and settlement here. We have appealed to their native justice and magnanimity, and we have conjured them by the ties of our common kindred to disavow these usurpations, which, would inevitably interrupt our connections and correspondence. They too have been deaf to the voice of justice and of consanguinity. We must, therefore, acquiesce in the necessity, which denounces our Separation, and hold them, as we hold the rest of mankind, Enemies in War, in Peace Friends.

We, therefore, the Representatives of the United States of America, in General Congress, Assembled, appealing to the Supreme Judge of the world for the rectitude of our intentions, do, in the Name, and by Authority of the good People of these Colonies, solemnly publish and declare, That these United Colonies are, and of Right ought to be FREE AND INDEPENDENT STATES; that they are Absolved from all Allegiance to the British Crown, and that all political connection between them and the State of Great Britain, is and ought to be totally dissolved; and that, as Free and Independent States, they have full Power to levy War, conclude Peace, contract Alliances, establish Commerce, and to do all other Acts and Things which Independent States may of right do. And for the support of this Declaration, with a firm reliance on the protection of divine Providence, we mutually pledge to each other our Lives, our Fortunes and our sacred Honor.

The Constitution of the United States of America*

We the People of the United States, in Order to form a more perfect Union, establish Justice, insure domestic Tranquility, provide for the common defence, promote the general Welfare, and secure the Blessings of Liberty to ourselves and our Posterity, do ordain and establish this Constitution for the United States of America.

Article. I.

Section. 1. All legislative Powers herein granted shall be vested in a Congress of the United States, which shall consist of a Senate and House of Representatives.

Section. 2. The House of Representatives shall be composed of Members chosen every second Year by the People of the several States, and the Electors in each State shall have the Qualifications requisite for Electors of the most numerous Branch of the State Legislature.

No Person shall be a Representative who shall not have attained to the Age of twenty five Years, and been seven Years a Citizen of the United States, and who shall not, when elected, be an Inhabitant of that State in which he shall be chosen.

Representatives and direct Taxes† shall be apportioned among the several States which may be included within this Union, according to their respective Numbers, which shall be determined by adding to the whole Number of free Persons, including those bound to Service for a Term of Years, and excluding Indians not taxed, three fifths of all other Persons.‡ The actual Enumeration shall be made within three Years after the first Meeting of the Congress of the United States, and within every subsequent Term of ten Years, in such Manner as they shall by Law direct. The Number of Representatives shall not exceed one for every thirty Thousand, but each State shall have at least one Representative; and until such enumeration shall be made, the State of New Hampshire shall be entitled to chuse three; Massachusetts eight; Rhode Island and Providence Plantations one; Connecticut five; New York six; New Jersey four; Pennsylvania eight; Delaware one; Maryland six; Virginia ten; North Carolina five; South Carolina five; and Georgia three.

When vacancies happen in the Representation from any State, the Executive Authority thereof shall issue Writs of Election to fill such Vacancies.

The House of Representatives shall chuse their Speaker and other Officers; and shall have the sole Power of Impeachment.

Section. 3. The Senate of the United States shall be composed of two Senators from each State, chosen by the Legislature thereof, for six Years; and each Senator shall have one Vote.*

Immediately after they shall be assembled in Consequence of the first Election, they shall be divided as equally as may be into three Classes. The Seats of the Senators of the first Class shall be vacated at the Expiration of the second Year, of the second Class at the Expiration of the fourth Year, and of the third Class at the Expiration of the sixth Year, so that one third may be chosen every second Year; and if Vacancies happen by Resignation, or otherwise, during the Recess of the Legislature of any State, the Executive thereof may make temporary Appointments until the next Meeting of the Legislature, which shall then fill such Vacancies.†

No Person shall be a Senator who shall not have attained to the Age of thirty Years, and been nine Years a Citizen of the United States, and who shall not, when elected, be an Inhabitant of that State for which he shall be chosen.

The Vice President of the United States shall be President of the Senate, but shall have no Vote, unless they be equally divided.

The Senate shall chuse their other Officers, and also a President pro tempore, in the Absence of the Vice President, or when he shall exercise the Office of President of the United States.

The Senate shall have the sole Power to try all Impeachments. When sitting for that Purpose, they shall be on Oath or Affirmation. When the President of the United States is tried, the Chief Justice shall preside: And no Person shall be convicted without the Concurrence of two thirds of the Members present.

Judgment in Cases of Impeachment shall not extend further than to removal from Office, and disqualification to hold and enjoy any Office of honor, Trust or Profit under the

---

*From the engrossed copy in the National Archives. Original spelling, capitalization, and punctuation have been retained.
†Modified by the Sixteenth Amendment.
‡Replaced by the Fourteenth Amendment.

*Superseded by the Seventeenth Amendment.
†Modified by the Seventeenth Amendment.

United States: but the Party convicted shall nevertheless be liable and subject to Indictment, Trial, Judgment and Punishment, according to Law.

Section. 4. The Times, Places and Manner of holding Elections for Senators and Representatives, shall be prescribed in each State by the Legislature thereof, but the Congress may at any time by Law make or alter such Regulation, except as to the Places of chusing Senators.

The Congress shall assemble at least once in every Year, and such Meeting shall be on the first Monday in December, unless they shall by Law appoint a different Day. *

Section. 5. Each House shall be the Judge of the Elections, Returns and Qualifications of its own Members, and a Majority of each shall constitute a Quorum to do Business; but a smaller Number may adjourn from day to day, and may be authorized to compel the Attendance of absent Members, in such manner, and under such Penalties as each House may provide.

Each House may determine the Rules of its Proceedings, punish its Members for disorderly Behaviour, and, with the Concurrence of two thirds, expel a Member.

Each House shall keep a Journal of its Proceedings, and from time to time publish the same, excepting such Parts as may in their Judgment require Secrecy; and the Yeas and Nays of the Members of either House on any question shall, at the Desire of one fifth of those Present, be entered on the Journal.

Neither House, during the Session of Congress, shall, without the Consent of the other, adjourn for more than three days, nor to any other Place than that in which the two Houses shall be sitting.

Section. 6. The Senators and Representatives shall receive a Compensation for their Services, to be ascertained by Law, and paid out of the Treasury of the United States. They shall in all Cases, except Treason, Felony and Breach of the Peace, be privileged from Arrest during their Attendance at the Session of their respective Houses, and in going to and returning from the same; and for any Speech or Debate in either House, they shall not be questioned in any other Place.

No Senator or Representative shall, during the Time for which he was elected, be appointed to any civil Office under the Authority of the United States, which shall have been created, or the Emoluments whereof shall have been encreased during such time; and no Person holding any Office under the United States, shall be a Member of either House during his Continuance in Office.

Section. 7. All Bills for raising Revenue shall originate in the House of Representatives; but the Senate may propose or concur with Amendments as on other bills.

Every Bill which shall have passed the House of Representatives and the Senate shall, before it become a Law, be presented to the President of the United States; If he approve he shall sign it, but if not he shall return it, with his Objections to that House in which it shall have originated, who shall enter the Objections at large on their Journal, and proceed to reconsider it. If after such Reconsideration two thirds of that House shall agree to pass the Bill, it shall be sent, together with the Objections, to the other House, by which it shall likewise be reconsidered, and if approved by two thirds of that House, it shall become a Law. But in all such Cases the Votes of both Houses shall be determined by yeas and Nays, and the Names of the Persons voting for and against the Bill shall be entered on the Journal of each House respectively. If any Bill shall not be returned by the President within ten Days (Sundays excepted) after it shall have been presented to him, the Same shall be a Law, in Manner as if he had signed it, unless the Congress by their Adjournment prevent its Return, in which Case it shall not be a Law.

Every Order, Resolution, or Vote to which the Concurrence of the Senate and House of Representatives may be necessary (except on a question of Adjournment) shall be presented to the President of the United States; and before the Same shall take Effect, shall be approved by him, or being disapproved by him shall be repassed by two thirds of the Senate and House of Representatives, according to the rules and Limitations prescribed in the Case of a Bill.

Section. 8. The Congress shall have Power To lay and collect Taxes, Duties, Imposts and Excises, to pay the Debts and provide for the common Defence and general Welfare of the United States; but all Duties, Imposts and Excises shall be uniform throughout the United States;

To borrow Money on the credit of the United States;

To regulate Commerce with foreign Nations, and among the several States, and with the Indian Tribes;

To establish an uniform Rule of Naturalization, and uniform Laws on the subject of Bankruptcies throughout the United States;

To coin Money, regulate the Value thereof, and of foreign Coin, and fix the Standard of Weights and Measures;

To provide for the Punishment of counterfeiting the Securities and current Coin of the United States;

To establish Post Offices and post Roads;

To promote the Progress of Science and useful Arts, by securing for limited Times to Authors and Inventors the exclusive Right to their respective Writings and Discoveries;

To constitute Tribunals inferior to the supreme Court;

To define and punish Piracies and Felonies committed on the high Seas, and Offences against the Law of Nations;

To declare War, grant Letters of Marque and Reprisal, and make Rules concerning Captures on Land and Water;

To raise and support Armies, but no Appropriation of

---

*Superseded by the Twentieth Amendment.

Money to that Use shall be for a longer Term than two Years;

To provide and maintain a Navy;

To make Rules for the government and Regulation of the land and naval Forces;

To provide for calling forth the Militia to execute the Laws of the Union, suppress Insurrections and repel Invasions;

To provide for organizing, arming, and disciplining, the Militia, and for governing such Part of them as may be employed in the Service of the United States, reserving to the States respectively, the Appointment of the Officers, and the Authority of training the Militia according to the discipline prescribed by Congress;

To exercise exclusive Legislation in all Cases whatsoever, over such District (not exceeding ten Miles square) as may, by Cession of particular States, and the Acceptance of Congress, become the Seat of the Government of the United States, and to exercise like Authority over all Places purchased by the consent of the Legislature of the State in which the Same shall be, for the Erection of Forts, Magazines, Arsenals, dock-Yards, and other needful Buildings;—And

To make all Laws which shall be necessary and proper for carrying into Execution the foregoing Powers, and all other Powers vested by this Constitution in the Government of the United States, or in any Department or Officer thereof.
Section. 9. The Migration or Importation of such Persons as any of the States now existing shall think proper to admit, shall not be prohibited by the Congress prior to the Year one thousand eight hundred and eight, but a Tax or Duty may be imposed on such Importation, not exceeding ten dollars for each Person.

The Privilege of the Writ of Habeas Corpus shall not be suspended, unless when in Cases of Rebellion or Invasion the public Safety may require it.

No Bill of Attainder or ex post facto Law shall be passed.

No Capitation, or other direct, Tax shall be laid, unless in Proportion to the Census or Enumeration herein before directed to be taken.

No Tax or Duty shall be laid on Articles exported from any State.

No Preference shall be given by any Regulation of Commerce or Revenue to the Ports of one State over those of another: nor shall Vessels bound to, or from, one State, be obliged to enter, clear, or pay Duties in another.

No Money shall be drawn from the Treasury, but in Consequence of Appropriations made by Law, and a regular Statement and Account of the Receipts and Expenditures of all public Money shall be published from time to time.

No Title of Nobility shall be granted by the United States: And no Person holding any Office of Profit or Trust under them, shall, without the Consent of the Congress, accept of any present, Emolument, Office, or Title, of any kind whatever, from any King, Prince, or foreign State.

Section. 10. No State shall enter into any Treaty, Alliance, or Confederation; grant Letters of Marque and Reprisal; coin Money; emit bills of Credit; make any Thing but gold and silver Coin a Tender in Payment of Debts; pass any Bill of Attainder, ex post facto Law, or Law impairing the Obligation of Contracts, or grant any Title of Nobility.

No State shall, without the Consent of the Congress, lay any Imposts or Duties on Imports or Exports, except what may be absolutely necessary for executing its inspection Laws: and the net Produce of all Duties and Imposts, laid by any State on Imports or Exports, shall be for the Use of the Treasury of the United States; and all such Laws shall be subject to the Revision and Controul of the Congress.

No State shall, without the Consent of Congress, lay any Duty of Tonnage, keep Troops or Ships of War in time of peace, enter into any Agreement or Compact with another State, or with a foreign Power, or engage in War, unless actually invaded, or in such imminent Danger as will not admit of delay.

Article. II.

Section. 1. The executive Power shall be vested in a President of the United States of America. He shall hold his Office during the Term of four Years, and, together with the Vice President, chosen for the same Term, be elected, as follows:

Each State shall appoint, in such Manner as the Legislature thereof may direct, a Number of Electors, equal to the whole Number of Senators and Representatives to which the State may be entitled in the Congress: but no Senator or Representative, or Person holding an Office of Trust or Profit under the United States, shall be appointed an Elector.

The Electors shall meet in their respective States, and vote by Ballot for two Persons, of whom one at least shall not be an Inhabitant of the same State with themselves. And they shall make a List of all the Persons voted for, and of the Number of Votes for each; which List they shall sign and certify, and transmit sealed to the Seat of the Government of the United States, directed to the President of the Senate. The President of the Senate shall, in the Presence of the Senate and House of Representatives, open all the Certificates, and the Votes shall then be counted. The Person having the greatest Number of Votes shall be the President, if such Number be a Majority of the whole Number of Electors appointed; and if there be more than one who have such Majority, and have an equal Number of Votes, then the House of Representatives shall immediately chuse by Ballot one of them for President; and if no Person have a Majority, then from the five highest on the List the said House shall in like Manner chuse the President. But in chusing the President, the Votes shall be taken by States, the Representation from each State having one Vote; A quorum for this Purpose shall consist of a Member or Members from two thirds of the States, and a Majority of all the States shall be necessary to a Choice. In every Case, after the Choice of the President, the Person having the greatest Number of Votes of the Electors shall be the Vice President. But if there should remain two or more who have equal Votes, the Senate shall chuse from them by Ballot the Vice President. *

The Congress may determine the Time of chusing the Electors, and the Day on which they shall give their Votes; which Day·shall be the same throughout the United States.

No Person except a natural born Citizen, or a Citizen of the United States, at the time of the Adoption of this Constitution, shall be eligible to the Office of President, neither shall any Person be eligible to that Office who shall not have attained to the Age of thirty five Years, and been fourteen Years a Resident within the United States.

In Case of the Removal of the President from Office, or of his Death, Resignation, or Inability to discharge the Powers and Duties of the said Office, the Same shall devolve on the Vice President, and the Congress may by Law provide for the Case of Removal, Death, Resignation or Inability, both of the President and Vice President, declaring what Officer shall then act as President, and such Officer shall act accordingly, until the Disability be removed, or a President shall be elected. †

The President shall, at stated Times, receive for his Services, a Compensation, which shall neither be encreased nor diminished during the Period for which he shall have been elected, and he shall not receive within that Period any other Emolument from the United States, or any of them.

Before he enter on the Execution of his Office, he shall take the following Oath or Affirmation:—"I do solemnly swear (or affirm) that I will faithfully execute the Office of President of the United States, and will to the best of my Ability, preserve, protect and defend the Constitution of the United States."

Section. 2. The President shall be Commander in Chief of the Army and Navy of the United States, and of the Militia of the several States, when called into the actual Service of the United States; he may require the Opinion, in writing, of the principal Officer in each of the executive Departments, upon any Subject relating to the Duties of their respective Offices, and he shall have Power to grant Reprieves and Pardons for Offences against the United States, except in cases of Impeachment.

He shall have Power, by and with the Advice and Consent of the Senate, to make Treaties, provided two thirds of the Senators present concur; and he shall nominate, and by and with the Advice and Consent of the Senate, shall appoint Ambassadors, other public Ministers and Consuls, Judges of the supreme Court, and all other Officers of the United States, whose Appointments are not herein otherwise provided for, and which shall be established by Law; but the Congress may by Law vest the Appointment of such inferior Officers, as they think proper, in the President alone, in the Courts of Law, or in the Heads of Departments.

The President shall have Power to fill up all Vacancies that may happen during the Recess of the Senate, by granting Commissions which shall expire at the End of their next Session.

Section. 3. He shall from time to time give to the Congress Information of the State of the Union, and recommend to their Consideration such Measures as he shall judge necessary and expedient; he may, on extraordinary Occasions, convene both Houses, or either of them, and in Case of Disagreement between them, with Respect to the Time of Adjournment, he may adjourn them to such Time as he shall think proper; he shall receive Ambassadors and other public Ministers; he shall take Care that the Laws be faithfully executed, and shall Commission all the Officers of the United States.

Section. 4. the President, Vice President and all civil Officers of the United States, shall be removed from Office on Impeachment for, and Conviction of, Treason, Bribery, or other high Crimes and Misdemeanors.

Article. III.

Section. 1. The judicial Power of the United States, shall be vested in one supreme Court, and in such inferior Courts as the Congress may from time to time ordain and establish. The Judges, both of the supreme and inferior Courts, shall hold their Offices during good Behaviour, and shall, at stated Times, receive for their Services, a Compensation, which shall not be diminished during their Continuance in Office.

Section. 2. The judicial Power shall extend to all Cases, in Law and Equity, arising under this Constitution, the Laws of the United States, and Treaties made, or which shall be made, under their Authority;—to all Cases affecting Ambassadors, other public Ministers and Consuls;—to all Cases of admiralty and maritime Jurisdiction;—to Controversies to which the United States shall be a Party;—to Controversies between two or more States;—between a State and Citizens of another State; *—between Citizens of different States,—between Citizens of the same State claiming Lands under Grants of different States, and between a State, or the Citizens thereof, and foreign States, Citizens or Subjects.

---

*Superseded by the Twelfth Amendment.
†Modified by the Twenty-fifth Amendment.

*Modified by the Eleventh Amendment.

In all Cases affecting Ambassadors, other public Ministers and Consuls, and those in which a State shall be Party, the supreme Court shall have original Jurisdiction. In all the other Cases before mentioned, the supreme Court shall have appellate Jurisdiction, both as to Law and Fact, with such Exceptions, and under such Regulations as the Congress shall make.

The Trial of all Crimes, except in Cases of Impeachment, shall be by Jury; and such Trial shall be held in the State where the said Crimes shall have been committed; but when not committed within any State, the trial shall be at such Place or Places as the Congress may by Law have directed. Section. 3. Treason against the United States, shall consist only in levying War against them, or in adhering to their Enemies, giving them Aid and Comfort. No Person shall be convicted of Treason unless on the Testimony of two Witnesses to the same overt Act, or on Confession in open Court.

The Congress shall have Power to declare the Punishment of Treason, but no Attainder of Treason shall work Corruption of Blood, or Forfeiture except during the Life of the Person attainted.

Article. IV.

Section. 1. Full Faith and Credit shall be given in each State to the public Acts, Records, and judicial Proceedings of every other State. And the Congress may by general Laws prescribe the Manner in which such Acts, Records and Proceedings shall be proved, and the Effect thereof.
Section. 2. The Citizens of each State shall be entitled to all Privileges and Immunities of Citizens in the several States.

A Person charged in any State with Treason, Felony, or other Crime, who shall flee from Justice, and be found in another State, shall on Demand of the executive Authority of the State from which he fled, be delivered up, to be removed to the State having Jurisdiction of the Crime.

No Person held to Service or Labour in one State, under the Laws thereof, escaping into another, shall, in Consequence of any Law or Regulation therein, be discharged from such Service or Labour, but shall be delivered up on Claim of the Party to whom such Service or Labour may be due.
Section. 3. New States may be admitted by the Congress into this Union; but no new State shall be formed or erected within the Jurisdiction of any other State, nor any State be formed by the Junction of two or more States, or Parts of States, without the Consent of the Legislatures of the States concerned as well as of the Congress.

The Congress shall have Power to dispose of and make all needful Rules and Regulations respecting the Territory or other Property belonging to the United States; and nothing in this Constitution shall be so construed as to Prejudice any Claims of the Untied States, or of any particular State.
Section. 4. The United States shall guarantee to every State in this Union a Republican Form of Government, and shall protect each of them against Invasion; and on Application of the Legislature, or of the Executive (when the Legislature cannot be convened) against domestic Violence.

Article. V.

The Congress, whenever two thirds of both Houses shall deem it necessary, shall propose Amendments to this Constitution, or, on the Application of the Legislatures of two thirds of the several States, shall call a Convention for proposing Amendments, which, in either Case, shall be valid to all Intents and Purposes, as Part of this Constitution, when ratified by the Legislatures of three fourths of the several States, or by Conventions in three fourths thereof, as the one or the other Mode of Ratification may be proposed by the Congress; Provided that no Amendment which may be made prior to the Year One thousand eight hundred and eight shall in any Manner affect the first and fourth Clauses in the Ninth Section of the first Article; and that no State, without its Consent, shall be deprived of its equal Suffrage in the Senate.

Article. VI.

All Debts contracted and Engagements entered into, before the Adoption of this Constitution, shall be as valid against the United States under this Constitution, as under the Confederation.

This Constitution, and the Laws of the United States which shall be made in Pursuance thereof; and all Treaties made, or which shall be made, under the Authority of the United States, shall be the supreme Law of the Land; and the Judges in every State shall be bound thereby, any Thing in the Constitution or Laws of any State to the Contrary notwithstanding.

The Senators and Representatives before mentioned, and the Members of the several State Legislatures, and all executive and judicial Officers, both of the United States and of the several States, shall be bound by Oath or Affirmation, to support this Constitution; but no religious Test shall ever be required as a Qualification to any Office or public Trust under the United States.

Article. VII.

The Ratification of the Conventions of nine States, shall be sufficient for the Establishment of this Constitution between the States so ratifying the Same.

done in Convention by the Unanimous Consent of the States present the Seventeenth Day of September in the Year of our Lord one thousand seven hundred and Eighty seven and of the Independence of the United States of America the Twelfth. *In witness* whereof We have hereunto subscribed our Names,

Articles in Addition to, and Amendment of, the Constitution of the United States of America, Proposed by Congress, and Ratified by the Legislatures of the Several States, Pursuant to the Fifth Article of the Original Constitution.

Amendment I*

Congress shall make no law respecting an establishment of religion, or prohibiting the free exercise thereof, or abridging the freedom of speech, or of the press; or the right of the people peaceably to assemble, and to petition the Government for a redress of grievances.

Amendment II

A well regulated Militia, being necessary to the security of a free State, the right of the people to keep and bear Arms shall not be infringed.

Amendment III

No Soldier shall, in time of peace, be quartered in any house, without the consent of the Owner, nor in time of war, but in a manner to be prescribed by law.

Amendment IV

The right of the people to be secure in their persons, houses, papers, and effects, against unreasonable searches and seizures, shall not be violated, and no Warrants shall

*The first ten amendments were passed by Congress September 25, 1789. They were ratified by three-fourths of the states December 15, 1791.

issue, but upon probable cause, supported by Oath or affirmation, and particularly describing the place to be searched, and the persons or things to be seized.

Amendment V

No person shall be held to answer for a capital or otherwise infamous crime, unless on a presentment or indictment of a Grand Jury, except in cases arising in the land or naval forces, or in the Militia, when in actual service in time of War or public danger; nor shall any person be subject for the same offence to be twice put in jeopardy of life or limb; nor shall be compelled in any criminal case to be a witness against himself, nor be deprived of life, liberty, or property, without due process of law; nor shall private property be taken for public use, without just compensation.

Amendment VI

In all criminal prosecutions, the accused shall enjoy the right to a speedy and public trial, by an impartial jury of the State and district wherein the crime shall have been committed, which district shall have been previously ascertained by law, and to be informed of the nature and cause of the accusation; to be confronted with the witnesses against him; to have compulsory process for obtaining witnesses in his favor, and to have the Assistance of Counsel for his defence.

Amendment VII

In suits at common law, where the value in controversy shall exceed twenty dollars, the right of trial by jury shall be preserved, and no fact tried by a jury, shall be otherwise reexamined in any Court of the United States, than according to the rules of the common law.

Amendment VIII

Excessive bail shall not be required, nor excessive fines imposed, nor cruel and unusual punishments inflicted.

Amendment IX

The enumeration in the Constitution, of certain rights, shall not be construed to deny or disparage others retained by the people.

Amendment X

The powers not delegated to the United States by the Constitution; nor prohibited by it to the States, are reserved to the States respectively, or to the people.

Amendment XI*

The Judicial power of the United States shall not be construed to extend to any suit in law or equity, commenced or prosecuted against one of the United States by Citizens of another State, or by Citizens or Subjects of any Foreign State.

Amendment XII†

The Electors shall meet in their respective States and vote by ballot for President and Vice-President, one of whom, at least, shall not be an inhabitant of the same State with themselves; they shall name in their ballots the person voted for as President, and in distinct ballots the person voted for as Vice-President, and they shall make distinct lists of all persons voted for as President, and of all persons voted for as Vice-President, and of the number of votes for each, which lists they shall sign and certify, and transmit sealed to the seat of the government of the United States, directed to the President of the Senate;—The President of the Senate shall, in the presence of the Senate and House of Representatives, open all the certificates and the votes shall then be counted;—The person having the greatest number of votes for President, shall be the President, if such number be a majority of the whole number of Electors appointed; and if no person have such majority, then from the persons having the highest numbers not exceeding three on the list of those voted for as President, the House of Representatives shall choose immediately, by ballot, the President. But in choosing the President, the votes shall be taken by states, the representation from each state having one vote; a quorum for this purpose shall consist of a member or members from two-thirds of the states, and a majority of all the states shall be necessary to a choice. And if the House of Representatives shall not choose a President whenever the right of choice shall devolve upon them, before the fourth day of March next following, then the Vice-President shall act as President, as in the case of the death or other constitutional disability of the President.—The person having the greatest number of

votes as Vice-President, shall be the Vice-President, if such number be a majority of the whole number of Electors appointed, and if no person have a majority, then from the two highest numbers on the list, the Senate shall choose the Vice-President; a quorum for the purpose shall consist of two-thirds of the whole number of Senators, and a majority of the whole number shall be necessary to a choice. But no person constitutionally ineligible to the office of President shall be eligible to that of Vice-President of the United States.

Amendment XIII*

Section. 1. Neither slavery nor involuntary servitude, except as a punishment for crime whereof the party shall have been duly convicted, shall exist within the United States, or any place subject to their jurisdiction.
Section. 2. Congress shall have power to enforce this article by appropriate legislation.

Amendment XIV†

Section. 1. All persons born or naturalized in the United States, and subject to the jurisdiction thereof, are citizens of the United States and of the State wherein they reside. No State shall make or enforce any law which shall abridge the privileges or immunities of citizens of the United States; nor shall any State deprive any person of life, liberty, or property, without due process of law; nor deny to any person within its jurisdiction the equal protection of the laws.
Section. 2. Representatives shall be apportioned among the several States according to their respective numbers, counting the whole number of persons in each State, excluding Indians not taxed. But when the right to vote at any election for the choice of electors for President and Vice-President of the United States, Representatives in Congress, the Executive and Judicial officers of a State, or the members of the Legislature thereof, is denied to any of the male inhabitants of such State, being twenty-one years of age, and citizens of the United States, or in any way abridged, except for participation in rebellion, or other crime, the basis of representation therein shall be reduced in the proportion which the number of such male citizens shall bear to the whole number of male citizens twenty-one years of age in such State.
Section. 3. No person shall be a Senator or Representative in Congress, or elector of President and Vice-President, or hold

---

*Passed March 4, 1794. Ratified January 23, 1795.
†Passed December 9, 1803. Ratified June 15, 1804.

*Passed January 31, 1865. Ratified December 6, 1865.
†Passed June 13, 1866. Ratified July 9, 1868.

any office, civil or military, under the United States, or under any State, who, having previously taken an oath, as a member of Congress, or as an officer of the United States, or as a member of any State legislature, or as an executive or judicial officer of any State, to support the Constitution of the United States, shall have engaged in insurrection or rebellion against the same, or given aid or comfort to the enemies thereof. But Congress may by a vote of two-thirds of each House, remove such disability.

Section. 4. The validity of the public debt of the United States, authorized by law, including debts incurred for payment of pensions and bounties for services in suppressing insurrection or rebellion, shall not be questioned. But neither the United States nor any State shall assume or pay any debt or obligation incurred in aid of insurrection or rebellion against the United States, or any claim for the loss or emancipation of any slave; but all such debts, obligations, and claims shall be held illegal and void.

Section. 5. The Congress shall have the power to enforce, by appropriate legislation, the provisions of this article.

Amendment XV*

Section. 1. The right of citizens of the United States to vote shall not be denied or abridged by the United States or by any State on account of race, color, or previous condition of servitude—

Section. 2. The Congress shall have power to enforce this article by appropriate legislation.

Amendment XVI†

The Congress shall have power to lay and collect taxes on incomes, from whatever source derived, without apportionment among the several States, and without regard to any census or enumeration.

Amendment XVII‡

The Senate of the United States shall be composed of two Senators from each State, elected by the people thereof, for six years; and each Senator shall have one vote. The electors in each State shall have the qualifications requisite for electors of the most numerous branch of the State legislatures.

When vacancies happen in the representation of any State in the Senate, the executive authority of such State shall issue writs of election to fill such vacancies: *Provided,* That the legislature of any State may empower the executive thereof to make temporary appointments until the people fill the vacancies by election as the legislature may direct.

This amendment shall not be so construed as to affect the election or term of any Senator chosen before it becomes valid as part of the Constitution.

Amendment XVIII*

Section. 1. After one year from the ratification of this article the manufacture, sale, or transportation of intoxicating liquors within, the importation thereof into, or the exportation thereof from the United States and all territory subject to the jurisdiction thereof for beverage purposes is hereby prohibited.

Section. 2. The Congress and the several States shall have concurrent power to enforce this article by appropriate legislation.

Section. 3. This article shall be inoperative unless it shall have been ratified as an amendment to the Constitution by the legislatures of the several States, as provided in the Constitution, within seven years from the date of the submission hereof to the States by the Congress.

Amendment XIX†

The right of citizens of the United States to vote shall not be denied or abridged by the United States or by any State on account of sex.

Congress shall have power to enforce this article by appropriate legislation.

Amendment XX‡

Section. 1. The terms of the President and Vice-President shall end at noon on the 20th day of January, and the terms of Senators and Representatives at noon on the 3d day of January, of the years in which such terms would have ended if this article had not been ratified; and the terms of their successors shall then begin.

Section. 2. The Congress shall assemble at least once in every year, and such meeting shall begin at noon on the 3d day of January, unless they shall by law appoint a different day.

---

*Passed February 26, 1869. Ratified February 2, 1870.
†Passed July 12, 1909. Ratified February 3, 1913.
‡Passed May 13, 1912. Ratified April 8, 1913.

*Passed December 18, 1917. Ratified January 16, 1919.
†Passed June 4, 1919. Ratified August 18, 1920.
‡Passed March 2, 1932. Ratified January 23, 1933.

Section. 3. If, at the time fixed for the beginning of the term of the President, the President elect shall have died, the Vice-President elect shall become President. If a President shall not have been chosen before the time fixed for the beginning of his term, or if the President elect shall have failed to qualify, then the Vice-President elect shall act as President until a President shall have qualified; and the Congress may by law provide for the case wherein neither a President elect nor a Vice-President elect shall have qualified, declaring who shall then act as President, or the manner in which one who is to act shall be selected, and such person shall act accordingly until a President or Vice-President shall have qualified.

Section. 4. The Congress may by law provide for the case of the death of any of the persons from whom the House of Representatives may choose a President whenever the right of choice shall have devolved upon them, and for the case of the death of any of the persons from whom the Senate may choose a Vice-President whenever the right of choice shall have devolved upon them.

Section. 5. Sections 1 and 2 shall take effect on the 15th day of October following the ratification of this article.

Section. 6. This article shall be inoperative unless it shall have been ratified as an amendment to the Constitution by the legislatures of three-fourths of the several States within seven years from the date of its submission.

Amendment XXI*

Section. 1. The eighteenth article of amendment to the Constitution of the United States is hereby repealed.

Section. 2. The transportation or importation into any State, Territory, or possession of the United States for delivery or use therein of intoxicating liquors, in violation of the laws thereof, is hereby prohibited.

Section. 3. This article shall be inoperative unless it shall have been ratified as an amendment of the Constitution by conventions in the several States, as provided in the Constitution, within seven years from the date of the submission hereof to the States by the Congress.

Amendment XXII†

No person shall be elected to the office of the President more than twice, and no person who has held the office of President, or acted as President, for more than two years of a term to which some other person was elected President shall be elected to the office of the President more than once.

But this Article shall not apply to any person holding the office of President when this Article was proposed by the Congress, and shall not prevent any person who may be holding the office of President, or acting as President, during the term within which this Article becomes operative from holding the office of President or acting as President during the remainder of such term.

Amendment XXIII*

Section. 1. The district constituting the seat of Government of the United States shall appoint in such manner as the Congress may direct:

A number of electors of President and Vice President equal to the whole number of Senators and Representatives in Congress to which the District would be entitled if it were a State, but in no event more than the least populous State; they shall be in addition to those appointed by the States, but they shall be considered, for the purposes of the election of President and Vice President, to be electors appointed by the State; and they shall meet in the District and perform such duties as provided by the twelfth article of amendment.

Section. 2. The Congress shall have power to enforce this article by appropriate legislation.

Amendment XXIV†

Section. 1. The right of citizens of the United States to vote in any primary or other election for President or Vice President, or for Senator or Representative in Congress, shall not be denied or abridged by the United States or any State by reason of failure to pay any poll tax or other tax.

Section. 2. The Congress shall have power to enforce this article by appropriate legislation.

Amendment XXV‡

Section. 1. In case of the removal of the President from office or of his death or resignation, the Vice President shall become President.

Section. 2. Whenever there is a vacancy in the office of the Vice President, the President shall nominate a Vice President who shall take office upon confirmation by a majority vote of both Houses of Congress.

Section. 3. Whenever the President transmits to the Presi-

---

*Passed February 20, 1933. Ratified December 5, 1933.
†Passed March 12, 1947. Ratified March 1, 1951.

*Passed June 16, 1960. Ratified April 3, 1961.
†Passed August 27, 1962. Ratified January 23, 1964.
‡Passed July 6, 1965. Ratified February 11, 1967.

dent pro tempore of the Senate and the Speaker of the House of Representatives his written declaration that he is unable to discharge the powers and duties of his office, and until he transmits to them a written declaration to the contrary, such powers and duties shall be discharged by the Vice President as Acting President.

Section. 4. Whenever the Vice President and a majority of either the principal officers of the executive department or of such other body as Congress may by law provide, transmit to the President pro tempore of the Senate and the Speaker of the House of Representatives their written declaration that the President is unable to discharge the powers and duties of his office, the Vice President shall immediately assume the powers and duties of the office of Acting President.

Thereafter, when the President transmits to the President pro tempore of the Senate and the Speaker of the House of Representatives his written declaration that no inability exists, he shall resume the powers and duties of his office unless the Vice President and a majority of either the principal officers of the executive department or of such other body as Congress may by law provide, transmit within four days to the President pro tempore of the Senate and the Speaker of the House of Representatives their written declaration that the President is unable to discharge the powers and duties of his office. Thereupon Congress shall decide the issue, assembling within forty-eight hours for that purpose if not in session. If the Congress, within twenty-one days after receipt of the latter written declaration, or, if Congress is not in session, within twenty-one days after Congress is required to assemble, determines by two-thirds vote of both Houses that the President is unable to discharge the powers and duties of his office, the Vice President shall continue to discharge the same as Acting President; otherwise, the President shall resume the powers and duties of his office.

Amendment XXVI*

Section. 1. The right of citizens of the United States, who are eighteen years of age or older, to vote shall not be denied or abridged by the United States or by any State on account of age.

Section. 2. The Congress shall have power to enforce this article by appropriate legislation.

*Passed March 23, 1971. Ratified July 5, 1971.

Admission of States

Order of Admission	State	Date of Admission	Order of Admission	State	Date of Admission
1	Delaware	December 7, 1787	26	Michigan	January 26, 1837
2	Pennsylvania	December 12, 1787	27	Florida	March 3, 1845
3	New Jersey	December 18, 1787	28	Texas	December 29, 1845
4	Georgia	January 2, 1788	29	Iowa	December 28, 1846
5	Connecticut	January 9, 1788	30	Wisconsin	May 29, 1848
6	Massachusetts	February 6, 1788	31	California	September 9, 1850
7	Maryland	April 28, 1788	32	Minnesota	May 11, 1858
8	South Carolina	May 23, 1788	33	Oregon	February 14, 1859
9	New Hampshire	June 21, 1788	34	Kansas	January 29, 1861
10	Virginia	June 25, 1788	35	West Virginia	June 20, 1863
11	New York	July 26, 1788	36	Nevada	October 31, 1864
12	North Carolina	November 21, 1789	37	Nebraska	March 1, 1867
13	Rhode Island	May 29, 1790	38	Colorado	August 1, 1876
14	Vermont	March 4, 1791	39	North Dakota	November 2, 1889
15	Kentucky	June 1, 1792	40	South Dakota	November 2, 1889
16	Tennessee	June 1, 1796	41	Montana	November 8, 1889
17	Ohio	March 1, 1803	42	Washington	November 11, 1889
18	Louisiana	April 30, 1812	43	Idaho	July 3, 1890
19	Indiana	December 11, 1816	44	Wyoming	July 10, 1890
20	Mississippi	December 10, 1817	45	Utah	January 4, 1896
21	Illinois	December 3, 1818	46	Oklahoma	November 16, 1907
22	Alabama	December 14, 1819	47	New Mexico	January 6, 1912
23	Maine	March 15, 1820	48	Arizona	February 14, 1912
24	Missouri	August 10, 1821	49	Alaska	January 3, 1959
25	Arkansas	June 15, 1836	50	Hawaii	August 21, 1959

Growth of U.S. Population and Area

Census	Population of United States	Increase over the Preceding Census		Land Area (Sq. Mi.)	Pop. per Sq. Mi.
		Number	Percent		
1790	3,929,214			867,980	4.5
1800	5,308,483	1,379,269	35.1	867,980	6.1
1810	7,239,881	1,931,398	36.4	1,685,865	4.3
1820	9,638,453	2,398,572	33.1	1,753,588	5.5
1830	12,866,020	3,227,567	33.5	1,753,588	7.3
1840	17,069,453	4,203,433	32.7	1,753,588	9.7
1850	23,191,876	6,122,423	35.9	2,944,337	7.9
1860	31,433,321	8,251,445	35.6	2,973,965	10.6
1870	39,818,449	8,375,128	26.6	2,973,965	13.4
1880	50,155,783	10,337,334	26.0	2,973,965	16.9
1890	62,947,714	12,791,931	25.5	2,973,965	21.2
1900	75,994,575	13,046,861	20.7	2,974,159	25.6
1910	91,972,266	15,997,691	21.0	2,973,890	30.9
1920	105,710,620	13,738,354	14.9	2,973,776	35.5
1930	122,775,046	17,064,426	16.1	2,977,128	41.2
1940	131,669,275	8,894,229	7.2	2,977,128	44.2
1950	150,697,361	19,028,086	14.5	2,974,726*	50.7
1960 †	179,323,175	28,625,814	19.0	3,540,911	50.6
1970	203,235,298	23,912,123	13.3	3,536,855	57.5
1980	226,504,825	23,269,527	11.4	3,536,855	64.0

*As measured in 1940; shrinkage offset by increase in water area.
†First year for which figures include Alaska and Hawaii.

Political Party Affiliations in Congress and the Presidency, 1789–1989*

Congress	Year	House Majority Party	House Principal Minority Party	House Other except Vacancies	Senate Majority Party	Senate Principal Minority Party	Senate Other except Vacancies	President and Party
1st	1789–1791	Ad-38	Op-26	—	Ad-17	Op-9	—	F (Washington)
2d	1791–1793	F-37	DR-33	—	F-16	DR-13	—	F (Washington)
3d	1793–1795	DR-57	F-48	—	F-17	DR-13	—	F (Washington)
4th	1795–1797	F-54	DR-52	—	F-19	DR-13	—	F (Washington)
5th	1797–1799	F-58	DR-48	—	F-20	DR-12	—	F (John Adams)
6th	1799–1801	F-64	DR-42	—	F-19	DR-13	—	F (John Adams)
7th	1801–1803	DR-69	F-36	—	DR-18	F-13	—	DR (Jefferson)
8th	1803–1805	DR-102	F-39	—	DR-25	F-9	—	DR (Jefferson)
9th	1805–1807	DR-116	F-25	—	DR-27	F-7	—	DR (Jefferson)
10th	1807–1809	DR-118	F-24	—	DR-28	F-6	—	DR (Jefferson)
11th	1809–1811	DR-94	F-48	—	DR-28	F-6	—	DR (Madison)
12th	1811–1813	DR-108	F-36	—	DR-30	F-6	—	DR (Madison)
13th	1813–1815	DR-112	F-68	—	DR-27	F-9	—	DR (Madison)
14th	1815–1817	DR-117	F-65	—	DR-25	F-11	—	DR (Madison)
15th	1817–1819	DR-141	F-42	—	DR-34	F-10	—	DR (Monroe)
16th	1819–1821	DR-156	F-27	—	DR-35	F-7	—	DR (Monroe)
17th	1821–1823	DR-158	F-25	—	DR-44	F-4	—	DR (Monroe)
18th	1823–1825	DR-187	F-26	—	DR-44	F-4	—	DR (Monroe)
19th	1825–1827	Ad-105	J-97	—	Ad-26	J-20	—	C (J. Q. Adams)
20th	1827–1829	J-119	Ad-94	—	J-28	Ad-20	—	C (J. Q. Adams)
21st	1829–1831	D-139	NR-74	—	D-26	NR-22	—	D (Jackson)
22nd	1831–1833	D-141	NR-58	14	D-25	NR-21	2	D (Jackson)
23rd	1833–1835	D-147	AM-53	60	D-20	NR-20	8	D (Jackson)
24th	1835–1837	D-145	W-98	—	D-27	W-25	—	D (Jackson)
25th	1837–1839	D-108	W-107	24	D-30	W-18	4	D (Van Buren)
26th	1839–1841	D-124	W-118	—	D-28	W-22	—	D (Van Buren)
27th	1841–1843	W-133	D-102	6	W-28	D-22	2	W (Harrison) W (Tyler)
28th	1843–1845	D-142	W-79	1	W-28	D-25	1	W (Tyler)
29th	1845–1847	D-143	W-77	6	D-31	W-25	—	D (Polk)
30th	1847–1849	W-115	D-108	4	D-36	W-21	1	D (Polk)
31st	1849–1851	D-112	W-109	9	D-35	W-25	2	W (Taylor) W (Fillmore)
32d	1851–1853	D-140	W-88	5	D-35	W-24	3	W (Fillmore)
33d	1853–1855	D-159	W-71	4	D-38	W-22	2	D (Pierce)
34th	1855–1857	R-108	D-83	43	D-40	R-15	5	D (Pierce)
35th	1857–1859	D-118	R-92	26	D-36	R-20	8	D (Buchanan)
36th	1859–1861	R-114	D-92	31	D-36	R-26	4	D (Buchanan)
37th	1861–1863	R-105	D-43	30	R-31	D-10	8	R (Lincoln)
38th	1863–1865	R-102	D-75	9	R-36	D-9	5	R (Lincoln)
39th	1865–1867	U-149	D-42	—	U-42	D-10	—	R (Lincoln) R (Johnson)
40th	1867–1869	R-143	D-49	—	R-42	D-11	—	R (Johnson)
41st	1869–1871	R-149	D-63	—	R-56	D-11	—	R (Grant)
42d	1871–1873	R-134	D-104	5	R-52	D-17	5	R (Grant)
43d	1873–1875	R-194	D-92	14	R-49	D-19	5	R (Grant)
44th	1875–1877	D-169	R-109	14	R-45	D-29	2	R (Grant)
45th	1877–1879	D-153	R-140	—	R-39	D-36	1	R (Hayes)
46th	1879–1881	D-149	R-130	14	D-42	R-33	1	R (Hayes)

*Letter symbols for political parties. Ad—Administration; AM—Anti-Masonic; C—Coalition; D—Democratic; DR—Democratic-Republican; F—Federalist; J—Jacksonian; NR—National-Republican; Op—Opposition; R—Republican; U—Unionist; W—Whig.
Source: *Historical Statistics of the United States: Colonial Times to the Present*, Various eds. Washington, D.C.: GOP.

Political Party Affiliations in Congress and the Presidency, 1789–1989* *(continued)*

| Congress | Year | House | | | Senate | | | President and Party |
		Majority Party	Principal Minority Party	Other except Vacancies	Majority Party	Principal Minority Party	Other except Vacancies	
47th	1881–1883	R-147	D-135	11	R-37	D-37	1	R (Garfield)
								R (Arthur)
48th	1883–1885	D-197	R-118	10	R-38	D-36	2	R (Arthur)
49th	1885–1887	D-183	R-140	2	R-43	D-34	—	D (Cleveland)
50th	1887–1889	D-169	R-152	4	R-39	D-37	—	D (Cleveland)
51st	1889–1891	R-166	D-159	—	R-39	D-37	—	R (B. Harrison)
52d	1891–1893	D-235	R-88	9	R-47	D-39	2	R (B. Harrison)
53d	1893–1895	D-218	R-127	11	D-44	R-38	3	D (Cleveland)
54th	1895–1897	R-244	D-105	7	R-43	D-39	6	D (Cleveland)
55th	1897–1899	R-204	D-113	40	R-47	D-34	7	R (McKinley)
56th	1899–1901	R-185	D-163	9	R-53	D-26	8	R (McKinley)
57th	1901–1903	R-197	D-151	9	R-55	D-31	4	R (McKinley)
								R (T. Roosevelt)
58th	1903–1905	R-208	D-178	—	R-57	D-33	—	R (T. Roosevelt)
59th	1905–1907	R-250	D-136	—	R-57	D-33	—	R (T. Roosevelt)
60th	1907–1909	R-222	D-164	—	R-61	D-31	—	R (T. Roosevelt)
61st	1909–1911	R-219	D-172	—	R-61	D-32	—	R (Taft)
62d	1911–1913	D-228	R-161	1	R-51	D-41	—	R (Taft)
63d	1913–1915	D-291	R-127	17	D-51	R-44	1	D (Wilson)
64th	1915–1917	D-230	R-196	9	D-56	R-40	—	D (Wilson)
65th	1917–1919	D-216	R-210	6	D-53	R-42	—	D (Wilson)
66th	1919–1921	R-240	D-190	3	R-49	D-47	—	D (Wilson)
67th	1921–1923	R-301	D-131	1	R-59	D-37	—	R (Harding)
68th	1923–1925	R-225	D-205	5	R-51	D-43	2	R (Coolidge)
69th	1925–1927	R-247	D-183	4	R-56	D-39	1	R (Coolidge)
70th	1927–1929	R-237	D-195	3	R-49	D-46	1	R (Coolidge)
71st	1929–1931	R-267	D-167	1	R-56	D-39	1	R (Hoover)
72d	1931–1933	D-220	R-214	1	R-48	D-47	1	R (Hoover)
73d	1933–1935	D-310	R-117	5	D-60	R-35	1	D (F. Roosevelt)
74th	1935–1937	D-319	R-103	10	D-69	R-25	2	D (F. Roosevelt)
75th	1937–1939	D-331	R-89	13	D-76	R-16	4	D (F. Roosevelt)
76th	1939–1941	D-261	R-164	4	D-69	R-23	4	D (F. Roosevelt)
77th	1941–1943	D-268	R-162	5	D-66	R-28	2	D (F. Roosevelt)
78th	1943–1945	D-218	R-208	4	D-58	R-37	1	D (F. Roosevelt)
79th	1945–1947	D-242	R-190	2	D-56	R-38	1	D (Truman)
80th	1947–1949	R-245	D-188	1	R-51	D-45	—	D (Truman)
81st	1949–1951	D-263	R-171	1	D-54	R-42	—	D (Truman)
82d	1951–1953	D-243	R-199	1	D-49	R-47	—	D (Truman)
83d	1953–1955	R-221	D-211	1	R-48	D-47	1	R (Eisenhower)
84th	1955–1957	D-232	R-203	—	D-48	R-47	1	R (Eisenhower)
85th	1957–1959	D-233	R-200	—	D-49	R-47	—	R (Eisenhower)
86th	1959–1961	D-283	R-153	—	D-64	R-34	—	R (Eisenhower)
87th	1961–1963	D-263	R-174	—	D-65	R-35	—	D (Kennedy)
88th	1963–1965	D-258	R-177	—	D-67	R-33	—	D (Kennedy)
								D (Johnson)
89th	1965–1967	D-295	R-140	—	D-68	R-32	—	D (Johnson)
90th	1967–1969	D-247	R-187	1	D-64	R-36	—	D (Johnson)
91st	1969–1971	D-243	R-192	—	D-58	R-42	—	R (Nixon)
92nd	1971–1973	D-255	R-180	—	D-54	R-44	2	R (Nixon)
93rd	1973–1975	D-242	R-192	1	D-56	R-42	2	R (Nixon, Ford)
94th	1975–1977	D-291	R-144	—	D-61	R-37	2	R (Ford)
95th	1977–1979	D-292	R-143	—	D-61	R-38	1	D (Carter)
96th	1979–1981	D-277	R-158	—	D-58	R-41	1	D (Carter)
97th	1981–1983	D-242	R-192	—	R-54	D-45	1	R (Reagan)
98th	1983–1985	D-266	R-167	2	R-55	D-45	—	R (Reagan)
99th	1985–1987	D-252	R-183	—	R-53	D-47	—	R (Reagan)
100th	1987–1989	D-258	R-177	—	D-55	R-45	—	R (Reagan)

Presidential Elections, 1789–1989*

Year	Voter Participation (Percentage)	Candidates	Parties	Popular Vote	Electoral Vote	Percentage of Popular Vote
1789		GEORGE WASHINGTON	No party designations		69	
		John Adams			34	
		Minor Candidates			35	
1792		GEORGE WASHINGTON	No party designations		132	
		John Adams			77	
		George Clinton			50	
		Minor Candidates			5	
1796		JOHN ADAMS	Federalist		71	
		Thomas Jefferson	Democratic-Republican		68	
		Thomas Pinckney	Federalist		59	
		Aaron Burr	Democratic-Republican		30	
		Minor Candidates			48	
1800		THOMAS JEFFERSON	Democratic-Republican		73	
		Aaron Burr	Democratic-Republican		73	
		John Adams	Federalist		65	
		Charles C. Pinckney	Federalist		64	
		John Jay	Federalist		1	
1804		THOMAS JEFFERSON	Democratic-Republican		162	
		Charles C. Pinckney	Federalist		14	
1808		JAMES MADISON	Democratic-Republican		122	
		Charles C. Pinckney	Federalist		47	
		George Clinton	Democratic-Republican		6	
1812		JAMES MADISON	Democratic-Republican		128	
		DeWitt Clinton	Federalist		89	
1816		JAMES MONROE	Democratic-Republican		183	
		Rufus King	Federalist		34	
1820		JAMES MONROE	Democratic-Republican		231	
		John Quincy Adams	Independent Republican		1	
1824	26.9	JOHN QUINCY ADAMS	Democratic-Republican	108,740	84	30.5
		Andrew Jackson	Democratic-Republican	153,544	99	43.1
		William H. Crawford	Democratic-Republican	46,618	41	13.1
		Henry Clay	Democratic-Republican	47,136	37	13.2
1828	57.6	ANDREW JACKSON	Democratic	647,286	178	56.0
		John Quincy Adams	National Republican	508,064	83	44.0
1832	55.4	ANDREW JACKSON	Democratic	687,502	219	55.0
		Henry Clay	National Republican	530,189	49	42.4
		William Wirt	Anti-Masonic	33,108	7	2.6
		John Floyd	National Republican		11	
1836	57.8	MARTIN VAN BUREN	Democratic	765,483	170	50.9
		William H. Harrison	Whig		73	
		Hugh L. White	Whig	739,795	26	49.1
		Daniel Webster	Whig		14	
		W. P. Mangum	Whig		11	
1840	80.2	WILLIAM H. HARRISON	Whig	1,274,624	234	53.1
		Martin Van Buren	Democratic	1,127,781	60	46.9
1844	78.9	JAMES K. POLK	Democratic	1,338,464	170	49.6
		Henry Clay	Whig	1,300,097	105	48.1
		James G. Birney	Liberty	62,300		2.3
1848	72.7	ZACHARY TAYLOR	Whig	1,360,967	163	47.4
		Lewis Cass	Democratic	1,222,342	127	42.5
		Martin Van Buren	Free Soil	291,263		10.1
1852	69.6	FRANKLIN PIERCE	Democratic	1,601,117	254	50.9
		Winfield Scott	Whig	1,385,453	42	44.1
		John P. Hale	Free Soil	155,825		5.0

Candidates receiving less than 1 percent of the popular vote have been omitted. For that reason the percentage of popular vote given for any election year may not total 100 percent.

Before the passage of the Twelfth Amendment in 1804, the Electoral College voted for two presidential candidates; the runner-up became Vice President. Figures are from *Historical Statistics of the United States, Colonial Times to 1957* (1961), pp. 682–83; the U. S. Department of Justice.

Presidential Elections, 1789–1989 *(continued)*

Year	Voter Participation (Percentage)	Candidates	Parties	Popular Vote	Electoral Vote	Percentage of Popular Vote
1856	78.9	JAMES BUCHANAN	Democratic	1,832,955	174	45.3
		John C. Frémont	Republican	1,339,932	114	33.1
		Millard Fillmore	American	871,731	8	21.6
1860	81.2	ABRAHAM LINCOLN	Republican	1,865,593	180	39.8
		Stephen A. Douglas	Democratic	1,382,713	12	29.5
		John C. Breckinridge	Democratic	848,356	72	18.1
		John Bell	Constitutional Union	592,906	39	12.6
1864	73.8	ABRAHAM LINCOLN	Republican	2,206,938	212	55.0
		George B. McClellan	Democratic	1,803,787	21	45.0
1868	78.1	ULYSSES S. GRANT	Republican	3,013,421	214	52.7
		Horatio Seymour	Democratic	2,706,829	80	47.3
1872	71.3	ULYSSES S. GRANT	Republican	3,596,745	286	55.6
		Horace Greeley	Democratic	2,843,446	*	43.9
1876	81.8	RUTHERFORD B. HAYES	Republican	4,036,572	185	48.0
		Samuel J. Tilden	Democratic	4,284,020	184	51.0
1880	79.4	JAMES A. GARFIELD	Republican	4,453,295	214	48.5
		Winfield S. Hancock	Democratic	4,414,082	155	48.1
		James B. Weaver	Greenback-Labor	308,578		3.4
1884	77.5	GROVER CLEVELAND	Democratic	4,879,507	219	48.5
		James G. Blaine	Republican	4,850,293	182	48.2
		Benjamin F. Butler	Greenback-Labor	175,370		1.8
		John P. St. John	Prohibition	150,369		1.5
1888	79.3	BENJAMIN HARRISON	Republican	5,477,129	233	47.9
		Grover Cleveland	Democratic	5,537,857	168	48.6
		Clinton B. Fisk	Prohibition	249,506		2.2
		Anson J. Streeter	Union Labor	146,935		1.3
1892	74.7	GROVER CLEVELAND	Democratic	5,555,426	277	46.1
		Benjamin Harrison	Republican	5,182,690	145	43.0
		James B. Weaver	People's	1,029,846	22	8.5
		John Bidwell	Prohibition	264,133		2.2
1896	79.3	WILLIAM McKINLEY	Republican	7,102,246	271	51.1
		William J. Bryan	Democratic	6,492,559	176	47.7
1900	73.2	WILLIAM McKINLEY	Republican	7,218,491	292	51.7
		William J. Bryan	Democratic; Populist	6,356,734	155	45.5
		John C. Wooley	Prohibition	208,914		1.5
1904	65.2	THEODORE ROOSEVELT	Republican	7,628,461	336	57.4
		Alton B. Parker	Democratic	5,084,223	140	37.6
		Eugene V. Debs	Socialist	402,283		3.0
		Silas C. Swallow	Prohibition	258,536		1.9
1908	65.4	WILLIAM H. TAFT	Republican	7,675,320	321	51.6
		William J. Bryan	Democratic	6,412,294	162	43.1
		Eugene V. Debs	Socialist	420,793		2.8
		Eugene W. Chafin	Prohibition	253,840		1.7
1912	58.8	WOODROW WILSON	Democratic	6,296,547	435	41.9
		Theodore Roosevelt	Progressive	4,118,571	88	27.4
		William H. Taft	Republican	3,486,720	8	23.2
		Eugene V. Debs	Socialist	900,672		6.0
		Eugene W. Chafin	Prohibition	206,275		1.4

*Greeley died shortly after the election; the electors supporting him then divided their votes among minor candidates.

Candidates receiving less than 1 percent of the popular vote have been omitted. For that reason the percentage of popular vote given for any election year may not total 100 percent.

Presidential Elections, 1789–1989 (continued)

Year	Voter Participation (Percentage)	Candidates	Parties	Popular Vote	Electoral Vote	Percentage of Popular Vote
1916	61.6	WOODROW WILSON	Democratic	9,127,695	277	49.4
		Charles E. Hughes	Republican	8,533,507	254	46.2
		A. L. Benson	Socialist	585,113		3.2
		J. Frank Hanly	Prohibition	220,506		1.2
1920	49.2	WARREN G. HARDING	Republican	16,143,407	404	60.4
		James N. Cox	Democratic	9,130,328	127	34.2
		Eugene V. Debs	Socialist	919,799		3.4
		P. P. Christensen	Farmer-Labor	265,411		1.0
1924	48.9	CALVIN COOLIDGE	Republican	15,718,211	382	54.0
		John W. Davis	Democratic	8,385,283	136	28.8
		Robert M. La Follette	Progressive	4,831,289	13	16.6
1928	56.9	HERBERT C. HOOVER	Republican	21,391,993	444	58.2
		Alfred E. Smith	Democratic	15,016,169	87	40.9
1932	56.9	FRANKLIN D. ROOSEVELT	Democratic	22,809,638	472	57.4
		Herbert C. Hoover	Republican	15,758,901	59	39.7
		Norman Thomas	Socialist	881,951		2.2
1936	61.0	FRANKLIN D. ROOSEVELT	Democratic	27,752,869	523	60.8
		Alfred M. Landon	Republican	16,674,665	8	36.5
		William Lemke	Union	882,479		1.9
1940	62.5	FRANKLIN D. ROOSEVELT	Democratic	27,307,819	449	54.8
		Wendell L. Willkie	Republican	22,321,018	82	44.8
1944	55.9	FRANKLIN D. ROOSEVELT	Democratic	25,606,585	432	53.5
		Thomas E. Dewey	Republican	22,014,745	99	46.0
1948	53.0	HARRY S. TRUMAN	Democratic	24,105,812	303	49.5
		Thomas E. Dewey	Republican	21,970,065	189	45.1
		J. Strom Thurmond	States' Rights	1,169,063	39	2.4
		Henry A. Wallace	Progressive	1,157,172		2.4
1952	63.3	DWIGHT D. EISENHOWER	Republican	33,936,234	442	55.1
		Adlai E. Stevenson	Democratic	27,314,992	89	44.4
1956	60.6	DWIGHT D. EISENHOWER	Republican	35,590,472	457	57.6
		Adlai E. Stevenson	Democratic	26,022,752	73	42.1
1960	64.0	JOHN F. KENNEDY	Democratic	34,227,096	303	49.9
		Richard M. Nixon	Republican	34,108,546	219	49.6
1964	61.7	LYNDON B. JOHNSON	Democratic	43,126,506	486	61.1
		Barry M. Goldwater	Republican	27,176,799	52	38.5
1968	60.6	RICHARD M. NIXON	Republican	31,785,480	301	43.4
		Hubert H. Humphrey	Democratic	31,275,165	191	42.7
		George C. Wallace	American Independent	9,906,473	46	13.5
1972	55.5	RICHARD M. NIXON	Republican	47,169,911	520	60.7
		George S. McGovern	Democratic	29,170,383	17	37.5
1976	54.3	JIMMY CARTER	Democratic	40,827,394	297	50.0
		Gerald R. Ford	Republican	39,145,977	240	47.9
1980	53.2	RONALD W. REAGAN	Republican	43,899,248	489	50.8
		Jimmy Carter	Democratic	35,481,435	49	41.0
		John B. Anderson	Independent	5,719,437		6.6
		Ed Clark	Libertarian	920,859		1.0
1984	53.3	RONALD W. REAGAN	Republican	54,281,858	525	59.0
		Walter Mondale	Democratic	37,457,215	13	41.0
1988	50.2	GEORGE H. BUSH	Republican	48,138,478	426	53.4
		Michael Dukakis	Democrat	41,114,068	112	45.6

Candidates receiving less than 1 percent of the popular vote have been omitted. For that reason the percentage of popular vote given for any election year may not total 100 percent.

Photo Credits

145 *Washington at Verplank's Point* by John Trumbull, 1790. (*Detail*. Oil on canvas 30″ × 20 ⅛″, rectangular) Courtesy Henry Francis Dupont Winterthur Museum
147 Washington University Gallery of Art, St. Louis
148 The Granger Collection
149 Valley Forge National Historic Park, National Park Service, U.S. Department of the Interior
150 Free Library of Philadelphia
151 Anne S. K. Brown Military Collection, Brown University Library

Chapter 10
154 Eastern National Park and Monument Association
156 Abigail Adams by Benjamin Blyth, *ca.* 1766. Courtesy, the Massachusetts Historical Society
164 New-York Historical Society
166 New York Public Library, Rare Book Room
167 New York Public Library Picture Collection
169 Alexander Hamilton by John Trumbull © Yale University Art Gallery
170 John Jay by John Trumbull © Yale University Art Gallery
171 Library of Congress

Chapter 11
174 *Election Day at Independence Hall* by John Lewis Krimmel, 1787. Courtesy of IBM Company
176 Metropolitan Museum of Art
180 HBJ Picture Collection
181 Edmond Charles Genet by Ezra Ames. Gift of George Genêt, collection Albany Institute of History and Art.
184 The Bettmann Archive
186 Indiana Historical Society
187 Brown Brothers
188 Library of Congress
189 John Adams by John Singleton Copley, Gift of Mrs. Charles Francis Adams. Courtesy, Museum of Fine Arts, Boston
190 The Granger Collection

Chapter 12
194 Library of Congress
196 Thomas Jefferson by Rembrandt Peale, New-York Historical Society
198 Maryland Historical Society
200 Chicago Historical Society
202 Missouri Historical Society
203 New-York Historical Society
204 The Bettmann Archive
206 Rhode Island Historical Society
209 (*l*) New York Public Library; (*r*) New-York Historical Society
210 (*l*) Courtesy of the Field Museum of Natural History, Chicago; (*r*) *The Open Door, Known as The Prophet, Brother of Tecumseh* by George Catlin, 1830. National Museum of American Art, Smithsonian Institution. Gift of Mrs. Joseph Harrison, Jr.
212 New-York Historical Society

Chapter 13
214 *Fairview Inn* by Thomas Ruckle, Maryland Historical Society
217 North Carolina Department of Archives and History
218–19 Smithsonian Institution
223 The Granger Collection
224 (*l*) All rights reserved. The Metropolitan Museum of Art, gift of I. N. Phelps Stokes, Edward S. Hawes, Alice Mary Hawes, Marion Hawes, 1937; (*r*) Bureau of Public Roads, Department of the Interior

227 *Flax Scutching Bee* by Linton Park, National Gallery of Art, Washington, D.C., gift of Edward William and Bernice Chrysler Garbisch
229 The Bettmann Archive
230 Library of Congress
232 Daguerreotype by Fantayne and Porter of Brooklyn. Cincinnati Public Library

Chapter 14
234 (*Detail*) *Fourth of July Celebration* by John Lewis Krimmel, 1819, Historical Society of Pennsylvania
237 Art Commission of the City of New York
239 Courtesy, The Shelburne Museum, Shelburne, Vermont
240 *Winter Scene, Brooklyn* by Francis Guy. 1817–1820. Oil on Canvas, 58 ¾″ × 75″, The Brooklyn Institute of Arts and Sciences
241 Culver Pictures
242 The Rhode Island Historical Society
245 New-York Historical Society
246 Courtesy, The Massachusetts Historical Society
247 *The Morning Bell* by Winslow Homer, 1866. Yale University Art Gallery, bequest of Stephen Carlton Clark, BA, 1903
248 The Bettmann Archive

Chapter 15
252 Robert Cruikshank's lithograph of *The President's Levee or All Creation Going to the White House*. White House Collection
255 University of Hartford, J. Doyle DeWitt Collection
256 Daguerreotype by Southworth and Hawes. All rights reserved, Metropolitan Museum of Art gift of I. N. Phelps Stokes, Edward Hawes, Alice Mary Hawes, Marion Augusta Hawes, 1937
257 Brown Brothers
258 Library of Congress
260 New-York Historical Society
261 Andrew Jackson by Thomas Sully. In the Collection of The Corcoran Gallery of Art, gift of William Wilson Corcoran
262 Culver Pictures
265 *The Cherokee Phoenix*, June 4, 1828. The New York Public Library, Rare Books Room
266 Courtesy of the Edward E. Ayer Collection, Newberry Library, Chicago

Chapter 16
268 *The Country Election* (*detail*) 1851 George Caleb Bingham. The St. Louis Art Museum
270 Photo by Matthew Brady. Library of Congress
271 New-York Historical Society
274 Library of Congress
275 Photo by Matthew Brady. Library of Congress
276 The Bettmann Archive
277 Chicago Historical Society
279 Mt. Holyoke College Library/Archives
280 (*t*) New-York Historical society; (*b*) Library of Congress
282 Library of Congress

Chapter 17
284 HBJ Picture Collection
287 Private Collection, Courtesy of Childs Gallery, Boston and New York
288 © Leonard Lee Rue, III, Animals, Animals
292 Utah State Historical Society
293 Utah State Historical Society
294 New-York Historical Society
295 The Bettmann Archive
296 Daguerreotype by J. J. Hawes. International Museum of Photography at George Eastman House

297 (l) The Bettmann Archive; (r) Museum of Fine Arts, Boston
298 The Bettmann Archive

Chapter 18
300 Museum of the City of New York
303 (l) Sophia Smith Collection, (Woman's History Archive), Smith College, Northampton, MA; (r) State Department of Archives and History, Raleigh, North Carolina
304 (t) The Bettmann Archive; (b) The Bettmann Archive
305 The Bettmann Archive
306 Library of Congress
307 Library of Congress
309 (l) The Bettmann Archive; (r) Sophia Smith Collection, (Woman's History Archive), Smith College, Northampton, MA
310 The Granger Collection
311 The Bettmann Archive

Chapter 19
312 Portraits in an Office by Edgar Degas, 1873. Musée de Beaux-Arts de Paul/Photographie Giraudon, Paris
316 National Archives
317 Sophia Smith Collection, (Women's History Archive), Smith College, Northampton, MA
318 Kansas State Historical Society/Kennedy Galleries, NY
319 The Last Moments of John Brown by Thomas Hovenden, 1884. All rights reserved. Metropolitan Museum of Art
320 Library of Congress
321 U.S. Army Military History Institute
322 Old Court House Museum, Vicksburg, MS
323 Brown Brothers
324 National Archives

Chapter 20
326 New-York Historical Society
328 New-York Historical Society
329 National Portrait Gallery, Smithsonian Institution
330 (l) Daguerreotype by Southworth and Hawes. All rights reserved, Metropolitan Museum of Art, gift of I. N. Phelps Stokes, Edward S. Hawes, Alice Mary Hawes, Marion Hawes, 1937; (r) New-York Historical Society
332 Library of Congress
333 Abbey Aldrich Rockefeller Folk Art Center
335 U.S. Department of Agriculture
336 U.S. Army Military History Institute
337 U.S. Army Military History Institute
339 Photo by Timothy O'Sullivan, Library of Congress

Chapter 21
342 Union League Club, Frick Art Reference Library
344 The Bancroft Library, University of California, Berkeley
347 Library of Congress
348 The Bettmann Archive
350 Association of American Railroads
352 Los Angeles County Museum of National History
353 The Granger Collection
354 Western Americana Collection, Beinecke Rare Book and Manuscript Library, Yale University
355 All rights reserved. The Metropolitan Museum of Art, gift of I. N. Phelps Stokes, and the Hawes Family, 1937

Chapter 22
358 Kansas State Historical Society
361 Kansas State Historical Society
363 San Diego Historical Society, Ticor Collection
364 California State Library
366 U.S. Army Military History Institute
368 Library of Congress

369 Photo by Matthew Brady, Culver Pictures
370 Franklin Pierce, by George Pater Alexander Healy. National Gallery of Art, Smithsonian Institution, Washington, D.C. Transfer from National Gallery of Art, Gift of Andrew Mellon
371 Library of Congress

Chapter 23
374 U.S. Army Military History Institute
377 (l) Library of Congress; (r) Print Collection, New York Public Library, Astor, Lenox and Tilden Foundation
378 New-York Historical Society
382 Sophia Smith Collection, (Woman's History Archive), Smith College, Northampton, MA
384 Photo by Matthew Brady, February 2, 1860. The Bettmann Archive
386 Library of Congress
387 National Archives
388 (l) Library of Congress; (r) Merserve Collection, Library of Congress
389 Kentucky Historical Society
390 The Bettmann Archive
391 Chicago Historical Society
392 New-York Historical Society

Chapter 24
394 Photo by James F. Gibson, Library of Congress
397 Photo by Timothy O'Sullivan, National Archives
398 Library of Congress
399 (both) U.S. Army Military History Institute
400 Photo by Matthew Brady, Library of Congress
401 Panic on the Road Between Bull Run and Centerville, probably July 21, 1861. Pencil sketch, Anonymous. Museum of Fine Arts, Boston. M. and M. Karolik Collection
404 Library of Congress
408 Library of Congress
409 (t) The Bettmann Archive; (b) Photo by Alexander Gardner, U.S. Military History Institute
410 U.S. Army Military History Institute

Chapter 25
412 Photo by Alexander Gardner, Library of Congress
415 Photo by Matthew Brady, Library of Congress
416 (l) Old Court House Museum, Vicksburg, MS; (r) Library of Congress
419 Photo by Timothy O'Sullivan. U.S. Army Military History Institute
420 Mary Boykin Chesnut by Samuel Osgood. National Portrait Gallery, Washington, D.C., on loan from Serena Williams Miles van Rensselaer
423 Library of Congress
424 Library of Congress
425 (l) New-York Historical Society; (r) Photo by Alexander Gardner, Library of Congress
426 (l) Photo by Alexander Hesler, June 3, 1860. Chicago Historical Society; (r) Photo by Alexander and James Gardner, April 8, 1865. Chicago Historical Society
428 Chicago Historical Society

Chapter 26
430 Library of Congress
432 All rights reserved. Metropolitan Museum of Art
433 Photo by Matthew Brady, 1865. Brady-Handy Collection. Library of Congress
435 The Valentine Museum, Richmond, VA
436 Western Reserve Historical Society, Cleveland, OH
438 Culver Pictures
439 Library of Congress
441 Library of Congress

Social Movements
Courtesy of the John Carter Brown Library at Brown University; Library of Congress; The New-York Historical Society; The Bettmann Archive; Museum of the City of New York; John Bryson, Life Magazine, © Time, Inc.; Bob Adelman/Magnum; Eugene Anthony/Black Star; UPI/The Bettmann Archive; Penelope Breese/Gamma/Liaison; © J. L.Atlan/Sygma

Rural vs. Urban
Detail of *Landscape* by Thomas Cole, The Minneapolis Institute of Art; The Historical Society of Pennsylvania; The New-York Historical Society; Library of Congress; Library of Congress; The Bettmann Archive; New-York Historical Association, Cooperstown; The Museums at Stony Brook, New York. Gift of Mr. and Mrs. Ward Melville; Museum of the City of New York; Dallas Museum of Art, Dallas Art Association Purchase; Art Institute of Chicago; Coit Tower, San Francisco Recreation and Park Department

Transportation
Museum of the City of New York; National Cowboy Hall of Fame, Tom McHugh/Photo Researchers; The Granger Collection; The New-York Historical Society; The Granger Collection; The Metropolitan Museum of Art, Bequest of Moses Tanenbaum, 1937; The Granger Collection; Coronado Press; Coronado Press; Memorial Art Gallery of the University of Rochester; James Pickerell; Tom McHugh/Photo Researchers; NASA

Index